KORANIC ALLUSIONS

EDITED BY

IBN WARRAQ

KORANIC ALLUSIONS

The Biblical, Qumranian, and Pre-Islamic Background to the Koran

Published 2013 by Prometheus Books

Cover design by Jacqueline Nasso Cooke

Inquiries should be addressed to
Prometheus Books
59 John Glenn Drive
Amherst, New York 14228–2119
VOICE: 716–691–0133
FAX: 716–691–0137
WWW.PROMETHEUSBOOKS.COM

17 16 15 14 13   5 4 3 2 1

Library of Congress Cataloging-in-Publication Data

Koranic allusions : the Biblical, Qumranian, and pre-Islamic background to the Koran / [edited by] Ibn Warraq.

pages cm

Summary: "For anyone with an interest in the early history of Islam, this erudite anthology will prove to be informative and enlightening. Scholars have long known that the text of the Koran shows evidence of many influences from religious sources outside Islam. For example, stories in the Koran about Abraham, Moses, Jesus, and other characters from the Bible obviously come from the Jewish Torah and the Christian Gospels. But there is also evidence of borrowing in the Koran from more obscure literature. In this anthology, the acclaimed critic of Islam Ibn Warraq has assembled scholarly articles that delve into these unusual, little-known sources. The contributors examine the connections between pre-Islamic poetry and the text of the Koran; and they explore similarities between various Muslim doctrines and ideas found in the writings of the Ebionites, a Jewish Christian sect that existed from the second to the fourth centuries. Also considered is the influence of Coptic Christian literature on the writing of the traditional biography of Muhammad"—Provided by publisher.

Includes bibliographical references.
ISBN 978–1–61614–759–4 (hardback)
ISBN 978–1–61614–760–0 (ebook)

1. Qur'an—Sources. 2. Qur'an—Criticism, interpretation, etc. I. Ibn Warraq

BP130.1.K675 2013
297.1'221—dc23

2013022370

TO MY COLLEAGUES AND FRIENDS AT THE
INARAH INSTITUTE, SAARBRÜCKEN, GERMANY.

Nullius In Verba.

Contents

PART 2. THE KORAN, THE BIBLE, AND THE DEAD SEA SCROLLS

PART 3. MUHAMMAD AND THE KORAN

APPENDIXES

Preface, Acknowledgments, and Advertisement for Myself

In 2004, I sent to Prometheus Books, along with my own longish introduction on variants and a short essay on pre-Islamic poetry, approximately forty-five articles by distinguished scholars in the form of photocopies, some barely legible, as they were copies from fragile journals dating from the early 1900s; many contained Arabic, Hebrew, Syriac, and Greek scripts. The staff at Prometheus Books made two decisions: first, they decided to divide the book into two; forty-five articles would have made for a book of over a thousand pages. The two volumes are *Which Koran? Variants, Manuscripts, Linguistics*, which came out in December 2011, and the present work, *Koranic Allusions*. Second, they insisted on keeping the house look and the house format and fonts; in other words, they elected to reset all the articles in a unified style; whereas I was ready to accept the tradition established by Ashgate–Variorum Press whereby the original articles are photographed and reproduced without any attempt to change any of the layout, font, or style, to the extent of keeping the original page numbers. There was, however, the unresolved problem of the original Arabic, Hebrew, and Syriac scripts. The staff at Prometheus elected to photograph each Arabic or Hebrew word as a separate individual image, which was then slotted, one by one, into the appropriate place in the reset text. There were several thousand such images. Such a procedure was time-consuming, which explains to some extent the delay in publishing the two anthologies, but it also posed special worries for me, the editor, since the chances for error were multiplied a hundred-fold. If it was difficult for the editor, it was a nightmare for the typesetters, in-house editors, and members of the art department, who handled the copying of the different scripts, treating each word as a separate piece of artwork. None of the latter knew the Semitic languages and scripts concerned. Hence their work was nothing less than heroic, and I should like to thank them for their extraordinary labors.

My anthologies continue to be of service to scholars and to anyone interested in the history of religions, providing access to scholarship neglected or almost forgotten, essays culled from hard-to-find journals. I hope the present collection will be of even greater usefulness, since it contains articles translated into English for the first time from the German and French. Recently, Professor David Cook[1] of Rice University in Texas had this say of my work:

> As a scholar of Islam myself, I find Ibn Warraq's attitude to be very refreshing, and his scholarship for the most part to be accurate and devastating in pinpointing weaknesses in Muslim orthodoxy. His third essay, "Some Aspects of the History of Koran Criticism, 700 CE to 2005 CE," could almost serve as a history of our field, and of its systematic failure to critique the foundational texts of Islam as those of other faiths have been critiqued.[2] It is an embarrassment for Islamic Studies that no critical text of the Qur'an has been produced.[3] However, even were this basic, elemental work done, there would be still a great more to be done in order to counter one of the most fundamental Muslim presuppositions—namely, that the text of the Qur'an has remained absolutely unaltered since the time of the Prophet Muhammad in the seventh century of the Common Era. Ibn Warraq counters this nonsense, which one hears on a regular basis even from educated Muslims who should know better, by demonstrating the prevalence of variant readings of the Qur'anic text.[4] That the existence of these variants, known as *qira'at*, demonstrates the falsity of the orthodox Muslim position vis-à-vis the Qur'an is obvious, and yet bizarrely rejected even by mainstream scholars.[5]

NOTES

1. David Cook, "Review of Ibn Warraq, *Virgins? What Virgins? and Other Essays*" (Amherst, NY: Prometheus Books, 2010) in *Reason Papers* 34, no. 2 (October 2012): 234–38.

2. David Cook's footnote: See for a discussion of this failure, F. E. Peters, "The Quest of the Historical Muhammad," *International Journal of Middle Eastern Studies* 23 (1991), pp. 291–315.

3. David Cook's footnote: Such work was begun in 1980, but stalled in 1989 due to lack of funding; see "Codex San'a I: A Qur'anic Manuscript from Mid-1st Century *Hijra*," accessed online at: http://www.islamic-awareness.org/Quran/Text/Mss/soth.html.

4. David Cook's footnote: It is further ironic that the existence of either seven or fourteen canonical "readings" of the Qur'an is accepted in Islam, and yet the implications of this fact for the "unaltered" nature of the text are not.

5. David Cook's footnote: See Hamza Andreas Tzortis, "Luxenberg & Puin: Origins & Revisions: Responding to Dispatches," accessed online at: http://www.theinimitablequran.com/respondingtodispacthes.pdf.

Transliteration and Other Technical Matters

There is no universally accepted system of transliteration (transcription) of the Semitic scripts. The authors in this anthology use two different systems for the Arabic alphabet. As some editors in whose journals the articles first appeared insisted that we not change one single letter as a precondition for allowing us to reproduce them, I was unable to standardize all the articles and adopt just one system. However, the two systems are not that difficult to come to grips with. For Arabic they are:

(1) ʾ, b, t, th, j, ḥ, kh, d, dh, r, z, s, sh, ṣ, ḍ, ṭ, ẓ, ʿ, gh, f, q, k, l, m, n, h, w, y. *Short vowels*: a, u, i. *Long vowels*: ā, ū, ī

(2) ʾ, b, t, ṯ, ǧ, ḥ, ḫ, d, ḏ, r, z, s, š, ṣ, ḍ, ṭ, ẓ, ʿ, ġ, f, q, k, l, m, n, h, w, y. *Short vowels*: a, u, i. *Long vowels*: ā, ū, ī

The journal *Studia Islamica* uses and recommends system (1). On the whole I have used this system in my own introduction and translations.

The journal *Arabica*, on the other hand, uses system (2); thus, the articles from this journal included in this anthology follow suit. (Readers are also likely to encounter, though not often in this anthology, the following variations: *dj* for *j*, and *ḳ* for *q*, for example, in *EI2* [the second edition of *The Encyclopedia of Islam*].)

For the Hebrew and Syriac, I use the following:

ʾ, b, g, d, h, w, z, ḥ, ṭ, y, k, l, m, n, s, ʿ, p, ṣ, q, r, ś/š, t

All long vowels are overlined. The small raised ^{e} stands for a hurried or neutral vowel. Underlined letters (as in bēṯ) are pronounced as fricatives, thus ṯ = English "th" as in "thin"; p̱ = "ph" as in "phial."

Right up to the 1930s, Western scholars used the edition of the Koran by Gustav Flügel (sometimes spelled Fluegel), *Corani Textus Arabicus* (1834), whose numbering of verses differs from what has now become the "official" or Standard Egyptian edition, first published in 1924. Again, not only was it obviously much easier for me to leave the original Flügel numbering in the pre-1924 articles included in this anthology, but in some cases it was even essential not to interfere with the original numbering, since some pieces only referred to Flügel's edition. As one scholar reminded me, attempting to change the numbering would only have increased the possibility of further errors.

TRANSLITERATION OF *UMAYYA B. ABĪ AṢ ṢALT*

Every editor of Arabic and Islamic texts, many of which must be translated from the German and French, and some of which date from the nineteenth and early twentieth centuries, is faced with the problem of the scientific transliteration of Arabic words and names. Conventions vary—there is still no absolute consensus on the best way to transliterate Arabic. I have not always kept the transliteration used in the original article. For instance, the name of the pre-Islamic poet, usually transliterated in modern times as Umayya b. abī aṣ-Ṣalt, has been transliterated in many different ways. Aloys Sprenger, writing in the nineteenth century, originally transliterated the poet's name as Omayya b. Aby-l-Çalt, which I changed to Umayya B. Abī al-Ṣalt. Clement Huart, writing in 1904, transliterated the name as Omayya ben Abi'ç-Çalt, which I have changed to Umayya B. Abī al-Ṣalt. Friedrich Schulthess, writing in 1906, transliterated the name in the German fashion as Umajja b. Abi-ṣ Ṣalt, which I have changed to Umayya b. abi-Ṣalt. I have kept E. Power's transliteration: Umayya ibn Abī-ṣ Ṣalt; D. S. Margoliouth's original transliteration: Umayyah b. Abi'l-Ṣalt; Tilman Seidensticker's Umayya Ibn Abī al-Ṣalt, and Gert Borg's Umayya b. Abī al-Ṣalt. It seems to me that despite the slight variations in the transliteration there is very little possibility of confusion as to which poet is being referred to.

TRANSCRIPTION/TRANSLITERATION

Consonants

ا	alif		ض	ḍā d	ḍ
ب	bāʾ	b	ط	ṭāʾ	ṭ
ت	tāʾ	t	ظ	ẓāʾ	ẓ
ث	thāʾ	th/ṯ	ع	ʿayn	ʿ
ج	jīm	j/ğ/dj	غ	ghayn	gh/ġ
ح	ḥāʾ	ḥ	ف	fāʾ	f
خ	khāʾ	kh/ḫ/x	ق	qāf	q/ḳ
د	dāl	d	ك	kāf	k
ذ	dhāl	dh/ḏ	ل	lām	l
ر	rāʾ	r	م	mīm	m
ز	zay	z	ن	nūn	n
س	sīn	s	ه	hāʾ	h
ش	shīn	sh/š	و	wāw	w
ص	ṣād	ṣ	ى	yāʾ	y

(ء hamza ʾ)

Vowels

ا	ā/â	َ	fatḥa	a
و	ū	ُ	ḍamma	u
ى	ī	ِ	kasra	i

Dipthongs : aw, ay

آ	ʾalif-madda	ʾā		لا lām-ʾalif lā
ة	tāʾmarbūṭa	-at-	ّ	shadda (doubling consonant)
ى	alif maqṣūra (pronounced like lengthening alif) ā			

Part One

Pre-Islamic Poetry as a Source for the Koran

1.1

The Consequences of Authenticity

Ibn Warraq

David Margoliouth warned us not to be too credulous about the authenticity of so-called pre-Islamic poetry. Two of his principal arguments were the probity, or rather the lack of probity, of the earliest compilers and editors of pre-Islamic poetry, and the fact that many putative pre-Islamic poems contained words, phrases, and religious concepts derived from the Koran, even though the authors had died long before the Koran can have been said to exist.

Margoliouth patiently hacks away at the certainties of the credulous by asking awkward questions. How was this pre-Islamic literature preserved? Orally? In written form? Did the profession of *rāwī* really exist? Was the so-called oral tradition of the Bedouins genuine or reliable? Is there any evidence for the existence of any written pre-Islamic literature? The history of Latin literature reveals a gradual organic development. Should we not expect the same in Arabic literature?

Ḥammād al-Rāwiya (694/5–772 CE) was responsible for the collection of the seven famous poems of the *Mu'allaqāt*, and the poetry of Imru' l-Qays ibn Ḥujr. By all accounts he was a charming rogue, given to carousing, drinking wine, but with a genuine delight in poetry, and he also professed to know the lore, rituals, and poetry of the Bedouins. Ḥammād remained a dilettante rather than a scholar, and he was somewhat cavalier in his attitude toward the question of authenticity and authorship. His contemporaries and later Arab scholars denounced him vehemently. The Baṣran Yūnus b. Ḥabīb attacked Ḥammād for not knowing grammar, prosody, or correct speech; and the Kufan Mufaḍḍal b. Muḥammad al-Dabbī "accused him of having ruined the tradition of Bedouin poetry beyond repair by his clever forgeries."[1] Abū Ḥātim al-Sijistānī quotes poems of al-Ḥutay'a from the *kitāb* of Hammād only to blame him for allowing spurious poems into the collection.

Other unreliable witnesses include Jannād, Barzakh, and Khalaf al-Aḥmar. The latter confesssed that he had circulated forgeries of his own in Kufa as ancient poems. Abū 'Amr b. al-'Alā (died AH 154) also owned up to having added at least one line of his own to a poem by al-A'shā. Al-Aṣma'i (died 828 CE) on his tour to Medina said he could not find a single sound poem. Abū 'Amr Shaybanī (died AH 205) was unable to find many genuine poems for his collection, and even those that got selected were said to be forgeries. The scholars took a dim view of each others' abilities; Ibn al-A'rābī did not think much of al-Aṣma'ī nor of Abū 'Ubaydah. Antiquaries of the third Islamic century are equally unreliable. Mubarrad (826–900 CE) was known to fabricate verses on demand practically. Doubts, uncertainties, suspicions, and improbabilities seem to plague all collections of putative pre-Islamic material.

In such a situation, we would do well to heed the caution advocated by Margoliouth, and repeated by M. Lecomte, who says, "the personality of the transmitters such as Ḥammād the presumed originator of the *Mu'allaqāt* and the uncertainties which surround their actions lead one to think that the attribution of these poems to persons duly classified and identified should be strongly regarded with caution. The faculties of adaptation, even of imagination, by these intermediaries—themselves poets—do not authorize us to see in the 'official' anthologies anything more than the reflection of an ancient poetical situation expressing itself by poems more or less arbitrarily taken from a much greater and more varied production, at least as representative in any case of the ancient poetic genius."[2] We now have an intermediate position on the *Mu'allaqāt*, but which perhaps can be extended to cover all pre-Islamic poetry, whereby "in their form and content and given that they comprise in part elements almost certainly apocryphal, the *Mu'allaqāt* [and perhaps all pre-Islamic poetry] must be considered as fixed, if not stereotyped, specimens of a poetic tradition—already very old—vigorously flourishing in different parts of the Arabian peninsula."[3]

We also know fr[illegible] hn Wansbrough[4] that so-called pre-Islamic poetry was often invented for polemical purposes:

Whatever may have been the original motives for collecting and recording the ancient poetry of the Arabs,[5] the earliest evidence of such activity belongs, not unexpectedly, to the third/ninth century and the work of the classical philologists. The manner in which this material was manipulated by its collectors to support almost any argument appears never to have been very successfully concealed. The procedure, moreover, was common to all fields of scholarly activity: e.g., the early dating of a verse ascribed to the *mukhaḍrami*[6] poet Nābigha Ja'dī in order to provide a pre-Islamic proof text for a common Quranic construction (finite verb form preceded by direct object), Mubarrad's admitted invention of a *Jāhilī* [pre-Islamic] verse as a gloss to a lexical item in the *hadith*, and Abū 'Amr b. 'Alā's candid admission that save for a single verse of 'Amr b. Kulthūm, knowledge of Yawm Khazāz would have been lost to posterity. The three examples share at least one common motive: recognition of pre-Islamic poetry as authority in linguistic matters, even where such contained non-linguistic implications. Also common to all three is another, perhaps equally significant feature: Ibn Qutayba, who adduced the verse of Nābigha to explain/justify Quranic syntax, lived at the end of the third/ninth century, as did Mubarrad; Abū 'Amr, of whom no written works were preserved, lived in the second half of the second/eighth century, but this particular dictum was alluded to only in Jāḥiẓ (third/ninth century) and explicitly in Ibn 'Abd Rabbih (fourth/tenth century). Now, that pre-Islamic poetry should have achieved a kind of status as linguistic canon some time in the third/ninth century may provoke no quarrel. That it had achieved any such status earlier must, I think, be demonstrated. The fact that it had not, in one field at least, can be shown: the absence of poetic *shawāhid* in the earliest form of scriptural exegesis might be thought to indicate that appeal to the authority of *Jāhilī* (and other) poetry was not standard practice before the third/ninth century. Assertions to the contrary may be understood as witness to the extraordinary influence exercised by the concept of *faṣāḥat al-jahiliyya*.

In other words, the putative eloquence of pre-Islamic poetry became commonplace only in the third/ninth century; there are no references to pre-Islamic poetry in the early, pre–third century, works of Koranic exegesis.

Margoliouth's second part of his argument is, I believe, fallacious, oft-repeated, and rests on a priori assumptions about the rise of Islam, the collection of the Koran, and the life of the Prophet. Margoliouth automatically dismisses any poem that echoes words, phrases, and even sentiments of the Koran as inauthentic. If a poem resembles a Koranic verse, then it must have been influenced by the Koran, and not vice versa. The Koran stands alone, heaven forbid that it should be inspired by profane poems!

For instance, Ibn Hishām gives the following lines as examples of Umayya b. Abī aṣ-Ṣalt's poetry:

> *kullu dīnin yawma l-qiyāmati 'inda l-lāhi illa dīna l-ḥanīfati būrū*
> In God's sight at the resurrection every religion
> but that of the ḥanīf is doomed to perdition.

Montgomery Watt immediately describes it as "presumably of Islamic inspiration."[7] And even Hamilton Gibb, who seems to accept, on the whole, the authenticity of Umayya's poems, confesses that he agrees with the view "that the poems ascribed to Umayya cannot be regarded as a source of Qur'anic materials or doctrine."[8] Carl Brockelmann tells us that "many passages of [Labīd b. Rabī'a's] *Dīwān* seem to owe their inspiration to the Qur'ān."[9] We know that Labīd b. Rabī'a died around about 660–661 CE. Can we truly say that the Koran as we know it today existed in 661 CE? The authenticity of any poem written at the beginning of the seventh century CE (i.e., by the so-called mukhaḍramūn poets, constituting the class of pagan poets who died after the proclamation of Islam, e.g., al-A'shā Maymūn, Labīd, Abū Dhu'ayb, and al-Ḥuṭay'a) poses grave problems for those who insist on following the traditional Muslim account of the collection of the Koran. If, for example, Umayya's poetry is authentic, and it does resemble verses from the Koran, then we must account for these resemblances by the normal mechanisms of human history, literary influence, and so forth. If we then combine the authenticity of the poems with a revisionist account of the rise of Islam and the collection of the Koran we arrive at a more plausible version of the similarities between the Koran, and certain poems by Umayya, but, of course, at the expense of everything that we have come to accept as the traditional account.

The revisionist position is very boldly set out by Nevo and Koran in their important but unjustly neglected work, *Crossroads to Islam*:[10] "The Qur'ān is a late compilation; it was not canonized until the end of the 2nd century A.H. or perhaps early in the 3rd. This conclusion, reached by Schacht and Wansbrough, is supported by an analysis of extant rock inscriptions and an examination of the references to the Arab religion in the works of the peoples with whom they came into contact." Wansbrough's achievement was to lay bare the canonization process. "Such a process differentiates between the composition of a text and its recognition as scripture, with all the implications of that term. In fact, the process is sometimes spoken of as having five stages: composition, circulation, revision, collection, and recognition. . . . [W]e cannot meaningfully talk about the Qur'ān as we know it today until that point of authority, acceptance, and stability has been achieved."[11]

But can we maintain the authenticity of the poems of Umayya while rejecting the authenticity of the Qur'ān? Do they stand or fall together? Uri Rubin writes, "As a rule, if one does not suspect the authenticity of the Qur'ān one does not have any immediate reason for rejecting the authenticity of other utterances containing a similar religious or ethical meassage."[12] Of course, they are independent issues, they do not fall or stand inexorably together. This is precisely why scholars like Tor Andrae[13] dismiss the poems of Umayya; their authenticity has consequences they do not wish to contemplate.

Certain eminent scholars have indeed accepted these consequences. R. A. Nicholson writes, for example, "Umayya's verses . . . are chiefly on religious topics, and show many points of resemblance with the doctrines set forth in the early Suras of the Koran. With one exception, all the Ḥanīfs whose names are recorded belonged to the Ḥijāz and the West of the Arabian peninsula. No doubt Muḥammad, with whom most of them were contemporary, came under their influence, and he may have received his first stimulus from this quarter."[14] Nicholson was still, of course, working with the assumptions of and within the framework constructed by Muslim tradition. H. H. Bräu[15] makes similar points: "The agreement between Umayya's poems and the Qur'ān may more easily be explained from the undoubted fact that about the time of Muḥammad's mission, and probably for some time before, currents of thought of a Ḥanīfi nature had attracted wide circles of the Ḥaḍarīs, especially in Mecca and Ṭā'īf, stimulated and nourished by Jewish haggadas and Christian legends, which were in circulation there and over South Arabia in many recensions—and this explains the occasional divergences between the Qur'ān and Umayya. Muhammad and Umayya like other *homines religiosi* (Zayd b. 'Amr, Waraqa, Maslama, etc.) drew upon common sources, whether written as Schulthess thinks or oral as Nöldeke holds."[16]

Christoph Luxenberg's work[17] has further complicated the picture. If his conclusions are anywhere near correct, then we have to revise our ideas of the collection of the Koran totally and radically. He is not simply making the obvious point that there is some Syriac in the Koran. Luxenberg further argues that we must look at some Palestinian Syriac liturgical works as the source of the Koran, or at the sacred scriptures of some heretical Judeo-Christian sect influenced by Ebionite and Elkesaite doctrines. He thinks that the Arabic Koran we know today must have existed as a Syriac text that was badly translated into Arabic, possibly going through a stage when it was in Karshuni (i.e., written in Syriac letters but in the Arabic language), before its conversion into its final form as the Arabic Koran. Thus, in a sense, he is arguing that parts of the Koran must have existed before Muḥammad, something that Günter Lüling[18] also argues for, and which Wansbrough, too, allowed for, as some sort of a proto-Koran: "Indeed, the text *must* have a prehistory for such a process to take place, a prehistory that brings strands of the earlier biblical and Arabian traditions together through the person of Muḥammad."[19] In that case, if pre-Islamic poetry were authentic, we would also expect it to manifest Syriac elements in its vocabulary, imagery, and ideas. In the case of Umayya, this is exactly what Professor Borg has found.[20]

Selected Bibliography on Pre-Islamic Poetry and the Koran

Anthologies

Al-Aṣma'ī [died 828 CE]. *al-Aṣma'iyyāt*, ed. Ahlwardt, *Sammlungen alter arabischer Dichter*, i, Berlin, 1902.

Abū Tammām [804–846 CE]. *Ḥamāsa*, ed. with commentary by al-Tibrīzī by G. Freytag, Hamasae Carmina cum Tebrisii scholiis, Bonn, 1828.

Al-Baghdādī, 'Abdal Qādir b. 'Umar [died 1682 CE]. *Khizānat al-adab wa-lubb lubāb lisān al-'arab,* 4 Bde, Būlāq, 1291.

Mu'allaqāt. Seven pre-Islamic poems collected by Ḥammād al-Rāwiya in the middle of eighth century CE. The Arab scholars are divided as to the authors of these poems, each scholar producing his own list. Imru' al-Qays, Ṭarafa, Zuhayr, Labīd, and 'Amr are common to all the lists. Some would add al-Ḥārith b. Ḥilliza and 'Antara b. Shaddād to the list.

Al-Iṣbahānī, Abū'l-Faraj 'Ali ibn al-Ḥusayn, *Kitāb al-aghānī*, 20 vols. Cairo, AH 1285.

Ibn Qutayba. *Shi'r* [ed., Shākir], Cairo, 1369/1950, *Liber poësis et poëtarum,* ed. M. J. de Goeje Lugduni Bat. 1904.

Al-Mufaḍḍal b. Muḥammad b. Ya'lā al-Ḍabbī [died 780 or 786 CE], *al-Muffaḍḍaliyyāt* [1], ed. A. M. Shākir and 'Abd al-Salām Hārūn, Cairo, 1942 CE, with commentary of al-Anbarī. [2] *The Mufaḍḍaliyāt*, an anthology of ancient Arabic odes, ed. C. J. Lyall, i, Arabic text, Oxford, 1921, ii, translation and notes ibid., 1918, iii, indexes to the Arabic text by A. A. Bevan, London, 1924.

Secondary Literature

Ahlwardt, W. *Bemerkungen über die Aechtheit der alten arabischen Gedichte*, Greifswald, 1872.

——. *The Diwans of the Six Ancient Arabic Poets*, London, 1870.

Andrae, Tor. *Les origines de l'Islam et le Christianisme*, Paris: A. M., 1955.

Arberry, A. J. *The Seven Odes: The First Chapter in Arabic Literature*. London, 1957.

Buhl, F. *Das Leben Muhammeds*, translated by H. Schaeder, Heidelberg, 1961.

Cheikho, Louis. *Poètes arabes chrétiens avant l'Islam*, Beirut, 1890.

Diem, Werner. "Das Kitāb al-jīm des Abū 'Amr as-Shaibānī: Ein, Beitrag zur arabischen Lexikographie," PhD diss., University of Munich, 1968.

von Grunebaum, G. E. "Pre-Islamic Poetry," in *MW* 32 (1942): 147–53.

Ḥusayn, Ṭāhā. *Fi l-adab al-jāhilī,* Cairo, 1345/1927.

Jacob, G. *Studien in arabischen. Dichtern, heft iii, Altarabisches Beduinenleben nach den Quellen geschildert*, Berlin, 1897.

Larcher, Pierre. *Le Brigand et l'Amant. Deux poèmes préislamiques de Ta'abbata Sharran et Imru' al-Qays traduits de l'arabe et commentés, suivis des adapta-*

tions de Goethe et d'Armand Robin et de deux études sur celles-ci, La Bibliothèque Arabe, collection Les classiques, dirigée par André Miquel, professeur honoraire au Collège de France. Paris et Arles: Sindbad/Actes Sud, 2012.

———. "Les incertitudes de la poésie arabe archaïque: l'exemple des Mu'allaqât," *La Revue des Deux Rives*, no. 1, 1999, pp. 121–35

———. *Le Guetteur de mirages. Cinq poèmes préislamiques d'al-A'shâ Maymûn, 'Abîd b. al-Abras et al-Nâbigha al-Dhubyânî*, traduits de l'arabe et commentés par Pierre Larcher, Petite bibliothèque de Sindbad. Paris et Arles: Sindbad/Actes Sud, 2004.

———. "La *Mu'allaqa* de 'Amr ibn Kulthûm. Introduction, traduction et notes," *Annales islamologiques* 33, 1999, pp. 105–20.

———. "La *Mu'allaqa* de 'Imru' al-Qays. Introduction, traduction et notes," *Arabica* 45, no. 3, 1998, pp. 249–60.

———. *Les Mu'allaqât : Les sept poèmes préislamiques*, préfacés par André Miquel, traduits et commentés par Pierre Larcher. Coll. Les Immémoriaux, Fata Morgana, 2000.

———. Le poème en dâl de al-Nâbigha al-Dhubyânî. Introduction, traduction et notes, *in L'Orient au coeur en l'honneur d'André Miquel, sous la responsabilité de Floréal Sanagustin,* Paris, Maisonneuve et Larose, 2001, pp. 35–44.

Lyall, C. Preface to *Mufaḍḍaliyyāt*. vol. ii., Oxford, 1921, ii, translation and notes, ibid., 1918.

———. *Translations of Ancient Arabic Poetry*. London, 1885.

Muir, William. "Ancient Arabic poetry: Its Genuineness and Authenticity," *JRAS* (1875): 75–92.

Nöldeke, T. *Beiträge zur Kenntnis der Poesie der alten Araber*. Hannover, 1864.

———. *Fūnf Mo'allaqāt übersetzt und erklärt*. Vienna, 1899–1901.

Nöldeke, T., and A. Müller. *Delectus veterum carminum arabicorum*. Carmina selegit et edidit T. Nöldeke, glossarium confecit A. Müller. Berolini, 1890.

Ruckert, F. *Hamāsa oder die ältesten arabischen Volkslieder übersetz und erläutert*. 2 vols, Stuttgart, 1846.

Sprenger, Aloys. *Das Leben und die Lehre des Mohammed*. Berlin, 1869.

Wellhausen, J. *Reste arabischen Heidentums*. 3rd. ed., Berlin, 1897.

Zwettler, Michael. *The Oral Tradition of Classical Arabic Poetry: It's Character and Implications*. Columbus: Ohio State University, 1978.

Individual Poets:

Ash Shanfarā, *Dīwān, in Dīwān al-ṣa'ālīk*, Beirut, 1413/1992. See F. Gabrieli (Sull' autenticità della *Lāmiyyat al-'Arab* in RSO, xv [1935], 361).

Ta'abbaṭa Sharran. *Dīwān*, ed. Yūsuf Shukrī Farḥāt, in *Dīwān al-ṣa'ālīk*, Beirut, 1413 /1992.

'Antara ibn Shaddād [sixth century CE]. *Dīwān*, ed. W. Ahlwardt, *The Diwans of the Six Ancient Arabic Poets*, London, 1870. See also Thorbecke, *Antarah*, Leipzig, 1867; H. Derenbourg, "Le Poète anté-islamique Antar," in *Opuscules d' un Arabisant*, Paris, 1905.

'Urwa b. al-Ward, ed. T. Nöldeke, *Die Gedichte des Urwa ibn Alward*, in Abh.KGW Göttingen, xi (1864.)

Ḥātim al-Ṭā'ī. *Der Dīwān des arabischen dichters Ḥātim Ṭaj*. ed. and trans, Fr. Schulthess, Leipzig, 1897.

Zuhayr ibn Abī Sulmā Rabī'a. See Fu'ād al-Bustānī, Beirut, 1929.

Imru' l-Qays ibn Ḥujr [died 550 CE]. Poems collected by Shaybānī, Khālid b. Kathūm, al-Aṣma'ī, Muḥammad b. Ḥabīb. Recensions by al-Sikkīt, al-Sukkārī. All of Imru' al-Qays poetry was transmitted by Ḥammād al-Rāwiya or Abū 'Amr ibn al- 'Alā'. *Dīwān*, ed. de Slane, Paris, 1837; W. Ahlwardt, London, 1870: 68 poems from al-Sukkārī plus some others from various sources.

Ṭarafa 'Amr b. al-'Abd b. Sufyān. *Dīwān*, ed. K. al-Bustānī, Beirut, n.d.

'Amr ibn Kulthūm. *Dīwān*, ed. F. Krenkow, in Machriq. 1922, 591–611.

Ḥārith b. Ḥilliza. *Dīwān*, ed. F. Krenkow, in Machriq. 1922. Considered inauthentic by Ṭāhā Ḥusayn. *Fi l-adab al-jāhilī'*, 'Cairo, 1345/1927, pp. 236–43.

'Alqama b.'Abada al-Tamīmī al-Faḥl. *Dīwān*, ed. A. Socin, Leipzig, 1867.

An-Nābigha al-Dhubyānī. *Dīwān*. Shukrī Fayṣal, Beirut, 1388/1988.

'Adī b. Zayd. J. Horovitz. *Adi ibn Zaid, the Poet of al-Hira*, IC, 1930, 31–69; F. Gabrieli, Adi b. Zaid, il poeta di al-Ḥīra, Rend. Lin, 1948, 81–96.

Al-Samaw'al b.'Ādiyā. J. W. Hirschberg, *Der Dīwān des as-Samau'al ibn 'Ādijā*, Cracow, 1931.

G. Levi Della Vida. "A proposito di as -Samaw al," in *RSO* 13 (1931): 53–72.

Labīd b. Rabī'a [died 660–61 CE]. *Dīwān*, des Lābid, *zweiter Teil, nach den Handschriften zu Strassburg und Leiden mit den Fragmenten, Übersetzung und Biographie des Dichters aus dem Nachlass des Dr. A. Huber*, ed. C. Brockelmann, Leiden, 1891.

Al-A'shā Maymūn b. Qays [570–625 CE]. *Dīwān*, ed. R. Geyer (Gibb Memorial N. S. VI), London, 1928.

Ka' b ibn Zuhayr. *Dīwān*, ed. T. Kowalski, Cracow, 1950.

Ḥassān b.Thābit [died circa 659 CE]. See W. 'Arafat, "Early Critics of the Authenticity of the Poetry of the Sīra," *BSOAS* 21 (1958). According to 'Arafat, 60–70 percent of the poetry attributed to Ḥassān is probably spurious.

Al-Ḥuṭay'a, Jarwal ibn Aws [died between 661 and 80 CE]. *Der Dīwān des Jarwal b. Aus al-Ḥuṭej'a*, ed. Ignaz Goldziher, *ZDMG* XLVI (1892), I ff., 173 ff., 471 ff.; XLVII (1893), 43 ff., 163 ff. [= Gesammelte Schriften, III, 50 ff.].

On Umayya b. abi aṣ-Ṣalt

Andrae, T. *Die Entstehung des Islams und das Christentum*, in Kyrohistorik Arsskrift, Upsala, 1926.

——. *Les origines de l'Islam et le Christianisme*, Paris, A. M., 1955

Borg, Gert. *The Divine in the Works of Umayya B. Abi al-Ṣalt*. In *Orientations: Representations of the Divine in Arabic Poetry*, edited by G. Borg and Ed de Moor.

Frank-Kamentzky, J. *Unters. über das Verhältnis der dem U. b. abi 'l-Ṣalt zugeschreibenen Ged. zum Qoran*, Kirchhain, 1911.

Gibb, H. A. R. "Pre-Islamic Monotheism in Arabia." In *The Arabs and Arabia on the Eve of Islam*, ed. F. E. Peters. Ashgate Variorum, G. B: Ashgate, 1999.

Hirschberg, J. W. *Judische und Christliche Lehren im vor-und frühislamischen Arabien*, Cracow, 1939.

Huart, Clement. "Une Nouvelle Source du Qoran." *Journal Asiatique* (July–August 1904): 125–67.

Power, E. "The Poems of Umayya ibn Abi-ṣ Ṣalt." In *Mélanges de la Faculté Orientale*, Université Saint-Joseph, Beyrouth, vol. 2, 1911–1912, pp. 145–95.

——. "Umayya ibn Abi- ṣ Ṣalt." In *Mélanges de la Faculté Orientale*, Université Saint-Joseph, Beyrouth, vol. 1, 1906, pp. 197–222

Rubin, Uri. *Ḥanīfiyya and Ka'ba: An Inquiry into the Arabian Pre-Islamic Background of Dīn Ibrāhīm*. In Peters, ed., *The Arabs and Arabia on the Eve of Islam*.

Schulthess, F. *Umajja b. Abi-ṣ-Ṣalt*. In *Orientalische Studien Theodor Nöldeke zum siebzigsten Geburtstag (2 März 1906) gewidmet von Freunden und Schülern und in ihren Auftrag herausgegeben von Carl Bezold*, 2 vols., Giessen, 1906, vol. 1, pp. 71–89.

——. *Umaija ibn Abi aṣ-Ṣalt, die Gedichtefragmente*. Leipzig, 1911. Reviewed by Nöldeke in *Z. A.* 28, 159ff.

Seidensticker, T. "The Authenticity of the Poems ascribed to Umayya Ibn Abi al-Salt." In *Tradition and Modernity in Arabic Language and Literature*, ed. J. R. Smart. Richmond (UK), Curzon Press, 1996, pp. 87–101.

Sprenger, Aloys. *Das Leben und die Lehre des Mohammed*. Berlin, 1869. Plus the articles in the present volume.

Notes

1. "Ḥammād al-Rāwiya," by J. W. Fück, *Encyclopedia of Islam*, 2nd ed., ed. H. Gibb et al. (Leiden: E. J. Brill, 1960 to present). Hereafter *E. I.*

2. *E. I.*, "Mu'allaqāt," by G. Lecomte.

3. Ibid.

4. J. Wansbrough, *Quranic Studies* (Amherst, NY: Prometheus Books, 2004), pp. 97–98.

5. [J. Wansbrough, footnote, "A not very convincing enumeration in Blachère, *Histoire de la littérature arabe*, Paris i–iii, 1952–66, pp. 94–95.]

6. Constituting the class of pagan poets who died after the proclamation of Islam, e.g. al-A'shā Maymūn, Labīd, Abū Dhu'ayb, and al-Ḥuṭay'a.

7. M. Watt, "Ḥanīf," *E. I.*

8. H. Gibb, "Pre-Islamic Monotheism in Arabia," *Harvard Theological Review* 55 (1962), reprinted in F. E. Peters, ed., *The Arabs and Arabia on the Eve of Islam* (Ashgate, Variorum, G.B., 1999).

9. C. Brockelmann, "Labīd b. Rabī'a," in *E. I.*

10. Yehuda D. Nevo and Judith Koren, *Crossroads to Islam: The Origins of the Arab Religion and the Arab State* (Amherst, NY: Prometheus Books, 2003), p.11.

11. Andrew Rippin, foreword to J. Wansbrough, *Quranic Studies, Sources and Methods of Scriptural Interpretation* (Amherst, NY: Prometheus Books, 2004), pp. xvi–xvii

12. Uri Rubin, "Ḥanīfiyya and Ka'ba: An Inquiry into the Arabian Pre-Islamic Background of Dīn Ibrāhīm," in *The Arabs and Arabia on the Eve of Islam*, ed. F. E. Peters (Ashgate, Variorum, G. B., 1999), pp. 277–78.

13. Tor Andrae, *Les origines de l'Islam et le Christianisme* (Paris: A. M., 1955), pp. 55–63.

14. R. A. Nicholson, *A Literary History of the Arabs* (Cambridge: Cambridge University Press, 1969), p. 150.

15. H. H. Bräu, "Umaiya b. Abi 'l-Ṣalt," in *Encyclopedia of Islam*, ed. M. TH Houtsma et al. (Leiden: E. J. Brill, 1913–1936).

16. [1] F. Schulthess, "Umayya b. Abi-as-Ṣalt," in *Orientalische Studien Theodor Nöldeke zum siebzigsten Geburtstag (2 März 1906) gewidmet von Freunden*

und Schülern und in ihren Auftrag herausgegeben von Carl Bezold, 2 vols., Giessen, 1906, vol. I, pp. 71–89; chapter 1.4 in present volume. [2] T. Nöldeke, in *Z.A.* 28, p. 159 sqq.

17. C. Luxenberg, *Die Syro-Aramäische Lesart Des Koran*, 2nd ed. (Berlin: Verlag Hans Schiler, 2004).

18. Günter Lüling, *A Challenge to Islam for Reformation* (Delhi: Motilal Banarsidass, 2003).

19. Rippin, foreword to *Quranic Studies*, p. xvii.

20. G. Borg, *The Divine in the Works of Umayya B. Abi al- Ṣalt*, chapter 1.9 in present volume.

1.2

On Umayya B. Abī al-Ṣalt[1]

Aloys Sprenger

I[2]

The most active and most excellent among the Ḥanīfs was Umayya b. Abī al-Ṣalt, a native of Ṭāyif, two daytrips south of Makka. He was ingenious and—just like his father—was distinguished by a poetic talent. Although he was condemned by the Prophet, the Muslims considered him one of the most celebrated poets of Arabia, and he certainly excelled above all poets of the Ḥijāz of his time. His hymns, only surviving in a few fragments, are said to have dealt with religious matters. They also contain allusions to the biblical story. In the year 624 he composed satires on Muhammad, whom he never accepted as Prophet. So he was not much older than the Prophet who was fifty-five years old at that time.[3]

Due to the lack of a literature or written tradition, the complete intellectual life of the Arabs found its expression in songs and poems. The influence of Umayya's poems, which were so popular that—regardless of the Prophet's prohibition to propagate them—they continued to be in everybody's mouth for a long time, must have been incalculably great.

In the Qur'ān VII, 174f. an important passage refering to Umayya can be found. This passage gave rise to a number of exegetic myths, when, in the first century, his relationship to Muhammad was only remembered vaguely.

VII, 174 *wa-tlu ʻalayhim naba'a llāḏī 'ātaynāhu 'āyātinā fa-nsalaḫa minhā fa-'atbaʻahu š-šayṭānu fa-kāna mina l-ġāwīna*

VII, 174 Recite to them the story of him to whom We gave Our signs, but he withdrew from them and Satan followed him up and he became one of the perverted.

[see Pickthall, *The Meaning of the Glorious Koran* (London: Allen and Unwin, 1948; 1st edition, 1930) for an alternative translation.] Recite unto them the tale of him to whom We gave Our revelations, but he sloughed them off, so Satan overtook him and he became of those who lead astray.]

We will find some accounts in the appendix, which describe exactly how a ghost or Satan (since Satan was a new personality for the Arabs, they did not make a big distinction between him and the evil jinn) followed him. And we will also find a long account on how he and his companions wandered about in the desert.

VII, 175: *wa-lawši'nā la-rafa'nāhu bihā wa-lākinnahū 'aẖlada 'ilā l'arḍi wa-ttaba'a hawāhu fa-maṯaluhū ka-maṯali l-kalbi 'in taḥmil 'alayhi yalhaṯ 'aw tatrukhu yalhaṯ ḏālika maṯalu l-qawmi llaḏīna kaḏḏabū bi-'āyātinā fa-qṣusi l-qaṣaṣa la'allahum yatafakkarūna*

VII, 175 Had We so willed We should have exalted him thereby, but he clung to the earth and followed his desire. So he is to be compared to a dog, which, if one attacks it, lolls out its tongue, and if one leaves it alone, lolls out its tongue. That is what the people who have disbelieved Our signs are like. So tell them the story, mayhap they will take thought.

Muḥammad admits that Umayya was inspired with God's spirit and that he knew the truth, but he lacked the purity of the heart in order to follow it. This is expressed figuratively by the exegetes in a legend according to which Umayya's heart was also opened by the angels, but since they did not find it pure, they did not ordain him Prophet. The idea that man is guided by the mercy of God and not by the power of his own intelligence is also pointed out in the following verses:

VII, 176–79.

176: *sā'a maṯalan-i l-qawmu llaḏīna kaḏḏabū bi-'āyātinā wa-'anfusahum kānū yaẓlimūna*

177: *man yahdi-l-lāhu fa-huwa –l-muhtadī wa-man yuḍlil fa'ūlā 'ika humu-l-khāsirūna*

178: *wa-la-qad ḏara'nā li-ğahannama kaṯīran mina l-ğinni wa-l- 'insi lahum qulūbun lā yafqahūna bihā wa-lahum 'a'yunun lā yubṣirūna bihā wa-lahum 'āḏānun lā yasma'ūna bihā 'ūlā 'ika ka-l-'an'āmi bal hum 'aḍallu 'ulā'ika humu l-ġāfilūna*

179: *wa-li-llāhi l-'amā'u l-ḥusnā fa-d'ūhu bihā wa-ḏarū llaḏīna yulḥidūna fī 'asmā'ihī sa-yuğzawna mā kānū ya'malūna*

VII, 176: Bad to be compared to are the people who have counted Our signs false, and who themselves have been wronging.

VII, 177: He whom Allah guideth is the (rightly) guided, and whom He sendeth astray—they are the Losers.

VII, 178: We have created for Gehenna many of the jinn and of mankind, hearts have they but they understand not with them, eyes have they but they see not with them, ears have they but they hear not with them. They are like the cattle, nay, they are further astray, these are the neglectful.

VII, 179: To Allah belong the most beautiful names, so call upon Him by them, and pay no attention to those who make covert hints in regard to His names. They will be recompensed for what they have been doing.

This verse has to be compared with Qur'ān XVII, 110—a similar verse—and this will show that it refers to the name Raḥmān which Muhammad used as a proper name for God. We will show that at first Christ, who will judge (the people) on the Day of Judgement, was called this way. Umayya knew it, but Muhammad, who had borrowed the term from the Christians, probably did not know it. Umayya revealed to the Qurayš the contradiction in which the Prophet was with himself, and he had to give up Raḥmān, and that after the formula "in the name [of Allah] the merciful Raḥmān" had already been generally adopted. Umayya introduced in his poems new and more suitable names for the goddess, like Silṭīṭ the sovereign. Instead of Muhammad's formula of invocation, he taught the Qurayš the more monotheistic one: "in Your name, o Allāhomm," which also came into common use and is still employed by Muslims nowadays.

VII, 180: Among those whom We have created is a community guiding by the truth, and thereby acting fairly.

180: *wa mimman ḫalaqnā 'ummatun yahdūna bi-l-ḥaqqi wa-bihī ya'dilūna*

This verse seems to refer to the accusation that he only teaches the belief of the *Ḥanīfs*, just as Umayya whom he condemned.

181: *wa-llaḏīna kaḏḏabū bi-'āyātina sa-nastadriğuhum min hayṯu lā ya'lamūna*
182: *wa- 'umlī lahum 'inna kaydī matīnun*
183: *'a-wa-lam yatafakkarū mā bi-ṣāḥibihim min ğinnatin 'in huwa 'illā naḏīrum mubīnun*

VII, 181: Those who have counted Our signs false We shall come stealthily upon from whence they do not know.
VII, 182: I shall treat them with forbearance, verily my craft is strong.
VII, 183: Have they not reflected? There is no madness in their friend, he is simply a warner clear.

The difference between Muḥammad and Umayya was to be found in the hysterical attacks which Umayya declared as obsession. But even if Umayya was rightly guided just as many others (v. 180), that is, he delivered the same doctrine, he more and more lost his way.

VII, 184: Have they not looked at the realm of the heavens and the earth and at the amount of things which Allah hath created, and that the possibility that their term may have drawn near? In what kind of discourse will they then thereafter believe?
184: *'a-wa-lam yanẓurū fī malakūti s-samāwāti wa-l-'arḍi wa-mā ḫalaqa llāhu min šay'in wa-'an 'asā 'an yakūna qadi qtaraba 'ağaluhum fa-bi-'ayyi ḥadīṯin ba'dahū yu'minūna*

Umayya seems to have been one of those jeering at Muhammad because of his claim to be sent in order to warn people against the upcoming punishment. Also verses 181 and 182 refer to this subject.

VII, 185: Whom Allah sendeth astray for him there is no guide, and he leaveth them in their arrogance blindly wandering.

VII, 186: They ask thee about the Hour, when it comes to port, say: etc.

185: *man yuḍlili llāhu fa-lā hādiya lahū wa-yaḏaruhum fī ṭuġyānihim ya'mahūna*

186: *yas'alūnaka 'ani s-sā'ati 'ayyāna mursāhā, qul . . . etc.*

When Muhammad says in verse 174 that God has given His signs to Umayya, this concession cannot be estimated high enough. This expression can be found many times in the Qur'ān, but only with reference to Abraham, Moses, and other admitted prophets, or refering to Muhammad himself, and it always means that God has given revelations. As we will see, the tradition says that Umayya hoped to become prophet of the Arabs. This passage seems to demonstrate that Muhammad compromises himself and that he recognizes him as a preacher of the true religion.

II[4]

From the *Kitāb al-Aghānī* vol. 1, p. 199: Umayya b. Abī al-Ṣalt 'Abd Allāh b. [Abī] Rabī'a b 'Awf b. 'Uqda b. Ghiyāra b. Qays (Thaqīf). His mother was Ruqayya, a daughter of 'Abd Šams b. 'Abd Manāf. Umayya had four sons: 'Amr, Rabī'a, Wahb and al-Qāsim.

"He was an excellent poet. Abū 'Ubayda says: The Arabs (Bedouins) are in agreement, that the residents of Yathrib (Madīna) are the most talented poets among all city-dwellers, second are the 'Abd al-Qays and third the Thaqīfites; among the latter Umayya was outstanding."

Al-Kumayt, who himself was a great poet, declared him the greatest of all the poets.

As all Arab master singers he made a living out of his art and composed hymns on rich people; among his benefactors he was singing the praise of Sayf b. Dhū-Yazan, ruler of Yaman; and 'Abd Allāh b. Ghud'ān from Makka is named.

From Ibrāhīm b. Ayyûb, from 'Abd Allāh b. Muslim:

> Umayya had read the old books of God (i.e., the revelations that preceded the Qur'ān) and he mentioned some things in his poems which the Arabs did not understand, e.g., the moon and Sāhūr are pulled out and put into the sheath.[5] He called God in his poems Salṭīṭ [from the same root as Sultān is derived from], e.g., the Salṭīṭ is almighty over the earth. Somewhere else he calles Him [God] Thoghrūr (according to a different manuscript Tho' rūr), e.g. may the Thoghrūr help him. Ibn Qutayba remarks that, since he chooses such arbitrary words, philologists do not take him into consideration.

From al-Zubayr, from Muṣ'ab b. 'Uthmān:

> Umayya had looked into the Bible and had read it and, in order to serve God, he put on a penitential robe. He was one of those speaking of Abraham and Ismael and the religion of the Ḥanīfs. He considered wine as prohibited, he doubted the idols, became a seeker (muḥaqqiq) and searched for *the* religion. He had a longing for being called to the office of the prophet, for he had read in the holy scriptures, that a prophet will rise among the Arabs and that they believed (according to a different manuscript "he believed"), that it would be him. When Muhammad had received his divine mission, Umayya was told: "It's him you have been waiting for and you have been talking about." But he envied him and said: "I have had the hope to be chosen." He is the enemy of God the Quranic words in Sūra VII, 174 refer to (see p. 78).

From Umayya are these words:

> On the day of Resurrection each religion will be a dread before God except for the religion of the Ḥanīfs ("dīn al- Ḥanīfa").

'Aṣma'ī says: "The most excellent theme of Umayya's poems is eternity; 'Antara sings war songs and 'Umar ('Amr?) b. Abī al-Rabī'a sings of the youth (i.e., love songs)."

From Zubayr, from Abū ʻAmr Šaybānī:

Abū Bakr, the Hudhaylite, asked ʻIkrima what he was thinking about the words which are put into the prophet's mouth: Umayya was a believer in his poems and an unbeliever in his heart. Ikrima answered: "This is true, what objection do you have to it?" The Hudhaylite replied that the following two verses were proving the opposite:

"The sun rises at the end of each night, first it is brown, then it becomes pink [because of anger]. Because it refuses to rise and only through harshness and force its hesitation can be overcome. It is certainly not true that the sun has to be stung like an ox." ʻIkrima answered: "I am swearing by Him, in whose power my life is, that 70,000 angels have to force the sun to rise, because it says: how should I shine on human beings who worship something else than God. And the devil tries to make it not rise. But God makes it float over the two horns of the devil, thus burning him. In the evening, when the sun sets, it first throws itself at God's feet in order to worship Him. The devil also appears, trying to alienate it, and God once again burns him under it. The words of the prophet allude to these circumstances: the sun rises between the two horns of the devil and it sets between the two horns of the devil."

From Aḥmad b. Muhammad b. al-Jaʻd, from Muḥammad b. ʻAbbād, from Sufyān b. ʻUyayna, from Ziyād b. Saʻd, from Ibn Ḥāḏir:

Ibn ʻAbbās and ʻAmr b. al-ʻĀṣī had a dispute in the presence of the Caliph Mu'āwiya. Ibn ʻAbbās asked his opponent: "Is that enough for you?" He replied "Certainly," and recited the verse:

At the end of each night (*sic!*) the sun dives into a hot spring and into stinking filth.

From Zubayr, from Muhammad b. Yaḥyā:

Umayya encouraged the Qurayš to fight after the battle of Badr and he composed epicedia [sad laments] on the killed. The following verse is from a poem which the prophet had forbidden to be transmitted: "Which Marzubān and great rulers are there near Badr and in the wide valley?"

> Umayya is claimed to have brought the expression "in your name, oh God (bismik Allāhomm)" to Makka, and the Qurayš put it at the beginning of their letters instead of [the expression introduced by Muhammad]: In the Name of Allāh, the merciful *Raḥmān*.

Ḥajjāj once said in a sermon: "The people, who knew the poems of Umayya, have passed away. In the same way this dispute will become silent."

From Zubayr, from 'Amr b. Abū Bakr Muammily and others:

> Umayya was searching for religion and had the desire to be chosen as prophet. One day he travelled together with several Arabs and Qurayš to Ṣām (Syria). They passed by a church and he said to one of his companions: "I have got something to do in this church, wait a little while." He entered and stayed in there for a long time. Finally he came out, and he was looking pale and grieved. He fell on the ground, and once he had recovered they continued their journey. After having completed their business in Syria they set out to return home. On the way he entered the same church again, and this time he also came out grieved, even worse than the first time. Then he told Abū Sufyān and his friends: "A Rāhib (ascetic) lives here, who told me, that there would be six periods (centuries?) after Christ, five of which had already passed and one was remaining. When this one is also completed, a prophet will rise from among the Arabs. I was longing to be this prophet. When I visited the Rāhib for the first time I was concerned that I would miss the prophethood. But the second time the ascetic told me that the sixth period had also been completed and that a prophet had already been chosen. So it was disappointed hope which made me so unhappy."

From Aḥmad b. 'Abd al-'Azīz, from 'Umar b. Šabba, from Khālid b. Yazīd:

> Umayya and Abū Sufyān made together a commercial trip to Syria (etc., as in the previous tradition, but with the addition): When he came back from the ascetic, he became grieved because of his questions. Abū Sufyān asked him about what had happened. He assured him that everything was all right, and he asked how old 'Utba b. Rabī'a was and how wealthy he was, and when he had answered his question he said: "I am subject to him." "No," Abū Sufyān remarked, "you are greater than him." "The man in question," Umayya said, "is neither old nor wealthy." The ascetic had

namely told him, that the prophet would be a Qurayš [and that is why he guessed it was 'Utba]."

Zuhrī says:

Umayya went on a journey. At one place he climbed a hill with a church on top of it. There was sittting a man, and when he saw Umayya he said: "A ghost (Rayy) visits you, from which side does he come to you, and which dress does he prefer when he comes to see you?" He answered: "He comes from the left hand side and he loves to be dressed in black when he comes to see me." The man remarked: "The one who comes to you is not the angel, but a *Khāṭir*, from the species of the jinn. For the angel approaches the prophet of the Arabs from the right hand side and is dressed in white clothes when he comes to see him."

Zuhrī also says:

Umayya came to Abū Bakr and said: "The matter looks suspicious, have you noticed something?" "No," Abu Bakr answered. "I have found out," Umayya replied, "that he will rise this year."

Abū al-Faraj, from his uncle, from Aḥmad b. al-Ḥāri', from Ibn A'rābī, from Ibn Dāb:

A Thaqīfī caravan travelled to Syria, and Umayya took part in it. On the way back they made a halt to have dinner. An Itzaya (some kind of lizard or chameleon) approached them, and one of the travellers threw something at its head and it ran away. After having finished their meal they wanted to continue their journey. Then an old woman came out from behind a sand hill, she leaned on her stick and said: "Why did you not feed the poor little animal?" They asked her who she was and she answered: "I've been a widow for years and I protect the insects in this pasture."

"But, o Lord of the servants in bands, let them be dispersed all over the lands."

Then she hit the ground with her stick and said: "Slow shall be your journey back home and your camels will not obey you any more."—There-

> upon the camels set off and, as if each one had a devil on its back, spread all over the valley. They managed to gather them the next evening. When they had prepared everything for the departure the old woman appeared again, saying and doing the same thing as she had said and done before, and with the same result. On the third day the same thing happened again. Then Umayya said to his companions that they should go and look for the camels, while he was going to deal with the old woman. He crossed the hill where she had come from and on the other side he discovered a church. Lamps were burning in it and a man with a white head and beard was lying at its entrance. When the man saw Umayya, he said to him: "Somebody follows you (i.e., you are possessed). From which side does your ghost come to you and which clothes does he tell you to wear?" Umayya said: "He comes to my left ear and tells me to dress in black." The old man answered: "The ghost is one of the jinn. A ghost, that brings pure revelations, always comes to the right ear and tells his man to dress in white." Then the old man told him, that the old woman was one of the Jewish jinn, whose husband had perished many years ago. "And she will continue with this prank until she destroys you if she can." "What can we do?" Umayya asked. He replied: "When she comes back, say seven times upwards and downwards: In your name, oh Allāhomm! And she will not be able to harm you." They did what he had told them to do, and the camels stayed calm. She said: "I know your man. Let him be white at the top and black down below." The next morning Umayya's cheeks were leprous and he was black down below. When they returned to Makka they told the story and since then the Makkans write in the beginning of their letters: In your name, o Allāhomm."[6]

Ṭabarī, from Ibn Ḥumayd, from Salama, from Ibn Isḥāq, from Ya'qūb b. 'Utba, from 'Ikrima, from Ibn 'Abbās:

> The prophet said: True are Umayya's words. Saturn is under his right and the Taurus under his left foot. The Eagle and the Lion are his viewpoint [German: warte].

This tradition is also told by Zuhrī, from 'Urwa, from 'Ā' iša:

Zubayr, from Ja 'far b. al-Ḥusayn Lahtī, from Ibrahīm b. Ibrahīm b. Aḥmad, from 'Ikrima:

> The prophet recited the following verses which are from Umayya:
>
> Praise to Allāh in the morning and in the evening. Our Lord has given as a happy morning and a happy evening.
>
> Lord of the religion of the Ḥanīfs, the principles of which will always be firm, the layers of the horizon are filled with your power.
>
> Is there not anywhere a prophet from among our midst who shall inform us about our limits, when to set out for our day-trip.[7]
>
> While our parents raised us, they passed away, and while we care for our children, we sink into the grave.
>
> We know (if only this knowledge would be of any use), that the current generation will soon be assembled with the elder generations.

Bukhārī, p. 540, from Sufyān Tawrī, from 'Abd al-Malik b. 'Umayr, from Abū Salama, from Abū Hurayra:

> The Prophet said: There is no word more true than the one that the poet said, the word of Labīd: "Is not everything vain except God? Umayya b. Abī al-Ṣalt was close to embrace Islam. He was a believer in his poems and an unbeliever in his heart."

From the *Kitāb al-Aghānī*:

> The Prophet said: "Umayya was close to Islam."

The external evidence proves the tradition as genuine. The close relationship between Umayya's and the Prophet's teaching on the one hand (the remembrance of which was preserved by this saying), and the enmity between them on the other hand, may have given rise to the legends according to which Umayya was influenced by a jinn—and not by an angel—and he hoped to be called to prophethood.

Kitāb al-Aghānī, from Aḥmad b. 'Abd al-'Azīz, from 'Umar b. Šabba, from Aḥmad b. Mu'āwiya, from 'Abd Allāh b. Abī Bakr, from Khālid b. 'Omāra. Also see Ḥamāsa p. 354:

Umayya reprimanded one of his sons in the following verses:

When you were a little child I fed you, and when you were a young man I looked after you.
Through my effort you had food and something to drink.
When the night brought pain to you, I could not sleep because of your suffering and I tossed and turned in my bed.
It was just as if it was only my concern, when misery hit you, and my eye dissolved in tears.
I feared evil could happen to you. I know that death will soon catch up with us.
After having grown up and reached that stage upon which I had pinned my hopes,
your behavior was full of harshness and rudeness just as if you would have been my benefactor.
If you do not bear in mind the demands, to which I have a right as your father, then you behave like a guest towards his protector, who harms him (the protector), as if it would be his assignment to impair righteous people.
You call me insane, whereas, if you have a real look at it, you yourself are guilty of insanity.

Zuhrī and also ʻAmr b. Abī Bakr, from a man from Kūfa, count:

Umayya was sleeping and two birds came. One of them sat down on the front door, the other one flew into the house and sat down on the sleeper's chest, opened it and pulled out the heart. The other one asked: "Is he mindful?" He answered: "Yes, but the heart is not pure (according to Zuhrī's version "is not receptive")." Both birds left after putting back the heart in its place.

In Zuhrī's version the story is more detailed. He is supposed to have said without waking up: "I am at your disposal and I am with you, I neither want to excuse myself nor call my relatives to help me against you." Thereupon one of the birds opened his heart and said: "It is not pure." This time Umayya said: "I am at your disposal, neither gold nor my relatives shall protect me from you." The birds looked at his heart two more times, and after each inspection he said similar verses.

From Ḥaramī, from his uncle, from Muṣ'ab b. 'Uthmān, from Thābit b. al-Zubayr:

> When Umayya was lying on his deathbed he said: "My last hour has come. I know that the religion of the ḥanīfs is true, but I am doubtful about Muhammad." He became unconscious, and when he had recovered, he said:
>
> "I am at your disposal, I am at your disposal, I am ready for you. Gold does not buy myself off and my relatives are not able to save me."
>
> Thereupon he fell unconscious again and the bystanders thought that it would be all over with him. Then he recovered and said:
>
> "I am at your disposal, I am at your disposal and I am ready for you. I am not free, so I could refuse, and I am not strong enough to resist."
>
> After he had fallen unconscious the third time he said: "I am at your disposal, I am at your disposal, I am ready for you. You have heaped me with acts of kindness. And if you have mercy, you have mercy upon everybody." Then he addressed to the bystanders and recited the following verses:
>
> "Each life, no matter how long it lasts, is short and has to come to an end.
>
> If I had only been on top of the mountains before this incident and herded wild goats.
>
> Face death and beware of the horrors of the time, for the time is a goblin."

Another story about Umayya's death is told by 'Abd al-'Azīz b. Aḥmad, Ubayy's uncle, from Aḥmad b. Yaḥya b. Tha'lab (in *Kitāb al-Aghānī*):

> When the prophet received his profession, Umayya took his two daughters and fled to the remotest region of Yaman. Then he returned to al-Ṭāyif, and while he was drinking hard with two of his brothers in the castle 'Aylān in al-Ṭāyif, a raven sat down on a battlement of the castle and croaked. Umayya said: "Dust in your throat!" His friends asked him about what the raven had said, and he answered, that it had announced him that once he would have emptied the cup he should die. The raven croaked again and

> Umayya repeated the same words and, at the same time, he indicated his friends that the raven would find a bone on the dung-hill underneath the castle and that he would choke trying to swallow it. This happened instantly, and when Umayya set down the cup he turned pale and said: "I am not free enough so I could refuse, neither I am strong enough to resist you"—and he passed away.

Zubayr b. Bakkār, from 'Abd al-Raḥmān b. Abī Ḥammād Minqarī:

> One time several people were sitting together with Umayya when a herd of sheep passed by. One of them bleated. Umayya said: "Do you know what it has said? It has warned its young one to beware of the wolf, so the wolf will not eat it, just as it ate its sister last year at the same spot." The persons present asked the shepherd if this ewe had a young one. He said: "Yes, and last year the wolf devoured one of its young ones right here."

'Abd Allāh b. 'Amr b. al-'Āṣ (d. 65), Sa'īd b. al-Musayyab, and Zayd b. Aslam claim that Qur'ān VII, 174 refers to Umayya b. Abī al-Ṣalt, the Thaqīfī. He had read the [holy] books and he knew that God would be sending a messenger at that time, and he hoped that he would be chosen. When Muhammad was sent, he envied him and continued to be an unbeliever. (Wāḥidī Asbāb VII, 174. Cf. also *Kitāb al-Aghānī*, vol. 1, p. 199, from al-Zubayr [b. Bakkār], from Muṣ'ab b. 'Uthmān.)

Baghawī, *Tafsīr* VII, 174, who also counts the above-mentioned words, adds:

> He had paid a visit to a king. On his way back he crossed the battlefield of Badr where there were still the dead lying around. When he heard that Muhammad had killed them he said: "May there be relatives of him among them!" After his death his sister Fārigha came to the Prophet, and he asked her about the death of her brother. She said: "When he was lying on his bed, two (angels) came down to him through the roof and one of them was standing by his feet and the other one by his head, and the first asked the latter one: "Does he remember? (i.e., does he know the truth?)" "He does remember." "Is his heart pure?" "He refuses—his will is malicious." Thereupon they left him, and after having recovered from his unconsciousness he said the following verses: "Any life, no matter how long it is, only lasts a while, then it ceases."

According to a more detailed version of this story,[8] the angels cut open his chest, examined his heart, and put it back in its proper place.

In order to appreciate the tendency of this myth and of those following it, it is necessary to compare them with the related myths about the purification of the Prophet's heart when he was still with his wet nurse Ḥalīme. That is, two angels came to the prophet when he was still a child, put him on the ground, pulled out his heart, and cleansed it of all sins. The purpose of the two myths is to point out that Muhammad's view was not different from that of Umayya, but Muhammad had a pure heart and not Umayya, and the difference between the two consisted in this fact. These legends are better evidence than any direct testimony that Islam had been preached in Mecca before Muhammad, that Umayya declared himself for it and propagated it strongly. But later Umayya revealed Muhammad's fraud.

Notes

1. [From A. Sprenger. *Das Leben und die Lehre des Mohammed nach bisher grösstenteils unbenutzen Quellen bearbeit*. Zweite Ausgabe. 3 Bände. Berlin, 1869. pp. 79–81; 110–19. Translated by Hans-Jörg Döhla].

2. [Part I: pages 76–81 of Sprenger, *Das Leben*.]

3. Single verses are preserved in several opus, and the reader can find some of them in the appendix. The only surviving complete poem—I know of—can be found in the Jamhara, Bibl. Spreng. 1215. The following verses are from Yaqūt's *Mu'jam* voce *Mujammas*: The signs of our Lord are visible. Only the unbelievers (kāfir) can doubt them. He chained the elephant in Mujammas, for on the Day of Resurrection all religions will perish before Allah except the religion of the Ḥanifs.

4. [A. Sprenger, *Das Leben*, pp. 110–19.]

5. During a lunar eclipse the moon is put into a sheath which is called Sāhūr. If this verse belonged to a poem that alludes to theology, the same idea may be expressed by this verse as we can read in the Qur'ān VI, 77. Sāhūr is an Aramaic form. In Arabic the first letter would be š, because in this language šar means "month, moon"; but in the north, in this case as in many others, s is put where the Arabs pronounce an š.

6. So far the traditions about Umayya are taken from the *Kitāb al-Aghānī*.

7. This verse is not clear to me and it could have a different meaning.

8. Cf. *Iṣāba* voce *Fārigha*.

1.3

A New Source of the Koran[1]

Clement Huart

Right from the beginning of research consecrated to the Koran, that is to say from the very dawn of Oriental Studies in Europe, it was quickly seen that it contained numerous passages obviously borrowed from the Old and New Testaments, but shortened, deformed, and mixed with stories from different sources. When one wanted to explain the manner in which these biblical texts had undergone these strange transformations and get rid of the fables with which the Middle Ages had surrounded the birth of Islam,[2] a mention of two journeys to Syria carried out by the future prophet was found in the histories; in Syria he had met a Christian monk named Bohaira or *Baḥīrā*,[3] whom one associated despite the difference in name with the Sergius preserved in the Christan tradition.[4]

It was in 583 that Muḥammad, while very young travelling in caravans for business with his uncle Abū Ṭālib, had met for the first time the monk at Bostra [Boṣrā], deep in central Syria. One presumed that this monk, it was not very well explained how, was his teacher, had introduced him to a knowledge of the two testaments, had recited to him the salient passages of the Bible, and that the memories of these Syrian conversations had come to light in the text[5] of the Koran in the form it was delivered to us by the Prophet's four secretaries and the commission for the revision of the time of the caliph 'Uthmān.[6] Later, during a second journey to Bostra [Boṣrā], Muḥammad, twenty-five years old at the time, just before his marriage to the rich businesswoman Khadīja, had had with the same monk new meetings whose result had been the definitive idea for a project for religious reform.[7]

The only conclusion that we can draw from the Arabic texts which have since been found, published, and studied is that the role attributed to the Syrian monk is but pure fantasy. Already, at the end of the 18 th century, we had the history of Abu'l –Fīdā', which J.J. Reiske had translated into Latin in Leipzig in 1754, while waiting for the edition of *Annales Muslemici*, published by Adler in Copenhagen between 1789 and 1794. Now, Abu'l –Fīdā' is content with expressing himself thus: "Baḥīrā said to Abū Ṭālib: Take this boy back (Muḥammad was then thirteen years old) watch over him with regard to the Jews for something important is going to happen to your nephew." In the second journey, there is no longer any mention of the monk.

The merit of having shown all that was legendary in the two journeys to Syria belongs to Aloys Sprenger,[8] and he went as far as asking himself if these caravans had really taken place.[9] First of all, he had encountered the name Baḥīrā in a list of delegates from the Negus, while Muḥammad was in Medina, about forty years later, and he concluded from this fact, as well as from a misunderstood sentence of the historian Wāqidī [747–823], that Baḥīrā had accompanied the caravan on its return to Mecca and had remained in this city.[10] The criticisms of Fleischer and Wüstenfeld[11] seem to have made an impression on Sprenger's mind, for he had another look at the question in a long note in his biography of Muḥammad, where he is led to consider the two journeys to Syria as one and the same legend,[12] which would have had as meager a foundation as the caravans accomplished by the future prophet when he was working for Khadīja, which did not take him beyond Sūq-Hobācha in the Tihāma and Ghorach in the Yemen. Besides, according to the traditionist Zuhrī, Baḥīrā was the name of a Jew of Tayma and not a Christian of Bostra [Boṣrā].[13] Meanwhile, all trace of the monk Baḥīrā is not lost; except it is not in Syria but in Mecca itself that we find him. We see Khadīja going to ask his advice after the first visions which announced the mission of Muḥammad. Sprenger even asked himself if it was not he [Baḥīrā] who had spread the doctrine of the *ḥanīfs*, or followers of the religion of Abraham in the Arabian capital.[14] A little later the same author portrays Baḥīrā as belonging to the Raḥmāniyya, that is to say, to those ascetic Christians who called God, ar-Raḥmān, the Compassionate.[15]

However seductive may have been the idea that the sight of the practice of the Christian religion had vigorously acted on the mind of the young reformer,[16] it was necessary to abandon it in the face of the uncertainty of the historical foundations. M. Nöldeke had, for his part, arrived at the conclusion that the fragments of the Old and New Testaments inserted into the Koran were due to the oral communications issuing from the Jews established in the towns of Arabia and from the Arab converts to Christianity more or less orthodox, who encountered each other while quite numerous, even in the nomadic tribes of the north of the peninsula.[17] But instead of being linked to Syria, this penetration of Arabia was connected above all to Mesopotamia. In fact, we now know the influence of the Christians of Ḥīra, the Arab town built on the edge of the Syrian desert, almost on the site of the later flourishing town of Kūfa (these two cities are today in ruins, and of them there is scarcely a trace), on the circulation of religious ideas in the interior of the Arabian peninsula. It was the 'Ibāds or Nestorian Christians of this town, of a mixed population, composed of Arabs of the most diverse tribes, who were the agents of this propagation. The Arab poets made their way readily to Ḥīra to which they were attracted by the celebrated generosity of Nu'mān and Mundhir, as they had been by the Ghassanids, the phylarchs of the Roman frontier of Syria. The poet 'Adi b. Zayd was an Ibadite. G. Jacob[18] and Wellhausen[19] have shown that the commerce in wine and the running of wineshops were the means by which Judeao-Christian ideas had penetrated the desert, for it was the Jews and 'Ibādite Christians of Ḥīra who dealt in wine and ran the wineshops. In this way the biblical legends were recounted in the bars, and we know, from a passage in the *Kitāb al-Aghānī*,[20] that the religious ideas of the pre-Islamic poet al-A'shā, one of their faithful clients, were acquired in this way.[21]

It was thus in the taverns that the Gospel was preached to uncouth minds who were just beginning to take an interest in intellectual life. The poet al-Nābigha al-Dhubyānī had sung the praise of Solomon, his dominion over the jinns who constructed Tadmur (Palmyra)[22] for him; he had the idea of the unity of God, and of His sublimeness in relation to other beings, and consciousness of the responsibility incurred by acts and oversights. It is undeniable that these ideas had prepared the way for Islam:[23] can one go further and recognize in the very text of the Koran traces of this influence?

Sprenger was the first to cite, among the oral sources where Muḥammad could have derived a part of his information, the pre-Islamic poets, and in particular Zayd b. ʻAmr b. Nufayl, who long before the Hijra had attacked the cult of idols in Mecca. But Sprenger encountered criticism which tried to show that he was deluding himself on this particular point. Nöldeke[24] thinks that he is going too far in concluding from a fragment of a sermon of Zayd which has survived and which resembles considerably the style of the Koran, that Muḥammad had borrowed not only his doctrine but also his expressions. For him the poems of Zayd cited in the biography of the Prophet by Ibn Hishām and in the *Kitāb al-Aghānī* are not authentic and bear the marks of the work of a Muslim who would have used passages from the Holy Book to rework them, and that with the intention of showing that the religion of Islam was not new in Arabia, only the logical conclusion of the religion of Abraham supposedly practiced from time immemorial by the monotheists of the Arabian peninsula. This criticism is specious, it merits our attention, we will come back to it shortly.

Among these poets, the influence of Umayya ibn Abī al-Ṣalt has always been considerable. Already Sprenger has said precisely the following: "The influence of the poetry of Umayya, who was so loved that the poems stayed for a long time on the lips of the people, despite the order of the Prophet not to spread it, must have been immeasurably large."[25] It is a personal idea; it is not a proof, not even the beginning of a proof. A recent publication is going to allow us to specify more precisely the ideas expressed by Sprenger.

I want to talk about the *Book of Creation and History* by al-Maqdisī,[26] a work written in Arabic probably in Sijistan, the ancient Sistan in East Persia, in 355 AH/966 CE, which has preserved no less than 135 verses of Umayya's, most of them totally unknown before. These verses are in the majority devoted to the poetical adaptation of passages from the Bible, and are going to allow us to study once again the question of the influence of pre-Islamic Arabic poetry on the composition of the Koran.

I.

Umayya, the son of Abī al-Ṣalt, belonged to the Thaqīf tribe and was originally from the town of Ṭāif, in the Ḥijāz, not far from Mecca. We do not have precise details about the period of his birth, but if take note with Sprenger that in 624 he was composing satires against Muḥammad who was then fifty-five years old, he could hardly have been older than the Prophet. He died in 630, eight years after the Hijra. Toward the year 572, Umayya himself, unless it was his father who also was a poet, was part of the delegation sent by the Qurayshites to the King of Yemen, Sayf, son of Dhū–Yazan, and had congratulated him for his victory over the Abyssinians. He wore a cilice out of devotion; he forbade the taking of wine and did not believe in idols. He had read the books and followed the Judeo-Christian doctrines; his poetry centered in general on religious subjects borrowed from the common foundation of these doctrines.[27]

One even wanted to consider Umayya a truly Christian poet. Reverend Father Louis Cheiko of the University of Saint-Joseph in Beirut tried to show that Umayya was one, but he did not succeed in providing a proof of it.[28] He cited among his authorities Wellhausen; the learned professor of Göttingen did in fact say: "Due to their turn of mind, Umayya and Labid (who later converted to Islam) were at least equally Christian";[29] but he does not quote a single source, and besides note that it is only "due to their turn of mind" that they are to be considered Christian; this is a judgment of literary criticism, not a scientific demonstration.

In the verses of Umayya that the author of *Book of Creation* has transmitted to us, there is a passage which could be decisive if one were sure of the moral to draw: "There is in *your* religion an edifying miracle, that of the Lord of Mary, whose servant Jesus was. . . ."[30] The poet is addressing the Christians, and is not their co-religionist. Only if the original reading were *wa fī dīni-nā*, "in our religion"; instead of *wa fī dīni-kum* (the two being prosodically equivalent), would it on the contrary be an explicit confession of his Christian beliefs. But how can one authorize such a correction? One cannot easily imagine a Muslim copyist, having in front of him a text showing that the poet was Christian, changing the lesson of this text in order to make one believe that he was not; what would be his interest in that?

The whole of the Muslim middle ages knew perfectly well that 'Adi b. Zayd, among others, was Christian; a copyist had never made this qualification disappear, a qualification which accompanied his name, for example, in *The Book of Creation*.[31] As to Umayya, "all the historians are agreed that he died pagan" wrote the author of *Khizānat al-Adab*.[32]

"The Arabs are agreed, "said Abu 'Ubayda, "that among town-dwellers, those who have the greatest gift for poetry are the inhabitants of Yathrib (Medina); then come the tribes of 'Abd al-Qays and Thaqīf; and by common consent also, the best poet of the latter is Umayya." Al-Kumayt has expressed this opinion: "Umayya is the best poet, for he has said the same things as us, and we have not said the same things as he."[33]

"Umayya," said Mus'ab b. 'Uthmān, "had looked at the books and had read them; he used to wear a cilice out of devotion. He was one of those who mentioned Abraham, Ismail and the religion of the ḥanīfs;[34] he forbade the use of wine, and had had doubts about the idols; he was looking for the truth and called for the true religion; he strongly desired to receive the calling of a prophet, for he had read in the books that a prophet would receive a mission among the Arabs, and he hoped that it would be him. When Muḥammad received this mission, they said to the poet, 'Here is the one you found so long in coming and of whom you used to talk about.'" When the enemy of God [Satan] made him envious, and made him say, "I alone wanted to be that." That is when this passage from the Koran was revealed, where it says [VII.174] "Recite to them the tale of him to whom We gave Our revelations, and who turned away from them."[35] It was also he who said :"On the day of resurrection, all the religions will be false in front of God, except that of the ḥanīfs."[36]

Umayya never compromised with the new religion preached by Muḥammad. "After the battle of Badr, he continued to rouse the Qurayshites for the struggle; he delivered the funeral oration for the dead killed in this battle. It is a poem whose recitation was forbidden by the Prophet."[37]

"It is also claimed that it was Umayya who suggested to the inhabitants of Mecca to put at the top of their letters the formula: "*Bi-ismika –llāhumma*, In your name, O Great God!" where the Muslims use the following: "In the name of God, the Compassionate, the Merciful."[38]

The life of Umayya is surrounded by legends. They depict him going to visit the churches in Syria: "Umayya was looking for the [real] religion and wanted to receive the prophetic mission. He became partners with some people from the bedouin tribes and the Quraysh, and together they set off for Syria to trade and do business. He came across a church, and said to his companions: 'I have business in this church, wait for me.' He entered and took time in coming out; then he came out all confused, his face altered; he dropped to the ground and his companions waited until his worries had passed. Finally, they all left, finished their business and got ready to head home. On passing near the same church, Umayya said to them, 'Wait for me,' and he entered the chapel, from which he re-emerged after a long wait in a worse state than the first time. Abu Sufyān b. Ḥarb then said to him:

"'You are putting your companions in an embarrassing position.'

"'Leave me,' replied the poet, 'for I want to go back alone. There is a learned monk here who has taught me that there will be six *returns*[39] after Jesus; five have passed and there is only one left; as it happens I want to be a prophet and I am afraid that the mission will slip through my fingers; that is why you saw me in such a state. On our return, I had been to see the monk who told me, "the return has just taken place, an Arab prophet has received the prophetic mission." Thus I was desperate to be a prophet, and you have seen what happened to me when I was certain that what I had desired had escaped me.'"[40]

The most extraordinary stories about him were circulating. It was claimed that he understood the language of animals. One day, he was sitting with some people; a herd of sheep passed by, a ewe began to bleat: "Do you know what the ewe said? No, they replied. She said to her little one: Come quick I am afraid that the wolf will come and eat you as he devoured your sister last year in the same place. One of those present got up, approached the shepherd and asked him: Tell us about this ewe which was just bleating; does it have a lamb? Yes, here it is, replied the shepherd. Did it have another one last year? Yes, he said, and the wolf ate it up in the same spot."[41]

His death is surrounded by circumstances no less strange. One version, which goes back to the traditionist al-Zuhrī, paints the poet as falling asleep on a seat, in a corner of the house of his sister; the roof opened, and two birds descended, one of which perched on his breast and tore out his heart and slit it, pronouncing the mysterious words that only the other bird understood.

"Has he remembered? asked the first one.—He has remembered—Has he accepted?—He did not want to." Then he put back the heart in its place and flew off; this scene was repeated three times, and each time Umayya cried: "Here I am at your call, here I am near you." Then, recounted his sister, the roof closed and Umayya sat up rubbing his chest. She said to him: "My brother, do you feel anything?" "No," he replied, "I just feel some heat." Then he composed the famous verse:

"Would to God that before anything happens to me I would be busy grazing the goats on the summit of mountains!

"Place death before your eyes and beware of troubled times, for the times have their misfortune."[42]

The verses of Umayya were above all consecrated to religious subjects; we have the testimony of grammarian al-Aṣma'ī, who used to say: "Umayya has dedicated the majority of his verses to the description of the future life; 'Antara to war, 'Umar b. abi Rabī 'a to juvenile passions." But these verses had the misfortune to disappear almost entirely, and to be extant only as isolated fragments in rare antholgies or in great works of lexicography. Nevertheless a diwan or a complete collection of his poetry, accompanied by a commentary of Muḥammad b. Ḥabib still existed before the year 1682: it was seen by 'Abd al-Qādir al-Baghdādī, who quotes it;[43] but we are not acquainted with it. We are obliged to keep to the great *qaṣīda* of thirty verses, classed in the category of *Mujamhara* by the *Jamharat ashār al-'Arab* of pseudo-Abū Zayd Muḥammad b. Abi'l Khaṭṭāb al-Qurayshī,[44] whose existence had been pointed out a long time ago by Sprenger, who had in his library a manuscript of this work;[45] to the elegy on the death of the Qurayshites fallen at the battle of Badr, to which we referred above; and to a quite large number of small fragments of poems and isolated verses that we come across in the *Kitāb al-Aghānī*, in the *Sīra* of Muḥammad by Ibn Hishām, and in some other works.

Now the extant fragments all have a common characteristic (except for a piece of verse on Luth and Sodom given by Yāqut and Qazwīnī and certain isolated verses quoted in the dictionaries), that is they do not have the least connection with the biblical legends.

On the other hand, all those verses that are included in the text of the *Book of Creation* deal precisely with these legends; and, if they are authentic, the long unknown author of this work has rendered us a great service by transmitting the verses of the old Arab poet fallen early into obscurity.

The objection of Nöldeke regarding the verse of Zayd b.'Amr that I quoted earlier is equally relevant for the verses of Umayya. Are the latter authentic? What guarantee do we have that they could go back to this pre-Islamic poet? Were they touched up by the grammarians of the school of Kūfa and of Basra? Were they even entirely fabricated, as the German critic thinks of the verses of Zayd b. 'Amr, by means of passages borrowed from the Koran, by some Muslim desirous of creating for the religion of Muḥammad titles of nobility, in associating it with the traditions that we know exsisted among the Jews and Christians, possessors of undeniably holy books? Here we have a problem whose terms should be closely examined.

II.

What proofs do we have of the authenticity of pre-Islamic Arabic poetry? Directly, none.[46] This poetry was not written, it circulated by word of mouth, and when one dared to go and look for them in durable form, it was already too late; a century had passed since the preaching of Islam had launched the nomads of the desert on the old states of Asia of former times. A century, three generations, that is a long time.

The confidence that we can have in those who went to collect the remains of this ancient poetry is most mediocre. Ḥammād al-Rāwiya was the son of a Persian of Daylam, made a prisoner during the wars, who called himself Sābūr (Sapor). Though born in Kūfa, Ḥammād betrays, by his faults of language, his foreign origin. But he had an extraordinary memory; he knew by heart thousands of Arabic verses and entire poems. His learning extended to the legendary history of the pre-Islamic Arabs, to genealogies of which the Bedouin were so proud, to various dialects. He knew how to distinguish between the ancient and modern style; he boasted of being able to recite a hundred long odes rhyming with each letter of the alphabet.[47] Now, this marvellous instrument of recitation himself composed verses; Mufaḍḍal al-Ḍabbi accused him of mixing his imitations with the verses of the ancient poets, in such a way that one could no longer distinguish between them, and it was even claimed that pressed by the Caliph al-Mahdi, he had confessed to his forgeries. Such was the man to whom we owe the preservation of a large part of pre-Islamic poetry; it is to him we are indebted for collecting into a book the seven poems of the Mu'allaqat.[48]

Khalaf al-Aḥmar was no less dubious. Said to be originally from Khurasan, he was descended from the captives of the time of the raids of General Qutayba b. Muslim, the conqueror of Turkistan; he was thus of Iranian origin like Ḥammād. He was experienced and skilled in writing verses; he produced them in the pure language of the bedouin, and he attributed them to the poets of the desert.[49]

Abū 'Amr Isḥāq b. Mirār al-Shaybānī, who lived more than a hundred years, died in 821 or 828 CE, collected the poetry of more than eighty different tribes, and was, for the traditions concerning Muḥammad, the master of the famous jurist Aḥmad b. Ḥanbal, the founder of the Hanbalite school. All the grammarians wanted to gather together the poetry of the desert: Khālid b. Kulthūm al-Kufi, al-Asma'ī and his student Abū-Sa'īd al-Sukkarī († 888), Ibn al-'Arabī and his disciple al-Ṭūsī (Abū-l Ḥasan 'Ali b. 'Abdallah b.Sinān al-Taymī), Ibn al-Sikkīt, and finally Muḥammad b. Ḥabīb, who collected and published the anthology of the poetry of Farazdaq, and who had also anthologized the poetry of Umayya. He was the student of grammarian Quṭrub and son of a freed slave (for Ḥabīb was the name of his mother) of the family of 'Abbās b. Muḥammad; he died in 861. He was considered a learned genealogist, well-versed in the history of the Ancient Arabs and their days or battles, and as a precise and truthful traditionist worthy of confidence.[50] He, at least, did not forge, it seems, verses of his own making in order to attribute them to the Pre-Islamic poets.

In short, everything rests on the confidence that we can have in the sincerity of such and such grammarian or storyteller, and we have just seen that, for the oldest, it is more than suspect. Thus we must look for another way.

To call in question the authenticity of the poems of Zayd b. 'Amr, we relied on their resemblance to passages in the Koran, and we concluded that they had been reworked or even entirely fabricated by a Muslim. This argument, if it is valid, will be entirely applicable to Umayya, for the passages in his poems which offer these resemblances. In that case a question arises: is it permitted for a Muslim to quote in his verses passages of the Holy Book, and under what conditions?

The polymath Suyūṭī has consecrated a section of chapter 35 of his marvellous work of Koranic exegesis, *al-Itqān*,[51] which is the basis of our knowledge in this matter, to plagiarism, that is to say to borrowings from the Koran that are permitted, either in prose or in verse; here is how he expresses himself: "Plagiarism consists in inserting, into pieces of verse or prose, parts of the Koran, on condition however that they do not form an integral part of the verse or prose and that they be separated from the text of the author by these words: "God on High has said," or other analogous expressions; otherwise it is prohibited, it is not an authorized quotation: *lā 'alā 'annahu minhu bi-'an lā yuqālu fīhi qāla l-lāhu ta'ālā wanaḥwa -hu*. It is well-known that the Mālikites forbid it absolutely and ostracize from the Muslim community anyone who was guilty of it; as to those of our school (Suyūṭī was Shāfi'ite, like the majority of Egyptians), the ancients did not indulge in it, neither did the majority of the moderns, although at that time these borrowings had been popularized and practiced by the poets, formerly and recently."

A little later, the authorities that he cites lead him to the conclusion that "this procedure is allowed in sermons, in acts of grace, in prayers, in prose, but nothing shows that it could be permitted in verse. There is in fact a difference, and the Mālikite *qāḍī*, Abū Bakr has established clearly that it is authorized in prose, but disapproved of in verse. The *Qāḍī* 'Iyāḍ used it also in several passages in the preface to *Shifā'*[52] (*khuṭbatu l- Shifā'i*). Sharaf al-dīn Ismā'īl b. al Muqri'al-Yamanī, author of *Mukhtaṣar al-Rawḍa* and other works, said in his commentary of his *Badī'iyya*: "What we come across in prayers, sermons, eulogies of the Prophet, of his family and his companions, is lawful, even in verse; otherwise it is to be rejected."

In the commentary of *Badī'iyya* of Ibn Ḥijja,[53] we find the following: "Borrowing is of three kinds; that which is acceptable, that which is permitted, and that which is rejected. What is acceptable is what we find in homilies, sermons, covenants; that which is permitted is what we find in erotic poetry, small treaties, short stories; as to what is rejected, there are two sorts: the first comprises the words of God where He Himself takes charge. May God preserve us from him who would attribute the words of God to himself, as was apparently the case with one of the *Marwānid* caliphs who added the following note on a document which contained a complaint against his agents: 'It is towards you that he should go back, then it is for us to settle the account.' (Koran LXXXVIII.25–26). The second is the insertion of a verse with the intention of mocking (May God preserve us from that!) 'This is a good classification, adds Suyūṭī, and I shall adopt it.'"

Suyūṭī was writing at a time when Islam had long since become rigid, which singled it out, and what he says of the legitimacy of the use of Koranic phrases in verse or in prose can scarcely elucidate the subject that concerns us. What could appear to be a condemnable sin in the fifteenth century was only a venial sin under the first 'Abbāsids, and if we were to go back as far as the Umayyads (and we know the bluntness with which they treated the Koran), we would quickly recognize that there was little understanding to be got from this exercise. But we have not finished with the *Itqān* yet.

Suyūṭī consecrated an entire chapter of his treatise on exegesis, chapter 36, to what Muslims call the "*gharīb*," the strange, that is to say strange expressions, rare, dialectical or even foreign that one meets with in the text of the Koran.[54] The second part of this chapter treats of the relationship between Arabic poetry and the Sacred Prose:

"Abū Bakr Ibn al-Anbārī says the following: 'Frequently the companions of the Prophet and their successors relied, to explain the difficult and strange expressions of the Koran, on the poetry; a crowd of ignoramuses denied the grammarians the right to do so, for the reason that if one employed this procedure one would be led to make of the poetry the source (or origin) of the Koran: "How can we use it to explain the Sacred Text, they said, when the poetry was the object of the disapproval of the Koran itself and of the traditions of the Prophet?"' 'But it was not like that,' continues Ibn al-Anbārī, 'for we did not make the poetry the source (or origin) of the Koran, but on the contrary we wished to explain by the poetry the strange expressions, for God Himself has said: "We have made a Koran (a recitation) in the Arabic language" (Koran, XLIII.2, and passim) and in another passage: "In a clear Arabic language" (Koran, XXVI.195). Ibn 'Abbās, moreover, has said: "The poetry is the register (*Dīwān*) of the Arabs." If then an expression seems to us obscure, we have to consult this register, demanding an explanation of which we have need.'"

After having established the legitimacy of turning to ancient poets to explain the difficulties of the Koranic text, Suyūṭī gives in their entirety a long series of examples drawn from the two works, the *Kitāb al-Waqf* of Ibn al-Anbārī[55] and the great dictionary of al- Ṭabarāni.[56] This passage is known under the name of "questions of Nāfi' b. al-Azraq," and here is how the scene is painted: "While 'Abd-Allāh b. al-'Abbās[57] was sitting in the parvis of the Ka'ba, the crowd surrounded him to pose him questions about the interpretation of the Koran. Nāfi' b. al-Azraq said to Najda b. 'Uwaymir: 'Let us get up and go and find this man who dares to interpret the Koran by things of which he does not know the first word.'" They got up and approached 'Abd-Allāh b. al-'Abbās and put to him some difficulties of interpretation that he resolved without any trouble; each time that Nāfi' asked him "if the Arabs [of the desert] know this expression," Abadallah replied by quoting a verse from an ancient poet. Now, among these verses, there were ten that were from Umayya b. Abi aṣ Ṣalt. All the same, we find this scene of open-air exegesis rather affected and artificial,—if it is not true, there is nothing unlikely about it, given the extraordianry memories of these people who wrote rarely,—one fact emerges from it which seems certain is that the verses which are quoted there do not appear to have been contrived for the needs of the cause, and that in all the cases one did not hesitate, at the time where this scene is placed, that is to say, the second half of the first century of the hijra, by authors who are of the third century, to go and look in the common treasure of bedouin poetry for the expressions which, in the text of the Koran, seem strange and difficult to explain.

All the preceding does not provide proof of the authenticity of the poetry of Umayya, but the presumptions in favor of this thesis are accumulating. To take a further step, it is time to pass onto the essential examination of the verses themselves.

III.

The history of the prophet Ṣāliḥ and his she-camel, placed at the site of Madāyin- Ṣāliḥ, in the heart of Arabia,[58] is recounted in the Koran; one had even thought that this legend was a creation of Muḥammad because we do not come across any trace of it earlier.[59] However, we now have, thanks to

The Book of Creation, some verses of Umayya that are consecrated to the same legend. If the latter blindly follow the text of the Koran, it is probable that they were fabricated later; if they offer noticeable divergences, there is a possibility that we find ourselves in front of an earlier document.

This legend is recounted in several places in the Koran. The oldest passage is chapter LIV (Mecca), verses 23–31, where the name of the prophet Ṣāliḥ is not given: "We shall send them a female camel as a test. . . . Inform them that the water in their cisterns must be shared between them and the she-camel, each drink to be taken in turn." The Thamūdis called one of their fellow tribesmen, who drew his sword and killed the she-camel. "We sent upon them one shout, and they became as the dry twigs of the sheep-fold builder."

Chapter XXVI (Meccan) speaks to us of the same legend in different terms, very concise. The Thamudis asked for proof of the mission of Ṣāliḥ; their prophet replied, v. 155: "Here is this she-camel. She shall have her share of water as you have yours, each drinking on an appointed day." Because the she-camel was drinking all the water destined for the tribe they plotted her downfall. The Koran does not say it expressly; but this explanation is in all the commentators and even in histrorians like Ṭabarī. In chapter XXVII (Mecca), verses 46–54, it is no longer a question of the she-camel at all; the people of Thamud are divided into two parties who are quarrelling with each other; nine individuals promise under oath to attack the prophet Ṣāliḥ and his family unawares during the night; but God foils their stratagems and destroys them.[60]

In chapter XI (Mecca), verses 64–71, the legend returns in more or less the same terms as in the most ancient version; it is a question of "the she-camel of God";[61] the time granted the Thamūdis is three days. Finally, in chapter VII (Mecca), verses 71–77, God sends to the Thamūd tribe the prophet Ṣāliḥ, who, as proof of his mission, indicates this "she-camel of God," which had been sent by the Deity. The chiefs, carried away by pride, killed the she-camel and asked [ironically] Ṣāliḥ to bring about the punishment that he had threatened them with; then they were overcome by a great shock, and in the morning they were found stretched out on the floor of their houses, dead.[62]

One realizes that nowhere is the legend explicit, but that Muḥammad procedes by means of allusions to a legend, already known before him; how could one have supposed that it had been invented by him? The commentators, to explain these obscure passages to some non-Arabs who had never heard of these lovely stories, must have supplemented them by details, which surely they did not invent either.

In Umayya,[63] the people of Thamūd "treat religion according to their fantasies, out of arrogance"; the reason for their destruction is the same as the one in the Koran (VII.73), but the word used is not the same. There are new features, which play an important part, as for example the young camel that accompanies its mother and that, after the death of the she-camel, "approached a rock and stood on it, emitting a cry to the sky which went beyond the rocks. It uttered a cry, and this cry of the young camel, directed against them, was the following: May you be destroyed!" This young camel, which plays a role in a later form of the legend, is nowhere mentioned in the Koran. As to the last three verses, they are difficult to understand, because the lessons of the only manuscript of *The Book of Creation* are visibly bad; but what emerges from it is that they have nothing to do with the Koran:

"They were all suffering, except the maid-servant (?) from the rapid walk, who escaped and who was earlier restive.

"It was the shell of a fruit (?) which was sent to give their news to the people of Qorḥ and to inform them that one evening they were scattered.

"They gave her something to drink after her tale, and she died: here our task is ended, that the humble servant has carried out."

We should note that

1. there is mention of a new character of whom there is no trace in the legend hitherto, neither in the shortened form of the legend to be found in the Koran nor in the elaborations added to it later; that this character be a slave or an animal is of no importance;
2. that the inhabitants of Qorḥ, the other town of Arabia, south of Al-Ḥijr, are named as having received the news of the destruction of the Thamūdis;
3. that the above-mentioned character dies at the end of the story.

We seem to have there a continuation of the legend, known to Umayya but of which Muḥammad and his commentators remained ignorant.

It should be noted that there is a point of contact between the verses of Umayya and the most ancient form of the Koranic legend (LIV.29): it is a sword that the Thamūdi uses to cut the tendons of the she-camel, whereas later it is an arrow that Qodar uses, for tradition has retained this name, which figures neither in the Koran nor in the verses of Umayya (where he is called "a little red man"; it is his traditional nickname, for the Thamūdis and Ṣāliḥ himself, their compatriot, had red skins[64]); the mention of the sword figures equally in a fragment of poetry that seems ancient, quoted without the author's name in *The Book of Creation*[65]; but one must add that the last verse mentions the time limit of three days, in such a way that the latter feature could well have been borrowed from the Koran.

In the Koran, the legend of Loth follows immediately that of Ṣāliḥ. In Umayya, it is part of a different verse. These two forms of the same story have a common feature in the punishment of Sodom: "A punishment" says Umayya, "which put the earth upside down, [*ja'ala l- 'arḍa sifla-hā 'a'lā-hā*] and He (God) unleashed on the earth a wind full of gravel [*biḥāṣibin*], then mud mixed with pebbles [*ḏī jurūfin*] (variant: with letters—*ḥurūf*—marked by a sign (*musawwam*)."[66] The Koran XI.84 says, "We turned it upside down, and We caused to rain on her bricks of baked earth, falling continuously and marked [*musawwamatan*], coming from God Himself "[*ja'alnā 'āliya-hā sāfilahā*]. In the underlined passages, the same words are used. The expression *biḥāṣibin* corresponds to *ḥāṣiban* in Koran LIX.34. In other passages of the Sacred Book, there is no more than: "We rained down on them a shower" [VII.81; XXVI.173; XXVII.59], and "We are going to bring down a punishment from the sky on the people" [XXIX.33]. Muḥammad had forgotten the details of the legend.

In the middle of the account of the flood, which appears twice in the Koran, Sura XI and Sura XXIII, we come across an odd expression that early on had attracted the attention of the commentators and had extremely embarrassed them. XI.42: "At length when our command came, and water welled out of the Oven, We said [to Noah] Take into this vessel two of each species. . . ." [*hattā 'iḏā jā'a 'amrunā wa-fāra t-tannūru qulnā ḥmil fihā min kullin zawjayni ṯnayni . . .*].

XXIII. 27: "Then when Our command comes and the oven gushes over, introduce into the ark a couple. . . ." [*fa-'iḏā jā'a 'amrunā wa-fara-t-tannūru fa-sluk fihā min kullin zawjayni ṯnayni. . . .*]

This oven that boils over, and from which comes forth the water of the deluge, is difficult to explain; notice how Muḥammad speaks of it as something already known. The commentator Bayḍāwī[67] says: "The water wells up from this oven and rises as in a saucepan which is boiling. It is a baker's oven where the water begins to rise up, unusally. This oven was at Kūfa, on the site of the mosque of this town, or in India, or in 'Ayn –Warda, in Mesopotamia. . . . It was said to Noah, apparently,[68] 'When the water will boil coming out of the oven, climb [into the ark] with your companions.' When the water began to well up from this oven, his wife averted him and he got on board. The site of this oven was in the mosque of *Kūfa*, to the right of the entrance, near the gate of Kinda. It is also claimed that it was at 'Ayn –Warda in Syria [read: in Mesopotamia], and they give further explanations which I have mentioned above."

This bizzare expression, which is repeated twice in the Koran, is encountered in Umayya, who has consecrated no less than three pieces of verse describing the Deluge. We come across this passage in the first piece of verse: "When God fanned the oven of the earth,[69] it began to boil while heavy rain swept over it." And in the second: "Its oven bubbled and boiled over, the mass of water covered the mountains and exceeded their summits."[70] The similarity is flagrant; nevertheless one cannot draw any conclusions from it to elucidate the question of the mutual priority of the two documents.

The expression *al-taġābun*, mutual cheating, to characterize the day of the Last Judgment, is found in the Koran only once: LXIV.9; later on one sought it out to make it the title of the Sura. This expression had been used by Umayya[71]: "On the day of mutual cheating, while the precautions will be of no use."

Umayya[72] has left us a long description of Heaven and Hell (23 verses) where one finds Koranic expressions. I am not talking of common words like *jahannum*, (Gehenna), and *'adn* (Eden), borrowed as such from Hebrew and that one finds in the Koran normally, but specific and strict resemblances. We note first of all that there are no points of contact between the two descriptions of hell, and that no expressions that are used in the Koran to depict it, for example in the older suras revealed at Mecca,[73] are to be found in the verses of Umayya; from which emerges the great probability of the authenticity of the latter, and which we cannot claim to have been refashioned in the manner of the Koran. In the Koran, the fire of hell consumes all and lets nothing escape it; it burns the flesh of man; nineteen angels are put in charge of it; the damned will drink boiling water and will not have any food other than the acrid fruit of a thorny shrub, which will emaciate them and will not calm their hunger; besides the boiling water, there will be pus. In Umayya, in the third verse, we find the grinding of the teeth that reminds one of the Gospel according to St. Matthew,[74] and in the fifth this explicit declaration: "The damned are swirling round in it like fine dust." The rest is too obscure for us to be able to turn it to account, but one sees clearly that there are traces of two different sources.

On the other hand, in the description of Paradise, the similarities are abundant. The chosen, according to Muḥammad, "are reclining on the couches; round among them are passed vessels of silver and cups of crystal, filled with a drink the admixture of which is ginger, drawn at the fountain of Salsabīl. They will be covered in garments of green satin and brocade, adorned with bracelets of silver."[75] In another passage,[76] "they are relaxing on couches adorned with gold and jewels, at ease and reclining facing each other; they are served by boys of perpetual youth with goblets, jugs and cups filled with a liquor whose vapour does not give a headache or befuddle their reason; they will have as much fruit as they desire and the flesh of birds to their hearts' content, near them will be houris with beautiful black eyes." A little further, it is a question of *men on the right* who will sojourn among the lotus trees without thorns and banana trees laden with fruit. To the banana trees are added palm trees and pomegranate trees.[77] In this garden flow rivers whose water never goes stale, and rivers of milk that do not alter in taste, rivers of soft wine, rivers of pure honey.[78] Such is the oldest description of Paradise in the Koran.

In Umayya we also find the houris: "Virgins with black eyes that do not see the sun, on figures of statues, but slim . . . tender on their nuptial bed, of narrow waists." The chosen are clothed in silk and brocade, adorned with bracelets of silver and precious stones. Finally, "there is a cup of wine which does not give any hangovers, and which the fellow-guest contemplates such is its beauty. This wine is refined in bowls of silver and gold consecrated and full to the brim." We find among the delights of Paradise honey, milk, and wine, among the fruit: dates, pomegranates, bananas; but there is more:

"some wheat, piled up on the site of production, some apples, and finally lamb's meat." In this raising of the stakes, the prize goes once more to the poet. But this last passage is essential to show the authenticity of the poems of Umayya contained in *The Book of Creation*. If they had been refashioned later under the influence of Muslim ideas and traditions, as one suspected for Zayd ibn 'Amr, one would not have introduced wheat, apples, and lamb's meat, which are not mentioned in the Koran, or in the commentaries on the Holy Book.

IV.

We had more or less agreed up to now to look for, since Sprenger, the origins of Muslim doctrine in Ebionism. Islam is related to Judeo-Christian sects, says Harnack, who has summarised previous research,[79] either popular Judeo-Christianity, more properly speaking Ebionism, or Gnostic Judeo-Christianity, above all the Elkesaites of Syria and Palestine, one of whose envoys, Alcibiades, had come to Rome at the time of Pope Calixte (c. 200 CE) where he had known St. Hippolyte and perhaps even Origen. The *Fihrist* still points to the existence of this sect in the tenth century, under the name *mughtasila* (so-called because they washed everything, even what they ate); the name of their founder was al-Ḥasīḥ.[80] This sect exists to this day, for they are the Mandaeans, Sabians, or Christians of John the Baptist, of which there are still some communities on the banks of the Euphrates and Tigris, as well as in the region of Basra.[81] The principle points of resemblance that connect the Ebionites to the Muslims were revealed by Harnack: not only do they allow marriage, they advocate it; the use of wine is forbidden; they replace the unique baptism by frequent washings and attach a great importance to it. Their founder boasted of a new revelation, consistent with earlier revelations that extend from Adam to Christ, but superior to the older ones, possessing a new book, fallen from the sky or brought by a huge angel (both versions exist in the sources). Al-Ḥasīḥ is the true prophet, who had already revealed himself in the person of the patriarchs. They have a special veneration for the members of the family of the founder. St. Epiphane speaks to us of the two sisters, Marthus and Marthana, worshipped like goddesses in their country because they belonged to al-Ḥasīḥ's family. This sect, for their prayers, turned not toward the East but always toward Jerusalem.

In this summary, it is easy to see that the history of the development of Muslim dogma is not taken sufficiently into account, and the connections that it offers us are not for this reason entirely convincing. Thus the veneration manifested with regard to the family of the Prophet is a specifically Shīʿī idea, whose development is due to the legitimism of the Iranians and their veneration for their former kings, and whose point of departure is historically the conquest of Persia by the Arabs; there is no question of such veneration within the confines of the Arabian peninsula at the time of the foundation of Islam. The successive incarnations of al-Ḥasīḥ in the person of various patriarchs is equally a Shīʿī idea that we find in the doctrines of the Nusayris. The propensity for frequent sexual intercourse, precisely the opposite of the Christian ideal of chastity, found among the Muslims, comes, it seems, rather from the example set by the Prophet than that the idea was taken by him from some earlier doctrine. As to the prohibition of using wine, the frequent ablutions (five times a day for the ritual ablution), the superiority of the new religion over the ancient ones, these are indeed traits of the Muslim religion, but they are not entirely original to it and are not enough to prove that the Muslim religion is connected to Ebionism. There is only one detail that connects primitive Islam to this Judeo-Christian sect, which is that both had taken Jerusalem as their direction for prayer, and not the rising sun.

Julius Wellhausen has taken up this question once again in his *Reste arabischen Heidentums*.[82] It is certain that the opponents of Islam right at the beginning of Muḥammad's preaching, applied to him and his proselytes the term "*ṣābi'*," Sabean, probably because of their frequent ablutions; it is a nickname that one gave them to mock this custom, which seemed extravagant to habitants of the desert. The Muslims are connected to the ḥanīfs and are quite happy that one gives them this title, but who are the ḥanīfs? This name designates during the Pre-Islamic period the ascetics, hermits or penitent Christians; the term was borrowed from them by the monotheist Arabs who wanted to distance themselves from the mass of the idolatrous population. One can understand that Muḥammad did not hesitate to call himself a ḥanīf, that is to say a follower of the original religion of Abraham. Such is, concludes M. Wellhausen, the means by which the Koranic revelations came: the relations of Muḥammad with the heterodox Christians of Mecca whose preaching and example had prepared for him the way.

In a celebrated passage in the Koran, LV:13, God says, "He created man from clay like pottery." [*khalaqa l-'insāna min ṣalṣālin kal fakhkhāri*] This expression is not to be found anywhere else in the Koran; it figures, on the other hand, in a verse of Umayya's that has been preserved for us by the *Djamhara*: *wa qāla 'ummayyat b.'abī l-ṣalt: kayfa l-juḥūdu wa -'inna-mā khuliqa l-fatā min ṭīni ṣalṣālin lahu fakhkhārun al-ṣalṣālu mā tafarraqa mina l-ḥ am'ati fa-takūnu lahu ṣalṣalatun 'iḏā wuṭi'a wa-ḥurrika wa-huwa qawlu-hu 'azza wa-jalla*: *'khalaqa l-'insāna min ṣalṣālin kal fakhkhārin* [Umayya said: "How can there be any doubt: it is from potter's clay that a young man is created; the *ṣalṣāl* is what separates itself from the wet clay and gets a ring to it after it is kneaded and pounded. This is as He is forever exalted and elevated: He created man from clay like pottery."]

But we must compare it to an analagous passage in the Coptic Apocrypha: "Having taken the virgin earth, we shaped it like potter's clay, we blew on his face."[83] That led me to check whether, in the Coptic Apocrypha, we could not find the origin of expressions common to the Koran and Umayya, and in particular whether the description of the delights of Paradise, even more developed in the latter than in the former, did not come from Coptic documents, but "in no Coptic Apocrypha is there a question of provisions in Paradise; the idea is much more elevated."[84]

At the time of Muḥammad, there was a small colony of Egyptians in Mecca, and one knows of the part played by a Coptic carpenter in the reconstruction of the Kab'a by the Qurayshites, but in the absence of conclusive documents, one must abandon the search for some elucidation in this direction.

V.

The preceding pages indicate that between the Ebionite, Mandaean, or Coptic ideas that flourished in the towns of Arabia, and the religion founded by Muḥammad, one must take into account an intermediate element on which we have up to now only some insignificant data, which is taking shape with the verses of Umayya conserved by *The Book of Creation*. These are the poets who have traced out the way to Islam among the pagan population of towns and desert, and who have supplied to the Koran if not the totality, at least a large part of the poetic expressions that it contains; the idea put forward by Sprenger and strongly criticized regains all its importance. Certain ideas of which we cannot find any trace in Christian literature, even apocryphal, are derived from these poets, who form the necessary link that was missing up to now, and which attaches the Judeo-Christian ideas to Islam.

CONCLUSIONS

The biblical poetry of Umayya, given by the author of *The Book of Creation*, are authentic, because they include details, notably in the description of Paradise, which are lacking in the text of the Koran.

The expressions that are common to *The Book of Creation* and the Koran come, in consequence, from Umayya; it seems then agreed that, as Sprenger thought, the pre-Islamic poetry of the ḥanīfs, and in particular that of Umayya, is one of the sources of the Koran.

It is possible that it was he who aspired to play the role of the Arab prophet who had given to the doctrines of the Ebionites a more decisive and more material than spiritual direction, out of which he created Islam; as it is also possible that he had only to translate into beautiful verse the ideas that were current in the sect to which he belonged, and that he wished to popularize among the Bedouin tribes.

The striking resemblance of those of Umayya's poems that were consecrated to religious subjects to the analogous passages in the Koran was the cause of the increasing disfavor that they encountered in the Muslim world, whose doctrines, very fluid at the beginning for everything that was not expressly foreseen by the text of the Holy Book, only crystalized little by little under the influence of writers and theologians whose authority culminated in being admitted, first by a more and more numerous group, finally by the quasi-totality of the believers.[85] These poems resembled the Koran far too much, which is what killed them.

NOTES

1. Paper read at a meeting of the Académie des Inscriptions et Belles-Lettres on 22 April 1904. [Published in *Journal Asiatique* 1904, July–August, pp. 125–67. Translated by Ibn Warraq. Footnotes in square brackets by I. W.]

2. See especially chapter VIII of *Historia mahumetica* of St. Pierre Paschasius [1296–1300], the martyr of the Order of Sainte-Marie du Rachat des captifs (c. 1300 CE) and the *Teatro della Turchia* of Michelis Febure [M. Febvre, *Théatre de la Turquie*, Paris, 1682], cited by Ludovico Maracci, *Prodromus*, t. I, p. 232 ff [*Prodromus*, first part of *Alcorani textus universus*, Padua, 1698, though the *Prodromus* was also published first in Rome in 1691]. Cf. Vincent de Beauvais, *Miroir historial*, ed. of 1531 CE vol. IV, fol. xlvii r°: "Sicome who was in the prime of life was a merchant who used to go often to Egypt with his camels, and to Palestine with Jews and Christians, from whom he learnt the Old and New Testament and became a perfect charmer."

3. The form Baḥīrā is already in Maracci, op. cit., Vita, p . 78 and t. I, pp. 245, 257; but J. Gagnier, *Vie de Mahomet*, 2 vols., Amsterdam, 1732, t. I, p. 121, has Bohaira.

4. Maracci, op. cit., t. I, p. 232; "As if Sergius the Monk had sinned seriously in his monastery, and was excommunicated and expelled for this sin; he arrived in the land of the Arabs as far as Mecca . . . [Muḥammad] learnt of this monk certain things of the Old and New Testament, and these he mixed with fables and lies in his Koran . . . ," Vincent de Beauvais, *Miroir historial*, vol. IV, ch. li, fol. IV. Cf. Joachim Mantzel, *Spicilegium . . . historia literarium Alcorani sistens*, Rostock, 1701 (unnumbered pages).

5. Abu'l –Fīdā', *Annales*, ed. Constantinople, t. I, p. 119. Cf. Ibn al-Athīr, *Kitāb al-Kāmil fi-ta'rīkh*, vols. 1–14, ed. C. J. Tornberg, Lugduni Batav, 1867–1876, t. II, p. 26, and Tabari, *Annales* [History] I, p. 1124 ff.; Mas'ūdī [died c. 956 CE], *Les Prairies d'Or*, ed. B de Meynard and P. de Courteille. 9 vols., Paris, 1861–1877, t. I, p. 146. Cf. Mas'ūdī, *Livre de l'Avertissement et de la revision*, trans. Carra de Vaux, Paris, 1896, p. 305. In the latter work Mas'ūdī mentions the two voyages in Syria; in the first took place the meeting with Baḥīrā; in the second the monk is called Nestor. This is an effort by the historian to reconcile the two pricipal versions of the legend.

6. Noel Desvergers [1805–1867], *Arabie*, Paris, p.138: "It is on this voyage, it is claimed, that Muḥammad, admitted into a Christian monastery was welcomed . . . by a Nestorian Monk . . . who . . . introduced him for the first time to the Old Testament, which Muḥammad later used as a base for his new religion."

7. Desvergers, *Arabie*, p. 139.

8. Aloys Sprenger, *Das Leben und die Lehre des Mohammad*, 2nd ed., 3 vols., Berlin, 1869.

9. Already these voyages had been denied or put in doubt by Erpénius in his *Oratio de lingua arabica*, p. 45, quoted by Maracci, *Prodromus*, t. I, p. 267; but J. Gagnier, *Vie de Mahomet*, t. I, p. 121 has shown in a note that this opinion of Erpénius' originated entirely from the silence of al-Makīn on this point. [George al-Makīn, 1205–1273 CE, *al-majmu' al mubarak*, translated into Latin by T. Erpénius, Leyden, 1625.]

10. A. Sprenger, *The Life of Mohammed*, Allahbad, 1851, p. 79.

11. *ZDMG*, t. III, p. 454, and t. IV, pp. 188, 457. See Sprenger's reply in the *Journal of the Asiatic Society of Bengal*, 1853.

12. Aloys Sprenger, *Das Leben und die Lehre des Mohammad*, 2nd ed., 3 vols., Berlin, 1869 t. I., p. 188.

13. Ibid., p. 192.

14. Ibid., p. 304.

15. A. Sprenger, *Das Leben* . . . , t. II, p. 210.

16. This idea was explored in detail by William Muir, *The Life of Mahomet*, 4 vols., Edinburgh, 1858–1861, vol. 1, p. 34ff.

17. T. Nöldeke, *Geschichte des Qorans*, Göttingen, 1860, p. 5ff. For the Jewish tradition compare Hartwig Hirschfeld, *Jūdische Elemente in Koran*, Berlin, 1878, p. 68. . . . This oral source could be 'Abdallah ibn Salām, Jewish scholar of Mecca, and those around him (op. cit., p. 25). On the latter see Ibn Hishām, *Sīrat Rasūl Allāh*, ed. F. Wustenfeld, 2 vols., Göttingen, 1858–1860, p. 387. One refers to, among the Christians of Mecca, two makers of sabres, Djabr and Yasār, who used to read the Torah and the Gospel, of whom the former is perhaps the same person as Djabr the Greek [Djabr al-Rūmī], the slave of 'Amr ibn al-Ḥaḍramī (Bayḍāwī, *Anwār al-tanzīl wa-asrār al-ta'wil*, ed. H. O. Fleischer, 2 vols., Leipzig, 1846–1848, t. I, p. 527). They had been accused of being the teachers of Muḥammad in matters of religion, and the Koran replies to them by Sura XVI, verse 105. Compare Baghawī in Sprenger, *Das Leben*, t. II, pp. 388–89. On the Jewish sources, see also the lecture of Dr. Werner on "Mohammed und das Judentum" given before the Oriental Society of Munich and summarized in *Asien*, t. II, 1903, p. 147. Dvorak, *Ueber die Fremdwörter im Koran*, Vienna, 1885, p. 24 (supplementary volume of *Sitzungsberichte de l'Académie des Sciences de Vienne*, 1885, t. CIX, 1 livr., p. 481ff.), and the new study of M. Hirschfeld, which unfortunately I was not able to consult, *New Researches into the Composition and Exegesis of the Qoran*, Asiatic monographs III, London, 1902 (reviewed in *JRAS*, Jan. 1903, p. 227).

18. G. Jacob, *Altarabisches Beduinenleben*, 2. Aufl, Berlin, 1897, p. 99.

19. J. Wellhausen, *Reste arabischen Heidentums*, Berlin, 1927, p. 231.

20. Al-Farag al-Isfahānī, *Kitāb al-Aghānī*, Cairo, 1905, t. VIII, p. 70 [*Aghānī*, hereafter].

21. G. Rothstein, *Geschichte der Laḫmiden* [G. Rothstein's *Die Dynastie der Lakhmiden in al-Hira*, Berlin, 1899], p. 26.

22. Wolff in *ZDMG*, t. XIII, p. 702.

23. G. Rothstein, *Geschichte der Laḫmiden*, p. 25.

24. T. Nöldeke, *Geschichte des Qorans*, Göttingen, 1860, p. 14.

25. Aloys Sprenger, *Das Leben und die Lehre des Mohammad*, 2nd ed., 3 vols., Berlin, 1869, t. I., p. 78.

26. Published and translated by M. Clément Huart, in the publications of the Ecole des langues orientales vivantes; 3 vols., 1899–1903. This work was for a long time attributed to the philosopher Abu Zayd Aḥmad ibn Sahl al-Balkhī; the name of the real author was established in the *Journal Asiatique*, IX série, t. XVIII, 1901, p. 16 [Al-Maqdisī, Muṭahhar ibn Ṭāhir (pseudo-Balkhī), *Al-Bad' wa'l-ta'rīkh (le Livre de la création et de l'histoire)*, ed. and trans. by Clément Huart, 6 vols., Paris, 1899–1919].

27. Cf. C. Huart, *Littérature arabe*, Paris, 1902, p. 24.

28. *Al-Machriq*, t. IV, p. 573; cf. t. VI, p. 573.

29. J. Wellhausen, *Reste arabischen Heidentums*, 2nd ed., Berlin, 1927, p. 233.

30. Al-Maqdisī, Muṭahhar b. Ṭāhir (pseudo-Balkhī) *Al-Bad' wa'l-ta'rīkh (le Livre de la création et de l'histoire)*, ed. and trans. by Clément Huart, 6 vols., Paris, 1899–1919, t. III, p. 123 of text, and p. 127 of the translation. [Referred to as *The Book of Creation* hereafter.]

31. *The Book of Creation*, t. I, p. 140 of translation.

32. Ibid., t. I, p. 122 of text: wa-lam yakhtalif 'aṣḥābu l-'akhbāri 'anna-hu māta kāfiran.

33. *Aghānī*, t. III, p. 187.

34. Monotheist Judeo-Christians who claimed to be of the religion of Abraham.

35. Cf. Bayḍāwī, *Anwār al-tanzīl wa-asrār al-ta'wil*, ed. H. O. Fleischer, 2 vols., Leipzig, 1846–1848, t. I, p. 35, where this passage is reproduced almost word for word.

36. *Aghānī*, t. III, p. 187.

37. *Aghānī*, t. III, p. 187. This poem is found in the biography of Muḥammad by Ibn Hishām, *Sīrat Rasūl Allāh*, ed. F. Wustenfeld, 2 vols., Göttingen, 1858–1860, p. 53; it is written in the same metre and same rhyme as a poem by the poetess al-

Khansa; cf. the remarks of Nöldeke, *Beitrage zur Kenntniss der Poesie der alten Araber*, Hanover, 1864, pp. 170, 174.

38. *Aghānī*, t. III, p. 187.

39. In Arabic *raja'āt*; a gloss in the margin of a manuscript carried over to the margin of the printed edition indicates that this term is the equivalent of six centuries.

40. *Aghānī*, t. III, p. 188; there are two versions of this legend, one coming from al-Zubayr (and that is the version we have just given), and the other from Khālid ibn Yāzīd. . . . A third, covered with the authority of the traditionist al-Zuhrī is different: the poet climbs a sand dune, sees behind it a church where he finds an old man who asks about his [the poet's] familiar demon (the djinn which inspired the poets of the desert) and explains to him [to the poet] that he [the poet] cannot become the Prophet of the Arabs because his demon is a djinn and not an angel, and because he prefers black clothes to white.

41. *Aghānī*, t. III, p. 188.

42. *Aghānī*, t. III, p. 190. In a second version, which cites the authority of Thābit ibn al-Zubayr, there are no birds but only the formula: Here I am, etc. His death took place after three fainting spells. It is perhaps the primitive form of the legend of the birds. In a third version, a crow explains to the poet that he will die when he will have drunk the cup that he had in his hand, while the bird choked itself with a bone that he took from a rubbish heap.

43. 'Abd al-Qādir al-Baghdādī [died 1682], *Khizānat al-adab wa –lubb lubāb lisān al-'arab*, 4 vols., Cairo, AH 1299/c. 1881 CE, t. I, p. 119.

44. *Jamharat Ash'ār al-'Arab* [collection of Bedouin poetry, complied under a fictitious name, but quoted as early as the eleventh century by Ibn Rashīq] Bulaq, AH 1308/c . 1890 CE, p. 106.

45. Sprenger, op.cit, t. I, p. 77 n. 1.

46. On this question, see Nöldeke, *Beiträge zur Kenntniss der Poesie der alten Araber*, Hanover, 1864, pp. I–XXIV, and W. Ahlwardt, *Bemerkungen über die Aechtheit der alten arabischen Gedichte*, Greifswald, 1872.

47. C. Huart, *Littérature arabe*, p. 58.

48. Cf. W. Ahlwardt, *Bemerkungen über die Aechtheit der alten arabischen Gedichte*, Greifswald, 1872, p. 13ff.

49. Cf. the *Fihrist* [the List], translated by de Slane, in Ibn Khallikan, *Biographical Dictionary*, 4 vols., Paris–London, 1843–1871, t. I, p. 572; Ibn Qutayba, *Kitāb al-Ma'ārif* [Handbuch], ed. F. Wustenfeld, Göttingen, 1850, p. 270; G. Flügel, *Die grammatischen Schulen der Araber*, Leipzig, 1862, p. 56; Ahlwardt, op. cit., p. 15.

50. *Fihrist*, p. 68.

51. [al-Suyūṭī, *al-Itqān fī 'ulūm al-qur'ān*, Cairo, 1306, Calcutta, 1852–1854.]

52. ['Iyāḍ b. Mūsā al-Qāḍī, *Kitāb al-Shifā'bi-Ta'rīf Ḥuqūq al-Muṣṭafā*, Constantinople, n.d., also 1329, Cairo, 1276, 1312, 1327.]

53. [Ibn Hijja, *Taqdīm Abī Bakr* (A Commentary on his *Badī'yya* called *Khizānat al-Adab wa-Ghāyat al-Arab*), pr. Calcutta 1230, Būlāq 1273, 1291, Cairo, 1301.]

54. An author of the beginning of the fourth century AH, Abū Bakr Muḥammad ibn 'Umar ibn Aḥmad ibn 'Uzayr as-Sidjistānī, who was still living in Baghdad in 330 AH [941 CE] composed a dictionary of these terms under the title *Gharīb al –Qur'ān* [the *Strange in the Quran*]. Cf. Josef Feilchenfeld, *Ein einleitender Beitrag zum gharib al-Kuran*, Vienne, 1982; De Slane, *Catalogue des manuscrits arabes de la Bibliothèque nationale*, I, pp. 590, 591.

55. The same work as *Kitāb al- īḍāḥ*; cf. C. Huart, *Littérature arabe*, p. 152.

56. Abū 'l-Qāsim Sulaymān, died 971 CE.

57. The cousin of the prophet, nicknamed "the Interpreter of the Quran" by Ibn *Mas'ūd*. Normally he is known as Ibn *'Abbās*; he is the sole authority for many traditions. Cf. Nawawī, p. 351; compare the appreciation of Sprenger, *Das Leben*, I, p. XVII, and III, p. CVI.

58. Al-Ḥijr, the ancient Egra. Cf. Philippe Berger, *L'Arabie avant Mahomet*, Paris, 1892, p. 10

59. T. Nöldeke, *Geschichte des Qorans*, Göttingen, 1860, p. 15, n. 2.

60. One can note in passing that in the two examples the history of Sāliḥ is followed by that of Loth; it is truly the habit of Arab poets, who pass from one subject to another without transition.

61. *Nāqatu l-lāhi a*; cf. *Nāqatu l-'ilāhi* [she-camel of Allah] in Umayya, "The Book of Creation," t. III, p. 41 of text, I. 1.

62. The City of Tombs of *Madāyin Ṣāliḥ* and its magnificent Nabataean tombs were taken for houses in the popular imagination. Cf. P. Berger, *L'Arabie avant Mahomet*, p. 18.

63. "The Book of Creation," t. III, p. 42.

64. Ibid., p. 39

65. Ibid., p. 41

66. Ibid., p. 60, and p. 59 of the Arabic text.

67. Bayḍāwī, *Anwār al-tanzīl wa-asrār al-ta' wil*, ed. H. O. Fleischer, 2 vols., Leipzig, 1846–1848, t. I, p. 434. Compare Ṭabarī, *Tafsīr*, 30 vols., Cairo, 1321, AH/ 1903 CE, t. XII, pp. 23–24, who gives three explanations: 1. the water began to flow

over the surface of the earth, the Arabs of the desert saying *tannūr l-'arḍi* to designate the surface of the earth; 2. the illumination in the morning, connecting *tannūr* to *tanwīr*, a simple popular etymology; 3. taking *tannūr* in the sense of "bread oven"; it is the latter that Ṭabarī prefers because this word is taken with its normal meaning, and is not forced.

68. Bayḍāwī, *Anwār al-tanzīl wa-asrār al- ta' wil*, ed. H. O. Fleischer, 2 vols., Leipzig, 1846–1848, t. II, p. 4.

69. The text reads "of his land," that is, of his country, that of Noah. However it is printed, "it began to boil," but it is the oven that is meant in the text and not the earth.

70. "The Book of Creation," t. III, p. 26 of the translation and pp. 24–25 of the text.

71. Ibid., t. II, p.133 of the translation and p. 145 of the text.

72. Ibid., t. I, p. 190 of the translation and p. 202 of the text.

73. Suras: LXXIV:26–34; LXXXVIII:1–7; LXXXVIII:21–30.

74. Matt. VIII:12; XIII:42; XXII:13; XXIV:51; XXV:30.

75. Sura LXXVI:12–21.

76. Sura LVI:12–39.

77. Sura LV:68.

78. Sura XLVII:16–17.

79. *Christliche Parallelen zum Islam*, Vortrag des Herrn Prof. Dr. Harnack, in *Leipziger akademische Docentenverein*, XVI, 1877–1878, p. 18.

80. *Al-Nadim al- Fihrist*, ed. G. Flügel, Leipzig, 1871, I. p. 340. The reading *al-Ḥasaīḥ* for *al-Ḥasīḥ* [Arabic] of the Arabic text is due to D. Chwohlsohn [Daniel Chwolson, born 1819], "*Die Ssabier und der Ssabismus*," 2 vols., St. Petersburg, 1856, t. II, p. 543, after the Greek Ηλχασαι.

81. The same communities as the Hemerobaptists of St. Epiphanus, an identification put forward already by Johan David Michaelis [1668–1738], *Syriaca Grammatica*, Halle, 1784, p. 17. Cf. also E. Babelon, *Les Mendaïtes*, extracts from *Annales de philosophie chrétienne*, 1881, p. 10ff.; J. Wellhausen, *Reste arabischen Heidentums*, 2nd ed., Berlin, 1897, p. 237.

82. J. Wellhausen, *Reste arabischen Heidentums*, 2 ed., Berlin, 1897, pp. 236ff.

83. Coptic documents quoted by E. Reveillout, *Journal Asiatique*, X ser., t. II, 1903, p. 167.

84. Personal communication from Mr. E. Reveillout.

85. See on this subject, my paper, "Sur les variations de certains dogmes de l'islamisme aux trois premiers siècles de l'hégire," read at the International Conference of the History of Religions in 1900 (Actes du ler Congrès, 2e part., p. 37 ff., and in *Revue de l'historie des religions*, 1901).

1.4

Umayya b. abi-Ṣalt[1]

Friedrich Schulthess

Sprenger tried, years ago, to collect through his reading of the tradition the relics of the *homines religiosi* before and at the time of the Prophet. He has had no successors, notwithstanding the material having accumulated and its incorporation in the research being a prerequisite for any serious endeavor to trace the origins of Islam. A historical-critical treatment of the indirect sources is insufficient, since the tradition had no interest in commemorating obscure or heretical believers, and even less in keeping alive the memory of their relations with nascent Islam. What has come down to us of their poems, our only direct source, is extremely scant, often forged, censored, or somehow arranged to fit Islam; coming from the circle close to the Prophet himself, they are, however, important enough to demand detailed research. Umayya heads the list of the men to be taken into consideration. He has not received much attention from us so far. Sprenger's view required immediate revision, the most recent of which, by Clement Huart,[2] I only agree with—to declare it immediately—to a very limited extent. He seeks to prove that "Umayya's" biblical or legendary poems quoted in Ps.-Balkhī's "Book of Creation"[3] are all genuine and, in their convergent passages, the Koran's direct source. There is much to take issue with in Huart's line of argument; it is possible to show that he gives too much authority to his source, al-Maḳdisī, to give his real name,[4] who adopted any obscure poem that came his way.—However, I do not intend to write a critique, but to examine, taking Huart's contribution into account, whether the tradition is capable of offering us any credible or concrete information[5] about the *ʾumayyatu l-badī'*.[6] The limited space must excuse the fact that I will confine quotations from the material to the strictly necessary and will generally be brief.

Information about U. is not scarce, but often of no value. The tradition's divergence in the assessment of U., which will be shown later on, is proof that genuine facts have always been a problem. Thus the *Dīwān* annotated by the well-known Muḥammad b. Ḥabīb (†245/859) is lost, apart from a few fragments preserved by al Bagdādī;[7] but it may be a consolation to know that it already contained serious false attributions.[8] Sources worth noting, alongside Ps.-Balḫī and the generally known works, include al Ǧāḥiẓ's *Book of Animals*, I. Kaṯīr's *Bidāja*,[9] which devotes an entire chapter to U., and the dictionaries that contain important special material.

The following biographical details are worth mentioning. U.[10] was born in Ṭāifer, the son of the locally renowned poet Abu-ṣ Ṣalt (ʿAbdallāh) and Ruḳajja bint 'Abd Šams b. ʿAbd Manāf, so closely related to the Meccan aristocracy and a cousin of ʿUtba and of Šaiba, Abū Sufyān's uncle, who were killed at the Battle of Badr. His sister 'Ātika, alias Fāriʿa,[11] was engaged by the Prophet in a memorable conversation after the surrender of the city of Ṭāif, while he had her brother Huḏail executed (Wāḳidī translation 369). U.'s four sons were ephemeral poets; the Prophet provided one of them, Wahb, with a property.[12] One of his grandsons obtained a position as a public official under ʿUṯhmān.[13] Authentic evidence for U. having been alive in 624 can be found in the laments (handed down by I. Isḥāk 531 et seq.) mourning respectively the Ḳurayshites[14] killed in action at Badr and the Asadites Zama'a and ʿAḳīl. According to tradition, he lived for several more years (8 or 9 AH).[15] Even if he reached a great age, in year two of the Prophet's birth (according to the genealogy given above) he was still too young to have been part of the Meccan deputation dispatched to congratulate Saif b. Ḏi-l Jazan, in the role of official orator or poet, alongside such notables as 'Abdal Muṭṭalib and Umayya b. 'Abd Šams. If there is any truth at all regarding this deputation, in which case at least the glorification of the Prophet's family *Aġ.* 16, 75[16] would have been a later addendum, U. should probably be replaced by his father or grandfather, the former with several, the latter with Masʿūdī,[17] unless there has been a simple confusion with the Umayya mentioned, to whom is attributed (*Aġ.*, Azrāḳī) the verses *Aġ.* 16, 77 that are linked with the congratulatory poem[19] Hiš. 44 = *Aġ.* 16, 75. The poems do not provide any biographical or other historical details. Only a few personalities feature in them. Like al-Ḥuṭai'a,[20] he repeatedly[21] sings of the generosity of 'Abdallāh b. Ǧudʿān, whose fabulous adventures (Damīrī I, 214) had made him as powerful in Mecca as his debauchery had made him notorious.[22] It appears that the Prophet himself took advantage of this man's great hospitality without being put off by the prospect of his damnation.[23] Further on, he mourns Ḥarb b. Umayya,[24] who died of malaria in peculiar circumstances while travelling for business, or, as one imagined, was killed by the startled djinns of the swamp.[25] The (Muslim) Umayya legend also includes this, making him part of the caravan and having Ḥarb slain by the djinns in revenge for the killing one supper time of a troublesome reptile. The main point, however, is U.'s formulation of باسمك اللهم on this occasion and its subsequent introduction by him to Mecca.[26] He does not learn this from the Jews but from a Christian hermit as a charm to ward off the Jewish female djinns. According to the legend—which I take to be generally known—this journey was the defining event of his life. The Rāhib recognizes his inspiration, but the *tābiʿ* or *ṣāḥib* is no angel, but rather a djinn, since he whispers into his left ear and prescribes black instead of white clothing.[27] U's dismay grows as he learns from him that, according to the calculations (six centuries after Christ), the Prophet should already have been awakened. I. Kaṯīr attributes the following tradition to Abū Sufjān, the eyewitness: at their staging posts, U. would read to his companions from his religious books. In a Christian village he goes to talk with the inhabitants—he had brought a black gown especially for this purpose—but returns to his quarters filled with remorse. This happens again two months later on their way home from Damascus; and at this point a Christian sheikh tells him of the imminent coming of the Prophet. Five months later, Abū Sufjān returns from a business journey to Jaman; he is bewildered by Muḥammad's limited interest in his share of the profits, and, upon his inquiries, learns that he has in the meantime declared himself a follower of the Prophet. He brings the news to U. in Ṭāif, who refuses, however, to follow him, out of consideration for the Ṯakafiten who believed in his own claims, and out of fear of, in particular female, malicious gossip.[28] He is even supposed to have had a personal and official interview with the Prophet in Mecca, having avoided him for eight years while living in Baḥrain:[29] Their conversation—cf. Ḫuṭba Sağ‘ and his poems on the one hand, and Basmala and sura 36 on the other—did not have a positive outcome. U. wants to see outward success first and goes to Syria, while the Prophet accomplishes the Ḥeğra. On the news of the victory at Badr, he hurries home in order to join Muḥammad's following and to formally give up his vocation in favor of the latter.[30] But then he learns at Badr the names of those in the cistern, mourns them in word and deed—and renounces Islam.[31] He later dies in Ṭāif.[32] According to both traditions, his estrangement from Islam is due to personal reasons: on the one hand, to his wounded self-esteem (it is often said "he envied him"), on the other, to his hatred of his relatives' murderer. Both are plausible. The meeting at the Ka‘ba, however, is not credible, for the manner in which, years later, the Prophet questions U.'s sister about him (see above) seems to preclude any previous acquaintance. He is not familiar with the poems she recites to him. He is enthusiastic about them and thinks that U. "was almost a Muslim"—according to another Ḥadīṯ, regarded admittedly as apocryphal by I. Sa‘īd,[33] "he is a believer in his poems, but in his heart a Kāfir." The tradition was also divided with regard to this ambiguous statement. On the one hand, it poses the question of why he didn't become the Prophet, since he shared the same belief, and answers it by having him have an experience similar to Muḥammad's,[34] a calling of the heart. Here it turns out that he agrees with him deep down, but doubts his mission.[35] "I know the Ḥanīfīja to be true, but doubt has crept into me about Muḥammad," he says on his deathbed. Alternatively, the term "Muslim" is emphasized in that convenient statement, and the tradition seeks to furnish proof by attributing to him poems similar to Ḥassān's, to the point of characterizing him as a Ḳorānic exegete. Conversely, "Kāfir" is emphasized. Just as Baḥīrā had Muḥammad, the ascetic finds U. inspired, but inspired by the djinns, i.e. the devil, which is why the tradition plainly calls him the "Kāfir"[36] and seeks to eradicate his memory.

What do U.'s poems tell us about all of this? First of all, we cannot be happy with the declaration that U.'s closest compatriot al Ḥağğāğ, once made in a Ḫuṭba:[37] to the effect that at his time the real connoisseurs of U.'s poems had already passed on, and with them their authentic interpretation. Moreover, his reputation as a poet, despite receiving all kinds of praise, is hardly based on his secular poems, but rather on his "religious" ones, which are, however, the poems the tradition most seriously impinged on. Thus the question of authenticity is necessarily linked to any investigation of the history of the tradition.[38]

As well as the historical poems mentioned above, there are some small fragments, e.g. of poems eulogizing the Ṯaḳīf tribe (Reğezvers[39] L'A عيط, etc.; I. Qut. *Dichterb.* 282,[40] etc.; Bakrī 451; Bakrī 838),[41] and the description of the Ijād's emigration to 'Irāḳ (Bakrī 45 + Addād 81,[42] cf. Wüstenfeld, *Wohnsitze* 63[43]). The lament about the son who turned out badly stands completely apart: *Ḥamāsa* 354,[44] *Aġ.* 3, 191, complete in cod. Goth. 532, fol 7r, and is probably of a later date (cf. Tebrīzī).

Of the main corpus, the "religious" poems, the following should be excluded as inauthentic because of their literary dependence on the Koran:[45]

a) Most of the verses quoted in Sujūṭī's *Itḳān* 285ff.[46] They are meant to establish certain peculiar words in the Koran as already existing in pure Arabic. Even Huart (*F. As. l. c.* p. 30) does not dare to, and rightly so, draw any final conclusion regarding authenticity from Sujūtī's study. Particular attention should be paid to the fact that some of those verses either have several of the same words in common with certain Koranic verses or are pieced together from several such words. Is it possible that the Prophet was unwise enough to include in his revelation material belonging specifically to U.? For a common source would have been known to those concerned with religious matters and immediately cast doubt on the originality of the revelation! On the contrary, the current of the tradition mentioned above has attributed it to U., and not even successfully, for these verses have hardly been handed down anywhere else than in Ṭabarī's *Tafsīr*, where Sujūṭī evidently found them, with neither the dictionaries nor the Koran's glossary including them.[47] The same is true of the verses quoted in this context in the introduction to the Jamhara's,[48] all of which depend on the Koran.

b) The poem I. Kaṯīr 287v. (shorter in Damīrī 2, 473 and above), a vision of paradise and hell—on the occasion of the exploration of the heart—in consideration of suras 19, 62. 88, 15, etc.[49]

c) The completely Koranized poem about the frailty of all creatures: Cheikho, *Naṣr*. 226f. (from a Muslim, now lost).[50]

d) The poem in praise of Muḥammad: *Ḫiz*. 1, 122f., (re. V. 3 cf. sura 9, 33, re. V. 12 sura 33, 40, etc.), which is incidentally, typical in its rejection of the belief in Muḥammad's immortality, V.13![51]

e) The description of heaven and hell: Ps.-Balḫī 1, 202f et seq., directly based on sura 56, 15 et seq.; 76, 21; 37, 41 et seq., etc.[52]

f) On the Annunciation and Conception and the birth of Christ: Ps.-Balḫī 3, 123 (cf. Jāq. 2, 587, 4), an adaptation of sura 19.

g) About Lot and the destruction of Sodom: Jāq. 3, 59 (cf. Ps.-Balḫī 3, 58, Ḳazwīnī 2, 135) based on sura 11, 15, 59; which implies excluding as well the verses on the Flood and the saving of Noah: Ps.-Balḫī 3, 24 et seq.

h) The verses about the *jaum al taġbāun* (sura 64, 9) and the retaliation: Ps.-Balḫī 2, 145, full of Koranic expressions, as well as idem 1, 207 (cf. sura 7, 44).[53]

i) The long poem in Naṣr. 227 (from a ms. held in the Middle East), an imitation of the one mentioned in sub 5), incidentally strongly reminiscent of Ḥassān 23, 4 et seq.

k) The fragment *Ḫiz*. 1, 120 (from *Aġ*., but only partially surviving in the printed version and cod. Goth). Note the postulation of the Ṣalīt (originally) taking place twice (v. 1) and the opposition between them: *ḳāfir* and *īmān* (7 et seq.). This could be established with even greater certainty as inauthentic if it included, as it possibly does, the verses Ps.-B. 2, 145 (cf. sura 7, 186, etc.).[54]

l) Aḍḍād 51, 10 et seq. (sura 39, 6).

m) I. Ḥağar 4, 723, more complete in Ṯa'labī's *Ḳiṣaṣ* [al-Tha'labī, died 1035, Qiṣaṣ al-Anbiyā' (Cairo, 1297)] (1306), p. 150: a paraphrase of sura 19, 62 et seq.[55]

n) Hiš. 146 (cf. below, Nr. 3).

o) The double verse Lisān al-'Arab ليط,[56] deriving from a (fake) poem by 'Adī b. Zaid (Ps.-B. 1, 151, more complete in Maḳrīzī, *Ḫiṭaṭ* 1, 22 [*Al-Mawā'iz wa'l-i'tibār bi-dhikr al-khiṭaṭ wa'l-āthar*, 2 vols., ed. G. Wiet, Bulaq, AH 1270]).

p) The verses in Ṯā'ālibī's *Kanz al Kuttāb* 27 v. [Tha'ālibī died 1038] an imitation of the authentic poem *Aġ*. 8, 3, 8 et seq. (cf. note 20), as well as the fragment *Ḫiz*. 4, 4 (cf. sura 11), which corresponds in rhyme and metre. Other examples must be omitted here.

There is no doubt that these poems contain genuine elements and were composed at an early period when the prohibition on imitating the Koran was not yet known, with the intention of attributing them to Umayya, but also partly to Waraqa, Zaid b. ʻAmr and others, in order to correct them by giving them a Muslim reading. Yet we have no way of distinguishing and will, for the time being, take the precaution of abandoning them all.

As far as we can tell, the following passages are free from this suspicion (of being dependent on the Koran):

1) The fragment Ps.-B. 3, 25 (Wāfir[57]): the sending out of the dove from Noah's Ark and its reward of the necklace. The initial position of verses 9 and 12 in Ǧāḥiẓ *Ḥaiw*.[58] (Vindob.) 112 v. 212 v. is probably correct. To judge from disparate verses,[59] the original poem was lengthy and included the description, among other things, of heaven and earth, and the worlds of stars and angels.

2) Baghdādī Ḫiz. 2, 542 et seq. says on the subject of a Khafīf[60] fragment about the sacrifice of Isaac that the last verse occurs more frequently, but according to prevailing, and correct, opinion, it belongs to a Ḳaṣīde of 79 verses by U., in which various prophets, including David, Solomon, Noah, Moses, Abraham, and Isaac are mentioned. A third of it can be reconstructed and, lacunae apart, divided into the following sections: the lightning progress of the Ark: Zamaḫš. *Asās al-Balāgha* [Cairo 1299 AH] 1, 82; on the animals therein: Haiw. 396 b. (excerpts in Mašriḳ 1894, 560); the sending out of the dove: Nuwairī's *Nihāja* 109 v.;[61] the sacrifice of Isaac: *Ḫiz*. l. c. 543;[62] the prayer of Solomon, the inventor of the coat of mail, to win God's blessing for any undertaking (or for this craft): Ǧawālīḳī, *Muʻarrab*,[63] *ZDMG* 33, 213; a verse about Solomon's autocracy: Lexx. شطن (etc.), and possibly single verses such as T.ʻA. 5, 450.[64]

3) The fragment (Ṭawīl[65]) in I. Hiš. 146 is controversial, the praise of the eternal God from whom nothing is hidden; following on from that, Abraham's and Aaron's mission to the Pharaoh, also the deliverance of Jonah, and a prayer for absolution. I. Isḥāḳ attributes it to Zaid b. ʻAmr, I. Hišām to U. (except v. 1.2.5.). According to Bagdādī 1, 119, who attributes it along with two other fragments to U., it belongs to a long Kasīde, in which he also spoke of Noah, Joseph, David, and Solomon. According to him, moreover, the مطلع is the rhyme on فانيا . On the other hand, I. Hiš.'s first

verse has an internal rhyme, and is the beginning of the poem according to ʿAinī (4, 243). However, precisely this verse is attributed to Zaid by I. Isḥāḳ, as well as several of the following verses by Ps.-B. (1, 62–75), whereas others are thought to be the work of U. (ibid. 2, 24, etc.). According to Ibn Isḥāḳ (149), one of the verses comes from Waraḳa. So the tradition was obviously contaminated, which could easily happen with poems by these men of similar tendencies. It is impossible to distinguish between them. However, twenty-seven of the verses quoted under U.'s name by Ǧāḥiẓ, *Kitāb al-Ḥayawān*. 11 r., and partially by Nuwayrī 94 v. 109 v., may have belonged to the authentic poem. They tell of the Ark's journey and landing on Mount Ǧūdī, the sending out of the dove and the dove's reward, the cock's betrayal of the raven. A poet's repetition of the same subject-matter is hardly unusual.

4) We know the following parts of a long Ḫafīf poem (about 45 verses): The praise of God, the description of his throne: I. Kaṯīr 5 r. 289 v. (Ps.-B. 1, 165); the Creation, the enumeration of all kinds of animals: *Kitāb al-Ḥayawān*. 113 r. 397 v. (based on this, *Mašriḳ* 11, 535); Pharaoh's punishment by famine and a plague of insects: ibid. 188 r.; his perishing in the sea: Ps.-B. 3, 82; destruction of the Tamūd (legend of Ahmar): ibid. 3, 40;[66] also the description of a drought and a rainmaking spell: *Kitāb al-Ḥayawān*, 245 v. (shorter in Damīrī 1, 888, and above); lastly, single verses such as *Kitāb al-Ḥaiw*. 230 v., Hiš. 598, 6, Ṭab. *Tafsīr* 1, 226, Qut. *Dicherb*. 280, 16.

5) The vestiges of a Kämil poem were probably arranged in roughly the following (indirect) order: the creation of heaven and earth: *Kitāb al-Ḥaiw*. 163 v.; the seven heavens, with a description of the first and the second: Ps.-B. 2, 7; of the third and fourth: Tāj al-ʿArüs: صقر حقر respectively; of the moon: Lisān alʿArab: سحر and the stars: Lisān alʿArab : صيدق (12, 66) مها (20, 169); the Cherubim: Ps.-B. 1, 165, 6 et seq.; the demons cast out from heaven: *Ḥaiw* 341 v.; God's majesty on the throne: Naṣr. 235.[67] Then the fasting angels': *Ḳāmūs* in Fleischer, *K. Schr.* 1, 60;[68] the messenger service of the angels: Ps.-B. 1, 169. It can be proved that this last part was immediately followed by the description of the Seraphim, the figures about the throne, and the lashing of the sun: Ps.-B. 1, 168 + I. Kaṯīr 289 r. This was probably followed by that of the earth as man's dwelling place: Ṭab *Tafsīr* 30, 26, and sustainer: Lisān alʿArab: طوط. Finally somewhere the legend of

the hoopoe (see below): *Kitāb al-Ḥayawān*. 183 v. (abridged Qut. Dichterb. 279 and elsewhere).[69]

6) The beautiful momento mori (Khafīf): I. Kaṯīr 288 r.[70] belongs to the corpus of the U. tradition generally considered incontestable.

7) The Ḫafīf poem Hiš. 40 is usually attributed to either U. or to his father, at least it stays in the family. Finally, all kinds of disparate verses must here remain unexamined.

This essentially sums up the tradition's corpus. The historical poems could have been composed by someone else, since their style is very conventional. The fact that the "religious" poems (to sum them up in this way) show the author in a completely different light is understandable. Incidentally, at least one fragment has survived where he (or possibly his father) combines both genres, illustrating God's character and omnipotence with his personal story of the elephant, already embellished in the manner of legend. Yet, can U. really be considered as the author of these poems? The poetry of his like-minded peers who share his sentiments has been too little studied to provide a yardstick;[71] we are forced to rely on mere clues. To begin with, it should be taken into account that U.'s religious poems never had the status of the Dīwāns of other well-known poets among those passing them on,[72] and were consequently less subject to the hazards of scholarly tradition and criticism. His poetry was partly suppressed, partly tendentiously imitated, but it may have lived on unofficially, off the beaten track. Who knows, maybe al Ǧāḥiẓ, for instance, to whom we owe many rarities, used excerpts of the Dīwān that I. Ḥabīb (who died only ten years before him: I. Ḥabīb died in 245 AH) annotated.[73] Thus the dictionaries' special material may fare better than material deriving from official editions of the Dīwān. In addition, the remains confirm the tradition's assessment of its distinguishing features: "He spoke of Abraham, Ishmael, the Ḥanīfīja, the hereafter" (*Aġ*. 3, 187, 188; I Raḳīḳ, *Ḳuṭb assurūr* cod. Vindob. I, 87 v.); they contained "wise sayings" (Damīrī, 2, 210 ult.). Ibn 'Abbās used to quote from the scroll of I. Abi-ṣ Ṣalt: Zamaḫšarī, *Asās* 1, 86, 22—and "reinforce monotheism" (Dam. l. c.). Our poems come, at least indirectly, from U. or his circle. The scholars were less interested in U.'s theology than in his stories and descriptions, but it seems preferable to have preserved more of the latter than of the former. I add to the following outline of their content some references to Jewish sources and other parallels; unfortunately the space available does not allow for further details.

The Flood is a popular subject.[74] Since the raven, coming across carrion, forgets his mission,[75] Noah sends out the dove to find a landing place (variant: a spring). Covered in excrement (as in the Babylonian account), it returns with a vine branch and receives the stipulated reward, that is, a band cast to adorn, like a *sikhāb*, the dove's neck and that of all its descendants.[76] Before the Flood, there was a Golden Age, where people went about naked, the stone slabs were soft,[77] animals and things had the power of language,[78] and where the raven betrayed the cock by taking off after a drinking binge with him, leaving him as security in the hands of the innkeeper.[79] The Ark's journey lasts seven days and eight nights, steered safely in spite of the deepest darkness, till it lands at Mount Gūdī. The sacrifice of Isaac: He asks his father to bind him fast, so that he won't tremble and to spare his coat from being spattered with blood. At the moment the father draws his knife, God turns Isaac's neck into "bronze."[80]—Apart from the dubious verses mentioned above under (3), only two of altogether hardly ten verses about Pharaoh[81] remain: the Egyptians' plague of locusts, ants, and famine,[82] and Pharaoh's perishing in the sea, including the well-known expression that he cries out to God at the very last moment,[83] but his "appeal, after all his idolatry, was futile." Here the fragment ends. According to the tradition, the single verse Lexx. شطن speaks of Solomon: "He puts all evil and rebellious (demons?? cf. Nābiġha 5, 22–25) in chains and dungeons. He probably also spoke the prayer mentioned under (2).[84] Arabic legend is represented by the detailed narration of Ahmar's crime and the fall of Ṯamūd it provokes;[85] maybe, in addition, by the note on the building of the dam in Ma'rib I. Hiš. 9 (a contested verse). The animal fable is represented by the tale of the hoopoe who offers his head as his mother's tomb.[86] We also owe to Umayya the detailed account of a kind of a rainmaking spell in ancient Arabia. In times of drought they tie firebrands to the tails of cattle and drive them up the hills, and water is sent from the skies.[87] Ǧaḥiẓ, handed down this passage in its most complete form and also the (seriously spoiled) verses on the snake charm (*Ḥaiw.* 211 r.) according to which the snake was punished by God (in Paradise) by the loss of its feet[88] and obeys man's magical words out of fear.—cosmological concepts.[89] Number 1: The canopy of heaven is the vault of a bowl cast without a crack, so smooth that the sun slips off it (at sunset). Heaven serves as a resting place for angels. God's servants, formerly fallen angels, live on the earth. Other passages speak of stars and of weather clouds racing along, ridden by the wind; of lush meadows that endow the cattle with fertility and an abundance of milk. Number 5: God made the earth kneel down to mate with the (rain)water.[90] Angelic servants (تلامذة) stand on the peaks of the Earth, carrying on their trembling shoulders the metal canopy of heaven that never wears out or buckles and is so smooth that not even the disobedient Kurād insect can get a foothold on it.[91] Having completed the six heavens, built like storeys one on top of the other, God created the seventh, the highest one. The first heaven بُرْقِع، resembles a "calm," "smooth" "sea" (سَدِر),[92] and is surrounded by angels. The second heaven is خَضْراء, looks like زُجاجة القَسْول and shades the heads of those angels. The third, صاقورة is hard, is melted down and hardens again (جمد). The fourth, حاقورة, borders on the fifth. God dwells in the highest, seventh heaven. He has put covers and saddles on the backs of the riding animals, whose legs are bound, and a palanquin adorned with rubies on their necks, on which he sits enthroned as the king, adored by angels. A blazing fire separates the lower spheres from him. Millions of light-winged angels, his تلاميذ, fly across the heavens as his messengers. His throne is borne by the four Seraphim, a man and a bull under the throne's right leg, an eagle and a lion under the left. A few comments may be in place here. Whereas the idea of أَطْباق (in the Koran طِباق) existed for the Jews, and perhaps for the Babylonians even with the same designation, the few surviving names of the heavens are quite unique. However, they may not be as mysterious to us as to the Arabic philologists,[93] if we avoid looking for them in the Assyrian dictionary.[94] بِرْقِع (variation in T'A رَقِع) is either בֵּי(ת) רְקִיעַ [Hebrew],[95] or בִּרְקִיעַ [Hebrew] which was used by Jews reciting e.g. Ψ 150, 1 [Psalms 150, 1] in Hebrew or Aramaic (Hebrew/Aramaic: a בִּירְקִיעָא),—rather than the term by itself in the casus rectus. It was understood as One Word.[96] Moreover: خَضْرَاء seems to be an attribute in the verse ("glass-colored" cf. Ez. 1, 22, Apoc. 4, 6), not actually a noun. The same may be true for صاقورة and حاقورة. If صاقور (in modern Arabic: شاقور) "hatchet" = סִיקוּרָא [Hebrew] (Dt. 19, 5 Jer. Tg.) equals syqwr

(ܣܡܩܘܪܐ): [Syriac],[97] then صاقورة = סְקוֹרָא; red color may mean "the color red" (Levy,[98] *T. W.* 2, 186 a.).[99] This explanation is supported by Ps.-Balḫī 2, 2, according to which some consider the third heaven to be the color hyacinth, that is, red.[100] If they are right in maintaining that the first heaven (برقع) is green (خضر), and others in holding that the substance of heaven موج مكفوف is a matter hardened by fire (جمد), there is an obvious connection with the expression خضراء, "smooth, calm sea" and the image of the hardening used in the poem, but assigned to the heavens with a somewhat different distribution.[101] That is why the names (attributes) apart from برقع (or رقع) do not correlate with the names elsewhere attested, at least half of which are the Jewish ones.[102] A typical concept is the combined image of God both riding the Cherubim and sitting on the throne: Ezekiel's throne chariot (c. l.). The figures of throne bearers also are the same as there (as well as in Apoc. 4).[103] The angel-messengers are clearly still conceived as flashes of lightning, for it is said that they are lying [on the ground] having been struck down by them (cf. Ψ 103. 104). The angels bearing the (first and fifth) heavens stand on the peaks of the Earth: a possible reference to the two hilltops of Land Mountain [Länderberges][104] in Babylonian cosmology? Another couplet about the expulsion of the Satans from heaven (*Ḥaiw*. 341 v., cf. Wellhausen, *Reste*² 137) is part of this, as well as the two oft-quoted assertions: the sun needs a lashing in order to rise every morning,[105] and the crescent moon (new moon) is sheathed like a sword and unsheathed again.[106]

What is the origin of these concepts, to which no other poet before and at the time of the Prophet gave such comprehensive expression? The usual answer is that they come from Syria or Iraq, as in al Aʿšā's work, who, being Christian, knew and made use of biblical-Jewish legends. But al Aʿšā' was also known in Neğrān, where he frequently travelled and thus must have come into contact with Judaism. Furthermore, it has recently been pointed out again, quite rightly, that, at the time of Muḥammad, the Ḥiğāz was still in touch with southern Arabic culture, whereas the Jewish influence from the north had faded away long before. The legend has the Ḥanīf U. study with the Christians and Jews of Syria. It seems to us that the legend thereby reveals that it really did not know anything about Ḥanīf culture anymore, just as it has (that is certain) always played with this concept and linked the Ḥanīf to northern Syrian Arabic Christianity by forging verses and whole poems. It has long been established that Zaid b. ʿAmr was given this treatment, but by seeing the term Ḥanīf through Aramaic spectacles, i.e. regarding the etymological link with a حَنِيف [Hebrew חֲנִיפָא] as historical,[107] the false tradition was unwittingly reinforced; Ḥanīf is a genuine Arabic word and means "secessionist."[108] We do not know whether the *homines religiosi* in question used this term to refer to themselves—in any case they did not form an organized community—they merely called their faith (or rather, their morality) الحنيفة. The Koran closely links the term حنيف to Abraham's religion, i.e. to Judaism (for how old is the Arabic Abraham legend?), which is certainly correct. The tradition made up a specifically new name for the confession حنيفيّة (*Aġ*. 3, 187, and elsewhere) and حنفية (I. Ḥağar, 1, 261, 264) possibly only inspired by the Koranic text. If, furthermore, the Ḥanīf Umayya's poems mentioned above are, if only partly, genuine, they lead us southward. They have exactly the coloring of all that was handed down by Wahb b. Munabbih († 110 H)[109]—to the extent that he could have been the author, had he emerged as a poet. He was, however, a southern Arab, from Yemen, the country where Christianity and Judaism faced one another over centuries and which displays as many traces of the old Babylonian culture as northern Arabic culture. There is no need for the tradition to confirm that U. had been to Yemen (*Aġ*. 3, 192), it being a matter of course for a noble and educated Ṭāifan. If the verses concerned addressed to I. Ğudʿān[110] are genuine, U. visited, in particular, the ʿAbd al Madān in Nağrān—as did al Aʿšā. The "theology" of the Ḥanīfs probably hardly differed from Jewish theology (and southern Arabic monotheism): they emphasized God's unity and otherwise mainly moral obligations, such as abstinence from alcohol. It was apparently part of their customs to tell Arabic and biblical-Jewish legends.[111] As attested by the glimmer of various ancient mythological references in U.'s work (see above), this implies a long and continuous mythological tradition, similar to the one attributed to the Arabs in the first century after Christ.[112] It would be of utmost importance to find linguistic indications pointing to the south.[113] I do not wish to attach any importance to فُرَيْعٌ (note 81). But according to old and unanimous testimony "seat" وِثَاب is Yemenite, and Jewish at that: ותב (as opposed to Ethiopic: ומב). The philologists attest the same for certain *fāʿul*'s, such as *kābūl*, *ġādūf*, and equally for باقور,

"cattle," which is identical with U's (and other poets') بَيْقُور (*bēqūr*). That is why ساهور might have been formed there (for why should U. and the Ṭayyite have distorted סַהֲרָא, סִהרָא gratuitously?), and maybe صاقورة and حاقورة as well, and who knows how many other *fā'ul*s!

The little theology the verses teach holds no surprises. Before the creation of the world God (ربّ, رَبُّنا, ربّ كريم, Var. رحيم)[114] seated himself on the heavenly throne (in accordance with Jewish belief in his pre-existence, as sura XI, 9), faithful (مُهَيْمِن sura 5, 52 etc., i.e. מְהֵימְנָא, מְהֵימָן , πιστός), adored by angels. He is our only protector and survivor (Ṭab. *Tafsīr 1*, 365); without his guidance we would go astray and would have to long for our grave. A reliable leader (صَيْدَق, الأمين الأرشد), he reigns in heaven and dictates the stars' orbit (L'A 12, 66). The angels, the bearers of heaven, are called his "servants."[115] The Ḥanīfa[116] alone will stake its claim at the Resurrection, all other "religions" are illusory. We should carry the sign of Death, who spares no one, not even the game in the remotest areas, as a reminder on our foreheads;[117] the Earth, "our mother," has to take us in again, but God will raise us from the dead.

We do not know how far removed from Islam U. was, nor whether his estrangement from it was really solely due to personal reasons. In spite of all of the tradition, we cannot consider him a serious contender for the honor of Prophet. Being a Ḥanīf, he was an outsider and inactive. It can be assumed that the Prophet, who after his emergence as such lost touch with the Meccan and Ṭāif's nobility—and hardly met with U. after his failure in the latter city—did not know him personally. It is even less credible that he directed certain damning prophesies (such as sura VII, 174; LXVIII, 12) against him (which is already clearly contradicted by the expression الآيات). Only after U.'s death does he hear several of his poems recited by his sister: they are entirely new to him, and if any of his comments on them are authentic, it is the following—with which we unfortunately have to a certain extent to concur:

> عند اللّه علم اميّة بن ابى الصلت UMAYYA b. ABI aṣ-Salt
> With God is the Knowledge of UMAYYA b. ABI aṣ ṢALT .
> [Only God knows UMAYYA b. ABI aṣ-ṢALT]

NOTES

1. [F. Schulthess "Umayya b. Abi-Ṣalt," *Orientalische Studien Theodor Nöldeke zum siebzigsten Geburtstag gewidmet von Freunden und Schülern und in ihren Auftrag herausgegeben von Carl Bezold*, 2 vols., Giessen, 1906, vol. I, 71–89. Translated by Anon. Footnotes in square brackets by I. W.]

2. *Mémoires de l'Acad. des Inscr. et Belles-Lettres,* 1904, April 22, and in particular *Journal Asiatique*, 1904, pp. 125–67. (I quote from the special edition which has its own pagination.)

3. [al-Maqdisī, Muṭahhar ibn Ṭāhir (pseudo-Balkhī), *Al-Bad' wa'l-ta'rīkh* (*Le livre de la création et de l'histoire*, ed. and translated by Clément Huart, 6 vols., Paris, 1899–1919.]

4. See Huart's edition, vol. 3, preface, *Journal Asiatique*, 1901 (vol. 18), p. 16. According to Goldziher, *ZDMG* 55, 702, he wrote only in the fifth century.

5. The material I have accumulated over many years has been significantly enriched by Dr. R. Geyer's kindness, mainly from mss. from the Vienna Hofbibliothek. I hope to present this in detail at a later date. Thorbecke's estate also provided some new material.

6. I. Kaṯīr 1, 289.

7. *Ḫizāna* 1, 119 paen., etc. ['Abd al-Qādir b.'Omar al-Baghdādī, *Ḫizānat al-adab*, Bd. I–IV, Būlāq, 1299]. It can be proved that, as well as him and al-'Ainī (2, 348), I. Jinnī (ibid.) and al Khafāgī (*Šarh. aš šifā*, cod. Vindob. 40r) used the Dīwān.

8. For instance, the song in praise of the Prophet.

9. Brockelmann, *Lit.G.* 1, 49. [Carl Brockelmann, *Geschichte der arabischen Litteratur*, 2 vols., Weimar, 1898; Berlin, 1902.] Used by me (at R. Geyer's kind suggestion) in the Vienna Codex (vol. 1).

10. One often reads U. b. aṣ Ṣalt in the texts, but this is certainly a careless mistake on the part of the scribes

11. Cf. e.g. I. Ḥağar, *Al-Iṣāba fî tamyîz al-ṣaḥāba* (*A Biographical Dictionary of Persons Who Knew Muḥammad*), ed. A. Sprenger et al., 4 vols., Calcutta, 1856–1888. See also Ibn al-Athīr; *Usd al Ghāba fi ma'rifat al-ṣahāba*, 5 vols., Cairo, AH 1285–1286]; Damīrī 2, 212, 1, as opposed to 2, 473 [al-Damīrī, *Muḥammad ibn Mūsā. Ḥayāt al-ḥayawān al-kubrā*, 2 vols., Cairo, 1319 AH (circa 1901 CE); also 2 vols., Cairo 1284 AH.]

12. I. Duraid 184 N. [Schulthess could be referring to any of the four following works: al-Jamhara (Haydarābad, 1344); *Kitāb al-Ishtiqāq*, ed. Wüstenfeld, Göttingen, 1854; *kitāb al mujtanā*, ed. Krenkow, Ḥaydarābād, 1342; *kitāb al-wishāḥ*, J. Kraemer *ZDMG*, CX 259–73], cf. I. Ḫağar 3, 1320.

13. I. Duraid, l. c., but different in Balādurī 205.

14. The authenticity of this elegy is not called into question by its reliance on the Ḫansā's lament for Ṣaḫr. The Prophet prohibited it from being passed on because of the invective directed at his followers contained within it, thus I. Ḫiz. suppresses such a couplet (532, 16. Cf. *Ḫiz.* I, 121, 8 from the bottom, 2, 43, 8 from the bottom; Bajān I, 113 bottom and other occurences; also Baġawī in Sprenger 1, 118. [*Das Leben und die Lehre des Muḥammad*, 3 vols., Berlin, 1861–1865] Abu Ḏarr edit., Brönnle 32, 1 [see Abu Ḏarr, *Monuments of Arabic Philology*, 2 vols.: Commentary on Ibn Hishäm's Biography of Muḥammad according to Abu Ḏarr's Mss. ed., P. Brönnle, Cairo, 1911.]

15. I. Ḥaǧar I, 1035; 3, 437 [Ibn Ḥaǧar al-'Asqalānī Abū'l-Faḍl Aḥmad ibn 'Alī, *Al-Iṣāba fi tamyīz al-ṣaḥāba* (*A Biographical Dictionary of Persons Who Knew Muḥammad*), ed. Aloys Sprenger et al., 4 vols., Cairo, 1307 AH, circa 1889 CE.

16. [*Aghānī = Kitāb al-aghāni*, ed. by al-Iṣbahānī Abū'l-Faraj, 20 vols., Cairo, AH 1285, 1868 CE.]

17. 3, 171 where Abū Rabi 'ah should be read as Abū Zam'ah.

18. [Azraḳī, *Die Chroniken der Stadt Mekka . . .* , ed. F. Wüstenfeld, Bd. I: el-Azraki's *Geschichte und Beschreibung der Stadt Mekka*, Leipzig, 1858.]

19. [Ibn Hishām, *Das Leben Muhammed*, ed. F. Wüstenfeld, Bd. I. II, Göttingen, 1858–60.]

20. *ZDMG* 46, 7. [The Dīwān of al-Huṭay'a was published in Istanbul in 1890, and subsequently by I. Goldziher (in *ZDMG*, xlvi–xlvii and reprint, Leipzig, 1893. Al-Huṭay'a, a famous pre-Islamic poet, was born some forty years before the Hijra.] I have not come across these verses under U.'s name.

21. *Aġ*. 8, 2 et seq. and apparently in various disparate verses. Cf. also below p. 70 under p. It can be assumed that *Aġ*. 8, 5, 2 sqq. was not only addressed to the dying man either (Ḥalabī, *Insān*, 1, 173 [*A Biography of the Prophet; Insān al-'uyūn (al-sīra al-Ḥalabiyya)*, Būlāq, 1292, Cairo, 1280. Ḥalabī, died 1635 CE] Balawī, *Alif -bā* 2, 84, and other occurences.

22. *Aġ*., Hiš., also Ḥalabī l. c., I. Ḥaǧar 2, 706, etc., and Ḥassān's Dīwān [Tunis, 1281 AH] 118, 11 et seq.

23. Ḥadith

24. Bakrī 735 = Dīwān Khansā 196 et seq. (N.)

25. *Aġ*. 20, 135. Rhodokanakis, al Khansā 7 [N. Rhodokanakis, *Al- Khansā und ihre Trauerlieder, in SBKAW* (*Sitzungsberichte der Kaiserliche Akademie der Wissenschaft*), cxlvii (Vienna, 1904).] W. Robertson Smith, *Religion of the Semites*, Edinburgh, 1889, 125.

26. For details cf. *Aġ*. 3, 189; Damīri 2, 211; Balawī 2, 508; I. *Kaṯīr* 288 v.

27. Like angel-devil the opposition, this prescription betrays its Muslim invention. The hermit, belonging to some sect or other, probably wore a black garb himself (cf. Rabbūa in Barhebr. *Nomok.* 110 [P. Bedjan, *Nomocanon Gregorii Barhebraei*, Leipzig, O. Harrassowitz, 1898; also Barhebraeus / Giuseppe A. Assemani, (*Nomocanon*) *Ecclesiae Antiochenae Syrorum nomocanon*, 1838]; G. Hoffmann, *Auszüge*, p. 125. [G. Hoffmann, *Auszüge syrischen Akten persischer Märtyrer*, Leipzig, 1880]; Braun, *Synhados* 67 and *Or. Ltz.* 1903, col. 337 [Oscar Braun, ed., *Das Buch der Synhados oder Synodicon orientale*, Die Sammlung der nestorianischen Konzilien, zusammengestellt im 9. Jahrh. Nach der Syrischen Handschrift, Museo Borgiano 82 der Vatikanischen Bibliothek. Übersetzt und erläutert von Oscar Braun, Stuttgart-Wien, 1900].

28. I. Ḥağar 1, 263, cf. 3, 437. I. Kaṯir 287 r.

29. I. Kaṯīr 288 r. (az Zuhrī).

30. *wa-'alqā 'ilayhi maqālîda hāḏā 'amri* [he sent him the keys to the matter; cf. R. Dozy, *Supplément aux dictinnaires arabes*, 2 vols., Leiden, 1881; s.v. *miqlād*].

31. Apparently he also incited the Qu'rayshites to revenge: *Aġ*. 3, 187, cf. top p. 73, A. 4.

32. According to one legend, while carousing at Ghailān Castle (*Aġ*, etc.).

33. In I Kaṯir 289 r.

34. See Sprenger 1, 162 et seq.

35. *Aġ*. 3, 188, 190. I. Kaṯir 287 r. Like Muḥammad's opening of the heart, U.'s exploration is fixed, characteristically, partly at a point in his youth (Balawī 2, 508), partly later, (usually) just before his death. In another critical study, U. receives the muse in this way (Goldziher, *Abhandlungen zur arabischen Philologie*, Leiden, 1896, 1, 213, cf. Damirī 2, 210 below).

36. Damirī l. c. Nawawī, p. 164.

37. *Aġ*. 3, 187.

38. We must also be careful of mix-ups. There were several poets called Umayya (cf. Khiz. 1, 122). He has even been confused with U. b. Abi-ṣ-Ṣalt al Maghribī, even more often with the Huḏailite.

39. [It is worth enumerating the Arabic metres here as Schulthess refers to them at various points throughout the article. There are normally taken to be sixteen metres: 1. rajaz, 2. sarī', 3. kāmil, 4. wāfir are the four iambic metres. There is one antipastic metre, namely 5. hazaj. The amphibrachic are three in number: 6. mutqārib; 7. ṭawīl; 8. muḍāri'. The anapaestic metres are four in number: 9. mutadārik; 10. basīṭ; 11 munasariḥ; 12 muqtaḍab. The ionic metres are also four in

number: 13. ramal; 14. madīd; 15. khafīf; 16. mujtaṯṯ. Source: W. Wright, *A Grammar of the Arabic Language*, Camridge University Press, 3rd ed., 1967, vol. 2, pp. 358ff.]

40. [I. Qutayba, *Liber poësis et poëtarum*, ed. M. J. de Goeje, Leiden, 1904.

41. The Wāfir poem in the Ǧamhara is not genuine, as recently proven by my colleague who just marked his anniversary (*Fünf Mo. all.* 1, 19 et seq. [T. Nöldeke, "Fünf Mo'allaqät, übersetzt und erklärt," *SKAW*, Vienna, 1899, 1900, 1901]).

42. [Abu Bakr ibn al-Anbāri, *Kitāb al-Addād*, ed. T. Houtsma, Leiden, 1881.]

43. [F. Wüstenfeld, "Die Wohnsitze und Wanderungen der Arabischen Stämme," in *Abhandlungen der Königlichen Gesellschaft der Wissenschaften*, Göttingen, 1872.]

44. [*Hamasae carmina cum Tebrisii scholiis integris edidit, indicibus instruxit, versione latina et commentario illustr.*, G. G. Freytag, 2 vols., Bonn, 1828–1847 (collected by Abū Tammām, died 231 AH/845 CE; commentary by at-Tabrīzī, died 502 AH/1108 CE. Other editions: Būlāq, 1296; Cairo, 1322, 1325, 1331. Cf. Volkslieder, collected by Abū Tammām, translated by Friedrich Rückert, 2 vols., Stuttgart, 1846.]

45. I do not take into account the numerous verses that can be proved to belong to other poets and appear in their poems.

46. Some of them are beyond suspicion, such as qiṭmīrā on p. 299, which should be corrected following Suyūṭī's *Tafsīr* 5, 248).

47. At least not the one by al Ispahānī cod. Berol. 675 (viele Verse, auch solche U.'s zitierende).

48. [*Jamharat aš'ār al-'arab: Gedichtsammlung* by Abu Zaid Muḥammad ibn al-Khaṭṭāb, Büläq, 1308.]

49. Incidentally, concerning critical studies and authorship, cf. 'Ainī 2, 187 and again Kāmil 43, 194.

50. According to L. Cheikho's communication by letter.

51. The verses in De Goeje's [and P. de Jong] *Fragmenta historicorum Arabicorum* [Leiden, 1869] 2, 33 were possibly part of this, if not of the poem Hiš. 39, 9 et seq. which has also been attributed to U.

52. Cf. incidentally 'Ainī 2, 346. It can be proved that it also included one of the verses of [the] *Itqān*, p. 289, discussed above; maybe also those in Ǧaḥiẓ Bukhalā' 236 et seq., [*Kitāb al-Bukhalā'*, ed. G. Van Vloten, Leiden, 1900], etc.

53. This may also include the verses in Lexx. √kfr; qassa and some others, as well as the much cited verse on *mustaṭir Lisān al-'Arab* [Arabic lexicon of Ibn Manẓūr, 20 vols., Cairo, 1308]; *Tāj al-'Arūs* [Arabic lexicon of as-Sayyid Murtaḍa,

10 vols. Cairo, 1307] √slṭ; Aġ. 3, 187, I. Qut. *Dichterb.* 280, I Ğinnī's *Khaṣā'iṣ* 134 r. (cf. below p. 88 A.1).

54. N.B., e.g., the Iranian word *dusfān* "messenger"!—cf. also Lexx. *dqt* (*dqẓ*), Khiz. 4, 70.

55. Including verses occurring somewhere in the Jamhara (sura XIX, 72).

56. Cf. Ṭabarī 1, 1122?

57. [An iambic metre. See note 39 above.]

58. [Ğaḥiẓ, *Kitāb al-Ḥayawān*.]

59. Lisān al'Arab *ḥll, qrq, rkb, qām, wṯb, r 'b*, Khiz. 3, 286 roughly in this—indirect—order.

60. [An ionic metre; see note 39 above.]

61. [Nuwayrī, *Nihāyat al-Arab fī Funūn al-Adab*, Cairo, n.d.]

62. Cf. Nasr. 230. Ps.-B. 3, 65. Other occurrences of single verses.

63. [Jawālīqī, *Kitāb al-Mu'arrab min al-Kalām al-'Ajamī'alā ḥurūf al-Mu'jam*, ed. F. Sachau, Leipzig, 1867, a lacuna filled from Cairo, discussed by Ms. Spitta in *ZDMG*, xxxiii, 208 ff.]

64. The verse in Suyūṭī's *Tafsīr* 4, 120 cannot be genuine (sura XVI, 54).

65. [An iambic metre. See note 39 above.]

66. U. is confirmed as the author of all these fragments by single verses occurring elsewhere.

67. Source? Verses 1 and 2 attested elsewhere.

68. [H. L. Fleischer, *Kleinere Schriften*, Bd. I–III, Leipzig, 1885–88.]

69. The following poem mentioned above is obviously an imitation of this one: Nasr. 227, which possibly includes the verses *Bayḍāwī*. 1, 555 and T'A 2, 511. [Tāj al-'Arūs, *Arabic Lexicon of as-Sayyid Murtaḍa*, 10 vols., Cairo, 1307/circa 1889 CE.]

70. Abridged in *Aġ*. 3, 192. However, the poem cannot be genuine if the preceding verse in Maš. 1, 138 is authentic. (Cf. also Aus b. Ḥağar n. 40.)

71. Cheikho's material in *Mašriq* 1904 lacks a critical approach. An examination of A'šā's poems could shed much light on the matter.

72. There is no evidence for them ever having been popular, let alone to the extent Sprenger 1, 78 claims.

73. Unfortunately, proof to the contrary cannot, for the time being, be given.

74. Cf. the enumeration of the fragments above.

75. Cf. *Pirqē R. Eliezer c*. 23. *Bienenbuch*, ed. Budge, p. [ܠܗ] Ṭab. 1, 188, etc., *Muḥāḍarāt* 2, 396.

76. The origin of the proverb: "As long as the ringdove is adorned by a necklace."

77. Cf. Ruba's famous verse (Ahlw. III, n. 46 [*Sammlungen alter arabischer*

Dichter, ed. W. Ahlwardt, vol. 3: *Der Dīwān der Rejezdichter Ru' ba b. al 'Ajjāj*. Ebd. 1903]), Provv. 2, 341, etc., and Maqrīzī, *Khiṭaṭ* 1, 160.

78. Jewish references for this generally accepted vision, e.g., *Jubiläen* 3, 28, Joseph. *Ant*. 1, 1, 4.

79. Mentioned as a curiosity by I. Qutayba (*Dichterb*. 279).

80. Jewish sources and Arabic legend in Grünbaum, *N. Beitr* [Grünbaum, *Neue Beitr. zur Semiet. Sagenkunde*, Leiden 1893], 112 et seq. Cf. also *Tha'labī's Qiṣaṣ* (1306) p. 59, 8 from bottom, Weil, "Biblische Legenden der Muselmänner, aus arabischen Quellen," Frankfurt, 1845, p. 89.

81. I only came across the form *furay'*, which U. "habitually used," according to Sprenger 1, 66, in the single verse T'A 5, 451 (*Muḥīt* 1595). A hypocoristic of *fir'awn* (like *sulaym*, *salām* Muzhir 2, 251, 7. 9 of *sulaymān*), it possibly comes from the southern Arabic tradition (see below).

82. Cf. Tha'labī l. c. 119 sq.

83. *P. R. Eliezer c*. 45. Sūra 10, 90, etc. (cf. Grünbaum l. c. 164 sq.)

84. However, the poem possibly refers to David as well, initially credited with the invention of the coat of mail.

85. In greater detail in Huart, *J. As*. l. c. p. 30 sqq., also Nöldeke, *Mo'all*. 3, 31. (The verse in I. Hiš. 483, which was possibly part of it, is suspect because of *saluma* and the more recent construction of *'anāba* with *li*).

86. Cf. De Goeje's note on Qut. 279, footnote. I leave it to others to discover the mythological reference.

87. See Robertson Smith (translated by Stübe), note 355. The custom is also attested by a Ṭayyite (Damīrī 1, 184. 188. Rasmussen, Add. Vε). Its supernatural and rational explanations in Spätern cf. Dam. l. c. 188 and L'A *bqr* compared to Yāq. 3, 118 [Yāqūt, *Mu'jam al-Buldān*, ed. F. Wüstenfeld, 6 vols., Leipzig, 1866–1870.]

88. As in the Jewish legend (and later, e.g., in Aphraates).

89. N. 1) and 5) and all of the disparate verses that belong to it (see above).

90. Like the camel with the stallion. The expression, according to Freytag in the Koran s. v. *nawwakha* presumably existed in the Hadith. Unlike Lane's erroneous translation 1370 a., cf. U's verse in L'A, T'A √'tm where he again has vegetation spring from the mating of earth and rain.

91. The poet here compares it to the back of a camel (cf. *Delect*. 112, 2).

92. *sadir* here means "sea" according to commentators (cf. Lane). Basically this entirely singular word probably has a foreign connotation; I do not wish to presume more at this point.

93. I Qut., *Dichterb*. 279.

94. Cf. Weissenbach, *Fā'ūl* p. 70 top. (school of Hommel).

95. According to De Goeje, Qut. Gloss.; Huart *J. As.* 1904, p. 341, A. Yet this composed form is not recorded. Also, in such cases the Hebrew בֵּי(ת) was written *bā* (even though pronounced *bē*). Winckler's explanation of √brq' (*Ar.-Sem.-Or*, p. 205) does not take into account the connection with Hebrew reqiya'.

96. Also Wahb: Ps.-Balkhī 2, 6., 5.

97. Cf. Brockelm, *Lex.*, Bedjan 5, 534, 12.

98. [J. Levy, *Chaldäisches Wörterbuch über die Targumim*, 2 vols., Leipzig, 1867.]

99. An adjective *sāqōrā* [Hebrew] (like *sāmōqā* [Hebrew]) is not attested.

100. Originally the different heaven was conceived of as precious stones, symbols of the zodiac.

101. According to Test. Levi c. 3, ὕδωρ κρεμάμενον should be placed, like in the poem, between the first and second heavens.

102. Cf. Lidzbarski, *De proph . . . legendis* [M. Lidzbarski, *De propheticis, quae dicuntur legendis arabicis*, Leipzig, 1893], p. 51, 52, N. Incidentally, even those lists are incomplete. *rq'* also designates the seventh heaven (T 'A 5, 361), etc.

103. There is no indication of why this verse met with Muḥammad's approval (*Aġ.* 3, 190, and elsewhere)—but certainly not because it reminded him of the four Evangelists (Winckler l. c. 137)!

104. Cf. Winckler l. c. 92, A. Jeremias, *Babylonisches im N.T.*, Leipzig, 1905, p. 64.

105. According to the Hadith, because it refuses to shine for its worshippers (I. *Kaṯīr* 289 r./v.).

106. The verse is only complete in L'A *shr*. Cf. Grünbaum, *ZDMG* 31, 288, Winckler l. c. 136.

107. *ḥanep, ḥanpā* [Hebrew] could have been adopted as *ḥanīfun* but not as ḥanīfun.

108. In Ethiopian the word (in its various forms) only existed as a literary term, taken from Syrian texts! Winckler, l. c. 79 et seq. completely failed to see this.

109. Cf. Huart's article about him in *J. As.*, 1904, p. 331 et seq. He is the source for Ṭabarī, I. Aṯīr, and also Ṯa'labī for his legends.

110. Suyūṭī, *Waṣāil* 44 r., cf. I. *Kaṯīr* 284 r., Ḥalabī 1, 173, Balawī 2, 84.

111. Cf. Waraqa b. Naufal. Unfortunately, the philologists mostly discarded the stories' "moral."

112. Cf. Winckler l. c. 135.

113. The remains of southern Arabic grammatical forms found in the Koran by Grimme, *Muḥammad* (1904), p. 49, are nothing but schematic rhyme and pausal forms. However, Muḥammad naturally did not walk on different ground from Umayya and the whole of central and southern Arabia.

114. If the verse quoted above on p. 78, A1 belongs to this poem, it is not genuine even though it has always been associated with U.'s name. Incidentally, instead of *mustaṭir* (in this form, not in the passive as in sura LIV, 53) *muqtadir* has been passed on as well, and instead of *as-salīṭaṭ* the forms *al-saluṭīṭ, al-salṭuliṭ, al-salṭalīṭ*—all that is missing is something like *al-saṭulṭ* = *šiṭluṭu*—and *waw* instead of *huwa*. Therefore the metre is not certain either.

115. For the believers this term is only used in the Rajaz verse "If you, o Lord, forgives," etc., *Aġ*. 3, 191, which is also attributed to others (cf. Khiz. 1, 358, Balawī 2, 309, and *Aġ*. 10, 146).

116. This name occurs only once: *Ḥiš*. 40 paen. (Elsewhere in the inauthentic poem *Khiz*. 1, 120, v. 2).

117. Unfortunately, these verses cannot be established with certainty as genuine, cf. above Nr. 6).

1.5

Umayya ibn Abī-ṣ Ṣalt[1]

Rev. E. Power, S. J.

I took as the subject of my thesis for the Doctorate in Oriental Science in this University the poems of Umayya ibn Abī-ṣ Ṣalt. My intention was to publish a critical text, with notes and commentary, of such of these poems as remained to us. A discussion of their authenticity and some considerations on the personality of Umayya and his connection with Muḥammad would naturally form the introduction. It seems, however, that such a publication would have now very little value. The most interesting and exhaustive article of Professor Schulthess[2] has not only made known to scholars where these poems are to be found, but has even given a *résumé* of their contents. Moreover, the daily-expected publication of Ǵâḥiẓ's *Kitâb al-Ḥayawân* will set at the disposal of everybody the chief part of such of Umayya's known poems as still remain in manuscript form. Some scattered verses, often of doubtful authenticity, and a collection of variant readings would, then, add little to present knowledge. A few brief remarks, however, on the personality of Umayya, as it manifests itself in his certainly genuine poems, may not be unwelcome. They will, at all events, be of utility in explaining the connection between our poet and Muḥammad, and in solving the question of the authenticity of the so-called "Koranical" poems. Most, no doubt, will accept the criticism of Schulthess; but some may wish to modify it in its details, more especially as the signs of Koranical influence are not equally evident in all the poems he rejects.

* * *

In the second half of the sixth century of our era the district of the Ḥiĝâz was peopled, almost exclusively, by tribes descended from Muḍar, the most idolatrous of all the tribes of pagan Arabia. Its two chief cities and centers of worship were Mekka and Ṭâʾif.[3] By one of these strange coincidences that manifest themselves so frequently in the world's history, at that time and in these cities appeared, almost simultaneously, two strenuous teachers of monotheism, Muḥammad and Umayya. Are we right in considering Umayya a religious teacher? While moral teaching entered occasionally within the sphere of pre-Islamitic poetry, it was not usual in ancient Arabia that a poet should propose to himself, as an end, the instruction of his contemporaries in sacred history and the mysteries of the seen and unseen world. True, but Umayya, like Suhail amid the planets, refused to march with the common herd:[4] and we learn from a certainly authentic fragment of his poetry, preserved to us in the unpublished manuscript of *Al-Ḥamâsat al-Baṣîya*,[5] that his originality displayed itself in end as well as in execution. These verses I subjoin as an appendix to this article. In all probability, they formed the conclusion of the famous Kâmil poem, in which Umayya described the construction of the heavens.[6] It is in the last two verses that the poet manifests himself to us, not as a prophet like Muḥammad, but as a simple religious teacher, expecting a reward, only from the God whom he serves, in the life to come. "And, as surely as clans will forget what I say, so surely will He who is not poor remember it. Pardon, then, a servant; it is drinking and gambling, joined with amusements, that have been the beginning of his sin."

The subject-matter of Umayya's religious teaching need not detain us long. It consists, first of all, of pious interpretations of natural phenomena such as the sun's redness in the morning,[7] the moon's disappearance at the end of each month,[8] the shooting stars,[9] the hoopoe's tuft of feathers[10] and the white collar of the dove.[11] Then we have descriptions of the throne of God,[12] of the angels and their ministry,[13] of the seven heavens and their construction,[14] of the state of the universe before the earth's creation,[15] of the condition of primitive man.[16] Finally, come the poet's accounts of Biblical events like the deluge,[17] Abraham's sacrifice,[18] Pharaoh's discomfiture,[19] and Jewish or Arabic legends such as Solomon's empire over the evil spirits[20] and the destruction of Ṯamūd.[21] Let us examine now the personal characteristics that display themselves in our poet's treatment of these varied subjects. These may, to my mind, be grouped under four heads. Umayya views God as a rewarder, and sets in relief His mercy rather than His justice; he shows considerable materialistic tendencies; he preserves interesting relics of idolatrous beliefs; and he has a great love for animals. The citations in proof of these facts shall be taken only from the undoubtedly authentic poems.

Umayya views God especially as a rewarder. Thus, in the verses that treat of Abraham's sacrifice, the poet tells us that the patriarch "fulfulled a vow in order to gain thereby a heavenly recompense."[22] The son, when about to be sacrificed, is made to say:—"Father, verily do I pray that God may reward you for your piety to Him under all circumstances."[23] Isaac, himself, is rewarded for his courage, for "God made his neck be of brass when He saw him brave among the brave."[24] Finally, God says:—"I am not displeased with what you two have done."[25] "And they bore away therefrom 'says the poet' the renown of a noble deed."[26]

In the long Kâmil poem, the concluding verses of which we give in the *Appendix*, the piety of the hoopoe, who would not leave his mother without burial, is said to have been rewarded by the tuft of feathers which distinguishes him from the other birds.[27] Here, too, as we have seen, the poet speaks of his own expected recompense.[28] It is worth remarking that, in the latter of these passages, God is represented by the paraphrase "He who is not poor": while, in the former, the subject of جزى is omitted, as if the very mention of reward with Umayya supposed at once God as the rewarder.

In the Wâfir poem on the deluge, we are told that the white collar of the dove is the recompense of her fidelity.[29] Here, too, the poet tells us that:—

"The most glorious God awarded the man Noah the reward of the just, in which there is no falsity,

Consisting of what his ship carried and saved, the morning sudden death came upon them."[30]

Indeed, it is especially in his poems on this subject that he praises the mercy of God "who put an end to the deluge."[31] Nowhere do we find denounced, as so frequently in the Koran, the crimes of the wicked who perished in the waters. In one verse only—and there the reading is doubtful—is God's vengeance spoken of.[32] The mention of the overthrow of the nations in the same poem is obviously intended to heighten the effect produced by the description of the ark and the security of its occupants.[33]

Umayya, again, in describing the enforced servitude of the angels does not forget to add that the bonds which bind them are the benefits of God.[34] When he speaks of the tempter of our first parents, he seems to make a distinction between the serpent and Satan, who entered into his body, and declares that the nourishment of the former is ever the object of God's care.[35] What a contrast with the malediction pronounced against the serpent in *Genesis*, III, 14, and reproduced by the christian poet ʿAdî ibn Zaid in a verse that has been falsely attributed to Umayya![36] It may be remarked too that the poet does not disapprove of the superstitious practices by which the Arabs sought for rain in time of drought. He contents himself with laying stress on the fact that it is God who sends the rain.[37] Muḥammad, on the other hand, emphatically condemns the whole proceeding.[38]

The materialistic tendencies of Umayya are never more evident than when he speaks of the angels. Listen to his description of the Seraphim[39] who bear the throne of God:—"Our Lord hath girt with saddle-cloths the *beasts of burden*, each one of them bound by the munificence of God . . . and on the saddles is extended a lofty throne fixed firmly on their shoulders with gems of ruby."[40] The angels keep guard in turn before the Almighty.[41] Their service, in general, is a forced servitude.[42] Some of them who were refractory have been tamed.[43] They sustain[44] and defend[45] the heavens, which are regarded by the poet as smooth walls built around the fortress in which the Divinity dwells.[46] The weapons which they make use of against the demons are the shooting stars.[47] They fight battles, conquer when they assist one another, and have wings like those of ostriches which bear them along with the rapidity of the west wind.[48]

Analogous tendencies may be observed, for instance, in Umayya's crude explanations of natural phenomena. The sun is red in the morning because the angels have scourged him unto blood.[49] The tuft on the back of the hoopoe's head was originally his mother's tomb.[50] The ring on the dove's neck was once a real collar framed "as a child's necklace is strung."[51] The Arabs, in time of drought, got rain by lighting fires on the tails of cattle which they drove up the mountain, because these fires acted as lightning, at the appearance of which rain fell.[52] The poet even considers it necessary to explain God's vision of things by the presence of "streaks and colouring, and delineating marks" which He perceives though they may be invisible to us.[53] Interesting, too, in this connection, is the extraordinary manner in which he insists on the smoothness of the heavens.[54]

Umayya is a strenuous teacher of monotheism; yet, even on him, nature-worship has left its mark. The sun and moon, if not divinities, are still possessed of reasoning power. The former refuses to rise in the morning, owing to his unwillingness to receive the adoration of idolators.[55] The latter, for a similar reason, hides herself for the last two or three nights of each month: and the bright stars, lending their aid, place themselves in front of her to conceal her from the vision of her worshippers.[56] The stars, in general, are beasts of burden, obedient to God their Master,[57] travelling alike day and night, and rushing to the place of their setting like race-horses to their goal.[58] The winds are the beasts on which the clouds ride[59] as well as the limbs or supports of the sea.[60] The latter when agitated mounts upon them, so that its calmness can be indicated by saying that "its limbs abandon it." The earth also is an animal.[61]

That many of the expressions, in which materialistic and analogous tendencies, as well as traces of nature-worship, are displayed, admit of a different explanation is, of course, evident. They may be merely the fruit of a poet's and, more especially, an Arabic poet's imagination. Yet, when we have made ample allowance for that important factor, it seems to me that the greater part will *still* remain to be accounted for only by the poet's own personal characteristics.

Umayya seems to have had a special love for animals. Nor did this point in his character escape the notice of his contemporaries, who even ascribed to him a knowledge of the language of beasts.[62] To it also we may, perhaps, ascribe the legendary tales of his adventure with a serpent in one of his Syrian voyages,[63] and with crows or eagles or other birds at the time of his death.[64] Hence it is, too, that we have his poetry so frequently cited in the *Kitâb al-Ḥayawân* of Ǵâḥiẓ. We have already seen how frequently he employs, in describing the angels and the forces of nature, expressions borrowed from the animal world. It can be safely said, I think that in this he goes far beyond the metaphorical language of other Arabic poets. Moreover, in the four most important and certainly authentic poems of which we possess more or less lengthy fragments, special mention is made of animals. Several verses of the Kâmil poem in ذ are devoted to the hoopoe's act of filial piety and its reward.[65] In the Wâfir poem in ب , where the deluge is described, the cock, the crow[66] and the dove find a place.[67] When treating of the same subject in his Ḫafîf poem in ل the poet calls our attention to the birds, beasts of prey and elephants that cry out within the ark as it pursues its course amid the waves.[68] It is in the Ḫafîf poem in را , however, that the animals take the most prominent part. Here their creation is described in no perfunctory manner.[69] Four species of bovine antelopes are ennumerated:[70] and even the ass has two or, perhaps, three mentions.[71] Umayya is not contented with saying that God sent the ants and the locusts with other plagues on the Egyptians, but takes care to add:—"He remembered that the ants were doers of evil and that the locusts were a destructive pest."[72] The important part played by the little camel in the destruction of Ṯamûd[73] will be referred to later on. The abandonment of the little beast by his mother, in consequence of the ill-treatment she received at their hands, seems, almost, to have been, in the eyes of Umayya, the cause of all their woe. In this poem, too, the cattle, laden with ʿUśar and Salaʿ, and driven up the mountain-side with fires lighted on their tails, are sympathetically described. "Salaʿ and ʿUśar are heavy and they oppress the cattle" says the poet.[74]

Umayya belonged to a transition period of religious life in Arabia, when paganism was preparing to pass over into Islâm: and the man is characteristic of his epoch, as the apparent contradictions in his religious teaching show. An exalted idea of the Divinity combats with materialistic tendencies: a rigid monotheism struggles against remnants of nature and animal worship.[75]

Nor can we be surprised that this teaching was a failure, as, indeed, the poet himself foresaw.[76]

The aspect of the Divinity which he loved to exhibit was not likely to produce a very vivid impression on the gross minds of the idolatrous Arabs. He himself, as far as we can see, was neither soldier nor statesman. He gathered together no powerful partisans and made no appeal to arms. He effected no conjunction of patriotism and religion, no oblivion of tribal factions in a common confederacy for dominion. He was, moreover, too sincere to lay claim to a gift of prophecy which he did not possess. He must have, however, at least, prepared the way for a more illustrious rival. May he also be regarded, in some degree, as the inspiring angel, the *Gabriel* of Muḥammad? In order to deserve this appellation, he must have previously treated of Koranical subjects in his poems, and these poems must have come to the knowledge of, and been utilized by the author of the Koran.

* * *

We have already spoken, in general, of the subject-matter of Umayya's poetry, and we refer the reader to the most interesting article of Professor Schulthess in the *Orientalische Studien* for further information as to its contents and the sources from which the poet has drawn. The Arabic authors agree in celebrating his learning and, especially, his knowledge of Biblical history and Jewish legends.[77] All that it is necessary for our purpose to remark here is, that the fragments of his poems which remain to us amply confirm this tradition. Umayya, then, certainly treated of Koranical subjects. Did he treat of them before Muḥammad? It seems most probable that he did, though we have no absolutely conclusive evidence in the matter.

The period of Umayya's birth is unknown: but his death occurred some time between the second and the ninth years of the Hegira.[78] His elegy on the slain at Badr in the former year and the fact that we hear nothing of him at the capture of Ṭâʾif in the latter confirm this assertion of the historians. In their disaccord as to the precise date, and in the absence of other proofs, we had better make no attempt to come to a decision on the point. As for his age, a verse preserved in one of the Mss. of the *Ḥamâsa* of Abû Tammâm, and forming part of the poem in which he complains of his son's ingratitude, tells us that he was then close on his sixtieth year.[79] The intimate relations that existed between him and Ibn Ǵudʿân seem to couple him with the generation that preceded Muḥammad.[80] But the illustrious Taimite was also panegyrised by Ḥuṭaiʾa, who was still alive under the Umayyad dynasty.[81] A tradition, cited by Ibn Ḥaǵar,[82] tells us that Umayya despaired of obtaining the gift of prophecy for two reasons. Firstly, the chosen one was to be a Quraiśite and secondly he was to receive his mission at the age of forty. The giving of the second reason implies that the originator of this tradition considered Umayya over forty at this period and, consequently, older than Muḥammad. The same author goes on to tell us that Umayya, when invited to become a disciple of the prophet, replied that he would become the laughing-stock of the women of Ṭâʾif if he gave up his own claims in favor of a youth (غلام) of the Quraiś. This implies, at least, that our poet's position as a religious teacher was well established before the appearance of his rival. The conclusion is confirmed by the fact that, while Muḥammad was more than forty years of age when he commenced his prophetic career, the poetic inspiration of Umayya can hardly have been of such tardy growth. Indeed, the supposition, that the bulk of his religious poetry was composed in the last ten or fifteen years of his life, would be very gratuitous. The manner, in which some of his verses are cited in the *Muḥâḍarât*, shows also that they were considered anterior to the Koran.[83] On the whole, then, we seem perfectly justified in concluding that Umayya's religious teaching belonged to an earlier period than that of Muḥammad.

In discussing the question as to whether Muḥammad was or was not influenced by the poetry of Umayya, we must not forget that our poet's native city was only a day and a half's journey from Mekka. There lived his maternal relations, the Urnayyad merchants, in whose company he made journeys into Syria, if tradition is to be believed.[84] There, too, lived ʿAbdallah ibn Ǵudʿân, his patron and friend, in whose honor most of his non-religious verses were composed. Umayya's poetry, then, must have been frequently heard in Mekka. Let us consider, on the other hand, Muḥammad, himself uneducated, about to compose a Koran, which was to treat largely of those matters which formed Umayya's favorite theme. He would, certainly, have been a stranger to the ability which distinguished him, if he made no attempt to utilize our poet's learning and to seize the inspiration within his grasp. The fact, that he sometimes asked others to recite Umayya's poetry,[85] shows a desire to increase his knowledge much more than a total ignorance of it. The accounts given of the supposed interview between Muḥammad and the poet's sister are of no worth.[86] The words of the latter are so evidently a later fabrication[87] that we are forced to form a similar conclusion as to the part played by the former. All that we can safely conclude from such an interview, if it ever took place, is that Muḥammad was well acquainted with Umayya's poetic fame.

While we have ground for supposing that a certain influence was exercised by Umayya's poetry on the author of the Koran, it must be admitted that the fragments of that poetry which remain to us offer no confirmation of such a hypothesis. There is no Koranical narrative that displays undoubted traces of our poet's handiwork. One might, indeed, cite the story of "The Seven Sleepers."[88] Poetical treatment and the love of animals peculiar to Umayya would well explain the seemingly objectless presence of the dog in the unskilfully copied version of Muḥammad. But, the fact that *Ar-Raqîm* is made to fill exactly the place occupied by كلبهم in the Koran, shows that the verse was simply fabricated to support one of the many explanations of that difficult word. We have a similar forgery, made with a similar object, in Abû 'Ubaida's definition of the black and white threads.[89] The conversion of falling stars into missiles, with which the demons are pelted,[90] accords well with the pious and, at the same time, naïve interpretation of natural phenomena that distinguished the teaching of Umayya. We cannot be sure, however, that the poet did not, in this instance, draw from a source to which Muḥammad also had access. The oven of the deluge admits of a similar explanation. It appears twice in the Koranical narrative:[91] and in four poems, in which Umayya speaks at length of the deluge, it is mentioned either expressly or implicitly.[92] It probably owes its origin, as Halevy suggests, to a Rabbinical legend.[93] That Muḥammad borrowed this feature of the deluge story from Umayya is rendered less probable by their otherwise different manner of treating that great event.[94]

A still more remarkable instance of independant treatment is to be found in their versions of the destruction of Ṯamûd. The Koranical account of this event is manifold;[95] but it contains one element never absent, the personality of Ṣâliḥ, and another element present in three of the longer versions,[96] a party of the Ṯamûdites who hearkened to the advice of Ṣâliḥ and were saved with him. These two elements represent, naturally enough, Muḥammad and his followers, and, consequently, have no reason to appear in Umayya's version.[97] The fact that the latter makes a servant-maid escape, expressly in order to tell the tale,[98] shows that he did not contemplate the existence of a Ṣâliḥ, who would perform this duty so natural for and even incumbent on him. Umayya, too, brings a new element into the story, the little camel deprived of his mother and calling upon the Ṯamûdites the wrath of heaven.[99] This is a good instance of poetical treatment and the love of animals which distinguished him. It is worth remarking that the main features of the legend, the destruction of the Ṯamûdites for their impiety,[100] and the deed of the ill-starred Aḥmar,[101] are referred to by pre-Islamitic poets in a manner which shows that they were well known. Umayya and Muḥammad fill in the outlines of the picture each after his own fashion.[102]

There is another connection between Muḥammad and Umayya about which we are better informed. The Arabic historians are unanimous in asserting that the latter remained to the end an open enemy of the former.[103] The cause of this enmity would be two-fold for Umayya, his rivalry in teaching and his alliance with the Quraiś. His sympathy with the Banî Asad and the other Quraiśites, who fell fighting against Muḥammad at Badr, is evidenced by his elegies, in one of which, according to the testimony of Ibn Ḥiśâm, he attacked the prophet's companions.[104] We find, moreover, in the extant poetry attributed to Umayya, two verses which seem to contradict Koranic doctrine, and that, in reproducing peculiar Koranical expressions. *T^c A, s. v.* قصّ gives the following verse as by our poet: قالت لاخت له قصيه عن جنب وكيف يقفو بلا سهل ولا جدد.[105] The verse must be set beside *Koran*, XXVIII, 10: وقالت لاخته قصيه فبصرت به عن جنب.[106] The reference is to the directions given by the mother of Moses to his sister, when she had placed him in the Nile, as she had been ordered to do.[107] The similarity of expression, the fact that قصّ, like its synonym قفا, is properly used of following the foot-prints of somebody, and the question as to how one might follow foot-prints where there was no ground to receive them, that is, in the water, make it possible that this verse is part of a satire on the Koran. Again, Ǵâḥiẓ in his *Kitâb al-Buḫalâ'*, p. 236, as well as *Tᶜ A* and *Lᶜ A, s. v.* عسم, give the following verse of Umayya's famous poem on Paradise: ولا يتنازعون عنان شرك ولا اقوات اهلهم العسوم.[108] In the Koran, LII, 23 we find, with equal reference to the blessed, the words: يتنازعون فيها كأسا.[109] Thus we have a second contradiction of Koranical doctrine and the employment, in its more usual and proper sense, of a word, which, in the similar Koranical context, is used in a rare sense capable of being misinterpreted.[110] Accordingly, it seems fair to regard this verse also as a possible instance of an attack on the Koran. It is evident that both of these seeming contradictions can be otherwise explained.[111] We give them only for what they are worth. They at least show what kind of treatment Koranical teaching and Koranical expressions would be likely to receive at the hands of Umayya. On the other hand, to turn into verse, without any notable alteration or expression of disapprobation, the contents of the Koran, using even its very language, would be the best way of spreading the teaching of Muḥammad, and would thus be the work, not of his foe, but of his friend.

* * *

The spuriousness of some of the poetry attributed to Umayya is proved by its frequent reproduction of Koranical expressions. Obviously our poet could have no possible motive for a servile imitation of the very words of the author of the Koran and vice versa. Such a procedure would be fatal to the imitator, since it would manifest, as source of knowledge in the one case, and of inspiration in the other, that which each would be most anxious to disavow. Besides, we can scarcely suppose in Muḥammad so great a familiarity with Umayya's verses, or, in Umayya, so precise a knowledge of the Koran, as would render such a similarity of expression possible. Indeed, it would be an absolute impossibility for the author of the Koran to scatter broadcast into Sûras, written at long intervals, expressions taken from any single poem.[112] We have remarked above how unlikely our poet would be to versify and disseminate Koranical doctrine without submitting it to any change or modification. Only a later writer, thoroughly familiar with the language and sentiments of the Koran, would naturally reproduce its very expressions in his religious poetry. When, however, the ideas set forth in the verses attributed to our poet are to be called "Koranical," is a different question; and the answer to it may vary with the individual. It is for this reason that, while quite in accord with the spirit of Schulthess's criticism,[113] I should feel inclined to modify some of its details. Such a modification will, in some cases, confine itself to an attempt to distinguish the later importation from the genuine stock on which it has been grafted, and the existence of which Schulthess himself admits.[114]

In the first place, the four verses on the deluge (Ps-Balḫ, III, 24) seem to me to have every claim to authenticity. The deluge, if a Koranical subject, is admittedly a favorite one with Umayya also, and his treatment of it here is exactly similar to his treatment of it elsewhere. Noah's salvation in recompense for his goodness,[115] the oven,[116] the terrible voyage,[117] and the landing on the mountain[118] are all to be found in the other poems in which our poet treats of that subject. There are no expressions peculiar to the Koran except فار التنور, which, as we have seen, is still more peculiar to Umayya. The sole reason, then, for condemning these verses is that they are in the same rhyme and metre as the spurious verses on the destruction of Sodom.[119] Rhyme and metre, however, form no necessary connection between two fragments that treat of different subjects. Besides, there is a decided metrical difference between these two fragments, to which I should like to call attention.

It may be seen, from a perusal of the verses given in the *Appendix*, that the style of Umayya's poetry is diffuse and flowing. It is thus that, following a more genuine inspiration, he often sets aside that rule of Arabic poetry which would make the sense end with the verse.[120] The same tendency shows itself in his use of the Ḫafîf metre, where the first half-verse, in most cases, ends in the middle of a word. The elegy on the Banî Asad was, on this account, even considered faulty in metre.[121] Now, the fact that this caesura is found in two of the four verses in question, while it is not found in any one of the seven verses on the destruction of Sodom,[122] ought to be sufficient to differentiate these two poems as far as metre is concerned.

The Wâfir poem, rhyming in مُ, which treats of hell and paradise,[123] seems to me to be largely authentic, but to contain an interpolation, namely v. 14–21 of the poem as given by Ps-Balḫî.[124] The spuriousness of these verses is clearly demonstrated by the striking Koranical parallels. This makes it all the more remarkable that the rest of the poem, as preserved to us by Ps-Balḫî, ʿAinî, Ǵâḥiẓ, Ǵauharî, *Tʿ A* and *Lʿ A*, etc., possesses few or no echoes of the Koran: There, too, we may observe strange words or meanings of words,[125] a well-known peculiarity of the poetry of Umayya. To this we may add the local color evidenced by the mention, among the joys of paradise, of all the fruits for which Ṭâʾif, Umaayya's native place, was so remarkable.[126] Still more noteworthy is the "Wheat cut down in the places where it grew."[127] How much this latter element of food appealed to the Ṭâʾifite Umayya may be seen from his satirical verses on and subsequent panegyrics of ʿAbdallah ibn Ǵudʿân.[128] Again, we have hell compared to a sea of fire,[129] a comparison not found in the Koran but figuring in another poem of Umayya,[130] about which we shall speak later on. We have also the race-course metaphor,[131] a favorite one with our poet.[132] Since Umayya wrote verses on hell and paradise,[133] and in this rhyme and metre, to judge from some certainly genuine ones preserved to us by authorities like Sîbawaihi, Gauharî and Ǵâḥiẓ, why should we not conclude that these are they? It is worth remarking that only in Ps-Balḫî does the undoubtedly genuine verse وفيها لحم ساهرة وبحر وما فاهوا به لهم مقيم precede the interpolation, and thus preserve its proper and original position. The mention of the meats comes naturally after the description of the fruits and bread, and should not be separated from it by verses that treat of quite a different kind of pleasures. Some transcribers thought it better to let the greater part of the interpolation precede this verse.[134] Some again fused its second hemistich into one with the first hemistich of an interpolated verse.[135] The difference of opinion as to its position, which these traditions manifest, seems to me to strengthen the proofs of interpolation in this poem.

There does not seem to me to be much reason for doubting the authenticity of the Basîṭ poem in انا, at least as it appears in the *Ḫizâna*, I, 120. The reference to the sect of the Ḥanîfites, whom Umayya is known to have celebrated in his verses, is certainly in its favor. The third verse with its "نبي منا" is, in my mind, the only one which is calculated to raise any doubts. The personal nature of the demand, however, that each one might learn the length of his own life, information which he could not so easily ask of a stranger, seems to justify the expression. Nor would a Mussulman interpolator be likely to assign this as a reason for, or object of Muḥammad's mission. Indeed, the proper parallel for this and the immediately following verses is to be found, not in the Koran, but in Psalm XXXIX, 5–6, where the Psalmist begs God to inform him of the length of his days, and then goes on to say that he knows well himself how short they are. The possibility of a connection between this poem and the Koran does not seem to be strengthened by the supposed "Voraussetzung der ursprünglichen zweimæligen Ṣalât"[136] in the first verse. By praising God morning and evening is meant simply praising Him all day long, at all times, as is proved by the second hemistich, where the reason for this praise is given in similar terms. Needless to say, God bestows his blessings on us, not twice a day, but continually. Morning and evening, as the two extremes, include all that is between them. We have a precisely similar mode of expression employed by Umayya when he calls his patron Ibn Ǵud'ân "a friend whom neither morning nor evening finds a stranger to noble qualities."[137] The scholiast, it is true, finds an express reference to the raid in the morning and the hospitality in the evening: for which he is rightly censured by Freytag, since it is much more natural to suppose that Ibn Ǵud'ân is thus represented as invariably noble and good than to see in these words such a far-fetched allusion.[138] As for the opposition between *kâfir* and *îmân*,[139] we are told in the first verse of the poem on the battle of the Elephant that it is only the *kafûr* who doubts the signs of God.[140] From this to a juxtaposition of *kâfir* and *îmân* the passage is easy and has no need of being bridged over by the Koran.

As regards the two poems in *'Su'arâ'an-Naṣrânîya*, pp. 226–27, that derive their origin from a Mosul manuscript, it is more difficult to come to a decision. The Koranical parallels are not very striking, especially if we take into account the religious nature of the poems. I must confess to not understanding why the idea of the mortality of creatures should be considered so peculiarly Koranical as to inevitably arouse suspicion.[141] The same idea is to be found in the first verse of the undoubtedly genuine fragment given in the *Appendix*, as well as in the fifth and sixth verses of the Basîṭ poem, of which I have just tried to establish the authenticity, and in some other possibly, though not certainly, genuine verses attributed to Umayya.[142] In the shorter of these two poems we may remark, moreover, the reference to hell as a sea of fire[143] and stars as missiles:[144] both of which doctrines are elsewhere propounded by our poet. In the longer, the celebration of the throne of God and the angels,[145] both favorite topics with Umayya, and the double occurrence of the so-called poetical fault,[146] to which we have referred above as frequent in his poetry are worthy of notice. On the other hand, it must be confessed that both poems appear less rude and ancient than other undoubtedly genuine fragments of his religious poetry. Yet, a similar difference may be observed between some of his non-religious poems.[147] Such a variety of poetical style finds its counterpart in the apparent contradiction which characterised his religious teaching. Both find their explanation in, and lend additional interest to the personality of him, who, animated by the hope of a future reward, strove by his religious verses to raise up the minds of his idolatrous contemporaries to higher things.

APPENDIX

Extract from *Al-Ḥamâsat al-Baṣrîya*, Ms. of St Joseph's University, Beyrout, II, 269.

وقال امية بن ابي الصلت

حيا وميتا لا ابا لك انمــا   طول الحياة كزاد غاد ينفد
والشهر بين هلاله ومحاقه   اجل لعلم الناس كيف يعدد
لا نقص [148] فيه غير ان خبيئةً [149]   قمر وسَاهُورٌ يسل ويغمــد
خرق يهيم كهاجع في نومه   لم يقض ريب نعاسه فيهجد
فاذا مَرَتهُ ليلتان وراءه [150]   فقضى سراه او كراه يسأد

لمواعد تجرى النجوم امامــه   ومُعَتَمٌ بجذائهن مسوّد
مستخفيا وبنَاتُ نعش حوله   وعن اليمين اذا يغيب الفرقد
حال الدرارى دونــه فتجنه   لا ان يراه كل من يتلدّد
والشمس تطلع [151] كل اخر ليلة   حمراء [152] يصبح [153] لونها يتورد [154]
ليست بطالعة لهم [155] في رسلها [156]   الا [157] مُعَذَّبَةً [158] والا [159] تُجلَدُ
لا تستطيع بان تقصر ساعة   وبذاك تداب يومهــا وتشرد
ولسوف ينسى ما اقول معاشرٌ   ولسوف يذكره الذى لا يزهد
فاغفر لعبد ان اول ذنبــه   شرب وايسار يشاركها دد

"Living and dead! Length of life, in very truth,[160] resembles only a traveller's provision-store that is consumed:

And, that men may know how it is to be measured, between the new moon and the end of the month is a fixed period.

There is no deficiency in the moon; but a hidden thing is she and the envelope from which she is drawn and in which she is sheathed.

Bewildered, she wanders about like a sleeper in his slumber, who has not satisfied the need of his drowsiness and who slumbers on.

And, while two nights behind her drive her on, and she puts an end to her night-journeying or her drowsiness, marching along

By appointed stages, (the stars hastening before her and opposite them their crowned chief

In disguise, with *Banât Na'ś* around her and *Al-faryad* on her right hand, when she is hidden,)

The bright stars come in front of her and conceal her, that none of the idolators[161] may behold her.

And the sun rises at every night's end, ruddy and purple in hue.

Nor does he rise for them of his own accord, but only when tortured and scourged.

He is unable to shorten his course by a single hour, and thus does he march and is he driven all day long.

And as surely as clans will forget what I say, so surely will He Who is not poor remember it.

Pardon then a servant; it is drinking and gambling,[162] joined with amusements, that have been the beginning of his sin.

Notes

1. E. Power, "Umayya ibn Abi-Ṣ Ṣalt," in *Mélanges de la Faculté Orientale de L' Université Saint-Joseph*, Beyrouth, vol. 1 (1906), pp. 117–202.

2. *Orientalische Studien*, pp. 71–89.

3. Ṯaqif, the tribe that inhabited Ṭâ'if, was probably not descended from Muḍar. Among the aristocrats, at least, the family of our poet and that of Mas'ûd ibn Mu'attib, both closely allied with Quraigś, traced their lineage to lyád. Cf. poetical citations i Bekrî, 51: to which add *Aḍdād*, 81, and *Aḡâni*, III, 187 (verses of Umayya's son Rabî'a). Their geographical position and the fact that they made common cause with the Hawâzin in their wars gave genealogists a reason for considering them a branch of that clan. The descendants of Iyâd, however, formerly

inhabited this part of the Arabian peninsula, nothing is more probable than that some should have held their ground in so strong a position and so fertile a district.

4. *Aḡânî,* II, 18.

5. Ms. of Oriental Library, St. Joseph's University, Beyrout, II, 269. This man-nuscript consists of two parts, of which the first contains 249 and the second 270 pages. It contains also fragments, to be found elsewhere, of seven other poems attributed to Umayya. It is copied from the Ms. of the Khedivial Library at Cairo, for an account of which consult *Catalogue* (ed. 1301-8 H.), 229.

6. *LʿA*, XII, 386.

7. See *Appendix*.

8. See *Appendix*.

9. *Al-Muḥâḍarât*, II, 369; Ǵâḥiẓ, *Kitâib al-Ḥayawdn*, Ms. of Vienna 341 v., (Cf. *WZKM*, VIII, p. 67, n. 4). — My citations from this manuscript are taken from some notes which Rev. L. Cheikho S. J. has had the kindness to lend me.

10. *Ḥayawân*, 183 v.; Ibn Qutaiba, *Book of Poets*, 279.

11. Ps-Balḫî, III, 25; *Ḥayawân*, 212 v.; At̲-T̲aʿlibî, *ʿImâd al-Balâḡa*, chap. XXXIX.

12. Ps-Balḫî, I, 165.

13. Ps-Balḫî, I, 169.

14. Ps-Balḫî, II, 7; *LʿA*, VI, 20; IX, 356; XII, 386; *TʿA*, III, 153, 262, 339; *Muzhir*, I, 286, etc.

15. *Ḥayawân*, 183 v.; Ibn Qutaiba, 279. The poet speaks of the "mist, darkness and thick clouds" that characterized the period when the hoopoe's mother died. We learn from Aristophanes, *Aves*, 471–75, that this was before the creation of the earth.

16. *Ḥayawân*, 212 v.; Ps-Balḫî, III, 25; Maqrīzī, *Ḫiṭaṭ*, I, 160; *ʿImâd al-Balâḡa*. chap. LVII.

17. Ps-Balḫî, III, 24–25; *Ḫizâna* IV, 4; *Ḥayawân*, 212 v., etc.

18. Ṭabari, I, 308; *Ḫiz*., II, 543; Ps-Balḫî, III, 65; At̲-T̲aʿlibi, *ʿArâ'is*, 82; Soiûtî, *'Saw. Muḡnî*, 241.

19. Ps-Balḫî, III, 82; *Ḥayawân*, 112 v. (Cf. *WZKM*, VIII, p. 61).

20. *TʿA, LʿA, s. v.* شطن ; *Naqd aś-S̲iʿr*, 86; Ibn Duraid, *Iśtiqâq*, 228.

21. Ps-Balḫî, III, 40; Yâqût IV, 54; ʿAinî, IV, 377; Sîrâfî (Jahn's Sîbâwaihi, I, 2, p. 29).

22. *ʿArâ'is* 82, v. 1: الموقي بنذر احتسابا. For sense of احتسابا , cf. Lane, *s. v.*

23. *Ḫiz*., II, 543, v. 3: ابقي النبي جزيتك بالله تقيًّا به على كل حال .

24. Ps-Balḫî, III, 65, v. 4: جعل الله جيده من نحاس اذ رآه زولا من الازوال.

25. Ṭabari, I, 308, v. 7: انّي للّذي قد فعلتما غير قالِ .

26. *Ibidem*, v. 8: فطارا منه بسمع فعال .

27. *Ḥayawân*, 183 v., cf. especially v. 8: فجزى بصالح حملها ولدًّا .

28. *Appendix*, v. 12.

29. *Ḥayawân*, 212v., v. 6–7; Ps-Balḫî, III, 25, v. 4–5; *ʿImâd al-Balâġa*, chap. XXXIX, v. 3–4 of a four-line fragment of this poem, for a translation of which cf. *ZDMG*, VIII, p. 511.

30. Ps-Balḫî, III, 25, v. 6–7.

31. *LʿA, TʿA, s.v.* شرجم : وينقّد الطوفان نحن فداوْه .

32. *Ḥiz*., IV, 4, v. 1. But cf. *LʿA, s. v.* قدم where it is said that God will take vengeance on the prince of evil " امير السوء " not the servants of evil "عبيد السوء" of *Ḥiz*. This reading, that of Ibn Barri, one of the best authorities for Umayya's poetry, is confirmed by the sense تقدّم there given to قدم. Only the rich and proud are threatened with vengeance; and, indeed, the "prince of evil" may be simply Satan.

33. *Ḥiz*., IV, 4, v. 4.

34. Ps-Balḫî, I, 165, v. 1: كل بنعماء الاله مقيّد .

35. *Ḥayawân*, 212v. Such, at least, seems the general sense of this badly corrupted test.

36. *TʿA, LʿA, s. v.* lāṭ. (The verse is cited with several others of the same poem). Magri: *Ḥiṭaṭ*, I, 22 and Ǵâḥiẓ, *Ḥayawân*, 213 r. (cf. *Maŝriq*, 1904, 535–36). Schulthess (p. 78) doubts the authenticity of these verses. But, cited by so good an authority as Ǵâḥiẓ and echoing *Genesis* rather than the *Koran*, they seem to me much more probably the composition of a learned christian poet like ʿAdi ibn Zaid than that of a Mussulman interpolator.

37. Cf. *Ḥam. Baṣ*. II, 257, v. 8; *Ḥayawân*, 245 v., v. 6–7:

فرآها الاله توشم بالقطر   واضحى جنابهم ممطورا

فسقاها نشاطه ....

(For the first verse I have taken the text of *Ḥam. Baṣ*. which is preferable).

38. Cf. Margoliouth's *Life of Muḥammad*, p. 459, and reference there.

39. Ps-Balḫî, I, 168: حبس السرافيل. Umayya has assigned to the Seraphim the office of the Cherubim in the Bible, *Psalms*, XVIII, 11; LXXX, 2; XCIX, 1; *Eccles*, XLIX, 10.

40. Ps-Balḫî, I, 165, v. 1–3.

41. Ps-Balḫî, I, 169, v. 1: في الف الف من ملائك تحشد   ينتابه المتنصفون بسُخرة. For سُخرة (which I read instead of Ms. سجرة) = تسخير cf. Lane, *s. v.* The textual corrections in the first and last word are after *Maŝriq*, 1904, p. 533.

42. See preceding citation. Cf. also Ps-Balḫî, I, 168: حبس ; *T‘A*, III, 339: مصقّدين.

43. *L‘A, T‘A, s. v.* قوم : ملائك ذُلّلوا وهمِ صعاب .

44. *T‘A*, III, 339: عليهم صاقورة . Cf. also citation at end of note 54 in following فبنى الاله عليهم مخصوفة .

45. *T‘A, s.v.* رقيم : ومن دون علم الغيب كل مسهّد . See also below note 47.

46. *T‘A*, III, 262; *L‘A*, VI, 20; IX, 356; XII, 386; Al-‘Ukbarî, *Śarḥ al-Matanabbî,* II, 3.

فاتمّ ستّا فاستوت اطباقها　　　واتى بسابعة فانّى تورد

The question « How shall it (the seventh heaven, God's abode) be reached? », as well as the stress laid on the smoothness of the heavens, of which we shall speak later on, reveal the poet's idea.

47. *Ḥayawân*, 341v. (ccf. *WZIC*, VIII, p. 67); *Muḥâḍarât*, II, 369, where the text is better.

وترى شياطينهم تروغ مضافة　　　وزواغها صبر اذا ما تطرد
تلقى عليها في السماء مذلّة　　　وكواكب ترمى بها فتعرد

48. Ps-Balḫî, I, 169.

49. *Appendix*, v. 9–10.

50. *Ḥayawân*, 183 v., v. 6-7: فبنى عليها في قفاه يمهد

مهدًا وطيًا

51. Ps-Balḫî, III, 25, v. 4: صاغوا لها طوقًا كما عقد السخاب.

52. *Ḥam. Baṣ.*, II, 257, v, 8: فرآها الاله توشم بالقطر واضحى　　　جنابهم مطورا . Cf. also *Ḥayawân*, 245 v., v. 6.

53. *Ḥayawân*, 183 v., v. 2–3: وبكل منكرة له معروفة　　　اخرى على عين بما يتعهد
جدد وتوشيم ورسم علامة

54. Ps-Balḫî, II, 7, the first heaven is said to be smooth, like a waveless sea, in v. 1 (where we must read, اجرد , سدر, after *T‘A*, III, 262; *L‘A*, XII, 386; *Muḫaṣṣaṣ*, IX, 6; X, 16, etc.). In v. 2 the second heaven "is even not bent" (reading تخضد for يحصد), and it is compared with glass in the next verse obviously in smoothness as well as in colour. In *T‘A*, III, 339, the third heaven is compared to a crystal sea. It is the smoothness of the fourth and fifth heavens that is referred to in the difficult verse cited *T‘A*, III, 153: وكأنّ رابعة لها حاقورة　　　في جنب خامسة عناصٍ تمرد . "It seems as if the fourth heaven, the Ḥâqûra, though hairless, had little locks of hair in comparison with the fifth." That is to say, though the fourth heaven is smooth, the fifth is far more so. The surface of the heavens is described as smooth, without cracks, so that the sun slides along it, in a verse cited by Ǵauhari, I, 53; II, 505 (var. سراة صلاية خلقاء صيغت . تُزلّ الشمس ليس لها رئاب (اياب . And similarly Umayya informs us that the heavenly vault, resting on angel-shoulders

never becomes worn or bent, and that, if it were not so smooth that even the Qurâd-insect could find no hold thereon, God would destroy it and build another possessing perfection.

والارض معقلنا وكانت أمّنا　　فيها معاقلنا وفيها نُولَدُ
فيها تلامذة على قذفاتها　　حَسَرَى قياماً والفرائض تُرعَدُ
فبنى الاله عليهم مخصوفةً　　خلقاء لا تَبْلَى ولا تتأوّد
فلو انّه يَجدُ (Ms يخد) البرامَ لمتنها　　لبنى والقاها التي لا تُقْرَدُ

The verses are taken from a Ms. of the Oriental Library, St. Joseph's Univesity, Beyrout, entitled *Śarḥ Abyât al-Iḍâḥ* by Abû'l Ḥaǵǵâǵ Yûsuf ibn Sulaimân al-Qurṭubî better known as Aś-Śantamarî al-A'lam, ff. 61 v. There seems to be no mention of composition among the works of the writer, unless it be identical with the *Śarḥ Abyât al-Ǵumal* ascribed to him by Ḫâǵǵî Ḫalifa, II, 627. For the author, cf. Brockelmann, I, p. 139; Ahlwardt, *Six Arabic poets*, XVIII. For معاقلنا of v. 1, At-Ṯa'libî, *'Arâ'is*, 8 gives مقابرنا and Ibn Sayyidihi, *Al-Muḫaṣṣaṣ*, XIII, 180: معايشنا. The latter also replaces by منها the second فيها .

55. See *Appendix*, v. 10–12. The reason of the sun's unwillingness is obviously the same as that assigned to the moon in v. 10.

56. *Ibidem.*

57. Cf. verse cited by *L'A* and *T'A*, *s.v.* صيدق .

58. Cf. *Muntaḫab Rabî al-Abrâr*, Ms. of Vienna, 84 v. : —

تامل صنع ربك غير شك　　بعينيك كيف تختلف النجوم
فما يجرى (sic) سوابق ملجمات　　كما تجري ولا طير يحوم
دوابّ في النهار فما تراها　　ويمشي (sic) مشي ليلتها تعوم

Also the oft cited verse *T'A*, V, 185; VII, 43, 57; *L'A*, XII, 198; *Muḫaṣṣaṣ*, IX, 35, etc:—

واعلاق الكواكب مرسلات　　كخيل القرق غايتها النصاب

"And the suspended stars, sent forth like steeds in a race-course, their goal being the place where they set."

All the lexicographers understand by قرق the game of that name. But the context (نصاب , غاية , خيل , مرسلات), the parallel passage just cited, the derivation of the word (ܩܘܪܩܘܣ, χίρχος, circus), as attested by its other form قرقوس and its other meaning قاع واسع كثير الحصى , lastly the difficulty of understanding by it here the game of the same name (in which stones have to be moved backwards and forwards until they are got into a straight line), all prove that this is another of the words by which our poet puzzled the lexicographers, and that it was employed here by him in the sense of "race-course."

59. *L'A*, I, 416: تردد والرياح لها ركاب

60. *T'A, L'A, s. v*, سدر , برقم, etc.—سَدِر = متحير , غير راشد ,·is an epithet of the sea when it is agitated. A propos of برقم , I do not know if it has been remarked what support De Goeje's derivatio gets from such names of Syrian villages as Bikfaya = ڪَد ڪفًا "Rockhouse," Brummâna = ڪد ؤومنًا "Pomegranate-house", = ڪد سَعدِنو "Ḥamdûn's house."

61. Umayya calls it طروقة . Cf. *L'A, T'A, s. v.* عتم and سقد.

62. *Agânî*, III, 188–89: he understands the language of sheep; *ibid.*, 192: he understands the language of crows.

63. *Alif-Bâ*, II, 508; Damîrî, II, 195, etc.

64. *Agânî*, III, 192; *Alif-Bâ*, II, 508; *Agânî*, III, 188–89, 189–90, etc.

65. *Ḥayawân*, 183 v., v. 5–9.

66. Ps-Balḫî, III, 25, v. 12; *Ḥayawân*, 212 v., v. 2; *'Imâd al-Balâga*, chap. LVII; *Ḫiz.*, 1, 120; Ibn Qutaiba, 279.

67. Ps-Balḫî, III, 25, v. 1–5; *Ḥayawân*, 212 v., v. 3–7; *'Imâd al-Balâga*, chap. XXXIX.

68. *Ḥayawân*, 396 v.

69. *Ḥayawân*, 397 v.

70. *Ibidem*, v. 2 and VA, XIII, 86, where the text is better.

71. *Ibidem*, v. 3. We may understand by Ms. صواحنا either ضواحيا or صواحنا . The latter would be plural of صحون=صاحنة "kicking she-ass." The former could mean "dwelling in the plain" and thus go with the immediately preceding نعام . Such an epithet is supported by the proverb given in *L'A*, XIII, 61, *s. v.* نعام; من يجمع بين الاروى والنعام applied to him who tries to unite things that are incompatible with one another.

72. *Ḥayawân*, in *WZICM*, VIII, p. 61: وان الجراد كان ثبورا ذكر الذرّ انه يفعل الشرّ , which Van Vloten translates: "Er machte die Ameise Bœses thun and die Heuschrecke zur Zerstœrung." But would not such a rendering require يكون instead of كان in the second hemistich?

73. Ps-Balḫî, III, 40.

74. *Ḥam. Baṣ.*, 257, v. 6; *Ḥayawân*, 245 v., v. 8; Damîrî, I, 170, v. 5; Ǵauharî, II, 220, v. 5; *L'A*, XIII, 516, v. 5, etc.:

سلع ما ومثله عشر ما عائل ما وعالت البيقورا

75. This expression is justified, if not by Umayya's frequent mention of animals in his religious poetry, at least by reference to the sacred camel (ناقة للاله , Ps-Balḫî, III; 40, v. 2) in the story of the destruction of Ṯamûd.

76. *Appendix*, v. 12.

77. *Aḡânî*, III, 187; Ibn Ḥaǵar, I, 261; Ibn Qutaiba, 279; *Ḥiz*. 121; *Alif-Bâ*, 508, etc.

78. The historians Abû'l-Fidâ, I, 137; Diârbakrî, *Al-Ḫamîs*, I, 412; Ibn Al-Wardî, I, 117, and others assign his death to the former date. For the latter, cf. Ibn Ḥaǵar, I, 262; *Ḫiz*., I, 121, etc.

79. Ms. Goth., 532, f° 17r., where the poet says: ولم يأتني من سنّ ستّون كمّلُ . Unfortunately the authenticity of this poem is doubtful. Cf. Freytag, *Ḥamâsa* (Arabic text), p. 354.

80. *Aḡânî*, VIII, 2–5, etc.

81. Cf. Goldziher, *ZDMG*, 1892, p. 31. The poem (*ZDMG*, 1893, p. 82) is attributed to Umayya himself: but the third verse

: كلّ أمرٍ ينوبُ عَبسًا جَميعًا   أنتَ فيه المُطامُ فيما تقولُ

shows that either the panegyrist or the panegyrized was of the tribe of 'Abs. That the verses were addressed to Ibn Ǵudʿân, however, rests solely on the Scholiast's authority.

82. I, 262–63. The general falsity of the substance of these traditions does not, of course, deprive them of their value in fixing the age of Umayya, as it appeared to those who who had means of knowing it that we do not possess.

83. *Muḥâḍarat*, II, 369.

84. *Prairies d'or*, I, 136, 139; *Aḡânî* III, 190, 191, etc. We learn from Aṯ-Ṯaʿlibi, *ʿArd'is*, 208 and Al-Ḫâzin, *Tafsîr*, II, 177, that Umayya visited certain kings shortly before Badr: and Ṭabarî, I, 1121 preserves to us a verse he is supposed to have addressed to Heraclius. A connection with Syria, thus supported by tradition, is hard to be denied in the case of Umayya, inhabitant of the trading town of Ṭâ'if and closely allied with the Umayyads.

85. Damiri, II, 195; *Ḫiz* I, 120; Ibn Hagar, I, 261; Ibn Qutaiba, 279; Aḡânî, III, 190; Iqd, III, 123.

86. Cf. *ʿArâ'is*, 208; Damirî, II, 441; *Alif-Bâ*, II, 508.

87. She gives a legendary account of the poet's death and recites some of his spurious verses to Muḥammad. No wonder the latter showed no previous knowledge of them.

88. Cf. Umayya's verse, *Kaśśâf*, I, 722; Baiḍâwî, I, 555 and *Koran*, XVIII, 8: والرقيم , 17: كلبهم باسط ذراعيه بالوصيد .

89. *LʿA*, *TʿA s. v.* خيط ; Ṣoiûtî, *Itqân*, 159. Cf. Koran, II, 183. The commentator might have found a genuine support for his explanation of the two threads in Labîd (ed. Brockelmaun, 64) where the poet says he reached his destination in the early morning :— قبل تبيّن الالوان .

90. *Ḥayawân*, 341 v.; *Muḥâḍardt*, II, 369. Cf. *Koran*, XXXVII, 7–10; LXVII, 5; LXXII, 8–9.

91. *Koran*, XI, 42; XXIII, 27.

92. Expressly in the third and fifth verses cited by Ps-Balḫî, III, 24. Implicitly, Ps-Balḫi, III, 25, in the word تسعار of the second last verse, and *Ḫiz.*, IV, 4, v. 5 in the word دخان , the fire and smoke proceeding from the oven or furnace.

93. *Journal Asiatique*, Janv.–Fev. 1905, p. 141. Cf. Talmudic legend which says that the hot springs near Tiberias are remnants of the eruptions of the deluge.

94. Muḥammad emphasizes God's justice in destroying, Umayya His mercy in saving. See above. . . .

95. *Koran*, VII, 71–77; XI, 64–71; XXVI, 141–59; XXVII, 46–54; LIV, 23–31; XCI, 11–15.

96. *Koran*, VII, 73; XI, 69; XXVII, 46. Only once (XCI, 14) is it expressly stated that they were *all* destroyed.

97. Ps-Balḫi, III, 40.

98. *Ibid.*, v. 8.

99. *Ibid.*, v. 5–7. "He prayed a prayer, and the prayer of the little camel against them was: — 'May they be utterly destroyed!'" —As the utterance of the little camel is expressed in words, I read دعا دعوة rather than رغا رغوة , the Ms. دعا رغوة leaving us free to read one or the other.

100. Labîd (ed. Brockelmann), 25. Cf. also ʿAdî ibn Zaid in *Śuʿarâ' an-Naṣrâniya*, 471.

101. Zuhair's *Muʿallaqa* (ed. Hausheer), 22.

102. It is noteworthy that Umayya's verses on the plagues of Egypt (cf. *Ḥayawân*, in *WZKM*, VIII, p. 61 and *ʿArâ'is*, 166), which probably formed part of this poem, also show independent treatment. Of the four plagues mentioned by Umayya, only two, the drought and the locusts, those most commonly experienced and most sensibly felt in the East, are given by Muḥammad, who adds several others (*Koran*, VII, 127, etc.). Both Al-Ǵâḥiẓ and At-Taʿlibî call special attention to our poet's mention of the ant plague.

103. Cf. *Aḡânî*, III, 187; *Ḫiz.*, I, 121, where Muḥammad forbids the recitation of his Badr elegy. He died an unbeliever: Ibn Ḥaǵar, I, 264; *Aḡânî*, III, 192; Al-Ḫâzin, *Tafsir*, I, 29, etc.

104. *Sîrat ar-Rasûl*, 532.

105. "She said to his sister, 'Follow him at a distance'; and how will she follow the track where there is no ground rough or smooth?"

106. "And she said to his sister, 'Follow him'; and she gazed on him from distance."

107. *Koran*, XXVIII, 6.

108. "And they pull not the reins of partnership, nor is the food of their people pieces of hard, dry bread."

109. "Handing around a cup to one another therein." The partnership, implied by this expression, is denied by Umayya.

110. "Snatching a cup from one another" is a possible rendering.

111. The former verse would be part of a Koranical commentary. The difficulty in Koran is there propounded as a question, to which we should perhaps find an answer in the following verses, if we had them. The resemblance and contradiction, in the second case, are too slight to suggest any necessary connection between that verse and the Koran. They are, more probably, purely accidental.

112. For instance, the nine verses in Ps-Balḫî, II, 146 contain expressions to be found in three times that number of Koranical sûras, and the same may be said of the six-line poem given at p. 209 of Aṯ-Ṯaʿlibâ's *ʿArâ'is*, where, by the way, the Koran (XIX, 83, 95) is expressly cited in the third verse: يوم تأتيه مثل ما قال فردًا.

113. *Orientalische Studien*, pp. 76–78.

114. *Ibidem*, 78, near end of page.

115. Cf. Ps-Balḫi, III, 25, v. 6–7; 24, v. 2; Al-Bekrî, 219.

116. See citations given above, note 96.

117. Cf. *Asâs al-Balâġa*, I, 82; *Ḥayawân*, 396 v.; *Ḫiz.*, IV, 4.

118. Cf. *Ḫiz.*, IV, 4, v. 6; Al-Bekrî, 219, where لهبطه (cf. اهبط here) is obviously to be preferred to the corrupt لشيعته of Ps-Balḫî, III, 24, v. 2.

119. Yâqût, III, 59; Ps-Balḫi, III, 58; III, 58; *Qazwînî*, *Aṯâr al-Bilâd*, 135. Cf. also *Orientalisch Studien*, p. 78 *g*.

120. Cf. especially the verses on the hoopoe, *Ḥayawān*, 183 v.; *Appendix*, v. 5–8. Also Ps-Balḫi, I, 165, v. 2–3 and v. 6–7 (where جديرا بالبناء الأعلى should be translated "worthy of the most lofty building"); III, 25, v: 10–11; *Śuʿara' an-Naṣrânîya*, 221 (end of page), v. 2–3, 6–7.

121. Ad-Dumâmînî, *Al-ʿUyûn al-fâḫira 'al-ġâmiza ʿalâ ḫabâyâ ar-râmiza*, 90. It is not, of course, meant to be implied by the above remarks that the presence of this caesura in the Ḫafif metre is peculiar to Umayya, but that its absence from his poetry, in a marked degree, would be surprising.

122. The same is true of the certainly spurious six-line poem in *ʿArâ'is*, p. 209 and of the four doubtful verses on the poet's own death (*Prairies d'or*, I, 138; *Aġânî*, III, 190, etc.).

123. Ps-Balḫi, I, 202. Cf. also ʿAinî, II, 346. The lexicons *s. v.* تنفّث, حتم, وزيم, شرم, عسم, فاه, ساهرة, حفض; *Muntaḫab Rabiʿ al-Abrâr*, Ms. of Vienna, 16 v.; *Ǵanzhara*, 8; *Itqân*, 154, 161; *Ǵâḥiẓ, Buḥâlâ'*, 236, etc. add verses and help to correct text.

124. See above, n. 123.

125. Cf. the words cited in note 123.

126. Ps-Balẖî, I, 202, v. 11–12.

127. *Ibidem*, v. 10 : وقمح في منابته صريم.

128. Ḥalabî, I, 173; Ibn Ḥiśâm, 369; *Śuʿcarâʾ an-Naṣrânîya*, poem at end of p. 221, v. 7.

129. Ps-Balẖi, I, 202, v. 5; *Muntaẖab Rabiʿ al-Abrâr*, 16 v., v. 3.

130. *Śuʿarâʾ an-Naṣrânîya*, 226, v. 11.

131. Ps-Balẖî, I, 202, v. 22. The text is perhaps corrupt: but التي stands for, not one of the houries, nor yet the wine-cup, but غاية or جنّة, the only term allowed by the context. تقبلهم, if not corrupt, has this word as subject; and the being dispensed from fasting follows the arrival in paradise, the end of this life's suffering. Translate, then: —"When they reach that (namely the goal or garden) to which they have been made to run, it receives them, and the faster is dispensed from his fast."

132. See above, note 58; cf. also *Ḫiz.*, I, 120, v. 3, where the reading as مجرانا as against محيانا of *Aḡânî*, III, 190 is supported by the context and by Sibawaihi (ed. Derenbourg), I, 385 and ʿAinî, IV, 412.

133. *Alıf-Bâ*, II, 508; *Prairies d'or*, I, 137, etc.

134. ʿAinî, II, 347; Al-Ḫuḍârî's, *Ḥâśiyat to the Alfîyat*, I, 221.

135. *Prairies d'or*, I, 137; Ibn ʿAqîl's *Commentary to the Alfîyat* (ed. Cairo, 1279 H.), p. 103; *TʿA*, IX, 405; *LʿA*, XIV, 272; XVII, 422.

136. *Orientalische Studien*, p. 78 *k*.

137. *Śuʿarâʾ an-Naṣrânîya*, p. 220, v. 3. خليل لا يغيره صباح عن الخلق الجميل ولا مساء.

138. *Hamasae Carmina*. Pars Posterior, II, 654.

139. *Orientalische Studien*, p. 78 *k*.

140. *Śuʿarâʾ an-Naṣrânîya*, p. 229, v.1: لا يماري فيهن الا الكفور.

141. *Orientedische Studien*, p. 77 *c*.

142. *Ḫiz.*, I, 119, v. 1–3. Cf. also the verses composed on his deathbed, *Aḡânî*, III, 192, etc.

143. *Śuʿarâʾ an-Naṣrânîya*, p. 226, v. 11; cf. Ps-Balẖi, I, 202, v. 5.

144. *Ibidem*, v. 4 :مراميها اشدّ من النصال. Cf. *Muḥâḍarât*, II, 369.

145. *Śuʿarâʾ an-Naṣrânîya*, 227–28 passim. Cf. also *Appendix*, note to translation of v. 8.

146. *Ibidem*, v. 14–15, 28–29.

147. Contrast, for instance, the two poems on Ibn Ǵudʿân (*Śuʿarâʾ an-Naṣrânîya*, pp. 220 and 222). The delicacy of the former is rendered all the more remarkable by the fact that it is the earlier of the two, the latter having been composed at Ibn Ǵudʿân's death.

148. Ms.: نقض.

149. *T'A*, II, 286; *L'A*, VI, 50; XII, 386: خبيئة, Ǵauharî, I, 336: جبينه.

150. Ms. ورائه.

151. *Ḫiz.*, I, 121; Ps-Balḫî, II, 22: تصبح.

152. *'Iqd*, III, 123: فجراو.

153. *Aḡânî*, III, 191: معظم; Ps-Balḫî, *l. c.*: تضحى.

154. *Aḡânî*, *l. c.*: متورد; Ps-Balḫî, *l. c.*; *'Iqd, l. c.*: يتوقد.

155. *Aḡânî*, *l. c.*: تأبى فلا تبدو لنا; Ps-Balḫî, *l. c.*; Damîrî, II, 194: تأبى فما تطلع لنا; *'Iqd*, III, 123, 157: تأبى فما تطلع لهم.

156. *'Iqd, l. c.*: وقتها.

157. Ps-Balḫî, *l. c.*; اما.

158. Ibn Qutaiba, 280: معذبةً (a preferable vocalization, though that of the Ms. may be defended by understanding وهي after the first الا).

159. Ps-Balḫî, *l. c.*; اما.

160. For this rendering of لا ابا لك, cf. Nœldeke, *Fünf Mo'allaqât*, III, 35. See also Fischer in *Orientalische Studien*, p. 50, note 1, and reference there given.

161. Lane gives تلدّد the meaning "wait in expectation," which would suit the cotent here. I prefer, however, to adopt the root meaning "turn aside from something," understanding the implied "something" as a line of conduct or religious belief. This meaning is supported by قومًا لُدًّا of Koran, XIX, 97, as well as by the use of لَدَّد as an equivalent of تلدّد in the third last verse of the poem given in *Śu'arâ' an-Naṣrânîya*, p. 227, where the sense of اعمى يلدد is determined by the الاعمى المميط عن الهدى of v. 29. Needless to say, employment of the same verb in a rare metaphorical sense in both these poems supports the tradition that ascribes them to the same author.

162. Cf. *Koran*, II, 219; V, 92–93, where الخمر والميسر are jointly condemned. Though the lexicons do not give أيسار or إيسار as an equivalent of ميسر, the meaning here must be the same as in the Koran. أيسار "the gamblers" may be used for ميسر "the game."

1.6

The Poems of Umayya B. Abī-ṣ-Ṣalt

Additions, Suggestions, and Rectifications[1]

E. Power, SJ

Professor Schulthess by his recent publication[2] has earned the gratitude of all who are interested in the early religious history of Arabia, for the poems ascribed to Umayya b. Abī-ṣ-Ṣalt, especially such of them as happen to be authentic, are of considerable importance in this respect. It is not an easy task to collect and interpret the verses of a poet, when there is no substratum, containing a number of more or less complete poems, on which to build. Besides the tedious labor of reading through an enormous amount of published and manuscript Arabic literature in vain or fruitful search of new material, there is a special difficulty in translating fragmentary verses of which the context is unknown and the textual correctness ill-assured. Professor Schulthess has mastered these difficulties and produced a work the completeness of which can be best appreciated by one who had previously set himself the task of collecting, translating, and commenting on these same poems. If we had any subsequent regrets for not then publishing the results of our labors, they are more than counterbalanced by the satisfaction of seeing the same work so much better performed in many respects by another. It is not, of course, to be wondered at, that, in comparing the published poems with our manuscript, we found that the two collections overlapped each other. The contrary would be strange, since every such collection, however diligently made, necessarily contains a certain element of haphazard, determined by the books and manuscripts that evade the collector's notice, even if he devotes an utterly disproportionate length of time to the search. The same is true, to a certain extent, with regard to the interpretation of verses hard to explain in themselves and rendered still more difficult by detachment from their context. The importance of the subject and the study of completeness, which Professor Schulthess has had in view in his work, induce us therefore to publish text and translation of the few verses we possess, which are not to be found in the published dīwān, and to suggest what appear to us to be improvements in the text and interpretation of more or less doubtful and difficult passages. A few considerations with regard to a new theory as to the religion of Umayya, calculated to modify the relations between the poet and Muḥammad, or, at least, our conception of them, will conclude our study.

While desirous to imitate Professor Schulthess's wise reserve in not pronouncing on the authenticity or spuriousness of the verses we are adding—their very fragmentary character makes it particularly difficult to form an opionion—we should like to call special attention to the fragments preserved to us by the great traditionalist of the West, Ibn 'Abd al-Barr an-Namarī al-Andalūsī,[3] especially number LXIX which has every appearance of authenticity,[4] all the more so as these verses belong to a class of poetry which must have been cultivated by Umayya,[5] though scarcely any other specimens have survived. For convenience sake we have continued the numeration of Professor Schulthess in the poems we have added. We have not given all references to or citations from already published poems that we possess, but only such as seem to be of some importance. The spurious verses are not of course essential to a study of Umayya's poetry and some, if not all, of them must have been already known to Professor Schulthess. Still, they serve to show at least how he has been confused with other poets of the same name, and thus throw light, indirectly, on cases in which that confusion still persists. Finally, we wish to thank Fr. Cheikho for having kindly placed his notes at our disposal. To them we owe the fragments 14, 16, and 17, containing additions to numbers VIII, XI, and XIII.

TEXTS

LXV.

Basīṭ.

Ibn ʿAbd al-Barr, *Muḫtaṣar gāmiʿ bayān al ʿilm wa faḍlihi wa mā yanbaǧī fī riwāyatihi wa ḥamlihi*; ed. Cairo, p. 40.

إِنَّ ٱلْغُلَامَ مُطِيعٌ مَن يُؤَدِّبُهُ   وَلَا يُطِيعُكَ ذُو شَيْبٍ بِتَأْدِيبِ

LXVI.

Basīṭ.

Ibn ʿAbd al-Barr, *Muḫtaṣar*, etc., p. 43.

وَلَيْسَ ذُو ٱلعِلْمِ بِالتَّقْوَى كَجَاهِلِهَا   وَلَا ٱلْبَصِيرُ كَأَعْمَى مَا لَهُ بَصَرُ
فَٱسْتَخْبِرِ ٱلنَّاسَ عَمَّا أَنْتَ جَاهِلُهُ   إِذَا عَمِيتَ فَقَدْ يَجْلُو ٱلْعَمَى ٱلْخَبَرُ

LXVII.

Kāmil.

Ṭabarī, *Annales*, I, 1122.

إِنَّ ٱلصَّفِيَّ بْنَ ٱلنَّبِيتِ مُمَلَّكًا   أَعْلَى وَأَجْوَدُ مِن هِرَقْلَ وَقَيْصَرَا

LXVIII.

Mutaqārib.

Al-Ḫāzin, *Tafsīr*, IV, 421.

دَحَوْتَ ٱلْبِلَادَ فَسَوَّيْتَهَا   وَأَنْتَ عَلَى طَيِّهَا قَادِرُ

LXIX.

Ṭawīl.

Ibn ʿAbd al-Barr,[6] *Kitāb bahǵat al-maǵālis wa uns al-maǵālis*. Manuscript of British Museum. Nr. 726, f. 33r.

إِذَا ٱكْتَسَبَ ٱلْمَالَ الفَتَى مِن وُجُوهِهِ   وَأَحْسَنَ تَدْبِيرًا لَهُ حِينَ يَجْمَعُ
وَمَيَّزَ فِي إِنْفَاقِهِ بَيْنَ مُصْلِحٍ   مُعَايَشَةً فِيمَا يَضُرُّ وَيَنْفَعُ
وَأَرْضَى بِهِ أَهْلَ ٱلْحُتُوفِ وَلَمْ يَضَعْ   بِهِ ٱلذُّخْرَ زَادًا لِلَّتِي هِيَ أَنْفَعُ
فَذَاكَ ٱلْفَتَى لَا جَامِعُ ٱلْمَالِ ذَاخِرًا   لِأَوْلَادِ سُوءٍ حَيْثُ حَلُّوا وَأَوْضَعُ

LXX.

Kāmil.

Mufaḍḍaliyāt aḍ-Ḍabbī, ed. Constantinople, 1308, p. 184.

أَحْلَامُ صِبْيَانٍ إِذَا مَا قُلِّدُوا   سُخُبًا فَهُمْ يَتَعَلَّقُونَ بِمَضْغِهَا

LXXI.

Munsariḥ.

Alex. Abkarius, *Rawḍat al-adab*, ed. Beyrouth, 1858, p. 35.

كَأَنَّمَا ٱلْوَرْدُ ٱلَّذِي نَشْرُهُ   يَعْبَقُ مِن طِيبِ مَعَانِيكَا
دِمَاءُ أَعْدَائِكَ مَسْفُوكَةً   قَدْ قَابَلَتْ بِيضَ أَيَادِيكَا

LXXII.

Ṭawīl.

L. A. XIII, 160. Ascribed to Umayya.

أَدَاحَيْتَ بِرِجْلَيْنِ رِجْلًا تُغِيرُهَا   لِتَنْجَى وَأَمْطٌ دُونَ ٱلْأُخْرَى وَحَزْجَلُ

LXXIII.

Ṭawīl.

L. A. XIII, 95. Ascribed to Umayya.

لَهُ نَفَيَانٌ يَخْفِشُ ٱلآكُمَ وَقْعُهُ   تَرَى ٱلتُّرْبَ مِنْهُ مَاثِرًا يَتَنَثَّلُ

LXXIV.

Ṭawīl.

L. A. XIX, 341. Ascribed to Umayya.

وَإِنِّي بِلَيْلَى وَٱلدِّيَارِ ٱلَّتِي أَرَى   كَٱلْمُبْتَلَى ٱلْمُعْنَى بِشَوْقٍ مُوَكَّلِ

LXXV.

Kāmil.

L. A. XIX, 341; T. A. X, 258. Ascribed to Umayya.

عَنْسًا تُعَنِّيهَا وَعَنْسًا تَرْحَلُ

LXXVI.

Basīṭ.

Ibn ʿAbd al-Barr, *Muḫtaṣar*, etc., p. 43.

لَا يَذْهَبَنَّ بِكَ ٱلتَّفْرِيطُ مُنْتَظِرًا   طُولَ ٱلْأَنَاةِ وَلَا يَطْمَعْ بِكَ ٱلْعَجَلُ
فَقَدْ يُزِيدُ ٱلسُّؤَالُ ٱلْمَرْءَ تَجْرِبَةً   وَيَسْتَرِيحُ إِلَى ٱلْأَخْبَارِ مَنْ يَسَلُ

LXXVII.

Ṭawīl.

Ibn ʿAbd al-Barr, *Muḫtaṣar*, etc. , p. 43.

وَقَدْ يَقْتُلُ ٱلْجَهْلَ ٱلسُّؤَالُ وَيَشْتَفِي   إِذَا عَايَنَ ٱلْأَمْرَ ٱلْمُهِمُّ ٱلْمُعَايِنُ
وَفِي ٱلْبَحْثِ قِدْمًا وَٱلسُّؤَالِ لِذِي ٱلْعَمَى   شِفَاءٌ وَأَشْفَى مِنْهُمَا مَا تُعَايِنُ

Fragments

Fr. 13 (cf Nr. III).

Asās, II, 144. Ascribed to Umayya.

دَارُ قَوْمِي فِي مَنْزِلٍ غَيْرِ ضَنْكٍ   مَنْ يُرِدْنَا يَكُنْ لِأَوَّلِ فُوقِ

Fr. 14 (cf Nr. VIII and Fr. 9).

Ḥamāsa Ms.

زَعَمْتَ أَنِّي قَدْ كَبِرْتُ وَعِبْتَنِي   وَلَمْ يَنْضِ لِي فِي ٱلسِّنِّ سِتُّونَ كُمَّلُ
وَسَمَّيْتَنِي بِٱسْمِ ٱلْمُفَنَّدِ رَأْيُهُ   وَقُلْتَ وَلَمْ يصدق أَنَكَ أَفْضَلُ
تُرَاقِبُ مِنِّي عَثْرَةً أَوْ تَنَالُهَا   هَبِلْتَ وَهٰذَا مِنكَ رَأْيٌ مُضَلَّلُ
وَإِنَّكَ إِذْ تَبْغِي لِحَامِي مَوَائِلًا   بِرَأْيِكَ شَابًّا مَرَّةً لَمُغَفَّلُ
وَمَا صَوْلَةُ ٱلْحِقِّ ٱلضَّئِيلِ وَخَطْرُهُ   إِذَا خَطَرَتْ يَوْمًا قَسَاوِرُ بُزَّلُ
تَرَاهُ مُعِدًّا لِلْخِلَافِ كَأَنَّهُ   بِرَدٍّ عَلَى أَهْلِ ٱلصَّوَابِ مُوَكَّلُ

1b. So Ms. My citation in *MFO*, I, 209, n. 1 is therefore inexact.
2. Meter requires مَا صَدَّقْتَ instead of لم تصدق.

Fr. 15 (cf. Nr. IX).

Al-ʿUbāb fī Šarḥ al-ādāt,[7] Ms. of British Museum Sup. 1111 f. 50r.

بَنَاهُ مَكَارِمٌ وَأُسَاةُ كَلْمٍ   دَمَا وَهُمُ مِنَ ٱلْكَلْمِ ٱلشِّفَاءُ

Ms. اساه for اساة; الكلب for الكلم.

Fr. 16 (cf. Nr. XI).

Maḳrīzī, *Kitāb al-Muḳaffa*, Ms. of Paris 2144, f. 195 v. (Br. II, 39).

فَمَا لَاقَيْتُ مِثْلَكَ يَا ٱبْنَ سَعْدٍ   لِمَعْرُوفٍ وَخَيْرٍ مُسْتَفَادِ

Fr. 17 (cf. Nr. XIII).

Maḳrīzī, *Kitāb al-Muḳaffa*, f. 196 r.

وَكَأَنَّمَا يدعا عُرَيْنَةٌ فِي طَوَائِفِهَا وَهَاجِرْ

. . . . .

آبَاءُكَ ٱلشُّمُّ ٱلْمَرَاجِيحُ ٱلْمَسَامِيحُ ٱلْأَخَايِرْ
وَإِذَا تُشَامُ بُرُوقُهُمْ جَادَتْ أَكُفُّهُمُ ٱلْبَوَاطِرْ
لَا يَحْتَوِيهُمْ جَانِبٌ نَائِي ٱلْمَحَلِ وَلَا مُجَاوِرْ
قَوْمٌ حُصُونُهُمُ ٱلْأَسِنَّةُ وَٱلْأَعِنَّةُ وَٱلظَّوَافِرْ
نَزَلُوا ٱلْبِطَاحَ وَفُضِّلَتْ بِهِمِ ٱلْبَوَاطِنُ وَٱلظَّوَاهِرْ

1. يدعا sic perhaps يُدْعَى | or بِدُعَا. For هاجر also هاطر in margin.

5. For الظوافر also البواتر in margin.

Fr. 18 (cf. Nr. XIX).

Asās, II, 355. Ascribed to Umayya.

لَا نَخَافُ ٱلْمُحُولَ إِنْ هَرَشَ ٱلدَّهْرُ   وَلَا نَنْتَوِي لِأَهْلٍ سِوَاكَا

Fr. 19 (cf. Nr. XXXV).

Tibrīzī, *Šarḥ kitāb iṣlāḥ al-manṭiq li Ibn Sikkīt*, Manuscript of Beyrouth, f. 86.

يَا لَذَّةَ ٱلْعَيْشِ إِذْ دَامَ ٱلنَّعِيمُ لَنَا   وَمَنْ يَعِشْ يَلْقَ رَوْعَاتٍ وَأَحْزَانَا

Fr. 20 (cf. Nr. XLI).

Az-Zamaḫšarī, *Rabîʿ al-Abrār*, Manuscripts of British Museum 728, f. 17 r; 1124, f. 12 v.

هُوَ ٱلْمُجْرِي سَوَابِقَهَا سِرَاعًا   كَمَا حَبَسَ ٱلْخِيَالَ فَمَا تَرِيمُ

Spurious Verses

1.

Munsariḥ.

Ibn Manẓūr, *Kitāb niṯār al-azhār fīl-lail wan-nahār*, etc., ed. Cairo, p. 53.

يَا لَيْلَةٌ لَمْ تَبِنْ مِنَ ٱلْقَصَرِ   كَأَنَّهَا قُبْلَةٌ عَلَى حَذَرِ
لَمْ تَكُ إِلَّا كَلَا وَلَا وَمَضَتْ   تَدْفَعُ فِي صَدْرِهَا يَدُ ٱلسَّحَرِ

2.

Mutaqārib.

Ibn Sīda, VII, 15; L. A. XIX, 361. Ascribed to Umayya.

يُرِنَّ عَلَى مُغْزِيَاتِ ٱلْعِقَاقِ   وَيَقْرُو بِهَا قَفَرَاتِ الصِّلَال

3.

Mutaqārib.

ʿAinī, I, 441–42.

أَلَا إِنَّ قَلْبِي لَفِي الظَّاعِنِينَ   حَزِينٌ فَمَنْ ذَا يُعَزِّي حَزِينَا

4.

Ibn Duraid, *Ištiqāq*, 280; cf. Brockelmann, *Labīd*, p. 16.

فَصَلَقْنَا فِي مُرَادِ صَلْقَةً   وَصُدَاءِ أَلْحَقَتْهُمْ بِالثَّلَلْ

5.

Ḫafīf.

Z. D. M. G., 47, 82–83.

إِنَّ عَمْرًا وَمَا تَجَشَّمَ عَمْرٌو   كَأَبْنِ بِيضٍ غَدَاةَ سُدَّ السَّبِيلُ
لَمْ يَجِدْ غَالِبٌ وَرَاءَكَ مَغْدًى   لِتِرَاثٍ وَلَا دَمٌ مَطْلُولُ
كُلُّ أَمْرٍ يَنُوبُ عَبْسًا جَمِيعًا   أَنْتَ فِيهِ ٱلْمُطَاعُ فِي مَا تَقُولُ
قَدْ تَحَمَّلْتَ خَيْرَ ذَاكَ وَلِيدًا   أَنْتَ لِلصَّالِحَاتِ قِدْمًا فَعُولُ

6.

Wāfir.

Z. D. M. G., 47, 164.

أَبُوكَ رَبِيعَةُ ٱلْخَيْرِ بْنِ قُرْطٍ   وَأَنْتَ ٱلْمَرْءُ تَفْعَلُ مَا تَقُولُ
أَشَمُّ كَأَنَّمَا حَدِبَتْ عَلَيْهِ   بَنُو ٱلْأَمْلَاكِ تَكْنُفُهَا ٱلْقُيُولُ
تَصُدُّ مَنَاكِبَ ٱلْأَعْدَاءِ مِنْكُمْ   كَرَاكِرُ مِنْ أَبِي بَكْرٍ حُلُولُ
كَرَاكِرُ لَا يَبِيدُ ٱلْعِزُّ فِيهَا   وَلٰكِنَّ ٱلْعَزِيزَ بِهَا ذَلِيلُ

7.

Manuscript of the *Ǵamhara* in British Museum, 1662 (Or. 415), f. 132.[8]

غَدَا جِيرَانُ أَهْلِكَ ظَاعِنِينَا   لِدَارٍ غَيْرِ ذٰلِكَ مُنْتَوِينَا
وَسَاقَكَ ٱلْحُدُوجُ حُدُوجُ سَلْمَى   وَقَدْ بَكَرَ ٱلْخَلِيطُ مُزَايِلِينَا
رَمَيْتَهُمُ بِعَيْنِكَ وَٱلْمَطَايَا   خَوَاضِعُ فِي ٱلْأَزِمَّةِ يَعْتَلِينَا
فَهَيَّجَ مِنْ فُؤَادِكَ طُولَ شَوْقٍ   فِرَاقُ ٱلْجِيرَةِ ٱلْمُتَصَدِّعِينَا
أَرَى ٱلْأَيَّامَ قَدْ أَحْدَثْنَ بَيْنًا   بِسَلْمَى بَغْتَةً وَنَوًى شَطُونَا
فَإِنْ تَكُنِ ٱلنَّوَى شَطَّتْ بِسَلْمَى   وَكُنْتُ بِقُرْبِهَا وَبِهَا ضَنِينَا
لَقَدْ كُنَّا نُرَى بِأَلَذِّ عَيْشٍ   وَأَفْضَلِ غِبْطَةٍ مُتَجَاوِرِينَا
لَيَالِيَ تَسْتَبِيكَ بِمُسْبَكِرٍّ   لَهَا مِنْهُ ٱلْغَدَائِرُ يَنْثَنِينَا
عَلَى مَتْنَيْ مُنَعَّمَةٍ حَصَانٍ   يَرُوعُ جَمَالُهَا ٱلْمُتَأَمِّلِينَا
أَفِي سَلْمَى يُعَاتِبُنِي أَبُوهَا   وَإِخْوَتُهَا وَهُمْ لِي ظَالِمُونَا
تُرِيكَ إِذَا وَقَفْتَ عَلَى خَلَاءٍ   وَقَدْ أَمِنَتْ عُيُونَ ٱلنَّاظِرِينَا
ذِرَاعَيْ عَيْطَلٍ أَدْمَاءَ بِكْرٍ   هِجَانِ ٱللَّوْنِ لَمْ تَقْرَأْ جَنِينَا
وَأَسْوَدَ مُدْلَهِمَّ ٱللَّوْنِ حَشْلًا   بِدُهْنِ ٱلْبَانِ وَٱلْغَالِي غُذِينَا
فَإِنَّكِ قَدْ شَعَفْتِ ٱلْقَلْبَ حَتَّى   بَلِيتُ وَلَا أَرَاكِ تَغَيَّرِينَا
أَجُودُ وَتَبْخَلِينَ إِذَا ٱلْتَقَيْنَا   يَلِينُ لَكِ ٱلْفُؤَادُ وَتَغْلُظِينَا

Manuscript of the *Ǵamhara* in British Museum, ... (*continued*)

كَأَنَّ ٱلمِسْكَ تَخلِطُهُ بِفِيهَا   وَرِيحَ قَرَنْفُلٍ وَٱليَاسِمِينَا

أَلَمْ تَرَى أَنَّ حَظِّي مِن سُلَيْمَى   أَمَانِي قَدْ يُرُحْنَ وَيَغْتَدِينَا

مُبَتَّلَةٌ يَضِيقُ ٱلمِرْطُ عَنْهَا   عُشَارِيٌّ بِأَيْدِي ٱلدَّارِعِينَا

أَلَا قُلْ لِلْقَبَائِلِ إِنَّ بَكْرًا   وَتَغْلِبَ بَعْدَ حَرْبِهِمِ سِنِينَا

أَطَاعُوا ٱللهَ فِي صِلَةٍ وَعَطْفٍ •   وَأَضْحَوْا إِخْوَةً مُتَجَاوِرِينَا

أُسَاةٌ شَاعِبُونَ لِكُلِّ صَدْعٍ   وَكُلِّ جَرِيرَةٍ فِيهِمْ وَفِينَا

مَتَى مَا أَدْعُ فِي بَكْرٍ يُجِبْنِي   قَبَائِلُهَا بِأَكْثَرِ نَاصِرِينَا

وَإِنْ هَتَفَتْ بَنُو بَكْرٍ أَجَبْنَا   إِلَيْهِمْ بِٱلصَّنَائِعِ مُعْلِنِينَا

نُجَالِدُ دُونَهُمْ وَتَذُودُ عَنَّا   كَتَائِبُهُمْ يَرُحْنَ وَيَغْتَدِينَا

فَلَسْنَا فِي مَوَدَّتِنَا أَخَانَا   إِلَى ٱلْأَعْدَاءِ بِٱلْمُتَعَذِّرِينَا

وَلٰكِنَّا وَإِيَّاهُمْ مَدَدْنَا   لِوَصْلِ قَرَابَةٍ حَبْلًا مَتِينَا

هُمُ ٱلإِخْوَانُ إِنْ غَضِبُوا غَضِبْنَا   وَإِنْ نَزَلُوا بِدَارِ رِضًى رَضِينَا

وَبَكْرًا إِنَّ فِي بَكْرٍ فَعَالًا   وَأَحْلَامًا بِهَا يَتَفَاضَلُونَا

تَمِيدُ ٱلْأَرْضُ إِنْ رَكِبَتْ تَمِيمٌ   وَإِنْ نَزَلُوا سَمِعْتَ لَهَا أَنِينَا

وَكَأْسٍ قَدْ شَرِبْتُ بِمَاءِ ثَلْجٍ   وَأُخْرَى قَدْ شَرِبْتُ بِقَاصِرِينَا

كَأَنَّ أَكُفَّهُمْ عَذَبٌ مُلَقًّى   وَحُمَّاضٌ بِأَيْدِي مُغْلِنِينَا

فَجَاؤُا عَارِضًا بَرِدًا وَجِينًا   كَمِثْلِ ٱلسَّيْلِ يَمْنَعُ وَارِدِينَا

وَشِيبُ ٱلرَّأْسِ أَهْوَنُ مِن لِقَاهُمْ   إِذَا هَزُّوا ٱلْقَنَا مُتَقَابِلِينَا

كَأَنَّ رِمَاحَهُمْ سَيْلٌ مُطِلٌّ   وَأَمْسَاكٌ بِأَيْدِي مُورَدِينَا

فَلَمَّا لَمْ تَدَعْ قَوْسًا وَنَبْلًا   مَشَيْنَا ٱلنُّصْفَ ثُمَّ مَشَوْا إِلَيْنَا

فَذَادُونَا بِبِيضٍ مُرْهَفَاتٍ   وَذُدْنَاهُمْ بِهَا حَتَّى ٱسْتَقَيْنَا

وَأَنْزَلْنَا ٱلْبُيُوتَ بِذِي طَلَالٍ   إِلَى ٱلنَّسَمَاتِ تَبْغِي مُوعِدِينَا

l.	14	Ms	سعفت	for	شعفت
»	26	»	طنينا	»	ضنينا
»	30	»	احر	»	اخرى
»	31	»	ملغًا	»	ملقى
»	34	»	إمساك	»	أمساك
»	35	»	مشونا	»	مشينا

Translation.

LXV.

The youth obeys him who corrects him, but the gray-haired heeds you not when you reprove.

LXVI.

He who hath cognizance of devotion is not like him who is ignorant of it, nor is he who sees like the blind man without sight.

Ask men, then, for information concerning the things thou art ignorant of, if thou art blind, information sometimes enlightens blindness.

Compare Koran, Sura 35, 20; 40, 60 مَا يَسْتَوِي ٱلْأَعْمَى وَٱلْبَصِيرُ and Nābiğat ed. Derenbourg, p. 81, 1. 11 .لَيْسَ جَاهِلُ شَيْءٍ مِثْلَ مَنْ عَلِمَ

LXVII.

Ṣafī son of An-Nabīt, when possessed of sovereign power, was more exalted and more generous than Heraclius and Caesar.

For this Ṣafī or Ṣafan, famed for his generosity, see Ṭabarī I, 1115 and 1122.

LXVIII.

Thou didst spread out the earth and make it level and Thou art able to fold it up again.

The verse is cited a propos of Sura 79, 30 والارض دحاها. For the second half cf. Sura 21, 104 يوم نطوي السماء كطي السجل للكتب.

LXIX.

If a youth acquires wealth in the various ways it may be acquired and manages it properly when he collects it,

And discriminates in spending it what is advantageous for his manner of life in regard to the things that injure and benefit,

And pleases with it the dead and does not store it up as provision for occasions of greater advantage,

Such a youth does not treasure up the wealth he collects for wicked children where they halt and where they journey.

L. 2. The grammatical relation between مصلح and معايشة is somewhat strained, but meter requires the tanwīn in the former word.

L. 3. It seems possible that Ahl al Ḥutūf could mean the author or authors of the death-sentences, or the possessor or possessors of the death-decrees. The second part of the verse of Ummayya given by Schulthess in the textual notes on XLI (p. 53, 1.13) is cited by Baṭalīūsī, *Al-Iqtiḍāb*, p. 405 with the v. 1. بكفيك المنايا والحُتوف. This however is against the rhyme and has no value against the numerous other citations with the reading حتوم (ʿAinī, II, 346; L. A. XV, 2; T. A., VIII, 236; Ǵawharī, II, 263; Ibn Sīda, XII, 210; Suiūṭi, Itqān, Cairo ed. 161; *Šārḥ al-Mufaḍḍaliyāt*, Beyrouth Ms. II, 137, and (after Schulthess l. c.) Ṭab. *Tafsīr*, XII, 109). As to the word اهل, while the nearest approach to its being used of God in a similar sense in the Koran is the expression هو اهل المغفرة Sura 74, 55, it is exactly so used by Umayya himself once, viz. XLI (2a), p. 53, 1. 20. Lane says s. v. "Frequently also اهل signifies the author or more commonly authors of a thing like صاحب and اصحاب; as in اهل البدع the authors or authors of innovations; and اهل الظالم the author or authors of wrong." But these considerations scarcely authorize us to depart from the natural sense of the expression which is completely in accord with the context. We should gratify and not dishonor our dead in our way of spending money, says the poet and not act like " the wicked children" of the following verse.

L. 4. اوضعوا seems to bear the same relation to حلوا as ينفع does to يضر in 1. 2. At any rate, the ordinary meaning of the fourth form is to travel or make travel quickly, applied to a camel.

These verses strongly support the authenticity of VIII.

LXX.

Intelligences of children who, when adorned with necklaces, apply themselves to chewing them.

For سِخَاب singular of سُخُب cf. XXX, 1. 4. and Professor Schulthess's note.

LXXI.

The rose, whose perfume is redolent of the sweet odor of thy good qualities,
Seems like the blood of thy enemies poured forth, meeting thy fair white hands.

LXXII.

Hast thou spread out two troops making one descend to Naǵna while before the other is Amṭ and Ḥazǵal?

The proper names are names of unknown localities. A marginal note in L. A. reads Taǵna instead of Naǵna.

LXXIII.

He raises clouds of dust dispersing the sand-hills when he jumps on them, you see the dust-heaps driven to and fro by him demolished.

LXXIV.

And verily am I, through Laila and the houses I see, like one tormented and tortured by love which has been committed to him.

LXXV.

A robust camel you use for laboring and one you use for riding.

LXXVI.

Let not remissness carry you off that you should wait long and languidly, and let not overhaste run away with you.

For inquiry at times increases a man's experience, and he who asks finds rest in the information he seeks.

LXXVII.

And sometimes questioning destroys ignorance, and the man is cured who inspects at close quarters the matter which troubles him.

And in inquiring and questioning is there from of old healing for the blind, but inspection at close quarters is more healing than either of them.

★
★★

Fragment 13 (cf. Nr III).

The home of my people is in no narrow dwelling place, he who attacks us shall be the first shot and dying.

So Lane under the word فوق after *Asās* وكان فلان لاوّل فوق أي أوّل مرمي وهالك. Perhaps we should render the latter part of the verse "shall belong to, i.e., shall fall before, our first discharge of arrows." So numerous are the defenders (cf. غير ضنك) that they will not have to shoot a second time.

Fragment 14 (cf. Nr VIII and Fr. 9).

(a) Thou thought'st me grown old and did'st repute it to me as a fault, whilst in age sixty full years have not yet passed over me.

(b) And thou did'st call me by the name of dotard and did'st say, but untruthfully, that thou wert the more excellent.

(c) Thou dost watch for a slip in me or dost seize upon one, thou art foolish and this is an erring judgment of thine.

(d) And verily thou, young as thou thinkest thyself while my flesh expecteth a resting place, shalt one day be a simpleton.

(e) And as a weak three-year-old camel jumps and lashes with his tail, when strong full-grown camels lash some day with their tails,

(f) You see him ready to contradict, as if he were charged with refuting people of sound judgment.

The Ḥamāsa Ms., from which the above has been taken, contains twelve verses of this poem in the following order *a–e*, 1, 5, 6, 2–4, *f*. But *e* fits in extremely well before *f*, which explains the comparison and which is given last by Ḥamāsa, while v. 16 according to Aḡānī and Ḥamāsa and v. 8 according to Ḥamāsa precede *b*, which is only a doublet of v. 7. Hence we may conclude that v. *a–e* have been misplaced and that the order 1–6, 8, *a–f*, has the best chance of being correct. We have reprinted *e* and *f*, already given by Professor Schulthess, to show their connection with each other and with the rest of the poem.

Fragment 15 (cf. Nr IX).

Noble qualities and those who heal a wound with blood have borne him, and they are the remedy for a wound.

The reading كلب for كلم is explained by the fact that this verse, though immediately preceded by v. 7 as the sense requires, is followed by v. 4, which contains the word كلب written directly underneath but having the v. 1. ضب written above it.

Fragment 16 (cf. Nr XI).

I have met none like to thee, O son of Sa‘d, in the gifts and benefits to be gained from him.

This is given as the concluding verse.

Fragment 17 (cf. Nr XIII).

(a) And it seems as if ʿUraina in all its divisions and Hāǵir (v. 1. Hāṯir) were invited (?).

(b) Thy forefathers are the high-nosed, the dignified, the generous, the best of men.

(c) And when their lightning flashes are observed their hands rain forth gifts.

(d) A land holds them, neither near to which nor far from which is there drought.

(e) A people are they whose strongholds are their spears and the reins and hoofs of their steeds (v. 1. for hoofs, sharp-edged swords).

(f) They settled in the Meccan valleys, and by them has the high ground as well as the low ground been ennobled.

a immediately precedes v. 6. *b–f* immediately precede v. 9. ʿUraina is a tribal name derived from عُرَّن = itch, camel disease, according to Ibn Duraid, *Ištiqāq*, p. 314. Hāǵir is probably Baḥrein, another form of Haǵar, since the inhabitant of that district is called Hāǵiri and Haǵari. يُدْعَى seems the easiest correction of the corrupt يدعا. . One might also suggest بِدُعَا for بِدُعَاء and suppose that the noise of the cooking pots, after having been compared with the camel's deep note in the preceding verse, is here likened to the war cry of these tribes; but that is less natural.

Fragment 18 (cf. Nr XIX).

We fear not droughts when the season is severe, and we have recourse to none but thee.

Fragment 19 (cf. Nr XXXV).

Oh! the happiness of life did but our pleasures last, and he who lives meets with fears and sorrows.

The verse is said to have immediately followed v. 1.

Fragment 20 (cf. Nr XLI).

It is He who makes the racers of them run quickly, just as He checks those that change their position, and they cease not their course.

This verse follows the last three of XLI, but the position of v. 25 and v. 26 is inverted in both manuscripts, correctly enough insofar as this additional verse is concerned, which comes much better after v. 25 (cf. مجري referring to preceding تجري). Both manuscripts read as the first word ذَوَائِبُ of v. 26, while the British Museum Manuscript of the *Muḫtār Rabīʿ al-Abrār*, 729, f. 6 v. reads ذواهبُ. Either the latter word or ذوائبُ (cf. XXV, 48) seems to be the correct reading. For حال used of stars cf. also XXV, 45.

★
★ ★

Spurious Fragments

1.

O night thou didst not appear at all, so short thou wert, short as a stolen kiss.

It was only as a very nothing and passed away, the hand of dawn thrusting at its breast to repel it.

This fragment is evidently not ancient, perhaps by the Andalusian Umayya.

2.

He brays after the she-asses that are not pregnant, and traverses with them the deserts, where, here and there, the rain has fallen.

From the fact that Ibn Sīda XV, 197, attributes to Umayya a verse describing a camel in the same meter and qāfiya which we find Maqṣūr wa Mamdūd p. 153 attributed to Umayya ibn Abi ʿAʾiḏ, we may conclude as most probable that the above verse is also by the Huḏail poet. There is another verse in the same meter and qāfiya ascribed to Umayya in L. A. III, 516 under the word كوثر which is said to be a Huḏail form.

3.

Is not my heart with those who are departing, sad, and who will console the sad?

This verse is given in Ḥizāna, I, 421, as the first of a qaṣīda addressed by the Hudail poet Umayya b. Abī ʿAʾid, an Umayyad panegyrist, to ʿAbd-al-ʿAzīz b. Marwān in Egypt whither he had gone to visit him. Three other verses are added from the same poem in one of which the Umayyad prince is mentioned by name.

4.

Against Murād and Ṣudā we raised a war cry which made destruction overtake them.

We may suppose that Ibn Duraid was led into error by the fact that this verse of Labīd and that of Umayya, given above by us, stood one immediately after the other in some lexicographical work, as they do at present in L. A. Thus the addition "Ibn Abī-ṣ-Ṣalt" of Ibn Duraid slightly favors the attribution of LXXIII, which L. A. gives as by Umayya, to Umayya b. Abī-ṣ-Ṣalt.

5.

Amr resembles in his undertakings Ibn Bīḍ, the morning the road was blocked.

No conqueror and no blood unavenged has found a means of passing over after thee to thy heirs.

In every matter that comes upon the whole tribe of ʿAbs, thou art obeyed in what thou sayest.

Thou didst charge thyself with the best of these things as a child; from of old thou art a doer of good deeds.

The reference to ʿAbs proves that the ʿAbside Ḥuṭaiʾa, and not Umayya, is the author if the panegyrized be Ibn Ǵudʿān.

6.

Thy father was Rabīʿa of the benefits, son of Qurṭ, and thou art the man who does what he says.

Haughty as if the sons of kings, helped by princes, had nursed him.

Breasts of those descended from Abu Bakr, who dwell among you, avert from you the shoulders of your enemies.

Breasts in which glory perishes not, but which make the glorious man become of no account.

7.

The neighbors of thy people have gone forth, mounted on camels, departing for a home other than that yonder.

And the camel saddles, the camel saddles of Salma, have led thee forth, when the company at early morning departed.

Thou didst cast thy eye upon them, while the beasts of burden bent down their heads in the reins as they ascended.

And separation from the neighbors, thus severed from thee, stirred up long yearning in thy heart.

I see that time hath suddenly caused a parting from Salma and a long separation.

And if it be that parting hath borne away Salma, after I had been near her and loath to leave her,

Yet we used to be seen enjoying a most pleasant life and most excellent happiness conversing together.

The nights she used to captivate thee by her long hair, whose plaited tresses (fell)

On the shoulders of a maiden refined and chaste, whose beauty frightens those who reflect thereon.

Does her father upbraid me for Salma and her brothers doing me wrong?

She shows thee, when thou standest where she observes thee not and she is without fear of the eyes of the beholders.

The arms of a long-necked, white, young camel, clear in color, that hath never borne offspring;

While we are swartly, dark-hued in our wretchedness, though nourished on bān-oil and fat flesh-meat.

For, verily, thou hast consumed my heart until I have become wasted away, and I do not see thee changed.

I am generous and thou art miserly when we meet, my heart softens to thee and thou art hard.

She seems to blend musk in her mouth with the odor of the qaranful and the jasmine.

Saw'st thou not that my lot in Sulaima are desires that come and go?

A woman of perfect make, whose waist-wrapper is too narrow for her—(a lance) ten cubits long in the hands of mail-clad men (?).

Say to the tribes that Bakr and Taḡlib, after their war lasting for years,

Have obeyed God by union and friendship, and have become brothers, living near each other.

When I call upon Bakr their tribes answer me with the fullest muster of auxiliaries.

And if the Banū Bakr call out we answer them, manifesting ourselves by our deeds.

We fight on their behalf and their squadrons defend us morning and evening.

And we are not such as make excuses to our enemies for loving our brother.

But they and we have stretched forth a strong rope for kinship's bond.

They are our brothers; if they are angry, we are angry, and if they halt in a home where they are contented, we are contented.

And in Bakr, verily, are there noble deeds, and among them intelligences that contend for superiority.

The earth shakes when the Banū Tamīm mount their steeds, and when they alight you hear it groan.

Many a cup have I quaffed at Mā' Ṯalǵ and many another have I quaffed at Qāsirīn.

Their hands remind one of floating weeds collected together and water-sorrel in the hands of those who display them (?).

And they came, as a broad cloud, laden with hail, and, at times, like a torrent that repels the water-drawers.

And there were gray-haired men, the easiest part of their encounter being when they brandished their spears facing their opponents;

Their lances like a dripping torrent and water-barrels in the hands of water-drawers.

And when we had not neglected bow and arrow, we marched halfway and they marched to meet us.

And they repelled us with bright keen swords, and we repelled them with the same till we had drunk enough.

And we visit the houses in Ḏū Ṭalāl as far as Nasamāt, seeking them that threaten us.

V. 13. Grammatical construction is not clear, but the poet seems to describe himself.

V. 18b. as it stands seems to describe Salma's commanding stature, but the text is probably corrupt. The lexicons give عشاري here as a garment ten cubits long, but that does not suit what follows.

V. 34. امساك is probably plural of مَسْك "grande outre en peau de œuf, carrée, pour porter l'eau à dos de chameau ou de mulet" (Dozy, II, 592 s. v.). Possibly however, إمساك is the proper vocalization "a restraining the hands of water-drawers." The sense would then be similar to that of 32b. The manuscript favors this reading as it has the hamza under the alif.

★
★★

Some Remarks on the Poems Already Published.

III. Also cited in *Asās*, II, p. 144, where رتوق is explained as = حصون ممتنعات from رَتْق = closing up or repairing of a gap or rent (فتق (cf. Eng. "fastness"). Hence Bekrī's شرف should be understood in a local sense and the last words rendered "in high ground and inaccessible places."

VIII, v. 3. For اذا read انا with all our authorities (cf. Wright, *Arabic Grammar*, II, 265).

Cf. Nr LXIX, which, by its mention of children's ingratitude toward their parents, strengthens the case for the authenticity of this poem, all the more so that tradition has nothing to say about this ingratitude of Umayya's child or children.

XI, v. 4. Render: "Ma'add knows the exaltation which is his, for the tent is lifted up by the tent-poles," that is, Ma'add is the tent and must therefore be conscious of the elevation of its pole Ibn Ǵuḏ'ān which is the measure of its own. For خيف = المكان المرتفع compare *Asās* under the word.

XIII. As كراكر of v. 4 certainly = "breasts of animals" كسور must mean "limbs." The taking of the latter word in the sense of "Sprünge" has led to an incorrect rendering of this and the following verse where ضرائر is plural of ضرة = udder. It seems preferable to translate:

In them the limbs and breasts appear when the boiling bursts forth and discloses them.

They seem in their heat and in their fulness like camels' udders.

XV. The first verse is also cited by Az-Zamaḫšarī (*Kaššāf*, I, 188; *Šarḥ Kaššāf*, 91) with وللسع بنات الدهر من راق, as the second half. For بنات الدهر = صروف الدهر = الليلي compare *Labīd* ed. Brockelmann, p. 80, 1. 3. In the *Kitāb Ǵamharat al-amṯāl* of Al-'Askarī, Cairo, 1310, p. 208 a very similar line

هل للفتى من بنات الدهر من واق　　ام هل له من حمام الموت من راق

is ascribed to Yazīd b. Ḥaddāq.

XXIII, v. 6–7. بُهَم is not "rocks," which does not suit the context, but مشكلات الامور (cf. T. A. s. v.). Thus حل المشكلات = فرج البهم (cf. XXIX, 1. 21 فرج = حل). On the other hand, به of v. 7 is not connected with دعا, which verb, here as in v. 7 and v. 10, Muḥammad not God for subject, but with فرج that is' "God has solved a difficult matter by means of him (Muḥammad)": compare v. 4 خص به, v. 12 به خاتم.

V. 14–15. Why does the writer of these verses assert so emphatically that the prohpets dwell in Paradise "without breaking the oath," and that Muḥammad "taught writing with the pen?" Perhaps to refute the contradictory assertion of Umayya that "oaths come to an end" in heaven (XLI, v. 23). Compare however, the tradition given by Lane under the word لا يموت: حل

للمؤمن ثلاثة اولاد فتمسه النار الا تحلة القسم where the last words, "save enough to expiate the oath, refer to the oath" implied in Sura 19, 72: "There is not any of you that shall not come to it, i.e. to hell-fire." It is more natural to connect the verse with this tradition and suppose that a prophetic privelege is alluded to. V. 15b may refer to Umayya's boastful attribution of "writing with the pen" to his tribe of Iyyād (I, v. 4). The word جميعا , which is somewhat awkward in v. 15, may have been copied directly and rather unskilfully from I, v. 4, where it immediately precedes the reference to writing. This latter gets added significance from the fact that Muḥammad had a Ṭaifite attached as scribe to his person. Moreover, the poet has in view all through those who attacked, not so much Muḥammad's doctrines, as his person and his prophetic claims. This, joined with the presence of the poem in Umayya's dīwān, tends to show that it is Umayya himself who is attacked, and thus explains the peculiar character of the "panegyric," while proving, at the same time, that Umayya never wavered in his hostility to Muḥammad.

XXV, v. 1–4. We propose an explanation of these verses somewhat different to that given by Professor Schulthess. Their whole object is, not to describe the creation, to which they do not refer at all, but to introduce the story of the hoopoe. This is evident from the word ملحد in the first verse. After declaring that God knows every burial place, the poet tells us in what way He knows them, and adds that He reveals the treasures of His knowledge, not sparingly but abundantly, to those whom He chooses—these latter, of course, may then communicate the matter to others, as the poet proceeds to do, with a moral purpose. We should thus translate v. 2–4:

"In all things unknown to us God has other things known and manifest to Himself when He renews His acquaintance with any of them (reading يتعهد of Vienna Manuscript),

Namely, streaks and coloring and delineating marks, and He has treasures (of hidden knowledge) which are open to, and not shut against, those for whom He desires them.

And He cuts out their riches (perhaps غناءها but عنانها expresses the same sense figuratively), not merely in full proportion to, but exceeding the measure required."

V. 1. As تعلم = لِتعلم is not uncommon in poetry and is probably Koranical also (Wright, *Arabic Grammar*, II, pp. 35–36), this verse is above suspicion, notwithstanding the reading of the very imperfect Cairo edition.

V. 3. The close connection of خزائن with v. 3a and the Koranic parallels (Sura 11, 33, where Noah says لا اقول لكم عندي خزائن الله ولا اعلم الغيب; 6, 50, where Muḥammad expresses himself similarly; and 6, 59 عنده مفاتيح الغيب cf. Umayya's لا تنفد) prove that the reference is to God's knowledge rather than to the treasures displayed in the creation as Frank Kamenetzky (*Untersuchungen über das Verhaeltniss der dem Umajja b. Abī-ṣ-Ṣalt zugeschriebenen Gedichte zum Qoran*, p. 9) understands it, though, of course, this latter sense is also Koranical.

V. 4. The metaphor is derived from leather-cutting (خلق = measure, فرى and جاب = cut) and should not surprise us in Umayya when we remember that the leather trade was one of the chief industries of his native Ṭa'if. The comparison goes beyond the similar one of Zuhair, cited in Lane, under the word خلق: ولانت تفرى ما خلقت وبعض القوم يخلق ثم لا يفري.. There is probably another reference to this industry in XXXIV, 34, compare our note *ad loc*.

V 8. This verse is unmetrical as vocalized by Professor Schulthess, and if, to correct the meter, we read كَلَّفَ and تَفقِدُ his rendering is no longer possible. The accusative ولدا, which is not naturally explained as *ḥāl*, the indefinite use of تفقد as second person singular, scarcely justified by the following تراه quite common in this sense, and the somewhat straightened interpretation of بصالح are also difficulties to his view. We should suggest reading in all cases with manuscript authority:

مِنْ أُمِّهِ فَجَزَى بِصَالِحِ حَمْلِهَا وَلَدًا وَكَلَّفَ ظَهْرَهُ مَا يَفْقِدُ

"(By his mother), and He (God) rewarded a child for his good deed in carrying her and charged his back with what he seeks." ما يفقد refers to يبغي القرار of v. 6, while صالح is thus used by Umayya in the Badr elegy v. 14. The only difficulty is the omission of the subject of جزى, but God, as subject, is often omitted in Arabic and this is less surprising in the present case as Umayya especially regards God as the recompenser of good deeds, compare v. 47 of this poem and our note there; also XXXV, v. 4, for a somewhat similar omission.

V. 27. Probably صَبْرٌ = constraint, compulsion, that is, the turning away of the demons is constrained not voluntary. Cf. expressions like حلف صبرًا = he was compelled to swear.

V. 49. The vocalization given to the last word of this verse يَزْهَدُ and the translation of الذي لا يزهد "wer sich nicht wie ein Asket von der Welt zurückzieht" is scarcely possible. If clans are to forget the poet's teaching, why should those who are not ascetics remember it? One could understand an opposition between clans and nonascetics. Moreover, to suppose that the ancient Arabs generally were blind to natural phenomena, and that, in this blindness, they could be said to resemble ascetics, is unwarranted in itself and has no analogy in the other verses of Umayya. On the other hand, our rendering "He who is not poor," that is, God, the rich Rewarder, and the implied vocalization يُزْهِدُ, though not judged worthy of mention by Professor Schulthess, is quite natural and seems alone possible here. For ازهد "be poor" cf. Lane under the word, and for its use in this sense by a contemporary poet Aʿša, cf. *Kāmil*, II, 19 (Cairo ed.).[8] Umayya uses an exactly equivalent expression for God as the rich Recompenser of the blessed لا مولى عديم = no needy Master, Fragment 11, 2, and frequently designates a concrete object by a descriptive relative clause, compare XLI, 22 (where Professor Schulthess accepts our correction of Huart's translation), XXV, 15, LXIX, 3. The following verse here, which begins "Pardon then a servant . . . ," supposes an immediately preceding reference to Him who pardons. Moreover v. 38–50 are obviously meant by Umayya to dissuade idolatrous worship of the heavenly bodies. We need not appeal to tradition nor to the religious nature of his poetry to prove this, as it is clearly implied by the verses themselves. When, then, in the opening part of the poem XXV, he traces his teaching, as we have seen, to communications coming to him from God, it is not strange that he should end by expressing a conviction that he should be rewarded for that same religious teaching and that he should desire this reward to consist, partially at least, in the pardon of his sins. The fact that he views God especially as a Rewarder (*MFO*, I, 200–201) makes still more natural such a conclusion.

XXVIII, v. 11. The verb تقتحم = "rush rashly into peril" should be taken not with ارواح but with سفينة, "adventuring with the winds on every surging wave."

V. 13. لكل ما استودعت = "withall that had been entrusted to it," rather than "ganzbestimmungsgemäss."

XXIX, v. 3b. lit. "between the backs of mountain-like waves." This seems better than "zwischen berggleichen Kamelrücken," compare Koran S. 11, 44 تجري في , الموج كالجبال . For ظهر of waves, compare XXXII, 25.

V. 6.The construction is difficult. As حاسبا takes up again the subject of اوفى it cannot form part of the circumstantial clause beginning with الناس and necessarily ending with كالعيال. Moreover جوفه "darin" is impossible as فلك is feminine, and the grammatical construction of رسولا "mittelst eines Boten" is problematic. Hence we should read with manuscript authority خوفه and render "Shutting in through His (God's) fear for his (Noah's) safety a messenger" that is, the dove.

V. 9–22. Frank Kamenetzky, *Untersuchungen*, etc., p. 2, n. 2, remarks on the fact that our fragments contain nothing about Ishmael, who, according to traditionalists, was celebrated in Umayya's poems. The Muḥammadan writers in question seem to refer to these verses, as they believed it was Ishmael, not Isaac, Abraham intended to sacrifice.

XXX, v. 4 (= 2). Ǵāḥiẓ explains this verse by saying that the dove was sent to seek a harbor, which makes Professor Schulthess substitute مينا for manuscript عينا and give up the second half of the verse as corrupt. We prefer to keep عينا and pointing to the next word عانِنَةً or عانِيَةً follow the reading of Ḥayawān, which thus gives a satisfactory sense. The dove is sent forth to seek "a spring and a flowing stream containing abundant water," that the ark may anchor in the stream and the voyagers have spring water to drink. The necessity of both is due to the fact that the ark was in danger, as the waters abated, of coming to grief on the precipices (cf. v. 3 = 1), and the water of the deluge was not drinkable (cf. v. 12 = 11).

V. 11 (= 10) ليس له جراب is an interesting parallel to Psalm 33: 7, which supports the reading כְּנֹד (= כְּנֹאד) of almost all the versions as against the vocalization כַּנֵּד of the Massoreths, as well as the probability that the waters of the heavens are there referred to. Compare Baethgen, *Die Psalmen*, 92.

If Professor Schulthess's interpretation of the serpent verses, which in Ḥayawān follow v. 5., be correct, we must consider them spurious, as Umayya has quite a different conception of the relations between God and the serpent. Compare XXVIII, 1–3; LXI.

XXXII. The arrangement of this collection of fragments is not the best possible. Verses 7–23 form a complete poem, as the first and last two verses show (allowing of course for omissions), the authenticity of which, from the double point of view of tradition and contents, is very doubtful. They should not then be inserted between two fragments better supported by tradition, containing no Koranical echoes and treating of the same subject—a favorite one with our poet—the deluge. The importance of this is that the authenticity of the second fragment is somewhat supported by its connection with the fourth, a connection whz ich is less evident in Professor Schulthess's arrangement.

V. 2. ولي is not "Beschützer" but successor, as is clear from Koran Sura 19, 5 فهب لي من لدنك وليا يرثني and ميراث of the preceding verse.

V. 22–23. Compare the last verse of XXV, also a prayer for the pardon of sin, and the poet's words at his death according to *Agānī*, III,192, لا بري فاعتذر..

XXXIV. 2. Compare Koran Sura 2, 22; 66, 6 where the fuel of hell is said to be men and stones الناس والحجارة, that is, idolators and idols. These may be the stones God is here said to resuscitate. But compare note to XLI, 3 and Matthew 3:9 Isaiah 51:1 for the idea of a creation from stones.

13. Our objection to Van Vloten's rendering of this verse (which seems to have escaped Professor Schulthess, cf. Dīwān p. 100, n. 4) was, that it supposes after ذكر two purpose clauses introduced by أَنْ. This use is late and requires imperfect in both cases. (Cf. Wright, *Arabic Grammar*, II, p. 24 D.) Accordingly, we took أنْ as introducing nominal clauses, in which case يكون = كان is not only possible but quite Koranical (Wright, *l. c.*, p. 266 B), and indeed supposed in every rendering. Some proofs that the Arabs regarded the male ant—incorrectly, of course—as particularly destructive would be to the point. In the

absence of this we prefer to suppose that the ants are taken generically *like the locusts* and that this verse begins with a verb having God as subject *like the two preceding verses*. The same verb is elsewhere used of God by Umayya, compare XXV, 49 and our note to that passage.

14. The manuscript reading تساق is correct. For ساق in this sense compare Koran, Sura 32, 27 نسوق الماء الى الارض الجزر, 7, 55 سُقناه (of a rain cloud). ماء being regarded as a plural may have its verb in the feminine singular, compare Lane under the word هلّا with the perfect generally expresses blame. Hence render "And Pharaoh when the water was brought to him (after the drought سنين mentioned v. 12) why was he not grateful to God?

30. من جواريهم is partitive, جرور literally "dragging," applied to a horse or camel means restive, stubborn; but applied to a woman means crippled مُقْعَدَة according to the dictionaries. "Only the fast one of their young women escaped and even she was crippled (with fatigue)."

There seems hardly sufficient reason to reject سنفة, a beanpod which alone remains when the bean has been consumed, a not inept comparison for the maid who alone survived to tell the tale of her companions' destruction.

34. The incorrect reading يسقون بالرحيق of Ibn Qutaiba, *Kitāb Adab al-Kātib*, ed. Grunert, Leyden, 1900, p. 548, shows how Koranical reminiscences (Sura 83, 53 يسقون من رحيق) have introduced variants into our text. Compare our note to XLI, 18 for another instance.

The word فطير in its ordinary sense, "unleavened," is difficult, because the context requires "dry, unsaturated with liquid" (cf. v. 34a), while unleavened bread is usually wet. But the word فطير is also applied to the dry leather before it is saturated with the tanning liquid: hence it probably means here "unsaturated with liquid." The vague شيئاً favors this sense. Compare our note XXV, 4 for another probable allusion to this great Tā'ifite industry.

V. 35. Read تبورا with V., L. A., as باقر is a collective noun and the plural مهازيل shows it is not treated as a singular.

V. 33–40. *Al-Ḥamāsat al-Baṣriya*, II, 257 contains these verses except 39 (but including 33a) with some important variants. It reads الطود للسهل instead of السهل للطود in v. 35 (a reading supported by Ḥayawān), استوت for اشتوت and هاجت for هاج in v. 37, and places v. 40 immediately after v. 36. As v. 40 has no connection with those preceding it at the end of the poem, while it explains very well the materials of the fires kindled on the tails of the cattle in v. 36, its position immediately after this verse is preferable. The variants of v. 37 seem also correct. "All of them (the fires) rise up and stir up high above them once again cloud after cloud." Thus هاجت has the same subject (fires) and object (rain or rain cloud) in 36 and 37, while, on the other hand, شوى roast for other than cooking purposes is unsatisfactory. As to the variant of v. 35, it would, of course, have been impossible to drive the cattle up the mountainside after fastening on them and igniting the ʿUšar and Salaʿ branches, and the effect of the magical ceremony, the assimilation of the first to lightning lashes, would be augmented by the wild rush of the cattle down the mountainside. They could, however, have been first driven up from the plains and the introduction to these verses in Ḥayawān suggests that hypothesis, though the verses themselves, which join closely together the driving and the lighting of the fires, are more favorable to that suggested by the variant given above.

XXXV. v. 10b. Compare Koran, Sura 2, 38 لا تشتري بآياتنا ثمنًا قليلًا and similar passages, whence we conclude to the meaning "desired not earthly prizes instead of God's reward." The use of ب to express price or equivalent is common.

V. 12. Compare Koran, Sura 46, 27 اتخذوا قُرْبانًا آلهةً which proves that قُرْبان here = intimates, associates, not offering. The word مقرّبون is frequently used in the Koran in this sense, Sura 3, 40; 4, 170; 7, 12; and so on. For ودّ as a collective noun = friends, beloved ones, see dictionaries.

V. 13b. The interpretation of Professor Schulthess, that the Messias is sent to discover the information sought in v. 11, that is, the time of the general judgment, is rendered difficult by v. 12, which puts the meeting with the Messias on the last day itself, so that he evidently does not return beforehand to announce it. Moreover, v. 13 refers to the Apostles, v. 11 to the desires of the poet's contemporaries six centuries later. Hence we had better read غيث and suppose with Fr. Cheikho an allusion to John 14:3, all the more so as v. 15 and v. 16 of this poem contain also Gospel allusions.

V. 15. There can be no reference to Potiphar's wife here as اخلع ثيابك منها cannot mean "gib ihr dein Kleid preis" but "cast off thy garments consisting of them" (i. e., the evil things خبيثات) divest thyself of them, cast them off though they cling to thee as a garment. The allusion in v. 15b to Mark 14:52 is obvious.

V. 16. Here as in v. 15 while the first part of the verse is Koranical the second is evangelical and alludes to Matthew 7:2.

XXXVI. Compare Koran, Sura 18, 49 ما كنت متخذ المضلين عضدا which shows that له probably refers to الله not سلم.

XXXVII. v. 1, 2, *a*, *b*, *c*, *d*. These verses are also cited in whole or in part with numerous variants by Zamaḫšārī, *Kaššāf*, I, 137; Al-Ḫāzin, *Tafṣīr*, III, 247; Maḳrīzī, *Ḫiṭāṭ*, I, 147; Ibn al-ʿAnbarī, *Aḍdād*, 190; and especially Alūsī, *Bulūg al arab fī maʿrifat aḥwāl al ʿarab*, II, 286–87. All these except *Aḍdād*, where the citation is anonymous, ascribe them to Tubbaʿ in (تبع *Dīwān*, p. 104 is a misprint), as do the best authorities cited in T. A. and L. A. Šammār, Ibn Barrī, Al-Azharī. Besides the citation under the word ثاط , compare also T. A. II, 335; L. A. IV, 125.

XXXVIII. v. 2. There is no reason for correcting سبّح which means "remove," regularly enough, as it is the causative of the verb of motion سبح. This sense is also Koranical and has given origin to the secondary sense "praise," that is, remove, or declare removed, from imperfections نزّه as the dictionaries explain it.

V. 4. To Professor Schulthess's connection of دمدم with ديوم we may add the following consideration. ديومة = desert, level ground without trees or water, is evidently connected with دممت على شي = I made the ground level over a thing. This expression is synonymous with دمدمت على شي and we find the latter used in the Koran, Sura 91, 11, of the punishment of Ṯamūd فدمدم عليهم . ربهم بذنبهم فسواها perhaps meaning "stretched them prostrate," compare Sura 7, 76; 51, 45.

V. 6. The contradiction between this verse and v. 4, where the going into the desert is represented as taking place before the Annunciation, shows how closely the poet depends on the Koran Sura 19 where the going into the desert is mentioned twice, both before the Annunciation, v. 16, and after it, v. 22.

V. 13b. Compare Koran, Sura 23, 52 آويناهم الى ربوة said by God of Jesus and Mary. Hence the text is probably correct and may be rendered, "He (God) sheltered them (Jesus and Mary) from their blame and from regret." The direct obejct is replaced by هم for metrical reasons.

XL. *Ḥam. Baṣ*. II, 269 has all the second recension except v. 2.

XLI. (1).We prefer to render "Stainless art Thou our Lord, in every crime." This is the original sense of سلامك as well as سبحانك , that is, declaring God sound or free from imperfection (cf. note to XXXVIII, 2, and Koran, Sura 4, 169; 6, 100, etc.), and is commended by the context here.

1. The reading تبغي تقيا is closer to the manuscript and more likely to be correct as it gives same sense as (4) of which 1 seems to be a doublet. *Rabīʿ-al-Abrār*, manuscript of British Museum. f. 28b, reads the second part of (4) وعدن لا يطالعها الاثيم.

2b. Perhaps "and hell refuses a light to those who ask it." This is more in accord with the sense of قبس and Koran Sura 57, 13, where the damned ask a light of the blessed.

3. We should read بجندل for بصندل. It is the reading of all the *Rabīʿ-al-Abrār* manuscript of British Museum. The epithets are generally applied to rocks (cf. variants of Ṯaʿālibī to XXX, 1 (=9)), and to جندل in particular, for example, in the Muʿallaqa of Imru'l-Qais. The Koran says that the fuel of hell is "men and stones," compare note to XXXIV, 2.

4. The v. l. سموم was probably suggested by the Koran, Sura 59, 41; 52, 27 and gives a good sense. For cooling breeze all they have is the fiery samūm.

6. For the peculiar دانية compare Koran, Sura 76, 14 دانية عليهم ظلالها "close down upon them (the blessed) shall be its shadows," where دانية refers directly to جنة. As an epithet, designating the latter word, it can scarcely be original here.

8. Cf. XXX, 10b for an exact parallel to من غير ضرع.

9. The explanation of this verse given by Professors Schulthess and Geyer is admittedly unsatisfactory. We propose the very slight correction of عرق to غرف. The poet describes the channels of milk that form one of the joys of Paradise; "In them the hands are free to move about, their milk flows forth without any udder to restrain it, is no sickness or satiety so that it should be forbidden to them, and, at every handful they drink, there is a glad cry not interrupted nor unaccompanied. Thus, غرف = lap up with the hands is confirmed by ايدى of v. 7, and محرم as applied to the milk by محالة of the same verse. The continuation of the sense beyond the limits of the verse is quite in the style of Umayya. We should, of course, read either فيه in v. 8 or تحرم in v. 9.

18. كريم is impossible, owing to the rhyme, and because it must, if genitive, agree with either عسجدة or اساور and so cannot be masculine singular. Evidently the Koranical parallel passage Sura 76, 21 has produced the reading وحلوا for وحلي, which gives the same sense, continues the construction of v. 17, and

has كريمٌ masculine singular in agreement with it.

21. We should vocalize مباركةٌ رذومُ (both fem. sing. agreeing with كاس of v. 20) for metrical reasons. The form فَعول as is well known, when equivalent to present participle can be masculine or feminine

22–23. Compare our note to XXIII, 14.

XLIII. فومان plural of فوم more probably means "wheat," as the word is certainly used in that sense XVIII, I, which is cited by Ibn Hišām to prove that فوم of Koran, Sura 2, 48 means "wheat." The citation given from Abū-Miḥǵān in L. A. and T. A., under the word فوم and Suyūṭī., *Itqān*, 162 goes to show that in Ṭā'if, at all events, the word meant wheat. The Ṭā'ifites were thought the most intelligent of the Arabs because they lived on bread as well as milk. Umayya frequently refers to wheat or bread: Badr elegy, v. 14; XI, v. 6; XXII, v. 3; XLI, v. 10; XLIII, v. 1; F 6. v. 1.

LV. v. 15. [mina l-ḫawfi] are better taken with v. 14. The fear of God is cause of the physical emotions of the Angels (v. 6), and not of their service, which is attributed to a higher motive (XXV, 23). There is an exactly similar prolongation of the grammatical construction beyond the limits of the verse in v. 28–29.

V. 23. XXVII, 8 supports the manuscript reading جِدّة "newness" against the proposed emendation.

LVII. Compare *Aš-Šu'arā' an-Naṣrāniya*, p. 616 for the poem (there attributed to Waraqa b. Naufal) of which this verse forms part.

LVIII. This verse is not by Umayya b. Abī-ṣ-Ṣalt but by Umayya b. Ḫalaf, and is part of a satire directed by him against Ḥassān b. Ṯābit whose father was a blacksmith. It is cited with two others by 'Ainī, IV, 563, and alone in L. A. XVII, 357; T. A. IX, 371. All these authorities attribute it to Umayya b. Ḥalaf (T. A. curiously adding al-Haḏalī) and read the first half of the verse عانيا يظل يشدّ كيرًا. Ḥassān's reply is given by 'Ainī l. c. and in his dīwān, Tunis ed. p. 58. These versions and the one verse of the reply given by Ibn Hišām p. 234 contain the word همزة, which is said to be an allusion to a Koranical malediction addressed to Umayya b. Ḥalaf, namely, Sura 104, 1 and 2.

LX. Mu'attib is not a lame she-camel nor a woman but the well-known Ṭā'if clan of that name. To them belonged the guardianship of the idol Al-Lāt (Ibn Hišām, 55; Wāḳidī-Wellhausen, 384), and the leadership of the Aḥlāf, which party, with that of the Banū Mālik, formed the population of Ṭā'if (Ibn al-Aṯīr I, 514–17). Other Ṭā'ifite poets use such expressions as ال معتب (Umayya b. al-Askar al-Kinānī in Ibn Ḥagar, I, 127) and شنت معتب بغارتها (Rabīʿ b. Ṣufyān in Ibn al-Aṯīr, I, 517), speaking of the same clan. As Umayya, being of the Banū ʿAuf b. ʿUqda, thus belonged to the Aḥlāf (Ibn al-Aṯīr, I, 516), and was also, like the chief of the Muʿattib clan, closely connected with Quraiš, the calamities referred to are not the mere boast of an opposing tribesman. There may be a reference to the treacherous slaughter of thirteen of the Banū Mālik by al-Mugīra before he fled to Muḥammad with whom we find him in AH 5. ʿUrwa, chief of the clan and Mugīra's paternal uncle, though he had earned the praise of the poet Al-Aʿša for paying 1300 camels as blood-money, declared in AH 6 at Hudaibiya, where he acted as mediator between Muḥammad and the Quraiš, that this act had brought upon the Banū Muʿattib the eternal hatred of the Ṯaqīfites. Wāḳidī-Wellhausen, 250–51). An allusion to ʿUrwa's tragic death, early in AH 9, at the hands of one of his townsmen, owing to his open profession of Islam, is just possible, if Umayya only died later in that year.

Professor Geyer's rendering of اعتبت "besserte sich" seems certainly correct, as it not only suits the context but also the explanation of the proper name given by Ibn Duraid, *Ištiqāq*, 1, 42: عاتبتُ فلاناً فأَعتبني اي استرضيتُه فأَرضاني . Thus here the calamities admonish Muʿattib and demand improvement as a favor, but Muʿattib does not accept the admonition and refuses to make the improvement that is demanded, contrary to what one would expect from the bearer of such a name.

LXI. The verse almost certainly refers to the temptation of Adam and Eve by the serpent and may be rendered: "Then (the serpent) made them acquainted with sin, ad they had previously been ignorant of it, and constrained them to a foolish cou rse, the folly of which they knew not."

LXIII. The verse is also cited *Kaššaf*, II, 69 (cf. *Šarḥ Kaššāf*, 28) a propos of Koran Sura 23, 4 الذين هم للتزكوات فاعلون, compare also Sura 76, 8 يطعمون الطعام.

★
★★

Fragment 1:1.2. Professor Schulthess interprets this verse after Geyer : "Die Hängestricke (d. h. Strahlenfaden) der Sterne, niederhängend, gleich der Schnur des Kreisels; ihre Enden in gerader Richtund Ǵ.The idea of the motion of the stars underlying this interpretation is dlearly expressed in the poetical joust between ʿUbaid b. al-Abraṣ and Imruʾl-Qais, *Maǵānī*, VI, 145.

قال عبيد   ما مرتجات على هول مراكبهـــا   يقطعن طولَ المدى سيرا وامراسا

قال امرو القيس   تلك النجوم اذا حالت مطالعها   شبهتها في سواد الليـــل اقباسا

There is a constant alternation for the stars of journeying, (سيرا) and having their strings readjusted on the pulley (اِمراسا), when the journey is completed. Nevertheless that idea has such difficulties here as make us prefer the following rendering (reading خيل for حبل which has at least equally good anuscript support): "The suspended stars sent forth like steeds in a race-course their goal being the place where they set" (or "the place whence they started"). Linguistically, مرسلات = sent forth to run of stars or steeds, is much better than "niederhängend" of strings, غاية = a goal of a race, is preferable to "Enden" of strings—the latter meaning seems hardly possible; نصاب according to the lexicons does not mean "in gerader Richtung," but اصل "origin," مغيب الشمس "place where the sun sets," جُزأة السكين "handle of a knife" (from the root meaning, "plant a pole upright by sinking it in the ground," it is easy to see how the same word means place in which a thing sinks or is set up or originates); قِرق = κρίκος קורקסא, if possible, is quite unsupported and philologically less likely than قِرق = κίρκος, circus, ܩܘܪܩܣ , which is a certain Arabic borrowing, as is shown by the double form it has and its connection with racing in the following extract from the *Šarḥ al-Mufaḍḍaliyāt* (manuscript of Cairo), note to Thorbecke, IX, 1. 27, where the commentator says: كقول نفيلة الاسجع

كان اوب يديها وهي لاهيه   اذا المطايا غشين السرنج القِرَقا

and adds explaining the concluding word : يقال قاع قرق وقاع قرقوس اذا كان واسعا كثير الحصى.

Our interpretation, thus linguistically preferable, is confirmed by the fact that Umayya loves the race-course metaphor and uses it, mostly in express connection with غاية, of the course of Noah's ark, XXXII, 27 (cf. also XXIX, 1); of the course of human life, with maturity as goal, VIII, 5; with death as goal, XXXV, 3; with paradise as goal, XLI, 22; and especially of the stars, which course along, XXV, 43, never resting, XXV, 21, travelling day and night XLI, 26, swifter than racehorses (the very same comparison we have here), 25. This interpretation admits equally well the v. 1 اعلاط. Compare *MFO*, I, p. 205.

Fragment 2: 1.4. Also cited *Naqd*, p. 76. The verse is given as an instance of bad division. "Lord of men and of savage men." Others render من يتأبد "men who feed on wild beasts," Professor Schulthess "Einsiedler." We should prefer to render "Lord of men and of those who are eternal, that is, angels," as Umayya likes to express a person or thing by a descriptive relative clause (cf. XXV, 49 ; XLI, 22 ; LXIX, 13; etc.), the dictionaries give تأبّد = صار ابديًّا and this interpretation could never have occurred to the commentator as the mortality of angels is a Muḥammadan dogma. That Umayya considered the angels eternal is evident from XXV, 26 where مخلّد is predicated of them while it is denied of men LV, 33; compare XXXIV, 2; XLVII, 1; XL, 13; and so on. Thus the verse is not an instance of bad division as it enumerates the two classes of rational beings who worship God.

Fragment 3: 1.2. A propos of كفر "mountains" there is a slip in Freytag's lexicon where the singular of this word is rendered "aquila" apparently through a confusion of عُقاب and عِقاب. We should propose حص for خص as it means "cut, destroy" and is a close equivalent of قطع usually joined with دابرهم.

Fragment 4: 1.2. We should read سِواها with V. and translate: "The main body (or foremost part) of the nightly raid rode down upon them without their perceiving anyone to warn them of it except itself."

Fragment 5: 1.1. *Naqd*, p. 86, cites this verse and says it belongs to the same poem as XXIX, 1. 23 also there cited.

Fragment 7: 1.2. The reading of the Paris manuscript pointed أُبْقِيَ "he would have been left (exposed to the sun)" seems better than أُلْفِيَ he would have been found (exposed to the sun)."

Fragment 8: 1.1. كلّ certainly refers to the angels "everyone is watchful to prevent secret knowledge becoming known," that is, to the Ǵinn (cf. XXV, 27–28).

1.3. There seems to be no reference here to the fulfilment of prophecies. Umayya simply says, describing the last day: "In it you shall receive visible tidings of past generations, and information about hidden things shall appear at the resurrection."

★
★★

WAS UMAYYA A MUSSULMAN?

We do not intend here to reopen the question of the authenticity or spuriousness of the religious poems attributed to Umayya. Now that these have been made so easily available, they will probably attract as they certainly merit the attention of more capable critics. Our object is to discuss a new and important element introduced into the subject by Professor Schulthess in his introduction, pp. 7–8, namely that Umayya may have been a Mussulman, one of that devout class of early believers from whom the spurious poems ascribed to him must have emanated, and, at the same time, to point out how exactly our opposing theory, that Muḥammad may have utilized the poems of Umayya[10]—very briefly and as an almost necessary consequence inaccurately described and rejected by the same writer—stands in the light of recent studies of these poems.

The hypothesis that Umayya was a Mussulman is important from several points of view. It would explain how the characteristic treatment of our poet may be combined with indubitable Koranical reminiscences in certain poems, for example, XLI, and thus supply whatever may be wanting in the theory of a common source. Again, it would throw light on the question of the Ḥanīfs. Umayya's religious poetry, if dependent on the Koran, would no longer impose a certain limitation to a recent theory which sees in the Ḥanīf movement a Mussulman invention intended to provide precursors to Muḥammad and a preparation for his doctrine. Finally, it would diminish the importance of Umayya himself, by depriving his religious teaching of much of its originality and his character of much of its relief. The matter is, therefore, worth investigating.

Tradition is so notoriously diligent in chronicling the early successes of Islam, even when nonexistent, that we should expect the conversion of so remarkable a personage as Umayya not to pass unnoticed. Nevertheless, the explicit testimonies about his religion which have been handed down to us, while affirming that Umayya possessed and professed most of the material elements of the Muḥammadan creed or, in other words, "was a believer in his poems,"[11] declare that he rejected what we may call its formal element, remaining always an enemy of Muḥammad and never acknowledging his prophetic mission.[12] The traditions recording these two facts, perfectly reconcilable with each other and quite in accordance with the extant poems of Umayya, are not, in so far, representative of different tendencies. Nay, their very varieties in accounting for the one is the best proof that they were convinced of both. It is precisely because Umayya was a believer in his poetry that they sought out different personal and unworthy motives to explain his recalcitrant attitude toward a fundamental dogma of Islam, an attitude which they never attributed to other doctrinal divergencies.[13]

Notwithstanding these explicit declarations that Umayya never went over to Islam, Professor Schulthess has been able to find three probable indications to the contrary.[14] The first of these is of particular importance, "as Umayya is therein claimed as a Muslim by the oldest historical tradition." His name is, in fact, given in an *isnād* by Ibn Isḥāq, as an authority for a specifically religious tradition. While we are sure that the later tradition-collectors would never have cited a non-Muslim in such an *isnād*, we cannot say the same for Ibn Isḥāq in whose time the *isnād* was very little developed and the tradition-criteria nonexistent.[15] Nevertheless, the mention would, at all events, prove a certain interest of Umayya in Islam and Muḥammad and thus justify, to some extent, the inference of Professor Schulthess if the *isnād* in question were historic. But the *isnād* is not historic, at least as far as the inclusion in it of Umayya b. Abī-ṣ-Ṣalt is concerned. To prove this all that is necessary is an attentive perusal of the tradition in the Arabic text.[16]

A woman of the Banū Ǧifār relates an interview that took place between herself and Muḥammad at the conquest of Ḫaibar in HA 7. From the accident that occurred to her then, for the first time, we may conclude that she was about fourteen years old. When, subsequently, she relates the story, she is, evidently, considerably older, as she deems it necessary to inform her interlocutor that she was a young girl then. Accordingly that interlocutor cannot have been Umayya b. Abī-ṣ-Ṣalt, whose death took place before that of Muḥammed in AH 11, to judge from the stories told the latter about him which either describe or suppose it and not after AH 9 according to all the historians. But our tradition is still more explicit, as it declares that the interlocutor of the Banū Ğifār woman was not a man but a woman. This point, which does not appear in Weil's translation, is quite evident in the Arabic text. The woman says: "And he took this necklace, which thou see'st (fem. تَرَيْنَ) on my neck, and gave it to me and fastened it on my neck and, by God, it will never leave me." She said (i.e., the interlocutor, قالت is not translated by Weil) : "And it was on her neck until she died. . . ." The latter sentence implies that Umayya, if interlocutor, lived on until the death of the Banū Ğifār woman, who was a young girl in 7 CE and who, from the story, does not appear to have died prematurely. Of course the سمّاها لي at the beginning of the narration refers to Sulāiman b. Suhaim, the subject of حدثني in the preceding line, and not to Umayya b. Abī-ṣ-Ṣalt. If the *isnād* be otherwise historical, the error in it is not difficult to explain. One might attribute it to the fact that Ibn Isḥāq, whose *isnāds* are notoriously indeterminate, wrote Umayya, *sine addito*, and that the poet, here as elsewhere, was confused with some other Umayya through the unwarranted addition of b. Abī-ṣ-Ṣalt to that name. Fortunately, however, we can here go beyond a simple hypothesis as Wāqidī has preserved to us the very same tradition, in a form so similar to that of Ibn Isḥāq that it supposes a literary dependence of one on the other or of both on a common source, and, at the same time, with an *isnād* which perfectly explains the unauthorized introduction of our poet into the story.[17] His *isnād* is "Ibn Abī Sabra from Sulaimān b. Suḥaim fromUmm ʿAlī bint Abī-l-Ḥakam from the Ğifār woman Umayya bint Qais b. Aṣ-Ṣalt, that of Ibn Isḥāq "Sulaimân b. Suḥaim from Umayya b. Abī-ṣ-Ṣalt from a woman of the Banu Ğifār." Thus the fact that the interlocuator of the Ğifār woman was also a woman and the Umayya in question was not the poet is assured. The loss of the second link of the chain in the *isnād* of Ibn Isḥāq was supplied by the name of the Ğifār woman herself, and that was identified with and transformed into the very similar name of the more famous poet. It is true that Umayya is usually a man's not a woman's name, but we have at least two other instances of women so designated, namely, the poetess Umayya bint Ḫuwailid in the Ḥamāsat al-Buḥturī, ed. Cheikho 1910 (cf. Index) and Umayyah bint Qais b. ʿAbdallāh, one of the returned Abyssinian exiles, Ibn Hišām 784 (whom Caetani seems to identify with Umayyah bint Qais b. Aṣ-Ṣalt, though they not only have different patronymics, but belong to different tribes, Asad, Ḫuzaima in the former case and Ġifār a branch of Kināna in the latter). We need scarcely add that the conclusion drawn from this *isnād* that Umayya was certainly alive in AH 7. (Schulthess *B. A.* VIII, 3, p.8 , n.1) is unjustified.

A second indication that Umayya was a Muslim is found in the declaration that he was the first to read "the Book of Allah,"[18] and the tradition that he was a believer in his poems, an unbeliever in his heart. If "the Book of Allah" is to be interpreted as Muḥammad's earthly Koran, or rather some part of it, such an inference is not unwarranted. But since suppositions about the first believers and the first Koran readers have always preoccupied the traditionalists, we may be sure that this belief, if it ever existed, would have been handed down to us by several channels and in a more unequivocal form. The declaration in question admits of a more natural and well-supported interpretation. It is an equivalent of the rather common traditional exegesis which explains Sura 7, 174 as referring to Umayya.[19] Thus Ibn Kaṯīr tells us "And it is said that he was a prophet and had the faith in the beginning but subsequently turned aside, and he it is whom God designated when He said: Read to them the declaration of him to whom we brought our signs, and who stepped away therefrom, and Satan followed him and he was of those who were beguiled."[20] To read the "Book of Allah" and to receive the prophetic call are equivalent expressions, as is evident from the way in which Muḥammud is supposed to have received his first revelation.[21] Indeed this declaration, when properly interpreted and compared with other similar ones, if it proves anything, proves that the religious teaching of Umayya was prior to that of Muḥammad, one of the fundamental elements of a theory proposed by us,[22] but rejected by Professor Schulthess.[23]

The tradition that Umayya was a believer in his poetry but an unbeliever in his heart proves exactly the contrary to that which is inferred from it. The first part is a declaration, universally acknowledged by tradition and abundantly proved by the verses that remain to us, that Umayya's poetry contained Koranical doctrines, while the second part, far from insinuating that he submitted to Islam, gives the supposed reason why he did not. The same is true of the traditions which treat him most favorably like that which represents him saying on his deathbed "I know that the Ḥanīfīya is true but I have my doubts about Muḥammad."[24] Those which liken him to Muḥammad, that of the heart-purification, for instance, are a direct consequence of the supposition that he was a prophet in the beginning and not unlikely owe their origin to the exegesis of Sura 7, 176, given above. They are thus on a par with so many traditions about Muḥammad himself, mere apocryphal developments of Koranical texts, as P. Lammens has abundantly demonstrated.[25]

Another argument is drawn from the fact that poems, which are mere interpretations of the Koran, nay even, a panegyric of Muḥammad himself, have been attributed to Umayya. But this does not give us any good reasons for believing that the poet either was or was considered a Muslim. The panegyric in question, like the similar one ascribed to Imru-l-Qais, or the prophetic verses attributed to one of the Himyarite princes, is obviously spurious, and seems to have imposed on nobody, to judge from the existence of so many contradictory and not a single confirmatory tradition. It is only found in the *Ḫizānat-al-Adab* and there Al-Baḡdādī tells us, evidently with some surprise, that he found it in Umayya's dīwān.[26] If it was expressly written to answer the latter's attacks on Muḥammad, as we have some reason for thinking,[27] it could have got into the dīwān without being once attributed to the poet. As for the other Koranical poems, the Mussulman authors who have preserved them to us, while ascribing them to Umayya, do not hesitate to affirm at the same time that he died a kāfir; and we need not suppose that their predecessors, who believed, no doubt, in a certain preparation of Islam and knew that Umayya had actually treated similar religious subjects, were more critical than they in this respect. Indeed all modern critics have not found the dependance of these verses on the Koran so very obvious.

Since then we have not the slightest reason to reject the unanimous declarations of the Muḥammadan writers that Umayya never submitted to Islam, we cannot suppose that he posed as an interpreter of the Koran, declaring it to be God's word (XLVI, 3) or using expressions like الداعي (XLIX, 6) and عجوز (XXXI, 5); which supposed in his hearers a close acquaintance with the Koranical text if they were to understand them, whatever may be said of the possibility of his contradicting himself in the effort to reproduce its incoherencies (see our note to XXXVIII, 4–6), or of his copying it word for word (XLI, 14–21). This is even more unlikely than that a pious Mussulman versified the Koranical account of the Ṯamūd legend without any mention of Ṣāliḥ[28] or his partisans. What then was the origin of the spurious Koranical poems? Why and when were they attributed to Umayya? Two explanations, not mutually exclusive, are possible and have both a certain foundation in the texts. Composed or not at an earlier date, these poems were only attributed to Umayya after the period when Koranical imitations began to be tabooed. Was not he, a precursor of Muḥammad and a believer in his poetry, their most probable author in the opinion of the orthodox? Such an attribution, moreover, was the best means to save the poems from destruction and their Mussulman authors from the charge of irreverence toward the sacred text. This hypothesis is confirmed by the fact that we find no trace of the spurious Koranical poems and no citation from any one of them before the composition of Pseudo-Balḫī's "Book of the Creation" in AH 355,[29] while the great bulk of the other religious poems attributed to Umayya and citations from nearly all of them are to be found in earlier authors of the second and third centuries, Sībawaihī, Ibn Hišām, Abī Tammām, Ibn Sikkīt, Al-Gāḥiẓ, Ibn Qutaiba, Al-Mubarrad, Aṭ-Ṭabarī, and so on.

This explanation, whatever it is worth,[30] does not exclude a second that the spurious poems owe their origin to attempts made by pious Mussulmans to islamize the religious verses of Umayya. The frequency of interpolations, due to reciters and with a much less appreciable motive, in Arabic poetry is well known. In the present case, owing to the fragmentary nature of Umayya's poetry, we cannot convict these interpolations of disagreeing with the context, since the context is nearly always missing. It is significant, however, that we have, in almost always all cases, verses in the same rhyme and meter which have every appearance of authenticity. Thus XLIX, 4–15 may be compared with v. 1–4, v. 16 and fr. 3 as سليطا of v. 16[31] and قساوسة of fr. 3 v. 1 favor their authenticity, XXXVIII, with fr. 12, which refers to a biblical, if also a Koranical, subject and one that would attract a lover of animals like Umayya, XXXI, 1–7 with 8–11. Part of XXXII is certainly authentic; part of XXXV, namely v. 15–16, is very probably Koranical.[32] The probability of an interpolation in XLVI has been already discussed. But there is nothing more striking in this respect than to compare the double recension of XL with the Koranical parallels collected by Frank-Kamenetzky, *Untersuchungen*, pp. 22–23. All the parallels belong to the new verses, contained only in the longer recension, while the non-Koranical verses of the shorter recension are testified by more numerous, and in some cases far more ancient, authorities, Sībawaihī and Al-Mubarrad.[33]

We have, however, one case in which the context of the Koranical passage is not missing and where we can catch the interpolator in the act. According to the investigation of Frank-Kamenetzky the parts of XLI preceding and following v. 10–21 are not Koranical and have every right to be considered authentic, while v. 10–21 are spurious.[34] This criticism is correct, except in as far as it condemns v. 10–13. Verse 10 declares like the Koran that honey, milk, and wine are among the drinks of the blessed, and v. 12 adds clear, sweet, wholesome water. But we find Umayya in XXXIV, 22 enumerating together milk and honey and pure water as special earthly benefits bestowed by God. What is more natural than that the poet should unite them here in describing the promised land "flowing with milk and honey?" Nor is the addition of the wine anything extraordinary. Jewish descriptions of Paradise contain similar elements.[35] Moreover v. 10 is completely differentiated from the Koran and appropriated to the Ṭaifite Umayya by the mention of "wheat cut down in the places where it grew."[36] Verses 11, 12, 13 have each one word found in Koranical descriptions of Paradise and these are, respectively, نخل dates, رمّان pomegranates, and لحم meat. These generic terms, so natural in an Arab's and especially a Taifite's description of Paradise, ought not to be regarded as Koranical. On the other hand, the borrowings of v. 12–21 seem even more abundant than they are represented by Frank-Kamenetzky.[37] Here, then, we find eight consecutive verses, taken almost word for word from the Koran, in the very center of a poem, which, treating all though of the same Koranical subject, is without trace of Koranical influence and has every reason to be considered authentic. Professor Schulthess will not admit that we are justified in suspecting an interpolation, but offers no alternative explanation. We prefer Frank-Kamenetzky's solution within the limits assigned above.

That our criticism of Professor Schulthess's condemnation of some verses as unauthentic was not altogether unjustified is proved by his own admission: "Es ist mir zum mindesten zweifelhaft geworden, ob sich das

Qoranisieren in der Weise mit der Unechtheit deckt, wie ich in Or. Stud. angenommen hatte."[38] This admission—which appears to have been divined at least as probably by Professor Geyer in 1907[39]—seems scarcely in accord with the reference to our "Befangenheit wegen der Echtheitsfrage."[40] As a matter of fact, there were only five poems or fragments of poems in which we ventured to differ with Professor Schulthess in 1906. As regards two of these, XXVII and LV, we expressed ourselves doubtful (and the doubt has if anything since increased, especially with regard to XXVII). Our conclusions as to two others, XXXVI and XLI, have been confirmed by the investigations of Professor Schulthess's pupil Frank-Kamenetzky.[41] Accordingly, there only remains a four-line fragment, XXXI, 8–11, the spuriousness of which we declared unproven to illustrate our "Befangenheit."[42] While this difference of opinion with regard to the question of authenticity, whether existing or not in a notable degree, is of little consequence, we wish to rectify two other points in which our theory of a probable dependence of Muḥammad on Umayya has been misrepresented, unintentionally of course, in the note in question. We have not been influenced in proposing this theory by our supposed "Befangenheit wegen der Echtheitsfrage," as we expressly declared "While we have ground for supposing that a certain influence was exercised by Umayya's poetry on the author of the Koran, it must be admitted that the fragments of that poetry which remain to us offer no confirmation of such an hypothesis."[43] Neither is our theory based on the argument that "dieser (Muḥammad) junger sei als jener (Umayya). It has a double foundation which we thus stated before attempting to establish it. "He (Umayya) must have previously treated of Koranical subjects in his poems and these poems must have come to the knowledge of and been utilized by the author of the Koran."[44] Such a theory can from the nature of the case never be more than probable, but in supplying whatever may be wanting in the theory of a common source drawn from by both, whether that be the *Ahl aḏ-ḏikr* or the Jews and Christians, it accords much better with the facts than does the opposing one of Professor Schulthess that Umayya was a Muslim and made use of the Koran. As we have seen his proofs are not convincing, and one of them, the tradition "dass Umayya als erster das Buch Allahs gelesen habe," favors our contrary hypothesis, that Umayya was a prophet or religious teacher before Muḥammad. Moreover, we have shown that his supposition that Umayya was certainly alive in AH 7 is unfounded, so that the poet may have died in AH 2, as several historians assert, in which case he is little likely to have utilized the Koran. Again, while recent investigations as to the age of Muḥammad make him out to have been about fifty at the time of his death,[45] it is more probable than ever that our poet was alive when close on sixty, since the verses given above (cf. LXIX) strongly support the authenticity of VIII (cf. fr. 14, v. 1). To resume then the arguments we have given fully elsewhere, Muḥammad, to judge from the materials at our disposal, was younger than Umayya; was considered posterior to Umayya as a religious teacher; wrote the Koran; as a matter of fact, late in life, had means of becoming acquainted with Umayya's religious poetry, which must have been known in Mecca; had the need as well as the inclination to make use of such materials, indeed was actually accused, and not unjustly, of having utilized similar ones. Accordingly, if a borrowing took place, we are far safer in asserting that the indebtedness lay on the side of Muḥammad. But the question is more theoretical than practical because, as we already said, the materials at our disposal do not enable us to decide if such a borrowing really took place. A common source, we think, sufficiently explains all genuine resemblances, especially if, with Professor M. Hartmann, we suppose that source to have been the *ahl aḍ-ḏikr*.

NOTES

1. E. Powers, "The Poems of Ummaya B. Abī-ṣ-Ṣalt," in *Melanges de la Faculté Orientale de L'Université Saint Joseph, Beyrouth*, vol. 2 (1911–1912), pp. 145–95.

2. Umajja ibn Abī-ṣ-Ṣalt, *Die unter seinem Namen überlieferten Gedichtfragmente gesammelt und überstezt* [Beiträge zur Assyriologie und semitischen Sprachwissenschaft, VIII, 3] (Hinrichs, Leipzig, 1911).

The reference made by Professor Schulthess to the literary relations of our previous article to his (*B. A.*, VIII, 3, p. 1, n. 3), which might be misinterpreted, obliges us to say here that our materials were collected and our conclusions come to before we read his study. This we utilized in avoiding to say again what had been already said by him, and confining ourselves to those points, in which our views differed from his, or which, we thought, deserved fuller treatment than the necessarily limited nature of his article allowed. Not a single reference of his was then of any use to us, as any, that might have been so, were to manuscripts not at our disposal.

3. He apparently possessed Umayya's dīwān, to judge from his remark that XL contained about thirteen verses, (*Istiʿāb*, Manuscripts of the British museum 1624, f. 317 v., copied by Damīrī, II, 473).

4. Cf. the manner in which the sense runs on throughout after the end of the verse, the peculiar expression اهل الحتوف —reminding one of another singluar use made of that word by Umayya الحيّة الحتفة XXVIII, 1, and the connection of the subject matter with VIII or, at least, with its attribution to Umayya.

5. Cf. Schulthess in *Orientalische Studien*, p. 87, on the moral character of the poetry of the Ḥanīfs.

6. Brockelmann, I, 367–68, speaks of two poetical anthologies by this writer in the manuscript collection of the British Museum, which he numbers 333 and 726, respectively, but there is only one at p. 333, nr. 726 of the catalogue.

7. An anonymous commentary on the *Kitāb al-Adab* of Al-Ḫilāfa.

8. The transcriber of Or. 415, who gives this poem, says it is said to be a forgery in the name of Umayya b. Abī-ṣ-Ṣalt (مصنوعة عليه) or according to others of ʿAmr b. Kulṯūm والله اعلم.

9.

وقال الاعشى لسلامة ذي فائش الحميارى

وقومك ان يضمنوا جارة   وكانوا بموضع انضادهـا
فلن يطلبوا سِرَّها للغنى   ولن يُسْلِمُوها لِازْهَادهـا

في هذا قولان احدهما انهم لا يطلبون اجبارها اليهم على زعم اولياءها من اجـل مالها غصبا للجوار ولا يسلمونها اذا انقطع رجاؤهم من الثواب والمكافأة والاخر انهم لا يرغبون في ذوات الاموال وانما يرغبون في ذوات الاحساب اختياراً للاولاد وصيانة للاصهار ان يطمع فيهم من لا حسب له

10. *MFO*, I, 208–11.

11. Ibn Haǵar, I, 263; *Aǵānī*, III, 191; etc.

12. ولم يختلف اصحاب الاخبار انه مات كافرًا "The traditionalists are unanimous in declaring that he died a Kāfir," Ibn Ḥaǵar, I, 262; *Ḫizāna*, I, 121–22, thus resume their predecessors' accounts.

13. Cf. Schulthess, *Orientalische Studien*, pp. 75–76, for references.

14. *B.A.* VIII, 3, pp. 7-8.

15. Caetani, *Annali*, Introduction, p. 32 sq.

16. References in *MFO*, I, n. 3 and 4. Add Ibn Kaṯīr, Manuscript of British Museum 276, 40 r., 40 v., 42 r; *Istī'āb*, of Ibn 'Abd al-Barr, Manuscript of British Museum 1624, f. 317–18.

17. We give the text of Ibn Hišām with the variants in Wāqidi, manuscript of British Museum Or. 1617, f. 156 r.

قال ابن اسحاق حدثني سليمان بن سحيم عن امية بن ابي الصلت عن امراة من بني غفار قد سماها لي (a) قالت اتيت (b) رسول الله صلعم في نسوة من بني غفار فقلنا يرسول (sic) الله اردنا (c) ان نخرج معك الى (d) وجهك هذا وهو يسير الى خيبر (e) فنداوي الجرحى ونعين المسلمين بما استطعنا فقال (f) على بركة الله قالت فخرجنا معه وكنت جارية حدثة (g) فاردفني رسول الله صلعم على حقيبة رحله قالت (h) فوالله لنزل رسول الله صلعم الى الصبح واناخ ونزلت عن حقيبة رحله واذا بها دم مني وكانت اول حيضة حضتها قالت (i) فتقبّضت الى الناقة واستحييت فلما راى رسول الله صلعم ما بي وراى الدم قال ما لك لعلك نفست قالت قلت نعم قال فاصلحي من نفسك ثم خذى اناء من ماء فاطرحي فيها ملحاً ثم اغسلي ما اصاب

الحقيبة من الدم ثم عودي لمركبك (j) قالت فلما فتح رسول الله صلعم خيبر رضخ لنا من الفي واخذ هذه القلادة التي ترين في عنقي فاعطانيها وعلّقها بيده في عنقي فوالله لا تفارقني ابداً قالت فكانت في عنقها حتى ماتت ثم اوصت ان تدفن معها وكانت لا تطهر من حيضة الا جعلت في طهورها (m) ملحاً واوصت به (n) ان يجعل في غسلها (o) حين ماتت (p)

a) W — حدثني بن ابي سبرى عن سليمان بن سحيم عن ام علي بنت ابي الحكم عن امية بنت قيس بن الصلت الغفارية
b) W — جت
c) W — انا نريد يا رسول الله
d) W — في
e) W omisit وهو يسير الى خيبر.
f) W addidit رسول الله صلعم
g) W inseruit السن
h) W — فنزل الصبح فاناخ واذا انا بالحقيبة عليها دم مني
i) W omisit قالت
j) W — ففعلت
k) W — فلما فتح الله خيبر
l) W addidit ولم اسهم
m) W — طهرها
n) W omisit به
o) W addidit ملحاً
p) W — غسلت.

18. *Aġānī*, III, 187. We have not seen this form of the tradition elsewhere.

19. Al-Ḫāzin, *Tafsīr*, II, 171; Baiḍāwī, I, 351; *'Arā'is*, 208; *Aġānī*, III, 187; *Ḫizana*, I, 122; etc.

20. Manuscript of British Museum 276, 37 v.

21. Cf. S. 96, 1–4 and the traditions connected with it (Nöldeke-Schwally, *Geschichte des Qorans*, pp. 78 sq.).

22. *MFO*, I, 288, sq.

23. *B. A.* VIII, 3, p. 7, n. 1.

24. Ibn Ḥaǵar, I, 264.

25. Cf. article "Qoran et Hadith" in *Recherches de Science Religieuse* (1 January–February 1910).

26. *Ḫizāna*, 1, 122, ورايت في ديوانه قصيدة مدح بها النبي صلعم "And I saw in his diwan a poem in which the prohpet was panegyrised." We may and must vocalize مُدِحَ unless we wish to put the author in contradiction with his immediately preceding declaration that Umayya died a kāfir.

27. See above, note to nr. XXIII.

28. Nöldeke-Schwally, *Geschichte des Qorans*, p. 20, n. 1, consider Ṣālīḥ a creation of Muḥammad Cf. *MFO*, I, 212ï23.

29. An exception is XLVI said by Ibn Ḥaǵar IV, 722 to have been taken by At-Ṯa'ālibī from Fāqihī's Meccan chronicle composed about AH 275. But of the three verses given by Ibn Ḥaǵar two are wholly and one partially un-Koranical and the last mentioned v. 2, which looks like a doublet of v. 3, may have originally formed with it a single un-Koranical verse. The poem given by At-Ṯa'ālibī himself not in the *Tafsīr* to which Ibn Ḥaǵar refers but in the *'Arā'is* is much more Koranical and may be a later form not taken from Fāqihī. We have also earlier testimony for individual verses cited in Ṭabarī's *Tafsīr* and in the *Ǵamhara* to support Koranical interpretations, but these form a different category and could have been early invented for the purpose. Cf. Schulthess *O.S.*, p. 77.

30. The weak point in it is that Koranical imitations were objected to at a very early date.

31. Notwithstanding this strange word which the Lexicons and *Aǵānī* notice as a peculiar formation of Umayya, Frank-Kamenetzky, *Untersuchungen*, p. 30 condemns the verse owing to the not necessarily Koranical مستطر or مقتدر .The presence of interpolated Koranical words in the text or variants is common in Umayya's poetry: cf. our note to XXIV, 34; XLI, 4, 6, and the v.1.طير in XLI, 13.

32. Cf. Frank-Kamenetzky, *Untersuchungen*, pp. 48, 43–44.

33. Of course the reference to the cup of death in v. 13 is no exception, as it cannot be called Koranical.We already find it in the pre-Islamic poet Muhalhil, *Aššu'arā' an-Naṣrānīya*, p. 177, l. 15 اراهم سُقُوا بكأس حلاق .

34. *Untersuchungen*, pp. 24–26, 45.

35. Ibid., p. 24, n. 1.

36. Cf. our note to XLIII and *MFO*, I, 217.

37. We might add for v. 14–15, Sura 56, 13 على الارائك لا يرون الشمس; for v. 16, Sura 83, 24 نضرة النعيم; Sura 86, 11, نضرة 20, ثَمَّ نعيم (which shows we should vocalize ثُمَّ not ثَمَّ) and for v. 20, S. 43, 71 صحان من ذهب . . . تلذ الاعين

38. *B. A.* VIII, 3, p. 3.

39. Cf. *W. Z. K. M.* XXI, p. 396.

40. *B. A.* VIII, 3, p. 7, n. 1.

41. *Untersuchungen*, p. 48. He also decides in favour of part of LV.

42. Our remark on the use of the Ḫafīf meter in these verses was of course not meant to prove directly their authenticity but to counterbalance the even weaker argument of Professor Schulthess that they should be considered spurious because in the same rhyme and meter as the Sodom verses. The argument since drawn from Koranical resemblances (Frank-Kamenetzky, *Untersuchungen*, p. 15) shows a certain amount of special pleading. مرساها place of anchorage in a poem treating of a ship's voyage and rhyming in اها is considered a borrowing. سيرها ومرساها are considered Koranical because two different nouns are thus united with reference to the ark in the Koran though مرساها is most natural as a rhyme-word and is used elsewhere by Umayya in an admittedly authentic poem about the deluge, XXXII, 25 where also special reference is made to the night and day journey. The reference to the *tannūr* is also Koranical but of Talmudic origin and present in other genuine poems (cf. *MFO*, I, p. 211 and n. 5). The قيل فاهبط of v. 11 are alone remarkable but hardly sufficient to prove a literary connection. Of قال similarly used XXIX, 19 and إهبط a technical term in this sense represented by the v. 1 اهبطه in XXXII, 6a.

43. *MFO*, I, 211.

44. *MFO*, I, 208.

45. Cf. H. Lammens, "L'âge de Mahomet et la chronologie de la Sira," *Journal Asiatique* 17 (1911): 2.

1.7

The Origins of Arabic Poetry[1]

D. S. Margoliouth

The existence of poets in Arabia before the rise of Islam is certified by the Qur'an, which contains one Surah named after them and occasionally alludes to them elsewhere. Among the descriptions of the Prophet given by his opponents there was "a Jinn-ridden poet" (xxxvii, 35), to which he replies that he has brought the truth. In another passage (lii, 29) the suggestions that he was a kāhin, a jinn-ridden man, and a poet are offered as alternatives. Since those who described him as a poet said they would wait to see what would happen to him (lii, 30), it might be inferred that poets were in the habit of foretelling the future. Elsewhere he asserts that his language is not that of a poet, but rather of an honorable messenger (lxix, 41), and that God had not taught him poetry, which would have been of no use to him (xxxvi, 69); his utterances were "statement and clear lesson," whence we should infer that poetry was obscure. These hints about the poets are summarized in the Surah that bears their name (xxvi, 224f.), where we are told that they are followed by the misguided, rave in every valley, and say what they do not do. The sequel might seem to except certain pious bards from this condemnation, but the style of the Qur'an renders it uncertain whether this exception really applies to bards. From what precedes it might be inferred that the demons descend on every guilty fabricator, to whom they communicate rumor, mostly mendaciously. This seems to refer to the practice ascribed elsewhere to the demons (xxxvii, 10) of eavesdropping at the heavenly councils, an offense for which they are punished by being fired at with shooting stars. And this again brings the poets into connection with prophecy.

If by poetry the same be meant as in the later literature, we are confronted with a slight puzzle: Muḥammad, who was not acquainted with the art, was aware that his revelations were not in verse; whereas the Meccans, who presumably knew poetry when they heard or saw it, thought they were. We should have expected the converse. Perhaps we might infer that a poet was in general known rather by his matter than by the form of his utterances; whence the repudiation points not to the absence of regularity in the form of the utterances, but to the nature of the matter communicated. Yet the text "we have not taught him poetry" certainly implies the existence of some artifice which distinguished the poetic style, and which had to be learned.

However, the tone of this last text seems decidedly different from that of the others. In the others the poetic gift is repudiated; the Qur'an is thought to be poetry, and the charge is rebutted. But here it would rather seem as though the absence of poetic artifice was excused; it is no longer something which the audience finds there when it ought not to be there, but something which they desiderate, and whose absence is justified.

The passages cited are to some extent at least in accordance with later ideas. Poets at times repudiated solemn engagements on the ground that the Qur'an declared them to be liars by profession.[2] They not only admitted that they were inspired by Jinn, but could at times name these internal monitors.[3] Though the words "they rave in every valley" are probably metaphorical, and mean "they exercise their imagination on all subjects indiscriminately,"[4] they can also be rendered "they philander in every valley," and in accordance with this, most poems commence with an erotic situation wherein the poet does what has been described. The Prophet himself is represented in some stories as displaying the very crassest ignorance of the poetic art,[5] and according to one tradition asserted that a man's inside had better be filled with anything rather than with poetry;[6] yet verses were actually attributed to him,[7] occasionally he appears as a critic of poetry,[8] and a reciter of it,[9] and there is a familiar tradition wherein he bestows his approval on it.

In the very considerable mass of pre-Islamic inscriptions which we now possess in a variety of dialects, there is nothing whatever in verse; a fact which is especially noteworthy in the case of the funereal inscriptions, since most literary nations introduce verse into compositions of this sort. Thus Latin literature commences with the epitaphs of the Scipios which are in Saturnian meter. Of the recently discovered though at present unintelligible Lydian inscriptions a goodly number are in meter. From the old Arabic inscriptions then we should not have guessed that the Arabs had any notion of meter or rhyme, though in many respects the civilization which they represent was highly advanced. When, however, the Qur'an speaks of poetry as something requiring teaching, it is reasonable to suppose that it refers to these artifices, which imply acquaintance with the alphabet, since the Arabic rhyme means the repetition of the same group of consonants, and with a grammatical system, since the meter depends on the difference between long and short syllables and the association of certain termination with certain senses.

Perhaps then what the evidence of the Qur'an entitles us to assume is that before its appearance there were among the Arabs certain fortune-tellers, known as "poets"; their language would be likely to be obscure, as is always the case with oracles; and since the earliest Delphic oracle which we possess commences:

"I know the number of the sand and the measures of the sea"

the accuracy of these persons' statements might be sufficiently questionable to justify the description of them given in the Qur'an.

Now the view of the early poetry taken by the poet and antiquarian Abū Tammām at the beginning of the third century of Islam is very different. In words which are somewhat obscure, yet not unlike some used by Horace, he asserts that with the primitive Arabs no glories were retained save such as were securely fettered by odes; that they were the guardians of battles and other scenes of importance, and were even called "limited monarchy," a phrase which perhaps means that within certain limits the tribe which had the best poet dominated the others.[10] The poets according to this are not unintelligible oracle-mongers, but the recorders of events, which their talent enables them to immortalize. And this view is maintained by Abū Tammām's contemporary, the polygraph Jāḥiẓ of Basrah.[11] It is not quite easy to reconcile this theory with the statements, and indeed the general attitude, of the

Qur'an. It applies very well to Abū Tammām's own Dīwān, which immortalizes the exploits of his patrons, such as the storming of Amorium by Mu'taṣim; and fairly well to the fragments collected by him in his Ḥamāsah, since many of these are historical or autobiographical in character. So far from poets saying what they do not do, they are here supposed to be recording what they have actually done or seen done; and indeed if any Arab from the time of Ishmael onward does anything he appears to perpetuate the memory of it in an ode. But a body of odes wherein history is perpetuated constitutes a literature such as by no means merits the contemptuous language used by the Qur'an, and whose existence, as we shall see, other passages of the Qur'an seem absolutely to exclude.

The Muslim archaeologists, however, who commence toward the end of the Umayyad period, not only maintain that there was a body of classical literature of this sort in pagan Arabia but claim to produce large portions of it. There is reason for thinking that those who first produced it had to encounter some skepticism; when Khalīl (ob. 170) produced his metrical system, learned, he averred, from the Arab tribes, one of his contemporaries wrote a book to prove the whole system a fiction.[12] When the Arab versification is supposed to have commenced is far from clear; one of our authorities can trace it to Adam;[13] another can produce Arabic odes of the time of Ishmael.[14] Though the South Arabian monarchs compose their inscriptions in their own languages and dialects, the verses in which, according to the Muslim archaeologists, they frequently indulged were in the Arabic of the Qur'an.[15] The general view seems, however, to be that Arabic poetry at any rate in the forms which were afterwards stereotyped commenced at most a few generations before the rise of Islam. Père Cheikho[16] accepts the view of the *Aghani*[17] that Mulhalhil, brother of Kulaib, whose *floruit* was 531 CE, and who is mentioned as one of the glories of the Bakr b. Wā'il,[18] was the first to compose long poems and introduce love into them. What is meant by a *long* poem is not clear; it would seem to be something over twenty lines, since a poet, al-Barrāq, whom Cheikho dates 470 CE, is credited with an ode of that length.[19] We get something more precise in the case of al-Aghlab, who is said to have been the first to compose long poems in *rejez*; by long it is explained that more than a couple of verses is meant.[20] This person is said to have died at the battle of Nihawand in AH 23. As he was aged ninety at the time, his birth would synchronize with the *floruit* of Muhalhil. Nevertheless, a high authority asserted that the first composer of more than a couple of verses in *rejez* was al-ʻAjjāj, who lived in Umayyad times.[21] Muhalhil's claim is also by no means uncontested; on the one hand, poems with erotic prologues are cited from far earlier times;[22] on the other, there is high authority for the assertion that the first poet was Imru'ul-Qais, who is somewhat later than Muhalhil.[23] Similarly A'shā of Qais, whose death date according to Cheikho was 629 CE, is said to have been the first poet who devoted his muse to mendicity;[24] but ʻAbīd b. al-Abraṣ, who is far earlier, is quite a master of this form of art,[25] and ʻAntarah of ʻAbs, who is somewhat earlier, is by no means averse from or unacquainted with the practice.

It is probable that Mulhalhil's claim is based on his name, which means "maker of fine textiles," interpreted as "poetical fabrics," while the interpretation of the name as "fabricator" led to the remarkable view that he was the first poet who departed from the strict truth.[26]

If we regard the story which ascribes to him the invention of the *qaṣidah* as historical, it must be admitted that he found numerous imitators. For we possess an imposing row of volumes containing the collected works of a very large number of poets who belong to the period which separates his invention from the hijrah. The reputed authors of the ten *Muʻallaqāt* are all authors of *dīwāns* or "collected Odes" most of which have been published and run into a considerable number of pages. There are, besides, several poets equally prolific, who are not included among the ten Immortals. Further, the odes emanating from the poets of particular tribes were collected into *Corpora*, and one such Corpus has been printed. Since these odes from their nature imply acquaintance with the alphabet, and frequently allude to writing, the pre-Islamic Arabs who used the dialect of the Qur'an must have been a highly literary community; ancient Greece can scarcely exhibit so many votaries of the Muses.

Our first question must be: Supposing this literature to be genuine, how was it preserved? It must have been preserved either orally or in writing. The former seems to be the view favored by the indigenous authorities, though, as will be seen, not universally held. The second Caliph is quoted for the assertion that though the pagan poetry was neglected during the early days of Islam and the years which were crowded with conquests, when more peaceful times came, the Muslims returned to the study; they had, however, no written books or collections to which they could refer, and as most of the Arabs—that is, those who had been converted from paganism—were either killed or had died a natural death, most of the poetry had perished, and only a little survived.[27]

It is clearly an anachronism to ascribe this statement to the second Caliph; the quiet time did not come till the reign of the first Umayyad, some thirty years after his death. It is also absurd to say that only a little survived, if what is meant be a whole row of volumes. If, however, numerous odes of considerable length were orally preserved, this can only have been because there were persons whose business it was to commit them to memory and hand them on to others. We have no reason for thinking that such a profession existed or that it could have survived the early decades of Islam.[28] "Islam cancelled all that was before it"; the Qur'an states that those who follow the poets are misguided, and its language about them is harsh and contemptuous. There was then a strong reason for forgetting the pre-Islamic poetry, if any existed, and yet another that was likely to work powerfully. The deeds which the ballads are supposed ordinarily to have commemorated were intertribal victories; Islam, which aimed at uniting the Arabs and greatly succeeded in achieving this, discouraged all such recollections; ballads of this kind could only stir up bad blood. And indeed such ballads, unless they are committed to writing, have a tendency to be forgotten. Further, the Bedouins were regarded as untrustworthy and indeed reckless in their assertions about verses;[29] whence an oral tradition maintained by them could claim little credibility.

There remains the other possibility, that the odes were preserved in writing. If, as one of them asserts, such verses shone over the world, and when they were recited people asked who could have composed them,[30] the probability that they would be committed to writing would be considerable; for it would have been a profitable business to multiply copies. Now allusions to writing are very common in this literature,[31] and some poets even speak of it in connection with their own verses. A pre-Islamic versifier in the Hudhail collection desires that "a message wherewith new scrolls gleam, wherein there is writing for him that will read,"[32] be conveyed for him;

doubtless referring to his own ode. The commentators suppose him to mean Ḥimyari writing on palm-leaves. And indeed it is actually recorded that certain Arabic verses were written by one Qaisabah in the Ḥimyari script on the back of his saddle;[33] while two others were written by a courtier of a Ḥimyari prince, Dhu'l-Ru'ain, in a sealed document, though the nature of the script is not stated.[34] The Ḥimyari king Dhū Jadan, whose skeleton of enormous dimensions was discovered at Ṣan'ā, had above his head a tablet where there was an inscription in rhymed prose, in classical Arabic, only in the Ḥimyari character.[35] Most likely then his verses were also committed by him to writing.[36] The pre-Islamic poet Laqīṭ composed a poem, with the title "Writing on a scroll from Laqīṭ to the Iyādites in the Jezirah," to warn them against a punitive expedition by some Persian king.[37] A pre-Islamic poet even quotes a maxim which is read off a parchment by one who dictates.[38] Perhaps then there would be nothing inconsistent with the statements of these odes if we imagined them to be regularly circulated in writing.

Yet the existence of a pre-Islamic classical literature in the dialect of the Qur'an in the Ḥimyari, or indeed in any other script, seems too flagrantly at variance with the statements and assumptions of the Qur'an to be entertained. "Have ye a book wherein ye study?" it asks the Meccans (lxviii, 37); "Have they the mystery and do they write?" it asks of its opponents (ibid., 47). Those to whom it is addressed were a people whose fathers had received no warning (xxxvi, 5); "to whom no previous admonisher had come" (xxxii, 2; xxviii, 46); only two communities, the Jews and Christians, had revealed books (vi, 157); the pagans had nothing of the kind. This is a matter on which it is difficult to suppose that the Qur'an could be mistaken; a missionary to the Hindus might condemn their books as valueless and pernicious; he could not well deny their existence. And if the pre-Islamic poetry was written, the pagans had plenty of books (and, indeed, "inspired" books) which perhaps were unedifying—though, as we shall see, they were by no means exclusively so—yet sufficient to give the affirmative answer to the questions which have been cited, but which the Qur'an certainly assumes will be answered in the negative.

Further, the process of literary development is normally, perhaps invariably, from the irregular to the regular. Latin literature begins with what Horace calls *horridus ille numerus Saturnius*; presently Greek meters are adopted, but the adaptation is at first very rough; after a century and a half Virgil and Horace set an example of regularity which others have to follow. The Arabic literary styles, rhymed prose and verse, both bear some resemblance to the style of the Qur'an; there are parts of the Qur'an which only the extremely orthodox deny to be in "rhymed prose," and of many a meter the Qur'an offers an occasional illustration.[39] The process from the Qur'anic style to the regular styles would then seem to be in accordance with analogy; and if the Qur'an were the first work in the language which displayed literary art, its claim to miraculous eloquence would be something which people could easily understand; it would not be very different from that which is claimed for or by others who have for the first time introduced versification into a language. But if the audience had already been accustomed to rhymed prose and verse of the finish and elaboration which is displayed in the ostensibly pre-Islamic performances in these styles, the claim would at the least have been harder to substantiate.

Still it may be said that this last argument is a priori, and that where the Muslims themselves impugn the veracity of the Qur'an others are not justified in believing it. Thus the author of the *Aghani*, who is a Muslim, quotes as a genuine ode by the precursor of Muḥammad, Waraqah b. Nufail, one wherein he declares that he is an admonisher, bidding them worship none but their Creator.[40] This flatly contradicts the Qur'an, which, as has been seen, asserts that the Meccans had had no such admonisher before Muḥammad. Qudam b. Qādim (400–480 CE) in the poem which bears his name anticipates the warnings of the Qur'an in many details, and claims to have given religious guidance to his people in the Muslim sense.[41] Hence when the Qur'an declares that the pagans had no books, even a Muslim apparently is not bound to believe it; what, however, we propose to show is that those who maintained the existence of such written literature were considerably less worthy of credence than the Prophet, even if we reject the Muslim view of his character.

Before we believe in the stories about Arabic verses written in the Ḥimyari character, it would be desirable to see some specimens. One would like to see how the caligrapher in this script dealt with the Mu'allaqah of Ḥārith, in which numerous words are divided between the two hemistichs. It is a principle of the South Arabian scripts to mark the end of a word by a perpenducular line; this would not look elegant in verse, where cæsura is common; further, the ordinary Arabic script seems well suited to Arabic verse on the ground that the caligrapher can easily extend or contract his words so that the whole composition is "justified," but the process would scarcely be possible in the South Arabian writing. Still a specimen, if such could be discovered, might silence this objection.

In the history of Islam we come across notices of written volumes of poetry before prose works are mentioned; according to Ṭabari someone in the year 83 found in a castle in the desert of Kirman a volume of poems by Abū Jildah al-Yashkurī; a Kufan fellow-citizen had written the book.[42] He also quotes at length a poem by A'shā of Hamdān referring to the events of the year 65, which was concealed at the time; it is scarcely possible to conceal anything but a material object. The jurist Abū Yūsuf, who compiled a code for the use of Hārūn al-Rashīd (180–93 = 788–809), mentions among articles in which there is no property, that is the theft of which is not punishable by the ordinary process, the Qur'an and the leaves whereon are verses;[43] the most natural interpretation of this rule is that the only books in familiar use at the time besides the Qur'an were volumes of verse; and the rule is given as having been formulated by Abū Ḥanīfah, whose death date is 150. Ṭabari records that a little after this date a collection of Arabic (probably pre-Islamic) poetry was made by order of the Caliph Mahdī (158–69).[44] The Ḥamāsah of Abū Tammām, which is about a generation later, was made from written materials.[45] Perhaps it was this early association of poetry with writing which led some who produced pre-Islamic poetry in great quantities to favor the supposition that their sources were written documents. Ḥammād al-Rāwiyah (AH 95–155), who was one of these benefactors of the community, is supposed to have asserted that the Lakhmid Nu'mān (580–602 CE)[46] ordered that the poems of the Arabs should be copied on boards,[47] and buried in his White Palace in Ḥīrah. When the adventurer Mukhtār b. Abi 'Ubaid came to Kufah in 65 AH, he was informed that there was a treasure buried in this Palace; he dug it up and this collection of poetry was brought to light. Supposing this story really goes back to Ḥammād, its purpose was doubtless to account for the fact that he knew quantities of pre-Islamic poems and verses which were known to no one else. In the *Aghani* he is charged with shameless forgeries;[48] and his contemporary Mufaḍḍal Al-Ḍabbī declared that he had corrupted poetry beyond the hope of recovery.[49] In one of the anecdotes, he and Mufaḍḍal are summoned by the Caliph Mahdī—the occasion must have been before his Caliphate, since that began in 158, whereas Ḥammād died—and asked to explain a verse of Zuhair, which begins with an ode with the words *quit this*. Mufaḍḍal explained the difficulty as well as he could; Ḥammād declared that the ode did not begin with that line, but with three others which preceded it. Presently under oath he confessed that these lines had been fabricated by himself. They figure, however, in our editions.[50] The antiquarians of Kufah maintained the genuineness of verses known to have been composed by this Ḥammād for the entertainment of the governor Khālid al-Qasrī, and assigned to earlier poets.[51] It is asserted by Yāqūt, on the authority of al-Naḥḥās (ob. AH 331), that the seven Mu'allaqāt were collected by this Ḥammād; one could wish their discovery had been made by someone more respectable. The other authority in Kufah for the early poetry, Jannād,[52] was one who, like Ḥammād, recited much, but had little knowledge.

Like Ḥammād, the early collectors of poetry were for the most part persons whose scruples in the matter of forgery were slight. One Barzakh, a contemporary of Ḥammād and Jannād, when asked on whose authority he recited certain verses ascribed to Imru'ul-Qais, replied on his own, which he regarded as sufficient.[53]

Somewhat later than Ḥammād was Khalaf al-Aḥmar, whose death date was about 180 and who was the instructor of the most eminent antiquarians. He too has a bad reputation, and in a story which Ibn Khallikan gives on the authority of Abū Zaid confesses that he circulated forgeries of his own in Kufah as ancient poems; alarmed by an illness, he acknowledged his guilt to the Kufans, but like many another man found it easier to "bamboozle" than to "de-bamboozle." A contemporary of his, Abū 'Amr b. al-'Alā, ob. 154, who has a great name as an antiquary, confessed that he had inserted a line of his own in a poem of al-A'shā;[54] one wonders whether he had not inserted more than one. A disciple of Khalaf, al-Aṣma'i, who made one of the best-known collections of early poetry, asserted that he had stayed in Medinah, and failed to see there a single sound poem; those which were not corrupt were spurious.[55] Yet he does not seem to have been overcritical. It was recorded of one Kaisān that he used to go to the Bedouins and hear their recitations. He would take them down on his tablets and transfer them in altered form to his notebooks; he would alter them again before he committed them to memory, and yet again before he communicated them to others. Clearly not much of the original would by this time have been left. Yet al-Aṣma'ī regarded him as a good authority.[56]

The great collector Abū 'Amr Shaibanī (ob. 205) was found to possess a case containing only a few pounds' weight of books; when someone wondered at the paucity, he replied that for a genuine collection they were numerous.[57] Yet even this small collection was not free from spurious matter; the author of the *Aghani* quotes from a work of his a lengthy ode ostensibly by a pre-Islamic poet, and declares it to be clearly an Islamic fabrication.[58]

It may be added that the opinion which these eminent antiquarians had of each other was often by no means high. Ibn al-A'rābī thought neither al-Aṣma'ī nor Abū 'Ubaidah was any good at all;[59] they probably returned the compliment, and certainly took the same view of each other.

The standard of the third century seems to have been no better than that of the second. We have two stories of Mubarrad, an antiquary of this period, on whom the warmest encomia are lavished. He visits a man of eminence, who asks him the meaning of a word in the Tradition; not knowing it, Mubarrad makes a guess, for which the great man solicits an authority. Mubarrad without hesitation produces "the verse of the poet" as a proof passage. Then another learned visitor arrives, who is asked the same question. He happens to know the right answer, and gives the word its true meaning; when Mubarrad's verse is brought out by the great man, Mubarrad confesses that he had composed it for the occasion.[60] Another time some people who suspected Mubarrad's proof-passages fabricate a word and send to ask Mubarrad the meaning; he replies without hesitation that the word means *cotton*, and proceeds at once to cite a verse to prove it. The performance wins the admiration of the questioners, equally whether the answers be true or not.[61]

It is in accordance with the facts that we occasionally get highly disconcerting information about quite important collections of verse. It has been seen that we are in possession of the Corpus of the works of the poets of the tribe Hudhail, and this tribe was thought to be the most poetical of all the tribes;[62] the grammarian Aḥmad b. Fāris of the fourth Islamic century visited the tribe in its home and could not find that any member of the tribe knew the name of one of these poets; at best those among the tribesmen who possessed any poetical taste could recite some commonplace lines which had no connection with their tribe.[63] Sukkarī, the collector of the Corpus, lived a century before; one would have thought that the compilation would have led to increased study of the odes among the tribe whence they emanated, but apparently it had the opposite effect. At an earlier period, though the names of the poets were known, there was great uncertainty as to the attribution of the odes.[64] There was a considerable amount of poetry attributed to a poet known as the Majnūn of the Banū 'Āmir. An antiquary took the trouble to consult every family of this tribe, but found no one who had ever heard of him.[65] For all that, it was possible somehow to find out his name or names and even to trace his ancestry to the tenth generation, and to discover a whole quantity of biographical detail, including quite lengthy conversations. The names of two of the romancers are in this case recorded.[66]

In some other cases we are told not only the names of forgers, but those of the works which they forged. Yazīd b. Mufarrigh was the fabricator of the story of the Ḥimyari king Tubba' and of the poems attributed to him.[67] The verses incorporated in the Life of the Prophet by Ibn Isḥāq, probably the earliest prose work in classical Arabic, were made to order;[68] in several cases the editor Ibn Hishām notices their spuriousness, but there is little, if any, reason for supposing any of them to be genuine. The poet Nuṣaib began his poetical career by composing verses which he attributed to celebrated members of the tribes Ḍamrah b. Bakr b. 'Abd Manāt and Khuzā'ah. When these verses had won the admiration of leading men in these tribes, Nuṣaib felt confident of his poetic gift.[69] Doubtless the experiment indicated a scientific mind, but if the admiration of the tribal leaders was genuine, it is likely that the verses would be cherished as the work of the ancient bards; it would scarcely have been in Nuṣaib's power to undeceive them. Similarly, the poet Ja'far b. al-Zubair, brother of the anti-Caliph 'Abdallah, is said to have attributed his own verses to Omar b. Abī Rabī'ah, and these verses were in consequence, we are told, introduced into the diwan of the latter.[70]

It must be added that good encouragement was given by Caliphs and others to forgers. When Mufaḍḍal and Ḥammād acted to Mahdi in the way described above, the former got the higher reward, but Ḥammād, who had forged and lied, was well paid also. Hārūn al-Rashīd offered ten thousand dirhems to anyone who could recite an ode by al-Aswad b. Ya'fur; it is most surprising to read that though all the Arab chieftains from Syria, Arabia, and Mesopotamia were present, no one responded.[71] On some other occasions readiness to recite an ode that a Caliph wanted led to an immediate rise of stipend.[72]

Muwaffaq, brother of the Caliph Mu'tamid, and even more powerful than he, who desired his vizier applied, declared that he knew of none. But a rival scholar, Tha'lab, to whom appeal was then made, was in the fortunate position of having been collecting Jewish poetry for the last fifty years. He produced his Corpus, and his fortune was secured.

Owing to the bad faith of those who gave publicity to the odes, they were very variable quantities. The author of the *Aghani* produces an ode of Dhu'l-Aṣba' in six lines; presently it is increased to twelve; next we learn that in the opinion of a most notable antiquary only three of the lines were genuine; and we wind up with seventeen.[73]

That in spite of temptations some of the antiquaries may have been scrupulous, and even critical, can be admitted; they did not themselves fabricate, and admitted into their collections what they believed to be genuine monuments of antiquity. But this brings us back to the question of their sources. The mission of Muḥammad was a tremendous event in Arabia; it involved a breach with the past to which history furnishes few analogies. From all parts of the peninsula men left their homes to establish themselves in regions whereof few of them had even heard; and within the peninsula the rise of Islam was accompanied and followed by civil wars. The attitude of Islam toward the old paganism was not one even of contemptuous toleration, but one of the fiercest hostility; it offered no compromise of any sort with it. If the poets were the spokesmen of paganism, who were the persons who preserved in their memories and transmitted to others those compositions which belonged to a dispensation which Islam terminated? We can trace the consciousness of this difficulty in the solution which Ḥammād is said to have offered; the poems had been buried during the years when Islamic fervor was at its height, and were casually unearthed after it had somewhat cooled. The other explanation with which we shall now deal was that the poets were not spokesmen of paganism. They were Muslims in all but in name.

If we turn our attention to internal evidence, there are some features about these poems which at least occasionally surprise. The poets of most nations leave no doubt at all about their religion, and the Arabs of the inscriptions are equally candid on this subject; most of the inscriptions mention one or more deities and matters connected with their worship. Marzubānī devoted a work of over five thousand pages to an account of the pre-Islamic poets, their religions, and their sects;[74] one would fancy that the materials for these subjects were very scanty, as allusions to religion in the odes which we possess are far from common. One poet, indeed, asserts that his religion agrees with some other people's;[75] only he does not tell us what it was. The polytheistic atmosphere of the inscriptions is simply absent. This is perhaps what suggested to Père Cheikho his theory that they were all Christian, but it does not seem that this theory will work. Some of these supposed Christians express themselves in a manner which shows clearly that they belonged to a different community; thus A'shā of Qais, who is on Cheikho's list, speaks of petitioners making the circuit of some patron's gates even as Christians make their circuit round the house of their idol;[76] and one of the few cases wherein we find an oath by a pagan deity is in a verse ascribed to him.[77]

Christians wherever they are have their sacred books, and their language and thought are greatly affected by the phraseology of the Gospels, Epistles, and Psalms. Their poetry most frequently takes the form of hymns. But in the supposed pre-Islamic poetry, there is a dearth of allusions to the Scriptures and institutions of Christendom even among those poets who are supposed to have flourished at Christian courts. The expert author of the *Aghani* argues that a certain poet who flourished toward the end of the first Islamic century must have been a Christian because he swears by the Gospel, the Monks, and the Faith, which he rightly says are Christian oaths.[78] Though the pre-Islamic poets very frequently swear, it is almost invariably by Allah; this oath indeed pervades their diwans. The pre-Islamic 'Abīd b. al-Abraṣ even says in Qur'anic language, "I swear by Allah, verily Allah is bountiful to whom He will, and is forgiving and gracious."[79] And their view of the operations of Allah is such as no monotheist could disapprove; it anticipates the statements of the Qur'an in almost every detail. Allah "opens and closes the world";[80] He is invoked to reward benefactors;[81] and to gather those who are dispersed;[82] He it is whose orders are carried out;[83] His pity is implored by women in bereavement;[84] His blessing is invoked on wells.[85] Imprecations are made in His name.[86] He who asks of Allah is not disappointed like one who asks of men.[87] Guilt in Allah's eyes in what they feared.[88] Allah is the witness to whom they appeal.[89] He knows what is hidden from others.[90] He is called the Lord of mankind.[91] A pagan poet says: "By Allah does the traveller know, when the earth conceals him, what Allah is about to do?"[92] Sometimes the name Raḥmān is substituted for Allah, as is the case in the Qur'an.[93]

Indeed, the only religion with which these pre-Islamic poets can be credited is the Muḥammadan. They are not only, as has been seen, strict monotheists—for they very rarely mention any deity save Allah, and such mention is at times not respectful[94]—but they show themselves quite famililar with matters which the Qur'an asserts were unknown to the Arabs prior to its revelation. Thus in Surah xi, 51 it is stated that neither Muḥammad nor his people had previously heard the story of Noah; and this statement is in accordance with what we should infer from the inscriptions, which make no allusion to the Biblical genealogies of the Arabs, which involve it. However, Nābighah of Dhubyān, whose *floruit* is given by Cheikho as 604 CE, a year which is also given as his death date, is not only familiar with the story of Noah, but even knows something about the patriarch for which the Qur'an appears to be the sole authority. He says *I found fidelity which thou didst not betray, even thus was Nūḥ, he did not betray.*[95] There is here an evident reference to the epithet *faithful*, which in the Qur'an is applied to Nūḥ (xxvi, 107). The poet 'Antarah of 'Abs, whose diwan occupies 284 pages, evidently knew the revelations of the Qur'an and the technicalities of Islam before the appearance of Muḥammad; in an address to the Persian king Anushirwan, who died about AD 580, this poet calls the king the *Qiblah* of Suppliants,[96] using a technicality of Islam for the direction of prayer, which perhaps ought not to surprise us since according to the *Aghani* the pre-Islamic Medinese had a *masjid* with a *qiblah*,[97] which are ordinarily regarded as Islamic innovations. This same poet is familiar with the Islamic postures of prayer, inclination, and prostration,[98] and with the Stone of Standing, that is that whereon Abraham stood, whose connection with the

Meccan sanctuary is quite certainly an Islamic innovation.[99] He also knows the Qur'anic names for Hell, *jaḥīm* and *jahannum*,[100] and those which that work employs for the Day of Judgment.[101] He uses with favor Qur'anic expressions.[102] Hence there is no reason for doubting that he was a good Muslim, except that his life was passed before Islam had appeared.[103]

This pre-Islamic bard perhaps parades his Muḥammadanism somewhat excessively; but many others give glimpses of theirs. We should have gathered from the Qur'an that the distinction between the present and the future life had been introduced to the Arabs by Muḥammad; for his opponents are represented as treating the notion of a future life with contempt. Hence we should assume that the usage of the phrase *the nearer* in the sense of "the world" must have been introduced by the Qur'an, where sometimes it is used alone, but more frequently with the substantive "life." The person who thinks of the world as "the nearer life" must have in mind a more distant life, the doctrine which Muḥammad's audience at first regarded with scornful bewilderment. But the pre-Islamic poets are thoroughly familiar with the expression. 'Abīd b. al-Abraṣ, who lived many decades before the preaching of the Qur'an, speaks in Qur'anic language of "the goods of the nearer,"[104] meaning the goods of this world, and Dhu'l-Aṣba', who is also pre-Islamic, quotes from the Qur'an the phrase *wishing for the goods of the nearer*.[105] The former, in addressing a remonstrance to the father of Imru'ul-Qais, refers to the Resurrection day,[106] and has an expression which implies acquaintance with the Muḥammadan Law of Inheritance;[107] while the latter knows the dinstinction between the *sunnah* and the *prescription*, that is the text of the Qur'an. The phrase *al-dunyā* for "the world" is also found in the Mu'allaqah of 'Amr b. Kulthūm, who is supposed to have died in the year 600 CE, more than twenty years before the Flight. When these poets wish to illustrate the relentlessness of the divine power, they regularly take the Qur'anic cases of Iram, 'Ād, and Thamūd;[108] and several of them confuse the two latter,[109] for which there can scarcely be any reason except their juxtaposition in the Qur'an whence indeed the story of the three was in all probability obtained. Even the supposed founder of the *Qaṣīdah*, Muhalhil, who, as has been seen, flourished a whole century before the Prophet, is sufficiently in advance of his time to quote the Qur'an. *They told us Kulaib was dead, and I said: has the earth swayed with us or have its anchors swayed?*[110] This is evidently to be explained from Surah xvi, 15, where we read: *And he flung upon the earth anchors lest it should sway.* Another Surah (lxxix, 32) makes it clear that mountains are meant. Similarly Ta'abbaṭa Sharran in his dirge on Shanfara quotes the Qur'an.[111] A prehistoric Persian king, according to Tha'ālibi, does the like.[112]

Sometimes the obvious use of the Qur'an in these odes is too much for the Muslim critics; thus we are told that doubts were held about the genuineness of a poem ascribed to Labīd, wherein the story of the Elephant is told, and the defeat of the foreigner attributed to Allah precisely as the Qur'an tells the story.[113] The author of the *Aghani* argues that Ḥaṣīn b. al-Humām was Islamic on a similar ground.[114] Others were less critical; Muṭahhar b. Ṭāhir, who is of the fourth century of Islam, notices that the pre-Islamic Zaid b. 'Amr b. Nufail preached monotheism in a set of verses which are a mere cento of Qur'anic texts about Mūsā and Hārūn in their relations with Fir'aun and went so far as to declare himself a Muslim in the phrase *aslamtu wajhī*.[115] Umayyah b. Abi'l-Ṣalt, who speaks of the Christians as though he were not one of them, uses for the Day of Judgment a phrase which we should have supposed to have been introduced by the Qur'an,[116] even if we could accept the view that the pagan Arabs were thoroughly familiar with the notion of such a day. The poetess Khansā is familiar with the *Zabāniyah*, which would seem to be a Qur'anic technicality.[117] Ḥātim Ṭā'ī, who is a Christian, is acquainted with the Islamic exclamation *Allāhu akbar*.[118]

It is quite conceivable that Muḥammad may have had "forerunners" in the sense that some persons before his time in Central Arabia may have revolted against the pagan worships. Christianity, moreover, seems clearly to have obtained a hold over parts of the peninsula. If the pre-Islamic poets had composed like Christians, assuming the doctrines of Christianity and showing familiarity with its institutions, we might be confronted with some difficulties in their odes and the question of their transmission, only their religion would not be one of them. But when we find them talk like Muḥammadans, being as rigid monotheists as the followers of the Prophet afterwards were, and so far as they echo any sacred book, echo the Qur'an, it seems most difficult to believe in their genuineness. Why should the Arabs of the inscriptions have their various local deities in their thoughts, and the poets of the same regions know of no God save the deity whose unity Muḥammad proclaimed? Even if we suppose the inscriptions to have emanated from communities other than those of the poets, what becomes of Muḥammad's mission if those whom he "warned" were believers in One God and expecting a Day of Judgment? If we are guided by the inscriptions, it must be admitted that the polemic of the Qur'an is rightly directed; the cults of the Meccans and their neighbors may not have been identical with those of the regions to which the inscriptions belong, but they had a family likeness to them. But the views of the pre-Islamic poets on religious subjects seem to be similar to or even identical with those taught in the Qur'an.

A second line of internal evidence is that of the language. All these poems are in the dialect of the Qur'an, though here and there a word or form may be employed which is said to belong to some particular tribe or region. If we suppose the imposition of Islam on the tribes of Arabia to have unified their language, because it provided them with a classic of indisputable correctness in the Qur'an, analogies occur; the Roman conquest did the same for Italy, Gaul, and Spain. But it is difficult to imagine that before Islam provided this unifying element there was a common language, different from those of the inscriptions, spread over the whole peninsula. The individual tribes, or at least the groups of tribes, would have had easily recognizable differences of grammar and vocabulary. Père Cheikho's collection commences with the poets of South Arabia; they compose in the dialect of the Qur'an. Within South Arabia itself the inscriptions are in a variety of dialects, and some of these come near the Prophet's time; they can only be interpreted with difficulty, because the help which the classical Arabic gives is scanty. Yet when the Muslim archaeologists produce verses by a king of Ḥaḍramaut, and written by him, they say, in the Ḥimyari character, they are in the dialect of the Qur'an, which he expected his people to understand.[119] The authority for this story is Ibn al-Kalbi, one of the foremost of the antiquaries. A Ḥimyarite, who belongs to a period before the Abyssinian invasion, writes and seals a couple of verses, not in the language of the contemporary or somewhat later inscritptions, but in Qur'anic Arabic.[120] In these cases few will even doubt that the verses are fabrications and the events wherewith they are connected at best legendary. Yet we have to remember that the authorities for these pre-Islamic poems are either the same as or not less trustworthy than those for Cheikho's poets of Yemen; and the author of the *Aghani*, who occasionally practices criticism, produces them without suspicion. He very likely does so in good faith, like those Muslim controversialists who assert that the Christian doctrine of the Divinity of Christ was occasioned by the misreading of two points on a word in the second Psalm; it should have been read *nabiyyun*, but was misread *bunayya*. They are not aware that this doctrine was held many centuries before the Arabic alphabet was invented, an invention at least a century earlier than that of the diacritic points. And the ascription of verses in the classical Arabic to pre-Islamic bards of Yemen appears to be an error of the same sort. There is no evidence that South Arabia had any poets; if, however, there were any, they must have sung in one of the South Arabian dialects.

And having this decided evidence of bad faith in a group of cases, we do not know what we can accept in other cases. In North Arabia one or two inscriptions have indeed been discovered in the Qur'anic dialect, but others exhibit a wealth of dialects similar to that found in the South; and here again verse is non-existent in the present state of our knowledge. Since Islam originated in the Ḥijāz, the Muslims might be expected to know more about the history of that part of Arabia than about the South; in fact, they know somewhat more about the South, because events of greater importance for the peninsula had happened there than elsewhere. Yet their knowledge of South Arabia was so vague that they ascribe verses to South Arabian potentates in a language which we know on epigraphic evidence was not theirs. When the antiquaries made their compilations, the language of the Qur'an had, owing to Islam, become the classical language in South Arabia; but there was the same reason for its predominance in other parts of the peninsula; we have as yet no ground for supposing that it counted as a literary language anywhere until the Qur'an was produced.

Now, if we were dealing with prose documents, we might acquiesce in the hypothesis that they had been either translated, or at least gradually shifted, from one stage of the language to another; somewhat as changes in orthography get gradually introduced into printed works, in accordance with later usage, without any violation of good faith. But in Arabic poetry, of which the artifice is more complicated than any other known style, such a proceeding would be simply impossible. The works would have to be recast. And it may be observed that just as the converts to Islam turned their backs on their old religion, so that the Qur'an knows more about it than any of the later Muslims, similarly in Arabia they turned their backs on their old languages and dialects, so that help for the understanding of the inscriptions can now be obtained from two authors only, whom the late Professor Hartmann justly termed eccentric. And just as the occurrence of Islamic ideas in ostensibly pagan works is a clear proof of spuriousness, so the employment of the dialect which the Qur'an rendered classical furnishes ground for grave suspicion.

That the language of the Ḥijāz was the court language of Ḥirah is not impossible, but the evidence for this apart from the "early poems" seems wanting; vast deserts separate these regions. The Muslims who produce poems from all parts of the peninsula in the same dialect seem to be acting consistently with their practice of making many or most of these poets worshipers of Allah and of no other god; they project into past times the phenomena with which they are themselves familiar. Something like this seems to be the case with the geography of these poems; 'Amr b. Kulthūm, the author of a Mu'allaqah, states that he has drunk wine in Baalbek, Damascus, and Qāṣirīn; that which he solicits is of Andarin. The last two places are said to be in the neighborhood of Aleppo. Doubtless in the 150 years which this person is supposed to have lived, he had time for extensive travels; but acquaintance with these places as well as with the provinces and tribes of Arabia such as this ode displays reminds the reader of the time when the Muslim empire included Syria and Arabia rather than of the time when the Arabs were in the condition depicted in the Chronicle of Joshua the Stylite, about 500 CE.

A third line of evidence is to be found in the *content* of the odes. If they regularly commence with erotic passages because the Qur'an says poets philander in every valley; if they proceed to describe their wanderings and their mounts because the Qur'an, says poets are followed by those who go astray, which certainly implies that they go astray themselves; and if they proceed to dilate on their achievements, often immoral in character, because the Qur'an says they say what they do not do; we can at least trace to the source this monotony, which led some critics to declare that all that mattered in poems was the language, since they all repeat the same ideas.[121] But if this stereotyped form is earlier than the Qur'an it must go back to certain acknowledged models; and the search after these leads us, as has been seen, back to Adam. It is true that the odes show remarkable acquaintance with the anatomy of the horse and camel, and perhaps with the habits of other animals; but these, as we know, were studied by grammarians as well as by poets. That some Bedouin poet may have started an ode with a lament over the ruined dwelling of his beloved, or with an account of her wraith, and may have proceeded to describe his livestock, is quite possible, but we can name with precision no classic whose work formed the basis of education and whose example had to be followed by all aspirants to the poetic art. If there had been such a classic or classics, the polemic of the Qur'an must have taken account of such, because they would have been the authoritative source of current ideas. Their guidance might be stigmatized as bad; but it could not well be denied that the people had books which they studied.

The main odes which are ascribed to the early poets are what are called occasionals, and are records of experiences which would have interested themselves only or at best some of their tribesmen. The possibility cannot indeed be denied that an Arab who divorced a wife or raided camels or slaughtered an enemy might compose an ode on the subject; and where several persons were involved in such transactions, each of them might record his experience in this way. But Horace is quite accurate when he says *neque Si chartae sileant quod bene feceris mercedem tuleris*; the record must be on paper or its equivalent, or such compositions have no chance of being preserved. When what the antiquaries communicate is something that takes the form of a dialogue, that is, a series wherein poet replies to poet, the probability that the whole is romance becomes especially great; for we cannot well credit the rival poets with taking steps to preserve each other's performances, so that the intervention of a third party is required; whereas if we suppose the whole to have emanated from one mind, we at least have something before us that is simple and easily paralleled.

The hypothesis of romance further accounts for cases wherein the anecdotes associated with the verses contradict experience; so the author of the *Aghani*, who introduces a number of verses improvised in a poetical competition wherein the poets Nābighah Ja'dī, al-'Ajjāj, and al-Akhṭal took part,[122] calculates that this Nābighah must have been 220 years old at the time, and declares himself satisfied with this conclusion. Others had made him reach the age of 180, but as he had quite certainly celebrated his 180th birthday in the time of the Prophet, this was a serious understatement. Now when we read the poetical competition between Homer and Hesiod, chronology does not trouble us, because we know that the whole story is imaginary. Only if the same person who told it in good faith were also our chief authority for the history of the poets, we could not be too skeptical.

This is only one example; but there are many others. We can perhaps trust the statements of the *Aghani* so far as it is clear that they are based on written materials; whence, if we had the collection of poems made by order of the Caliph Mahdi, we could be confident that those poems were in existence as early as the year AH 158. And if the collector seemed a reasonably veracious and critical person, we might trust him if he informed us that he got his material from much earlier documents. But if in lieu of sobriety and veracity we had tall stories about men who lived for a couple of hundred years, and collections of poems buried under palaces, and gigantic skeletons with inscribed tablets on their heads, we should be justified in dismissing everything as a fabrication. And if in lieu of written materials we found our author relying on oral transmission through a period when anything which had been remembered would, if possible, have been forgotten, we could feel doubly sure that his statements were not to be trusted on any subject.

If then the ostensibly pre-Islamic poetry is suspect on both external and internal grounds, we are brought back to the question of the commencement of Arabic versification; is it of high antiquity, though the monuments which we possess are for the most part post-Islamic? Or is it altogether post-Islamic, being a development of the styles found in the Qur'an? This question appears to be of great difficulty.

On the one hand, we seem to have continuity; the Umayyad poets come after those of the time of the Prophet and his Companions, whereas these follow on the pagan poets. Some of the earlier diwans, for example, that of Ḥassān b. Thābit, the Prophet's encomiast, inspire little confidence; but it would be difficult to shake the genuineness of those of the Umayyad poets. Further, a few of the technicalities of verse seem to lie behind phrases of the same sort which occur in the Old Testament, whence the hypothesis that the Arabs composed odes, only we cannot be sure whether we actually possess any lines that are earlier than Islam, is attractive.

On the other hand, besides the absence of verse in the inscriptions we notice that the Qur'an has no allusion to music.[123] In Dr. Stanton's most useful Index to the Qur'an we look in vain for the items *Music* and *Singing*. The word *rattil* in that book cannot really mean "to chant," since it is used of the Divine Being (xxv, 34); it must mean something like "set in order." The Psalms, which from their Syriac and Greek names clearly mean words accompanied by wind or stringed instruments, in the Qur'an have become *Zubūr* "texts," "books." Indeed the dates for the introduction of music into Muslim communities are given in the *Aghani*, and these take us into Umayyad times. About the year 65, we are told, one Ibn Misjaḥ introduced *barbiṭiyyah* and *istuchusiyyah* from the Greeks, having started his musical studies by hearing Persian builders humming tunes when the Ka'bah was rebuilt after its destruction in that year.[124] One songstress, Rā'iqah, introduced singing into Medinah about the same time.[125] There are, however, other claimants. The first of the two words mentioned clearly means "harp-playing"; the second is obscure. Mr. Farmer, a high authority on these matters, thinks it means the system of Aristoxenus.

These statements of the *Aghani* seem to correspond well with the phenomenon which has been noticed—the absence of allusion to music in the Qur'an, though with most communities it is an important adjunct of public worship, and with a military community like that of the Muslims we should have expected that its importance for the operations of war would have been recognized. But if music was an introduction of Umayyad times, can we imagine that meter existed among the Arabs before in the regularity and copiousness which their versification displays? The more usual order of origin would seem to be dance, music, verse; and the emancipation of verse from music is ordinarily a lengthy process. Some of the Arab meters seem to suggest either the dance or music or both.

The existence of the Qur'an, containing the rudiments of rhymed prose and of meter, would account for the development of when both the theory and the practice of music had been introduced; and the projection of the art into pre-Islamic antiquity would not be unthinkable. The dialect of the Qur'an had become a court language, and with the establishment of a court the profession of court poet arose. The encomia of the second 'Abbasid by Ru'bah are in *rejez* meter, a halfway house between poetry and prose; and, as has been seen, a leading antiquary asserted that this poet's father was the first to compose more than a couple of lines in this, the least artistic of the meters. It seems remarkable that long poems should have been composed in the more difficult rhythms at an earlier period.

An inquiry into the genuineness of the diwans of the period of the pious Caliphs and of the Umayyads would exceed the limits of this paper. The evidence that is before us on the main question seems sufficient to render all ostensibly pre-Islamic verse suspect, and perhaps all pre-Umayyad verse. The pre-Islamic kingdoms which are known to us from the inscriptions were highly civilized, but do not appear to have had poetry; can we believe that the uncivilized Bedouin had it, in anything like the elaborate form wherewith the Muslim archaeologists credit them? On the whole the probability would seem to lie on the side of the supposition that both poetry and rhymed prose are in the main derived from the Qur'an, and that such literary efforts as preceded that work were less, not more artistic.

The tribal bard may perhaps be compared to the Pastoral poet and bear a similar relation to reality. The author of Ecclesiasticus is unnecessarily plainspoken when he says (xxxviii, 25):

> *How can he get wisdom* (the Greek σοφισθήσεται might
> well be rendered *become a poet*) *that holdeth the plough,*
> *And that glorieth in the goad,*
> *That driveth oxen and is occupied in their labours,*
> *And whose talk is of bullocks?*

Yet his opinion seems to be sound. No one thinks of Virgil or Theokritus as real shepherds or goatherds; they are clearly men of learning and culture who "simulate" shepherds and goatherds. And this is evidently the case *mutatis mutandis* with the author of the Mu'allaqāt. Ṭarafah, for example, is clearly a learned man; he knows about Byzantine bridges, and navigation on the Tigris, as well as that in the Persian Gulf, or more probably the Red Sea. Although he died some seventy years before the Hijrah, he takes a phrase from the Qur'an, which he misunderstands. In Surah xxvii, 44, the Queen of Sheba, fancying that she is stepping into a pool, lifts her skirt; but Solomon explains that it is *ṣarḥ mumarrad* out of glass. Some Muslims naturally suppose this to mean "a tower erected (or raised high) out of pieces of glass"; but it seems clear that the true sense is *polished smooth*, an epithet which would apply to Solomon's supposed crystal palace, but not to any ordinary palace. When, therefore, Ṭarafah compares the thighs of his camel to the two gates of a منيف ممرّد (line 19), it is difficult to avoid the conclusion that he is thinking of the verse in the Qur'an, where the word *mumarrad* belongs to the special palace which Solomon constructed; his education, therefore, includes the study of the Qur'an. This work, however, was revealed some sixty years after the supposed Ṭarafah's death. It is like the *dunyā* of 'Amr b. Kulthum, whose death date is given as 600 CE, but who by the use of this word displays acquaintance with the doctrine of the Qur'an, first promulgated some twelve years after his demise.

If on the question whether Arabic versification goes back to immemorial antiquity or is later than the Qur'an it seems wisest to suspend judgment, the reason lies in the bewildering character of the evidence that is before us. We are on safe ground when we are dealing with inscriptions; and the Qur'an can be trusted for the condition of the Arabs to whom it was communicated in the Prophet's time. But for the history of Arabic verse we have to go to other authorities, who for the most part treat of times and conditions of which they themselves had no experience, and whose training had caused them to assume much that necessarily misled them. In judging their statements we can carry skepticism too far, but we also may be too credulous.

Notes

1. [D. S. Margoliouth, "The Origin of Arabic Poetry," *Journal of the Royal Asiatic Society* (1925), pp. 417–49.] The subject of this paper was treated by Ahlwardt in a monograph called *Bemerkungen über die Aechtheit der alten arabischen Gedichte*, Greifswald, 1872, and by Sir C. Lyall in the preface to vol. ii of his *Mufaḍḍaliyyāt*. The former is not very confident, and calls attention to some of the matters which have been discussed rather more fully below; Sir C. Lyall deals chiefly with the character of the transmitters, which he rates rather more highly than the present writer.

2. *Aghānī*, ed. 2, xiii, 48, 23.

3. *Letters of Abu'l-'Alā*, 66 25.
4. Rāghib Ispahānī.
5. *Agh*. xiii, 64; xx, 2.
6. *Musnad* of Ibn Ḥanbal, ii, 331.
7. Baiḍāwī on xxxvi, 69.
8. *Agh*. xi, 76, 23.
9. *Talbīs Iblīs*, 240.
10. Dīwān, Beyrut, 1889, p. 83.
11. *Bayān*, ii, 184.
12. *Irshād*, ii, 366, 5.
13. *Murūj al-Dhahab*, i, 65.
14. *Agh*. xiii, 104.
15. Tabarī, i, 906; *Agh*. xiii, 118; xx, 9.
16. *Poetes Arabes Chretiens*, p. 160.
17. iv, 148, 11.
18. *Agh*. xx, 15, 27.
19. *PAC*. 142.
20. Cf. *Agh*. xviii, 164.
21. *Muẓhir*, ii, 243.
22. *Agh*. xi, 154 (Khuzaimah b. Nahd).
23. Jāḥiẓ, *Bayān*, ii, 184 (after Abū 'Amr b. al-'Alā).
24. *Agh*. viii, 75.
25. Ed. Lyall, 57, 9.
26. *Agh*. iv, 148.
27. *Muẓhir*. i, 121.
28. Tha'ālibī, *Histoire des Rois des Perses*, 556, mentions Sawwār b. Zaid as the *rāwiyah* of the people of Ḥirah. He recited Arabic verses by a Persian king. The *Rāwī* of the people of Kufah (Mubarrad, *Kāmil*, i, 358) is Islamic.
29. *Agh*. xi, 100, 3.
30. *Agh*. xii, 123, 4.
31. Ḥārith, *Mu'allaqah*, 67, speaks of treaties written on *mahāriq*, parchments?
32. Kosegarten, 13, 6.
33. *Agh*. xi, 125, 21.
34. *Agh*. xx, 8, 13.
35. *Agh*. iv, 37.
36. *Agh*. xii, 112, Shamardal *writes* a poem.
37. *Agh*. xx, 24.

38. *Diwan of Hudhail*, ed. Kosegarten, 115, 2.
39. See Wright's *Grammar*, ii, 359.
40. iii, 15.
41. See Griffini, *Il Poemetto di Qudam ben Qādim*, Rome, 1918.
42. ii, 1102, 6.
43. *Kitāb al-Kharāj*, 105.
44. ii, 841, 21.
45. Tabrīzī's preface.
46. See Rothstein, *Die Dynastie der Lakhmiden*, 1899.
47. Ibn Jinni, *Khaṣā'iṣ*, Cairo, 1914, i, 393; he wrongly renders *ṭunūj* by "quires."
48. v, 172, ed. 1; 163, ed. 2.
49. *Agh.* v, 172.
50. *PAC.* 540; Ahlwardt, p. 81, etc.
51. *Agh.* xiii, 4, end.
52. *Irshād*, ii, 426, 3.
53. *Irshād*, ii, 366, 18.
54. *Agh.* iii, 23.
55. *Irshād*, vi, 110.
56. *Irshād*, vi, 215.
57. *Irshād*, ii, 236, 5.
58. *Agh.* xiii, 4.
59. *Irshād*, vii, 5, 13.
60. *Irshād*, i, 126.
61. *Irshād*, vii, 138.
62. *Muzhir*, ii, 242.
63. *Irshād*, ii, 8, 5.
64. *Agh.* xx, 19, 3 a.f.
65. *Agh.* i, 161, 10.
66. Ibid., i, 170.
67. *Agh.* xvii, 52.
68. *Irshād*, vi, 40, 1.
69. *Agh.* i, 126.
70. *Agh.* xiii, 102, 16.
71. *Agh.* xi, 129 med.
72. *Agh.* iii, 4.
73. *Agh.* iii, 2, 4, 10.

74. *Fihrist*.
75. 'Amr b. Qami'ah, ii, 9.
76. Sukkari. *Comm. on Ḥuṭay'ah*, p. 38.
77. *Agh*. xx, 139, 4 a.f.
78. A Muslim swears by the Torah and the Qur'an, ibid., xii, 72, 9.
79. Diwan, 67, 1.
80. Dhu'l-Aṣba'. *Agh*. iii, 9.
81. *Agh*. xiii, 5.
82. Ibid., 4.
83. Ḥārith, *Mu'allaqah*, 44.
84. *Agh*. iv, 151, 6.
85. 'Abīd b. Abraṣ, 19, 8.
86. Ibid., 66, 12.
87. Ibid., 8, 23.
88. Ibn Qutaibah, 44, 10.
89. *Agh*. iv, 144, 15.
90. 'Abīd b. Abraṣ, 50, 17. Ḥārith, *Mu'allaqah*, 55.
91. *Agh*. xi, 132, 6 a.f.
92. *Agh*. xiii, 7.
93. Ibid., near the end.
94. 'Abīd b. Abraṣ, 13, 14.
95. *PAC*. 730, 4 a.f.
96. Cairo ed., 254.
97. xiii, 116, 12.
98. Cairo ed., 101, 154.
99. Ibid., 232.
100. Ibid., 237, 204.
101. *Qiyāmah*, 83, 247; *maḥshar*, 127.
102. So *jabbār 'anīd*, 191, 206, 231.
103. *Agh*. iv, 128, 4 a.f.
104. 80, 28.
105. *Agh*. iii, 9, 8. Sirah viii, 68.
106. Ibn Qutaibah, 37, 15.
107. *Dhū suhmah*, for "a relation," Lyall.
108. *Agh*. xi, 61, 11; 'Amr b. Qami'ah, 64, 4.
109. Zuhair, *Mu'allaqah*, 32; *Hudhail*, Kosegarten, 80.
110. *PAC*. 166, 6 a.f.

111. Surah xl, 18; *Agh.* xxi, 89.

112. *Histoire des Rois des Perses*, 47, 2.

113. Labīd, ed. Brockelmann, xxxiv.

114. xii, 123.

115. *Livre de la Création*, i, 75.

116. Ibid., ii, 145, *Yaum al-taghābun*, Surah lxix, 9.

117. *Agh.* iv, 136, 7.

118. Ed. Schulthess, 51, 15.

119. *Agh.* xi, 125, 4 a.f.

120. *Agh.* xx, 8, 13.

121. Ibn Rashīq, *'Umdah.*

122. *Agh.* iv, 129, 131.

123. Three texts are supposed to refer to music (xvii, 66, xxxi, 5, liii, 61), *Talbís Iblīs*, p. 246. The reference is obscure.

124. *Agh.* iii, 84.

125. Ibid., xvi, 13.

1.8

The Authenticity of the Poems Ascribed to Umayya Ibn Abī al-Ṣalt[1]

Tilman Seidensticker

Umayya Ibn Abī al-Ṣalt is a personality of some relevance both for religious and for literary history. As for the realm of literature, the poems ascribed to him are markedly different from what else is known of Arabic poetry of the early seventhth century AD with respect to form and content: the polythematic *qaṣīda* with its typical sequence of topics is missing completely; instead he deals with such subject matters as the creation of the world, the angels' service, the deluge, the resurrection of man, and so on. These latter topics, on the other hand, are not likely to be dealt with by a pre-Islamic pagan poet and, as there is no evidence at all that the Ṭā'ifī Umayya was a Jew or a Christian,[2] one has to ask what else he could have been.

From a Muslim point of view, this question is easily answered: he must have been a *ḥanīf*, a member of the small group of monotheists on the Arabian peninsula who followed the monotheism of Abraham. Abraham's belief is attested to in the Qurʾān where it is connected with the Kaʿba ub Necca; according to the Qurʾān, this first monotheism was corrupted later, which fact led to the predominance of *shirk* in Arabia. In Western research, some doubts have been cast on this concept of *Heilsgeschichte*, as there is no biblical or extra-biblical evidence of Abraham's connection with Arabia, and these doubts[3] naturally affect the *ḥanīfs*. In 1990, however, Uri Rubin[4] tried to rehabilitate the *ḥanīfs*, arguing that some of them are described as enemies of the prophet Muḥammad and that they therefore can hardly have been invented for apologetic reasons. Convincing as this argument sounds, the problem still remains that the reports on these *ḥanīfs* are contained in quite heterogeneous sources and that Ibn Isḥāq's *Sīra* from which Rubin repeatedly quotes poetry is an unreliable source for poetry even in the eyes of ancient Arab scholars.

The aforementioned characteristics of the poems ascribed to Umayya have drawn considerable attention to this figure. Besides three editions, seven articles and two doctoral dissertations have been devoted to him, 1700 pages altogether, which is quite a lot for someone of whom less than 900 lines have been preserved. But as it seems, this trouble is out of all proportion to the role he plays in modern research. The reason for this neglect is the quarrel about the authenticity of his poetry for, whereas some scholars maintain that there is a hard core of possibly authentic poems of a religious coinage, others are willing only to accept about two dozen uninteresting fragments with nonreligious themes. This state of affairs has resulted in a sort of agnosticism: Umayya is simply not mentioned in, for example, *Der Islam* by Watt and Welch[5] or in the first volume of the *Cambridge History of Arabic Literature*.[6] Tilman Nagel, on the other hand, in his monograph on the Qur'ān,[7] goes to the opposite extreme in quoting Umayya's poetry from Arabic sources without worrying about the fact that four of the seven pieces adduced by him are—with good reason—regarded as suspect in the studies on Umayya.

In what follows, I would like to examine the controversy about Umayya once again. First of all, some remarks on his biography, his poetry and its transmission: these facts are more or less undisputed in literature.[8]

Umayya stems from the city of al-Ṭā'if, situated some 50 miles to the southeast of Mecca in the mountains, and he belonged to the Thaqīf tribe who dominated the area. Through his mother Ruqayya bt. ʿAbd Shams, he was related to Meccan aristocracy, and close relations to Mecca are also reflected in eulogies on the Meccan celebrities ʿAbdallāh b. Judʿān and Ḥarb b. Umayya. An elegy on the Meccans killed at the battle of Badr in the year 2 AH is generally accepted as authentic. On the one hand, this poem shows Umayya's political loyalties at that time, and on the other hand, it is the last datable sign of his life. He must have died before the Muslim occupation of al-Ṭāʾif in 8 AH because he is not mentioned in the historical reports about this event. A eulogy on the prophet Muḥammad is generally regarded as a forgery, 18 lines in the *mutaqārib* metre composed in an awkward style out of Qurʾānic phrases and in fact hardly suitable to a poet who is supposed to have lived in pagan al-Ṭāʾif until his death.

The well-known philologist Muḥammad b. Ḥabīb, who died in 859 AD, is said to have collected Umayya's poetry in a *dīwān* and commented on it, and in the eighteenth century, the compilator of the monumental dictionary *Tāj al-ʿarūs* still had a copy of this *dīwān* at his disposal.[9] Today, it seems to be lost, but of some consolation to us is the fact that, as can be judged from quotations, it contatined some very doubtful poems and thus would not have been of great value in dealing with the question of authenticity.[10] Instead, we have at our disposal three collections of fragments, the first (containing 530 lines) compiled by Friedrich Schulthess in 1911, which is quite voluminous, considering the small number of printed source works available at that time.[11] Second, there is the edition by ʿAbd al-Ḥafīẓ al-Saṭlī, published in Damascus in 1974,[12] and third, the Baghdad master thesis by Bahja ʿAbd al-Ghafūr al-Ḥadīthī, published in 1975 (=al-Ḥadīthī [1975]). These editions contain 895 and 857 lines respectively.[13] The lesser part of the poetry in all these editions is devoted to profane topics we are familiar with from Umayya's contemporaries; the greater part bears a religious stamp.

The course of research on Umayya has followed a zig-zag line since he was, so to speak, discovered in the middle of the last century by Alois Sprenger.[14] Sprenger placed him among the group of *ḥanīfs* without, however, discussing the authenticity of Umayya's poems. This question was raised only in the present century by Clément Huart who, in 1904, got off to a dramatic start in his article *Une nouvelle source du Qurān* (=Huart [1904]). As the editor of al-Maqdisī's *K. al-Badʾ wa-l-tārikh*, which contains a large number of poems ascribed to Umayya, Huart had noticed that the content of Umayya's poems is often of greater informational value than that of Qurʾānic passages dealing with the same subject matter. One of his examples is the story of the extinction of the people of Thamūd who disregarded God's command to give pasture and watering to a female camel consecrated to him but who slaughtered her. In the Qurʾān, this story is mentioned in five places, and it is the prophet Ṣāliḥ who warns the Thamūd and finally escapes the punishment. Umayya does not mention Ṣāliḥ but gives some details not mentioned in the Qurʾān: he knows the name of the man who hamstrung the camel and tells us about the camel's young calling down upon the Thamūd the warth of heaven, and about a girl who escaped and brought the message of the Thamūd's extinction to the neighboring people of Qurḥ before she died. From additional information of this kind Huart concludes that the common traits between Umayya and the Qurʾān must go back to Umayya.

Huart's uncritical attitude toward the poems ascribed to Umayya was not accepted in the ensuing period. His article provoked six publications[15] whose authors agreed insofar as they all admitted that poems which do not contain a substantial surplus of information and show a clear lexical agreement with the Qurʾān are the products of later Muslim forgers. The most important and detailed discussion is Israel Frank-Kamenetzky's Königsberg doctoral dissertation published in 1911 under the title *Untersuchungen über das Verhältnis der dem Umajja b. Abi ṣ Ṣalt zugeschriebenen Gedichte zum Qorān*. He is willing to accept as authentic, besides pieces or lines without any resemblance to the Qurʾān, free improvisations in Qurʾānic style and Qurʾānic expressions as well as poems showing isolated reminiscences of the Qurʾān among ideas known from Umayya's unsuspect poems (Frank-Kamenetzky [1911] p. 47). In this way, Frank-Kamenetzky came to consider some 225 lines with a religious subject as authentic.

In a review of Frank-Kamenetzky's book, Theodor Nöldeke, otherwise known to be highly critical of the authenticity of ancient Arabic poetry, puts his view as follows: "With no. 23 [of the Schulthess edition] begin those poems which we *a potiori* may call 'religious' or 'pious.' At a glance, one is inclined to regard them all as Muslim forgeries. But in some of them, a more thorough study reveals so many strange or even odd traits that we cannot help ascribing them to a poet original in his way, and as several of them resemble each other, there is reason enough to ascribe them to Umayya." (Nöldeke [1912] p. 163). Nevertheless Nöldeke accepts a smaller number of lines as genuine than does Frank-Kamenetzky.

In order to give examples of the poetry in question, I would like to quote from two poems. The first one deals with the annunciation to Mary and the birth of Jesus; as it is quoted to show a case of obvious use of the Qurʾān, I have picked out only five lines out of a total of seventeen.

Umayya 38/1.4.9.11–12 SCHULTHESS = 79/1.4.9.11–12 AL-SAṬLĪ = 119/1.4.9.11–12 AL-ḤADĪTHĪ (from al-Maqdisī, *Badʾ*, line 4 also in Yāqūt, *Muʿjam al-Buldān*):

1. *wa-fī dīnikum min rabbi Maryama āyatun*
munabbiʾatun wa-l-ʿabdi ʿĪsā bni Maryamī
"In your religion is an announcing sign from the Lord of Mary and of the servant Jesus, the son of Mary."

With this compare the following quotations from the Qurʾān:
wa-li-najʿalahū [i.e. *ʿĪsā*] *āyatan li-l-nāsi*: Qurʾān 19/21; *wa-jaʿalnā bna Maryama wa-ummahū āyatan*: Qurʾān 23/50; *qāla* [i.e., *ʿĪsā*] *innī ʿabdu llāhi*: Qurʾān 19/30; *lan yastankifa l-masīḥu an yakūna ʿabdan li-llāhi*: Qurʾān 4/172; *ʿĪsā bnu Maryama*: Qurʾān, passim.

4. *wa-laṭṭat [i.e. Maryamu] ḥijāba l-bayti min dūni ahlihā taghayyabu ʿanhum fī ṣaḥāriyyi Damdamī*
"She dropped the veil of the tent before her people, hiding from them in the deserts of Damdam."

Cf.: *idhi ntabadhat min ahlihā makānan sharqiyyan fa-ttakhadhat min dūnihim ḥijāban*: Qurʾān 19/16–17.

9. *fa-qālat* [i.e., *Maryamu*] *lahū* [i.e., *li-l-malʾaki*] *annā yakūnu wa-lam akun baghiyyan wa-lā ḥublā wa-lā dhāta qayyimī*
"Mary said to the angel: Whence shall this be, as I am not a whore, not pregnant and not married?"

Cf.: *qālat annā yakūnu lī ghulāmun wa-lam yamsasni basharun wa-lam aku baghiyyan*: Qurʾān 19/20; *qālat rabbi annā yakūnu li waladun wa-lam yamsasni basharun*: Qurʾān 3/47.

11. *fa-sabbaḥa thumma ghtarrahā fa-ltaqat bihī*
ghulāman sawiyya l-khalqi laysa bi-taw'amī
"The angel praised God and then came over her unexpectedly, and she conceived from him a well-proportioned boy, no weakling."
sabbaḥa said of angels: Qur'ān, passim.

12. *bi-nafkhatihī fī l-ṣadri min jaybi dir'ihā*
wa-mā yaṣrami l-raḥmānu mil-amri yuṣramī
"by his breathing into her breast through the bosom of her garment, and what the Merciful decides is decided."

Cf.: *ka-dhālika llāhu yakhluqu mā yashā'u idhā qaḍā amran fa-innamā yaqūlu lahū kun fa-yakūnu*: Qur'ān 3/47; *wa-kāna amran maqḍiyyan*: Qur'ān 19/21.

The last two lines show that the Qur'ān is not only quoted or paraphrased but occasionally interpreted in agreement with the *tafsir*. Whereas in the Qur'ān the creative breath seems to come directly from God (*wa-Maryama bnata 'Imrāna llatī aḥṣanat farjahā fa-nafakhnā fīhi min rūḥinā*: Qur'ān 66/12), the commentators of the Qur'ān, apparently from a desire to avoid anthropomorphism, make Gabriel, at God's command, breathe into Mary's garment, which is what Umayya's line seems to imply.[16]

The second example does not contain any borrowings from the Qur'ān at all; it consists of two fragments (taken from an ensemble completely composed of fragments) both showing the same rhyme and probably belonging together. The first fragment is quoted in several sources, the oldest of which date from the third/ninth century. Variant readings abound, and the text is difficult to understand. I therefore give the sources, the text in Arabic characters, and the critical apparatus in an appendix.

Umayya 25/10–14 SCHULTHESS = 10/10–14 AL-SAṬLĪ = 23/1–3.5–6 AL-ḤADĪTHĪ:

10. "God made the earth kneel down like a she-camel to be covered by the water until every fire drill was lent (as there was no more dry wood)."[17]

11. "The earth is our refuge and was our mother, in it are our graves, and on it we are born."

12. "On it, there are angel-servants[18] on its summits, held in custody standing, their jugular veins trembling (with strain)."

13. "And God built upon them (heavens) one covering the other and smooth, which do not vanish nor bend."

14. "And if you tried to drive a louse over its back, the louse would drop from what is not matted."

The second fragment is preserved only in al-Maqdisī's *K. al-Badʾ wa-l-tārikh* (Umayya 25/32–37 SCHULTHESS = 10/32–37 AL-SAṬLĪ = 23/21–26 AL-ḤADĪTHĪ); again, there are some difficult passages:

32. *yantābuhu l-mutanaṣṣifūna bi-suḥratin*
fī alfi alfin min malāʾika tuḥshadū
"The servants (i.e., the angels, or: those appealing for justice) come to him (i.e., God) consecutively at the beginning of dawn among a million of gathered angels."

33. *rusulun yajūbūna l-samāʾa bi-amrihī*
lā yanẓurūna thawāʾa man yataqaṣṣadū
"Messengers traversing the heavens at his command who do not mind that those who have been broken to pieces (or killed) remain (dead)."

34. *fa-humū ka-awbi l-riḥi baynā adbarat*
rajaʿat bawādiru wajhihā lā tukradū
"They are like turning wind: he has hardly turned his back when his fore-runners return and cannot be driven away."

35. *ḥudhdhhun manākibuhum ʿalā aktāfihim*
ziffun yaziffu bihim idhā mā stunjidū

"Their shoulders have scanty feathers, on their shoulder blades there is plumage which carries them swiftly when they are asked to help."

36. *wa-idhā talāmidhu l-ilāhi taʿāwanū*
ghalabū wa-nashshaṭahum janāḥun muʿtadū
"And when God's angel-servants assist each other, they are victorious, and a well-prepared wing strengthens them."

37. *nahaḍū bi-ajniḥatin fa-lam yatawākalū*
lā mubṭiʾun minhum wa-lā mustawghidū
"They rise with the help of wings without being indifferent (to their duties), are neither sluggish nor weaklings."

In these fragments, there is not much reminiscent of the Qurʾān. Of course, the concept of God as the cause of rain in line 10 is compatible with the Qurʾānic message, but the comparison is not Qurʾānic, nor are the angelology and cosmology and the concept of "mother earth" in the remaining lines. Although there was some disagreement in borderline cases, research in the time prior to World War I generally accepted poems like this one as genuine.

The confidence that at least some of the poems ascribed to Umayya might well be authentic was shaken by Tor Andrae, a historian of religion and for a time bishop of Linköping, and it seems to be due to his influence that nowadays nobody in the Western world dares to be serious about Umayya. In his book *Der ursprung des Islams und das Christentum*, published in 1923–25, Andrae devoted seven pages to Umayya, focusing his attention on those cases in which Umayya seems to display a greater extent of knowledge than the Qurʾān. He managed to adduce passages from commentaries to the Qurʾān that, for their part, contain more information than Umayya's poetry.[19] In dealing with the extinction of the Thamūd, we have heard that Umayya on the one hand does not mention the prophet Ṣāliḥ but on the other hand knows the name of the evil-doer who hamstrung the camel, tells of the camel's young crying for punishment, and is informed about a girl who escaped and brought the message of the catastrophe to the neighbors before she died. Andrae quotes a report from al-Ṭabarī's commentary to the

Qurʾān that contains details about the evil-doer's origin and of the sacrilege and mentions that the girl's father was called al-Silq (Andrae 52f. [200f.]/59f.). He quotes two more examples of this kind and then concludes that the poems ascribed to Umayya must be pseudepigraphic versifications stemming from the exegetes called *quṣṣāṣ*, whose contribution consisted in providing more detailed reports on Qurʾānic narrative themes. They sometimes were renegades of Jewish origin or at least had Jewish informants.

Andrae's skepticism has made a lasting impression on scholarship. In the entry on Umayya in the first edition of the *Encyclopaedia of Islam*, for example, Andrae's "noteworthy arguments" are mentioned; Brockelmann accepted Andrae's views as well as Blachère who, in his *Histoire de la littérature arabe*, is willing to accept as genuine only the poems dealing with profane matters.[20]

Yet, in 1939, Joachim W. Hirschberg cast his vote against Andrae. Hirschberg, in his Cracow doctoral dissertation entitled *Jüdische und christliche Lehren im vor- und frühislamischen Arabien*, tries to show that there is a reason enough to assume that Umayya had drawn his information from pre-Islamic Haggada and therefore is independent of Islamic exegesis; as a matter of fact, he is able to adduce Jewish texts that no doubt can corroborate this theory (Hirschberg [1939]). Regrettably, his monograph is somewhat ill-constructed, and certain arguments are not very convincing. Johann Fück wrote a gruff review,[21] and Hirschberg's contribution was dismissed.

Nevertheless, the material he presents is very useful. One of Andrae's three examples for Qurʾānic exegesis as a source for pseudo-Umayya is a report on the sacrifice of Abraham's son that goes back to al-Suddī. Here, the son asks his father to fasten his shackles so that he will not wince. This is exactly what Umayya reports:

Umayya 29/15 SCHULTHESS = 62/15 AL-SAṬLĪ = 87/7 Al-ḤADĪTHĪ

(fa-ajāba l-ghulāmu . . .) wa-shdudi l-ṣafda an aḥīla ʿani l-sikkīni ḥayda l-asīri dhi l-aghlālī

"(and the son answered:) 'and fasten the shackles because I might dodge the knife, as does the captive caught in chains.'"

In the Qur'ān, on the other hand, these details are not mentioned. Hirschberg (1939) (p. 126f.) quotes several pre-Islamic Haggadic passages that give the reason for these requests: according to Talmudic regulations, a sacrificial animal must not twitch when slaughtered; if this happens, the sacrifice is not valid.[22] There are some other cases where Hirschberg adduces Haggadic material that explains certain lines of Umayya that are otherwise difficult to understand. To give just one more example: without giving any explanation, Umayya mentions that the sun has to be forced to rise in the morning:

Umayya 25/47 SCHULTHESS = 10/29 AL-SAṬLĪ = 22/12 Al-ḤADĪTHĪ

laysat (i.e., *al-shamsu*) *bi-ṭāliʿatin lahum fi rislihā illā muʿadhdhabatan wa-illā tujladū*

"The sun rises for them slowly only after it has been punished and flogged."

The Haggadic reports tell us that the sun would rather not rise because it is ashamed that mankind adores it (Hirschberg [1939] p. 91).[23]

Summarizing Hirschberg's contribution, we can note that there are some pre-Islamic Jewish sources that might very well represent Umayya's background. Parallels between Umayya and Muslim exegesis do not therefore prove that "Umayya" is forgery based on the latter; they can just as well be explained assuming that both are dependent on the same tradition. Moreover, we cannot exclude the possibility that Muslim *tafsir* presents Haggada-like reports on the Qur'ān *and* Umayya even in cases where the latter's name is not mentioned. As for Umayya's possible informants, it is interesting to read in al-Balādhuri that there were Jews living in the district of pre-Islamic Ṭā'if; according to him, they were expelled from Yathrib and the Yemen.[24]

So far, we have heard about two stages in research: the first one took place in the years 1904 to 1912 and was devoted to editing and sorting out cases of obvious dependence on the Qur'ān, the second one consisted of Andrae's skeptical attack with its aftermath in the statements of Brockelmann and Blachère and in Hirschberg's answer, which was presented in insufficiently clear terms and therefore inadequately taken note of by other scholars. The third and so far last phase of scholarly preoccupation with Umayya took place in the seventies in the Arab world. The editions of al-Ḥadīthī and al-Saṭlī mentioned above contain introductions of 150 and 330 pages respectively. While al-Ḥadīthī gives only a general statement on the question of authenticity,[25] al-Saṭlī explains in detail which poem he considers for what reasons as a) genuine or forged very well, b) questionable but not definitively forged, or c) definitively forged. In this, he follows a comparatively skeptical course. In some cases, he is overly critical, for example when he summarily dismisses the *kāmil* "poem" rhyming in *-dū* (Nr. 25 ed. Schulthess/Nr. 10 ed. al-Saṭlī) from which we quoted above. The 50 line "poem" consists, to say it again, of several fragments collected from a number of sources. These 50 lines are rejected altogether because he regards line 15 and line 27f. as containing purely Islamic elements. In line 15, the seventh heaven is called inaccessible, in line 27f. shooting stars are explained as missiles launched in order to chase away eavesdropping devils (*shayāṭin*). Al-Saṭlī quotes reports from al-Ṭabarī's commentary on the Qurʾān that states that the heavens were not regulated in the time before the prophet Muḥammad; he furthermore points to the fact that in Qurʾān 72/8–10 (which speaks about some demons, *nafarun mina l-jinni*) this "shooting star myth" is told as something unheard of by the *jinn* (al-Saṭlī [1977] p. 190f.). Even if we accept this argument, one could still ask whether the possibly Islamic origin of lines 27f. (which are transmitted in isolation) must necessarily affect the status of the remaining fragments bearing the same rhyme and metre.

Nevertheless, a comparison of his results with those reached by Frank-Kamenetzky is quite interesting. The latter came, as we have heard, to consider 225 lines with a religious thematic as genuine, while al-Saṭlī regards only 104 lines out of a larger number on religious matters as authentic. The most important point is that these 104 lines, with the exception of six, are regarded as authentic by Frank-Kamenetzky *as well*. As al-Saṭlī arrived at his results more or less independently of Frank-Kamenetzky, this shows that there must be criteria that can be objectivized.

However, we have not heard the last of Umayya. Laudable as the editions of al-Ḥadīthī and al-Saṭlī are, they contain incomplete or erroneous explanations, do not give all variant readings, and could be enlarged with the help of the numerous editions of primary sources published since the seventies. Further, the possible motives of forgeries should be examined.[26] Finally, neither al-Ḥadīthī nor al-Saṭlī has made use of the analysis of Frank-Kamenetzky and the material presented by Hirschberg. The task of an authoritative edition and translation and a balancing of all arguments about authenticity against each other still has to be carried out. What I have tried to show is that there might well be some authentic material among the nearly 900 lines ascribed to Umayya. Also there is a very early testimony to Umayya's fame as an author of a special sort of poetry, namely a line by Surāqa al-Aṣghar who died about 700 AD:

(wa-dhkur Labīdan . . .) wa-Umayyata l-baḥra lladhī fī shiʿrihī ḥikamun ka-waḥyin fī l-zabūri mufaṣṣalī

"(Remember Labīd . . .) and Umayya, the 'sea' (of knowledge) in whose poetry are pieces of wisdom like a detailed revelation (or: book?) in the Psalter."[27]

Appendix: Umayya 25/10–14 SCHULTHESS = 10/10–14 AL-SAṬLĪ = 23/1–3.5–6 AL-ḤADĪTHĪ

V. 10–11: Jāḥiẓ, *Ḥayawān* III 363 ult. – 364, 1

V. 11–14: Jāḥiẓ, *Ḥayawān* V 437, 8 – 438, 2; al-Shantamarī, *Sharḥ abyāt al-Īḍāḥ* (?), manuscript of the Oriental Library, St. Joseph's University, Beirut (as quoted by Power [1906] p. 204, footnote 9)

V. 11–12: Baghdādī, *Tilmīdh* 222, 4f.

V. 10: Jāḥiẓ, *Ḥayawān* III 365, 10; b. Qutayba, Mushkil 68 pu.; *Lisān al-ʿarab* 3, 218 b 7f. (*sfd*) = *Tāj al-ʿarūs* 2, 380, 3 (*sfd*) = Lane 1370 a (*sfd*)

V. 11: b. Qutayba, *Mushkil* 76 ult.; Thaʿlabī, *Qiṣaṣ* 7, 17; *Mukhaṣṣaṣ* 13, 180 apu.; Qurṭubī, *Jāmiʿ* I 112, 9

V. 12: *Qāmūs*, Turkish translation (as quoted by Fleischer [1885] I 62, 19)

V. 14: b. Qutayba, *Maʿānī* 633, 4

١٠ وَالأَرْضُ نَوَّخَهَا الإِلهُ طَرُوقَةً ... لِلْمَاءِ حَتَّى كُلُّ زَنْدٍ مُسْفَدُ

١١ وَالأَرْضُ مَعْقِلُنَا وَكَانَتْ أُمَّنَا ... فِيهَا مَقَابِرُنَا وَفِيهَا نُولَدُ

١٢ فِيهَا تَلَامِيذٌ عَلَى قُذُفَاتِهَا ... حُبِسُوا قِيَامًا فَالْفَرَائِصُ تُرْعَدُ

١٣ فَبَنَى الإِلهُ عَلَيْهِمُ مَخْصُوفَةً ... خَلْقَاءَ لَا تَبْلَى وَلَا تَتَأَوَّدُ

١٤ فَلَوَ/انَّهُ تَحْدُو الْبِرَامَ بِمَتْنِهَا ... زَلَّ الْبِرَامُ عَنِ الَّتِي لَا تُقْرَدُ

Lisān, Tāj, Lane مسيّرها : Jāḥiẓ *Ḥayaw.*, b. Qut. *Mushkil* نوّخها . 10

:Jāḥiẓ *Ḥayaw.* III, b. Qut. *Mushkil*, Thaʿl. *Qiṣaṣ*, Qurṭubī *Jāmiʿ* مقابرنا . 11

:*Mukhaṣṣaṣ* معايشنا : Jāḥiẓ *Ḥayaw.* V, Shant. *Sharḥ* معاقلنا

*Baghd. *Tilmīdh* مقامتنا

:Jāḥiẓ *Ḥayaw.*, b. Qut. *Mushkil*, Thaʿl. *Qiṣaṣ*, Shant. *Sharḥ* وفيها

**Mukhaṣṣaṣ* ومنها

Baghd. *Tilmīdh*, *Qāmūs* ديها : Jāḥiẓ *Ḥayaw.*, Shant. *Sharḥ* فيها .12

Jāḥiẓ *Ḥayaw.*, Baghd. *Tilmīdh*, *Qāmūs* تلاميذ على قذفاتها

Jāḥiẓ *Ḥayaw*, variant تلامذة على قدماتها

*Shant. *Sharḥ* تلامذة على قذفاتها

:Jāḥiẓ *Ḥayaw.*, Baghd. *Tilmīdh*, *Qāmūs* حبسوا

*Shant. *Sharḥ* حسرى : Jāḥiẓ *Ḥayaw.* variants حسر ، خسرا

:Jāḥiẓ *Ḥayaw.*, Baghd. *Tilmīdh*, *Qāmūs* فالفرائص

*Shant. *Sharḥ* والفرائض

*Jāḥiẓ *Ḥayaw.* variant محصوفة : Jāḥiẓ *Ḥayaw.*, Shant. *Sharḥ* مخصوفة .13

*Jāḥiẓ *Ḥayaw*, variant فلا : Jāḥiẓ *Ḥayaw.*, Shant. *Sharḥ* لا

:Jāḥiẓ *Ḥayaw.* variant يحدو : Jāḥiẓ *Ḥayaw.* تحدو . 14

:Shant. *Sharḥ* Ms. يخد

*b. Qut. *Maʿānī* يجد : ed. Schulthess (conj.) يجدو : Shant. *Sharḥḥ* تجد

:Jāḥiẓ *Ḥayaw.*, Shant. *Sharḥ*, b. Qut. *Maʿānī* البرام

*Jāḥiẓ *Ḥayaw*, variant البزام

*Shant. *Sharḥ* لمتنها : Jāḥiẓ *Ḥayaw.*, b. Qut. *Maʿānī* بمتنها

:Jāḥiẓ *Ḥayaw*, variant لبنى والفاها : Jāḥiẓ *Ḥayaw.* زلّ البرام عن

ib. Qut. *Maʿānī* صعدا لاالفاها | : Shant. *Sharḥ* لبنى والقاها

Abbreviated Literature

Andrae (1923): Tor Andrae, *Der Ursprung des Islams und das Christentum* (Uppsala/Stockholm, 1926 [originally published in *Kyrkohistorisk Årsskrift* 23 [1923] pp. 149–206, 24 [1924] pp. 213–92, 25 [1925] pp. 25–112])/*Les origines de l'Islam et le Christianisme*, transl. Jules Roche (Paris, 1955)

Bustānī (1942): Buṭrus al-Bustānī, "Umayya b. a. al-Ṣalt al-Thaqafī," *al-Mashriq* 46 (1942) pp. 201–20

Fleischer (1885): Heinrich Leberecht Fleischer, *Kleinere Schriften*, 3 vols. (Leipzig, 1885–88)

Frank-Kamenetzky (1911): Israel Frank-Kamenetzky, *Untersuchungen über das Verhältnis der dem Umajja b. Abi ṣ Ṣalt zugeschriebenen Gedichte zum Qorān* (Diss. Königsberg: Kirchhain N.L., 1911)

al-Ḥadīthī (1975): Bahja ʿAbd al-Ghafūr al-Ḥadīthī, *Umayya b. a. al Ṣalt, Ḥayātuhū wa-Shiʿruhū* (Baghdad, 1975)

Hirschberg (1939): Joachim W. Hirschberg, *Jüdische und christliche Lehren im vor- und frühislamischen Arabien. Ein Beitrag zur Entstehungsgeschichte des Islams* (Cracow, 1939) (Polska Akademia Umietności. Prace Komisji Orientalistycznej 32)

Huart (1904): Clément Huart, "Une nouvelle source du Qorān," *Journal Asiatique*, Sér. 10, 4 (1904) pp. 125–67

Ḥusayn (1927): Ṭāhā Ḥusayn, *Fī al-Adab al-Jāhilī* (Cairo, 1927; here used in the 12th ed. 1977)

Lane: Edward William Lane, *Arabic-English Lexicon*, 8 vols. (London, 1863–93)

Nöldeke (1912): Theodor Nöldeke, "Umaija b. AbiṣṢalt," *Zeitschrift für Assyriologie* 27 (1912) pp. 159–72

Power (1906): E. Power, "Umayya Ibn Abi-s Salt," *Université Saint-Joseph Beyrouth. Mélanges de la Faculté Orientale* 1 (1906) pp. 197–222

Power (1912): E. Power, "The poems of Umayya B. Abî-ṣ-Ṣalt. Additions, Suggestions and Rectifications," *Université Saint-Joseph Beyrouth. Mélanges de la Faculté Orientale* 5, 2 (1912) pp. 145*–195*

al-Rabīʿī (1979): Aḥmad al-Rabīʿī, "Umayya b. a. al-Ṣalt," *al-Balāgh* 7, 10 (1979) pp. 38–44

Rubin (1990): Uri Rubin, "*Ḥanīfiyya* and *Kaʿba*. An inquiry into the Arabic pre-Islamic background of *din Ibrāhim*," *Jerusalem Studies in Arabic and Islam* 13 (1990) pp. 85–112

al-Saṭlī (1977):, ʿAbd al-Ḥafīẓ al-Saṭlī, "Umayya b. a. al-Ṣalt," (Damascus,[2] 1977)

Schulthess (1906): Friedrich Schulthess, "Umajja b. Abi-ṣ-Ṣalt," *Orientalische Studien Theodor Nöldeke zum siebzigsten Geburtstag gewidmet . . . herausgegeben von Carl Bezold* (Giessen, 1906), vol. 1 pp. 71–89

Schulthess (1911): Friedrich Schulthess, *Umajja ibn Abi ṣ Ṣalt. Die unter seinem Namen überlieferten Gedichtfragmente gesammelt und übersetzt* (Leipzig, 1911) (Beiträge zur Assyriologie 8, 3)

Vallaro (1978): Michele Vallaro, "Umayya ibn Abi ṣ-Ṣalt nella seconda parte del *Kitāb az-Zahrah* di Ibn Dāwūd al-Iṣfahānī (manoscritto di Torino)," *Atti della Accademia Nazionale dei Lincei, Memorie. Classe de Scienze morali, storiche e filologiche* 22, no. 4 (1978): 180, 423.

Arabic Sources

Baghdādī, *Tilmīdh* ʿAbd al-Qādir al-Baghdādī, *Risālat al-Tilmīdh*, ed. ʿAbd al-Salām Muḥ. Hārūn, *Nawādir al-Makhṭūṭāt* (Cairo,[2] 1973) pp. 217–25

Jāḥiẓ, *Ḥayawān* a. ʿUthmān ʻAmr b. Baḥr al-Jāḥiẓ, *K. al-Ḥayawān*, ed. ʿAbd al-Salām Muḥ. Hārūn, 7 vols. (Cairo, 1938–45)

Lisān al-ʿarab Jamāl al-Din a. al-Faḍl Muḥ. b. Mukarram al-Ifrīqī, *Lisān al-ʿArab*, 15 vols. (Beirut, 1955)

Mukhaṣṣaṣ a. al-Ḥasan ʿAlī b. Ismāʿīl b. Sīda, *K. al-Mukhaṣṣaṣ*, 17 vols. (Būlāq, 1898–1903)

Qurṭubī, *Jāmiʿ* a. ʿAbd Allāh Muḥ. b. Aḥmad al-Qurṭubī, *al-Jāmiʿ li-Aḥkām al-Qurʾān*, 20 vols. (Beirut, 1985 [repr.])

b. Qutayba, *Maʿānī* a. Muḥ. ʿAbd Allāh b. Muslim b. Qutayba, *K. al-Maʿānī al-Kabir fi Abyāt al-Maʿānī*, 3 vols. (Hyderabad, 1949–50)

B. Qutayba, *Mushkil* id. *Taʾwīl Mushkil al-Qurʾān*, ed. al-Sayyid Aḥmad Ṣaqr (Cairo, 1954)

Tāj al-ʿarūs a. al-Faḍl Muḥ. Murtaḍā b. Muḥ. al-Zabīdī, *Tāj al-ʿArūs*, 10 vols. (Bengasi, n.d. [repr.])

Thaʿlabī *Qiṣaṣ* a. Isḥāq Aḥmad b. Muḥ. al-Thaʿlabī, *K. Qiṣaṣ al-Anbiyāʾ al-Musammā bi-l-ʿArāʾis* (Cairo,[2] 1951)

Notes

1. Tilman Seidensticker, "The Authenticity of the Poems Ascribed to Umayya Ibn Abī al-Ṣalt," in *Tradition and Modernity in Arabic Language and Literature*, ed. J. R. Smart (Richmond, UK: Curzon Press, 1996), pp. 87–101.

2. Cf. the discussion in Huart (1904) pp. 135 f.; al-Ḥadīthī (1975) pp. 57–64; al-Rabīʿī (1979) pp. 40–42; al-Saṭlī (1977) pp. 55–68. That Umayya at some time of his life adopted Islam is quite unlikely. Schulthess (1911) p. 7 f. seems at least willing to take this into consideration, but it was rejected by Power (1912) pp. 183*–190*; cf. Vallaro (1978) p. 430 f. footnote 45; Rubin (1990) p. 96; al-Saṭlī (1977) p. 40. In the years 1993 and 1994 I read papers on Umayya at the Oriental Institutes of the Universities of Berlin (FU, Semitistik—Arabistik), Kiel, Saarbrücken, and Hamburg. I would like to thank those present on these occasions, as well as the participants in the 2nd Shaban Memorial Conference for their comments and suggestions.

3. Inaugurated by Christiaan Snouck Hurgronje in his doctoral dissertation *Het Mekkaansche Feest*, generally accessible in id., *Verspreide Geschriften*, vol. 1 (Bonn/Leipzig, 1923).

4. Rubin (1990) pp. 85–112.

5. W. Montgomery Watt and Alford T. Welch, *Der Islam* I (Stuttgart, etc., 1980).

6. A. F. L. Beeston et al., *Arabic Literature to the End of the Umayyad Period* (Cambridge, etc., 1983).

7. *Der Koran. Einführung—Texte—Erläuterungen* (München, 1983).

8. The most extensive treatment of Umayya's "biography" is al-Saṭlī (1977) pp. 33–85 (Addenda p. 697); cf. also al-Ḥadīthī (1975) pp. 46–70; Schulthess (1906) pp. 72–76; Power (1906) pp. 208–10.

9. See al-Saṭlī (1977) pp. 86–92 (and in addition the reference in Power [1912] p. 146 footnote 1). On a collection of 300 of Umayya's poems in a "book" (*kitāb*) by Jarīr b. Ḥāzim al-Baṣrī or his son Wahb b. Jarīr cf. ʿAbd al-Malik b. Qurayb al-Aṣmaʿi, *Fuḥulat al-shuʿaraʾ*, ed. Charles Torrey, *Zeitschrift der Deutschen Morgenländischen Gesellschaft* 65 (1911) p. 500/ed. Muḥammad ʿAbd al-Munʿim Khafāji and Ṭāhā Muḥammad al-Zaynī (Cairo, 1953) p. 33.

10. See Schulthess (1906) p. 72 and Saṭlī (1977) pp. 121–24.

11. Schulthess (1911). Additional material was published by Power (1912).

12. A second edition was published in 1977 that contains an appendix (pp. 673–95) with seven poems or fragments (46 new lines) (= al-Saṭlī [1977]).

13. Independently of al-Saṭlī and al-Ḥadīthī, Vallaro (1978) published material not contained in Schulthess's edition from Ibn Dāwūd's K. *al-Zahra* that is, however, included in the edition of al-Ḥadīthī and the second edition of al-Saṭlī. Vallaro abstains from developing his own ideas about the issue of authenticity while confessing that he instinctively feels more attracted by Andrae's critical approach (Vallaro [1978] pp. 471 f.).

14. *Das Leben und die Lehre des Moḥammad nach bisher grösstentheils unbenutzten Quellen bearbeitet* (Berlin, 1861–65), vol. 1, pp. 76–81 and 110–19.

15. Schulthess (1906); Power (1906); Schulthess (1911), introduction; Frank-Kamenetzky (1911); Nöldeke (1912); Power (1912).

16. Cf. Thomas J. O'Shaughnessy, *The Development of the Meaning of Spirit in the Koran* (Rome, 1953) p. 63.

17. This is the explanation given in *Lisān al-ʿarab* (and *Tāj al-ʿarūs* and Lane), cf. the quotations given for line 10 in the appendix. A different explanation is proposed by b. Qutayba, *Mushkil* p. 69, lff.; he takes the two woods used to make fire as the parents and the fire as the child. A third explanation is given by Schulthess [1911] p. 85 in his translation "*bis jedes (kleinste) Feuerholz begattet war*," obviously implying that the rain makes the wood grow (cf. his footnote 6). But *zand* means the fire drill and not the plant from which it is taken, and *asfada* means "to make cover," not "to cover."

18. Cf. *talāmidhu l-ilāhi* in line 36 below.

19. Andrae (1923) p. 48 [196]–56 [204]/55–63.

20. *Enzyklopaedie des Islām*, vol. 4 (Leiden/Leipzig, 1934) p. 1080 b (H. H. Bräu); Carl Brockelmann, *Geschichte der arabischen Litteratur*, Erster Supplementband (Leiden, 1937) p. 55; Régis Blachére, *Histoire de la litérature arabe* (Paris, 1952–66) p. 305f.

21. *Orientalische Literaturzeitung* 44 (1941) col. 76f.

22. The following line reads: *innanī ālamu l maḥazza wa-inni lā amassu* (or *amassa?*) *l-adhqāna dhāta l-sibālī*. On the interpretation cf. Schulthess' translation (Schulthess [1911] p. 93), H. Reekendorf's remark in *Orientalische Literaturzeitung* 15 (1912) col. 214; al-Saṭlī (1977) p. 442, footnote 5. Even if this line gives a reason for the son's request (which is not sure), this would not make Hirschberg's explanation superfluous.

23. Similar reports are found in Islamic sources, cf. Frank-Kamenetzky (1911) p. 42 footnote 3 (from p. 40); Hirschberg (1939) p. 91; al-Saṭlī (1977) p. 366 footnote 2.

24. Aḥmad b. Yaḥyā al-Balādhurī, *K. Futūḥ al-Buldān*, ed. M. J. de Goeje (Leiden, 1866) p. 56 line 10.

25. On p. 127, he accepts as probably genuine those poems in which there are traces of the *ḥanīfiyya* and the holy books of the Jews and Christians, whereas he dismisses poems showing influence of the Qurʾān and written in pallid style. This is acceptable in general, but there will be room for considerable disagreement where the classification of single poems is concerned.

26. So far, the following motives have been mentioned: the tabooing of imitating the Qurʾān (Power [1912] p. 190*f.; Werner Caskel, *Gamharat an-nasab. Das Genealogische Werk des Hišām ibn Muḥammad al-Kalbi*, vol. 2 [Leiden, 1966] p. 570b); attempts to improve the esteem of the tribe Thaqīf, unpopular by the role of al-Mughīra b. Shuʿba, Ziyād b. Abīhi, ʿUbaydallāh b. Ziyād, al-Ḥajjāj, and others (Nöldeke [1912] p. 161 footnote 1; Bustānī [1942] p. 210); attempts to make Umayya a Muslim (Power [1912] p. 190*f.); attempts to fabricate a pre-Islamic monotheism on the Arabian peninsula (Ḥusayn [1927] p. 145).

27. Cf. al-Rabīʿī (1979) p. 42; al-Ḥadīthī (1975) p. 50; Nāṣir al-Dīn al-Asad, *Maṣādir al-shiʿr al-jāhilī* (Cairo, 1982), p. 230. Cf. also S. M. Husain, "The poems of Surâqah b. Mirdâs al-Bâriqî—an Umayyad poet," *Journal of the Royal Asiatic Society* (1936) p. 610, 8f.

1.9

The Divine in the Works of Umayya B. Abī al-Ṣalt[1]

Gert Borg

The discussions that concerned the work of the poet Umayya b. Abî al-Ṣalt are dominated by the question of its authenticity. Seidensticker[2] meticulously discusses this subject and reaches a disappointing conclusion: we first need an authoritative edition of Umayya's work, before the discussion about this poet and his work can continue.

Of course we have every reason to be cautious in view of what is at stake: fragments of the work that is attributed to this poet show some kind of similarity with passages in the text of the Koran, so we are close to a minefield of historical and religious implications. Of course such implications cannot be the scope of this contribution; at this stage we can hardly do more than confine ourselves to less ambitious questions and propositions. The trap however is always there, so we are well advised to be careful to refer to a historical person "Umayya."

On the other hand if—in accordance with Seidensticker's point of view—we accept that the problem of the authenticity of Umayya's work should be solved first, before we could seriously discuss it, we are surely heading for a state of mute stagnation in our dealing with this poet's work, because an authoritative edition of it does not seem to be forthcoming shortly. Nonetheless, caution is the order of the day.

Authenticity is an ambiguous and often unruly problem. To illustrate this, we can refer to the following example: Seidensticker[3] argues against the authenticity of one poem ascribed to Umayya.[4] In this poem the archangel

Gabriel is made responsible for breathing Jesus into Mary's breast through her garment, which Seidensticker states is consistent with—later!—Islamic *tafsîr*, whereas in the Koran (Q. 66,12) God himself performed this creative act. At first glance this seems a convincing argument to shed doubts on the poem's authenticity, but we cannot definitely rule out the possibility that ideas about Gabriel's involvements in Jesus' conception circulated in the area before Koranic revelation, especially so because in Christian tradition Gabriel plays an important role in this process as well. Seidensticker's argument is sound and he is probably right, but a different state of affairs cannot be excluded.

Normally the way out of the authenticity problem would be to historically assess the biographical data of Umayya b. Abî al-Ṣalt himself, that is to say, the little we know about him, but this does not seem to bring us closer to any solution, because almost everything about this man is enigmatic.

Just as an example we could look at the end of his life: he is believed to have died around the year 631, that is 9 of the Hijra, and did *not* convert to Islam, although most sources regard him as an extremely religious person. Some sources—for what they are worth—describe a meeting Umayya had with the prophet Muhammad in person. After hearing some of Umayya's poetry, Muḥammad states that Umayya actually almost was a Muslim.[5]

The main reason that al-Ḥadîthî gathered from his sources for Umayya's nonconversion is that he apparently believed himself to be the chosen prophet of the Arabs.[6] Arab historians consider him to have been a *ḥanîf*—but we don't know what a *ḥanîf* exactly is. Does the word merely indicate that someone is monotheistic? Or does it also refer to actively preaching some form of religious ideas, as perhaps in Umayya's case?[7]

The first source to turn to for an answer to these questions would be the diwan of this poet, but as we have seen, things are not made any easier for us there, because the main part of his diwan seems to be lost and some of what remains of it is under severe suspicion of not being authentic. As for Umayya's identity, the essential question might be: How does Umayya present himself? The answer is simple: he is a poet. I know of no literary texts in *saj*ʿ or in any other prose that are ascribed to him.

All sources ascribe to him some traditional *marâthî* and some *madiḥ*-poetry, so we may at least assume that he knew and practiced some of the literary conventions of the time.

The poetry that was collected in a *Dîwân Umayya*, the main part of which is nowadays lost, and that has been gathered from several sources, consists of poems of four kinds:

- tiny fragments (one verse or even only half verses) without any context that can hardly be analyzed
- longer fragments that stand on their own, because they cannot technically be connected to other fragments
- longer fragments that, according to their rhyme and meter, may or may not belong to other fragments
- shorter and longer poems that seem more or less unaffected by the ravages of time, because they show some kind of thematical development or at least have some kind of beginning and end.

Thematically his poetry can be divided into two categories:

- traditional poetry, consisting of *madîḥ, fakhr* of his own tribe Thaqîf, and a few *marâthî*
- religious poetry, which—as I hope to show—partly has a vigorous public character, partly a distinctive personal character

The very fact that Umayya composed other poetry than the usual kinds that we know from *jâhilî* and *mukhaḍram* poets is in a way nothing unusual: as Jacobi has shown,[8] the poets of the era just before Islam tended to experiment within the framework of the traditional genres, like, for instance, in love poetry, but tried out some new ideas as well. On the other hand, we know of no other poet of this early age who took religious ideas as a theme for his poetry. In this respect Umayya seems to be standing quite alone.

Looking at the same phenomenon from an opposite point of view makes it even more intriguing: if we suppose that in that very age some individuals dwelled on religious topics or even acted as vagrant preachers—I have not been able to find any proof of such practices—they might have used ordinary language or even *sajʿ* as their vehicle—in the latter case continuing the tradition of the *kuhhân*—but to use *poetry* as a means of expression for these purposes seems to be quite unusual, because of its status in expressing the traditional core of poetic themes. On the other hand, it can be argued that poetry is the logical vehicle for preaching religious thought, if we think of poetry as the only "media" of the time.

It may be that this thematic originality had some influence on the quality of Umayya's poetry. From a technical point of view, in terms of medieval Arabic literary theory, Umayya probably was not a very strong if not weak poet: he often uses enjambment, reiterates rhyme words easily, uses strange and sometimes even obscure working, a partly non-Arabic vocabulary[9]—and his themes are of course contrary to the normal stock and pile that a pre-Islamic audience would expect.

Let us now turn to the texts:

Some notes on the text of poem 21:

In line 1B al-Ḥadîthî reads: *wa-lâ majdu*, but I prefer to read with Schulthess: *wa-amjadu*, because the last reading would be metrically correct.

In line 4B I suggest to read: *mu'abbadu* instead of *mu'ayyadu*, a reading in line with the *al-Zahra* manuscript, edited by Vallaro;[10] al-Ḥadîthî calls it a case of *taṣḥîf*.

Vallaro's edition of the *Kitâb al-Zahra*, written by Abû Bakr Muḥammad ibn Dâwud al-Ẓâhirî, who died in AH 297, contains a second part of the same poem.

Translation of the first part:

1. Praise to You and Grace and the Kingdom, O Lord, Nothing is higher than You and more praiseworthy
2. King on the Throne of Heaven, a Ruler, to whose Glory the faces bow and [people] kneel down
3. Over Him is the veil of light, the light surrounds him and rivers of light burn around him
4. No man rises towards him with a look of his eyes and beyond the veil of light are immortal (strong?) beings
5. Angels with their feet in His earth and their necks rising over the Heavens
6. Among them those who are bearing one of the legs of his Throne with their hands and if that were not so, they would become exhausted and fall to the ground (?)

7. Standing on their feet bowing under it (the Throne), their shoulder blades trembling from fear
8. They are with a Lord whose command they observe, they prick their ears to the Inspiration, standing still
9. Among them are his secretaries, the Holy spirited Gabriel and the strong spirited Michael, the steady one
10. Angels who will not stop being servants, Cherubs, some of them kneeling, others prostrated
11. The prostrated ones never raise their heads, they praise their Lord above them and glorify him
12. And the kneeling ones bow their backs to Him in fear, repeating God's benefactions and praising him
13. And amongst them are those who fold their heads in their wings and whose heads are almost sweating at the very thought of their Lord
14. out of fear, not tiring from serving Him and they do not consider it a burden to serve Him longtime
15. Behind them are the guards of Heaven's gates, standing near them, with their keys, watchful
16. Good servants they are, chosen for his command; behind them stands a strong, well equipped army
17. Under the water masses in the deep soil there are angels who descend and rise
18. And between the layers of the earth under its inner parts there are angels who go to and fro on His command
19. Praise be to the One whose power his creation does not know and Who is on the throne, alone and unique
20. The One Whose reign is not contested by his creatures and Who is unique even though his servants do not hold Him for that
21. King of the strong heavens and the earth below; there is nothing above us that will bend
22. He is God, the Creator of creation, and all of his creatures, male and female, are his servants in obedience
23. How can creation be like its Creator, Who is forever and eternal, whereas the created will vanish

24. The created has no access to the act of creating; who then can be eternal against the course of fate
25. So [the created] will vanish and only the overpowering One will stay, who produces Life and Death eternally and will not weaken
26. The birds concealed in their hiding praise Him and behold: they ascend in the open air of heaven
27. And out of fear of my Lord thunder above us praises him and the trees and wild animals, forever
28. The whales praise him and the sea, swirling, and all that it enclosed and holds together

What we see in the first part of the poem is an exalted vision, in which Umayya tries to present God's transcendency; He is an unapproachable ruler of Heaven with a strong command over his angels; they have the task to serve him, uphold his throne, and praise him continuously, and their main motivation to do so is fearful respect for their Lord.

Further away from Heaven, under the earth and sea, his angels are seen running errands on his command. (17–18)

What kind of place is this Heaven? What strikes us first of all is that Umayya never mentions any room for the souls of the righteous in this perfectly organized fortress: obviously they will have no share in Heaven's glory, which in itself is a strange image for Umayya, because elsewhere in his poetry he articulates that the sinners will be punished in hell, whereas the righteous will dwell in the comfort of Heaven.

Furthermore it seems that what inspires Umayya to present this kind of Heaven, looks like the very ideal of an *earthly* court: it is strongly organized with God at the head of its hierarchy assisted by his secretaries Gabriel and Michael. They appear to be some kind of middlemen between God and his angels, although this is not mentioned explicitly: probably it would not be fitting to put anyone in a commanding or even subcommanding position in the presence of the Lord and in such a kind of organization.

It is strange to see that humans are hardly mentioned in this part of the poem, but Umayya of course implies them in the whole of creation. In verse 20 Umayya refers to failing belief in the Oneness of God, and this must necessarily be a reference to human failure to do so.

Umayya stresses the difference between the Almighty who is one and eternal, whereas all of his creation is mortal and cannot possibly reach His overwhelming state of being.

Finally, he presents a pastoral scenery in which several creatures in nature—even thunder—by the essence of being what they are, praise their Creator.

One of the remarkable things is the epithet of God that is missing: in this text God is never mentioned as being *raḥîm*, an epithet Umayya uses frequently in other poems, at one time even for the Prophet.

The second poem that I would like to discuss can in my view only be interpreted correctly if we assume that it was actually performed before a live audience.

Translation:

1. In front of (in the face of?) the Owner of the Throne, before Whom THEY will be shown, the One Who knows what is in the open, and also the hidden word
2. on the day WE will come to Him—he is a merciful Lord—what he promised always came true
3. on the day YOU[11] will come to Him, as He said: INDIVIDUALLY when He will not forget righteous nor sinner
4. Will I be blessed? It is blessing I hope for;[12] or will I be blamed for what I obtained in a shameful way
5. My Lord: *If* you forgive me, forgiveness is *all I can hope for* (?) or if you punish me, You will not punish an innocent
6. If I will be blamed for what I have committed, then I will surely face an abominable punishment . . .
7. My Lord, You have destined for everyone to descend to the fire of hell, you have imposed a book, firm in its judgement
8. My Lord, do not withhold from me eternal paradise but be merciful, my Lord, and forgiving to me

In this poem Umayya also starts with a reference to God Almighty, an opening with which Umayya seems to legitimize his performance. As if in soliloquy he then refers to humanity as a whole by using the personal pronoun THEY. He does so, however, in front of an audience, in which everyone knows—or is supposed to understand—that he or she will be among those who will be judged.

In verse 2 he knits a bond between his audience and himself by using the first person plural WE, a bond that seems even more intimate when he describes God as a merciful Lord; the thought behind it is: we are united and we can be assured of God's steadfastness.

But in verse 3 he is pointing a finger at YOU, meanwhile opposing a Lord of wrath and vengeance to the merciful one in verse 2. He even goes so far as to stress the individual judgment: *fardan*.

Now we come to an important question: Whom does Umayya mean by "I," bearing in mind that Umayya is performing for an audience. He is enacting a person addressing God and asking to be forgiven. We might even go as far as to assume that the "I" here stands for every individual in his audience: the "I" is every individual for him- or herself, or—to put it another way—the "I" is the person for his audience to identify with. A modern equivalent might be the "I" that a priest will use in praying during service: if he prays for "his" salvation, it is not only his own personal salvation—although he's not excluded—but the individual salvation for everyone present. The "I" in this context might be used by Umayya as a rhetorical device, for which I was not able to find an appropriate technical term, but "identificational I" comes close to what I think would be appropriate.

With this in mind we may be able to understand the rather peculiar expression *fa-al-muʿâfâtu ẓannî* in verse 5, which I translated provisionally as *forgiveness is all I can hope for*. A better translation would perhaps be: Forgiveness is what I'm guessing at, what I'm counting on. To grasp the full meaning of this passage we probably have to suppose that here Umayya does not speak for himself, but for the individual, who will think in everyday life, that things won't be that bad after all, that everything will be all right in the end.

In the remaining part of this poem Umayya enacts the repenting individual, almost falling to his knees in awe, begging to be forgiven. In short, I think that this poem can be characterized as a sermon that gradually becomes a prayer.

If we now return to the second part of the first poem, we will find that it also is a kind of prayer:

29. Oh you, heart of mine, dwelling on desire, how long will you be so stubborn
30. Oh verily the world offers sufficiency to live, and whilst a man may become a respected sayyid in it
31. Behold! It will turn away from him and its loveliness will cease and he will have made from the dust of graves his cushion
32. He will be split from his soul that lived in his body and be a neighbor to corpses whose property proved to be unstable
33. Which man have you seen before me, living forever, who posessed in ancient times that what could keep him alive
34. Whom Fate torments with stumbling, will keep stumbling and the fates of time are unstable
35. The earth will not be well, even if its inhabitants will think it to be well: fate may always reveal itself
36. Have you not seen in what has passed a warning for you? Stop now! Don't be, heart of mine, [like] a blind man, erring to and fro
37. Because guidance has come that knows no doubt and only a liar will reject the truth
38. Be fearful of death and of resurrection after it and do not belong to those, who are deceived by today or tomorrow
39. Because you are in a world that deceives its inhabitants; in it there is an enemy, full of hate, who kindles a fire
40. who lives in the regions of heaven above the air and is without the knowledge of what is hidden, he will be completely without sleep [?]
41. If not for the bond with God, we would be wandering and lost and it would make us happy to be thrown to the ground to be buried alive
42. In this bond you will see the stories of ages passed and the stories of what is hidden, will be clear at resurrection
43. [There is nothing in them except the dog nearby and their booty and the ones in the cave are weakened?] (a reference to the *Ahl al-Kahf*)
44. (*missing*)
    because my Lord said to the angels: bow down

45. for Adam when God completed his creation and they threw themselves down for him in obedience, prostated, and they stayed that way
46. And God's enemy spoke out of pride and evil nature "is it a piece of loam (?) on the fire of the hot winds? Go ahead: Make it your master!"
47. Thus disobedience drove him (Adam) away from the best of dwellings and that was what caused in ancient times his wrath
48. with us (primordial sin?); we will spare ourselves no folly nor trick to lead it (our soul) to a fire, that will be brought to it (?)
49. A hell that is burning and will not be made lukewarm for one moment and its heat will not become cold until the end of time
50. You have no example of how the devil and hell will be when you are being burned in the fire; you will be lost
51. He (the devil) is a leader, always calling you to the Fire, to bring us near it, without going there himself
52. You will have no excuse nor the (false) obedience of the sinner and you will have no influence on the fire when you are burning in it.

Although this is a kind of prayer, it completely lacks the vigor and rhetoric devices of text 140. Nonetheless, it is rather personal in tone, because the poet starts by addressing his own heart. Umayya soon however turns to a number of *ḥikam* on the transitory nature of rank and personal glory and of all earthly possessions. His observations of the ruling of Fate are at least still very much inspired by pre-Islamic concepts: a verse like 34, for example, would easily fit in any pre-Islamic poem.

In verse 36 Umayya starts to urge his heart to turn away from idle disbelief and follow new guidance, that has come. The word used in verse 37 for "guidance" is *hudâ*, but it is hard to see what he means by it. Does it refer to the new mission by Muḥammad, or to what Umayya's concept of the *dîn al-aḥnâf*? The preceding verse 36 and the following verses 41 and 42 may give a clue: Umayya points to a warning from the past, with which he probably means the history of the prophets, and he explicitly mentions the bond with God. From verse 44 onward we can also notice an orientation toward stories from the Old Testament: creation, paradise, and the primordial sin, so my best guess would be that it is not early Koranic revelation that is at stake here, but biblical inspiration, unless of course this message of his is inspired by the corresponding Suras, and he semi-quotes them, so to say.

As usual Umayya ends his poem with vivid images of eternal punishment in hell, the destiny of all sinners.

If we compare these two poems we can point at the following differences

- The longer poem 21 consists of two very different parts: I would call the first part a hymn to God, whereas the second part might best be described as a personal prayer.
- This poem, 21, is rather formal in character, shows some connections to pre-Islamic poetry, and, as far as Umayya's religious ideas are concerned, it refers mainly to the Old Testament.
- Its religious perspective is rather rigid, because it mainly focuses on two ideas: God is almighty and the individual, confronted with this glory, should repent.
- Apart from resurrection, when the hidden will be revealed, it holds no promise whatsoever for us humans.
- Seen this way the poem creates an enormous distance between God and us, mortals, if only for the ranks of servants who are put in between and who, though more lofty than we are, are seemingly only motivated by fear. In other words: in this vision we, humans, are hardly more than worms.

In contrast to this, the shorter poem 140

- shows many more features of a vivid performance, mainly by its quick changing of personal pronouns
- this makes it sound much more like an act of preaching in front of a live audience
- it offers us humans much more of a perspective to share in the glory of God
- it does so by clearly making a distinction between the righteous and the sinners

- in verse 7 it clearly refers to the Koran
- in short: this poem offers a perspective of hope

Based on the comparison of these two poems, I would be tempted to put an earlier date to the longer of the two, although it is clear that Umayya in both of these texts acts as a *nadhîr*.

This relative dating, if convincing, can be a contribution to the question of the authenticity of Umayya's work: if we can detect a development in religious convictions that would run parallel to a possible development on a personal level, and to a development in historical facts as we know them, we would have a strong indication for the intertextual authenticity of these poems.

Anyone might argue the other way around: that the shorter poem preceded the longer, and I would be curious for the arguments given. I can even think of some arguments myself, but in the end, the result would be the same, in the sense that the difference between the two can be attributed to mental change or development and would be an indication for changing religious attitudes.

I argued earlier that Umayya b. Abî al-Ṣalt should first of all be seen as a poet. We can now modify his position some more: he probably started as a conventional pre-Islamic poet, but in the religious poetry that he started to make, he is a *nadhîr* who uses poetry as a medium for his religious message. This offers a curious parallel, because as far as I am aware the prophet Muḥammad started off the same way: as a *nadhîr*.

Texts

Poem 21

1. *Laka al-ḥamdu wa-al-naʿmâʾu wa-al-mulku rabbanâ*
fa-lâ shay'a 'aʿlâ minka jaddun wa-lâ majdu
2. *malîkun ʿalâ ʿarshi al-samâ'i muhayminun*
li-ʿizzatihi taʿnû al-wujûhu wa-tasjudu
3. *ʿalayhi ḥijâbu al-nûri wa-al-nûru ḥawlahu*
wa-anhâru nûrin ḥawlahu tatawaqqadu
4. *wa-lâ basharun yasmû ilayhi bi-ṭarfihi*
wa-dûna ḥijâbi al-nûri khalqun mu'ayyadu (mu'abbadu? B.)

5. *malâ'ikatun 'aqdâmuhum taḥta 'arḍihi*
wa-'a'nâquhum fawqa al-samawâti ṣu''adu
6. *fa-min ḥâmilin 'iḥdâqawâ'imi 'arshihi*
bi-'aydin wa-lawlâ dhâka kallû wa-balladû
7. *qiyâmun 'alâ al-'aqdâmi 'ânîna taḥtahu*
farâ'iṣuhum min shiddati al-khawfi tar'adu
8. *fa-hum 'inda rabbin yanẓurûna li-'amrihi*
yuṣîkhûna bi-al-a'smâ'i li-al-waḥyi rukkadu
9. *'amînâhu rûḥu al-qudsi Jibrîlu minhumâ (minhumû?* B.*)*
wa-Mîkâlu dhû al-rûḥi al-qawîyu al-musaddadu
10. *malâ'ikatun lâ yaftirûna 'ibâdatan*
karûbîyatun minhum rukû'un wa-sujjadu
11. *fa-sâjiduhum lâ yarfa'u al-dahra ra'sahu*
yu'aẓẓimu rabban fawqahu wa-yumajjidu
12. *wa-râki'uhum yaḥnû lahu al-ẓahra khâshi'an*
yuraddidu 'âlâ'a al-'ilâhi wa-yaḥmadu
13. *wa-minhum muliffun fû janâḥayhi ra'sahu*
akâdu li-dhikrâ rabbihi yatafaṣṣadu
14. *mina al-khawfi lâ dhû sa'matin bi-'ibâdatin*
wa-lâ huwa min ṭûli al-ta'abbudi yajhadu
15. *wa-ḥurrâsu 'abwâbi al-samâwati dûnahu*
qiyâmun ladayhi (ladahâ? B.*) bi-al-maqâlîdi ruṣṣadu*
16. *fa-ni'ma al-'ibâdu al-muṣṭaffûna li-'amrihi*
wa-min dûnihim jundun kathîfun mujannadu
17. *wa-taḥta kathîfi al-mâ'i fî bâṭini al-tharâ*
malâ'ikatun tanḥaṭṭu fîhi wa-taṣ'adu
18. *wa-bayna ṭibâqi al-'arḍi taḥta buṭûnihâ*
malâ'ikatun bi-al-'amri fîhâ taraddadu
19. *fa-subḥâna man lâ ya'rifu al-khalqu qadrahu*
wa-man huwa fawqa al-'arshi fardun muwaḥḥadu
20. *wa-man lam tunâzi'hu al-khalâ'iqu mulkahu*
wa-'in lam tufarridhu al-'ibâdu fa-mafradu
21. *malîku al-samâwâti al-shidâdi wa-'arḍihâ*
wa-laysa bi-shay'in fawqanâ yata'awwadu

22. *huwa allâhu bârî al-khalqa wa-al-khalqu kulluhum*
'imâ'un lahu ṭaw'an jamî'an wa-'a'budu
23. *wa-annâ yakûnu al-khalqu ka-al-khâliqi alladhî*
yadûmu wa-yabqâ wa-al-khalîqatu tanfadu
24. *wa-laysa li-makhlûqin 'alâ al-khalqi juddatun*
wa-man dhâ'alâ marri al-ḥawâdithi yukhladu
25. *fa-yafnâ wa-lâ yabqâ siwâ al-qâhiri alladhî*
yumîtu wa-yuḥyî dâ' iman laysa yamhadu (yahmudu? B.*)*
26. *tusabbiḥuhu al-ṭayru al-kawâminu fî al-kafâ*
wa-'idh hiya fî jawwi al-samâ'i taṣa''adu
27. *wa-min khawfi rabbî sabbaḥa al-ra'du fawqanâ*
wa-sabbaḥahu al-'ashjâru wa-al-waḥshu 'abbadu

NOTES SOURCE:

1. Gert Borg, "The Divine in the Works of Umayya B. Abī al-Ṣalt," in Gert Borg and Ed de Moor, ed., *Representations of the Divine in Arabic Poetry* (Amsterdam: Editions Rodopi, 2001).

2. T. Seidensticker, "The Authenticity of the Poems Ascribed to Umayya Ibn Abî al-Ṣalt," in *Tradition and Modernity in Arabic Language and Literature*, ed. J. R. Smart (Richmond, Surrey, 1996), pp. 89–96.

3. Ibid., p. 91.

4. B. al-Ḥadîthî, 'A., *Umayya Ibn Abî al-Ṣalt Ḥayâtuh wa-Shi'ruh* (Baghdad, 1975, Dîwân), p. 292.

5. Al-Iṣfahânî, *Kitâb al- Aghânî* (Cairo, 1963), IV, 129; al-Ḥadîthî, pp. 66–67.

6. He is described as traveling to Iraq and entering a church. After some time he reappears, in total shock, but he and his party continue their journey to Iraq. On the way back Umayya enters the same church and after a while comes out as shocked as he was before. When asked for the reason of his anguish he claims to have heard at his first visit that he was to become the prophet of the Arabs, which seems a good reason to become nervous. The second time, however, he has learned that God decided against him and would not grant him this honor. See al-Iṣfahânî, *al- Aghânî*, IV, 123.

7. An interesting point might be that the same root in Hebrew (ḤNP) is associated with profaneness, pollution, desecration; could this be a case of adopting an honorary soubriquet?

8. R. Jacobi, *Die Anfänge der arabischen Ġazalpoesie: Abû Dhu'aib al-Hudhalî in Der Islam*, 61, 1984, pp. 219 ff.

9. See, for instance, Ibn Qutayba, *al-Shi'r wa-al-Shu'arâ'* (Beyrout, s.d.), I, 370–71.

10. Al-Ẓâhirî, *Kitâb al-Zahrah*, 2nd ed, ed. M. Vallaro (Napoli, 1985), pp. 14–16.

11. According to al-Ḥadîthî (*Umayya Ibn Abî al-Ṣalt*, p. 314: *yawma na'tîhî*) the translation would run: "on the day WE will come to him."

12. It was suggested to me by Mike Carter to read a *maf'ûl muṭlaq* here: "Will I be blessed in the way I hope to be blessed. . . ." This is a good solution, but I still prefer my own translation because of the parallel construction in 5a.

Postscript by B. Borg

In a way this contribution gained a different perspective by the theses put forward by Christoph Luxenberg in his hotly disputed study "Die Syro-Aramäische Lesart des Koran," Berlin, 2000. Together with a number of colleagues I regret the heat of this debate and the emotions it provoked. The debate seems hardly to consider the intended extent of this study: "Ein Beitrag zur Entschlüsselung der Koransprache": a contribution, not the final word.

Having studied Ugaritic, I am very skeptical about "root-hunting" in Semitic languages, and I believe that this is one of the main deficiencies of Luxenberg's study.

New Hanover County Public Library
Carolina Beach Library
4/24/2014

Thank you for using self-checkout!

**********7706

34200011893001
Unapologetic :
Date Due: 05/15/2014 11:59:00 PM

34200011812688
Sec- (BC): Koranic allusions :
Date Due: 05/15/2014 11:59:00 PM

Monday thru Thursday 9 A.M to 6 P.M.
Friday 9 A.M. to 5 P.M.
Saturday 9 A.M. to 1 P.M.
Telephone Renewals: 910-798-6320
Website: www.nhclibrary.org
Checked Out / # Not Checked Out
2 / 0

Part Two

The Koran, the Bible, and the Dead Sea Scrolls

2.1

The Gideon-Saul Legend and the Tradition of the Battle of Badr

A Contribution to Islam's Oldest Story[1]

Hans von Mzik

The number of Muslims in the Battle of Badr in the year 2 AH as it is handed down in Arab tradition varies. The smallest figure of 300 is to be found in the poems attributed to Ḥamza,[2] the largest emerges from Ibn Sa'd, who puts the number of Muḥammad's Meccan fighters at 86[3] and those of the Medina fighters as 238,[4] giving a total of 324 combatants at Badr, without counting those undecided. In general, the sources speak of 313 or 314, or "310 and several more,"[5] and also of 307, 317, or 318 fighters at Badr.[6] The details at first create the impression that we are dealing with a genuine historical account. We know, however, a tradition[7] according to which the number of fighters at Badr is as great as the number of people of Ṭālūt (Gideon-Saul).[8] According to a variant, the prophet is supposed to have said to his people on the day of Badr: "You are the same number as the people of Ṭālūt on the day that he clashed with Jālūt." If we now use this clue to examine the description of the Battle of Badr as given by Ibn Isḥāq, we find a whole series of traditions that contain motifs from the biblical Gideon-Saul legend.

1. The story of Badr is introduced by 'Ātika's dream: "I saw a rider who approached on his camel and finally stopped at Abṭaḥ. Then he cried in a loud voice: 'Heda, you dilatory ones, go out to your death-ground; within three days!' and I saw how the people gathered round him. Then he went up to the shrine, the people followed him and, while they were around him, his camel stopped with him on the roof of the Ka'ba. Hereupon he cried the same thing: . . . Then the camel stood still at the top of [Mount] Abū Qubays

and he cried (once more) the same thing. Hereupon he took a boulder, threw it down and it came rolling down until, reaching the foot of the mountain, it shattered; and there wasn't a house . . . left in Mecca that was not struck by a fragment."[9] A variant of the same motif is found in the dream of Juhaym ibn aṣ-Ṣalt: 'I was between sleeping and waking. There I beheld a man who approached on a horse and finally stopped. With him was a camel. Then he cried out: 'Utba ibn Rabī'a is dead, and Šaiba ibn Rabī'a and Abu-l- Ḥakam . . . and that man and that man' and listed the names of the noble Quraysh who (afterwards) were killed on the day of Badr. Hereupon I saw him slit his camel's throat. Then he made it run around the camp and there was not a tent left in the camp that was not spattered with blood."[10]—It is not hard for us to recognize the model in both dreams: the ominous dream of the Midianite before the great battle with Gideon: "Behold, I dreamed a dream; and lo, a cake of barley bread tumbled into the camp of Midian, and came to the [commander's] tent, and struck it so that it fell, and turned it upside down."[11] All three dreams have the rather unusual motif of movement in common: the "rolling" of the boulder, the "running round" of the camel, and the "rolling" of the barley bread, but the Muslim versions have been expanded and become more sensory as is typical of more recent emulations. 'Ātika and Juhaym ibn aṣ-Ṣalt's dreams are composed of two parts: the disaster is not only symbolically but also directly announced, in order to leave no doubt about the compelling relationship between prophecy and the event in question. The symbolism has become much coarser: the barley bread[12] becomes a piece of rock, the disaster that befalls the camp commander's tent in the Midianite's dream is now extended to include all of the houses in Mecca. In Juhaym's dream the effects are even more exaggerated: blood spatters the Meccans' tents and those who will fall first are already proclaimed dead. For the sake of effect, the original symbolism was also completely dropped in Juhaym's dream. The "barley bread" represents the enemy; with the "boulder" we may be uncertain as to whether the enemy or the disaster are signified; but in Juhaym's dream there is no trace left of the original symbolism.

2. It is less easy to analyze the motif of the historically unauthenticated anecdote of Muḥammad's reconnaissance ride with "one" of his companions[13] before the battle. ". . . And he (Muḥammad) and one of his comrades rode out,"—Ibn Hishām: the man was Abū Bakr aṣ-Ṣiddīq"[14]—Ibn Isḥāq:

"as Muḥammad ibn Yaḥya ibn Ḥabban passed on to me"—until he met a Shaykh of the Arabs. He asked him about the Quraysh, about Muḥammad and his comrades and what news he had of them. The Shaykh said: "I won't tell you anything until you let me know who you are!" God's envoy answered: "If you give us information, we will let you know."—"So, one after the other?"—"Yes."—The Shaykh spoke: "I have learned that Muḥammad and his comrades set forth on such and such a day and, if he who told me this spoke truly, he is today in such and such a place,"—in the very place where God's envoy actually was—"In the same way, I learned that the Quraysh set forth on such and such a day and, if he who told me this spoke truly, they are today in such and such a place"—in the very place where the Quraysh actually were. When he had finished his story, he asked: "Whence come the two of you?" So God's envoy spoke: "We are (or come) from a stretch of water." Hereupon he moved away from him, while the Shaykh asked: "What does that mean: from a stretch of water? From the water of Iraq?"—Ibn Hishām: "the Shaykh was Sufyān ad-Damrī"—. Ibn Isḥāq: "Hereupon God's envoy returned to his companion."—The story may have been told with the intention of presenting Muḥammad in the role of 'Aqīd,[15] as is certainly the case with Abū Sufyān and the anecdote of the date-stones.[16] On the other hand, it is reminiscent of the reconnaisance mission of Gideon and his servant Pura.[17] Since it is couched in extremely vague terms—one may note the formulation *kaḍā wa-kaḍā* that appears four times—and is devoid of any descriptive detail or precision, it is not possible to determine which motif it is based on. It is also possible that both motifs contributed to the shaping of the story.

3. Immediately before the battle, a crowd of Qurayshites approached until they came to the prophet's watering place. Among them was Ḥakīm ibn Ḥizām. Then the prophet spoke: "Let them [drink]! And no one drank at that time who would not be killed, except for Ḥakīm ibn Ḥizām, for he was not killed. . . ."[18] Wāqidī adds to this: "Twice Ḥakīm escaped ruin through God's mercy: once when Muḥammad, after the recitation of sura 36, threw dust at the heads of a number of Qurayshites that were hostile to him, among whom he was also to be found the second time at the Badr drinking place."[19] On its own, it is not possible to infer why simply "drinking" is supposed to have been wrong and entailed death. The reason originates from the *Ṭālūt* legend: he

who drank was an unbeliever, and the unbeliever deserved to die. In a further elaboration of this thought process, the "drinking ones" = the unbelievers, naturally had to be killed in the battle. The whole episode is nothing more than a reshaping and elaboration of Aswad ibn 'Abd al-Asad al-Makhzūmī's story corresponding to the prevailing mind-set, an event neutral in itself which is supposed to have taken place at the beginning of the Battle of Badr.[20]

4. In view of the findings of our investigation so far, the traditions that make a correlation between the number of Badr fighters and the number of people in *Ṭālūt* take on greater significance. Let us remind ourselves that Gideon had three hundred men with him. The figure of 318 that is cited in one tradition calls to mind another biblical battle: Abrahams's battle with the four kings.[21] It is therefore questionable whether one can accept at all that the number of Muḥammad's fighters, if not 300, 313 , 314, or 318, comprised at least roughly this figure. In view of all the circumstances, it is very improbable that an exact counting of the combatants was undertaken immediately before or after the Battle of Badr.[22] The assumption that *Ṭālūt* was only ascribed a particular number of warriors in view of the Battle of Badr—an assumption that would presuppose the repercussions of history on a legend—has little to recommend it either from a religious, historical, or psychological perspective.[23] The oldest historical document pertaining to the battle, 'Urwa ibn Zubayr's letter to the Caliph 'Abd al-Malik,[24] mentions no figure, whereas such a significant historical detail, if it had really survived up until the time of Ṭabarī, would hardly have been omitted from 'Urwa's letter. We are forced, therefore, to admit that we have no indication at all of a particular number. The lists of the Badr fighters in Ibn Hishām and so on, and Ibn Sa'd's collections of biographies are scarcely more than documents testifying to a compromise between the roll-call of fighters at Badr, the meaning of which had been lost over the course of time, and the claims to participation in this first battle of Islam. A comparison of the different lists gives rise to the impression that the number had first of all to be supplemented with fictitious persons. Other families came along later who reflected on the honor of having an ancestor who had taken part in the Battle of Badr. Now others had to be deleted from the list. Since, of course, these new inclusions and deletions were not carried through consistently, contradictions appeared as we discover looking at the different lists.

The *ḥadīths* under discussion in the context of our investigation are typical of religious creations by analogy. "The prophet had to take on the inheritance of his predecessors and don their holy mantle."[25] He had to gain legitimacy by "repeating" acts of the old prophets. The *Ṭālūt-Badr ḥadīths* run through the whole hierarchy of such creations by analogy with which we are sufficiently familiar from the history of Islam and from the history of religion in general: from the free emulation of an event in the sense of a passed-on intellectual model and the imagining of supposed happenings that were half-known before being appropriately reshaped down to fact "recounted with relish" or "accentuated."[26]

Told first of all as *Maghāzī-ḥadīths* "for entertainment and instruction,"[27] their content was subject to manifold changes, until it was adopted by the "collective memory" and thus fixed at least in its broad outline. Its setting down in writing may have occurred at the same time, at which point they, by virtue of the necessary chain of mediators, passed into the reservoir of "authenticated," "historical" stories. These processes can still be clearly observed in the construction of our *ḥadīths*.[28]

Going further back, the letter of 'Urwa ibn Zubayr, which a kind twist of fate has preserved for us, allows us to trace the whole development of the Badr legends. The letter is reproduced here in its entirety to aid closer analysis. "Miracles" (i.e., events occurring outside the laws of cause and effect) which had already been accepted, that is, recognized as historical events, appear in spaced type; *Maghāzī* stories, which for 'Urwa and probably for others did not yet count as "confirmed" and which in 'Urwa's letter are introduced with the very reserved sounding words za'amu, are in italics.

> 'Alī ibn Naṣr ibn 'Alī and 'Abd al-Wārith ibn 'Abd aṣ-Ṣamd ibn 'Abd al-Wārith have passed on to us,—and indeed 'Alī from 'Abd aṣ-Ṣamd ibn 'Abd al-Wārith (etc.)—'Abd al-Wārith: my father passed on to me of Ābān al-Aṭṭār from Hishām ibn 'Urwa from 'Urwa himself that he wrote in the following way to 'Abd al-Malik ibn Marwān: "You wrote to me about Abū Sufyān and his expedition and asked me about the course it took. So it happened that Abū Sufyān was approaching from Syria with 70 horsemen from various clans of the Quraysh—they had all been merchants in Syria and together were bringing their money and wares home. They were announced

to the prophet and his companions. War had already prevailed between the two parties before and it had come to deathblows. Ibn al- Ḥaḍramī had been slain with others at Nahla and prisoners were taken by the Quraysh, among them some of the Banu-l-Mugira, for example, their client Ibn Kaysān. ‘Abdallāh ibn Jaḥsh and Wāqid, a protégé of the Banū ‘Adī ibn Ka‘b, along with other companions of the prophet, who had sent out this company with ‘Abdallāh ibn Jaḥsh, had attacked them. This encounter ignited the war between the prophet and the Quraysh. It was the first warlike clash between the two parties and it took place before the expedition of Abū Sufyān and his people to Syria. But Abū Sufyān and the Qurayshite horsemen, who were returning home with him from Syria, were approaching—according to this story—and were travelling along the coastal path. When the prophet heard of them, he called his companions together and told them of the treasures they were bringing with them and of their small number. So the Muslims set forth and were only out to get Abū Sufyān and the caravan; they thought of the booty that would fall to them and did not think that it would end in a great battle when they met them. Here the Koran verse that God revealed in relation to this: . . . but it was your wish to take possession of the one that was unarmed.[29] When Abū Sufyān heard that the prophet's companions wanted to obstruct his way, he sent word to the Quraysh: Muḥammad and his companions are blocking your way! Protect your wares! When the news reached the Quraysh—in Abū Sufyān's caravan the clans of Ka‘b ibn Lu'ayy were represented—the people of Mecca set out to give them protection in the form of the contingent of the Banū Ka‘b ibn Lu'ayy. Of the Banū ‘Āmir there was not a single one among them, with the exception of the Banū Mālik ibn Ḥisl. Neither the prophet nor his companions heard any news of the Quraysh contingent until he came to Badr. The Qurayshite horsemen's route had occasionally (also in the past) been the coastal road to Syria. So Abū Sufyān turned away from Badr and chose the coastal road: he feared an ambush at Badr. The prophet advanced, finally rested in the vicinity of Badr and sent Zubayr ibn al- ‘Awwām with a company of his companions to the water of Badr. But they did not think that the Quraysh had set forth against them. Meanwhile the prophet paused in prayer. Then some of the water-carriers of the Quraysh came to the water of Badr and as one of these, who was a black slave of the Banū Ḥajjāj, climbed down to the watering place, the company of those men whom the prophet had sent to the water with az-Zubayr took him captive. Several of the slave's fellows fled back to the Quraysh. But those men took him with them and brought him to God's envoy who was in his hut and asked him about Abū Sufyān and his people, for their only thought was that he belonged to them. But the slave began to talk of the Quraysh and which of them had set forth and about their chieftains and gave them correct information. But for them the news was the most unpleasant thing for they had only anticipated Abū Sufyān's caravan. Meanwhile the prophet prayed, performed the rakas and prostrations and saw and heard what was taking place with the slave. They began to strike him when he told them the Quraysh had come, called him a liar and said: 'You are just disowning Abū Sufyān and his people.' When they thus set to him with blows and asked him about Abū Sufyān and his people, about whom he knew nothing, since he was the water-carrier of the Quraysh, the slave began to say: 'Yes, it's Abū Sufyān,' whereas at this time the caravan was in fact below (towards the sea), as God said: You were encamped on this side of the valley and the unbelievers on the further side, with the caravan below etc.[30] When the slave said to them: 'it's the Quraysh that have desended on you,' they struck him and when he told them: 'it's Abū Sufyān,' they let him go. When the prophet saw their actions, he stood up from his prayers. He had heard what information he had given them. *People claim that God's envoy said: 'By he in whose hand I lie: you strike him when he tells the truth and let him go when he lies.' They said: 'He told us that the Quraysh have arrived.' He said: 'He speaks the truth; the Quraysh have indeed set forth in order to protect their caravan.'* He called the lad to him, questioned him and the latter gave him news of the Quraysh and said: 'I know nothing of Abū Sufyān.' Then the prophet asked him. 'How great is their army?' The other said: 'I don't know; by God! they are very many.' *People claim that the prophet asked: 'Who fed them the day before yesterday?' and the other named the man. Then the prophet asked: 'How many camels did he slaughter for them?' The other said: '9 camels.'—'And who fed them yesterday?' The other named the man (once again). 'How many did he slaughter for them?'—'10 camels.' Then they claim that the prophet said: 'The army is between 900 and 1,000 strong.'* In fact the Quraysh contingent at the time numbered 950 men.[31] Hereupon, the prophet went away, descended to the water, filled up the watering holes and arranged his companions in battle rows before them, whereupon the enemy army advanced on him. When God's envoy climbed down to Badr, he said: 'This is their battleground.' The enemies found that

> the prophet had arrived at Badr before them and encamped there. *When they attacked him, the prophet is supposed, so people claim, to have said: 'That's the Quraysh, they come from there with their cries and their high spirits, to fight you and to brand your envoy as a liar. O God, I beg you for that which you promised me!'* When they approached, he went to meet them, scattered sand in their faces and God sent them fleeing. Before the prophet clashed with them, a horseman of Abū Sufyān and of the caravan, which was with him, had come to them (with the demand) that they turn back. The caravan, which the Quraysh had requested to turn back, was (at that time) in Juḥfah. (But) they said: 'By God, we will not turn back before we have come to Badr. We will stay there for three days and those of the inhabitants of Ḥijāz will see who will come to meet us. Forsooth, no Arab will see us and our might and then (still) want to fight with us.' It was they of whom God speaks: those who left their homes elated with insolence and vainglory. . . .[32] Then they and the prophet met one another and God bestowed victory on his envoy and ruined the leaders of the unbelievers and delivered the faithful from them."

The letter was obviously written with the aim of countering the *Maghāzī* stories in circulation about the events leading up to the Battle of Badr with an account that corresponded with the facts. At the same time the author of the letter uses quotations several times to stress that the events accord with the Koran and the occurrences it presupposes (or appears to presuppose). Even if the Battle of Badr itself is not therefore at the center of 'Urwa's preoccupations, being treated to a certain extent as of secondary importance, the type of "historical" details that he brings to bear on it are nevertheless very significant. First of all, we find the two miracles, which are given as historical facts. They concern—what is almost self-evident—the "miraculous" outcome of the battle, the element around which the construction of the legends first of all crystallized. The other unconfirmed anecdotes that are recounted are so colorless and uninteresting that one asks oneself how they found their way into the letter. Moreover, it contains an anecdote aimed at explaining sura VIII, 49, but with scarcely any details that might warrant being taken seriously. Might not the reason for this fact be that in Medina and generally at the time of 'Urwa's letter, people only paid attention to historical anecdotes inasfar as they served to elucidate passages of the Koran,[33] that otherwise people no longer knew of many details and, on the other hand, did not have very many "authenticated" details of the Battle of Badr? In itself it appears improbable that in the second third of the first century AH people did not know more about the Battle of Badr, the first and most important battle of Islam, but in fact people in the first period of Islam appear to have had little interest in the history of the prophet, unless it was required by the Koran or was necessary for its elucidation.[34] The lacuna that quickly formed around this was then filled by stories in the style of *ayyām al-'arab* and of popular legend. That the motifs for the latter were often provided, inter alia, by the Old Testament, I believe to have demonstrated here.

Notes

1. [Original title: Hans Mzik, "Die Gideon-Saul-Legende und die überlieferung der Schlacht bei Badr. Ein Beitrag zur ältesten Geschichte des Islam, in *WZKM* 29 (1915): 371–83. Anonymous translation. Footnotes in square brackets by I. W.]

2. Ibn Hishām, p. 516, line 3 from the bottom [Ibn Hishām, *Sīrat Rasūl Allāh*, ed. F. Wüstenfeld. 2 vols. (Göttingen, 1858–60]) The poem, which incidentally had already been declared apocryphal by the majority of Arab literary historians (l. c. lines 2, 3: *wa-'aktharū 'ahlu l-'ilmi bil-shi'ri yunkiru-hā*), bears all the hallmarks of later composition.

3. III, 1, Biographien der mekkanischen Kämpfer Muḥammads in der Schlacht bei Badr, etc. (Leiden, 1904). [Ibn Sa'd, *Kitāb al-ṭabaqāt al-kabīr*, ed. E. Sachau et al., 9 vols. (Leiden, 1904–1940)].

4. III, 2, Biographen der medinischen Kämpfer, etc.

5. *wa-biḍ'ah*

6. Ṭabarī I, pp. 1296–99, 1357, 1358 [Ṭabarī, *Ta'rīkh al-rusul wa-l-mulūk*, ed. M. J. de Goeje et al., 15 vols. (Leiden, 1879–1901)] ; *Tafsīr* II, p. 373 and following [*Jāmi' al-bayān fī tafsīr āy al-Qur'ān*, 30 vols. (Cairo, AH 1321)] ; Ibn Hishām, p. 506; *Wāqidī*—Wellhausen [J. Wellhausen, *Muhammad in Medina, das ist Vakidi's Kitab al Maghazi in verkürzer deutscher Wiedergabe* (Berlin, 1882)], p. 83 and following: 313, pp. 66 and 68: 313 + 4 (servants who had taken part in the battle but received none of the spoils).

7. Allegedly passed on by al-Barā' (Ṭabarī I, pp. 1296–99), who, because of his

youth with several others, was excluded by Muḥammad from the expedition to Badr.

8. Koran II, 250–52. That Muḥammad mixes together Gideon's campaign against the Midian (Judges 7:2–8), Saul's campaign against Goliath (I Sam. 17:1 and following) and perhaps also the episode in I Sam. 14:24 and following is perhaps less surprising than it might first appear, given that the Gideon and Saul legends do in fact display many parallels (see also Jensen, Gilgamesch-Epos I, p. 722 [P. Jensen, *Das Gilgamesch-Epos in der weltliteratur*, Band I (Strasburg, 1906)].

9. Ibn Hishām [IH henceforth], pp. 428, 429; *Wāqidī*—Wellhausen [W-W, henceforth], p. 40; Ṭabarī. [Ṭ, henceforth] I, pp. 1292, 1293. With respect to this story, in order to avoid misunderstanding, one should again underline what is actually self-evident, that in the development of each story other series of motifs have also been at work. Thus the boulder "whose fragments struck every house" appears to refer back to Koran VIII, 23. One should bear in mind that the eighth sura in its entirety *(bi-'asrihā* Ibn Hishām, p. 476, 6) is supposed to relate to the Battle of Badr. The rain of stones demanded by the Meccans had, however, somehow—at least in the dream—to be fulfilled as a punishment for the infidel (see also Koran XI, 84). Later the story evolved still further: Amr ibn al-Āṣ even saw a piece of the stone in his house (W-W, p. 40).

10. IH, p. 437; W-W, p. 45; Ṭ, I, p. 1306.

11. Judges 7:13.

12. The people of Israel being farmers.

13. IH, p. 435, 436; W-W, p. 47; Ṭ, I, pp. 1302, 1303.

14. A typical gloss from a later period. The same goes for the name of the Shaykh, which IH likewise knows.

15. Regarding the tasks of the 'Akid in relation to looting see A. Jaussen, *Coutumes des Arabes au Pays de Moab* (Paris, 1908), p. 166f.

16. IH, p. 437; W-W, p. 44; Ṭ, I, p. 1305.

17. Judges 7:10f.

18. IH, p.44; W-W, p. 51; Ṭ, I, pp. 1311, 1312. *Ḥizām*'s horse is a later addition.

19. W-W, l. c.

20. IH, pp. 442, 443; W-W, p. 53; Ṭ, I, pp. 1316, 1317.

21. Genesis 14:14.

22. The Koran III, 11 and VIII, 66, 67 also indicate that the exact number of Muslims at Badr was not known. The latter passage is certainly not only a promise for the future along the lines of 3, Leviticus 26:8, but also a reference to the present, including the Battle of Badr (*'al'āna khaffafa l-lāhu 'ankum*). We do not know the exact number of Meccans at Badr either, nor the number of Abū Sufyān's horsemen.

'Urwa speaks of 70, IH, p. 427, of 30 or 40.

23. It is also a matter of concern that we know the precise names of many of the Badr fighters, but otherwise know nothing, or at least nothing that warrants being taken seriously in historical terms. This gives rise to the strong impression that the names were invented.

24. Ṭ, I, pp. 1284–88. Inadequately translated by Sprenger III, pp. 142–44. The letter is perhaps only one part of a longer missive to the Caliph, which may have contained Muḥammad's story and which is passed on to us piecemeal by Ṭ. in various passages of his work. See for example Ṭ, I, pp. 1180, 1224 .

25. J. Horovitz in Islam V, p. 42.

26. To this last group belongs perhaps the report that Muḥammad had three standard-bearers in his army for the three groups of which it was composed: for the *Muhājirūn*, the Aus, and the Khazraj (W-W, p. 50). Gideon's throng also consisted of three companies (Judges 7:16). However, alongside this exist traditions that speak of only two standards (IH, pp. 432, 433; *Ṭ*, I, p. 1297).

27. See Goldziher, Muham. Studien II, p. 153f, 206f. [I. Goldziher, *Muhammedanische Studien*. 2 vols. (Halle, 1888–90).]

28. Regarding the distortion of the factual substratum in the oral tradition see K. v. Roretz, "Zur Psychologie des Gerüchts," in Ö. R. XLIV, p. 205f.

29. Koran, VIII, 7 (Dawood).

30. Koran, VIII, 43 (Dawood).

31. This sentence is perhaps not a remark by 'Urwa, but a later gloss. Incidentally, the Quraysh were, even if one accepts the traditional figure of 950, certainly not as strong in Badr as before, since in the meantime the Banū Zuhra and the Banū 'Adī ibn Ka'b Adi ibn Ka'b had turned back (IH, p. 438; W-W, pp. 45, 46; Ṭ. I, p. 1307). Sprenger III, p. 118 footnote, estimates them only as 600 in number and refers to Koran III, 11.

32. Koran VIII, 49.

33. It is not possible in this context to go into the question of the extent to which the Koran was generative of "history," i.e., whether and which stories arose in order to illustrate passages of the Koran, however tempting it might be to examine to what extent the Koran and *Tafsīr* on the one hand and popular legend on the other hand, which emerged from different circles and with different tendencies, contributed to the Badr tradition and so created an important chapter of the *Sīra*. I would just like to point out in passing that the story of Muḥammad throwing sand in the faces of the Quraysh is unhistorical (it is, moreover, recounted on another occasion). The anecdote was only invented in order to illustrate Koran VIII, 17 (*wamā ramayta*

'iḍ ramayta). And wrongly so, since this passage is nothing other than the repetition of a previously executed thought (*falam taqtulūhum walākinna—l-lāha qatalahum*) expressed with different words, and therefore to be translated: "it was not you who shot" (*'ani l-qawṣi, al- ḥajara, al-sahma*), etc. The "throwing of sand" was inserted by arbitrary *Tafsīr*.

34. See also I. Goldziher l. c. p. 207.

2.2

Some Literary Enigmas of Koranic Inspiration[1]

A. Regnier

The Koran abounds in passages that make rather overt and often very curious use of the Bible; rare are the books of the Old and New Testament that have no echo in Koranic inspiration, leave no trace in its Arabic expression. However, these traces are almost never in the faithful form of a direct quotation, as in sura XXI, 105, where we read: "And verily We have written in the Psalms [*Zabūr*], after the Reminder: My righteous slaves will inherit the earth"—these last words in fact come from Psalm 37:29 ("The righteous shall inherit the land").[2] Even here the correspondence is not rigorously exact, however. The Arabic gives us "My servants, the righteous, shall inherit the earth" [Arabic: *'anna l-'arḍa yariṯuhā 'ibādiya l-ṣālihūna*]; the Hebrew Psalm "the righteous will inherit the land" [Hebrew: *ṣedīqīm yirašū 'ereṣ*]. So we may conceive that the Hebrew text inspired the Koran only through approximate versions and that the linguistic kinship more or less explains the presence on both sides of two identical radicals [stems].

Outside this privileged space, the biblical influences on the Koran are transmitted through implicit and inexact quotations, by general references to the Torah, to the Psalms, to the Gospel, to the Book, through the transformation and often the distortion of stories, scenes, sentences, and proper names. I cannot summarize these parallels here, though Goldziher and others have done so.

But I must insist on the fact that these contacts with the Bible—often operating through different versions, apocrypha, Talmudic and Christian legends, Gnostic and heretical deviations—cannot be explained by conscious, erudite, and writerly composition, which is of, above all, a visual kind. Instead, one must suppose the intervention of a more total psychology, both more alive and more primitive, and then one must accept the possbility of rather unexpected phenomena of an auditory or verbal-motor kind, or else the imaginative and mnemonic fermentation of the subconscious.

Did this elaboration occur principally in the personal mentality of Muhammad? One might accept this hypothesis without excluding secondary sites, if one thinks for example of Umayya b. Abi Ṣalt, the Christian poet, or the famous monk Baḥīrā, or else Waraqa b. Nawfal, the cousin of Khadīja.

Concerning the latter, we read in Ibn Hishām that he was Christian, that he read books, that he had listened to the people of the Torah and the Gospel. And moreover, a hadith related by Bukhārī, according to 'Ā'isha, states that he made himself a Christian "in the time of ignorance," was writing the Hebrew book, was writing the Gospel in Hebrew, what Allah wanted him to write. The sense of this passage is undoubtedly that he knew how to read Hebrew writing [Arabic: *wa-kāna yaktubu l-kitāba l-'ibrāniyya*] and that he wrote in Arabic based on the Hebrew Gospel; but the meaning of the second part might be also that he was writing extracts from the Hebrew Gospel, or else that he was writing in Hebrew extracts from the Gospel [Arabic: *fa-yaktubu mina l-'injīli bil-'ibrāniyyati*]. Despite the vagueness of the information, this confirms the possibility of a fusion in an Arabic head contemporaneous with Muhammad's of certain biblical Hebrew texts with their Arabic equivalents.

Moreover, can anybody tell us that this head is not that of Muhammad himself? He had spent time with the Jews; he had a notion of spoken Hebrew, as we see in sura II, 98 (and parallels), where he knows that *naẓara* [Arabic = to see, perceive with the eyes, view, eye] translates ראה [Hebrew: *r 'h* = to see, etc.] and where he warns against *rā'ā* [Arabic] who profits from the ambiguity between רעע [Hebrew: *r ' '*][3] = broke to pieces and ראה [Hebrew, *r ' h*] = to see.[4]

Regarding the sometimes narrowly verbal character of these processes, we have a remarkable example—not from the Hebrew but from the Greek—in sura LXI, 6: "And when Jesus son of Mary said: 'O Children of Israel! Lo!

I am the messenger of Allah unto you, confirming that which was (revealed) before me in the Torah, and bringing good tidings of a messenger who cometh after me, whose name is the Praised One [*Aḥmad*].'" One sees here how the promise of Paraclete, John 15:26, is exploited. The name, a synonym of Muhammad, renders the Greek παράκλητος [parakletos], which has caused such problems for diverse translators, and which a Syriac or an Arabic version managed to render as "praised" or "illustrious," especially since some scholars suppose that Greek copies carried the variant παράκλυτος, "illustrious" [paraklutos]. In any case, it is upon this name that the whole application of the Koran is centered, and it is probably the principal reason why "the people of the book" are so often accused by it of having misunderstood or corrupted the texts announcing the coming of the Prophet.

Whatever the confusions reigning in the Koran and the Hadith relative to the language and nature of the biblical books, this should not prevent us from eventually discerning in the Koran before our eyes some literary enigmas whose key lies in biblical memories and even in one word or another from these biblical passages that have meandered in obscure and tortuous ways to the point of inspiring the author. We are going to investigate some cases of this kind.

I

1) Sura III, 96–97: "Lo! the first Sanctuary appointed for mankind was that at *Bakka*, a blessed place, a guidance to the peoples; Wherein are plain memorials (of Allah's guidance); the place where Abraham (*maqām Ibrāhīm*). . . ." Then a pilgrimage to this house of worship is recommended. It is acknowledged that *Bakka* equals *Makkah*, Mecca. The commentary of the *Jalālayn*, which represents current opinion, gives as the motive for this alteration the symbolic attachment to the root **bakka*, to crush, "Because Mecca crushes (or breaks) the neck of the proud"! Some philologists believe *Bakka* is a dialect pronunciation that confuses the two labials *b* and *m*. So be it, but it is strange that the other place where Mecca is mentioned in the Koran (sura XLVIII, 24), it takes the form Makka (in a passage concerning the conquest of the city).

It so happens that our *Bakka*, which one finds a single time in the Koran, in a context relating to the site of worship and pilgrimage, corresponds to a biblical word *Baca* [Hebrew בָּכָא, *bāḵā'*], which one finds a single time in the Bible, in Psalms 84:6–7, precisely in a song of pilgrimage! If we look more closely, we find this: "Happy are those whose strength is in you, in whose heart are the highways to Zion. As they go through the valley of Baca, they make it a place of springs; the early rain also covers it with pools." Thus the pilgrims arrive in the courts of Zion.

Thus there is a similarity of theme, on the one hand a Koranic hapax and on the other a biblical hapax, and finally, assonance of these two hapax. Let us add some secondary resemblances. First, the Hebrew בְּרָכוֹת *berāḵōṯ* some words after בָּכָא *bāḵā*, echoes *mubārakan* مُبَارَكًا [A] immediately after *bakkata* بَكَّةَ [A]. Then, the Greek version translated מעין [H] *m'yn* (*ma'yān*) (*spring, source*), as τόπος, [topos] having read מעון [H] *mā'ōn* (dwelling); so does the Syriac, and the Vulgate with its "*in valle lacrymarum, in loco quem posuit*" [in the vale of tears, in the place which he hath set . . .]: so precisely does the Koran offer us a few words after *bakkah* بَكَّة [A] (and making the latter more precise) its *maqām Ibrāhīm*, venerated site and monument of the sacred enclosure: *maqām* reflects τόπος, *mā'ōn* [H], dwelling.

Here are a few more observations: the versions translated *hbk'* [*ha-bāḵā*] הבכא [H] as if it were *hbkh* הבכה [H],[8] moreover found in some manuscripts, "valley of tears." But in order for *bk'* בכא [9] [H] to stick to the Arabic parallel **bk'* (to be deprived of milk, water, tears), it would signify on the contrary drought, supposing that *bk'* בכא [H] is a poetic and not a geographical term. In any case, someone reading the Hebrew could respect all the originality of this בָּכָא *bāḵā* [H] and keep its form and pronunciation as for a proper name, without either translating it or interpreting it. And, despite the difference in root, the word *bakkah* بَكَّة [10] [A] resembles it as a proper name with the same assonance.

Some will maintain that all this is pure chance, in which case it must be admitted that chance creates singular coincidences. But since we are on the subject, there is something even more strange that we cannot accept as a product of chance: while *b'mq hbk' –be-'emaq ha-bāḵā* בעמק הבכא [11][H] (*in valle Baca*) corresponds to *Bakkah* بكة [12] [A] for the characteristic element *Baca*, it happens that in Sura XLVIII, 24, it is the other element, to wit *b'mq –be-'emaq* [H] that corresponds to *bi-baṭni m.* ببطن م[13] [A] (the valley of Mecca), there where *makkah* [A] receives its normal *m* [letter *mīm*]! But we could also suggest that the two Koranic passages are allied in a certain dependence on the Hebrew verbal complex.

And so we retain the word Baca [H: בָּכָא *bāḵā*] as the radiant term of this first example.

2) In our second example, the star term will be *sullām* [H, סֻלָּם *sullām* ladder).

We read in sura XCVII, 1–5: "Lo! We revealed it on the Night of Power. Ah, what will convey unto thee what the Night of Power is! The Night of Power is better than a thousand months. The angels and the Spirit descend therein, by the permission of their Lord, with all decrees. (That night is) Peace [*salāmun*] until the rising of the dawn." This night of the decree immediately evokes the night of Jacob at Bethel, notably Genesis 28:12–13: "And he dreamed that there was a ladder [*sullām*] set up on the earth, the top of it reaching to heaven; and the angels of God were ascending and descending on it. And the Lord stood beside him."

Let us note parallels such as "the angels of God" = "angels and the Spirit." (We will set aside for the moment a possible influence here of the temptation of Jesus in which the angels serve him before the Spirit pushes him to Galilee.) Let us continue: "ascending and descending" = "descend"; "And the Lord stood beside him" = "by the permission of their Lord, with all decrees."

But there is something not quite right with the Koran's version: the absence of the ladder [H, *sullām*; A: *sullam(un)*], though it is there in a certain way, through the word of the same assonance [A: *salām*]. But, for the sake of the meaning, what is "peace" doing here, this peace that is night until dawn? The ladder on which the angels move until the morning—(Gen 28:16) "when Jacob awoke from his sleep" after the revelation of his destiny and the vision of the heavenly ladder—is missing in the Koran as a way of enabling the descent of the angels and the spirit who bear the revelation and the destiny until the break of day. And *sālam* in this theme seems out of bounds. Arabic commentary is reduced to maintaining a position that is pure fantasy: this night is characterized by health and peace, it asserts, because salvation multiplies by the passing of angels who salute each believer!

We will not go so far as to pretend that the primitive text might have carried *sullam* [A]. This word, making a brusque appearance and an incomprehensible allusion, might rather naturally have been the victim of its dynamism as the star and polarizing term; such a term, which works on the author's subconscious, is thrown out without sufficient attention: it has the bad luck to be evinced by a banal term that is its analogue, and thus *salām* [A] might have replaced *sullam* [A]. One might add that the latter word appears twice in the Koran: at LII, 38, where it concerns climbing a ladder to learn celestial secrets, and at VI, 35, where Muhammad is pushed to climb a ladder to the skies to bring back a convincing Sign. In both places, the ladder corresponds to Jacob's—and to the ladder that, by pure hypothesis, correctors might have replaced in our S. XCVII with *salām* [A], such a frequent word in the Koran.

But let us remain on firmer ground and argue simply that *salām* [A] was imported here by the occult and indecipherable influence of the biblical *sullām* and the koranic *sullam*, with the latter depending on the former.

3) In Sura LIV, we are reminded of the story of Noah and the flood. Let us read in particular verse 11 onward: "Then opened We the gates of heaven with pouring water / And caused the earth to gush forth springs, so that the waters met for a predestined purpose. / And We carried him upon a thing of planks and nails, / That ran (upon the waters) in Our sight, as *a reward for him who was rejected.* / And verily We left it as a token; but is there any that remembereth?" The words in italics are *jazā'an li-man kāna kufira*. They signify that Noah, saved by the ark, found compensation for being rejected by his entourage (v. 9). But another koranic reading, instead of having the passive *kufira* [A], moreover favored by neighboring rhymes (vv. 12, 14, 15 in *ir*, but 13 in *ur*), gives the active *kafara*; the meaning then becomes "in punishment for those who did not believe," that is to say, they were drowned while Noah was saved.

How can we explain this hesitation? Because in the Koran *kafara* occurs frequently, whereas *kufira* is found only here. It is a hapax. And moreover, the syntax, without a reflexive pronoun, is unexpected. While the active forms of this verb abound, one encounters only two passive constructions apart from the case under discussion: in III, 111, "And whatever good they do, they will not be denied the meed thereof" [*fa-lan tukfarū-hu*]; and in IV, 139, "When ye hear the revelations of Allah rejected and derided" [*yukfaru bi-hā*]. So, the latter has a passive impersonal with *bi* as sole object; while the former has a passive personal with the accusative of the second object, the first object of the active becoming the subject of the passive, and the verb *kafara* is then supposed to govern two accusatives: that of the person who is denied and that of the thing that is denied him.

Hence if we understand our *kufira* in the passive impersonal, one would expect *li-man kāna kufira bi-hi*; if we understand it in the passive personal, it would respond to an active voice governing not both accusatives but one, specifically an animate being. Does this active voice exist in the Koran? There is not one single example of the form *kafara*, to which we have confined our examination, the exact counterpart of our passive *kufira*. Everywhere it is used absolutely in the sense of being unbelieving or ungrateful (II, 96; II, 120, 254, 260; III, 92; V, 15, 19, 76, 77; XXIV, 54; XXX, 43; XXXI, 11, 22; XXXV, 37; LIX, 16). There are two exceptions: XVI, 108, where it is constructed with *bi-* and the complement of an animate object (to deny Allah), and XIX, 80, with *bi-* and the complement of an inanimate object (to deny our verses). Nowhere is there an active voice parallel to our *kufira* understood as a passive personal voice; in other words, one does not find a construction like "someone *kafara* someone"; therfore one cannot expect in the passive the construction "such a *kufira*" nor in our passage, *man kāna kufira*.

If *kufira* is thus a hapax in form and an anomaly in syntax, should we not prefer in its stead the lesson *kafara* that was offered us? On the contrary, we believe that *kufira* should be maintained. Not because of the rhyme, which is often undemanding in the Koran and which is often made, as here, in *ar* like *kafara* [A]; note that v. 29 *'aqara* rhymes *ir* and *ur*. Nor for the external and debatable reasons of reading traditions. Nor because in principle one ought to favor the most singular lesson *kufira*. Nor because *jazā'an li-* (a compensation favorable to someone) would be more suited, by avoiding the detour of irony, for a recompense than for a punishment. Nor because the true meaning of √kfr would here be supposedly "to cover," which would signify that Noah was covered by the ark: according to the text it is not important that he was covered by a roof but that he was carried on a solid raft.

So, then, why do we advocate conserving *kufira*? Because it arises from the influence of the inductive Hebrew term in the corresponding passage in the Bible, Genesis 6:14: "So make yourself an ark of cypress wood; make rooms in it and coat it with pitch inside and out." The ark of a resinous wood *gōp̄er* [H] composed of cells corresponds to the Koranic (thing) of planks and nails; and you will coat it with pitch *wə-ḵāp̄artā 'ōṯāh bakkōp̄er* [H] has no parallel, but *kōp̄er* [H], stressed by the regent of the same root *ḵāp̄artā* [H], and joined to the preceding *gōp̄er* [H], has induced a kind of Koranic paronymy *kufira* [A]. The word *gōp̄er* [H] is a biblical hapax (Assyr. *kupru*); it is accompanied by another hapax *kōp̄er* [H] (Assyr. *Kupru*, Arabic *kufr* [A], bitume); these two conjugated hapaxes have produced a koranic hapax *kufira* [A] in a koranic context of the same theme as their biblical context!

Of course, nothing in the form or syntax has changed, nor in the meaning of *kufira* [A]. But we now understand why this Koranic phenomenon is quite authentic; it proceeds from the inductive current emanating from *gōp̄er* and *kōp̄er* (*kprt*). Could anyone invoke chance for this third example?!

4) Sura XLVI contains a passage that appears anodyne and yet is quite difficult. Here are the literal verses 26 and 27:

[Regnier's French translation: Nous avons déjà détruit les villes autour de vous, et nous avions aménagé les signes afin qu'ils se convertissent. Et pourquoi ne les ont-ils pas aidés, ceux qu'ils prirent en dehors d'Allah *comme offrande dieux* (*l-laḏīna –t-takhaḏū min dūni-l-lāhi qurbānan 'ālihatan*)? Bien au contraire, ils (ces dieux) s'évanouirent loin d'eux; et c'était là leur illusion et ce qu'ils forgeaient faussement!"]

[Arberry] "And we destroyed the cities about you, and We turned about the signs, that haply they would return. Then why did those not help them that they had taken to themselves as mediators, gods apart from God? Not so; but they went astray from them, and that was their calumny, and what they had been forging. "

[Bell] "We destroyed the towns round about you, and We turned the signs about, if mayhap they might return. Why helped them not those whom they had chosen apart from Allah as neighbours[5] [*Qurbān* taken as plural of *qārib*, neighbour] gods [*'ālihatan*]? [Arabic: *l-laḍīna –t-takhaḍū min dūni-l-lāhi qurbānan 'ālihatan*] Nay, they went astray from them; that was their lie, and what they had been inventing."

The sense is that the ancient cities were, after warning, punished by Allah and not saved by the false gods that they had chosen for themselves. But the italicized words [*comme offrande dieux,* as "mediators" (Arberry) or as "Neighbors" (Bell)] cannot be satisfactorily explained. The conscientious but often debatable French translation in the Montet edition gives: "those they had taken for gods besides Allah (and which they had put) into his entourage"; but this interpretation does not take into account that *qurbānan* comes before *'ālihatan*, and it attributes to it the meaning "entourage, as for a prince." Goldschmidt's very faithful German version reads: "those who prayed outside Allah as offering and gods"; thus the meaning of *qurbān* as offering is kept, but without obtaining proper sense, unless one gratuitously lends *qurbân* (and *Opfer*) the acceptance of "a person to whom one sacrifices and makes offering."

The Arabic commentary already cited interprets as follows: "they took, outside Allah, as something that would bring them close to Him, gods who are idols." And from the syntactical standpoint the commentary explains: "those whom they had taken as an approach to Allah, to wit as gods," where the verb "take" has as first complement the pronoun and for second *qurbānan* and *''ālihatan* as permutative of the latter. One sees how all this remains awkward, just as much for the meaning as for the place granted *qurbānan* Let us ask first if *qurbān* figures elsewhere. Sura III,179, concerns an offering consumed by fire; Sura V, 30 refers to the sacrifice offered by Cain and Abel. By this route we return to the accepted meaning of "offering," which in no way supports the Arabic commentary and which accords with Goldschmidt's translation, though unfortunately stripped of meaning. And here we are once again in the presence of a hapax—not of form (since it is found twice elsewhere) but of meaning.

What is this meaning? Earlier in the same sura, we come upon a text on another theme, relating to filial duties. Here is verse 17: "And whoso saith unto his parents: Fie upon you both! [*'uffin lakumā*] Do you threaten me that I shall be brought forth (again) when generations before me have passed away? And they twain cry until Allah for help (and say): Woe unto thee! [*wayla-ka*] Believe! Lo! The promise of Allah is true. But he saith: This is naught save fables of the men of old." Parents want to convert their child but he will not listen to reason. It is the only dialogue in the Koran on this subject. There are two interjections, one of contempt, the other a threat. The former [*'uffin*] is also found in XXI, 67, in which adorers of false gods are blamed; and also in XVII, 23, a verse that reads: "Thy Lord hath decreed, that ye worship none save Him, and (that he show) kindness to parents. If one of them or both of them attain old age with thee, say not 'fie' [*'uffin*] unto them nor repulse them, but speak unto them a gracious word." This text is a reworking of XLVI, 16 and is inspired by the Gospel of Mark 7:11: "But you say that if a man should say to his father or mother 'What help you received from me is Korban [κορβαν] or gift of God'"; this term, which contrasts, under the color of devotion, the child's avarice with his filial duties is kept in the Aramaic form; it expresses a taboo in a brusque and energetic way, as an interjection or an imprecation.

To this word—the equivalent of "anathema" in its semantic evolution, become a cry of contempt or execration—our two Koranic texts, XVI, 24, and XLVI, 16, have added as a pendant the interjection *'uffin!* But in Sura XLVI the latent and subconscious influence of the inductive term κορβαν is not exhausted by this first and inadequate expression [*'uff*]; it has worked belatedly and some verses later, in verse 27, it is exercised, in the exact form of κορβαν in the Arabic *qurbānan*.

Now everything becomes clear: the *qurbān* of XLVI, 27 is a term of more or less magic malediction, exploiting the perjorative nuance taken by κορβαν, especially in the Gnostic writings, and designates the idols as an abomination, an anathema. The passage might therefore be translated: "those who outside Allah have taken as anathema, as false gods."

In summary, a biblical hapax, also an Aramaic hapax of the Gospel, has served as a term inducing the koranic hapax (of meaning) in verse 27, through a slightly earlier koranic context (verse 16), itself of Gospel inspiration and bearing an initial imprint (in *'uffin*) of the inductive term. By this route a difficulty of koranic exegesis gets a fitting solution. Naturally, anyone who has refused to follow us this far is free to admit only an influence from the biblical κορβαν in order to determine at this precise point in the Koran (XLVI, 27) the strange appearance of a *qurbānan* from which one would always reserve the definitive acceptance.

Before gathering these points for a conclusion, it is important to note two things. First, when we begin from the Hebrew or Aramaic (Greek) text of the Bible, we equally allow for an intermediary, whether Syriac or Aramaic or Arabic—in short, a Semitic version that would have reflected phonetically the biblical forms that we have placed in contact with certain literary phenomena of the Koran. Second, something more is at work here than the simple problem of exoticisms in the Koran, understanding thereby Hebraicisms, Aramaicisms, and other Semitisms and Hellenisms; consequently, it involves something other than realizing that Abraham has become *Ibrāhīm*, and that εὐαγγέλιον or διάβολος has given rise to *Injīl* and *Iblīs* (proper names); that *furqān* and *šekīnah* have been kept while changing meaning (technical nouns); or that אֶרֶץ and שָׁמַיִם correspond to *'arḍ* and *samā'* (common Semitic vocabulary). What we think we have discerned might really be formulated thus: it seems that certain "Hebrew" terms that, apart from proper names, are found in the Bible, are hapax, stellar or strange words, or especially evocative and synthetic words, that may have played an inductive role in the inspiration of the Koran, bringing or modifying certain phrases and certain expressions to the point of giving rise to Arabic homonyms or paronyms. Finding the inductive term would provide the key to the exegesis of certain passages.

II

We now refer to cases where the verbal tenor of the biblical passages has influenced that of the Koran, yet without it resulting in creating a phonetic resemblance between the koranic and biblical terms. This motor verbalism has played out more than once. We will confine ourselves to two examples borrowed from the New Testament.

1) In sura LXXV:6 ff we read: "He asketh: When will be this Day of Resurrection?/ *But when sight is confounded* [*bariqa l-baṣaru* [lit. *sight*

struck by lightning]/ And the moon is eclipsed/ And sun and moon are united, / On that day man will cry: ? Whither to flee? '" One recognizes the influence of Biblical eschatological descriptions, for example Mark 13:24 ff. The italicized expression especially corresponds to I Corinthians 15:52 [εν ριπη οφθαλμου/in the twinkling of an eye], and to Matthew 17:24 and 24:27 [ωσπερ γαρ η αστραπη/for as the lightning] It synthesizes the two elements, the lightning and the eye-blink in the somewhat hybrid formula: [*bariqa l-baṣaru*]. *Baraqa* is regularly said of clouds, the sky, etc. that shines with lightning; in the derived form *bariqa* it has given: to be stupefied, precluded by the dazzle; the same as *barq*, lightning, is close to *barqatun*, consternation. We have here this derived form [*bariqa*] applied not to a man but to his sight, to his eye [l-*baṣaru*].

Among the numerous eschatological passages of the first Meccan suras—including our sura LXXV—this is the only time the detail of the lightning and the confounded sight appears. Among later texts, sura II, 18 mentions a cloud that contains darkness, thunder and lightning, and in the following verse lightning snatches away sight [*al-barqu yakhṭafu 'abṣāra-hum*] from the disbelievers who walk by its light: this text is moral, not eschatological, and although more recent than sura LXXV, it can certainly not be considered as a decomposition of the formula examined in sura LXXV. With respect to the purely physical and astonishing phenomenon, one finds in XXIV, 43 a more analytical formula: "the flashing of His lightning all but snatcheth away the sight." Other uses of *barq* (XIII:13, XXX:23) are without interest. As for our expression "in the blink of an eye," it is found again only in XXVII, 40, in the form "before thy gaze returneth to thee" [*qabla 'an yartadda 'ilay-ka ṭarfu-ka*], to mark the rapidity of a movement, but without the least eschatological allusion.

In these circumstances, the singularity of the formula of LXXV, 7 allows us—if not constrains us—to think that it would lump together the two Biblical details (*sicut fulgur—in ictu oculi*): on the one hand, the rapid light of the lightning bolt that crosses the sky, and on the other hand, the beating or dazzling of the eye: to this effect *al-baṣaru* has become the subject of √*brq* vocalized *bariqa*.

2) In sura II, 168, we read: "He hath forbidden you only carrion, and blood, and swineflesh, and that which hath been immolated to (the name of)

any other than Allah. . . ." These four articles correspond in number to those of the Assembly of Jerusalem (Acts 15:20 and 15:28–29). The order of the enumeration differs, though, in the Koran and in each of the two passages in Acts. As for the nature of these interdictions, the third (pork meat) that translates the Jewish usage agreed to by Muhammad, is not found in Acts; on the other hand, the list there speaks of πορνεία / fornication, unchastity; and what the Koran expresses in the tormented form [*mā 'ahilla li-ghayri l-lāhi*], "that which has been immolated to any other than Allah," perhaps represents better the είδωλόθυτα [sacrificing to idols] of Acts 15:28 than the αλισγηματων των ειδωλων of 15:20 [pollutions of the idols].

One is inclined to ask what became of the interdiction of πορνεία in Acts, while the rest (completed by the interdiction of pork meat) has so thoroughly influenced the Koran's quartet. Even the forbidding of είδωλόθυτα [sacrifying to idols] has been maintained, in an apparently obscure form, since it was certainly not in season [commonly done] among Muhammad's entourage, to whom it is addressed (verse 167 "O ye who believe!" Can we acknowledge that the inductive current coming from Acts might have lost the Arabic equivalent for πορνεία? No, and in effect if we read a few lines above (verse 164), here is what we find: "[Satan] enjoineth upon you only the evil and the foul [*wal-faḥshā'i*]." This is a moral text that belongs to the theme of verse 168 and allows us to reconstitute the bundle of four articles, made dissimilar by the substitution of the forbidden pork. This one separated from the three others [*al-faḥshā* = πορνεία] is thus not too far away, encased in a preparatory phrase several lines above. It would be foolhardy to assert that its existence and its proximity are the pure effect of chance! All the more so in that the term *faḥshā*, which overall occurs six times in the Koran, appears only once more (verse 271) in this long sura II, and exactly repeats verse 164 ("The devil enjoineth on you lewdness"). Of course, we will omit, as without interest here, discussing the precise meaning, moral or symbolic, of *faḥshā* or of πορνεία. It suffices to have shown how the latter seems to have induced the Koranic term—in an unexpected place.

NOTES

1. [A. Regnier, "Quelques Enigmes Litteraires de l'Inspiration Coranique," *Le Muséon* 52 (1939): 145–162. Translated by Susan Boyd-Bowman.

2. [Cf. Psalms 37:9, 11, 29, 34, and Matt. 5.]

3. [A. Geiger, thinks that *Rā'inā* in Sura II, 98 is related to the Hebrew Rā', meaning "mean, nasty or villainous," whereas Hirschfeld suggests that the word Rā'*inā* is the first term in a Jewish prayer.]

4. [Sura II, 98 reads: O ye who have believed, do not say: "*Rā'inā*" but say "*Unẓurnā*," and hearken; for the unbelievers is (in store) punishment painful." (Bell). Bell's footnote reads: "Evidently an attempt to reproduce a Hebrew word meaning "regard us," for which the Arabic is to be used" (Bell. vol. I, p. 14).]

5. [Bell's footnote: "I.e., patrons or intercessors. The meaning of the word is uncertain; cf. Wensinck in *E. I.* s. v. 'Qurbān.' 'Gods' seems to be a later explanation or gloss."]

2.3

The Figure of Abraham[1]

At the Turning-Point of Muhammad's Development, Analysis of Sura II, 124–41

Edmund Beck

One of the few certain results of the efforts of Western critics toward the illumination of Muhammad's inner development from the primary source of the Koran is known to be based on the change that the figures of Ibrāhīm and Ismā'īl undergo.[2] The decisive passage for this is to be found in sura II, 124–41. This passage will be analyzed here not, of course, to contest the clearly apparent change and development, but where possible to make corrections to certain details or to give prominence to new points of view. The subject of the whole verse group can summed up as: *millatu Ibrāhīma*. This theme is pursued 1) in factual historical terms in verses 124–34, and 2) polemically against Jews and Christians in verses 135–41.

1A. Verse 124

That a new section begins with *wa'iḏ ibtalā Ibrāhīma rabbuhū bi-kalimātin* is beyond doubt. The two preceding verses, 122–23, which correspond almost word for word to sura II, 47–48, clearly have both a linking and concluding function.[3] The "words" with which God puts Ibrāhīm to the test and which Ibrāhīm fulfills can only be understood as the divine command to sacrifice his only son. This event is only mentioned once, in sura XXXVII, 101–13; but there the root of the verb from sura II, 124 appears: *inna hāḏā la-huwa l-balā'u l-mubīnu* (XXXVII, 106). The reward for obedience consists in sura II in *Ibrāhīm* being made the *'imām* of mankind, although not all of his descendants follow him on the right path. This latter point has its counterpart in sura XXXVII, 113. *Ibrāhīm* executed the words putting him to the test: *'atammahunna*. The verb *'atamma* has *ṣiyām* as its object in sura II, 187, in sura II, 196 *ḥajj*, and in sura IX, 4 *'ahd*. It is probably this that has led Islamic interpreters to look for series of individual rules in the *kalimāt*. The *kalimāt* in sura II, 35 speaks against such a conception.

The final clause of the *wa'iḏ* brings Allah's promise: *qāla 'innī jā'iluka li-n-nāsi'imāman qāla wa-min ḏurriyyatī*. I add Abraham's question straightaway[4] because the meaning of the ambiguous *an-nāsu* can be determined from it. Here it has a universal meaning (mankind) because in his question *Ibrāhīm* singles out his descendants as a subgroup of this *an-nās*.

In the Koran *'imām* has both the objective meaning of "model" and the personal meaning of "leader." The former occurs in passages such as suras XLVI, 12 and XI, 20, where the Book of Moses is called *'imām waraḥma*, as well as the well-known designation of the holy book as *'imām mubīn* (sura XXXVI, 12) and certainly also, if one considers the discrepancy of grammatical number in sura XXV, 74: *wa- j'alnā lil-muttaqīna 'imāman* and sura XV, 79: *wa'innahumā* (sodomites and wood-dwellers) *la-bi-'imāmin mubīnin*. However, it is without doubt the personal meaning we are looking at, not only in the following verses in the plural, sura XXI, 73: *waja 'alnāhum* (Abraham, Isaac, and Jacob) *'a'immatan yahdūna bi- 'amrinā* and sura XXXII, 24: *waja'alnā minhum (hum = banū Isrā' īla) 'a'immatan yahdūna bi- 'amrinā*, but also in the passage in the singular in sura XVII, 71: *yawma nad'ū kulla 'unāsin bi-'imāmihim*. That in sura II, 124 the personal meaning is intended is proved by the thematic similarity of this verse with suras XXI, 73 and XXXII, 24.

1B. Verse 125

The form of the second *wa'iḏ* sentence is obviously corrupted; the variation of the reading between *wattakhiḏū* and *wattakhaḏū*, neither of which are satisfactory, betrays the fact that the sentence got out of order. The verse needs to be compared with a closely related passage from sura XXII.

Sura II, 125	Sura XXII, 25–26
	(Beginning of the insertion about the *ḥajj*)
	’inna llaḏīna kafarū wayaṣuddūna ‘an
wa’iḏ ja‘alnā l-bayta maṯābatan	*sabīli llāhi wal-masjidi l-ḥarāmi*
lin-nāsi wa-’amnan	*llaḏī ja‘alnāhu lin-nāsi sawā’ani*
	*l-‘ākifu fīhi wal-bādī**
wattakhiḏū min maqāmi ’Ibrāhīma	(Verse 26) *wa’iḏ bawwa’nā li-*
muṣallan wa-‘ahidnā ’ilā ’Ibrā-	*’Ibrāhīma makāna l-bayti*
hīma wa-’Ismā‘īla ’an ṭahhirā	*’an lā tušrik bī šay’an wa-ṭahhir*
baytī liṭ- ṭā’ifīna wal –‘ākifīna	*baytī liṭ- ṭā’ifīna wal-qā’imīna*
war-rukka‘i s-sujūdi	*war-rukka‘i s-sujūdi *wa-’aḏ-*
	ḏin fī n-nāsi bil-ḥajji . . .

The comparison first of all clarifies the character of the *wa’iḏ*. In sura XXII follows a recitative *’an* which requires the imaginary completion of a verbum dicendi (except for *qāla*). In sura II this verb is present in the form of *‘ahidnā* (*’an*). The direct speech introduced by this *’an* is the same in both suras. This suggests that an attempt at emendation of sura II, 125 was made. The words *wattakhi(a) ḏū min maqāmi ’Ibrāhīma muṣallan wa* are unlikely to be original. If they are left out, we have the simple sentence: *wa’iḏ ja‘alnā . . . wa-’amnan ‘ahidnā ’ilā ’Ibrāhīma. . . .*

Furthermore, on comparison of the two texts it is striking that in sura XXII the *an-nāsu*, for whom the Meccan shrine of God was founded, through the addition of *sawā’an fīhi . . .* is limited to the Arabs only. Since in sura II these words are missing, the *an-nāsu* probably has the same comprehensive meaning as in the preceding verse, 124.

From the part that corresponds word for word, it should be emphasized that sura XXII has *al-qā’imīna* as a variant for *al-‘ākifīna*. The *‘ākif* is present in sura XXII in the already mentioned addition: *sawā’ani l-‘ākifu . . .* with the meaning of "settled," differing from that of sura II. The meaning that *‘ākif* has in sura II, 125 (perseverance in the worship of God, in practicing a cult) can also be found in the Koran in the following passages:

sura II, 187:	*wa-'antum ' ākifūna fī l-masājidi;*
sura XXI, 52:	*mā hāḏihi t-tamāṯilu llatī 'antum lahā ' ākifūna;*
sura XX, 91:	*lan nabraḥa 'alayhi* (*-hū* = golden calf) *' ākifīna;*
sura XXVI, 71:	*na'budu 'aṣnāman fa-naẓallu lahā ' ākifīna.*

In both texts, the second pair of participles are in the plural: *war-rukka'i s-sujūdi*, an inner plural therefore, in contrast to the outer ones of the first pair: *liṭ- ṭā'ifīna wal –'ākifīna*. It is striking that in the extremely close relationship between the two participles of the second pair—through the omission of the *wa* the expression even takes on a formulaic character—the form *sujjad* is not present, which would correspond to the *rukka'*, even though *sujjad* frequently appears alongside *sājidūna* in the Koran, notably in sura XLVIII, 29 where once again the inner plurals of *rāki'* and *sājid* crop up linked together: *tarāhum* (*-hum* = Muhammad's followers) *rukka 'an sujjadan*, while, conversely, *sujūd* only appears as a plural form in sura XXII, 27 = II, 125. Nevertheless, *sujūd* probably has to be retained as the original version on account of the rhyme. In both suras it stands at the end of the verse and in the second half of sura II constitutes the only exception—*ūd* to the reguler *-ūn*, just as the rare cases of *-īr* (*-īl*) (see sura II, 106–108) stand in contrast to the usual *-īn* (*īm*).

Sura XXII and sura II speak first of all of the "House" (the "holy place of worship") alone, of its character as a gathering place and refuge. Ibrāhīm is only mentioned after this; he (together with Ismā'īl in sura II) is (contractually) obliged[5] to cleanse Allah's house for devout visitors. That is why in Muhammad's view the shrine at Mecca was older than Abraham;[6] the position that Ibrāhīm takes on here is similar to the role that Muhammad would later play in this respect: the reformer of an (ancient) cult.

At this point a third passage should also be quoted, that of sura III, 96:

'inna 'awwala l-bayti wuḍi'a lin-nāsi (!Sura II and XXII) *la-llaḏī biBakkata mubārakan wa-hudan lil-'ālamīna *fīhi 'āyātun bayyinātun maqāmu 'Ibrāhīma* (Sura II) *waman dakhalahū kāna 'āminan* (Sura II!) *walillāhi 'alā n-nāsi ḥajju l-bayti* (Sura XXII!).

In sura III the founding of the shrine at Mecca is explicitly placed back at the earliest times of mankind. *Ibrāhīm* is only mentioned incidentally—in the formulation with which we are already familiar from the insertion in sura II, 125: *maqāmu 'Ibrāhīma*. This does not designate in the Koran the small part of a rock with (Ibrāhīm's) footprints. Some readers have added this meaning to sura III, 96 by reading the singular instead of the plural *'āyātun bayyinātun* and then perceived the following *maqāmu 'Ibrāhīma* as being in apposition. *fīhi 'āyātun bayyinātun* is, however, purely idiomatic and can be left out without disturbing the meaning of the sentence. *maqāmu 'Ibrāhīma* is the predicate of an elliptical sentence, the subject of which is to be completed in general terms by what goes before it, that is, the shrine at Mecca. The pronominal suffix in *waman dakhalahū* refers back to *maqāmu 'Ibrāhīma*; the expression therefore designates the whole of the holy district/precinct. Linguistically and in terms of its content, it corresponds to the *(bawwa'nā li-'Ibrāhīma) makāna l-bayti* of sura XXII, 25. In the insertion in sura II, 125: *wattakhiḏū min maqāmi 'Ibrāhīma muṣallan* the *min* should be emphasized in this context. Nevertheless, it could be understood as being purely tautologous. However, in that case the predicate *muṣallan* would not go with *maqām* in the sense of the later interpretation. But another Koranic use of the *ittakhaḏa min* emerges from the fact that *min* has a partitive meaning, that is, singles out a small part of a greater whole, as in sura XVI, 68: *wa'awḥā rabukka 'ilā n-naḥli ani ttakhiḏī mina l-jibāli buyūtan wamina š-šajari wamimmā ya'rišūna*.

1c. Abraham's Prayer. Verses 126–29

These verses also have striking similarities with verses 35–41 of sura XIV (Abraham), which stand out clearly from the surrounding text as a single unit.

Sura II, 126 et seqq.	Sura XIV, 35 et seqq.
wa'iḏ qāla 'Ibrāhīmu	*wa'iḏ qāla 'Ibrāhīmu*
rabbī j'al hāḏā baladan 'āminan	*rabbī j'al hāḏā l- balada 'āminan*
	. . . * *rabbī* . . . **rabbanā*
	'innī 'askantu min ḏurriyyatī

wa-rzuq 'ahlahū mina ṯ-ṯamarāti
man 'āmana minhum billāhi wal-
yawmi l-'ākhiri qāla waman kafara
fa'umatti'uhū qalīlan ṯumma
'aḍṭarruhū 'ilā 'aḏābi n-nāri . . .
wa'iḏ yarfa'u 'Ibrāhīmu l-qawā
'ida mina l-bayti wa'Ismā'īlu
rabbanā taqabbal minnā 'inna-
ka . . . rabbanā wa-j'alnā mus-*
limīna laka wamin ḏurriyyatinā
'ummatan muslimatan laka (wa
'arinā manāsikanā

bi-wādin ghayri ḏī zar'in 'inda
baytika l-muḥarrami rabbanā
li-yuqīmū ṣ-ṣalāta . . . wa-rzuqhum
*mina ṯ-ṯamarāti . . . * rabbanā*
*'innanka . . .**
al-ḥamdu lillāhi llaḏī wahaba lī
'alā l-kibari 'Ismā'īla wa'Isḥāqa
*. . . * rabbī j'alnī muqīma ṣ-ṣa*
lâti wamin ḏurriyyatī rabbanā
wataqabbal du'ā'ī (rabbanā*
ghfir lī wali-wālidayya . . .)

That there is a close relationship between the two texts there can be little doubt. The situation is the same. The introduction and the first petition of the prayer coincide word for word. In the petitions that follow, the *wa-rzug*, *taqabbal*, and *wa-j'alnā* (*j'alnī*) share the same forms. The most striking difference is that one prayer in sura XIV—through a short sentence where Allah speaks (the end of verse 126) and a second introduction that follows on (*wa'iḏ yarfa'u 'Ibrāhīmu . . .*)—becomes two prayers in the *al-baqara* sura [Sura II]. In the first prayer the salutation *rabbī* corresponds to the introduction, which only names Abraham. In the second one, we have *rabbanā*, which, conversely, agrees with the second introduction, which as well as *Ibrāhīm* also mentions Ishmael, whose name trails behind in quite a striking manner. In the prayer in sura XIV, *rabbī* and *rabbanā* appear indiscriminately next to one another. One could easily conclude from this that the division into two of the prayer in the *al-baqara* sura [sura II] stemmed solely from the attempt to divide the salutations *rabbī* and *rabbanā* into two different prayers. In that case the prayer in sura II would be secondary to that in sura XIV. In particular, the second introduction in sura II, 127 would be suspected of being a later insertion that perhaps does not go back to Muhammad himself at all. The form and content of this introduction might support such an interpretation: *wa'iḏ yarfa'u 'Ibrāhīmu l-qawā 'ida mina l-*

bayti wa'Ismā'īlu. The trailing behind of *Ismā'īl* has already been underlined. Moreover, this short sentence contains two other grammatically striking constructions: the imperfect in *yarfa'u* and the *mina l-bayti* instead of the simple genitive. One can compare the *al-qawā'id* to sura XVI, 26: Allah smites the houses of the infidels at their foundations and the roof collapses on their heads. *rafa'a l- qawā'ida* can therefore hardly mean anything other than that *Ibrāhīm* (and Ishmael) have just founded the shrine at Mecca, which contradicts suras II, 125, III, 96; and XXII, 25.

However, the form and content of the prayer in sura XIV also give rise to serious reservations. The alternation between *rabbī* and *rabbanā*, which for the moment is our concern, is so unmotivated, indeed pointless, that it can hardly be original. Thus we have in the second salutation, for example: *rabbanā 'innī 'askantu min ḏurriyyatī*. If one wishes to justify the *(rabba)- nā* with the *(in)-nī*, one can argue for the anticipatory effect of the *min ḏurriyyatī* that follows. However, we read in the same situation in the penultimate petition: *rabbī j'alni . . . wamin ḏurriyyatī* and not *rabbanā*. In the last petition: *rabbanā wa-taqabbal du'ā'ī*, the inconsistency between the *-nā* and the *– ī* is so glaring that it is scarcely possible to find any kind of justification for it.

The second point that arouses suspicion is the inconsistency of the rhyme scheme in the verses of the prayer XIV, 35–41. The rhymes are: . . . *'aṣnām* *. . . *raḥīm* *. . . *yaškurūn* * . . . *samā'** . . . *du'ā'* * . . . *du'ā'** . . . *ḥisāb* *. However, one should not attach too much importance to this fact, given that in this sura one often encounters a transition from *ī*- and *ū* syllables to *ā*-syllables in the rhyme; this can already be seen in verse 23.

In favor of the form of the prayer in sura XIV, one can refer to the fact that here the strikingly incomplete *rabbanā taqabbal minnā* of sura II has its expected object: *wataqabbal du'ā'ī*. Furthermore in sura XIV, the petition *wa-rzuq* is very well justified by the preceding *bi-wādin ghayri ḏī zar'in*. One could also see an argument for the greater age of the form of the prayer in sura 14 compared with that of sura II in the fact that in sura XIV the expression *muslim* is missing, which is used with great emphasis in II, 128: *rabbanā wa-j'alnā mus limīna laka wamin ḏurriyyatinā 'ummatan muslimatan*. In sura XIV the corresponding phrase is merely: *rabbanā j'alni muqīma ṣ-ṣalāti wamin ḏurriyyatī*.

Let us now move from these more formal details to consideration of the content. First of all, the last petition of the prayer in sura XIV can be used to argue again for its greater age, possibly its Meccan origins. It reads *rabbanā ghfir lī wali-wālidayya*. Certainly, this petition appears in the Medina sura: *illā qawla Ibrāhīma li-'abīhi la 'hima li'abihi la-'astaghfiranna laka*. However, here it contains the addition: *wa-mā 'amliku laka mina llāhi min šay'in*. Moreover, by means of the introductory *'illā*, *Ibrāhīm*'s intercession for his father is described as being an error rather than an example to be followed. Sura IX, 114 goes even further in this direction: *wamā kāna stighfāru Ibrāhīma li-'abīhi 'illā 'an maw'idatin wa'ada-hā 'iyyāhu fa-lammā tabayyana lahū 'annahū 'aduwwun lillāhi tabarra'a minhu*. The text is obviously striving to explain and excuse an offense on the part of *Ibrāhīm*. In sura XIV there is not the slightest trace of such a judgment of the prayer for an unbeliever.

A second important point in terms of the content of the prayer in sura XIV is without doubt the mention of the link between *Ibrāhīm* and part of his descendants with Mecca: *'innī 'askantu min ḏurriyyatī biwādin . . . 'inda baytika l-muḥarrami*. The prayer speaks not of the cleansing or the founding of the shrine but only of the settlement of a part of *Ibrāhīm*'s descendants in the Mecca valley. Is this the oldest form of the view of *Ibrāhīm*'s connection with Mecca, which Muhammad already held in the Meccan period? I regard this as both possible and probable since the prayer in sura XIV taken as a whole appears to be Meccan in origin and the words that are in question here (*'innī 'askantu*) are kept in the same form throughout the prayer.

The situation in this last point is quite different. Toward the end of the prayer (in sura XIV) there is a segment that already in terms of its form is strikingly different in that it abandons the *rabbī* (*rabbanā*) that is found throughout and begins instead with *al-ḥamdu lillāhi llaḏī*: verse 39: *allaḏī wahaba lī 'alā l-kibari 'Ismā'īla wa-'Isḥāqa*. These words raise the question of the figure of *Ismā'īl* in the Koran, which must now be looked at.[7]

In sura XIX, which is assigned by Nöldeke-Schwally to the second Meccan period, we read in verse 49: *wa-wahabnā lahū* (= *Ibrāhīm*, in the context of the *Ibrāhīm* story that starts in verse 41) *Isḥāqa wa-Ya'qūba wakullan ja'alnā nabiyyan*. According to this, at the time of sura XIX Muhammad regarded *Isḥāq* and *Ya'qūb* as *Ibrāhīm*'s two sons. That *Ismā'īl*

was at that time in Muhammad's eyes a prophet in his own right with no connection to *Ibrāhīm* is proved by the continuation of sura XIX. Verse 51:
waḏkur fī l-kitābi Mūsā . . . (this was also how *Ibrāhīm* was introduced in
verse 41). Verse 54: *waḏkur fī l-kitābi Ismā'īla 'innahū kāna ṣādiqa l-wa'di
wa-kāna rasū lan nabiyyan * wa-kāna ya'muru 'ahlahū biṣ-ṣalāti waz-
zakāti wa-kāna 'inda rabbihī marḍiyyan.* This is followed by the even briefer
mention of *'Idrīs* and with this the list of prophets in sura XIX is concluded.

In the *Ibrāhīm* story in sura VI, the words from XIX, 49 return: *wa-
wahabnā lahū* (= Abraham) *Isḥāqa wa-Ya'qūba* (VI, 84). An enumeration of
prophets follows, which however confines itself to giving the names only:
Dāwūd, Sulaymān, 'Ayyūb, Yūsuf, Musā, and *Hārūn.* This is followed by the
end of the verse: *kaḏalika najzī l-muḥsinīna.* Then the enumeration is continued: *Zakariyyā', Yaḥyā, 'Īsā,* and *'Ilyās,* with the verse ending: *kullun
mina ṣ-ṣāliḥīna * wa'Ismā'īla wal-Yasa'a wa-Yūnusa wa-Lūṭan.* There can
be no doubt here either that according to Muhammad's conception of the
time *Ibrāhīm's* sons were *Isḥāq* and *Ya'qūb,* whereas *Ismā'īl* stands quite
alone and could be placed at any point in the list.

We encounter the same circumstances, moreover, in sura XXI, 52–85.
We read again of *Ibrāhīm* in verse 72: *wa-wahabnā lahū 'Isḥāqa wa-
Ya'qūba* and again *Ismā'īl, Idrīs,* and *ḏul-Kifl* are only mentioned in verse 85
with their own introduction after the verses in between have spoken of *Lūṭ,
Nūḥ, Dāwūd, Sulaymān,* and *'Ayyūb.*

A final passage that separates *Ismā'īl* from *Ibrāhīm* in a similar manner
is sura XXXVIII, 45-48: *waḏkur 'ibādanā Ibrāhīma wahima wa 'Isḥāqa wa-
Ya'qūba . . . * . . . * . . . * waḏkur Ismā'īla wal-Yasa'a wa ḏā-l-Kifli
wakullun mina l-'akhyār*.*

All of these passages from suras VI, XIX, XXI, and XXXVIII therefore
support the same view that *Ibrāhīm's* sons were *'Isḥāq* and *Ya'qūb;*
according to them, *Ismā'īl* is an unclearly drawn figure among many other
Jewish and Christian prophets, who were certainly not regarded as having a
closer connection with *Ibrāhīm.*

There is, however, in the Koran a second group of enumerations of the
prophets that is just as coherent—in suras II, III, and IV—which place
Ismā'īl quite differently. One need only compare sura IV, 163:
'inna 'awḥayna 'ilayka kamā 'awḥaynā 'ilā Nūḥin . . . wa'awḥaynā 'ilā

*'Ibrāhīma wa- 'Ismā'īla wa-'Isḥāqa wa-Ya'qūba wal-'asbāṭi wa 'Īsā wa'Ayyūba wa-Yūnusa wa-Hārūna wa-Sulaymāna wa'ātaynā Dāwūda zabūran *.*

In sura III, 84, and also identically in verse II, 136, to be discussed in the next section, we find the same order with the programmatic words:

'āmannā billāhi wamā 'unzila 'alayna wamā 'unzila 'alā 'Ibrāhīma wa-'Ismā'īla wa- 'Isḥāqa wa-Ya'qūba wal-'asbāṭi wamā 'ūtiya Mūsā wa 'Īsā wamā 'ūtiya n-nabiyyūna min rabbihim.

In sura II the formally established group: *Ibrāhīm -' asbāṭi*, with which we are above all concerned, returns and again a few verses later in verse 140: *'am taqūlūna 'inna 'Ibrāhīma wa-'Ismā'īla wa-'Isḥāqa wa-Ya'qūba wal-'asbāṭa kānū Hūdan 'aw Naṣārā.*

The change in the order in which *Ismā'īl* is placed could not therefore be given clearer or more unambiguous expression. One is obliged to conclude from these passages alone that Muhammad had learned in the interval separating these two groups that *Ismā'īl* was not just another prophet among others, but that he and Isaac were the two sons of *Ibrāhīm*. For the fact that Jacob is further separated from *Ibrāhīm* by the positioning of *Ismā'īl* and becomes more closely linked with the *asbāṭ* could likewise be gathered from the lists of prophets that are cited. However both of these elements can be verified elsewhere in the Koran. The first point brings us back to the verse that was our starting point—sura XIV, 39: *al-ḥamdu lillāhi llaḏī wahaba lī 'alā l-kibari 'Ismā'īla wa-'Isḥāqa. 'Isḥāqa* and *Ya'qūba* were designated as *Ibrāhīm*'s sons with the same verb (*wahabnā lahū*) in suras XIX, 49, VI, 84; and XXI, 72. The addition in sura XIV of *'alā l-kibari* does not change the situation since the story for which this *'alā l-kibari* forms the basis is provided in sura XI, 71 (*'a-'alidu'ana 'agūzun wa-hāḏā ba'lī šaykhan*) and we nevertheless still have the older view in the words of the angel: *fabaššarnā-hā bi-Isḥāqa wamin warā'i 'Isḥāqa Ya'qūba.*

There is consequently no doubt: sura XIV, 39 is clearly and unambiguously on the side of the Medinan passages; the verse is an insertion from the Medinan period.

The second point, that is, the change in *Ya'qūb*'s position, which is very closely related to the new ordering of *Ismā'īl*, will necessarily be touched on when we now, after this rather lengthy digression, return to the elucidation of the section sura II, 124–34.

At the beginning of this section only *Ibrāhīm* is spoken of. *Ismā'īl* is mentioned for the first time in verse 125. Here *Ibrāhīm* and *Ismā'īl* are given the task of cleansing Allah's House in Mecca. In the parallel verse of sura XXII, 26 the same order is issued to *Ibrāhīm* alone. In sura II also, the following verse (126), the introduction to *Ibrāhīm*'s prayer, speaks again only of *Ibrāhīm*. It is only in the resumption of the prayer in verse 127 that *Ismā'īl* is added belatedly and unorganically. If one removes the second introduction (and therefore *Ismā'īl* from the text), we are left with the unity of the prayer as we find it in sura XIV.

All of this, in spite of the difficulties mentioned, gives rise to the conclusion that our extract from sura II also seems originally to have spoken only of *Ibrāhīm*; *Ismā'īl* was here, as in sura XIV, only added later. In other words, *Ibrāhīm*'s connection with Mecca is older than *Ismā'īl*'s connection with *Ibrāhīm*. The latter is certainly of Medinan origin; the former appears to go back to the Meccan period.

The last part of *Ibrāhīm*'s prayer in sura II, that is, the end of verse 128 (*wa-'ari-nā manāsikanā* . . .) and verse 129, is an amplification of the prayer in sura XIV. There is no mention of *manāsik* in sura XIV; however, we find the word and the matter in great detail in sura XXII, 25 et seqq. in the description of the pilgrimage (sacrificial) customs. There we read in verse 34: *walikulli 'ummatin ja'alnā mansakan li-yaḏkurū sma-llāhi 'alā ma razaqnāhum*. The plural *manāsik* is found elsewhere in the Koran in sura II, 200, in a verse from the group 196–203, which like XXII, 25 et seqq. contains regulations regarding the pilgrimage.

Verse 129 has three parallels in the Koran:

Sura II, 129	Sura II, 151	Sura III, 164
rabbanā wa-b'aṯ	*kamā 'arsalnā*	*'iḏ ba'aṯa*
fīhim rasūlan minhum	*fīkum rasūlan minkum*	*fīhim rasūlan min 'anfusihim*
yatlū 'alayhim 'āyātika	*yatlū 'alaykum 'āyātinā*	*yatlū 'alayhim 'āyātihī*
wayu'allimuhumu	*wayuzakkīkum*	*wayuzakkīhim*
l-kitāba wal-ḥikmata	*wayu'allimukumu*	*wayu'allimuhumu*
wayuzakkīhim	*l-kitāba wal –ḥikmata*	*l-kitāba wal-ḥikmata*

The second passage from sura II (a verse from the *qibla* section) stands in the same relation to the first as the granting of the prayer does to the prayer itself. In sura III the words *laqad manna llāhu 'alā l-mu'minīna* come first, which themselves belong to a short self-defense on the part of the Prophet (verse 161: *wamā kāna li-nabiyyin 'an yaghulla*). In the third and final parallel in sura LXII, 2 these words are taken up in a short hymn: (*yusabbiḥu lillāhi . . .*) *huwa lladī ba'aṯa fī l-'ummiyyīna rasūlan min-hum yatlū 'alayhim 'āyātihī wayuzakkīhim wayu'allimuhumu l-kitāba wal-ḥikmata*. We see the fixed form of Muhammad's self-description, which he apparently often expressed in the time of suras II, III, and LXII, that is, in the first half of the Medinan period. It should be noted that here the universal character of Muhammad's mission is still missing.

1D. *Ibrāhīm*'s Religion and Its Heirs: Verses 128–34.

Verse 124 had already named *Ibrāhīm* as the religious leader of mankind. According to verse 125, the shrine at Mecca was also an object of his religion. *Ibrāhīm*'s prayer in the subsequent verses introduced the term *muslim-(ūna)* as well as the announcement of the (Meccan Arabs') own prophet, whose coming *Ibrāhīm* begs for and in this manner prophesies.

This is the preparation for and introduction of the *millatu Ibrāhīma* of verse 130: *waman yarghabu 'an milla'i ' Ibrāhīma 'illā man safiha nafsahū*. The Koranic passages containing the words *millatu Ibrāhīma* will be discussed in the course of the investigation that follows. Here it must be underlined that its broadening by *ḥanīf*, which seeks to describe *Ibrāhīm*'s religion more precisely, is still missing in our verse. If, moreover, we compare *man yarghabu 'an millati Ibrāhīma* with the words of sura III, 85 with the same meaning: *waman yabtaghī ghayra l-'islāmi dīnan*, we see how in sura III *islām* has already become an explicit designation for Muhammad's (= *Ibrāhīm*'s) religion. We have also found in sura II, in *Ibrāhīm*'s preceding prayer, that here the expression *muslim* is used with particular emphasis and in contrast to the form of the prayer in sura XIV: *waj'al-nā muslimīna laka . . . 'ummatan muslimatan laka*. However, at the same time the complement *laka* shows that the word has not yet become a proper noun. Incidentally, this part of the prayer (sura II, 128) is quoted by the Koran itself in a (necessarily) later passage with the reinterpretation of this *muslimūna* as a proper noun. These curious words are to be found in the Medinan appendix to sura XXII, verses 77–78: *yā 'ayyuhā llaḏīna 'āmanū* (of Medinan origin!) . . . *wajāhidū fī llāhi . . . huwa jtabākum wamā ja'ala 'alaykum fī d-dīni min ḥarajin millata 'abīkum 'Ibrāhīma huwa sammākumu l-muslimīna min qablu wafī hāḏā*, that is, and here in the Koran, apparently in sura II, 128.

With regard to the utilization of the word *milla* prior to the passage in question, the following should be said. The oldest passage in the Koran that uses milla appears to be sura XXXVIII, 7, where unfortunately the meaning of the expression *al-millatu l-'ākhiratu* remains unclear. In sura XIV, 13, the unbelievers speak, in a general description of the unbelieving peoples with regard to their prophets, of *millatunā* (we will drive you from our land if you do not return to our religion). Exactly the same is true of the Midian in the story of Shu'ayb in sura VII, 86; those converted by Shu'ayb retain the expression in their answer: *'in 'udnā fī millatikum. Milla* appears for the first time in connection with *Ibrāhīm* in sura XII, 37–38, where Joseph recounts in prison: *'inni taraktu millata qawmin lā yu'minūna billāhi . . . wattaba'tu millata 'ābā'ī 'Ibrāhīma wa-Isḥāqa wa-Ya'qūba*. As we can see, the passage belongs to the time before the new positioning of *Ismā'īl. Milla* is not yet linked exclusively to *Ibrāhīm* but through the designation *millatu 'Ibrāhīma*, sura XII, 38, unquestionably anticipates the monotheism proclaimed by Muhammad and in which regard he knows he is in agreement with all the great "apostles" of the past.

Ibrāhīm was from the start in Muhammad's eyes one of the greatest among God's apostles. His figure already appears in sura LXXXVII, of which the last verse refers to the authority of the books (*ṣuḥuf*) of *Ibrāhīm* and *Mūsā*. We see a similar situation in sura LIII, 37. Muhammad was therefore convinced right from the start of his career that his revelation (religion) accorded with that of *Ibrāhīm* and *Mūsā*. To these two is later added *'Īsā* as a third figure. Sura XLII (which is assigned by Nöldeke-Schwally to the third Meccan period), verse 13: *šara'a lakum mina d-dīni* (= Muhammad's religion) *mā . . . wamā waṣṣaynā bihī Ibrāhīma wa-Mūsā wa-'Īsā*. Thus Muhammad could also have called his religion *millatu (dīnu) Mūsā* or *millatu (dīnu) 'Īsā*. Why did the formulation *millatu Ibrāhīma* alone emerge? The reason for this is seen as stemming exclusively from the conflict into which Muhammad entered with Jews and Christians in Medina. But this conflict was only the final impetus. The actual cause has a deeper origin and goes back to the Meccan period. In sura X, 104, in an argument with his Meccan adversaries over his religion, Muhammad speaks the following words:

yā 'ayyuhā n-nāsu . . . 'in kuntum fī šakkin min dīnī falā 'a'budu llaḏīna ta'budūna min dūni llāhi walākin'a'budu llāha . . . wa'umirtu 'an 'akūna mina l-mu'minīna wa'an 'aqim wajhaka lid-dīni ḥanīfan walā takūnanna mina l-mušrikīna.

Sura XXX, 30 coincides with these words, sometimes word for word: *fa'aqim wajhaka lid-dīni ḥanīfan fiṭrata llāhi . . . ḏalika d-dīnu l-qayyimu.* In my analysis of sura XXX regarding the question of the period this section of sura XXX dates from, I was inclined toward an inclusion of Medinan origin, but only on the basis of the textual evidence that the claim that Muhammad's religion was the immutable ancient religion probably went back to the dispute with the Jews and Christians.[8] If, however, one considers passages like the quoted final verse of sura LXXXVII, where Muhammad asserts *Ibrāhīm*'s and *Mūsā*'s authority as his own, one is compelled to admit that the idea of the *ad- dīnu l-qayyimu* was implied from the beginning. Sura XXX, 30 has in common with sura X, 104 the meaningful term *ḥanīf* as a more exact characterization of Muhammad's religion. The same word is used in the same (late) Meccan period to characterize *Ibrāhīm*'s religion, namely, in sura VI, 78–79 where *Ibrāhīm* says: *yā qawmī 'innī wajjahtu wajhī lillaḏī faṭara s-samawāti wal-'arḍa ḥanīfan.* What common feature does this *ḥanīf* express which in this way is only associated with Muhammad and *Ibrāhīm*? The passages quoted themselves give the answer to this question: the situation in which Muhammad and *Ibrāhīm* found themselves is the same. They both stand for the religion of monotheism in a polytheistic environment. In this, *Mūsā*'s and *'Īsā*'s mission differed from that of *Ibrāhīm* and Muhammad. The *ḥanīf* in suras X, 105 and VI, 78–79, which can only arbitrarily be explained as a later insertion, proves therefore that already before the argument with the Jews (and Christians) in Medina, Muhammad saw his religion as having a special connection with that of *Ibrāhīm*. If, moreover, one accepts the conclusive nature of the reasons that have prompted me here to see *Ibrāhīm*'s association with Mecca as going back to the Meccan period, then all of the fundamental elements of the Medinan figure of *Ibrāhīm* are already present in their essential form in the Meccan period.

Now back to sura II, 130. In the verse's statement that only foolish people (*man safiha nafsahū*) can renounce *Ibrāhīm*'s religion, one can already detect a polemic; but it remains general and indefinite.

In the second half of sura II, 130 Allah speaks unexpectedly and very briefly. *Walaqadi ṣtafaynā-hu (-hū = Ibrāhīm) fī d-dunyā wa-'innahū fī l-'ākhirati la-mina ṣ-ṣāliḥīna*. In the insertion in sura XVI, verses 120–23 still to be discussed, we have the same statement: *ijtabāhu* (*-hū = Ibrāhīm* = Abraham, here in the third person, but switching straightaway to the first!) *wa-'ātaynā-hu . . . wa'inna-hū fī l-'ākhirati la-mina ṣ-ṣāliḥīna*.

The short verse 131 once again links the verb *'aslama* with the person of *Ibrāhīm*: *'iḏ qāla rabbuhū 'aslim qāla 'aslamtu li-rabbi l-'ālamīna*. For Muhammad and *'aslama* (as an expression for his religion), we can compare sura III, 19: *inna d-dīna 'inda llāhi l-'islāmu . . . fa'in ḥājjūka fa-qul 'aslamtu wajhiya lillāhi*. However, the use of this *'aslama* is not confined to *Ibrāhīm* and Muhammad. The Queen of Sheba, for example, speaks in a Meccan prophet story in the following manner: *rabbī innī ẓalamatu nafsī wa-'aslamtu ma'a Sulaymāna lillāhi rabbi l-'ālamīna*. (sura XXVII, 44).

The first words of verse 132: *wa-waṣṣā bi-hā 'Ibrāhīmu banīhi (wa-Ya'qūbu)* refer back to the *millatu 'Ibrāhīma* of verse 130. To this we can compare sura XLII, 13: *šara'a lakum mina d-dīni mā waṣṣā bihī Nuḥan wallaḏī 'awḥaynā 'ilayka* (Muhammad in Mecca; cf. verse 7, which speaks of the Arabic Koran and Mecca) *wamā waṣṣaynā bihī 'Ibrāhīma wa-Mūsā wa 'Īsā 'an 'aqīmū d-dīna walā tafarraqū fīhi*. The significance of this verse as a preliminary stage of the *millatu 'Ibrāhīma* has already been underlined. The mention of *wa-Ya'qūbu* that trails behind can certainly be deleted here. It anticipates the following verse.

The words of *Ibrāhīm*'s legacy read: *yā baniyya 'inna llāha ṣtafā lakumu d-dīna falā tamūtunna 'illa wa'antum muslimūna*. Muhammad speaks in exactly the same way to his community of believers in sura III, 102: *yā 'ayyuhā llaḏīna 'āmanū . . . walā tamūtunna 'illā wa-'antum muslimūna*.

The two verses that follow (133–34) were probably only added at a later date. Verse 133 reports what verse 132 told of *Ibrāhīm*, but putting *Ya'qūb* in his place. Here the introductory words *'am kuntum šuhadā'a 'id̲ ḥaḍara Ya'qūba l-mawtu* arouse suspicion. Where does the second person in this context come from with the scornful tone that we also find in the same expression in VI, 144: *'am kuntum šuhadā'a 'id̲ waṣṣākumu llāhu?* Here the words come at the end of an argument with the people of Mecca about their (pagan) sacrificial customs.

Based on its content, verse 133 belongs to the Medinan period in which Muhammad learned that *Isḥāq* and *Ya'qūb* were not the sons of *Ibrāhīm* but rather *Ismā'īl* and *Isḥāq*. For here *Ya'qūb*'s sons answer their dying father's question as to what they would worship after his death: *'ilāhaka wa'ilāha 'ābā'ik Ibrāhīma wa'Ismā'īla wa'Isḥāqa*. This is entirely the biblical genealogy, but even more clearly stated than in the Medinan list of prophets: *Ibrāhīm wa'Ismā'īl wa'Isḥāq wa Ya'qūb wal-'asbāṭ*.

The closing verse (134) returns in identical form as the closing verse of the next section but one in verse 141. As to the assessment of the question where the original place of the verse is, one can refer to the fact that the *lakum* of the address is completely disconnected from the structure of section 124–34. In verse 141 a formal link with what immediately precedes it is not hard to establish. There, however, the content presents difficulties.

2. Verses 135–41

The second verse group on the theme of *millatu Ibrāhīma* leads us, in contrast to the first, into the heart of the argument that led to the expression's full elaboration. In verses 135–38, Muhammad's adversaries are only spoken of in the third person; in the verses that follow, the Prophet turns to address the Jews and Christians directly.

2a. Verses 135–38

Verse 135: *waqālū kūnū Hūdan aw Naṣārā tahtadū qul bal millata Ibrāhīma ḥanīfan wamā kāna mina l-mušrikīna*. The form *waqālū . . . qul . . .* dominates the section sura II, 75–121. A verse group from this section is closely related to our verse, namely, verse 111 et seq.: *qālū lan yadkhula l-jannata 'illā man kāna Hūdan aw Naṣārā . . . qul . . . balā man 'aslama wajhahū lillāhi.*

Likewise verse 120: *walan tarḍā 'anka l-Yahūdu walā n-Naṣārā ḥattā tattabi'a millatahum qul 'inna hudā llāhi huwa l-hudā.* There is no doubt that verse 135 with the fully developed term *millatu Ibrāhīma ḥanīfan* belongs to a later period than verses 120 and 111. In other words: in the argument with the Jews and Christians, Muhammad did not claim *Ibrāhīm*'s religion for himself alone right from the start. It also appears that the initiative for the religious dispute came from the Jews and Christians, who declared that as a heretic Muhammad had forfeited his right to Paradise and openly demanded that he convert to Judaism or Christianity. With this, the question of the age of different religions was bound to come up, and more precisely: who could lay claim to the patriarchs for his religion? This point of the dispute is reflected by sura II, 140: *'am taqūlūna 'inna 'Ibrāhīma wa'Ismā'īla wa-Ya'qūba wal-'asbāṭa kānū Hūdan 'aw Naṣāra.* Or, concentrating on the person of *Ibrāhīm*, we read in sura III, 65: *yā 'ahla l-kitābi limā tuḥājjūna fī 'Ibrāhīma wamā 'unzilati t- Tawrātu wal-Injīlu 'illā min ba'dihī . . . mā kāna 'Ibrāhīmu Yahūdiyyan walā Naṣrāniyyan walākin kāna ḥanīfan musliman wamā kāna mina l-mušrikīna.*

In the reconstruction of the development of this argument, it is of crucial significance how one judges the fact that the Koran speaks throughout not only of Jews but also of Christians. To say that the mention of Christians was only added later would be a purely partial form of textual criticism, given that on our subject there is not a single place where Jews alone are spoken of. Moreover, it can be proved that Christians also made *Ibrāhīm* a representative of their religion and occasionally in a manner that corresponds exactly to Muhammad's practice. One only need compare the following sentences from Eusebius, *Demonstratio evangelica*: "*Christianity is neither a form of Hellenism nor of Judaism, but it has a peculiar stamp of its own. . . . Judaism would be correctly called the polity ordered according to the law of Moses. . . . What would you say about those pre-Mosaic or pre-Judaic saints . . . such as Enoch . . . and in addition Abraham, Isaac, and Jacob*?" (I, 2; publ. by Dindorf [Teubner], pp. 8–9). The equation of Christianity with the religion of *Ibrāhīm* is given clearer and more explicit expression in I, 5 (Dindorf, p. 29):

"If you should wish to compare Christian life . . . and worship with the way of those who with Abraham are witnessed to for piety and righteousness, you will discover one and the same thing; namely, thay they had abandoned polytheism [lit.: a wandering among many gods] (compare this to the Koranic *ḥanīf*) . . . *no longer deifying the sun or the moon, they turned toward the one supreme God* (see sura VI, 77–78) . . . *creator of the heavens and the earth*." In exactly the same way as Muhammad, therefore, the Christians see in the rejection of polytheism and the turning toward monotheism the proof of the identification of their religion with that of *Ibrāhīm*. The resemblance extends as far as the following detail. We saw that Muhammad pointed out the similarity between the names of the followers of *Ibrāhīm*'s religion and those of his own (*muslimūna*). Exactly the same is found in Eusebius when in I, 5 (pp. 32–33) he analyzes the psalm quotation *nolite tangere Christos meos* [Do not touch My anointed ones] (Psalm 105 [104]: 15) in the following manner: "The entire passage shows that the same inquiry (must) be made of Abraham, Jacob, and Isaac, the result being that they shared equally with us in the name of Christ." One can with good reason object to this surprising parallel by saying that Eusebius does not prove much about the Christians that Muhammad encountered. Nonetheless, this, in my view coincidental, detail strengthens the overall impression that also in the formulation of the figure of *Ibrāhīm* Muhammad did not act creatively, i.e., consciously deliberating and constructing, but rather further elaborated, under the constraint of the Jewish and Christian initiative, already existing elements of his teachings.

The phrase *millatu Ibrāhīma ḥanīfan* from sura II, 135 can be found in two further Medinan verses, sura III, 95: *ṣadaqa llāhu fattabi'u millata Ibrāhīma ḥanīfan wamā kāna mina l-mušrikīna*, and sura IV, 125: *waman 'aḥsana dīnan mimman . . . wattaba'a millatu Ibrāhīma ḥanīfan*. We also find it in two verses of Meccan suras, in which however the inclusion of a Medinan addition is very probable—sura VI, 162: *'innī hadā-nī rabbī 'ilā ṣīratin mustaqīmin dīnan qayyiman // millata Ibrāhīma ḥanīfan wamā kāna mina l-mušrikīna*. Likewise sura XVI, 120: *'inna 'Ibrāhīma kāna 'ummatan* (cf. the *imām* of sura II, 124) *qānitan lillāhi ḥanīfan walam yaku mina l-mušrikīna * . . . . * // ṯumma 'awḥaynā 'ilayka 'ani ttabi' millata Ibrāhīma ḥanīfan wamā kāna mina l-mušrikīna*. The two slashes indicate the presumed start of the Medinan supplements.

Verse 136 corresponds word for word to sura III, 84. Here intra-Koranic variants are to be found: in the place of the plural in the introductory *qūlū*, sura III has the singular *qul*, which in sura II stands in the preceding verse. In spite of the *qul*, sura III continues in the plural: *'āmannābillāhi wamā 'unzila 'ilaynā* (sura III. *'alaynā) wamā 'unzila 'ilā ('alā) 'Ibrāhīma . . . wamā 'ūtiya Mūsā wa 'Īsā wamā 'ūtiya* (in sura III this second *mā 'ūtiya* is missing*) n-nabiyyūna min rabbihim lā nufarriqu bayna 'aḥadin minhum wanaḥnu lahū muslimūna*. Muhammad refers here to the all-encompassing character of his religion in answer to the demand by the Jews and Christians to convert to their religion. It is not Muhammad and his followers but the Jews and Christians that are the schismatics to be condemned: *fa'in' āmanū faqadi htadaw wa'in tawallaw fa-'innamā hum fī šiqāqin* (verse 137).

Verse 138 begins abruptly with the exclamation *ṣibghata llāhi*. It can be linked to the *qul bal millatu 'Ibrāhīma* of verse 135, because that first *qul* ends here, of which the *qūlū* (or *qul*) of verse 136 constitutes only a further elaboration. The following section begins with a new *qul*. The Koran provides no other passages that clarify the meaning of *ṣibghatun*. However, the association with *milla*, even if a distant one, reveals that *ṣibgha* baptism (a fundamental religious practice, an initiation) here stands for religion in a more general sense.

2B. VERSES 139–41

Verse 139: *qul'a-tuḥājjūna-nā fī llāhi*. The object of the dispute in this second part, in which the Prophet turns to address the Jews and Christians directly, is first of all only vaguely indicated. However, the *fī llāhi* is probably closely related to *ṣibghata llāhi* so that here too the meaning would be: do you want to argue with us about Allah's religion? In sura III, 65 the same verb leads straight to the central point: *yā 'ahla l-kitābi limā tuḥājjūna fī 'Ibrāhīma*. In sura II the preliminary answer to the *'a- tuḥājjūnanā* remains general and is composed strikingly of Meccan formulations. One only need compare sura XLII, 15: *walā tattabi' 'ahwā'ahum waqul . . . allāhu rabbunā warabbukum lanā 'a'mālunā walakum 'a'mālukum* with *wahuwa rabbunā warabbukum walanā 'a'mālunā walakum 'a'mālukum*. The last segment: *wanaḥnu lahū mukhliṣūna*, stands alone in the Koran to the extent that here *mukhliṣūna* has no object. Nevertheless, it certainly belongs alongside the frequent Meccan formulation: *mukhliṣan(-īna) lahū d-dīna*.

Verse 140: *'am taqūlūna 'inna Ibrāhīma wa'Ismā'īl . . . wal-'asbāṭa kānū Hūdan 'aw Naṣārā*. The list of prophets (patriarchs) *Ibrāhīm . . . al-' asbāṭ* has already been discussed. The *'am . . .* pursues the question of the preceding verse *'a-tuḥājjūna* and makes it specific. The Jews and Christians contradict Muhammad and claim for themselves the right to represent *Ibrāhīm*'s religion. Muhammad, however, has the knowledge of Allah on his side: *qul 'a-'antum 'a'lamu 'ami llāhu*. The accusation follows that the Jews and Christians are withholding the truth, which is also known to them: *waman 'aẓlamu mimman katama šahādatan 'indahū mina llāhi*. Elsewhere in the Koran, *šahāda* means (legal) testimony. The argument over *Ibrāhīm* therefore takes on the form of a trial before God.

This is followed by the closing verse 141, which is identical to verse II, 134, as has already been underlined: *tilka 'ummatun qad khalat lahā mā kassabat walakum mā kasabtum walā tus'alūna 'ammā kānū ya'malūna*. If one links these words with what precedes them, *'ummatun* would then be a résumé of the generations from *Ibrāhīm* up to the *'asbāṭ*, and *lakum* would be used to address the Jews and Christians. In purely formal terms, there are no objections to be made to this, but in terms of content the following difficulty must be pointed out: how is the cool, almost chilling tone of *lahum mā kasabat* possible when it refers to *Ibrāhīm* and his descendants who, as the representatives of the true religion, were at the center of the argument? The verse appears, therefore, to be original neither here nor in sura II, 134. We have apparently before us, similarly to verses II, 122–23 = II, 47–48, which come before our section, a fragment of the Koran which originally had no fixed place or context and which, because of its formal character, was used in the writing of the canonical text to make a particular structure emerge. For, in any case, there can be no doubt here in sura II, 141 that we are looking at a conclusion, since the beginning of the next verse (*sa-yaqūlu s-sufahā'u mina n-nāsi mā wallāhum 'an qiblatihim*) unambiguously introduces a new theme: the argument over the direction of prayer.

* * *

To conclude this analysis of sura II, 124–41, I should like to underline the two main points again. 1) Muhammad saw Mecca as linked with *Ibrāhīm* before the reordering of *Ismā'īl* and this already in the Meccan period. 2) The emergence of the term *millatu Ibrāhīma* does not date exclusively from the early Medinan polemic with the Jews (and Christians) either. The concept and expression stem from a development that reaches far back into the Meccan period. This development took place organically, encouraged and accelerated by Muhammad's Jewish-Christian adversaries, whose arguments Muhammad managed skillfully to use for himself.

Notes

1. [Original article: Edmund Beck, "Die Gestalt des Abraham. Am Wendepunkt der Entwicklung Muhammeds. Analyse von Sure II.118 (124)–135 (141)," *Le Muséon* 65 (1952): 73–94. Translated by Anon.]

2. See Snouck Hurgronje, *Het mekkaansche Feest*, in *Verspreide Geschriften* (Bonn-Leipzig, 1923), vol. I, p. 23 et seqq.; Nöldeke-Schwally, *Geschichte des Qorans* (Leipzig, 1909), vol. I, p. 146 et seq., 152; Buhl-Schäder, *Das Leben Muhammeds* (Leipzig, 1930), p. 229 et seqq.

3. One can understand the address in verse 122 as being a link between the two parts. This was probably what prompted R. Bell (*The Qur'an*, I, 17) to attach these two verses to the section with which we are concerned. However, the much clearer conclusion that is expressed in the subsequent verse following Koranic tradition in the warning of the "day" speaks against such a division of the text. The fact, moreover, that both verses also appear with only minor divergences in sura II, 47–48 and have there the same double function is a strong argument against their originality: they seem in both places to have been inserted at a later date.

4. The *min (ḏurriyyatī)* is probably influenced by Allah's subsequent answer: *fa-lā yanālu 'ahdī ẓ-ẓālimīna* (to be completed with *min ḏurriyatika*).

5. For the construction and meaning of the *'ahida*, see sura III, 183: *inna llāha 'ahida 'ilaynā 'an lā nu'mina . . .*

6. In sura XXII we read later (verses 29 and 33) twice: *al-baytu l-'atīqu*.

7. See Snouck Hurgronje, *Het mekkaansche Feest*, p. 24.

8. See *Orientalia* 14 (1945): 124–26.

2.4

The Prophet's *Kunya* and Sharing the Spoils

A Midrash on Joshua?[1]

Jean-Louis Déclais

In an "essay on the Arab proper name," Jacqueline Sublet[2] analyzed the different elements of the complete "posthumous name" of deceased persons who entered with the "status of ancestors" into the pantheon of biographical books:

- the "personal name" of each (*ism*),
- the "surname" (*laqab*) that might be a nickname or an honorific title,
- the "relational names" (*nisba*) that connect a person to an ethnic group or a place and whose sequence sometimes allows us to retrace the itinerary of someone's existence,
- and that element specific to the Arab world, the *kunya*, which primarily affirmed that someone had realized himself by becoming a father or mother (*Abū 'Umar* = "father of 'Umar"; *Umm Muḥammad* = "mother of Muḥammad"); logically, the *kunya* could not be carried until after the birth of a first son, but it had such social and affective value[3] that one could attribute it to someone from birth by way of good omen, and certain people carried it as a decoration (Abū *l-Faḍā'il*, "man of virtues"), as a precious memory (*Abū Turāb*, "man of dust," a term that 'Alī received from the Prophet one day when he fell asleep covered with dust), or as a curse (*Abū Lahab*, "man aflame," fated to hellfire).

We know that Muḥammad bore the *kunya* Abū l-Qāsim,[4] because he had had from the *Khadīja* a son named al-Qāsim who died at the age of two. Several traditions say that the prophet himself had forbidden others after him to bear the same name (Muḥammad) associated with the same *kunya* (Abū l-Qāsim). And Sublet notes (p. 52) that "the reasons for this interdiction remain unknown."

Without claiming to discover the ultimate reason that led an authority to promulgate this ban, I propose to examine the reasons that are provided by the ancient texts themselves. They may perhaps lead us along unexpected paths.

Some Hadiths [Ḥādīṯ] on the Kunya *Abū l-Qāsim*

First let us read some examples of these traditions. I take them from the chapter that Ibn Sa'd devotes to the "*kunya* of the Messenger of God"[5] and from Bukhārī's *Ṣaḥīḥ*, where one may find these traditions in the "Book of Sales" (K. al-Buyū'), the "Book of the Obligation of the Fifth" (K. farḍ al-Khums) and the "Book of Good Manners" (K. al-Adab).

Ibn Sa'd:

1. of Abū Hurayra: God's Messenger said: "Do not put together my name and my *kunya*. I am Abū l-Qāsim, it is God Who gives and it is I who distribute [Fr: *répartis*]."

2. of Anas B. Mālik: The Prophet found himself in the *Baqī'*[6] when someone called "Abū l-Qāsim!" The Prophet turned toward him but the other said: "I was not addressing you!" He then said: "Take my name but do not take my *kunya*."

3. of Jābir, who said: A boy was born in the home of a man of the *Anṣār*, who called him Muḥammad. The *Anṣār* were angry and they said: "[Wait] until we have consulted the Prophet!" They spoke to him about it and he said: "The *Anṣār* have done rightly." He then said: "Take my name but do not take my *kunya* because I am only Abū l-Qāsim, I distribute among you."

4. of Jābir b. 'Abdallāh: A man of the *Anṣār* had taken the *kunya* Abū l-Qāsim; the *Anṣār* said: "We cannot give you this *kunya* before having asked God's Messenger." They spoke about it to God's Messenger, who said:

"Take my name, but do not take my *kunya*." And Sa'īd [one of the transmitters] says: Qatāda found it blameworthy that someone take the *kunya* Abū l-Qāsim, even if his name were not Muḥammad.

Bukhārī's *Ṣaḥīḥ*:

**Book of Sales* (title 34, chapter 49):

5. of Anas b. Mālik: The Prophet found himself in a market. Someone said: "Abū l-Qāsim!" The Prophet turned toward him. But the other said: "It was that one I was calling." Then the Prophet said: "Give my name, but do not take my *kunya*."

**Book of Obligation of the Fifth* (title 57, chapter 7: on the verse VIII, 41: "A fifth [of the spoils] is *for Allah, and for the Messenger*, that is, the Messenger has division of it. The Messenger of God has said: "Me, I am only a distributor and a guardian. It is God who gives."

6. of Jābir b. 'Abdallāh: "A boy was born to someone of our place, the *Anṣār*, and he wanted to call him Muḥammad. (*According to one of the transmitters, the father said:* "I will carry him on my shoulders and I will bring him to the Prophet." The latter said: "Give my name, but do not take my *kunya*, because I am only the distributor, I allot among you").

7. of Jābir B. 'Abdallāh al- Anṣārī: A boy was born to a man of our town and he called him al-Qāsim. The *Anṣār* said: "We will not give you the *kunya* Abū al-Qāsim, we will not give you that pleasure." The Prophet said: "The *Anṣār* have done well. Give my name, but do not take my *kunya*, because I am only a distributor."

8. of Abū Hurayra: The Messenger of God said: "It is not I who gives to you or refuses you. I am a distributor, I place only there where I have received the order."

**Book of Good Manners* (title 78, chap 109): Those who give the names of prophets).

9. of Jābir b. 'Abdallāh al- Anṣārī: The Messenger of God has said: "Give my name but do not take my *kunya* because I am only a distributor, I distribute among you."

Several observations arise from these nine examples:

1) The text of the hadith includes a *sentence* in the imperative, eventually followed by a *motivation* in the indicative (*because* . . .), and is preceded by an *anecdote* supposed to furnish the occasion for pronouncing the sentence. Sometimes the anecdote is not reported (1, 8, and 9). In 3, 4, 6, and 7, the sentence is pronounced on the occasion of a birth among the *Anṣār*; in 2 and 5 it is during a call in a public place of Medina. Visibly, the sentence exists independently of the anecdotes created to give it a frame that embeds it in a moment of Muḥammad's life.

2) The sentence's enunciation offers various formulas:

- **Give my name** (*sammū* . . . verb in the 2nd form) **and do not take my *kunya*** (either in the 8th form: *wa-lā taktanū*, 2 and 9, or in the 5th form, *wa-lā takannaw,* 5, 6, and 7).
- **Take my name** (*tasammaw*, in the 5th form) **and do not take my *kunya*** (3 and 4).
- Other examples (not cited here) place the negation at the beginning of the sentence so that it applies to both verbs (*lā tasammaw . . . wa-taktanū* . . .): **Do not take together my name and my *kunya*.**
- This is what is clearly said by this other formula: **Do not put together** (*lā tajma'ū*) **my name and my *kunya*** (1).

The 3rd and 4th formulae offer the simplest meaning: You may call yourself Muḥammad, you may take Abū l-Qāsim as *kunya*, but do not do the two things at once, because there should be only one "Abū l-Qāsim Muḥammad," and that is the Prophet. The 2nd formula has an analogous meaning if we understand it as: Take my name without taking my *kunya*, or, If you take my name do not take my *kunya*. It is a question of *adab*, of right conduct with respect to the Prophet. Some like 'Umar, it was said, condemned the custom of giving children the names of prophets; because one could thereby avoid an insult or curse against sacred names occurring during the anger of a quarrel, since such a name should always be followed by a blessing (*Abraham, on whom be peace!*).

The 1st formula is more strange. In fact, the one who gives his son the name "Muḥammad" does not risk taking his *kunya* since he would be "Abū Muḥammad" and not "Abū l-Qāsim."

Note (no. 4) that some were pushing the scruple to the point of condemning those who took the Prophet's *kunya* even if they did not bear his name. And so could the *kunya* "Abū l-Qāsim" have had another connotation than the simple identification of an individual?

3) If we now examine the logical link between the *sentence* put into Muḥammad's mouth and the *anecdotes* on the occasion of which it might have been pronounced, we may make the following findings.

To understand the hadiths of Anas b. Mālik (nos. 2 and 5: the call in a public place and the confusion that follows), one must remember that the *kunya* was a more customary usage than the "name" (*ism*). One called someone more easily by his *kunya* or by another surname than by his personal name; hailing someone in the market by crying his *kunya* ("Yā Abū l-Qāsim!") was normal, but it was less common to call out the "name" ("Yā Muḥammad!"). In this context, the Prophet's response signified: "You can always give my name, it has no importance since it will not be called out in public, so there will be no confusion between myself and another; but avoid taking my *kunya* so that there will not be several of us turning our heads when it is called in the markets." This is a matter of delicacy toward the person of Muḥammad and one understands that certain jurists could have thought that this was only valid during his lifetime.

Jābir's hadiths (3, 4, and 7) show that, in the case of Muḥammad at least, the *kunya* seemed more sacred than the name itself; it should be protected against any banalization. This was because it was more honorable and more gratifying (cf. no 7: "We will not give you this pleasure!"). The affair of the birth among the *Ansār* results in the same sentence as the misunderstanding in the market: a father may call his son by the name "Muḥammad" but he should not call him "al-Qāsim" in order not to lay claim himself to being called "Abū l-Qāsim."

4) Examining the link between the *sentence* and *its motivations* allows us to suspect in which context the ancient Muslim schools speculated on the *kunya* of the founder of Islam.

Numbers 2 and 5 pose no problem: Do not take my *kunya*. There should be no other Abū l-Qāsim so as to avoid any confusion.

Other passages are more curious. The ban on the Prophet's *kunya* is tied to the meaning of the name itself. In Arabic, distribution is called *taqsīm*; the person who performs the distribution is called *qāsim*. Muḥammad *kunya* underlines, therefore, that he has a certain role to play in the "distribution" of the goods of this world among members of his community:

- no. 3: I am *only* Abū l-Qāsim, I distribute (*aqsim*) among you.
- nos. 7 and 9: I am *only* a distributor (*qāsim*).
- no. 6: I was constituted *only* as distributor.

There is a major difference between "do not call yourself Abū l-Qāsim because I *alone* have that right" and "do not call yourself Abū l-Qāsim because I am *only* a *qāsim*." The *innamā* (*only*) of nos. 6, 7, and 9 do not contrast Muḥammad with other men, but with God, as shown by example 1 ("It is God who gives and it is I who distribute") and 8 ("It is not I who distribute to you and refuse you, I am a distributor, I place where I have received the order").

5) But was this ban respected? Examining the classic biographical collections tells us it was not. One the one hand, companions as authoritative as Abū Hurayra and Anas. B. Mālik assure us that the Prophet had asked that nobody after him be called "Abū l-Qāsim Muḥammad." On the other, a collection edited in the tenth century was amused to count ninety-four Abū l-Qāsims in the first two generations of Islam![7] Ibn Khallikān[8] enumerates some who are sons of the foremost companions: 'Alī, his brother Ja'far, Ṭalḥa his adversary, killed in the battle of the Camel (656), Abū Bakr, 'Abd ar-Raḥmān b. 'Awf, Sa'd b. Abu Waqqāṣ. . . . This list is all the more piquant in that Ibn Sa 'd reports an altercation on this subject between 'Alī and Ṭalḥa:

> There were words between 'Alī and Ṭalḥa. Ṭalḥa says to him: "There is no shamelessness like yours toward God's Messenger! You gave his name and his *kunya* while the Messenger of God had forbidden that anyone of his Community after him bear the two together!" 'Alī says: "The shameless one (*jarī'*) is the one who undertakes (*ijtara'*) something against God and

> his Messenger. You, go call someone from the Qurayshites." The latter arrived. "What did you witness?" he said. "We were witnesses when the Messenger of God said: 'After me there will be born to you a boy to whom I attribute my name and my *kunya*, whereas it is not permitted to anybody in my Community after me.'"[9]

According to Ibn Khallikān, though, Ṭalḥa could have done the same thing as 'Alī. When one knows the role that Alī, Ṭalḥa, and even the son of 'Alī at issue (in effect Muḥammad b. 'Alī ibn al- Ḥanafiyya) played in the power struggles that followed the assassination of 'Uthmān, one suspects that this problem of names concealed something else that relates to power.

Sharing the Spoils, or: "I Am only the Distributor"

Bukhārī puts us on the right track by classifying these hadiths in the *Book on the Obligation of the Fifth* under a title in which he cites sura 8 that, for classical exegesis, is the Koran's echo of the battle of Badr (cf. nos. 6, 7, and 8 above).

After a raid or a conquest, it is in the nature of things that the sharing of the spoils provokes friction and rivalries among warriors. Several verses of the Koran are concerned with this question:

- some declare that the whole booty should go into the public Treasury, entrusted with sharing it among a certain number with a right to it:

> LIX, 6–7: And that which Allah giveth[10] as spoil unto His messenger from them,[11] ye urged not any horse or riding-camel for the sake thereof, but Allah giveth His messenger lordship over whom He will. Allah is able to do all things. That which Allah giveth as spoils unto His messenger from the people of the townships, it is for Allah and His messenger and for the near of kin and the orphans and the needy and the wayfarer, that it become not a commodity between the rich among you, take it. And whatsoever he forbiddeth, abstain (from it). And keep your duty to Allah. Lo! Allah is stern in reprisal.
>
> (Verses 8 to 10 enumerate the various recipients of the spoils.)

VIII, 1: They ask thee (O Muḥammad) of the spoils of war. Say: The spoils of war belong to Allah and the messenger, so keep your duty to Allah, and adjust the matter of your difference, and obey Allah and His messenger, if we are (true) believers.

- another affirms that only 20 percent (from whence "the obligation of the fifth") goes into the public Treasury, the rest being shared among the combattants:

VIII, 41: And know that whatever ye take as spoils of war, lo! A fifth thereof is for Allah, and for the messenger and for the kinsman (who hath need) and orphans and the needy and the wayfarer. . . .

- another (IV, 94) tackling the question from a quite different angle, encourages accepting the offer of peace from a possible adversary, even if this would deprive people of anticipated spoils, because the better booty is with Allah.

Commentators and jurists have been able to harmonize these divergences by relating the various verses to battles that were waged in different conditions (Badr, the expulsion of the Jews Banū Naḍīr from Medina, etc.) and by explaining that the spoils were not divided in the same fashion depending on whether the adversary surrendered without a fight or whether he was defeated by force of arms.[12]

But one may also hear in these divergent verses an echo of debates and rivalries that at Islam's beginnings sentenced different groups from the nascent authority and from each other. Ibn Isḥāq states that this had begun with the battle of Badr:[13]

Revelation on the sharing of spoils after the Muslims had differed on this subject:

Ibn Isḥāq said: When the Badr affair was ended, Allah revealed to his subject the entire sura *Al-Anfāl* [= 8 "Spoils of War"] of the Koran. Here is what was revealed about their differences on the subject of spoils, when they had differences on this subject: "*They ask thee [O Muḥammad] of the spoils of war. Say: The spoils of war belong to Allah and the Messenger.*

Fear Allah. Adjust the matter of your differences, and obey Allah and His Messenger, if you are believers" (VIII, 1).

According to what I learned, when one asks about *al-Anfāl*, 'Ubāda b. al- Ṣāmit[14] says: It was revealed to us, the group of Badr people, because we had differences about the spoils, the day of Badr. Allah took them out of our hands because our arrangements were bad and he gave them to the Messenger of God who allotted them [*qasama*] between us in parity (*he also said:* in equality); in this there was fear of Allah, obedience to Him and to his Messenger and mutual accord.

Sublet distinguishes the *kunya* of filiation (Muḥammad is called Abū l-Qāsim because in fact he had a son called al-Qāsim) and the *kunya* of emphasis that functions as a title or nickname: thus Abū l-Nabāt ("man of the plants") for someone who bore the name Rabīʿ ("of Spring"), Abū l-Alf ("thousand man") for a former slave bought for a thousand (*alf*) dinars. We see here the *kunya* of Muḥammad shift from the first usage (father of a son called al-Qāsim) to the second usage (person entrusted with distribution). Simultaneously it acquires a political significance. It is God himself who gives,[15] the Prophet is only a *qāsim*, distributor (the same as the authority who succeeds him); he applies a set of rules decided by an incontestable authority. And he is the only distributor, the others must stand aside; there is no place in the community for a second Abū l-Qāsim.

Former Prophets and the Spoils, or: "I Am the Distributor!"

Allah gives. . . . In fact, the question bounces back to us, since this is not a matter of an atemporal and universal affirmation of the generosity of the Creator who dispenses the gifts of nature to all people. This "gift" is a new divine disposition, a change with respect to previous dispositions: Allah decides to allow us to profit from the spoils, whereas he had forbidden it to communities that came before us.

A tradition affirms: "The Messenger of God said: For me, the booty has become licit."[16] One sometimes finds this in a slightly more developed form that makes its bearing precise: "The Messenger of God said: For me, the booty has become licit, *although it was not so for any prophet before me.*"[17] This is one of the Prophet's *faḍā'il*, one of the "characteristics"[18] that distinguish him from other prophets.

This phrase presupposes a debate occurring no longer just among Muslims over the modes of sharing and hence over power inside the Community, but between Islam and ancient scriptures on the legitimacy of sharing. Several texts permit us to grasp the problem:

1. Just after the hadith of Jābir b. 'Abdallāh that I have just cited, Bukhārī offers an astonishing midrash:

> Muḥammad b. al-'Alā'[19] reported to us: Ibn al-Mubārak[20] reported to us, having it from Ma'mar,[21] who had it from Hammām[22] b. Munabbih, who had it from Abū Hurayra, who said: The Messenger of God said:
>
> Leaving on a raid, a prophet told his people: "The following may not follow me:
>
> - one who, having contracted marriage with a woman, wants to consummate the union and has not yet done so;
> - one who has built rooms and has not yet placed the roof;
> - one who, having bought sheep or camels in foal, is waiting for them to drop."
>
> He went on the raid and approached the town at the moment of the afternoon prayer or a little after. He said to the sun: "You are a subordinate, and I also! O my God, stop it above us." And it stopped. Allah gave victory to the prophet. He gathered the booty. And it [fire] came to devour it but it did not consume it.
>
> [The prophet] says: "There are defrauders among you. Let a man from each tribe come to touch my hand." The hand of one of them remained stuck to his hand, and he said: "The defrauders are among you. Let the tribe come and touch my hand." The hands of two or three men remained stuck to his, and he said: "The defrauders are among you." And they brought a head resembling a cow's head, in gold, and they put it down. Then the fire came and devoured [the booty]. After this, Allah allows us to have booty; he sees our weakness and our powerlessness, and he allows us to have it.

The same text is found in the *'Arā'is al-Majālis* of Tha'labī, after the story of the taking of Jericho by Joshua with which it is twinned, as it were. It is cited by Ibn Kathīr, who says he had read it in several collections of hadiths, in particular the *musnad* of Ibn Ḥanbal.

From the outset one recognizes the various biblical passages that entered into the composition of this page.

1) Deuteronomy's code regulates recruitment of soldiers (20:5–9): it stipulates that someone who has built a house without having yet dedicated it, someone who has planted a vineyard but not yet enjoyed its fruit, someone who has not yet married his fiancée, and even someone who is afraid are all dispensed from going into combat.—In the Koran, the planter of the vineyard is replaced by the buyer of livestock.

2) Constructed according to the canons of holy war, the story of the taking of Jericho (Joshua 6) recounts that the town was totally destroyed, the inhabitants put to death (with the exception of Rahab and her family), and all objects thrown into the fire. But a certain Akān [Achan] kept for himself a beautiful "Sumerian" mantle as well as gold and silver. Because of this, Joshua's army no longer benefited from divine protection and the men he sent to take Ai, situated about ten kilometers north of Jerusalem, suffer a severe defeat. God reveals the cause of this and demands that Joshua discover the guilty party by the process of elimination, tribe by tribe, clan by clan, family by family. Achan, of the tribe of Judah, of the clan of Zarḥi [*sic*] was thus discovered; having admitted his crime, he is stoned to death and thrown into the fire, along with his family, the booty that he had purloined, and his own livestock. This happened in the Valley of Achor, "that is, Trouble." Then they marched against Ai and this time it was taken without problem (Joshua 7–8).

In the Bible, it is the defeat of the Israelites that reveals that someone has infringed against the rule of totally destroying the booty; here, the crime is revealed when the fire refuses to consume the booty of the conquered "town," just as in I Kings 18:20–29, it refuses to take the sacrifices of the priests of Baal.—In the same manner as Joshua, the "prophet" leads his inquiry tribe by tribe, proceeding by elimination. In Joshua 7:21, Achan's fraud concerned a lovely foreign mantle, as well as silver and gold; here, to make things more "biblical," the gold has been fashioned into a cow's head (cf. "the Golden Calf" of Exodus 32).

The book of Joshua continues by recounting that the people of Gibeon submitted to alliance with the Israelites (Joshua 9). Seeing this, five "Amorite kings" of the region went to lay seige to Gibeon. Joshua rushed to rescue his allies. God got into the battle by sending huge [hail]stones that killed more of the enemy than the sword of the Israelites. And on this occasion Joshua ordered the sun and moon to stand still to give him time to complete his victory (Joshua 10:12–14). Tracked to the cave where they were hidden, the five kings were finally executed.

The story transmitted by Tha'labī is more fleshed out than the simple schema above. Joshua, having succeeded Moses as prophet, receives the order to attack the "Giants." He takes the Ark of the Covenant and lays seige to Jericho for six months. The seventh month, he blows a great blast on the trumpet and the walls of the town crumble. Then the massacre of the Giants begins. But it was Friday afternoon. The Israelites ought to cease combat at sunset and the Giants might escape. This is why Joshua performs the miracle of the sun.[23] After that, the five kings of the "Armenians" form a coalition against Joshua. Pursued by the sword of the Israelites and the divine hailstones, they try to take refuge in a cave from which they are pulled to be executed. It is then that the spoils are gathered and that the fire of heaven refuses to descend to consume it. Thus was revealed the crime of the miscreant who ultimately perishes with the booty itself. —After which, Tha'labī gives in more or less identical terms the short text of Hammām b. Munabbih and Abū Hurayra that we read above.

The page of Tha'labī is again rather concrete, although several different episodes are blended into a single one and several locations are telescoped. Again, there are the proper names, although just those of Joshua and Jericho, as well as the "Armenian" kings who have replaced the Bible's Amorites. With Abū Hurayra's schema, the precision of proper names (personal or geographic) has disappeared. The story of Joshua and Achan is no longer recounted, nor the taking of Jericho, but a "prophet" approaches the "town" and detects two or three cheats in a "tribe." Above all, one is speaking of a previous, outmoded situation; the important word is "since then" [*par la suite*]: in fact, God has now changed the rules concerning booty, out of mercy for *our weakness*.

2. A Text by 'Ibn Isḥāq[24] Commenting on Koran VIII, 67

Revelation about the booty and the prisoners:

Then, Allah remonstrated with him about the prisoners and the seizure of the booty, since before him no prophet had consumed booty coming from one of his enemies.

Ibn Isḥāq said: Muḥammad[25] Abū Ja 'far b. 'Ali-Ḥusayn b. 'Alī said: The Messenger of God said:

- "I was assisted by fright;[26]
- For me, the earth was constituted as mosque and pure place;
- I received what contains all discourse [= the Koran];
- For me, the booty has become licit, although it was not for any prophet before me;
- I received [the privilege of] intercession.

Five things that no prophet has received before me."

Ibn Isḥāq said: [God] said: *It was granted to no other prophet* (meaning, before you) *to take prisoners* (among his enemies) *before imposing oneself on the land* (meaning, to vanquish one's enemies in order to chase them from the land). *You want the good things of this world* (meaning, the objects, the ransom after having taken men), *but God wants the last life* (meaning, that they are killed so that the religion may appear that He wants to appear and by which one obtains the last life). *If a Scripture coming from God had not already intervened, you would have warranted, because of what you have taken* (meaning, the prisoners and booty), *a great punishment* (that is to say, if I had not already warned that I punish only after having prohibited[27]—but He had not prohibited them to have them—I would have punished you for what you have done). Then, He declared them

> licit for him and for them, out of mercy on His part and by indulgent return of Clemency and Misericord: In the booty that you have taken, eat what is licit and good and fear God. God Pardons, he is merciful. Then He said: O Prophet, tell the prisoners who are in your hands: If God recognizes the good in your heart, He will give you a better good than He took from you and He will pardon you. God pardons, He is merciful.

God wants the last life: Ibn Isḥāq's commentary is expressed with objectivity and professionalism and it has become classic. In Ṭabarī's *Commentary,* one reads on this verse:

> *God wants the last life:* that is, God wants to grant you the beauty of the final life which he has prepared in his paradises for believers and those who recognize his authority, if you execute [the enemy prisoners] and if you impose yourselves on the land. He says to them: Search for what God wants to grant you, work for that, and not for what is offered by the desires that attach you to this world. . . .

We know that after the battle of Badr, Muḥammad discussed with his Companions the fate reserved for prisoners. It is an obligatory chapter of the literature of the *Maghāzī*. Let us cite only the two stories reported by Ṭabarī in the same place of his *Commentary*.

According to a tradition passed down by Abū ʻUbayda, the son of ʻAbdallāh b. Masʻūd, to the question posed by Muḥammad: "What do you say about these prisoners?":

> *Abū* Bakr replied: "Messenger of God, they are of your people and kin; let them live and be patient with them, God will perhaps come back to them." ʻUmar said: "Messenger of God, they treated you as a liar and they exiled you. Bring them and have them decapitated." ʻAbdallāh b. Rawāḥa said: "Messenger of God, find a ravine full of dry wood, put them in and set it on fire." . . .

Muḥammad then remarks that each solution can claim a prophetic example:

> God may soften the hearts of men so that they may be sweeter than milk; and God may harden the hearts of men so they are harder than rock. Abū Bakr, you resemble Abraham when he said: "Whoso followeth me, he verily is of me. And whoso disobeyeth me—Still Thou art Forgiving, Merciful" (14:36). Abū Bakr, you also resemble Jesus when he said: "If thou punish them, lo! They are Thy slaves, and if Thou forgive them . . . Thou, only Thou art the Mighty, the Wise" (5:118). 'Umar, you resemble Noah when he said: "My Lord! Leave not one of the disbelievers in the land" (71:26). Ibn Rawāḥa, you resemble Moses when he said: "Our Lord! Destroy their riches and harden their hearts so that they believe not till they see the painful doom" (10:89). And the Messenger of God says: "Today, you are in need. Let not one of them be released without a ransom, or else he be decapitated."

The story that follows in Ṭabarī is attributed to Ibn 'Abbās and stresses how daring the decision was. One has the impression that the defeat that struck Joshua's troops because of Achan's fraud is still present as a threat (the *punishment* Koran VIII, 68 speaks of). Above all, the story recounts that Muḥammad adopted the proposal of Abū Bakr and not that of 'Umar. The next day, finding the Prophet and Abū Bakr in tears, 'Umar asked them the reason for their tears, adding:

> "If I find that there is something to cry about, I will cry; if not, I will appear to!" The Messenger of God replied: "I cry over the one who proposed to the others to impose the ransom; since the *punishment* that was destined for you has been shown to me and it is closer than that tree." . . . And then God revealed: *It was granted to no other prophet to take prisoners before imposing himself on the land* . . . until: *what is licit and good*. And God declared licit that they take booty.

Moreover, Ṭabarī cites several traditions about the "biblical custom" that insisted that any booty taken from the enemy be thrown on the fire.

In a primary sense, as we have seen, by issuing a ban on the *kunya* Abu l-Qāsim, the clerics of Islam affirmed that the Prophet (and hence power claiming legitimacy from him) was the *only one* authorized to allot the profits from conquests. In a secondary sense, they affirm that he was historically the *first one* to be able to do so, a way of stating both Islam's continuity with and difference from the stories of the Ancients (*asāṭīr al-awwalīn*).

The Clerics and Sacralized Violence

Thus the permission to take prisoners and to liberate them in return for ransom was a concession to the weakness of those who saw no further than "*the good things of this world*"; but the true will of "God" would have been that the prisoners be executed; religion would be strengthened by this, and the way to eternal life would have been more distinct. Finally, if God conceded that prisoners' lives be saved, it was not out of mercy for them, but out of mercy with respect to the warriors of Badr, for whom he pardoned the error of not having killed them and whom he allowed to profit from the spoils.

We may be permitted to speculate about the clerics' discourse, especially when it touches on politics and makes a transcendent actor intervene in conflicts among men. The reflections that we have just read are directly in line with the celebrated biblical passages that attribute a similar attitude to God or to his representative; they belong to a value system that is very distant from the one to which our contemporaries customarily adhere:

- In Numbers 31, Moses is furious because in the war of vengeance against the Madianites the Israelites have killed only the men, while making prisoners of the women and children.
- In Joshua 6:21 and 8:20–29, the taking of Jericho and of 'Aï are followed by the extermination of the inhabitants (with the foreseen exception of Rahab and her family); and this continues in chapter 10 with the impressive litany of the conquests of Makkedah, Lachish, Eglon, Libnah, Hebron, and Debir.
- In I Samuel 15, Samuel declares to King Saul that God has definitively rejected him because he proved guilty of weakness in the "ethnic purification" against the Amalekites.

Of course, like everyone else, ancient Israel profited from booty taken in combat. Several pages in the Bible testify to this: Deuteronomy 20:14;

21:10–14; II Samuel 12:30–31. And while David's troops leave no survivors (I Sam. 27:9), their intention is not to obey a sacred law but to prevent the survivors from revealing to Achish, the Philistine king of Gath, that David is betraying him. But the stories that speak of the extermination of entire cities doomed under the ban (*ḥèrèm*) struck the imagination of readers and commentators on the Bible even more forcefully. We have seen that the Muslim narrators seem to have remembered only such stories.

Again, the historian and exegete may discern that the text is more complex than it seems. Many think that stories of this kind were developed during an era of restoration. People wondered why they had suffered so much misery. The "religious" replied that the cause was clear: they had yielded too much to Canaanite sirens by going to celebrate pagan rites under the green trees (II Kings 17:10). It was easy to conclude: "Ah, if we had only exterminated all the Canaanite men and women at the time of the conquest! This was surely what God wanted and our ancestors did not know enough to obey."

> At the time these texts were written, it was already possible for the best in Israel to hear in this only that the attraction to the Canaanite gods is radically condemned, rather than to hear it as an appeal to spill the blood of their idolators.[28]

This is no doubt true, and it is reassuring to think that Israel behaved like everybody else in the various phases of its destiny, neither better nor worse, that the texts about extermination do not correspond to historical practice, and that perhaps they were written in an era when the community did not possess armed forces. But the text is there and it raises at least two questions:

First, someone had the temerity to write this. "Sages," reflecting in peacetime on what they knew of their history, advanced without batting an eyelid the hypothesis that "God" wanted a final solution for the Canaanites and other pagans.[29] Herein lie violent drives that ought to be examined.

Second, everyone can read it for himself—not only "the best of Israel." Experience shows that when circumstances lend themselves to it, such texts may demolish the last barriers that try to curb instincts toward violence and death. Why have scruples if "God" spoke thus to the "prophets"?

Conclusion

In the same way that one may climb up a mountain wall that has neither fissure nor bump, so one may open a text that is perfectly smooth. But the texts we cited at the beginning of this essay presented at least two flaws that allow us to suspect that something more profound is hidden underneath the apparent meaning:

1) the Prophet forbade anyone to bear the same names (*ism* and *kunya*) as himself; but it appeared that this interdiction was far from being respected;

2) the *innamā* of certain formulas is at the very least awkward: Do not take my *kunya* because I am *only* a distributor.

What is hidden derives from a collective patrimony that is always more present than one sometimes believes; it reveals to us that the issue being debated was not really an onomastic problem. It was not a matter of avoiding taking for oneself some name or other, or giving them to one's sons, out of reverence for the person of the Prophet. The clerics' reflections bear on more serious matters: the unique place of prophetic power in the alotting of the riches of this world, and foremost goods that had been taken from the infidel enemy, and the novelty that Islam brought on this point in comparison with preceding religions.

There remains one question: in which direction did the movement go? Was there first the ban on taking the *kunya* of the Prophet out of respect for his person, and then clerical reflection on the role of the Prophet in the Community and on the comparison between the Prophet of Islam and previous prophets? Or else was it the other way around: this reflection came first and the ban on bearing the *kunya* was a secondary and theoretical decision?

In other words, are we dealing with an event in the life of Muḥammad in which the clerics of Islam subsequently discovered a meaning that exceeded the simple onomastic problem? Or else is this a construction elaborated by the same clerics on the basis of ancient Scripture and of the practices of their time, which was then displaced back to the *Ḥijāzan* past in order to furnish an element in the writing of the founder's biography? The question merits being asked.

Notes

1. [Jean-Louis Déclais, "La kunya du Prophète et le Partage du Butin. Un midrash sur Josué?" *Arabica* 1999, Tome XLVI, pp. 176–92. Translated by Susan Boyd-Bowman.]

2. Jacqueline Sublet, *Le voile du nom: Essai sur le nom propre arabe* (Paris, PUF, 1991).

3. This is "proof that one is integrated into Arab society, that one is free and a Muslim," ibid., p. 56.

4. It has become the name (*ism*) Belkacem, rather current in the Maghreb.

5. Ibn Sa'd, *Aṭ-Ṭabaqāt al-Kubrā* (Beirut: Dār Ṣādir, n.d., vol. I, pp. 106–107).

6. "*Baqī'* al-Garqada" (the field of brambles) is the first Muslim cemetery of Medina.

7. Sublet, *Le voile du nom*, p. 52.

8. *Wafāyāt al-A'yān*, ed. Iḥsān 'Abbās (Beirut: Dār Ṣādir, 1977), vol. IV, p. 170.

9. Ibn Sa'd, *Aṭ-Ṭabaqāt al-Kubrā*, vol. V, p. 91.

10. The verb *afā'a* (from which comes the word *fay'*, "spoil") signifies *to make return, to bring back,* from which *render to the Muslims the infidels' spoils that belong to them by right.*

11. *From them:* The People of the Scripture referred to in the preceding verses.

12. Cf. Si Boubakeur Hamza, *Le Coran, traduction nouvelle et commentaires* (Fayard-Denoël, 1972), vol. II, p. 1092.

13. Ibn Hishām, *al-Sīra al-Nabawiyya*, ed. Ṭaha 'Abd ar-Ra'ūf Sa'd (Beirut: Dār al-*Jīl*, 1991), vol. III, p. 218.

14. One of the *Anṣār*, of the tribe of Khazraj; he participated in the negotiations that preceded the hijra and all the Prophet's battles, he died in Palestine in 656 or shortly after.

15. Note that in Koran LIX, 7, it is the *Messenger* who is presented as the *giver* whose decisions must be accepted.

16. Of Jābir b. 'Abdallāh, classed by Bukhārī in the same *Book of the Obligation of the Fifth*, in chapter 8, as someone who follows the series of hadiths on the *kunya* of the Prophet.

17. Cf. the text of Ibn Isḥāq on Koran VIII, 67.

18. The scholars of Islam have classified what distinguishes the prophets from each other (not what distinguishes them from ordinary men); this work has given rise to the literature of the *faḍā'il*. Thus Abraham is the only one who enjoys the title of *Khalīl* (Friend of God), David is the only one who could mold iron with his bare

hands, Adam and Jesus are the only ones who are born without a father. In this sense, permission to amass spoils of war distinguishes Muḥammad from other prophets.

19. Refers to Abū Kuryab, traditionalist of *Kūfa* who died in 860.

20. 'Abdallāh ibn al-Mubārak, resident in Khurāsān, died around 797.

21. Ma 'mar b. Rāshid al- Ṣan'āni (died 770), of the generation of the first authors of complete books in Islam.

22. Hammām (died around 720) is the elder brother of Wahb b. Munabbih, one of the writers who worked hardest to adapt the stories of the biblical tradition to Islam. In this case, was Hammām content to transmit a text that he would have received from Abū Hurayra, or else did he have a more active role in the elaboration of the hadith, he who belonged to a family that knew the Bible and Judeo-Christian apochryphal literature?

23. Tha'labī then interrupts the story to insert a tradition concerning Muḥammad that has him, too, making the sun hold back so that Ali might perform in his own time a prayer that he had omitted.

24. Ibn Hishām, *al-Sīra al-Nabawiyya*, vol. III, p. 231.

25. Here, Muḥammad al-Bāqir, great grandson of 'Ali, fifth imām for the Twelver Shi'ites, died in 731.

26. The fright that destroyed the adversary's forces after the supernatural intervention is a habitual theme in holy war. Cf. Koran III, 151; VIII, 12; XXXIII, 26; LIX, 2; and, in the Bible, Deut 2:25.

27. In his commentary on Koran VIII, 67, Bayḍāwī (d. 1286) gives the following paraphrase: *Whether a decision of God has not been previously inscribed on the (heavenly) Tablet, to wit:*

he does not punish one who commits an error by making a personal interpretation;
or else: he does not punish the combattants of Badr;
or else: . . . nor a people for that which was not declared prohibited;
or else: the ransom that they took, he made it licit for them.

28. P. Beauchamp, in *Cahier Evangile no. 76 (Violence in the Bible)* (Paris, 1991), p. 37. See also Pierre Gibert, *La Bible à la naissance de l'Histoire* (Paris: Fayard, 1979), p. 126.

29. For its part, the *Book of Wisdom*.

2.5

Dave and the Knave in the Cave of the Brave[1]

Qur'ān 9.40: Ḥākim al-balad ma'a l-walad fī ġār al-ġabbār

Michael B. Schub

> Only the future is certain;
> the past is constantly changing.
>
> Polish proverb[2]

Faithful Muslims will forever believe that Q 9.40, "If ye help him not, still Allah helped him when those who disbelieve drove him forth, the second of two; when they two were in the cave, when he said unto his comrade: Grieve not. Lo! Allah is with us. Then Allah caused His peace of reassurance to descend upon him and supported him with hosts ye cannot see, and made the word of those who disbelieved the nethermost, while Allah's word it was that became the uppermost. Allah is Mighty, Wise,"[3] refers to the Prophet Muḥammad and Abū Bakr, although not one word of the Qur'ānic text supports this.

There are a number of reasons to hold this belief suspect:

1. Ṭabarī[4] supplies the following overly pietistic Ḥadīṯ: While preaching in a mosque (*ḥīna xaṯaba*) Abū Bakr asked for a volunteer to recite Sūrat al-Tawba. When the fellow reaches the words "then he said to his companion," Abū Bakr broke down in tears and said: "[That's] me, by God! [I am] his companion (*'anā wa-llāhi ṣāḥibu-hu*)."
2. Zamaxšarī[5] goes to such an extreme as to presage a Nixonian "there

> goes the presidency" scenario by fabricating [*sic*] a Ḥadīṯ in which he has Abū Bakr warn the endangered Prophet: "If you are struck down now, that's it for God's religion (*'in tuṣabi l-yawma ḏahaba dīnu l-lāhi*)."

If the "historical"[6] Qur'ān assumes on the basis of wishful thinking the protagonists to be Muḥammad and Abū Bakr, what might the "historic" Qur'ān "originally have had in mind?"

The truth may never be known (scil. *'al-lāhu 'a'lam*). But we may hypothesize that Muḥammad's muse conflated some biblical passages that he had heard from Jewish and/or Christian sources.

Most important is the passage 1 Samuel 23:16ff. Saul is out to kill David (the founder of the Messianic line for both Jews and Christians), but David and his companion Jonathan, Saul's son, have already become a metaphor for brotherly love (cf. 1 Samuel 18:1).

The relevant passage is:[7] 1 Samuel (15) "[. . . David was in the Wilderness of Zīf] *fīl-ġāb* (in the thicket). (16) *fa-qāma yūnāṯānu bnu ṣā'ūla wa-ḏahaba 'ilā dāwūda 'ilā l-ġābi wa-ṣaddada yada-hu bi-l-lāhi*. (17) *wa-qāla la-hu: lā taxaf li-'anna yada ṣā'ūla 'abī lā taġidu-ka wa-'anta tamliku 'alā 'isrā'īla wa-'anā 'akūna la-ka ṯāniyan* . . . (18) *wa-'aqāma dāwūdu fī l-ġābi*. . . ."

When we compare the original Arabic of Q 9. 40 to this biblical passage, we have:

1. most strikingly: *ṯāniya l-iṯnayni* corresponds to Jonathan's being *ṯāniyan*, i.e., David's "second-in-command."[8]
2. *l-ġār* ("the cave") corresponds to *l-ġāb* ("the thicket") three times [in this biblical version]. A few years later on, 1 Samuel 24:2ff. concerns a pivotal *cave* incident between David and Saul. Note that the Qur'ānic text does *not* use the synonymous *kahf* (the title of Sūra 18) here. In this instance Speyer's[9] dictum is most appostie: "dass, . . . wie so oft im Qoran, Mohammed gehörte Dinge verwechselt oder vermischt hat."
3. *lā taḥzan* stands for *lā taxaf*. Cf. Ṭabarsī:[10] *lā taḥzan* 'ay lā taxaf [*sic*].

4. *fa'anzala sakīnata-hu 'alay-hi wa-'ayyada-hu* corresponds closely to *wa-ṣaddada yada-hu bi-l-lāhi*.
5. ". . . He brought low the word of the unbelievers and exalted the word of god" is the result of ". . . the hand of my father Saul can't touch you, and you [David], will rule over Israel. . . ."
6. The commentaries ("In its allusiveness and referential style, the Qur'ān behaves precisely like a commentary, presuming that the audience knows the situation being commented upon and the characters and stories being referred to"),[11] including Ṭabarī and others, relate the myth about a spider spinning its web at the entrance of the cave to protect the fugitive(s) both at Q 9.40 and at an incident when David takes refuge from Saul in a cave.[12]
7. ". . . and in Sūra 21.105 he [i.e., Muḥammad] quotes from this *zabūr* Psalm 37:29, in an almost literal translation . . . moreover the majority of the passages in the Qur'ān that remind us, by sense or sound, of the Bible, are from the Psalms."[13]

Psalm 57 begins with the words: "To the chief Musician, Altashchith, Michtam of David, when he fled from Saul in the cave"; Psalm 142 begins with the introduction: "Maschil of David; A prayer when he was in the cave." Both of these are references to David's meeting with Jonathan in the cave at 1 Samuel 23:14ff.

Given Muḥammad's certain knowledge of (some) Pslams especially, and of other Jewish religious texts and customs in a more general way, his conflation of the relevant biblical passages into Q 9. 40 is readily understandable.

Nöldeke's well-known contention that the Isrā'īliyāt function as models of God's support for the believers[14] is borne out well here; a diachronic re-identification of Abū Bakr with David's alter ego Jonathan could only strengthen Abū Bakr's historic claim as first Caliph.

I concede that this hypothetical exegesis is not a conclusive proof; but it is hardly an exiguous eisegesis. Cf. Q 13.43: *kafā bi-l-lāhi šahīdan bayn-ī wa-bayna-kum wa-man 'inda-hu 'ilmu l-kitābi*.

Notes

1. Michael Schub, "Dave and the Knave in the Cave," *Zeitschrift für Arabische Linkguistik* 38 (2000): 88–90.

2. Quoted from C. G. Starr, *A History of the Ancient World* (New York: Oxford University Press, 1991), p. viii.

3. M. M. Pickthall, *The Meaning of the Glorious Koran* (New York: New American Library, n.d.), p. 149.

4. Ṭabarī: *Jāmi' al-Bayān* . . . vol. 10, p. 137 in initio. 1954–68.

5. Zamaxšarī: *Al-Kaššāf* . . . ad. loc. Q 9.40.

6. Cf. D. A. Madigan, SJ, "Reflections on Some Current Directions in Qur'ānic Studies," *MW* 85, nos. 3–4 (1995): 345–62.

7. United Bible Society, Cambridge 1965, p. 467 in medio (The verse numbering in this version differs slightly from the standard.)

8. Sic. P. K. McCarter Jr. *I Samuel*, in *The Anchor Bible* (Garden City, NY: Doubleday, 1980), p. 373.

9. H. Speyer, *Die biblischen Erzählungen im Qoran* (Hildesheim, 1988), p. 396 in medio.

10. Abū l-Faḍl al Ṭabarsī, *Mağma' al-Bayān fī Tafsīr al-Qur'ān*, vol. 5–6 (Tehran, ca. 1965), p. 31 in fine.

11. Madigan, "Reflections on Some Current Directions in Qur'ānic Studies," p. 354 in fine.

12. B. C. De Vaux, art. Dāwūd, in: *Shorter EI* (Ithaca, NY: Cornell University Press, 1953, 1974), p. 72, col. 2, in initio.

13. J. Horovitz, Art. Zabūr, in: *Shorter EI*, p. 649 in initio and in fine.

14. Cf. B. Heller, Art. Ṭālūt, in ibid., p. 571, col. 2, in medio.

2.6

Qumran and the Preserved Tablet(s)[1]

E. F. F. Bishop

The following paragraphs should be considered as in the nature of an appendix to the exhaustive article by Dr. F. Nötscher, which appeared in 1959 in the *Revue de Qumrân*. This dealt with the "Heavenly Tablets and Fatalism."[2] There are references to those passages in the Old Testament, the Apocrypha and Pseudepigrapha, as well as "Qumrân," which make mention of "The Tablets" or "The Books." Between, however, the Babylonian Tablet of Fate and the ideas behind the Book of Remembrance or the Book of Life, there are similarities in detail, deserving of attention, as well as significant differences; with fatalism less prominent in biblical contexts. This is more questionable in "Qumrân," but so far as the literature of the Settlement is concerned "the end is not yet." The material here presented may perhaps be allowed to carry the vaster researches of F. Nötscher a stage further, since the broad ideas reappear in the Surahs of the *Qur'ân*. We are grateful to add this little.[3]

In the concluding chapter of his *Qumrân Studies* Professor Rabin discusses "Islam and the Qumrân Sect," listing some dozen affinities of varying significance—matters of specific detail rather than more general Semitic ideas. But he does not think his list final.[4] Others are likely to find further parallels; and perhaps one of these occurs in the first of the Qumrâni *Hodayot* (rendered "Thanksgiving Pslams"). This is in reference to things "engraved" or "inscribed" from the "eternal years." This phraseology has been translated differently, but the idea seems constant. This may well have passed into Islamic thinking through Jewish rather than Christian sources, even if no Qumrânic connection can be established. There is, however, the remarkable allusion in 2 Corinthians to the "law (Torah) engraved letter by letter upon stone."[5] Other New Testament references in Luke, Hebrews and the Apocalypse are examined by F. Nötscher, who also mentions *Hodayot* 1, 23–24, the various English renderings of which are as follows:

> Everything is engraved before thee with a pen of
> remembrance for all the everlasting periods. (Millar Burrows).[6]
> All things are inscribed before thee
> in a recording script,
> for every moment of time. (T. H. Gaster).[7]
> All is inscribed before thee, engraved as a memorial
> For all times of eternity. (E. F. Sutcliffe).[8]
> All things are graven before thee
> on a written reminder
> for everlasting ages. (G. Vermes).[9]
> Everything is engraven in Thy presence with
> the ink of remembrance unto all appointed
> times of eternity. (Svend Holm-Nielsen).[10]

More than one of the above translations is reminiscent of the language of Malachi 3, 16. In his note on the passage, Holm-Nielsen besides calling attention to the possibility of "ink" coming into the picture, for the *Hodayot* were written in ink by the Qumrânis, mentions, as Nötscher, the "heavenly tablets of fate," and adds: "This concept, which can be traced back to Babylonian mythology, is also known from the Late Jewish literature." It is here that the transition is made to the Quranic inheritance from Qumrân or some other Jewish source. There is the one famous allusion to "a guarded tablet." This seems to have been reckoned to contain (among other things) "the story of the hosts, Pharoah and Thamûd."[11] The full narrative (as the Prophet heard it) of Moses' experiences with Pharoah and what happened afterwards with the Lord "on the mountain" occurs in the Seventh Surah (Battlements). In this narrative there are three allusions to the "Tablets" (plural):

> We wrote for him on the Tablets of everything, an admonition and a distinguishing of everything. When Moses returned to his people, angry and sorrowful, he said: "Evilly have you done in my place, after me; what, have you outstripped your Lord's commandments?' And he cast down the Tablets. . . .
>
> And when Moses' anger was abated in him, he took the Tablets; and in the inscription of them was guidance and mercy unto all who hold their Lord in awe.[12]

Commenting on the mention of "a guarded Tablet," the adjective meaning that it was free from "corruption" ("*al-tahrîf*"), al-Baidâwi says that the Tablet which contained the *Qur'ân* was situated above the seventh heaven. One grammarian preferred to read "guarded" in the nominative case, thereby making it synonymous with *Qur'ân*.[13]

Then there are the three occasions when the Tablets are mentioned. What "we wrote for him" is explained by al-Baidâwi to mean what people are in need of in the matter of religion ("*din*") whether for admonition or distinguishing of everything.[14] There is a difference of opinion as to the number of the Tablets—ten or seven—and they were either emerald or topaz or sapphire or hard stone, which God made pliable for Moses, so that he was able to manipulate them. They contained the Torah or something else. This latter phrase is interesting, if speculative, because of the information in the second reference when the Tablets were broken, and Moses had to gather them up. The Torah, inscribed on them, was in seven parts; and when they were recovered, it was found that six-sevenths comprised the "distinguishing of everything," while one-seventh was devoted to the admonitions and regulations. In the third context where there is mention of "inscription" ("*nuskha*"), al-Baidâwi interprets the *nusakh* as meaning books, like "discourses" for the clarification of truth and guidance for what is seemly and good; with the further interesting statement that they were intended for those who held their Lord in awe, that is virtually, people who were apprehensive of rebellion or disobedience towards their Lord.[15] It is perhaps only coincidental that the Quranic word for "hold in awe" is connected with the Arabic for "monk," curiously reminiscent of the (more or less) monastic Qumrânis.[16] Be that as it may, do we not have another link between Qumrân and the *Qur'ân*, both for those who approve the suggestion of Professor Rabin, and those who would not commit themselves to more than acquiescence in a general Semitic outlook in which nascent Islam shared with the Judaism of seventh-century Arabia? The references to the "discourses" as making for the clarification of what is seemly and good, might even be an echo, if faint, of the passages in Daniel and the Apocalypse, considered by F. Nötscher. In the *Interpreter's Bible* Jeffery mentions the "Babylonian texts . . . the tablet of good deeds and the tablet of sins," when commenting on the passage in Daniel.[17] Rist similarly discusses the "books" in the relevant contexts in the Apocalypse.[18]

Whether or not we accept the "ink of remembrance," as in the translation of Qumrâni *Hymn* I, 23–24 by Holm-Nielsen, or prefer "the finger of God,"[19] whatever the implication, we should be thankful both for the research initiated by F. Nötscher into another of those concepts in some sense cardinal in each of the Monotheistic religions—the "books"; and for the light shed backwards and forwards on the great Corinthian passage: "a letter written not with ink but with the Spirit of the Living God, written not on stone tablets,[20] but on the pages of the human heart" (New English Bible).

Notes

1. E. R. F. Bishop, "Qumran and the Preserved Tablet," *Revue de Qumran*, No. 18 Tome 5, Fasc. 2, April 1965, pp. 253–56.

2. The books mentioned in F. Nötscher's well-documented article include *Jubilees*, *Enoch*, and the *Testaments of the Twelve Patriarchs*.

3. A preliminary study of "The Qumrân Scrolls and the Qur'ân" appeared in the *Muslim World* in July 1958.

4. Chapter VIII. On page 112 Rabin says: "It seems not unlikely that the number of correspondences could be increased."

5. II Corinthians 3, 7, as in the *New English Bible*. The *Interpreter's Bible* (10, p. 307) refers to "the Decalogue carved in letters of stone used as the symbol of the entire law."

6. *The Dead Sea Scrolls*, p. 400.

7. *The Scriptures of the Dead Sea Sect*, p. 133.

8. *The Monks of Qumrân*, p. 185.

9. *The Dead Sea Scrolls in English*, p. 152.

10. *Hodayot: Psalms from Qumran*, p. 18.

11. Surah 85 (*The Constellations*), (Arberry: *The Koran Interpreted* 2, pp. 332–33).

12. Surah 7 (Arberry 1, pp. 189 ff).

13. Commentary of al-Baidâwi, Book 4, p. 181.

14. Commentary of al-Baidâwi, Book 3, pp. 27, 28, 29.

15. The Tablets in this Surah would appear to be records of good deeds, as in some biblical passages.

16. "*Râhib*" ("*ruhbân*") is the ordinary word for "monk" and occurs three times in the *Qur'ân* in the plural; while monasticism comes once, as a phenomenon forbidden in Islam.

17. Volume 6, pp. 458–59.

18. Volume 12, p. 526.

19. *Hodayot: Psalms from Qumran*, note 47 on page 25.

20. Arabic versions use the same word for "tablets" as the *Qur'ân*.

2.7

Qumran and "The Companions of the Cave"[1]

Hugh Nibley

While Jewish and Christian writings have been diligently searched for possible references direct or indirect to the Qumran tradition, the Moslem commentators on the Koran have been neglected as a source of information, and that for the very quality that renders their work most valuable, namely their "uncritical" reluctance to omit from their profuse and repetitive notes any tradition, anecdote, or rumor that might conceivably cast light on a subject. Packed in among their jumbled baggage are many items that bring Qumran to mind. Whether these are significant or not remains to be decided after some of them have been examined.

The most promising place to begin a search for possible glimpses of Qumran is among the commentaries on the "Sura of the Cave" (*Sura* XVIII), and the most promising guide-book is that inexhaustible storehouse of oddities and surprises, Ahmad ath-Tha'labi's *Accounts of the Prophets*.[2] Following Tha'labi's lead, and eking out his reports with those of other commentators, we shall attempt to show that Moslem scholars were convinced that there had once been a singular community of saints living in caves in the Judaean desert, particularly in the region of Jericho, and that those Cave People had a portentous message for the human race.

As the most fitting commentary to the thesis that all things of this earth are but "dust and dry dirt," the Prophet refers us to the *Ashab al-Kahf wa-l'Raquim*, "The Companions (often rendered simply "People" or "Inhabitants") of the Cave and the Inscription" (*Sura* XVIII, 9–10). This was a group of holy men who had sought retreat in the wilderness in flight from a wicked and godless community and in the expectation that God would guide them in a proper way life, fill them with grace, and provide for their wants; in due time they were hidden from the knowledge of men and their bodies were miraculously preserved in a cave, where they were at length discovered when a youth, by the providence of God, circulated old coins in a nearby town and thereby brought a rush of treasure-seekers to the scene (*Sura* XVIII, 10–22). Such a tradition might well look back to the sectaries of the desert—but there is a catch, for most commentators are agreed that the People of the Cave were the Seven Sleepers of Ephesus. That would settle the matter were it not that the Ephesus tradition itself rests on the flimsiest of foundations, archaeologically and philologically.[3] It is "une de ces légendes vagabondes qui n'ont pas d'attache fixe et prennent pied sur les terrains les plus divers, sans qu'aucun fait connu semble justifier le choix."[4] Scholars ancient and modern who have tried to get to the historical kernel of the story have found themselves confronted by countless conflicting traditions, and the Koran and its commentators note that every essential element of the history of the Companions is a subject of hopeless controversy among the People of the Book, who cannot agree as to where the cave was, how many people were in it,[5] what their religion was,[6] how long they stayed there, or in what condition.[7] In short, nobody really knows their history.

The main source of the confusion is not far to seek: there was more than one cave story because there was more than one cave—as the extremely popular legend spread abroad in the world the tale had to be adjusted to the interest of local patriotism, which from Andalusia to Persia enthusiastically and profitably exploited local grottoes as the authentic and original sites of the Seven Sleepers or the Companions of the Cave.[8] But amid a welter of conflicting legends and claims two main traditions have always been recognized—an Occidental, containing clearly-marked pre-Christian Classical elements as its distinctive ingredient, and an Eastern or Arabic tradition, based principally on Jewish apocryphal lore.[9] The clearest distinction between the two versions is preserved by Tha'labi. He knows the Ephesus tradition as well as anybody: the pre-Christian legends of youthful sleeping heroes are well represented in his pages;[10] he knows the resurrection miracle-stories of the early Christian apocrypha;[11] he and the other Arabs give an accurate description of the state of the Church both when the Sleepers fell asleep and when they awoke;[12] and they know the name of the mountain near Ephesus where they slept—a name which Christian scholars apparently do not know.[13]

But knowing the Ephesus version as he does, Tha'labi still gives priority to an entirely different story about a party of three refugees who were looking for a place for their families to settle when "the sky smote them" and they took refuge in a cave, only to be trapped by a rock-slide that sealed the entrance. Being thus caught, each one of them recounted some pious deed he had done in this life-time, and with each successive story a fissure in the wall opened wider until they could all escape.[14] This tale has nothing to do with Ephesus—the men in the cave tell Jewish stories and do not even fall asleep.[15] The violence of the elements, the sliding down of the mountain, and the sequel is that the people settled on the spot, since they left their records there.

The story of the Three is an Arabic contribution, designated by Huber as the "Raqim" version, that being the uniquely Arabic name for the locale of the Cave.[16] Since it is a perfectly plausible tale, one wonders why the Arabs, who insist on placing al-Reqim in Syria or Palestine, bother with Ephesus at all. It is because Ephesus had loudly advertised its claim to the Seven Sleepers ever since the middle of the fifth century, and our commentators are not the men to leave anything out.[17] Ephesus, however, gets into the picture only by usurping the much older credentials of Antioch—a circumstance that has been overlooked by researchers. The hero of the Arabic accounts of the Sleepers is one Tamlikh, whose name does not appear in the standard Western lists of the Seven: When he turns up in the Syriac versions his name makes an eighth in the established list, so that the older Syriac and Arabic accounts uniformly insist that there were really eight Sleepers.[18] The origin of the intruder is indicated by the epithet that Tha'labi gives him of *Ibn Falastin*—the Palestinian.[19] His Greek name of Iamblichus usually appears in Latin sources as Malchus while the Arabic writers point it variously as Tamlikh, Yamlikh, and Namlikh: all that remains in Bamlikh to remind us that, as Huber long ago suggested, the name Iamblichus-Malchus is simply Alimelech.[20] What brought Huber to that observation was the long-established identity, or at least very close parallel, between the Seven Sleepers and Abimelekh, the friend of Jeremiah who slept for 70 or 100 years.[21] Abimelech in turn has long been identified with Onias-Honi the Circle-drawer.[22] Onias, Abimelech and Jeremiah all fell into century-long slumbers as they sat in the shade of a tree, and the tree is a peculiar detail which the Arabic writers introduce into their version of the Seven Sleepers;[23] and just as Onias was driven with his workment to seek shelter from a storm in a cave, so the Arabs say the Cave of the Companions was discovered by a shepherd escaping from a storm, who ordered two laborers to open the mouth of the Cave for him.[24] This Onias has in our day often been put forth as the leader of the Zadokite forerunners of the Qumran community in the days when they were being persecuted by Antiochus Epiphanes, and even as the founder of Qumran.[25] So we have Tamlikh the leader of the Companions of the Cave identified, through Abimelech, with Onias the leader of the Qumran society.

The earliest mention of the Seven Sleepers of Ephesus is in the *Itinera Theodosi*, 530 Anno Domini, which states that the Seven were brothers, and that their mother was Felicitas.[26] When one recalls that one of the first female martyrs was St. Felicitas, who heroically endured the extinction of her seven sons, and that these seven have been identified in ancient and modern times with the seven young Jewish heroes of IV Maccabees, martyred at Antioch by the brother of Antiochus Epiphanes,[27] and that Byzantine Christians also identify the Seven Sleepers with the martyrs of Antioch,[28] and when one further considers that Decius, the villain of the Ephesus story, goes by the name of Antiochus in an eastern version of it,[29] one begins to wonder if the fifth-century Ephesus story might not reflect a much earlier Syrian version. The confusion of Antioch and Ephesus is apparent in the strange insistence of our Arabic informants that the city of Ephesus changed its name to Tarsus after its conversion from paganism. Scholars have found no explanation for this strange aberration, and indeed it is hard to see how well-travelled men could have confused two of the best-known cities in the world.[30] But there is evidence that the name of Tarsus was indeed changed to Antiochia in 171 before Christ in honor of the pagan Antiochus Epiphanes, in which case it was back to Tarsus after his demise.[31] Zonaras in a rhetorical play on words calls the city Epiphanes,[32] and one wonders if the confusion of Tarsus-Epiphanes with Ephesus might not be a typical slip: the Arabs knew that the city had once had another name—and what could it have been but Ephesus, since they favored Tarsus as the site of the cave?[33] The year that the name was changed, 171 BC, also saw a migration of Jews to Tarsus,[34] and one Arabic commentator suggests that Tarsus got its name at the time of the Cave People from a group of colonists from Tripolis in Syria.[35] At about the same time, it is surmised, the Bene Zadok were first being driven by Antiochus Epiphanes under their leader Onias III.[36] Thus there is some evidence to associate the founding of the Cave community with persons, times, places and circumstances that have become familiar in the discussions of the founding of the Qumran community.

While quite aware that the Seven Sleepers story is Christian property, our Arabic informants are inclined to favor a *pre*-Christian date for the Companions of the Cave, explaining that they later became disciples of Jesus and flourished "in the days of the kings of Tawaif, between Jesus and Mohammed."[37] This implies that the society had a fairly long life, a thing entirely out of keeping with the brief and violent episode of the Ephesians. Another thing to note is the dependence of our Arabic informants, especially Tha'labi, on Jewish sources.[38] While it was Jacobite and Nestorian leaders arguing about the People of the Cave who first asked Mohammed's opinion on the matter,[39] those who really claimed a monopoly of knowledge on the subject were the Jews. According to one account the Quraish sent a delegation to Medina to father intellectual ammunition against the Prophet from the local Jews, who loudly insisted that they alone were qualified to speak on prophetic matters. They suggested some test questions to embarrass the new prophet, the prize one being about the People of the Cave.[40] In another version it is the skeptical Jews themselves who send the delegation to investigate Mohammed.[41] But the account favored by Tha'labi is that of a delegation of three holy men who came not to Mohammed but to Omar, looking for a true phophet. These were not the smart, proud, skeptical Jews of Medina but sincere and humble seekers, who gladly accepted the Prohpet as soon as they were made sure of his calling.[42] The impression one gets is that of Hasidic Jews interviewing the sympathetic Omar during his campaign in Palestine—he calls them "brothers," and he must send back home for Ali in order to answer their questions.[43] The peculiar questions they put to him moreover bear the characteristic stamp of the non-conformist sectaries: they ask about the keys of heaven, the moving tomb of Jonah, the warning minister who is neither spirit nor man, the things that walk the earth but were not created in the womb, the speech of animals and its spiritual message, and above all "about the people of a former age who died 309 years, and then God revived them—what is their story?"[44]

That the story of the devout delegates goes back to the early sectaries is indicated in a report attributed to Ibn Abbas, the nephew of the Prophet and the star witness in all matters concerning the People of the Cave. "The followers of Jesus remained on the sacred path for 80 years after his ascension," and then "Yunus the Jew came among the Christians wearing a hermit's or monk's gown (this well before the days of Christian monasticism). . . . His devout life produced great confidence among the Christians, and . . . he said, 'Send me three of your learned men . . . that I may divine a secret before each of them separately.'" As a result "the Christians were divided into three sects" forever after—the very sects that argued about the Cave People in the presence of Mohammed.[45] Here we have a counterpart both to the three malicious questions that the Jews put to Mohammed (in nearly all the commentators the questions are three) and the delegation of three pious Jews that came to him. The oldest Syrian version of the Seven Sleepers, which some hold to be the original, places their history around 60 Anno Domini, thus taking it entirely out of the later Ephesian setting and putting it in the orbit of the early sectaries.[46]

Tha'labi is quite at home with certain pre-Christian communities in the desert. He tells us among other things how the infant Mary was taken to be reared by "the priests of the sons of Aaron," and how the priestly society cast lots for her, standing on the banks of the Jordan to see whose rod would sink and whose would float, they being "the reeds with which they used to write the Torah." Zacharias, the father of John the Baptist, and, according to Tha'labi, "the chief of the scholars and their prophet," won the lottery; but when a famine came he could no longer support the child and it was necessary to have another casting of lots, won this time by Joseph the righteous carpenter.[47] Since "Brownlee argues that the mother of the Messiah is the 'Essene Community,'"[48] Mary's prominence in such a community as this may not be without significance. The story of Joseph's winning of Mary is told in the *Epistle of I Clement*, c. 43, and indeed Tha'labi's general familiarity with Clementine motifs should be studied in view of the importance of the latter in understanding the background of Qumran.[49] His tracing of Zacharias' genealogy through both a Ṣaduq and a Ṣadiq indicates access to early source material;[50] and is quite relevant to the Seven Sleeper investigation, since the oldest Western version, that of Gregory of Tours, reports on the authority of "a certain Syrian" that the mission of the Seven Sleepers was to correct certain errors not of the Christians but of the Sadducees—a term often confused with Zadokite in the early Middle Ages in designating nonconformist sectarians among the Jews.[51] Why should the Seven Sleepers of Ephesus be emissaries to the Sadducees, of all things? The Zadokite background of Qumran needs no demonstration.

A significant aspect of the Seven Sleepers' history as told by the Arabs is that nobody ever sees them alive.[52] Even in the Western legends the ruler merely embraces the youths as they sit on the ground and after a short and formal benediction by one of them they promptly fall asleep again.[53] The miracle that proves the resurrection is never the animation of their bodies, but only their preservation;[54] no capital is made of the rich store of Jewish and Christian apocryphal lore, the "Testaments" of various prophets, patriarchs, and Apostles who come to life to tell of wonderful things in the worlds beyond. This remarkable reserve suggests, what many students have pointed out, that the Sleeper stories may well have originated with the actual discovery of human remains in caves. The Mediterranean world had never been without local hero-cults and their grottoes: Arabic writers report visits to a center in Andalusia which had all the fixtures and purported to be the original home of the Companions of the Cave,[55] and such a shrine and cult survived at Paphos on Cyprus down to modern times.[56] But the cave best known to the Arabs was one near Tarsus, where 13 cadavers in a remarkable state of preservation were annually propped up and groomed—their clothes brushed, the nails manicured, their hair dressed—and then laid down to sleep for another year before a devout host of Christian pilgrims who believed they were in the presence of the Seven Sleepers.[57] This reproduces exactly the drama of the original Sleepers in the presence of Theodosius and his people, and strongly suggests a cult of the dead. In the "Hunting" version of the Sleepers story, which has all the marks of the Classical Endymion cycle, our Arabic informants comment on how the spring dried up and the trees all withered while the youths slept, only to be miraculously revived at their awakening.[58] Such obvious cult-motifs serve to set the Ephesian tradition apart from the more down-to-earth "Raqim" accounts of the Arabs, which indeed contain rather surprisingly nothing of a miraculous nature.

In a much-cited passage, Ibn Abbas tells how on a campaign with Mu'awiyah or Habib ibn Maslamah he passed by a cave containing bones which were said to be those of the Companions. His friend wanted to take a look, but Ibn Abbas protested that that would be sacrilege; some men who were sent to the cave to investigate were driven back in terror by a fierce wind.[59] Ibn Abbas is quoted as saying that the cave was "near Aelia," and Al-Qurtubi explains that they passed by it on the way to Rum.[60] The latter authority also reports that when Ibn Abbas made a few fitting remarks at the cave site a Syrian monk who was standing by observed with surprise, "I didn't think that an Arab would know anything about that!" to which the company proudly replied by introducing Ibn Abbas as their Prophet's nephew.[61]

The key to the location of the Eastern Cave is the mysterious name of *al-Raqim*. The great Ibn Abbas confesses that the word is one of the four things in the Koran which he cannot understand, but is quoted by Tabari as saying that Raqim is "a wadi between ʻAsfan and Aelia beyond Palestine; and it is near Aelia";[62] while Damiri has him say: "it is a wadi between Amman and Aelia, beyond Palestine between the Ghatfan (tribe) and the country beyond Palestine; and this is the wadi in which the People of the Cave live, but Kaʻab says it is their village."[63] Most Arabic authorities locate al-Raqim in the plain of Balq in southeastern Palestine, and the geographer Istakhri mentions a small town by that name in the area, apparently near the Dead Sea.[64] Some writers, however, favor the region of Damascus and others that of Amman.[65] Clermont-Ganneau noted that the village of al-Raqim 7 km. south of Amman is identified by Usama with a place called el-Kahf, where there are some remarkable tombs cut into the living rock—hence *Ashab al-Kahf wa l'Raqim*. In December of 1964 the writer visited this site with Mr. Rafiq Dajani of the Jordan Department of Antiquities, whose forthcoming book on the subject treats at length the features of the newly-excavated site which render it in our opinion by far the most likely candidate for the original Raqim. Even Huber concedes that this was probably the al-Raqim of the

Arabic commentators, but hastens to point out that it cannot possibly have been the cave of the Seven Sleepers of Ephesus.[66] But then no one says it was—our Arabic authors readily admit that they are dealing with other caves, and what interests us here is not the mythical cavern of Ephesus but real caves in the Judaean desert.

Distant candidates in Nineveh and Yemen need not detain us, though we should not overlook the suggestion that the Companions were originally wandering artisans (*ṣayāqala*).[67] Tha'labi reports that when writings inscribed on metal plates (and we shall presently see that the "Inscriptions" of the Cave were such documents) were found in a cave in Yemen no one could decipher them until one of these travelling smiths or artisans was consulted.[68] This is noteworthy because some scholars have seen in these nomadic craftsmen the descendants of the Rekhabites and hence the possible ancestors of the Qumran community.[69] The earliest Oriental versions of the Seven Sleepers stories actually do come from Nejran, the borders of Yemen. Massignon explains this by showing that the feast of the Martyrs of Nejran falls on the same day as that of the Seven Sleepers of Ephesus, making it easy if not inevitable for Jacob of Sarug to confuse the two; and since Ephesus was inconveniently far away, Massignon reasons, Eastern Christians simply moved the shrine to Nejran, whence it was transplanted to "military garrisons and the hermitages of anchorites on the fringes of the deserts."[70] The objection to this theory is that the men of Nejran will have nothing whatever to do with *Seven* Sleepers, but only three or five, which is strange indeed if they imported the magic Seven directly from Ephesus.[71] Plainly the Nejran version rests on another tradition.

Al-Raqim, so Lane informs us, means writings engraved or scratched on something, "a brass plate, or stone tablet, placed at the mouth of the cave," Sale suggests, though he is not sure,[72] or else it is two lead tablets in a sealed copper box—with silver seals,[73] or it is simply a book, or even a golden tablet,[74] or perhaps it is an inscription over the cave door,[75] or else the name of the cave itself, or of the wadi where it is,[76] or possibly the mountain,[77] or it may have been the stone that blocked the entrance,[78] or else it is the ruins near the cave or even the village where the Cave People lived;[79] or it may refer to water-holes or running water in the wadi.[80] On the other hand, it may refer to coins, or to an ink-stand or writing-desk found on the spot;[81] or it may be the dog that guarded the cave,[82] or any number of regions claiming to possess the Cave.[83] Strangely enough, no one seeking to locate the cave ever mentions the church or mosque that is supposed to have marked the spot with perpetual ritual observances—this most obvious clue of all has no place in the Raqim tradition. Instead we are confronted with a combination of caves, writings, bones, ruins, coins, ink-stands, wadis (there is no mention of a valley in any of the orthodox Ephesus stories), etc., suggesting that the would-be interpreters of al-Raqim all have in mind a type of archaeological site which the modern reader most readily associates with Qumran.

The general consensus is that al-Raqim refers to secret buried writings, containing the history and even the teachings of the Companions, but "whose meaning God has kept from us, and whose history we do not know."[84] These were deliberately hidden away to come forth in a later age when "perhaps God will raise up a believing people."[85] There was a tradition that Jeremiah with the same purpose had hidden such treasures in a cave near Jericho,[86] as Peter had done near Jerusalem (according to Baidawi it was Peter who discovered the documents of al-Raqim),[87] and the theme of buried holy books has a special appeal to Tha'labi, who carries the custom back to the remotest times.[88] The recently recognized possibility that the library of Qumran was deliberately buried in "a solemn communal interment," to come forth in a more righteous age thus supplies another link between Qumran and the Companions of the Cave and the Raqim, while putting a new stamp of authenticity on their existence.[89]

Let us recall how the question was put to Omar: "Tell me about the people of old who died 309 years and then God revived them—what is their story?" One wonders in passing why Jews should be so interested in a purely Christian story, and why they alone should claim to know its details, which according to Tha'labi were all to be found in Jewish books: plainly they were not asking about Ephesus at all.[90] The length of the famous sleep is reported at anything from 70 to 900 years. The Christians favor 372, while the Moslems accept the 309 years of the Koran.[91] The true meaning of the 309 is a great mystery, which only a true prophet can explain;[92] it comes from the beni Israel, and "the Christians of Nejran way, 'As for the 300 years we already knew about that, but as for the 9 years we know nothing about it.'"[93] But all are agreed that it represents the period of darkness during which the blessed Companions slept, like Onias, to awaken only at the dawn of a new age of faith.[94] Such was also, whatever the actual years may have been, the significance of the 390 years of the *Damascus Document* I, 5–6, "the Era of Anger" and darkness. Massignon shows the lengths to which Christians and Moslems will go to see significance in 309; it is the "anagram of the total of the 14 isolated initial letters of the Koran," namely 903, as also, of the name of Jesus: *'Isa* = 390.[95] The free juggling of figures does not draw the line at arranging them in any order, just as modern scholars are not embarrassed by the difference between 390 and 393 years or the necessity of adding or subtracting 20 or 40 to suit one's calculations. It has been recognized that the 390 of the *Damascus Document* is a symbolic number having "no more than a schematic value," and the same is held for the Koranic 309.[96] Since both have the same significance and are equally vague, distant, and mysterious, a possible confusion of the two may furnish yet another link between the two societies.

The consensus of opinion that al-Raqim were *metal* plates containing the writings of the Companions, as well as Tha'labi's preoccupation with metal documents in general, is moved from the realm of pure fantasy by the recent discovery of a number of metal documents in Palestine and Syria, the most notable being the *Copper Scrolls* from Qumran Cave 4. Tabari tells of a shepherd who discovered inscribed tablets which no one could read but an old holy man of the desert—like the Copper Scrolls, these tablets contained lists of buried treasure.[97] Another peculiarity of the Companions (which does not fit with the Ephesus scene) is the emphasis put on the formal organization of the society. After individually receiving enlightenment in the shade of a tree—like Onias, Abimelech, and the Buddha—the Seven discover to each other their like-mindedness and resolve to form a community with a near-by cave as their headquarters. They have a president and spokesman, Maximilianus, and a secretary and treasurer, Tamlikh, the star of the play.[98] Each member fetches his property from his father's house and after giving lavishly to the poor turns the rest over to a common fund, to be shrewdly administered.[99] Such a community of property is one of the best-known features of the Qumran society.

In taking to the wilderness, the Brethren set up (according to the Arabs, but not to the Greeks) at a place where there was a good spring and some fruit trees, subsisting as did many a pious anchorite in years to come on the water and dates of an oasis.[100] "They left their homes and lands, families and children . . . and entered the caves (plural) in the year of the prophets."[101] Here we have a definitive religious movement, as against the adolescent escapade of Ephesus: in the latter case the youths (who are very young) flee to the wilderness expressly to escape the Emperor, while in the former their society flourishes before the Emperor ever hears of it.[102] Part of the heroic allure of the Companions is that they are high-ranking officers in the Imperial army, which seeming inconsistency suits well with the image of the men of Qumran as "dedicated holy warriors."[103]

Considerable emphasis is placed by our Arabic authors on the North-south orientation of the Sleepers, who must face the north to preserve their bodies against the day of their arising. Here is a reminder of the North-south orientation of the burials as Qumran, whatever may be its significance.[104] The bodies of the Sleepers were turned from side to side by angelic ministers (to avoid corruption) every seven days, or seven years, or twice a year, or (in most writers) every year on New Year's Day.[105] Also, the sun shines into the cavern on just two days of the year—suggesting the Equinoxes, and it is the sun which finally awakens them.[106] The emphasis here on a solar (resurrection) cult and calendar is a reminder that the Qumran people were peculiar for their zealous adherence to an archaic solar calendar.[107]

It was in the ancient practice of incubation at healing shrines that E. Rohde sought the origin of the Seven Sleepers tradition, and indeed our Arabic and Syriac sources tell how God speaks to the Companions as they sleep, and how one calls upon their names for healing dreams.[108] It is just possible that Qumran itself may have been such a healing shrine: ". . . the idea of a place of healing by the Dead Sea was well established in Jewish tradition and gives added reason for the Essenes' ('Physicians') choice of Qumran (Mesillah) for their desert home."[109] In this connection, Allegro dwells on the ancient designations of Qumran as meaning "shady," "sheltered"—which puts one in mind of the elaborate arrangements described by the Arab scholars for keeping the sleeping Companions in the shade,[110] though admittedly far-fetched.

The one truly moving episode in the history of the Seven Sleepers as the Arabic commentators tell it is the manner of their falling asleep. The indefatigable Tamlikh returns from the town in tears of anxiety to report to his friends that the monster (*jabbar*, a Jewish word) has returned to Ephesus and is coming out against them. This calls for a general lamentation until Tamlikh tells the brethren to dry their eyes, lift up their heads, and "eat what God has given," an expression suggestive of an exhortation to martyrdom. Accordingly, we behold the Brethren of the Cave partaking of their last sorrowful supper as the sun sets (the setting of the sun receives special emphasis), and then, as they sit upon the ground, preparing and exhorting one another in holy conversation, quietly yielding up their souls to God.[111]

The celebration of a last supper and love-feast as the sun sets brings to mind Philo's account of an Egyptian branch of the Essenes holding their solemn feast at sundown,[112] as well as al-Biruni's report that the Jewish sect of the Maghariba celebrated their rites at sunset—a circumstance which could easily lead him to omit the single *nuqṭah* that makes the difference between Maghariba ("Sundown-people") and the familiar Maghariyah or "People of the Caves."[113]

The reference in *Sura* LXXXV, 4 to "the people of the pit" (*asḥabu 'l-ukhdud*) deserves mention because in the past it has commonly been interpreted as referring to the persecutors of the Christians of Nejran. This explanation was seriously questioned, and the now familiar designation of the "people of the pit" in the Dead Sea Scrolls indicates an earlier origin of the concept.[114] At the same time it vindicates the Christian Nejran tradition as an authentic echo of the old desert sectaries: it was the Christians of Nejran, it will be recalled, who first mentioned the Companions of the Cave to Mohammed.

The name given by the Companions to their settlement, according to the Arabic sources, was Hiram or Khiram, meaning "sectarians" or "separation," but also an appropriate designation for forbidden ground.[115] The wonderful dog that spoke with a human voice and faithfully guarded the threshold of the Cave usually goes by the name of Qatmir, though we also find him sharing the well-nigh universal name of Raqim, explained by Damiri's note that the Arabs often called a dog Raqmah, meaning a wadi with water in it, which he believes to be the source of the name Raqim.[116] Since the name of the dog is thus confused with that of the society, the cave, the valley and what-not, one wonders if the second commonest name of the dog might not represent a like confusion—for the name is Khumran, the closest parallet yet to "the meaningless Arabic name Qumran."[117]

Let us now briefly summarize some of the main points of ressemblance between Qumran and the Companions of the Cave. First of all, the experts favor a pre-Christian origin for both; each begins its history with a persecution and migration under (possibly) Antiochus Epiphanes, as a time when both societies seem to have the same leader; both have ties with wandering artisans—the ancestors and/or descendants of desert sectarian groups; they have the same apocalyptic-mystic teachings, familiar alike from the early Jewish and the early Christian apocryphal writings; both have connections with a priestly society on the Jordan before the birth of Christ; the activities of both are reflected in the Clementine writings; both are identified with the Zadokites by name; both are near Aelia and even nearer to Jericho; both left behind the same peculiar combination or archaeological litter; both engaged in the odd practice of burying sacred records to come forth at a later time as a witness; both make use of metal plates for such records; each thinks of itself as the righteous remnant; the numbers 309 and 390 have for the Companions and Qumran respectively the same significance; both societies are well organized and practice a community of property; each community has its buildings, spring, and fruit-trees as well as its caves; both were ritually oriented, dedicated to good works and religious exercises, controlled by special solar calendar; in both the dead were laid away facing the north; both practice healing and incubation and seem to have had a solemn ritual feast at sundown; the members of both are dramatized in a military capacity; both sites are linked in later times with the mysterious word Khumran-Qumran. In both cases everything is very vague, far away, and strangely portentous.

The great mystic and symbolic appeal of the Sura of the Cave, which is recited every Friday in every mosque, rests on the concept of the Seven as intercessors for man in a wicked and dangerous world.[118] But there may be more than abstract symbolism or allegory involved here. Scattered references in Jewish and Christian writings such as the Karaite texts and the letter of Bishop Timotheus, indicate at least a dim awareness down through the centuries of the existence and the peculiar significance of writings found in caves near Jericho. When the red herring of Ephesus is removed we are faced with the very real liklihood that the people who left those records were those very "Companions of the Cave and the Writing" who made such an indelible imprint on Islam.

The purpose of this brief exploratory study has been to raise rather than settle issues. The Arabic commentators cited are of course only a sampling, since the Arabic sources available at present in the far West are limited, though increasing very rapidly, thanks to the titanic efforts of Professor Aziz S. Atiya. But they have given us enough to indicate that many questions still await and deserve investigation. We have not even touched upon the knotty and intriguing question of the identification and status of the all-knowing Tha'labi, nor have we examined the possible paths by which the Qumran tradition reached him and other Arabic writers; nor have we considered the wealth of literary tradition and folk-lore that surrounds the wonderful dog Qatmir, nor sought to trace the mysterious and significant line of Zadok in the Arabic sources; nay, we have not even mentioned the many other possible references to the Qumran tradition in the Koran itself. What we have done is simply to indicate the possibility that echoes of Qumran still reverberate in the pages of many Moslem writers, who may yet prove valuable informants to students of the Dead Sea Scrolls.

NOTES

1. Hugh Nibley, "Qumran and the Companions of the Cave," *Revue de Qumran* No. 18 Tome 5, Fasc. 2, April 1965, pp. 177–98 [Nibley's orthography has been retained].

2. "Abu Ishaq Ibn Mohammed Ibn Ibrahim ath-Tha'labi of Nishapur, the celebrated commentator, was the outstanding (Koran) interpreter of his time; he composed a great commentary which was without equal for fullness. . . .": Ibn Khallikan, *Kitab wafayat al-aiyan* (Paris, 1842), I, p. 30. "Ein besonders heiss umstrittenes Feld waren altarabischen, jüdischen und christlichen Legenden des Korans und der Tradition. . . . So kommt es, dass der bedeutendste Korangelehrte deiner Zeit, der im Jahre 427/1036 gestorbene Ahmed eth-Tha'labi, als bedeutendstes Werk seine 'Prophetengeschlichten' erfasst hat": A. Mez, *Die Renaissance des Islams* (Heidelberg, 1922), p. 190. His "History of the Prophets gives all the stories in very great detail. . . ." *Encyclopedia of Islam* (1934), IV, p. 736. Cf. C. Brockelmann, *Geschichte der Arabischen Literatur* (Weimar, 1898), I, pp. 350–51.

3. Baronius and Tillemont both declared it spurious. The Austrian archaeologists working at the supposed site discovered "pas un nom ni un symbole, indice d'une tombe vénérée," *Analecta Bollandiana* 55 (1937), p. 351. Philology is no less nonplussed: ". . . il ne faut pas oublier que les noms de la grotte et de la montagne de la légende ne se retrouvent pas aux environs d'Éphèse," *Ibidem*, 24 (1905), p. 503.

4. *Analecta Bollandiana* 55 (1937), p. 351. Cf. *Ibidem*, 39 (1921), p. 176, commenting on the "systèmes déjà échafaudés autour de cette littérature foisonnante." There is no apparent reason why the legend should have become the special property of Ephesus, according to Bernhard Heller, *La Légende des Sept Dormants*, in *Revue des Études Juives*, 49 (1904), p. 216, note 6, though it is understandable that the city once in possession should exploit the legend to the fullest.

5. For location, see below, notes 62–66. The number of sleepers is a subject of endless debate: *Sura* XVIII, 22; al-Nasafi, *Tafsir al-Qur'an al-jalil* (Cairo, 1936–1942), 11, p. 286; al-Hijazi, *al-Tafsir al waḍiḥ* (Cairo, 1952), XV, pp. 53–54. It is one of the great mysteries, known to but a few, al-Tabari, *Kitab jami' al-bayan fi tafsir al-Qur'an* (Cairo, 1910), XV, p. 150; al-Nasafi, *loco citato*. The Jacobites said there were three sleepers, the Nestorians five, the Moslems seven: al-Qurtubi, *al-Jami' li-ahkam al-Qur'an* (Cairo, 1935?–1950), X, p. 382; al-Damiri, *Hayat al-hayawan* (Cairo, 1867), II, pp. 353–54 (pages are incorrectly numbered, but we follow the numbers given); al-Nasafi, *opus citatum*, 11, p. 285; al-Baydawi, *Anwar al-tanzil* (Cairo, 1899–1902), IV, pp. 98–99. Yusuf Ali, a modern authority, says that Mohammed "*suggested* that the youths were seven in number," *The Holy Qur-an* (New York, Hafner, 1946), 11, p. 730, note 2337.

6. Some say they lived before Christ and were idolaters, others that they were Christians, others that they were Moslems: Tabari, *Tarikh al-Ṭabari* (Cairo, 1961), 11, pp. 6–7, and *Jami' al-bayan*, XV, p. 137; some even that their people were *majus*: Damiri, II, p. 353. Yet the Jews have a special claim on them: Ibn Kathir, *Tafsir al-Qur'an al-asim* (Cairo, 1954), III, p. 74. See below, note 38.

7. See below, note 91, for the length of the stay. As to their condition, the main discussion is as to whether they were sleeping or dead, Baydawi, IV, pp. 97–98; Qurtubi, X, p. 388; Damiri, II, p. 358, etc. See Michel Huber, *Die Wanderlegende von den Siebenschläfern* (Leipzig, 1910), pp. 79–99.

8. Huber, *opus citatum*, pp. 17, 122. Thus after favoring Ephesus (though Ephesus is not mentioned in the Koran), Ibn Kathir, III, p. 75, concludes: ". . . we are not told what land the cave was in. . . . But Ibn Abbas says it was near Aelia, and Ibn Ishaq says it was near Nineveh, while others say it was in the land of Rum and others that it was in the plain of Balqā (south-eastern Palestine), but God knows." See below, note 60.

9. Discussed by Huber, *opus citatum* in note 6 above, pp. 552–56. The distinction is clear in Huber's classification of sources into the Classical Endymion and Epimenides legends (pp. 378–90), as against the Onias-Abimelech-Erra tradition (pp. 403–47) of the Orient. The arabic commentators themselves admonish against confusing the two traditions. Thus al-Shirbini, *al-Siraj al-munir* (Cairo, 1868), II, p. 350, assures us that the three pious refugees (below, note 14) are "another group entirely from the (traditional) People of the Cave." Cf. al-Qurtubi, X, p. 357, and Ibn Kathir, III, p. 75.

10. The Endymion motif, in which E. Rohde, *Die sardinische Sage von den Neunschläfern, in Rheinisches Museum für Philologie*, Neue Folge, 35 (1880), pp. 158–59, 162–63, sees the origin of the Seven Sleepers of Ephesus, is one of the four distinct versions of the Sleepers reported by Tha'labi and others. It is the "Hunting" story in which youthful nobles go forth to hunt and celebrate a great pagan festival only to end up falling asleep in a cave, guarded by their faithful dog. The fullest account of this is in Tha'labi, *Qissas al-anbiyah* (Cairo, 1921), pp. 289–90, 292–93. Cf. Ibn Kathir, III, pp. 74–75; al-Qasimi, *Tafsir al-Qasimi* (Cairo, 1957–1960), X, p. 4032. Typical of the cycle is Tha'labi's account of Saint George, pp. 299–300.

11. One of the four versions (see preceeding note) is the tale of the Bath Attendant (Tha'labi, p. 293; Tabari, *Tarikh*, II, p. 8, and *Jami' al-bayan*, XV, p. 136; Damiri, II, pp. 344–45; Qurtubi, X, pp. 359–60), which consists of familiar motifs from the early apocryphal *Acts of John, Thomas, Andrew, Peter*, etc., see Huber (*opus citatum* in note 6), pp. 306–10. Also the well-known talking-dog motif, found in all the above-named Arabic sources, is familiar from the pseudo-*Acts of Andrew, Thomas*, etc. Damiri, II, p. 344, says that the official story of the People of the Cave was written down by Andrew (Mandrūs) and Thomas (Dūmās), and others say that it was "a righteous ruler of the people called Peter (Bīdrūs)" who ruled for 68 years who discovered the document: Baydawi, IV, pp. 87, 90.

12. The moral decline of the Christians just before the Decian persecution, to which Eusebius and Cyprian attribute that persecution, is passed over in silence by Christian commentators on the Ephesus story, but is very well described by the Arabs: Tha'labi, p. 293; Tabari, *Jami' al-bayan*, XV, p. 133; Nasafi, II, p. 284; Shirbini, II, p. 351; Damiri, II, pp. 339–40. The state of things under Theodosius is equally well described, M. Huber (*opus citatum* in note 7), p. 567; *Analecta Bollandiana* 72 (1954), p. 265. The risen youths seem to the Emperor like the ancient disciples come to life, and he rejoices in the restoration of the old religion: Tabari, *Jami' al-bayan*, XV, p. 147; Shirbini, II, p. 362; Damiri, II, p. 319. The righteous leader who greets the saints on their awakening sometimes bears the name of Arius:

Tabari, XV, pp. 145–47; Shirbini, II, p. 361; Tha'labi, pp. 297–98, reads it *Armūs*.

13. In Greek sources it is Chaos, Chileton, Chileon; in the Latin, Chilleus, Celius, Mons Celeus, *Analecta Bollandiana* 41 (1923), p. 374; 55 (1937), p. 350. In the Syrian tradition it is always Mount Anchilos, of which Huber, pp. 222–23, notes that "um Ephesus herum kein einziger Berg einen auch nur halbwegs ähnlichen Namen trägt," surmising that the Christians could readily borrow the name of Mons Caelius near Rome for their Sleepers, "da der Berg selber nicht existierte . . . ," p. 58. The Arabs ring the changes on Anchilos with *Yanjilūs* (Baydawi, IV, pp. 85–86, 89), mispointed to read *Banāhīyūs* and even *Manhilūs* (Damiri, II, pp. 343, 350), but most commonly written as *Banjilūs* (Tabari, XV, p. 135; Shirbini, II, p. 353; Ibn Kathir, III, p. 73), this being nearest to the modern Turkish name for the real mountain east of Ephesus, Panajir-Dagh: *Analecta Bollandiana* 55 (1937), p. 350.

14. Tha'labi, p. 287, attributing the story to Mohammed. It was *thalātha nafrin*, which can mean either a party of refugees or a military detail. That it was the former may be inferred from the nature of their mission: *yartadūna li-ahlihim*, "looking about for some place for their families"—seeking asylum. See Damiri, II, p. 341.

15. The stories have been analyzed by B. Heller (*opus citatum* in note 4), pp. 199–202, and classified as Haggidic.

16. "So ist eine genaue *Scheidung* zwischen den Hö hlenleuten (of Ephesus) un den Genossen des Er-Raqim festzuhalten. . . ." Huber (*opus citatum* in note 7), p. 239. See below, notes 62 and 63.

17. It is now definitely established that the story was first fastened on Ephesus by a "pia fraus" of Bishop Stephanus of that city in the year 449 or 450, according to *Analecta Bollandiana* 72 (1954), p. 265, citing E. Honigmann, *Patristic Studies* (Rome, Vatican, 1954).

18. M. Huber (*opus citatum* in note 7), pp. 593, 503; *Analecta Bollandiana* 39 (1921), p. 177; 66 (1948), p. 195. The Arabs explain the discrepancy by having the Seven joined by a shepherd on their way to the Cave (Tha'labi, p. 293). Tabari, *Tarikh*, II, p. 6, Baydawi, IV, p. 48 and Damiri, II, p. 339, all tell straightforward stories of eight Sleepers, in spite of *Sura* XVIII, 22.

19. Tha'labi, p. 292.

20. "Schon der Name Abimelech weist den Jamlich-und-Malchus hin": Huber (*opus citatum* in note 7), p. 22.

21. Heller (*opus citatum* in note 4), pp. 207, 214.

22. Huber (*opus citatum* in note 7), pp. 418–26. See the article *Onias* (*Honi*) in *Jewish Encyclopedia* (1901), IX, pp. 404–405.

23. For the three Hebrews, see B. Heller (*opus citatum* in note 4) pp. 202–206.

For the tree episode, see Tha'labi, p. 292; Tabari, XV, p. 136; Baydawi, IV, p. 86; Ibn Kathir, III, p. 74; Qurtubi, X, p. 359; Shirbini, II, p. 355.

24. Heller, p. 206; Cf. Tha'labi, p. 295; Tabari, *Tarikh*, II, p. 8; Baydawi, IV, p. 87; Damiri, II, p. 357. Down to modern times the Seven Sleepers have been protectors against storms: *Analecta Bollandiana* 68 (1950), p. 248.

25. Whether a later Onias is preferred (R. Goossens, *Onias le juste . . . lapidé en 64 avant J.-C.*, in *La Nouvelle Clio*, 1–2 (1949f), pp. 336–53), or the earlier Onias III, *circa* 170 before Christ (M. Black, *The Scrolls and Christian Origins* [New York, Scribner's, 1961], p. 20), there is general agreement on a connection between Onias and Qumran: See H. H. Rowley, *The Zadokite Fragments, and the Dead Sea Scrolls*, in *Expository Times* 63 (1951/2), p. 382; M. H. Segal, *The Habakkuk "Commentary" and the Damascus Fragments*, in *Journal of Biblical Literature* 70 (1951), p. 145.

26. ". . . civitas Epheso ubi sunt septem fratres dormientes . . . quorum mater Caritina dicitur, graece, latine Felicitas," text in *Analecta Bollandiana* 41 (1923), p. 372. Cf. Gregory of Tours, in Migne *Patrologia Latina* 71, col. 787: "Septem vero germanorum. . . ."

27. The identification is recognized in *Analecta Bollandiana* 57 (1939), p. 39. Heller (*opus citatum* in note 4), p. 217, believes that the Seven heroes of Antioch are the most instructive of all parallels to the Seven of Ephesus.

28. Namely at Paphos on Cyprus, *Analecta Bollandiana* 26 (1907), p. 272. The Christians of Antioch built a basilica over the tomb of the Seven Jewish brothers, just as those of Ephesus did at the shrine of the Seven Sleepers: Heller, p. 217.

29. In an "Antiochus-Gedicht" of 1527, that ruler is designated throughout as Decius: W. Bacher, in *Jewish Quarterly Review* 16 (1904), p. 529. "Voilà la fusion des deux légendes," cries Heller, p. 218, commenting on this.

30. Tha'labi, p. 287. Some writers simply speak of Tarsus without even mentioning Ephesus: Nasafi, II, p. 282; Shirbini, II, p. 358; al-Zamakh-shabi, *al-Kashshaf* (Cairo, 1890), I, p. 469. Heller, p. 200, note 5, can make no sense of this.

31. Bohlig and Steinmann, in Pauly-Wissowa, *Realencyclopädie*, IV A, col. 2419.

32. *Ibidem*, col. 2431.

33. Below, note 57.

34. *Realencyclopädie*, IV A, col. 2420–21.

35. al-Qasmi, X, p. 4028.

36. H. H. Rowley, *The Covenanters of Damascus and the Dead Sea Scrolls*, in *Bulletin of the John Rylands Library* 35, no. 1, September 1952, pp. 137–45; P. Kahle, *The Cairo Geniza* (London, 1947), p. 19.

37. See Tha'labi, p. 288; Damiri, II, p. 349; Tabari, *Tarikh*, II, pp. 6-7: "Some say they worshipped Jesus . . . and some say their history . . . was before Christ, and that the Messiah taught his people about them, and that God woke them from sleep after he had raised up Jesus, in the time between him and Mohammed, but Got knows". Cf. Qurtubi, X, pp. 359, 388, and Huber (*opus citatum* in note 6) p. 21, citing Ibn Qutaiba. Damiri, II, p. 357, says they fell asleep, following one tradition, until the land became Moslem; and Ibn Kathir, III, p. 74, notes that if they had been Christians, the Jews, who do not mention such a thing, would certainly have reported it.

38. See B. Heller, *La légende biblique dans l'Islam*, in *Revue des Études Juives*, 98 (1934), p. 7, and *Ibidem*, 49 (1904), pp. 202–12. Tha'labi knows of specific Jewish informants of Mohammed, pp. 77, 137, and refers to his own Jewish teachers, pp. 137, 152, 241, 254, 257, etc. He often betrays a distinctly pre-Jewish and anti-Christian prejudice, as in the long story of Jesus' vain attempt to convert a Jew, pp. 276–79. He even knows the Pumbeditha scandal-story that Mary was once a ladies' hair-dresser, p. 131.

39. "The seyyid and the Jacobite and their Christian companions from Nejran were visiting (*kānū 'inda*) Mohammed" when the matter came up: Baydawi, IV, p. 98; Cf. Nasafi, II, p. 285; Damiri, II, p. 354.

40. Shirbini, II, p. 351; al-Hijazi, XV, p. 54; as-Suyuti, *Lubab al-nuqul* (Cairo, 1935), p. 144, emphasizes the boastfulness of the Jews.

41. Ibn Kathir, III, p. 74; as-Suyuti, *loco citato*; Sayyid Qutb, *Fi zilal al-Qur'an* (Cairo, 1953?), XV, p. 81.

42. Tha'labi, pp. 288–89. B. Heller (*opus citatum* in note 4) p. 200, believes this story to be a unique contribution of Tha'labi.

43. Ali and Omar in the story both address the delegates as "brothers of the arabs," who in turn are "the brothers of the Jews": Tha'labi, p. 289. The way in which Ali is greeted by Omar as he arrives wearing the robe of the Prophet suggests that he has been summoned from a distance, p. 288. As both the conqueror of Palestine and the would-be rebuilder of the Temple (H. Nibley, in *Jewish Quarterly Review* 50 [1959], pp. 118–220), Omar would be sympathetically received by the "Hasidic" sectaries of the desert.

44. The questions are given in full in Tha'labi, pp. 288–89. Most Arab writers mention only three questions: ". . . about the Spirit, the Companions of the Cave, and Dhu 'l-Quarnain," Hijazi, XV, p. 54. On the apocryphal-sectarian nature of the questions, see M. Huber (*opus citatum* in note 7) pp. 454–56; K. Ahrens, *Christliches im Qoran*, in *Zeitschrift der Deutschen Morenländischen Gesellschaft* 84 (1930), p. 163.

45. H. Wernecke, in *Monist* 15 (1905), pp. 467–68. They became "the three chief sects of Syria," pp. 466–67.

46. This is Jacob of Sarug, discussed by Heller (*opus citatum* in note 4), pp. 260–61, who is at a loss to explain the surprisingly early date.

47. Tha'labi, pp. 260–61.

48. M. Black (*opus citatum* in note 25), p. 149.

49. Tha'labi, pp. 122–23, also tells the Clementine story of the blossoming staff. On the influence of the Clementine writing on the Koran, see K. Ahrens (*opus citatum* in note 44), pp. 56–60, 64, 174; on their importance for Qumran, see H. J. Schoeps, in *Zeitschrift für Religions-und Geistesgeschichte* 3 (1951), pp. 333–34; 6 (1954), pp. 277–78; 10 (1958), p. 15, and especially *Das Judenchristentum in den Pseudo-klementinen* 11 (1959), pp. 72–77.

50. Tha'labi, p. 259. Onias, as the grandfather of John the Baptist, belongs to the same line, that of the Sadiqqim: R. Eisler, *Iesous Basileus ou Basileusas* (Heidelberg, 1930), II, p. 49.

51. Gregorius Turonensis, in *Patrologia Latina*, 71, col. 788. On the confusion of Sadducees and Zadokites, see H. H. Rowley (*opus citatum* in note 36), pp. 129–32. The Moslems designated non-conformist sectarians as *Zandakiyah*, and though the origin of the word is obscure, a *zindīq* is, according to Lane's *Arabic-English Lexicon*, I, p. 1285, "One of the thanawiyah [or asserters of the doctrine of Dualism]; or one who asserts his belief in [the two principles of] Light and Darkness: or one who . . . conceals unbelief and makes an outward show of belief." How well this applies to the dualistic theology and secretive policies of Qumran needs no illustrations. Our Arabic commentators often refer to the Companions of the Cave as *thanawiyah*. When a Moslem victor asked some sectarians, "Who are you?" they replied, "Harranites." "Christians or Jews?" Neither, was the reply. "Have you holy books or a prophet?" To this they gave a guarded and confusing answer *(jamjamū)*, whereupon the official observed, "You must be Zandokiyah. . . ." So in order to survive they changed their name to Ssabians. D. Chwolson, *Die Ssabier und der Ssabaismus* (St. Petersburg, 1865), II, p. 15. Sabaean denotes "irgend eine täuferische Sekte," according to K. Ahrens (*opus citatum* in note 44), p. 154. Could Zandokite and Zadokite not have been as easily confused as Zadokite and Sadducee?

52. The entire company falls asleep as soon as Tamlikh announces the approach of visitors; the entrance of the cave then becomes invisibles or else all who attempt entry are driven out in terror: Tha'labi, p. 292; Tabari, *Jami' al-bayan*, XV, p. 143. Some say the purpose of the shrine is to keep anyone from entering the cave: Nasafi, II, p. 284; Zamakhshari, I, p. 724; others that the youths walled themselves

in, or were killed in the city and taken to the cave for burial: Qasimi, X, p. 4051. Only one informant reports that they "arose and went out to the king and exchanged greetings" and then returned to the cave and promptly expired; but even he adds that "most of the scholars say" they died as soon as Tamlikh gave them his message: Qurtubi, X, p. 379.

53. So in the Syrian and Western texts supplied by Huber (*opus citatum* in note 7), pp. 118–27, 155–56. The same in Tha'labi, p. 298; Ibn Kathir, III, p. 77; Baydawi, IV, p. 90; Nasafi, II, p. 284. Tha'labi also tells this story, but quickly qualifies it by adding that "no man could enter into them," explaining on the authority of Ali that as soon as Tamlikh went in to his friends God took their spirits and concealed their hiding-place, p. 298. The most convincing of all Tha'labi's accounts is his vivid description of the greedy citizens and the wild-eyed and bedraggled youth who told them the fantastic story of his grizzly companions in a near-by cave—companions that nobody ever saw alive, pp. 296–97. Here we have a story that bears the marks of plausibility.

54. "And behold their bodies were completely unchanged, except that there was not breath *(arwaḥ)* in them. So the king said, "This is the sign which God has sent you": Tabari, *Tarikh*, II, pp. 9–10, and *Jami' al-bayan*, XV, p. 147; Damiri, II, pp. 349, 357. Much is made of their eyes being open, giving them a frighteningly lifelike appearance: Shirbini, II, p. 356; Baydawi, IV, p. 95; Nasafi, II, pp. 280–81; as-Sa'di, *Taysir al-karim al-rahman fi tafsir kalam al-mannan* (Cairo, 1954–1957), V, p. 10.

55. Qurtubi, X, p. 358. Huber, pp. 231–33, supplies translations of descriptions of this shrine by Idrisi, Qurtubi, and Yaqut.

56. *Analecta Bollandiana* 26 (1907), p. 272.

57. al-Biruni, *Kitab al-athar al-baqiya 'an al-qurun il-khaliya* (Leipzig, 1923), p. 290. Many other sources are cited by Huber, pp. 225–26, 228–31. The extra cadavers were readily accounted for as those of devout monks who had chosen to live and die in the presence of the Seven, *Ibidem*, p. 231. M. J. DeGoeje maintained that the story of the Seven Sleepers originated with the finding of human remains in a cave near Arabissas in southeastern Asia Minor, the place being known to the Arabs as Afsus—hence Ephesus: *De Legende der Zevenslapers van Efeze*, in *Verslagen en Mededeelingen der Koninklijke Akademie van Wetenschappen*, III (1909), pp. 9–33, of which there is a lengthy summary in Huber, pp. 233–38.

58. Tha'labi, pp. 291, 293; Huber, pp. 276–77.

59. Tabari, *Jami' al-bayan*, XV, p. 143; Damiri, II, pp. 338, 353; Shirbini, II, p. 365; Ibn Kathir, III, p. 77.

60. Qurtubi, X, p. 388; Damiri, II, p. 352. Though Ibn Kathir, III, p. 77, says the cave was in the *bilad* of Rum, he explains, "We are not told in what land the cave was. . . . But Ibn Abbas says it was near Aelia, and Ibn Isaac says it was near Nineveh," *ibidem*, p. 75. Ibn Isaac is a notoriously imaginative informant.

61. Qurtubi, X, p. 388. This may be an embellishment of an older version in which Ibn Abbas expresses some skepticism as to the possibility of recognizing bones 300 years old; Ibn Kathir, III, p. 77; Huber, p. 233, citing Tabari and Tha'labi.

62. Qurtubi, X, p. 356; Tabari, *Jami' al-bayan*, XV, p. 131.

63. Damiri, II, p. 342.

64. al-Qazwini, *Al-athar wa 'l-bilad* (Göttingen, 1848), I, p. 161; other sources in Huber, pp. 235–38, al-Istakhri, *Al-masalik wa 'l-mamalik* (Cairo, 1961), p. 47.

65. Huber, p. 224, citing Yaqut and Qazwini. About the year 751 there was great excitement throughout the East in anticipation of an immediate appearance of the Seven Sleepers in a cemetery of Damascus, according to al-Biruni (*opus citatum* in note 57) p. 285; cf. *Analecta Bollandiana* 68 (1950), p. 253. On Amman, Huber, p. 237.

66. Clermont-Ganneau, *El-Kahf et la Caverne des sept Dormants, in Comptes Rendus de l'Académie des Inscriptions et Belles-Lettres*, 4e série, XXVII (Paris, 1899), pp. 564–74. Huber, pp. 238–39, accuses Clermont-Ganneau of following a false scent, yet the latter specifies that he is NOT seeking the original cave of the Seven Sleepers but only the favorite Moslem site of it: *Analecta Bollandiana* 19 (1900), pp. 356–57. L. Massignon accepts his location of al Raqim: *Analecta Bollandiana* 68 (1950), p. 254.

67. Damiri, II, p. 340; Qurtubi, X, p. 367.

68. Tha'labi, pp. 102–103. Tabari (cited by Huber, pp. 254–55) tells of a shepherd who found an inscribed tablet in a cave, which no one could read but an old holy man of the desert.

69. R. Eisler (*opus citatum* in note 50), II, pp. 35, 182–84, 190–93, 197–99. On a possible Rechabite Background for Qumran, see H. J. Schoeps, *Theologie und Geschichte des Judentums* (Tübingen, 1949), pp. 247–54.

70. *Analecta Bollandiana* 68 (1950), p. 254. It was the leaders of the Nejran Christians who first questioned Mohammed about the Cave: Nasafi, II, p. 285, etc.

71. Above, note 5.

72. The quotation is from Sale's note to *Sura* XVIII, 8, though Sale is not sure of the explanation and leaves the word raqim untranslated. Tabari, *Jami' al-bayan*, XV, p. 131, says it was a stone tablet.

73. Tha'labi, p. 298; Baydawi, IV, p. 83 (lead or stone). The box was sealed

with a silver seal. Al-Bokhari, *Jami' al-Sahih* (Leyden, 1868), III, p. 276, says there was just one lead plate.

74. Tabari, *loco citato*, suggests a book, Qurtubi, X, p. 357, a golden tablet.

75. L. Massignon, in *Analecta Bollandiana* 68 (1950), p. 252, discusses the significance of this.

76. Hijazi, XV, p. 50; Qurtubi, X, p. 357; Ibn Kathir, III, p. 73 (it is the wadi); Tabari, *Jami' al-bayan*, XV, p. 131; Baydawi, IV, p. 83. Al-Raqim designates "the people of the Cave who were confined (or trapped) in it" *(ashāb al-ghāri alladhī inṭabaqa 'alayhim*): Qurtubi, *loco citato*.

77. Ibn Kathir, Tabari, Baydawi, *loco citato*.

78. Qurtubi, IV, p. 357, citing al-Saddi.

79. Baidawi, IV, p. 83, and Qurtubi, X, pp. 356–58, suggest both.

80. "It is said that al-Raqim is a wadi beyond Palestine in which is the Cave; (the name) is taken from Raqmah, a wadi with water-holes in it. . . . And Ibn Atiya says, "It is in Syria, according to what I heard from many people; it is a cave with dead people in it": Qurtubi, X, p. 357. It means running water in a wadi; Damiri, II, p. 341.

81. Qurtubi, *loco citato*, suggests both.

82. Qurtubi, *loco citato*; Hijazi, XV, p. 50; Nasafi, II, p. 277.

83. It was the name given to the Andalusian site (above, note 55), and to a region of Rum where there was a cave containing "twenty-one souls as if they were sleeping," Qurtubi, *loco citato*, who does not believe that this is *the* Cave.

84. Qurtubi, *loco citato*. Most commentatores (including those mentioned in the following note, no. 85) note that the tablets contained the names and history of the Sleepers, and Qurtubi *loco citato* would even include in the writings "the rule which they embraced from the religion of Jesus" (*al-shar' tamassakūhu bi-hi min dini 'Isa*).

85. Tha'labi, p. 295; Tabari, *Jami' al-bayan*, XV, p. 135; Baydawi, IV, pp. 86–87; Damiri, II, p. 344, according to whom the book itself is to come forth as a new revelation.

86. *II Maccabees* 2, 4–8. At the time of the First Crusade local reports located this cave near Jericho: Fulcher, *Historia Hierosolymitana*, edited by H. Hagenmeyer (Heidelberg, 1913), p. 289. When the Patriarch Timotheus was informed, about the year 800, of the discoveries of documents in caves near Jericho, he assumed that they were those buried by Jeremiah: J. Hering, in *Revue d'Histoire et de Philosophie Religieuse* 41 (1961), p. 160.

87. E. A. W. Budge, *The Contendings of the Apostles* (Oxford, 1935), pp. 394–96; Baydawi, IV, pp. 87, 90. See Above, note 11.

88. He takes the custom back to the burial of Aaron, p. 171. He tells of a book sent to David from heaven sealed with gold and containing thirteen questions to be put to Solomon, p. 202; of an apocalyptic writing sealed in an iron box, p. 246; of another buried in a mountain, p. 242; of gold tablets containing the history of a vanished empire found in a cave in Yemen, p. 102; of magic books dug up from beneath Solomon's throne, p. 35, etc.

89. M. Black (*opus citatum* in note 25), p. 12.

90. Tha'labi, p. 288. When Ali finishes his story, the most skeptical Jew confesses that he has not added or removed a single letter from the account in the Torah; p. 292.

91. Various estimates are given by Huber (*opus citatum* in note 7), p. 102. Cf. *Analecta Bollandiana* 72 (1954), p. 266; B. Heller, in *Revue des Études Juives* 49 (1904), pp. 205, 211.

92. It "belongs to the secrets of heaven and earth": Tabari *Jami' al-bayan*, XV, p. 152; Shirbini, II, p. 366. The Prophet spent 40 nights trying to comprehend it: as-Suyuti, *Lubab al-nuqul . . .* (1935), p. 145.

93. Qurtubi, X, p. 386, who quotes Tabari as saying that the Jews also could not agree about it. It could hardly have been a Christian invention, since no amount of manipulating can fit the conventional three centuries of sleep into the century-and-a-half interval between Decius and either Theodosius. Cf. *Analecta Bollandiana* 66 (1948), p. 195.

94. Heller (*opus citatum* in note 91) pp. 206–207. Onias slept from the destruction of the First Temple to the completion of the Second: ". . . the parallel with the Seven Sleepers . . . is of course obvious," comments *The Jewish Encyclopedia* (1901), IX, p. 405. Some say the Seven fell asleep until the land became Moslem: Damiri, II, p. 357.

95. *Analecta Bollandiana* 68 (1950), p. 351.

96. H. H. Rowley, in *Expository Times* 63 (1951/2), p. 381; M. H. Segal, in *Journal of Biblical Literature* 70 (1951), p. 146, note 59, and p. 130; Yusuf Ali, *The Holy Qur'an*, II, p. 720, note 2337. The 390 and the 20 years "belong to the remote past. . . . Their writers lack any real knowledge of the origin and early history of the sect; hence the: nebulous atmosphere pervading all the documents . . . the characters . . . appearing as types rather than individuals": E. Wiesenberg, in *Vetus Testamentum* 5 (1955), pp. 304–305.

97. Above, note 88. Tabari's story is discussed by Huber, pp. 254–55.

98. Tha'labi, p. 292. They say *nakūnu 'ala amrin wahadin*, Tabari, *Jami' al-bayan*, XV, p. 132, where the last word suggests the much-discussed "yaḥad" of the

Scrolls.

99. Nearly all Arabic sources mention this. Tha'labi, pp. 292–93, even notes that they gained the repute of being money-changers.

100. Tha'labi, p. 291. See above, note 80. Huber, p. 455, sees a Jewish tradition in the spring and the trees, and Heller (*opus citatum* in note 48), p. 201, notes that the society eschewed pork.

101. Qurtubi, X, p. 360; Nasafi, II, p. 278. Both mention caves in the plural. Cf. Tabari, *Jami' al-bayan*, XV, pp. 132, 151.

102. On al-Raqim as a going concern, Tabari, XV, p. 135; Ibn Kathir, III, pp. 74–75. In some Western versions Tamlikh is only 12 or 15 years old, and in all of them the youths must fetch all their food and drink from the city—they were NOT self-sustaining. There was a tradition that the activities of the Cave included even dancing, according to Qurtubi, X, p. 466, who describes the pious exercises of the community.

103. Tha'labi, pp. 289, 294; Ibn Kathir, III, p. 74, who mention the dramatic episode of the stripping of their military insignia by the enraged Emperor. This is a characteristic episode in the cycle of youthful military heroes who are martyred by the Emperor but then come alive to prove the resurrection. Such were St. Mercurius, St. Victor, and St. Sebastian. Tha'labi's St. George, pp. 299–305, clearly belongs to the cycle.

104. Tha'labi, p. 291; Qurtubi, X, p. 369; Ibn Kathir, III, p. 75; as-Sa'adi, V, p. 10, etc. On Qumran, M. Black (*opus citatum* in note 41), p. 141.

105. Once a week (Tabari, cited by Huber, p. 279); every seven years (Qurtubi, X, p. 370); twice a year (Baydawi, IV, p. 94); once a year at New Year's (Tha'labi, p. 291; Nasafi, II, p. 281; Qurtubi, *loco citato*).

106. Tha'labi, p. 291; Nasafi, II, p. 281; Qurtubi, X, 369; Baydawi, IV, p. 93. Ibn Kathir, III, p. 75, sees astronomical significance in these arrangements. Huber, p. 295, discusses the awakening by the sun.

107. S. Talmon, in *Revue de Qumran* 8 (1960), p. 475; E. Ettisch, in *Theologische Literaturzeilung* 88 (1963), pp. 186, 188, 191–92.

108. E. Rhode, in *Rheinisches Museum für Philologie*, Neue Folge, 35 (1880), pp. 157–59, 162–63. Their names have great "valeur prophylactique" throughout the Moslem world: Massignon, in *Anal. Boll.* 68 (1950), pp. 249–50; for their healing offices, *ibidem*, pp. 247–48, and dreams, Huber, p. 135.

109. J. M. Allegro, *The Treasure of the Copper Scroll* (New York: Doubleday, 1960), p. 73. The Essenes specialized in "Traumdeute- und Weissagejunst"; R. Eisler (*opus citatum* in note 50), II, p. 17.

110. Allegro, *opus citatum*, pp. 70–71. Cf. Tha'labi, p. 291; Nasafi, II, p. 280; Qurtubi, X, p. 369; as-Sa'adi, V, p. 10.

111. Tha'labi, pp. 294–95; Tabari, *Jami' al-bayan*, XV, p. 134; Damiri, II, pp. 339–40; Shirbini, II, pp. 352–53; Baydawi, IV, pp. 85–86: ". . . lift up your heads, eat, and trust in God." On the Hebrew origin of *jabbar*, see K. Ahrens (*opus citatum* in note 44), p. 19.

112. Epiphanius, *Adv. haer.*, Haer. 29, no. 5, in *P. G.*, vol. 41, col. 397.

113. Al-Biruni, *opus citatum* in note 57, p. 284. The added evidence of the Companions of the Cave tips the scales against the reading *maqariba*, favored by N. Golb, in *Journal of Religion* 41 (1961), pp. 42–44.

114. This expression puzzled Huber, p. 283, as the only purely Christian tradition in the Koran, where it is strangely out of place. But J. Horovitz, in *H.U.C.A.* 2 (1925), p. 178, showed that "it is by no means assured that . . . Mohammed really meant the martyrs of Najran," and that the only reason for such an assumption is lack of evidence as to what else the "People of the Pit" could refer to. The Dead Sea Scrolls now supply that evidence.

115. Baydawi, IV, p. 91 (Khīram); Damiri, II, p. 350 (Haram, Khadam); Qurtubi, X, p. 367 (Khiwam). The usual difficulty with pointing is apparent.

116. Damiri, II, p. 341. Nasafi, II, p. 285, also says the dog was Raqim. Tha'labi, p. 290, gives a list of suggested names, not including this one.

117. Ibn Kathir, III, pp. 73, 78; Qurtubi, X, p. 360. The quotation is from Allegro (*opus citatum* in note 109), p. 70.

118. This has been discussed by Massignon in *Anal. Boll.* 68, pp. 245–55.

2.8

Ebionite and Elkesaite Elements in the Koran[1]

Notes and Hypotheses (1971)*

Martiniano P. Roncaglia

EBIONISM AND ELKESAISM[2]

Alfred Bertholet in his classic *Dictionary of the History of Religion* (Freiburg, 1897), defined the Ebionites as follows: "Ebionites (Hebrew-Aramaic: "the poor") or Nazarenes (the two names are ones the original Christian communities gave themselves). The Christian-Hebrews leaving the Church at the end of the 2nd century. The Ebionites did not form a homogeneous sect. They did not recognize Saint Paul, holding to the Torah Law, and did not give the Messiah Jesus the title of Logos."

It is practically impossible to deduce from these few laconic lines the extent and depth or the cultural and religious importance of the complex movement called Ebionism. According to Epiphanius, the Christian heresiologist (ca. 315–403), the Ebionites "also receive baptism, apart from their daily baptisms. And they celebrate mysteries year after year, if you please, in imitation of the sacred mysteries of the church, using unleavened bread—and the other part of the mystery with water only. But as I said, they set two divine appointees side by side, one being Christ, but one the devil. And they say that Christ has been allotted the world to come, but that this world has been entrusted to the devil—by the Almighty's decree, if you please, at the request of both. And they say that this is why Jesus was begotten of the seed of a man and chosen, and thus named Son of God by election, after the Christ who had come to him from on high in the form of a dove. But they say he is not begotten of God the Father, but was created as one of the archangels, and that he is ruler both of angels and of all creatures of [the] Almighty; and he came and instructed us [to abolish the sacrifices]. As their so-called Gospel says: 'I came to abolish the sacrifices, and if ye cease not from sacrifice, wrath will not cease from you.'"[3]

For the Ebionites, Jesus is a prophet, assisted by the angel of good who had already come to Adam, then to Moses and other prophets.[4] They deny in the most categorical fashion the Virgin birth of Jesus; it was only during his baptism by John the Baptist that a heavenly power (δύναμις / power) from God descended on him. One has to connect this doctrine with the stress put by the Κηρύγματα Πέτρου [mandates of Peter] on monotheism, and the elimination of passages of the Old Testament that might suggest there is a plurality in God and which the Christians of the Great Church (ἡ μεγάλη ἐκκλησία / The Great Church) used in a Trinitarian sense. The Ebionites are radically anti-Trinitarian and reject the whole soteriological aspect of Christianity. For them, the mission of Jesus is reduced to teaching; Jesus is merely the successor to the other prophets who preceded him, maintaining the tradition of the true religion. Jesus succeeded Adam and Moses in order to reform Judaism and to bring it back to the purity of its origins.

And who were the Elkesaites? This name designates the sectarians of Elchasaï or Elxaï. They constitute a group of heterodox Jewish Christians to be situated within the Ebionite current; doctrinally, they present archaic Christian elements. Epiphanius[5] says that Elxai "came from Judaism and thought in the Jewish manner." Hippolytus of Rome[6] writes that "Elxaï proposes a way of life according to the Torah, repeating that the faithful should be circumcised and live according to the Torah."

Ebionites and Elkesaïtes are doctrinally and liturgically a Jewish Christian current very close to the Essenes of the Qumrân who seem to have embraced Jesus' teaching, especially after the fall of the Temple in 70 CE.[7] Ebionites and Elkesaites have much in common, as Origen reports with respect to the latter sect: "It rejects certain parts of Scripture, but elsewhere uses texts extracted from the whole Old Testament and the Gospels: it [the Elkesaite sect] rejects the Apostle [Paul], however."[8] For Jewish Christians in general, Saint Paul, because of his refusal to follow Judaizing practices, is defined as "the enemy man."

The most lucid of the Christian authors who speak of Ebionites is undoubtedly Origen; he clearly saw and established relations that connect Ebionism to Judaism on the one hand and to the early Church on the other. In addition, Origen, who closely follows the story in Acts of the Apostles, offers us a precise interpretation of the controversies between Hellenists and Palestinians at the very birth of the first Christian community. We find in Origen the exact historical perspective that was misunderstood by the majority of the ecclesiastical authors of antiquity.[9]

Locating the Problem

After this brief introduction, we may attempt to advance through the maze of problems raised by the more or less demonstrable dependence of Islam upon Judaism and Christianity. We think that historical sense obliges us to speak of the beginnings of a slow process of assimilation of disparate elements in order to express a message of the divine will that wanted to be new and original, specially adapted to the Arabs ([*'innā 'anzalnā qur'ānan 'arabiyyan*: "We have sent it down as an Arabic Qur'an"] Sura XII:2). Therefore I will not try to demonstrate a problematic dependence but rather to seek elements that constituted the raw materials upon which was raised the religious, cultural, and civil monument that is universally known under the name Koran. My conclusions will be somewhat different from the customary conclusions of either apologists and comparativists. I am in fact convinced that the moment has come to tackle the historical problems of other religions with the same methodology used to approach those of Judaism or Christianity. Science does not play favorites. And so, if we are trying to distinguish the Ebionite elements in the doctrine and practice of primitive Islam, it should not be interpreted as an attempt to dismantle a construction built on heterogeneous elements (if it may be put thus as concession to current ways of expressing these things). Any attempt made to discover either a Jewish or a Christian influence cannot be accepted en masse; the insufficiency of documentation and the particular frame of mind of someone convinced of belonging to a superior religion and of being concerned with an "underdeveloped" religion have not allowed this to be seen clearly; similarly, those who have wanted to be more Muslim than the Muslims have rendered no service to either the truth or to Islam, which, in effect, does without apologists to illuminate the minds of its believers. The simplest way is certainly not a compromise but to approach the texts without forcing their content.

THE NAṢĀRĀ

A preliminary requirement is as exact a knowledge as possible of the religious geography of the pre-Islamic Arab world at the time of the Prophet. Once this is in place, it will not be difficult to discover within earliest Islam the nascent crystallization of a form of Jewish Christianity in which various orthodox and heterodox tendencies must be included—among which Ebionism is certainly preponderant. This even leads us to modify the meaning of the term *Naṣārā*—which should no longer be translated as "Christians" in the absolute sense[10]—but should be attributed to members of the Christian community of Mecca and *Ḥijāz*, with all the historical, cultural, and religious nuances demanded by this specific denomination of a specific group. The milieu or the *Umweit* in which the Prophet's family and he himself grew up—it appears he had a bishop of the Naṣārā among his relations[11]—is formed not of Christians of the orthodox Church, nor of Jews of the Diaspora, but of these Naṣārā: they constituted the humus that fertilized the religious attitudes of the Prophet. Adolf von Harnack formulated this historical fact in terms that cannot help but astonish us, in view of when he was writing (1879). Through his historical and theological speculations, he came to define Islam as a form of Gnostic Jewish Christianity, itself based on a particular form of the Jewish religion that developed on the terrain of Arabism.[12] He justified his thesis in seven points,[13] bravely making a bridge between Islam and Elkasaïsm (another Gnostic and Ebionite sect that appeared on the West Bank of the Jordan around 101 CE). Let us set aside the Elkesaïte elements discovered by Harnack in the Koran—now a sufficiently solid historical fact, despite the contrary opinion held by Carl Clement, who prefered to see this as the influence of a Manichaean gnosis.[14] Instead let us open new avenues, working within the traditional historical method.

SABEANS

Let us start with the religious sect of Sabeans [*al-Ṣābi'ūn*], from צבא or the Mandaean *ceba* = to baptize, wash, purify. The Koran makes the Sabeans the third most important group, between Jews and Christians, all of them *Ahl al-Kitāb*, people who believe in God and in a revealed book and in the Judgement, and who do good (Suras II:59; V:73; XXI:17). In fact, by the denomination "Sabean" and in conformity with the meaning of the term, Muhammad apparently meant all of the baptist sects,[15] while others have wanted to identify them with the Mandeans,[16] and finally with the *Ḥanīf*, presenting the term *al-Ṣābi'ūn* as a synonym for Gnostics.[17] Much light has been shed on the matter by a hadith teaching that is found in the annals of Hamza al-Isfahānī, finished in the year 350 of the Hijra, or 961 CE;[18] there one reads that "the true Sabeans [i.e., those mentioned in the Koran] are a Christian sect that lives in desert or marshy zones; they are in disagreement with most Christians, who consider them heretics." The pagan adversaries of Muhammad accused him of being a "Sabean," an accusation that was meant to be understood by everyone, referring to some aspect visible to all,[19] such as, for example, the frequent daily ablutions before prayer—we know that such practices were current also among the Ebionites and Elkesaites.[20] But we know that even the Elkesaites were also designated by the nickname of Σοβίαι or Sabeans, precisely because of these frequent ablutions.[21]

It seems that one might deduce a supplementary proof from the name the Prophet gave to the Judgement: he calls it *yawm ad-dīn*, and we encounter the same terminology in the prayer formulae of Elchasai.[22] It is these Ebionites-Elkesaites that he identifies with the *mughtasila* or the baptist sect of which an-Nadīm speaks in his *Kitāb al-Fihrist*. One finds them mentioned again in the tenth century: the sect was still living between the Tigris and Euphrates, an occasionally fertile zone extending from the Arab desert to Maisan in Mesopotamia; this accords very well with another piece of information from the seventh century that we read in the *De heresibus liber* of St. John of Damascus, in chapter 53: "Σαμψαῖοι (the Sabeans) καὶ 'Ελκασαῖοι ἔτι δεῦρο τὴν 'Αραβίαν κατοικοῦντες καθύπερθν τῆς Νεκρᾶς Θαλάσσης κειμένην"[23] ["The Sabeans and the Elkesaites still now occupying that part of Arabia above the Dead Sea"] and with the citation from Hamza al-Isfahānī already mentioned. The accusation of "Sabean" made against Muhammad by his enemies would seem to indicate more exactly that, in his practices, he did not much differ from the Sabeans-Elkasaïts-Ebionites, designated by the Koran under the name *Naṣārā* and with whom the paleo-Muslims had in common the daily ablutions, perhaps their way of dressing, and also perhaps certain liturgical formulae.[24]

The Concept of "True Prophet"

Another Ebionite and Elkesaite element discernible in Islam is the concept of the "true prophet" ὁ ἀληθὴς προφήτης [The True Prophet], and more precisely, the typical series of seven "columns," ἑπτὰ στῦλοι [Seven Columns], that in Islam are identified with Noah, Lot, Moses, then three Arabs—Hûd, Ṣāliḥ, Shu'ayb—and finally, with Abraham, to whom should be added Muhammad—exactly as an eighth prophet-messiah is added by the Ebionites. Wensinck[25] has already observed that if Muhammad names persons who in the Bible are not considered prophets, this was not because he was as yet ignorant of the historical existence of prophets such as Elijah, Isaiah, Jeremiah, Ezekiel, etc., since he was not yet in contact with the Jews of Yathrib and later Medina, as Rudolf and others would have it,[26] but simply because the Ebionites did not recognize them.

Adam and Abraham

That Adam is not named among the prophets, despite the great esteem in which he was held by the Ebionites and Elkesaites, is perhaps not a matter of chance, although Sura III:59 puts Adam, in the Ebionite manner, on the same level as Jesus: "Lo! The likeness of Jesus with Allah is as the likeness of Adam. He created him of dust, then He said unto him: Be! And he is." The story of the creation of Adam through the infusion of the breath of Spirit of God (Suras XV:29, XXXVIII:72) relies on the Jewish Christian Haggada that establishes a parallel between Adam and Christ[27] already indicated in St. Paul's letters. Neither Adam nor Jesus had a man as father: this is found in the Haggada of Paul's era that the Ebionites transposed onto the pneumatic and prophetic plane. Abraham, by contrast, whether in the Jewish or the Jewish Christian Haggada (also in the Judaeo-Christian-Islamic one), is the *imâm* (=guide) to believers or, better still, *of all believers* (Sura II:118), being himself neither Jew nor Christian, but a *ḥanīf* (according to the Suras of the Medina period), synonymous with the pre-existing type of the *Muslim* or the *mu'min*; nor was he a polytheist (Sura III:60).

All these elements establish an extremely coherent consistency between Jewish Christianity and Islam.[28] The *millat Ibrāhīm* (Sura II:129), "the religion of Abraham" uniting all believers on an equal footing before the Torah and the *Injīl*, and their restoration to their authentic state, is considered by Muhammad as a mission that concerns him by right. This pre-Mosaic revelation is identical with that of Islam. Muhammad's participation in the revelation of the *Kitāb* (divine book) only confirms the parts previously revealed in this same *Kitāb* called first "Torah," then "*Injīl*," and finally "Qur'ân": "And unto thee have We revealed the *Kitāb* (i.e., the Koran) with the truth, confirming whatever *Kitāb* (the Torah=Pentateuch) and *Injīl* was before it, and a watcher over it" (Sura V:48).

This particular situation makes him a Prophet of tolerance *par excellence*: "So judge between them [Jews and Christians] by that which Allah hath revealed. . . . For each We have appointed a divine law and a traced-out way [*minhājan*]" (Sura V:48), and again, "So judge between them by that which Allah hath revealed" (Sura V:49).

The "Seal of the Prophets"

What is meant by the concept of a "chain" of prophets, stressed in the Koran as well as in the Hadith, as for example by Abdallaj b. Sābā? Today one might reply that we have here a "universalist" concept that is strictly related to Ebionism: the Prophets (note that the term *nabī* is more rigorous than *rasūl*) are representatives of the humanity with whom Allah concludes a *mīṯāq* or covenant. Noah, Abraham, Moses, Jesus, and Muhammad are strictly speaking the contractants in the divine alliance. Any *nabī* opens a new era or eon (αἰών), a concept current in the religious Orient. The Koran explicitly says that Allah sent to every *umma* a *rasūl* to bring a people the divine message (Suras VI:42; X:48; XVI:38, etc.). Muhammad himself, who closes his own cycle or eon as *khātama l-nabiyyīna* seal of the Prophets,[29] was sent to his own people, the Arab *umma*, who until then had not had any Prophets.

If we reinsert the concept of *khātama l-nabiyyīna* in its Jewish Christian context—which seems justified by the fact that this concept appears only once in the Koran (Sura XXXIII:40), though an extra-canonic variant appears in Ubayy (Sura LXI:6)—then it does not and could not indicate a chronological period that is necessarily definitive (as the official Muslim exegesis unanimously would have it, having always ignored the historical and cultural exegesis of this passage). The Jewish Christian author of the Letter to the Hebrews (attributed to Paul), expresses himself in analogous concepts: "Long ago God spoke to our ancestors in many and various ways by the prophets, but in these last days he has spoken to us by a Son, whom he appointed heir of all things, through whom he also created the world [αἰῶνας / worlds]" (I:1–2).

Exegesis of this passage as referring to Jesus' eschatological discourse and to the problems of Christian Parousia has created in us the mentality that accepts as evidence that which is merely a structure contingent upon a "forma mentis" that ignores the Jewish Christian substratum of Christian doctrines, as well as the late Jewish substratum of Jesus' doctrines. He was born and grew at a particular historical moment, saturated with apocalyptic elements that constituted the spiritual nourishment of any pious Jew living in the expectation of a liberation or a new cycle of the "Dispensation" (as one would say today).

The "Dispensation" and the Judgment

The importance in Jewish Christian and Koranic theology of the idea of judgment, dialectically linked to that of "Dispensation," cannot be stressed enough. In late Jewish apocalyptics (the *Spätjudentum*), in Jewish Christianity as well as the Koran, there seems to be a precise concept that the coming of any prophet is in itself a judgment, an end of the world. In the apocalyptics of the *Spätjudentum*, of original Jewish Christianity, of Elkesaite Ebionism of Arabia, as well as in the Koran, there is no shortage of passages that lead us to think that Muhammad—as had Jesus and as a consequence of that—thought of the most distant end of the world as a sign of a new prophetic cycle that would succeed their manifestation.[30]

Certain arguments should not be rejected because, from a Christian viewpoint, making such a parallel seems to lack respect; what interests us is the acknowledgement of the continuity of religious and cultural elements proper to a particular way of thinking, the Semitic way. Sabatino Moscati has more than once stressed elements of continuity in the domain of the comparative grammatical structures. It is within this structure peculiar to Semitic religious culture (which also appears in the thought structures articulated through language and in other existential manifestations) that one may understand a particular trait of Elkesaite Christology: "According to Elxaï," writes Hippolytus of Rome, "Christ was a man like all others. It would not be the first time during that period that he was born of a virgin; this coming has already been verified in the past; there have already been several times that he was born and is born."[31] In other words, we have here an "eonization" of History of a Gnostic kind: the various incarnations of the ἀληΘὴς προφήτης of which Adam would be the first.[32]

The Messengers of God

The specific function of a *rasūl Allah* is to be a messenger entrusted by God with transmitting a message, but even so he cannot claim to be a son of God or an angel (Sura VI:50). A hadith of Ibn Sa'd says: "I came from the best generations of men and from age to age I was sent anew by Allah, until I was finally sent in the period in which I am."[33]

If we substitute this hadith for the one that suits orthodox Muslim consciousness—setting aside our critique of authenticity—we see that Bausani's intuition (which we have paraphrased with new elements) is confirmed in

Ibn Sa'd's hadith, alongside the opening of the *Letter to the Hebrews* as well as what Hippolytus of Rome reported about Elxai and everything we read in the apocalyptic literature of the *Spätjudentum*. It is perhaps not a case of textual interdependence but certainly of an interdependence of a Semitic *forma mentis*, of a way of thinking of the divine οἰκονομία or the "Dispensation" in the governing of the world and the guiding of human beings.

The Semitic Concepts of Time and Eternity

Bausani's thesis is further illuminated when one recalls the idea of ἀνάπαυσις that is expressed in the Jewish Christian writings of pseudo-Clement.[34] But the Stoic concept of the Church Fathers coincides with that of the prophetic cycles of the Semitic type; one should not understand it in the sense of a cyclical repetition in time and space but in the sense of periods or eons, a Hellenized Semitic concept.[35]

Οἰκονομία and ἀνάπαυσις [Arrangement and Cadence (lit. resting)] in Jewish Christian writings, and in writings contemporaneous with the New Testament, imply the most simplistic and the most vigorously realist conception of *time*. If Plato's time, that *mobile image of eternity*, and Greek time in general finds its best image in the closed circle, then it is the straight and infinite line that represents Christian time, as well as time in Judaism and its derivatives. Along this line are situated the *times* (οἱ καιροί / the times) that humankind chooses for personal actions and those that God or Allah determines. God, like humans, has his "D Days" and those of God are not those of humans but are inscribed on the same continuous line—not outside time, in the beyond of an atemporal eternity.

These *times* divide up *Time*; the καιροί circumscribe upon the indefinite extension of duration, the eons (αἰῶνες), that is to say, periods that are both those of time and those of eternity: there is a αἰῶν οὗτος/this age, a "saeculum praesens" that runs from the day of creation to the day of the "end of time" (*usque ad consummationem saeculorum*); there is a αἰῶν before creation (designated by the expression ἐκ τοῦ αἰῶνος, or the "ante omnia saecula"); there is a αἰὼν μέλλων/age to come, a "saeculum futurum" or the eon to come after the end of time; finally, there are the αἰῶνες τῶν αἰώνων, the eons of eons, rendered in the Roman liturgy by "saecula saeculorum," that encompass the totality of this duration and are also coextensive with the eternity of God.

But if the eternity of God is thus conceived in simplistic fashion as the indefinite extension of time, its transcendence is manifest in Judaism, Jewish Christianity, and Islam in the fact that God is master of time. Divine lordship over time is made plain in many ways. All the manifestations of Allah's lordship over time merely develop the consequences of his principal intervention in duration, whether with Moses for Judaism, with 'Isa b. Maryam for Jewish Christianity (here, *nāṣāra*), or with Muhammad for Islam. As with Arab Jewish Christianity, so for nascent Islam the result was a *new division of time*: the manifestation living within the current eon had already virtually opened the αἰὼν μέλλων [future ages], since the decisive instant from which issues this ultimate eon is no longer to be awaited: it has already arrived. After the decisive day (*yôm furqônô*) of the *nāṣāra* (*yawm al-furqān* for the palaeo-Muslims), which coincides with the coming of the Messiah for the former and the coming of Muhammad for the latter, onward until the ultimate day, we are already in the "last time," whatever its duration.

Such a dialectic can only be grasped in the Arab Semitic context, since in the Hellenistic context "jede Epochentrennung bedeutet einen gewaltsamen Einschnitt in den ununterbrochenen Fluss der Entwicklung" ["every division of an epoch means a tremendous incision in the uninterrupted flow of development"], as Bodenwalt writes.[36] Therefore we have argued that only in connection with the Semitic conception of "Dispensation" is it possible to understand the profound meaning of the eonic continuity of revelation in Judaism, Jewish Christianity, and Islam: "And unto thee have We revealed the Scripture [*Kitāb* = *Qur'ān*] with the truth, confirming whatever Scripture was before it [=Pentateuch and Gospel], and a watcher over it" (Sura V:52).

"The Book" and "the Books"

We call the *Qur'ān* that part of the pre-existing *Kitāb* that was revealed by an angel to Muhammad. For Elxasai also, it was during a vision that his book was entrusted to him by an angel.[37] In the first century of the Christian era, we find angels in the context of the revelations of a book: an angel annunciates to Mary the coming of Jesus, angels announce that Jesus has arrived, an angel reveals one apocalypse or another, an angel reveals the Pastor of Hermas (a Jewish Christian Essene who lived in Rome), an angel bears revelation to Elkesai, etc. Messages, announcements, divine revelations are all made by the intermediary of an angel. More than a conventional literary framework, this seems to constitute the matter of any original vision.[38]

Just as the *Injīl* completes the Torah, so the Qur'ān completes both the Torah and the *Injīl*: it is part of a dialectic historical movement that transcends the existential element whose principle was stated by Aristotle: "Posterius generatione, prius perfectione." Nevertheless, theoretically, this does not necessarily exclude that in the time known only to Allah there might open another prophetic cycle that would complete the Torah, the *Injīl*, and the Qur'ān—not in a circular but in a linear movement (insofar as this is an accurate expression). Popular Muslim consciousness rejects such a possibility, not on the basis of a dialectic that is the very principal of Islam, but based on the refusal of the idea of the perfectibility of the Koran, which is an understandable sentiment. In fact, however, the possibility of a prophetic cycle subsequent to Muhammad is not apodictically excluded in Koranic texts as soon as we insert them into the current of ideas to which they belong and from which they emerge.

Just as the Torah, for Jewish consciousness and also for Philo of Alexandria, pre-existed the written text in the mind of Yahweh and was its Logos, and just as in Christian consciousness the Gospel was pre-existent in the incarnate Logos of God, so the Koran pre-existed in Allah. Adam, Moses, *'Īsā* (Jesus) and Muhammad transmitted the revelation issuing from a common course. The theory of the preexistence of revealed texts plays a considerable part in Elkesaite doctrine. With the Pentateuch, Moses perfected the Adamic revelation; Jesus perfected the Mosaic Revelation; Muhammad for his part perfected the preceding revelations, as well as the teachings of the rabbis[39] and Christian priests (Sura V:48–52 and 68).

"Prophet of the Arabs," Messiah and Paraclete

The Prophet Muhammad designated himself as an *an-nabî al-ummî* (Sura VII:156 and 158). Muslim exegesis developed this idea in an apologetic sense in favor of the Koranic "miracle," giving the term *ummî* the meaning "illiterate." Carolo Alfonso Nallino in a very learned thesis dealt at length with this question.[40] Reinserted in the Jewish Christian current, the aforementioned expression would correspond, on the contrary, to the concept of *nebi'e 'ummot ha-'olam*.[41] To go back to the source of the *Spätjudentum* that transmitted it by direct means to Jewish Christianity: the treatise Baba Batra 15b of the Talmud enumerates the seven prophets of the "peoples of the earth"; it is as such that Muhammad presents himself to his people, who, born and raised in contact with elements of Arab Jewish Christianity, did not have much difficulty in understanding and acknowledging such an attribution.

Ebionite hope in the coming of a new Moses, that is to say, in the expectation of the prophet "who was to come," influenced nascent Islam. According to the tradition of Ibn Ishāq, Muhammad was promised by Abraham, Moses, and 'Īsā (Jesus) as the prophet "who was to come," to whom one must grant faith. In Sura VII:157, Moses and Jesus had already predicted his coming: one speaks of those "who follow the Messenger, the Prophet of the [Arab] *umma*, whom they will find described [i.e., predicted] in the Torah and the Gospel." That the text of Deuteronomy 18:15 had some influence on this Sura is unlikely *if* one is thinking of a direct knowledge of the text, whereas it appears beyond doubt with respect to the idea, or rather, the Ebionite tendency to draw a parallel between Moses and Jesus.

The Ebionite influence on Muhammad in this respect has been sufficiently demonstrated by the internal critique of the Islamic tradition, which has accepted the Haggada of Maryam as mother of 'Īsā, a kind of preliminary concept to the idea of the Messiah.[42] In fact, Jesus, or 'Īsā the son of Maryam (who is still uniquely presented in his human aspect as Prophet, although of a superior rank), is not the fruit of the anti-Jewish polemic;[43] in effect, the theological doctrine of Jesus κτῖσμα καὶ ἐξ οὐκ ὄντων καὶ δοῦλον τὸν μονογενῆ υἱὸν τοῦ Θεοῦ εἶναι ["Jesus the only-begotten son of God created out of nothing being the servant of God"],[44] already put forward by

Arius and Eunomus, closely corresponds to what is said in Sura IV:171 and especially 172: "The Messiah will never scorn to be a slave unto Allah, nor will the favored angels." *'Īsā-Masīḥ-Malak* (in other words, Jesus-Messiah-Angel) are Jewish Christian terms that also passed into Eastern liturgy in the concept Χριστὸς-ἄγγελος-δοῦλος, which disappeared from the glorious and triumphal construction of Imperial Byzantine liturgy but is expressed in the Kenotico-Ebionite context. It is only our interpretation here that is able to conserve these terms and, by detaching them from their original cultural and religious context, insert them into current orthodoxy. Even the Roman liturgy transmitted to us by Hippolytus of Rome[45] contains the same kenotico-Ebionite concepts.

The designation of Jesus as "al-Masīḥ b. Maryam"[46] is specifically Jewish Christian. However, the term *al-Masīḥ*[47] (which inexperienced translators translate as *Messiah*, carrying the theological meaning that it bears in the Christological language of the councils) preserves a certain disillusionment once it is reinserted into its Koranic context, where it accentuates its specifically Jewish Christian, Ebionite, Elkesaïte content, usually unsuspected by translators.[48] My very scholarly friend, the Dominican father Jacques Jomier, wrote as follows:

> Faced with the problem of its Christian background, the Koran takes a position when it pronounces against the divinity of Jesus Christ. In that, it is close to Rabbinic Judaism, which in its turn has denied Christ's divinity. Still [continues Father Jomier, proving his solid Biblical exegesis and cultural history] this Judaism should not be confused with that professed by Orthodox rabbis. The Koranic tendencies are so Christianizing that the Koran contains something about the person of Jesus that goes beyond simple respect. In effect, who in the circles of Orthodox Jews would have been able to call Jesus *Word of God* and *Messiah*, when one knows the force of understanding lying beneath such titles?[49]

In reality, the Koran is Christianizing because it arose in the cultural and religious ambiance of Elkesaite Ebionism that used precisely the terms *Kalimat Allâh* and *al-Masīḥ* to refer to Jesus, but the force of these terms is much weaker than in orthodox Christianity, which charges them with a theological content that is always growing and in clear contrast to the kenotic value of the hierosolymitan [native to Jerusalem] catechesis of Saint James, "the Lord's brother."[50]

'Īsā b. Maryam, according to Sura LXI:6, prophesied the coming of Muhammad: "And when Jesus son of Mary said: O Children of Israel! Lo! I am the messenger of Allah unto you, confirming that which was (revealed) before me in the Torah, and bringing good tidings of a messenger who cometh after me, whose name is the Praised One [*Aḥmad*]," later developed as "*Muḥammad*."[51] It is quite possible that here an indirect allusion is being made to the Gospel of John 16:26; 15:7) in relation to the promise of a παράκλητος [paraclete] or intercessor, which was not unknown in Judaism, where the Greek term, transcribed into Hebrew in the Pirqe Avot 4:11 with the meaning "consoler,"[52] then passed into the translation of Aquila and Theodotian.[53] The meaning adopted by Christians, "advocate," comes from the speculations of Philo of Alexandria. One must think less of a Jewish tradition than of a tradition (or catechesis) of the *Nāṣāra* of *Ḥijāz* for whom the Gnosticizing doctrine of John's Gospel held a special interest,[54] as it did for all Gnostic circles, including those of Coptic Egypt,[55] not to mention Montanus and Mani,[56] who also claimed to have been predicted as "Paracletes."

We have already indicated that this doctrine is not in fact in contradiction with what Muhammad declares elsewhere on the subject of the prophets of ancient Arabia, of whom he acknowledges seven as his predecessors. 'Īsā b. Maryam was and still remained for him a simple *rasûl*, and even the term *al-Masīḥ* was for him merely a synonym for a *rasûl*, as he says in Sura IV:170): "The Messiah, Jesus son of Mary, was only a messenger of Allah." For the Koran, it would be a false interpretation of the scriptural texts that would lead to the divinization of Jesus (Sura III:72–74 and also 57–59). All that perfectly agrees with Jewish Christian doctrines. Moreover, the very image Muhammad uses for the crucifixion of Jesus (Sura IV:156) has forcefully undergone the influence of the schema of post-Ebionite Docetic Christology.[57]

The Doctrine of Salvation

The Christian theological terminology that passed into the Koran has been studied by Mark Lidzbarski,[58] who as a specialist in Mandean religion, tends to see Mandean influence amost everywhere. But once returned to its Jewish Christian context, the material acquires a considerable probative value and it also conforms more to the nature of things.

For example, the term *Salâm* in the sense of "salvation, redemption" that has a better equivalent in the Semitic ם ל ש and that the Greek texts of the New Testament translate by the words σωτηρία/salvation and σωτήρίον/ savior, would later find soteriological synonyms in λύτρωαις [deliverance, redemption] and in the Syriac *furqônô*, which finally passed into the Arabic *furqān*. We cannot go into a detailed enquiry, however interesting; it suffices to indicate the possibilities that are opened when one considers the Koran from the new, more critical viewpoints. It now seems certain that in Christian Arab circles the term *salām* was adopted for ασωτηρία, and that the verb *'aslama* from which came *'islām* would originally have had a different meaning from the one it later acquired: it would have been a soteriological and Ebionite concept.

The word *furqān* that among other meanings signifies "revelation," "knowledge," and in Greek γνῶσις [knowledge], also has a cultural origin in Gnostic Christianity. One knows the Gnostic parallelism: Knowledge-Redemption, Knowledge-Salvation, Redemption-Salvation, etc. Whether Muhammad was perfectly aware of the soteriological and Gnostic value of the word is doubtful, but that he received it from the Gnostic Christian milieu now seems beyond doubt. Thus Sura III:2, which says *wa-'anzala l-furqāna*, etc., must have this meaning, whether the expression refers to the Koran or to written revelation in general, whereas it is clear that in Sura VIII:42, on the day of Badr, *yawmu l- furqāni* signifies "the day of decision."

The concept of ἀληθὴς προφήτης [True Prophet], when put alongside that of the Sabeans, is the most certain sign of a historical relation between Muhammad and the cultural and religious milieu of Arab Jewish Christians, and such a relation is not accidental,[59] for the Muslim proselytes of the early days came in part from the Ebionite sects.[60] Their religious doctrines derived from a rich literature, in particular the "Predications of Peter" or Κηρύγματα Πέτρου, which we have already mentioned at the beginning of this article: this is a Jewish Christian text that should not be confused with another work of which Clement of Alexandria speaks and which, on the contrary, is the first apologetic treatise that we know of.

The first book of the Κηρύγματα Πέτρου deals with the true prophet, ἀληθὴς προφήτης and the veritable intelligence of the Torah in line with Moses' teachings. This first book is one of the most important, for we find there the notion of Jesus as the expected true prophet, and that of Adam as the first incarnation of the true prophet and a stranger to sin. The dualist conception of Good and Evil is explained in the sixth book and is expressed throughout this history in the theory of the *syzygy* or couple, according to which to any true prophet there corresponds a false one who precedes him. In reality, we have here a theory of Essenism of great consequence but with a superficial Christian coloring, since Christ becomes the last of the prophets, a kind of Jewish Christian *khātamu l-nabiyyīna*. In any case, for a better understanding of the dialectic movement immanent in the Koran, do not forget the basic doctrinal import of Essenism (the Qumrân texts are today the best known) in Ebionite tradition. On this question, the work to be done is difficult but would be interesting; and hence younger scholars have their work cut out for them.

"Monolatry"

The absolute unity of God defended by the Koran, a dogma that our Mario Martino Moreno thought it preferable to define as "monolatry" rather than monotheism, is the μοναρχία of the Christian heresy of the Monarchians, who excluded the idea of the Trinity in the same way as did orthodox Judaism, Jewish Christianity, and Ebionism. Similarly, a Jewish Christian writing widespread in the Church during the first half of the second century onward is anti-Trinitarian: Κηρύγματα Πέτρου [Predications/Preachings of Peter]. This work—which allows us to perceive the theology of Ebionism—seems to have had a missionary goal and, in view of the time when it was redacted and the milieux to which it was addressed, to particularly highlight the superiority of Christian monotheism—or, more exactly, Jewish Christian monotheism—over other religious movements. Origen in the third century took the work as authentic, at least in part, and even probably in its entirety.[61]

A correlation between the Koranic monotheist doctrine and that of

Kerygmata Petri has in fact been attempted.[62] The essence of the religion that Saint Paul synthesized from faith in a God the Creator who punishes the evil and rewards the good and from the belief that He had sent Christ as redeemer, is presented in the homilies of Pseudo-Clement of Rome (*Homel.* VII, 8) as follows: "θρησκεία ἐστὶν αὕτη τὸ μόνον αὐτὸν σεβεῖν καὶ τῷ τῆς ἀληθείας μόνῳ πιστεύειν προφήτῃ" ["Religious worship is in itself the revering of him alone and having faith in the prophet of truth alone"] and in this formula Islam could recognize elements of its *shahâda*. Muḥammad, as the ὁ τῆς ἀληθείας προφήτης, the prophet of truth, is according to Islam the legitimate successor of Musâ and of 'Isâ in the mission to enlighten humanity.

The idea of God in Islam remains closely related to the μοναρχικῇ θρησκείᾳ, "the divine monarchy" (*Homel.* VII, 12) of the Ebionites and the Monarchians, with the Christological implications that follow from this. Historians of the origins and diffusion of Islam believe they can discover in this religious situation a probable explanation of the rapidity with which the Christian populations of Arabia received the Koranic message. The religious structures were strictly similar, as was the psychology. Jewish Christianity, Ebionism, Elkesaism, Monophysitism, and Nestorianism all had an absolutely monotheistic basis that conditioned their Christology, the only stumbling block that would eventually divide them, while it is by no means impossible to suppose that if the *Nāṣāra* had possessed the Pauline Christology, then the Koran would have been Trinitarian.

JEWISH PRACTICES IN ISLAM

The problem of the relations between Islam and the Torah, setting aside the evident Ebionite infiltrations, as in the precise case of ablutions (more exactly, ablutions before the five daily prayers) would demand too vast a scientific enquiry to tackle here.[63] In any case, the very fact of the transmission of elements of the Torah into Islamic doctrine by means of the spreading of Ebionism and Elkesaism ought not raise serious difficulties, as might be proved by a particular practice like ritual ablution after the conjugal act,[64] the direction of the prayer or *qibla* that Jewish Christians directed toward

Jerusalem (as did all of Judaism in the Diaspora, moreover). It was only later that Muhammad, in conflict with the Jews of Yathrib (Medina), turned in the direction of the Ka' ba in Mecca:[65] in any case, we know from Epiphanius[66] that Elxai obliged his adherents to pray turned toward Jerusalem.

The alimentary restrictions imposed on Jews are presented by Muhammad as a divine punishment for their sins (Sura III:87; IV:158; VI:147; XVI:119): we know that the same opinion had already been circulated by an apocrypha esteemed among the Jewish Christians of Syria and Palestine, Egypt and Arabia, the *Didascalia Apostolorum*. The Koranic regulation of food is closely linked to these prescriptions of the *Ordinance of the Apostles*, as is the prohibition against smothering animals, the interdiction of blood, of pronouncing any other name than God's at the moment of immolation, the prohibition against pork meat, etc. We know that all these prescriptions have no declared or implicit pretension to be spreading asceticism, whether Jewish Christian or Muslim. On the contrary, it is a matter of a pure ritualism that consists in the observance of certain prescriptions but without scrutinizing their meaning or justification. It is certain that such observances create in the subject a *malaka* or *habitus* that realizes a certain religious state, no less than a certain interior freedom in face of the *dunyâ*, that is to say, in face of the exigencies of this "world below," and recalls the practices of Oriental Semitic Monachism.

As for the prohibition of wine, it seems of Elkesaite origin, if one thinks of the liturgical prescription of the use of water in the place of wine; similarly with the day of fasting of *Ashoura* (Leviticus 16:29; 23:27) passed from Judaism to Jewish Christianity and finally from there to Islam. The Jewish religious value attached to the duty of marriage also came into the Koran through Elkesaite teaching.[67]

The Alteration of Scripture

Also of Jewish Christian origin is the opinion crystallized in the Koran that Jews had altered their Scripture. In Sura II:75 we read: ". . . a party of them [the Jews] used to listen to the Word of Allah, then used to change it, after they had understood it, knowingly." Such falsifications are elsewhere attributed to the conscience of the Pharisees (Sura II:154, 169, 207; III:72; V:16, 45). The term Pharisees is rendered in the Koran by *munāfiqūna*, *hypocrites*, an expression specific to Christian preaching.

To better grasp the possible influence of Ebionism on the Koran, we should not forget what we read in Epiphanius:[68] "Nor do they [Ebionites] accept Moses' Pentateuch in its entirety; certain sayings they reject. When you say to them, of eating meat, 'Why did Abraham serve the angels the calf and the milk [that is to say, offer a sacrifice]?' . . ." This allows us to suppose that the Ebionites, out of principle, excluded from the Pentateuch everything that dealt with the prescriptions about sacrifice. But Jewish Christians did not act otherwise, not even the Essenes. On the other hand, from information about ecclesiastical heresies and by reconstructing Ebionite literature, we also know that they had a particular recension of the Gospel. Epiphanius goes on: "[The Ebionites] accept the Gospel according to Matthew, the only one they use. They call it *Gospel According to the Hebrews*. This *Gospel According to Matthew*, which is in their possession, is not complete, but false and mutilated."[69] Now, in another subsequent note on the Nazareans or *Nāṣāra*, Epiphanius records that the *Gospel According to Matthew* that they used was very complete. According to other sources such as Clement of Alexandria and Origen, the Ebionites had the same text as the *Nāṣāra*, but the latter had adapted it, at least partially, to their conceptions; thus theirs is known as the *Gospel of the Ebionites*.[70]

The historian Eusebius, bishop of Caesarea in Palestine, gives us supplementary information that might clarify the Islamic theory of false pericopes. Here is what he writes:

"One of the translators of the Bible, Symmachus was an Ebionite. The heresy that we call Ebionite is of those who (continues Eusebius of Caesarea) affirm that Christ was born of Joseph and Mary (in a manner common to all mortals), who think that he is a virtuous man and who insists energetically that one should observe the Torah absolutely like the Jews. They also show the commentaries of Symmach where he strives to prove the heresy in question (Ebionite) by means of the Gospel According to Matthew. Origen recounts that he received these works at the same time as the other glosses of Symmach on the Scriptures of a certain Juliana, which he had had from Symmach himself."[71]

On the other hand, the pseudo-Clementine Homilies—an eminently Jewish Christian work—contains the thesis of false Scriptural sayings (Homil. II:39), a thesis that we read in the *Letter to Flora* by the Gnostic Ptolemy; and we find again this same theory about the textual falsification of Scripture in the *Didascalie of the Apostles* (VI:20).[72]

Everything allows us to believe that the Islamic tradition about the falsification of the Bible comes from Jewish Christianity; at the very least its writings contain parallel conceptions that cannot help but attract the attention of scholars.

The opinion about false sayings assumed major importance in Muhammad's mind and in the later polemic of Islam; in fact, this theme surfaces more than once in the Hadith literature.[73] In the anti-Jewish polemic of Arabia, Jewish Christians and Muslims find themselves in agreement on the necessity of "restoring" Hebraic Scripture.[74] But were the texts accepted as authentic by the Synagogue really altered? Muhammad certainly could not have known if this were so, and the Jewish Christians had their own doctrinal reasons for asserting this. In any case, the Qumrân texts have shed sufficient light on certain falsifications that the apologist Justin Martyr offered in opposition to Tryphon: today we know that it was simply a matter of different textual recensions,[75] which *mutatis mutandis* may be compared with the *qirâ'ât* of the Koran.

Clues from Muslim Literature

After this very brief summary of what we argue was contributed by Ebionite and Elkesaite elements to the Koran, it is perhaps time to ask if Muslim literature has transmitted to us something that might confirm our hypothesis.

In fact, Muslim writers prove themselves much more informed about Jewish Christians and the sects deriving from them than we were formerly led to believe—not because they seem suspect to us, but in part because we cannot manage to locate the sources that they handed down to us, and in part because it is hard to destroy what has been tirelessly constructed by immense erudition upon foundations that until recently seemed unshakeable.

One of the first pioneers was J. W. Hirschberg[76] who analyzed all the texts at his disposal and could assert: "Soll auch der im Arabischen für Christen gebräuchliche Name *nāṣāra* ursprünglich eine Jüdische-Christliche Sekte bezeichnet haben" ("The name *nāṣāra*, commonly used in Arabic for Christians, is said to originally have identified a Jewish-Christian sect").[77] But we must remember the time (the 1930s), the documents, and the mental habits against which he was fighting, given such Orientalists as Sprenger, Nöldeke, Lammens, Nielsen, Andrae, et al. . . !

A more decisive step forward was taken by Shlomo Pinès,[78] who published testimony from one of the most important and last *Mu'tazilites*, the Qāḍī l-qudāt abū l-Hasan 'Abd al-Jabbâr b. Muḥammad b. 'Abd al- Jabbâr al-Hamadānī al-Astarabādī (died in January 1025 CE). This 'Abd al- Jabbâr in his *taṯbīt dalā'il nubuwwat sayyidinā Muḥammad*, inserted amidst other texts of Shi'ite polemic a Jewish Christian text against the ethno-Christians. The content is against St. Paul—an obligatory position of all convinced Jewish Christians, to whichever nuance they subscribed—and against an emperor that Pinès identified with Constantine, who in 325 summoned the Council of Naçârâ, where Monophysites, Nestorians, and Jewish Christians of all stripes were thrown into suspicion, which consequently obliged them to seek refuge elsewhere, in Arabia.[79] The sources used by 'Abd al- Jabbâr, after internal critical examination, seem to have been redacted around the fifth century, and maybe in the Syriac language. The author of the Jewish Christian source believes that the original language of the New Testament was Hebrew, which would indicate, in the absence of other evidence, the tendency of either redactor or the tradition being fixed by the text, to determine the relations between Jewish Christianity and Judaism by the means of the linguistic element.

In addition, one must not forget that among the late Muslim theologians like Al-Isfarā'inī al-Khorāsānī (born in 1241) in his *rasā'il al-nūr fi samā' 'ahl al-surūr* and Ash- Shahrastānī (born in 1071) in his work *kitāb al-milal wal-niḥal* (already studied in part by Giuseppe Gabriele[80]), we encounter a strong anti-Pauline current, exactly in the Jewish Christian vein. This finding is worthy of interest, because Muhammad never took Saint Paul into consideration, either directly or indirectly. In order to explain the existence of such a current in Islam, therefore, must one speak of a Koranic anti-Pauline polemic *ex silentio*? Such a hypothesis seems to make no sense.[81]

CONCLUSION

To conclude, we may remember that the exaggeration on the part of those who have seen in Islam a Jewish enterprise (like the Dominican G. Théry under the pseudonym of Hanna Zakarias)[82] has only been equaled by those who see in the Koran merely a pile of badly understood scraps of Christian teaching (and here the bibliography running from the School of Toledo to our days is immense). After what we have indicated or just implied due to the shortness of the lecture format, we may modestly propose the direction in which research should henceforth be directed: to discover in the Koran the crystallization of an Arabized form of Jewish Christianity that, received during its Ebionite and Elkesaite phase, had already entered into the dialectical movement of religious ideas that would lead to Islam. Therefore, it no longer is correct to speak of the Christian influence on the Koran in the usual way, but of an evolution of Jewish Christianity toward Islam.[83] The time was already ripe when Muhammad appeared on the Arab world scene.

Paradoxically, we may advance the idea that it is properly through encystment in the Koranic amber that the doctrine of a Church headed for gradual and ineluctable disappearance, that of the *Naṣārā*, was fixed as "unvarying" and so came all the way down to us practically intact in its content. "Return to the old and there will be progress" says an adage. In effect, when the old Christian apologists and heresiologues saw in Islam a Christian heresy, they were not far from the truth; their way of expressing themselves was somewhat simplistic, but they had grasped the kernel of truth of a religious phenomenon that they poorly understood. From the Ebionite standpoint, the dialectical movement that goes from Adam, Abraham, and Moses up to Jesus then found in Muhammad its culmination, historically and theologically.

Moreover, the theological role of heresies and of religious movements taken to be such (because, soteriologically, everything is recapitulated in the Christ in whom all have faith) can no longer be misunderstood. Detached from the trunk of the μεγάλη ἐκκλησία, they found themselves for various contingent reasons in the situation that Eberhard Otto defined as the *Endsituation* of a culture, that is to say, the cessation of all dialectical development still in vigor. The Koran conserved for us a Christian eschatological teaching that had disappeared within the official Church, at least in Alexandria, already in the time of Clement of Alexandria—and hence well before Constantine.[84] The "Enteschatologisierung," or process of de-eschatologization, had been halted only in the Eastern Churches, separated from the Western Scholastics, and within the Sects, it was absorbed into Semitic elements, where eschatologism belongs by right.[85]

Some in the West think that Islam, in its cultural expression,[86] represents a religious phase inferior to Christianity, but this is justified only in that our Western Christianity has been "re-elaborated" and re-thought within Greco-Roman culture. But if we reinsert Christianity within the historical and cultural framework that was originally its own, that is to say, within the Jewish Christian framework, if we set aside the Platonization of Christology[87] in order to return to the forms of the Mother Church of Jerusalem under the leadership of Saint James, "the Lord's brother," and if we reinsert the whole within the Semitic context, then Islam would appear to us in a more favorable light, even in the West. We know very well that what we are saying is a paradoxical position with respect to the "superior" culture of the West, whereas it is completely normal in the face of "under-developed" Semitic culture.

In truth, this whole way of thinking is not at all new, for Harnack expressed it in 1877 and reformulated it in 1909: "Der Islam ist eine Umbildung der von dem gnostischen Judenchristentum selbst schon umgebildeten jüdischen Religion auf dem Boden des Araberthums durch einen grossen Propheten" [Islam is a transformation of the Jewish religion already transformed by the gnostic Jewish-Christians on Arabic soil by a great prophet].[88]

Today, the renowned specialist in the theology and history of Jewish Christianity, Hans-Joachim Schoeps, has arrived at the same conclusions,[89] with the nuances imposed by progress in more recent research.

—Martiniano P. Roncaglia (1971)

NOTES

1. [Martiniano P. Roncaglia, "Elements Ebionites et Elkésaïtes dans le Coran," *Proche Orient Chrétien* 21 (1971): 101–26. Translated by Susan Boyd-Bowman]

*These "Notes and Hypotheses" were read in the form of a lecture on 12 February 1969 in Rome at the invitation of the *Istituto di Studi Islamici* of Rome University and the *Istituo per l'Oriente*. They were translated from Italian into French and published in their entirety in *Proche-Orient Chrétien* 21 in 1971. [The present translation is from the French]

2. [Note from *Encyclopaedia of Religion and Ethics*: "The Elkesaites are so named from an Aramaic formation which the Greek tradition represents as (Epiphanius). . . . Elkesai was in possession of a book of revelation. He required his adherents to practise circumcision, to observe the Sabbath, and, in general, to live according to the Jewish Law. . . ."]

3. Epiphanius, *The Panarion*, trans. Frank Williams, Leiden/New York, E. J. Brill, 1987, XXX:16, pp. 131–32.

4. Ibid., XXX:3, p. 121.

5. Ibid., IX:14, p. 44

6. Hippolytus, *Elenchose*, IX, 14.

7. Oscar Cullmann, *Die neuentdeckten Qumrrântexte und das Judencrhistentum der Pseudo-Klementinen, In Neutestamenliche Studien für Rudolf Bultmann,* Berlin, 1954, pp. 35–51.

8. Eusebius, *Hist Eccl.* VI, 38. Here are Origen's words (from *Homily on the Psalms 82*): the Elkesaïts "say that apostasy does not matter, and that someone who reflects may deny with his mouth if necessary but not in his heart." To juxtapose what P. H. Lammens wrote in *Syrie: Precis historique*, vol. I, p. 185): "Taking as authority the theology of the *taqyya*, which the *Nuṣayrīs/Alawites* interpreted much more widely than the *Shī'ites*, they thought it licit, like the Druzes, to conform in their attitudes to the dominant religion."

9. Origen, *Contra Celsum*, II, 1 and V, 61; *De principiis*, IV, 3, 8; *In Matth.* 16, 12 and 11, 12; *In Ierem. Homil.* 19, 12; *In Epist. Administration Titum* (Lomm, V, 286). On the complexity of the Ebionite movement, see Marcel Simon, *Versus Israel: A Study of the Relation Between Christians and Jews in the Roman Empire 135–425*, New York, Oxford University Press, 1986, 277–314.

10. Saint Jerome had met *Naṣārā* or Nazoraeans in Berea in Syria; Hieronymus, *Détente viris illustribus*, 3.

11. *Lisān al'Arab* [Arabic Lexicon of *Ibn Manẓūr* 20 vols., Cairo, 1308]

alludes to Waraqa ibn-Nawfal, cousin or uncle of Khadija, which the *Sirat al-Halabia*, relying on the *qāmūs*, calls *qaṣṣ l-naṣārā*. This fact was kindly pointed out to me by Professor Haddad, author of the book *al-qur'ān da'watun' naṣrāniyyatun* [*The Koran: A Christian Call*], an erudite work full of original perceptions. For him, for example, *ḥanīf, naṣrāni, muslim* are all three equivalent terms to designate the sect to which Muhammad's own grandfather belonged; and when the latter tells us (Koran sura VI:163): *'anā 'awwalu l-muslimīna* [*"I am the first of those who bows to his will"*], he allows us to understand that it is he, Muhammad, who had succeeded Waraqa as head of the Meccan community.

12. Adolf von Harnack, *Lehrbuch der Dogmengeschichte,* 4, Auflage, Tubingen, 1909, II, 537. Note that the English edition of *History of Dogma* does not contain the appendix on Islam that appears in the German edition.

13. Ibid., 534.

14. C. Clement, *Muhammeds Abhängigkeit von der Gnosis* (Harnack-Ehrung), Leipzig, 1922.

15. J. Horovitz, *Koranische Untersuchungen*, Berlin, 1926, 131.

16. B. Carra de Vaux, in *Enzyklopaedie des Islam*, IV, 22.

17. J. Pedersen, "The Sabians," in *A Volume of Oriental Studies Presented to E. Browne*, Cambridge, 1922.

18. Quoted by S. Chwolson, *Die Ssabier*, St. Petersburg, 1853, II, 205; other teachings are taken from Al-Bīrunī i and Al-Mas'ūdī and collected by J. Thomas, *Le mouvement baptiste en Palestine et en Syrie*, Gemblous, 1935, 197 ss.

19. Thomas, op. cit.

20. The documentation was gathered by Julius Wellhausen, *Reste arabischen Heidentums*, Skissen und Vorarbeiten, III, Berlin, 1888, 236 ff. [*Religio-Political Factions in Early Islam*, trans. Ostle and Walzer, Amsterdam, American Elsevier, 1975] and by Frants Buhl, *Des Leben Muhammeds*, Leipzig, 1930, 238.

21. H. Waitz, *Der Prophet Elchasai* (Harnack-Ehrung), Giessen, 1922, 103 ff.; K. Ahrens, *Muhammed als Religionsstifter*, Leipzig, 1935, 10.

22. Ahrens, op. cit., 59; Hans Joachim Schoeps, *Theologie und Geschichte des Judenchristentums*, Tübingen, 1949, 324, 325–34; Schoeps, *Jewish Christianity: Factional Disputes in the Early Church*, Philadelphia, Fortress Press, 1969.

23. Migne, *Patrologia Graeca*, XCIV, 709.

24. Father Joseph Haddad, an expert on the Koran, told me that many of the hymnic elements of Ebionite and Elkesaite liturgies were probably to be found in the Koran. This question is under study.

25. Arent Jan Wensinck, "Muhammad und die Prophetie," in *Acta Orientalia II* (Oslo, 1924), 178 ff.

26. Wilhelm Rudolf, *Die Abhängigkeit des Qorans vom Judentum und Christentum*, Stuttgart, 1922, 45 ff.

27. Epiphanius, *Panarion*, XXXVIII, p. 250.

28. On the importance of Abraham in the Islamic religion, see H. Speyer, *Die biblischen Erzählungen im Koran*, Gräfenheiniche, 1932, 120 ff., and in the "Massignon" movement, Y. Moubarac, *Abraham dans le Coran: L'Histoire d'Abraham dans le Coran et la naissance de l'Islam, Étude critique des textes coraniques suivie d'un essai sur la representation qu'ils donnent de la Relgiion et de l'Histoire. Avec un liminaire de Louis Massignon* (Études Musulmanes, V), Paris, 1958.

29. According to Ahrens, op. cit., 125, this is a Manichean expression.

30. Alessandro Bausani, *Postille a Cor. II*, 248—XXXIX:23—XX:15, in *Studi Orientalistici in onore détente Giorgio Levi della Vida*, Rome, 1956, I, 50–51. The problem of the Parousia has been studied by Johannes Timmermann, *Nachapastolishces Parusiedenken, ...*

31. Hippolytus, *Elenchos*, IX, 14.

32. Epiphanius, *Panarion*, LIII:1.8, p. 71.

33. Quoted by Ignaz Goldziher, "Neoplatonische und gnostische Elemente im Hadith," in *Zeitschrift für Assyriologie* (1909), 340. [The theories of the Imam's reincarnations, specific to Shi'ism and especially to Druzism, seem to belong to the same perspective.]

34. Goldziher, op. cit., 337 ff.

35. Michel Spanneut, *Le Stoïcisme des Pères de l'Eglise de Clément de Rome à Clément d'Alexandre* (Paris, Seuil, 1969); Philipp Vielhaver, "'Ανάπαυσις Zum gnostischen Hintergrund des Thomasevangeliums," in *Apophoreta*, Festschrift für Ernst Haenchen, Berlin, 1964, 281–99.

36. G. Bodenwalt, "Begrenzung und Dliederune der Spätantike," in *Serta Karazoviana*—Izvvestija na Bulgarskija Archaeologiceski Institut, 16 Sofija 1951, 53–58.

37. Hippolytus, *Elenchos*, IX, 13–15.

38. Jean Daniélou, *The Theology of Jewish Christianity*, trans. and ed., J. A. Baker, London, Darton, Longman & Todd, 1977, pp. 64–67.

39. Carlo Alfonso Nallino, *Raccolta di Scritti editi e inediti*, Roma, 1941, III, 11.

40. Ibid., II, 60–65.

41. J. Horovitz, *Qoranische Untersuchungen*, Berlin, 1926, 52.

42. G. Rosch, "Die Jesusmythen des Islams," in *Theologische Studien und Kritiken* (1876), 425.

43. As Karl Ahrens has already demonstrated in *Christliches im Qoram*, in *Zeitschrift der Deutschen Morgenländischen Gesellschaft* (1930), 153.

44. G. Hoffmann, *Verhandlungen der Kirchenversammlung zu Ephesus* 449, Kiel, 47 and 21.

45. Hans Lietzmann, *Die Entstehung der christlichen Liturgie nach den ältesten Quellen*, Darmstadt, 1963, 10, and Martiniano Roncaglia, *La vie liturgique en Egypte du 1er au IIIième siècle*, Beirut, 1969.

46. Karl Ahrens, *Muhammed als Religionsstifter* (Abhandlungen für die Kunde des Morgenlandes, XIX, Band, no. 4), Leipzig, 1935, 194–99.

47. George Graf, "Wie ist das Wort Al-Masīḥ zu übersetzen?" in *Zeitschrift der Deutschen Morgenländischen Gesellschaft* 104 (1954), 119–23, which repeats the same classical reflections on Muhammad's incomprehension of the problem of Christ's status as messiah, etc. However, he suggests translating *al-Masīḥ* by "messenger of God or *rasûl*," which is more in line with the Prophet's thinking and with the knowledge he had of the Christian religion. In effect we cannot accept the thesis offered in the usual manner of "ecclesiastical science" by Michel Hayek, "L'origine des termes 'Isâ-al-Masīḥ (Jésus-Christ) dans le Coran," in *L'Orient Syrien* 7 (1962), 223–54, who concludes the first part of his study as follows: "Muhammad seems a beneficiary, as much in his religious conceptions as in his technical vocabulary, of a diffuse and sporadic Christianity, carried into Arabia by 'humble people' [we would say, Ebionites] who had his first sympathies, wine and oil merchants from Syria, slaves, mercenaries, cupping glass users from Abyssinia, transplanted from their original locales to the bourgeois milieu of Mecca. They were the vehicles of their naïve religiosity, in this Arabia whose language they scarcely knew, therefore creating a vernacular that resembled a pidgin. To the already mangled names of their Biblical personages, they must have added a monstrous deformation, the Koranic name of 'the most beautiful of the children of men,' attached to the most disfigured face of all, 'Īsā, Jesus.'" See also, Hayek, *Le Christ de l'Islam*, Paris, Seuil, 1959. On the real situation of Arab Christianity when Islam appeared, cf. Ruth Stiehl, "Christliche Mission beiderseits des Roten Meeres," in *Die Welt des Orients* IV (1967), 109–27.

48. The meaning, or rather the sense given by J.-M. Abd-el-Jalil, *Marie et l'Islam*, Paris, 1950, 59, belongs to spiritual edification and is derived principally from a Muslim writer of the nineteenth century, Al-Alûsi.

49. Jacques Jomier, *Il Corano è contro la Biblia?* The Italian translation seems to contain the passage quoted above, which does not appear in the original French or in the English (*The Bible and the Koran*, trans. Edward Arbetz, Chicago, Desclee, 1964). See also Michel Hayek, *Christ et l'Islam*, Paris, 1957, and Geoffrey Parrinder, *Jesus in the Qur'an*, London, 1965.

50. W. Warren, "On "ἑαυτὸν ἐκένωσεν" in *Journal of Theological Studies* 12

(1911), 461–63, and K. Petersen, "ἑαυτὸν ἐκένωσεν [Gk]," in *Symbolae Osloenses* 12 (1933), 96–101.

51. O. Pautz, *Mohammade Lehre von der Offenbarung quellemässig dargestellt*, Leipzig, 1898, 126–27.

52. O. Betz, *Der Paraklet: Fürsprecher im häretischen Spätjudentum, im Johannes-Evangelium und in neu gefundenen gnostischen Schriften* (Arbeiten zur Geschichte des Spätjudentum und Urchristentum, II), Leiden, Brill, 1963.

53. S. Krauss, *Griechische und lateinische Lehnwörter in Talmud, Midrasch und Targum,* 1898–1899, I, 210; II, 496.

54. See the introduction to *Iohannis Evangelium Apocryphum Arabice* in lucem edidite, latine convertit, praefatione et commentario instruxit Ioannes Galbiati, (Antiquitatis Christianae ex Oriente Monumenta) Mediolani 1957, and the survey by Mariano Roncaglia, in *Oriens 15* (Leiden, 1962), 474–78.

55. Martiniano Roncaglia, "Essai d'Histoire de la Littérature Copte des origines à la fin du IIIème siècle," in *al-Machriq* 61 (1967): 103–34.

56. Karl Ahrens, *Muhammed als Religionsstifter*, 154–58.

57. Alessandro Bausani, *Persia religiosa*, Milan, 1959, 111–12.

58. Mark Lidzbarski, "Salâm und Islâm," in *Zeitschrift für Semitistik* 1 (1922), 85–86.

59. Tor Andrae, "Der Ursprung des Islams und das Christentum," in *Kyrkohistorisk Arsschrift* (1923), 153; (1926), 204.

60. H. H. Schaeder, "Die islamische Lehre von vollkommenen Menschen. Ihre Herkunft und ihre dichterische Gestaltung," in *Zeitschrift der Deutschen Morgenländischen Gesellschaft* (1925), 213, thinks that this doctrinal position of Muhammad's should be considered as deriving "auf mündliche Uberlieferung von Proselytes aus christlichen und jüdischen sektiererischen Kreisen" ["from an oral tradition of proselytes from Christian and Jewish sectarian circles"].

61. E. Klostermann, *Apocrypha*, I (Kleine Texte, III), Bonn, 1908, 13–16 (fragments of Clement of Alexandria), and E. von Dobschütz, *Das Kerugma Petri kritisch untersucht* (Texte und Untersuchungen . . . XI, Heft 1), Leipzig, 1893.

62. A. Siouville, "Introduction aux Homélies Clémentines," in *Revue de l'Histoire des Religions* (1930), 200.

63. The erudite elements one can gather from S. D. Goitein, *Studies in Islamic History & Institutions*, Leiden, 1960, still belong to the classical theses of Jewish influence on Islam, although less radical than those of C. C. Torrey, *The Jewish Foundation of Islam*, New York, 1933. That there is Judaism within Islam, granted; however, it does not come from Judaism but from Jewish Christianity.

64. A. J. Wensinck, "Die Entstehung des Islamischen Reinheitsgesetzgebung," in *Der Islam* 5 (1914), 68ff.

65. F. Schwally, *Geschichte des Qorans*, Leipzig, Weicher, 1909, I, 130–45, 175.

66. Epiphanius, *Panarion*, XIX:3.5, p. 46.

67. Ibid., XIX:1, p. 44.

68. Ibid., XXX:18.7, p. 134.

69. Ibid., XXX:3.7, p. 122.

70. Hans-Joachim Schoeps, *Theologie und Geschichte des Judenchristentums,* Tübingen, 1949, 25–33.

71. Schoeps, op. cit., 350–66.

72. Ibid., 179–87.

73. Theodor Nöldeke and F. Schwally, *Geschichte des Qorans*, 2, Auflage, Lepzig, 1919, II, 121.

74. Moritz Steinschneider, *Polmische und apologetische Litertur in arabischer Sprache swischen Muslimen, Christen und Juden: nebst Anhängen verwandten Inhalts mit Benutzung handschriftlicher Quellen* (Abhandlungen für die Kunde des Morgenlandes, Band VI, Heft 3), Leipzig, 1877, 320.

75. J. Smit Sibinga, *The Old Testatment Text of Justin Martyr, I: The Pentateuch*, Leiden, 1962.

76. J. W. Hirschberg, *Judische und christliche Lehren im vor—und frühislamischen Arabien: Ein Beitrag zur Entstehungsgeschichte des Islams* (Polska Akademia Umiejetonosci, Mémoires de la Commission Orientaliste No. 12) Krakow, 1939.

77. Ibid., p. 16.

78. Shlomo Pinès, "The Jewish Christians of the Early Centuries of Christianity according to a New Source," in *Proceedings of the Israel Academy of Sciences and Humanities* 2, no. 13, Jerusalem, 1966.

79. One is surprised to find Emperor Constantine and the Council of Nicaea associated with the mention of Monophysites and Nestorians, when we would instead have expected the name of the emperor Marcion who in 451 presided over the council of Chalcedonia, where monophysism was condemned, and who in 457 expelled from Byzantine lands the Nestorian theologians of the School of Edessa.

80. Giuseppe Gabrieli, *I prolegomeni dello Shahrastani alla sua opera su le Religioni et le Sette*, Rome, 1905.

81. G. Klinge, "Die Beziehungen zwischen christlicher und islamlischer Theologie," in *Anfang des Mittelalters*, in *Zeitschrift für Kirchengeschichte* 56 (1937), 43–58, especially pages 52–53.

82. Hanna Zakarias, *L'Islam: entreprise juive, De Moise à Mohammed,* Cahors-Paris, 1955–1964, 4 vols.

83. A. Schlatter, "Die Entwicklung des jüdischen Christentums zum Islam," in *Evangelischer Missionsmagazin* (1918), 252.

84. A. Oepke, "Parusie," in G. Kittel, *Theologisches Wörterbuch zum Neuen Testament, V* (Stuttgart, 1954), 856–57. The author, after examining forty-one texts by Clement of Alexandria relating to the Parousia, states that already at the end of the second century, eschatological sense was already well blunted among Christians of the Great Church.

85. Timmermann, op. cit., 125.

86. The thinking of the author should not be misunderstood. He by no means intended to compare the dogmatic content of the two religions. Here he speaks only of two different modes of expression, two ways of trying to express what is properly inexpressible. For centuries, our theological language, learned from Greek philosophy, especially Aristotle, has spoken in abstract concepts. The same was not true at the very origins of Christianity: "Jewish Christian theology," writes Jean Daniélou, "is a theology in the proper sense of the word, that is to say an attempt to construct a vision of the whole on the basis of the data that constitute the divine events of the Incarnation and the Revelation of the Word. This theology appears already in certain works of the New Testament, in St. Paul and St. John in particular . . . but this theology is, in many respects, the expression of a common speculation that is antecedent to it and of which Jewish Christian writings are a further attestation" (*Théologie judéo-chrétienne*, p. 433). Leaving aside the doctrinal content of this theology, not to mention the form in which it is presented, one must say that this kind of thinking in late Judaism, in proto-Christianity, in Jewish Christianity, and in Islam is by no means conceptual: it could be called a "mythic" kind of thinking, on condition of not giving the word "myth" the sense of "fable" but of "representation of the imaginative (not imaginary) structure with a grasp of values" (H. Duméry, *Philosophie de la religion*, I, p. vi). We find a perfect example in the *Pastor of Hermas*, the little book that disconcerted so many and caused so much foolishness on the part of those who attempted the exegesis of it with their Aristotelian categories or Cartesian logic. "This mode of expression is as valid as a metaphysical or existential mode," writes Daniélou (op. cit., p. 227). Today, contact with Symbolist poetry has made us a little less impermeable to this mode of expression with which, however, we are not yet familiar and which always leaves us ill at ease.

87. An example of the refusal to Platonize Christology is given by Denys of Alexandria who refused to use the term ομοούσος, suggested to him by Denys

Bishop of Rome, because the said expression was not found int he Bible. Ludwig Hertling, *Geschichte der katholischen Kirche*.

88. Adolf von Harnack, *Lehrbuch der Dogmengeschichte,* Zweiter Band: Die Entwicklung des Kirchlichen Dogmas, 4, Auflage, Tübingen, 1909, 529–38, pp. 537.

89. Hans-Joachim Schoeps, *Theologie und Geschichte des Judenchristentims*, Tübingen, 1949, 334–42. Here is how in his later *Jewish Christianity* he takes up Harnack's thesis: "Thus we have a paradox of world-historical proportions, viz, the fact that Jewish Christianity indeed disappeared with the Christian Church, but was preserved in Islam and thereby extended some of its basic ideas even to our own day" (p. 140).

2.9

An Essenian Rule in the Koran[1]

Marc Philonenko

Sura XXIV refers in verses 27–31 to various rules concerning decorum among the believers: that no one enter someone else's home without being announced first; that women be chaste and veiled. The subject is taken up again in verses 57 to 63. Verse 60 treats a related problem, that of a communal meal. One reads:

> XXIV.60 "There is no restriction [*ḥaraj*] *upon a blind or lame or a sick person*, nor upon yourselves in the matter of eating in your houses, or in the houses of your fathers, or the houses of your mothers, or the houses of your brothers, or the houses of your sisters, or the houses of your uncles or aunts either on the father's or the mother's side, or (houses) of which ye possess the keys, or of your friend; it is no fault upon you that ye eat together or in separate groups."[2]

Muhammad here allows believers to sit at the table of those to whom they are related, or to whom they have ties of friendship. This permission is extended to the blind, the lame, and the sick. It is clear that the latter extension fits badly in the context as much for style as for sense. The older commentators do not try to hide their embarrassment. According to Aḍ-Daḥḥāk, "Before the Prophet's apostleship the Medinans did not eat with the blind and sick. Some explain this by their fear of and disgust for uncleanliness; others by the fact that the sick do not imbibe food in the same manner as the healthy; the lame, being handicapped, can not hurry (with the others) to the food and the blind cannot see the choicest parts of the dishes. Then God revealed that there is no harm in sharing the food with the sick, the blind and the lame."[3]

Bayḍāwī realizes that the incriminating passage "did not go either with what precedes or that which follows."[4] In fact, as Blachère,[5] agreeing with Goldziher,[6] remarks, it is difficult to believe that the blind and the lame would be excluded from communal meals on the sole basis of their infirmity.

There is more. This morsel of the phrase "There is no restriction *upon a blind or lame or a sick person*" is found in another sura, Sura XLVIII. The Prophet takes to task some Bedouins who were hesitating about participating in a warlike expedition [XLVIII:16], "Say to the Bedouin who were left behind: 'You will be summoned to a people of vehement warlike spirit, whom you will fight or they will become Muslims; then if you obey, Allah will give you a good reward, but if you turn away, as you turned away before, He will inflict upon you a punishment painful.'" He [Muhammad] immediately adds however [XLVIII:17]: "There is no blame [*ḥaraj*] upon the blind, or upon the lame, or upon the sick [for abstaining from going to war]." This specification fits perfectly in this context. It is natural enough—one would think—that, from the fact of their infirmity, the blind, the lame, and the sick be excused from taking part in combats. One understands then if perceptive critics have considered the mention of the blind, the lame and the sick in Sura XXIV as coming from Sura XLVIII. Nevertheless, and Torrey[7] has underlined it, a difficulty persists. How does one decide if there was an accidental deplacement or an intentional interpolation?

The expedition invoked in Sura XLVIII is no ordinary razzia, but an episode in the Holy War. One knows the place of this warrior ideal in Islam.[8] Its prehistory remains however a little obscure. A comparison with the Old Testament forces itself upon us and even more with the Dead Sea Scrolls.[9] The scroll of "the Sons of Light against the Sons of Darkness" exalts, as never before, the holy war and describes in detail the tactics, the arms and the rules of the holy soldiers of God.[10] In this way one finds established the plan of mobilisation, and specified the moral and physical qualities of those who are combatants and those who are not. It is this latter category that interests us in the highest degree: "No one crippled, blind, or lame, nor a man who has a permanent blemish on his skin, or a man affected with ritual uncleaness of his flesh; none of these shall go with them to battle."[11]

The addition, in the *Military Regulations*, of other categories of disabled to those who were lame, blind and crippled does not suffice to mask a discovery that is too precise to be pure chance. The Prophet knew the Qumranian regulation. There is no good reason to be too surprised, if, as we have tried to show elsewhere, Muhammad had knowledge of Essenian traditions.[12] One needs to note once more that the Prophet seems to have changed the original import of the Qumranian rule. According to the Hebrew text, the blind, the lame or the crippled are excluded because of their impurity. According to the Arabic text, they have been exempted because of their incapacity.

One finds in the Appendix to the Rules a long list of persons excluded from the Assembly: "No man who suffers from a single one of the uncleannesses that affect humanity shall enter their assembly; neither is any man so afflicted to receive an assignment from the congregation. No man with a physical handicap—crippled in both legs or hands, lame, blind, deaf, dumb, or possessed of a visible blemish in his flesh—or a doddering old man unable to do his share in the congregation of the m[e]n of reputation. For holy angels are [a part] of their congregation. If [one] of these people has some[thing] to say to the congregation, let an oral [de]position be taken, but the man must n[ot] enter [the congregation,] for he has been smitten."[13]

Thus, the lame, the blind, the sick of all kind are excluded from the Assembly, with so much greater reason from the communal meal whose regulation is referred to again in the Appendix to the Rules a few lines later.[14] The blind, the lame or infirm, impure according to the Laws of Leviticus,[15] would irremediably defile the sacred meal by their presence. That explains the deplacement of a part of the phrase "There is no restriction *upon a blind or lame or a sick person*." This interpolation, of which the Prophet himself could have been the author, has for origins the willingness to admit to the communal meal the blind, the lame and sick. It is a rejection of the Essenian rule that certain Jews of Medina wanted, no doubt, to see respected.

Muhammad then does not simply and slavishly copy his attitude with regard to the blind, the lame and the sick from Qumranian practice. He keeps it for all that concerns war, he rejects it for all that concerns meals. The reason for this subtle position is clear. For Muhammad, the blind, the lame or the sick find themselves, by their infirmity, physically incapabable of taking part in the Holy War. They are not, nonetheless, smitten by ritual impurity: they can partake of the communal meal.[16]

Notes

1. [Marc Philonenko, "*Une règle* Essénienne dans le Coran," *Semitica* 22 (1972): 49–52. Translated by Ibn Warraq.]

2. [I have used R. Bell's translation: *The Qur'ān*, Edinburgh: T&T Clark, vol. 1, 1937. Philonenko used R. Blachère's French translation, *Le Coran*, Paris: G. P. Maisonneuve & Cie, vol. 2, 1951: XXIV: 60: "Il n'est nul grief (*ḥaraj*) *à l'aveugle, nul grief au boiteux, nul grief au malade*, à vous à ce que vous mangiez réciproquement dans vos demeures ou dans les demeures de vos pères, ou dans les demeures de vos mères, ou ou dans les demeures de vos frères, ou dans les demeures de vos soeurs, ou dans les demeures de vos oncles paternels, ou dans les demeures de vos tantes paternelles, ou dans les demeures de vos tantes maternelles, ou [dans le lieu] dont vous possédez les clefs, ou [dans la demeure] d'un ami. Nul grief à vous de manger ensemble ou séparément."]

3. Ṭabarī, [Commentary] *Tafsīr al-Ṭabarī* (*Al-Jāmi' al-bayān fī ta'wīl āy al-Qur'ān*), 30 vols., Cairo, AH 1323–1329, vol. 18, p. 115, line 14 ss. I owe the translation of this passage to my colleague T. Fahd.

4. Bayḍāwī, *Anwār al-tanzīl wa-asrār al-ta'wīl*, ed. H. O. Fleischer (Leipzig, 1846–1848), II, 31:6., quoted by I. Goldziher, *Introduction to Islamic Theology and Law*, trans. Andras and Ruth Hamori (Princeton: Princeton University Press, 1981), p. 30, end of footnote 37.

5. R. Blachère, *Le Coran*, Paris: G. P. Maisonneuve & Cie, vol. 2, 1951, p. 1020, footnote 60.

6. I. Goldziher, *Introduction to Islamic Theology and Law,* trans. Andras and Ruth Hamori (Princeton: Princeton University Press, 1981), p. 29, footnote 37.

7. C. C. Torrey, "Three Difficult Passages in the Koran," in *A Volume of Oriental Studies Presented to E. G. Browne*, Cambridge, 1922, pp. 459–64. Also in Ibn Warraq, ed., *What the Koran Really Says* (Amherst, NY: Prometheus Books, 2003), pp. 466–80

8. See, for example, M. Gaudefroy-Demombynes, *Mahomet*, Paris, 1969, pp. 518–33.

9. Cf. E. Nielsen, "La guerre considérée comme une religion et la religion comme une guerre. Du chant de Débora au Rouleau de la guerre de [1] Qoumran," *Studia Theologica* 15, 1961, pp. 93–112.

10. See Y. Yadin, *The Scroll of the War of the Sons of Light against the Sons of Darkness*, Oxford, 1962.

11. I QM 7, 4–5 in M. Wise, M. Abegg Jr., and E. Cook, *The Dead Sea Scrolls: A New Translation* (New York: HarperCollins, 1996), p. 157. [Philonenko used A. Dupont-Sommer's French translation, *La Bible: Ecrits Intertestamentaires*, ed. A. Dupont-Sommer and M. Philonenko (Paris: Gallimard, 1987), p. 204.]

12. M. Philonenko, "Une tradition essénienne dans le Coran," *Revue de l'histoire des relgions* 170, 1966, pp. 143–57; "Une expression qoumrânienne dans le Coran," in *Atti del III Congresso di Studi Arabi e Islamici*, Ravello, 1966; Naples, 1967, pp. 553–56; both translated into English by Ibn Warraq in I. Warraq, ed., *What the Koran Really Says* (Amherst, NY: Prometheus Books, 2003), pp. 268–87

13. M. Wise, M. Abegg Jr., and E. Cook, *The Dead Sea Scrolls: A New Translation* (New York: HarperCollins, 1996), pp. 146–47 [1 QSa 2, 3–10]; *La Bible: Ecrits Intertestamentaires*, ed. A. Dupont-Sommer and M. Philonenko (Paris: Gallimard, 1987), p. 51. Cf. a fragment of the Damascus Document found in Cave IV of Qumran and referred to by J. T. Milik, *Dix ans de découvertes dans le désert de Juda*, Paris, 1957, p. 76: "Stupid persons, the mad, the idiot, the demented, *the blind, the crippled, the lame*, the deaf, the adolescent, none of them shall enter the heart of the community, for Holy Angels [stand in the middle of it]."

14. 1 QSa 2, 17–22.

15. Leviticus 21:18.

16. The religious import of the Essenian rule is better understood in the Gospel according to Luke 14:11–14. To the question "Who to invite?" Jesus replies: "Call not thy friends, nor thy brethren, neither thy kinsmen, nor thy rich neighbours . . . call the poor, the maimed, the lame, the blind." Once the mention of the poor—and the rich—is detached, which corresponds to typically Lucanian preoccupations, there remain the maimed, the lame, and the blind. One recognizes there three categories of sick that the Appendix to the Rules excludes from the community and who, according to Luke, will be allowed into the messianic banquet, as indicated by the Parable of the Banquet.

2.10

David in Islamic Tradition in the Light of the Dead Sea Scrolls[1]

R. Stehly

It was recently shown that in the Koran as well as in Ṭabarī and Ḥujwīrī the figure of David presents major Orphic traits and that this David –Orpheus is that of the Essenian tradition. Here we propose to study new Islamic texts on David, in particular those from the hadith and to show that on the one hand if the Islamic David is indeed a David–Orpheus, he is also a Sufi David, and on the other that the Essenian tradition is not only the origin of the Orphic traits of the Islamic David but equally his Sufi characteristics.

Like other persons of the Jewish tradition,[2] David has attracted the attention of the Islamic tradition. Does the latter depend directly on the Old Testament or has it tapped into the vast reservoir of post-biblical Jewish literature? This problem has for a long time aroused the interest of Western critics. If A. Geiger,[3] H. Grimme,[4] J. Horovitz[5] stick principally to the Old Testament horizon, A. Sprenger[6] insists more on the Ebionite and Essenian heritage of Islam, while H. Hirschfeld,[7] H. Speyer,[8] D. Sidersky,[9] V. Aptowitzer,[10] and C. C. Torrey[11] show that Islam had knowledge of Jewish traditions or late Judeo-Christian ones. Whereas Tor Andrae[12] directed his attention to the Syrian churches, G. Widengren[13] turned his regard toward the Apocryphal writings and the old ideologies of the Near East (Mesopotamian, Iranian, Manichaean, Mandaean). More recently, M. Philonenko[14] has shown that the Koranic David presents traits borrowed from the person of Orpheus, and that this David–Orpheus is that of the Essenian tradition. This David–Orpheus is not only found in the Koran,[15] but equally in Ṭabarī[16] and Ḥujwīrī.[17] These two authors describe to us in poetical terms the enchanting effect of the voice of David on creation: on the mountains and on the plains, the wild animals and birds come to hear David; on hearing his voice the water ceases to flow and the birds fall from the sky.

This survey could be completed by other Arabic works. We propose to translate and examine some here, two of the most important being that of Tha'labī [died 1035 CE] and of Kisā'ī [possibly died eleventh century CE].

Tha'labī in his *History of Prophets* [*Qiṣaṣ al-anbiyā'*[18]] provides us with a splendid painting of David–Orpheus:

> [Among the gifts of God to David], there is a beautiful voice, melodious and with the right tone, the refrain, the musical accents. He used to recite the Psalms in seventy modes, to the point that made the feverish perspire and he who had fainted was revived.
>
> When David recited the Psalms, he used to retire to the country; he stayed there, and with him stayed the scholars of Israel, behind the scholars, the people, behind the people the jinn, behind the jinn the demons. The savage beasts and wild animals used to draw close to him. One could touch the napes of their neck.[19] The birds created a shade for him in the middle of the day, and running water froze.[20] The wind stopped.[21] The flutes, the luths and the harps were made only to harmonize with his voice. Now Iblis, that is to say, Satan (May God curse him!) was jealous of him and redoubled his efforts in regard to him. He said to his evil-doing demons:
>
> "Don't you see what has happened?"
>
> "Order us what you wish!" they replied.
>
> "Only the person who opposes him and fights him in a similar situation will turn the people away from David," he replied.
>
> They got hold of, then, the flutes, the luths, the stringed instruments and [other] musical instruments tuned to the melodies of David. The idiots among the people heard them; they appreciated them and were fooled by them.
>
> It is claimed that David (Peace be upon him!) when he recited the Psalms, after having committed a sin,[22] the waters no longer stoppped because of him; the wild beasts and savage animals no longer listened to him, neither did the birds as they used before; the right tone was lacking.

"My God, why all that?" he asked.

"That was the familiarity of obedience, this is the distance of disobedience!" God on High revealed to him.

"My God, then have you not forgiven me?" he demanded.

"Yes, but the loving trust and closeness that existed between you and me has been suppressed, you will never attain it again," He replied.

Abū Sa'īd b. Aḥmad b. Ḥamdūn has transmitted to us the following from Wahb b. Munabbih:[23] "the following has been transmitted to us from the Apostle of God (May God give him His benediction and Preserve him): 'God has made the Koran easy for David. He ordered his mount to be saddled. And he recited the Koran before saddling his mount. He only consumed the product of the work of his hands.'[24] The eminent imam said one must hear the Psalms by the Koran."

Abū Bakr al-Jawzaqī[25] quotes Abū Mūsā al-Ash'arī:[26] "The Apostle of God (May God give him His benediction and Preserve him) said to me, 'You have received a flute from among the instruments of David.' 'By God, O Apostle of God, if I knew that you allowed me to do it, I would recite in a most beautiful voice!' I replied."[27] Abū Bakr has transmitted to us that Abū al-'Abbās[28] quoted the following from Barā' b. 'Azib[29]:

The Prophet (May God give him His benediction and Preserve him) heard the voice of Abū Mūsā—One would think, He said, that this voice comes from the sounds of the instruments of David![30]

Among the gifts of God to David, there is the submission of the mountains and of the birds. When he praises God, they accompany him in his praise as the Most High says, "Certainly, we have done David a favour. O Mountains resume with him his hymns and [you also] O Birds!" For him, we softened iron.[31] And his words: "We have made the mountains submit to him, with him, glorifying [the Lord] evening and morning."[32] They said that David (Peace be upon him), when he penetrated the mountains to praise God the Most High, the mountains began to reply to him by praise after his own praise. Then he said in himself: How I adore God the Most High, with such an adoration that no one has ever adored Him like that. He climbed the mountain. When he was in the heart of the night, he was taken with a feeling of anxiety. And God the Most High sent this message to the mountains

> "Keep David company." They jostled one another in their praise, in sanctification and in jubilation David said to himself, "How will my voice be heard with all these voices?" Gabriel (Peace be upon him) descended and took him by the arm until they reached the sea. He gave the sea a kick: and it cleaved in front of him. Then he retuned to land, and gave the land a kick, and it split in front of him. Then he made his way to the Fish, and gave it a kick, it burst open and a worm came out of it making a rustling noise. Gabriel said to it, "Your Lord hears the rustling of this worm at this place."
>
> As to the words of Most High: "They glorify [the Lord] evening and morning,"[33] they mean, according to the commentators, the prayer of dawn and the prayer of those who return to God between the two evening prayers. According to Ibn 'Abbās,[34] David could understand the praise of stones, of trees and clods of earth.

In the *History of the Prophets* [*Qiṣaṣ al-anbiyā'*] of Kisā'ī[35] we can pick out the following passages where traits borrowed from Orpheus are applied to David:

"The angels asked their Lord permission to visit David; they descended in such a way that they encircled his sanctuary. They copied out his praise. The birds flapped their wings above him. The mountains accompanied his praise; the savage beasts and the wild animals his sanctification."[36]

"God revealed this to him: O David, I have heaped upon you vocal talents such as no one has had except your father Adam. I have ordered the mountains to recite with you [your hymns] and to make the responses to your melodies. I have softened iron for you and I have guided you in the fabrication of a coat of mail. I have ordered the birds to accompany you in your praise. I have ordered the sand and stones to accompany you when you sing my praises. I have established you as a judge on earth."[37, 38]

The hadith recounted by Ibn Kathīr[39] [died 1353] gives even more details about the beauty of David's voice. The Koranic theme of the effect of his voice on creation resurfaces many times.

(1) According to Muḥammad b. Isḥāq,[40] following certain scholars, and following Wahb b. Munabbih, David was small of stature, with blue eyes, short hair,[41] a pure and saintly being.

(2) From Wahb b. Munabihh: According to the wisdom of the family of David, it is a duty for an intelligent man[42] not to neglect four times: the hour when he prays to his Lord in a low voice; the hour when he introspects or looks into his soul (*iḥtasaba*);[43] the hour when he is in close consultation with his brothers who will let him know their sins and who will tell him the truth about his soul; and the hour when wisdom can give free rein to their desires within the limits of the licit and decent.

(3) According to ʻAbd ar-Razzāq,[44] following Ibn Jurayj:[45] I questioned ʻAtā'[46]on the reading of the Psalmody: There is no harm in that, he told me, I heard ʻUbayd b. ʻUmar s[47] ay: David (Peace be upon him) took the timbal, he was reciting in proceeding thus. The instrument replied to him in the same tone. By that, he meant that he was crying and that the instrument was crying.

(4) Awzā'ī[48] said ʻAbd Allāh b. ʻAmir[49] recounted: David was blessed with a voice so beautiful that no one else has ever had such a voice before, to the point that the birds and the animals submitted themselves around him, to the extent of dying of hunger and thirst, and that the rivers stopped.

(5) According to Wahb b. Munabbih no one listened to him without hopping about as though dancing. He recited the Psalms with a voice such that the ears had never registered before and that the jinns, the birds and the animals remained captive to the point of perishing of hunger.

(6) According to Mālik,[50] David (Peace be upon him) when he began to recite the Psalms, pearls split open.

During eschatological times, David will ravish the elect with his silky voice:

(7) From Jaʻfar b. Sulaymān:[51] I heard Mālik b. Dīnār[52] say on the subject of God's word "And truly he shall have a high rank with Us, and an excellent retreat in Paradise" [Koran XXXVIII, 24. Rodwell]. David (Peace be upon him) will stand on the Day of Judgement near the Throne. God will say: O David, extol me today in this soft and beautiful voice with which you used to exalt me in the world. How, he will say, but you have taken it away from me. I give it back to you, He will reply, may peace be upon you! And David will raise his voice to express the delights of the people of Paradise.

Ibn Kathīr[53] insists on the piety of David à propos of Koran XXVIII, 26:

(8) David was someone we used to imitate at this time, his fairness, the abundance of his acts of adoration and of the categories of his acts of worship, so that at any moment of the night or at the end of the day there were always members of his family in the act of adoration. As Most High said: Family of David, make acts of gratitude—rare, among your servants are those filled with gratitude.[54]

One should have noted that certain of these hadiths present David as an ascetic, in particular hadith [2] above, and the commentary of Ibn Kathīr, [8] above. The portrait of an ascetic David, devoting himself to fasts and vigils is already present in the great classic collections of hadith.[55] We shall translate below the hadith that seem to us to be the most noteworthy:

"Abū Hurayra[56] recounts that the Prophet (May God bless him and protect him) has said: Recitation had been made easy for David. Thus he gave the order to saddle his mount, and before it was saddled, he had finished the recitation. He only consumed the product of the work of his hands."[57]

"According to 'Abd Allāh b. 'Amr[58] the Prophet (May God Bless Him and Preserve him) said: The fast most pleasing to God was the one David practiced: he fasted one day over two. The prayer most agreeable to God is the one David used to offer: he slept half the night, prayed a third of the night and slept during the last sixth of the night."[59]

What one gathers from these texts is that David, as he appears in Islamic tradition, has little to do with the biblical personage. It is on all levels the tradition of a David–Orpheus, liturgist and ascetic.

The ensemble of Arabic evidence confirms thus the exegesis that sees Orpheus in David. But in regard to the Koran the Orphic traits of David have clearly increased. This amplification poses an important problem for literary criticism: to explain how the hadith as much as the Muslim authors, Arab or Persian, could have completed the Orphic color of the koranic David by new traits unknown to the Koran, but coinciding perfectly with the legend of classical antiquity. Nothing allows us to affirm that the Muslim authors had discerned the Orphic component of the koranic David: all the koranic commentators are silent on this point. They could not have consciously had recourse to ancient tradition to complete the koranic tableau. M. Philonenko has formulated the hypothesis that Ṭabarī had had access to truly Essenian sources.[60] One could also suppose that the Koran and the hadith were tapping into a common source of which the koranic revelation would give us so to speak the short version. The question of the authenticity of the hadith would find itself thus illuminated with the light of a new day. This common source is, according to us, no other than the Orphic reading of David born in the Essenian milieu as confirmed by Psalm 151 found in the caves of Qumran.

The figure of an ascetic David poses an analogous problem. Already the rabbinical tradition depicts David as the untirable bard of God: he sits up at night or even more gets up at midnight to play the harp and the psaltery[61] (Jerusalem and Babylonian Talmud, Berakhot I.1). But the Islamic tradition is even more explicit: David there presents major monkish and ascetic traits: he is a humble person, a beggarly one [*poverello*[62]], he only consumes the product of his own labor, he fasts one day on two, prays a third of the night, practices meditation, and submits himself to fraternal correction. These practices correspond trait by trait to those of Islamic supererogatory piety and of Sufism.

The vigil of a third of the night of Sufism and of Islamic piety[63] is founded on the Koran, LXXIII, 1–4: *You that are wrapped up in your mantle, keep vigil all night, save for a few hours; half the night or even less: or a little more—and with measured tone recite the Koran*. These verses are interpreted by the koranic commentators as an invitation to keep vigil less than half the night, generally a third, a practice systematized in the Davidic hadith.

The fast of one day on two was equally in use in Sufi communities as well as among pious Muslims. Ghazali in his *Ihya* recommends fasting three times a week: Mondays, Thursdays, and Fridays. Better to fast, he said, every other day like David than to fast daily.[64] The Prophet, in return, according to hadith, fasted Mondays and Thursdays;[65] that is the Pharisaic custom.[66]

Meditation or reflection is, after all, no less than the *ihtisab* of the Sufis.

But we can go even further. There is also a correspondance between the

Sufi practices and those of one of the two known monastic Jewish communities: the Essenians of Qumran.

The monks of Qumran practice in effect the vigil of a third of the night: Rule VI, 7–8, "And let many keep the vigil in common during a third of all the nights of the year to read and study law and to call down blessings in common."[67]

We know, moreover, that the vigils were also the custom in Karaite circles. N. Wieder[68] has shown their relationship to the Essenian customs of Qumran. These astonishing similarities lead us to think that the origin of the Sufi custom of vigils of a third of the night is to be found in the equivalent Essenian vigils that Karaism has perpetuated in the Jewish milieu. One remarks further that the similarity of the purpose assigned to the vigil: to chant the Preaching [i.e., the Koran] on the one hand, and to read the Book on the other.

The fast was also the custom at Qumran. The Damascus Document[69] [XI, 4–5] alludes to it if we allow the reconstruction by A. Dupont-Sommer:

> that a man may not deprive himself of food voluntarily during the Sabbath[70, 71]

If we must not starve ourselves during the Sabbath, it is certain that fasting was practiced on other days. Which ones? These days are most certainly not specified in the writings from Qumran. One can nevertheless formulate a plausible hypothesis on this subject. A. Jaubert[72] has shown that the calendar in use in the Qumran sect priviliged three days: the Sunday, the Wednesday, and the Friday. If there had to be a regular fast in Qumran, one can reasonably suppose that it fell on one, two, or the totality of these three days. Given the fervor of the monks of Qumran, one should not be at all astonished that the fast was practiced on Sundays, Wednesdays, and Fridays, which, if you do not count the Sabbath, makes three days out of six, in other words every other day, the figure of the Davidic hadith and Sufi practice. This sequence is in contrast to the custom of the Phariseans; the latter fast in effect on Mondays and Thursdays.[73] When one knows how much the Essenes were against Pharisaic Judaism on the question of the calendar, our hypothesis only becomes more plausible. The same opposition applies also to primitive Christianity. Doesn't the Didache[74] say:

> Let not your fasts coincide with those of the hypocrites; they fast in effect on Mondays and Thursdays; for you, fast Wednesdays and Fridays.

Now. Wednesdays and Fridays were precisely the two days revered in Qumran. Thus we are in the presence of the following schema:

Qumranian fast:	Sunday	Wednesday	Friday
Sufi fast:	Monday	Thursday	Friday
Christian fast:	Wednesday	Friday	
Pharisaic fas:	Monday	Thursday	
Prophet's fast:	Monday	Thursday	

If we allow the possibility of a historical filiation culminating in the practice of superogatory Islamic and Sufi fast, by which channel did the historical connection come about? At first glance the most logical hypothesis would be to suppose that early Islam increased the Pharisaic custom by adding Friday. It seems to us however that such an hypothesis does not take into account the point revealed in Sufi usage. What in effect counts for al Ghazali is not so much the days when this fast is practiced but the fact that for *three days per week* the fervent believer or the Sufi submerges himself in profound devotion, according to Davidic custom. This highlighting of three days is obviously Qumranian and the Sufi sequence could be explained by the repugnance to privilege Sundays, the holy day of the Christians. Or perhaps it more subtly manifests itself by the desire of Islam to distance itself from a Jewish practice felt to be recommendable in its essence but whose servile imitation was visibly repugnant. Sufi practice would thus have followed the same logic as in other cases: prayer in the direction of Mecca and not Jerusalem, celebration of Friday as opposed to the Sabbath. But in the Sufi practice of fasting, as in that of vigils, the origin is to be looked for in the Essenian component of Judaism, while the fast of the Prophet recounted in the hadith would continue the Pharisaic custom.

The economic autarchy of the Islamic David corresponds also with what we know of the Essenians. Do we not read in *Quod omnis probus liber sit* of Philo of Alexandria [died after 40 CE] at paragraph 76: "Among the Essenes, some work the land, others exercise diverse trades which contribute to the peace; thus they make themselves useful to themselves and to their fellow-creatures. They do not hoard money or gold, they do not make themselves the owners of vast territories with the desire to gain revenue from them, but they procure for themselves only what is essential to live?"

The economic ethic of Islam scarcely teaches otherwise.

As for fraternal correction that according to the hadith of Wahb b. Munabbih was in use in the family of David, it is also attested in Sufism as in the Rule V. 24–25: "They reproach one and other in truth and humility and affectionate charity in regard to each."

Thus a double authentication imposes itself:

1. The David of hadith is a Sufi David.
2. This Sufi David presents major Essenian traits.

This double face of the Islamic David goes well beyond a simple literary fact. It crystalizes a historical reality. Already Aloys Sprenger[75] had remarked the presence of Essenian traits in Islam, although the hiatus between the epochs of the two religions posed a difficult problem. In fact the hiatus between the apparent disappearance of the Essenians and the seventh century, the period of birth of Islam, is not impossible to overcome. Judeo-Christian sects such as the Elkesaites were able to gather together at least a part of the Essenian heritage and to pass on certain practices. According to Epiphanius,[76] in effect, the Elkesaites, also called Sampseans,[77] finished their prayers at sunrise; now we know that already the Essenians used to recite "certain ancestral prayers addressed to the sun as though they pleaded with it to rise"[78] Thus, the Elkesaites only perpetuated Essenian custom. Moreover, when Muhammad instituted the Islamic prayer, one of his first measures was to decide that neither the morning prayer nor the evening prayer could be said facing the rising or setting sun.[79] They are still only performed to this day before or after the rising or the setting of the sun, as the case may be. If the Prophet took such a measure, it is really obvious that at his epoch there were people who performed prayers at sunrise like the Elkesaites and the Essenians. Otherwise such a measure would be incomprehensible. From clues of this kind[80] one can legitimately conclude that at the time of

Muhammad, there remained at least traces of customs and Essenian doctrines that, depending on the case, were integrated and refounded in Islam. The ascetic traits of the Islamic David and the permenance of the specific monachal practices of the Essenians in Sufism are a new piece in the file of the Jewish context of Islam.

Notes

1. [R. Stehly, "David dans la Tradition Islamique a la lumière des Manuscrits de Qumran," *Revue d'Histoire et de Philosophie Religieuses* LIX (1979), pp. 357–67. Translated by Ibn Warraq.]

2. Aaron, Abraham, Adam, Elias, Elijah, Esdras, Goliath, Enoch, Isaac, Jacob, John the Baptist, Jesus, Job, Jonah, Joseph, Lot, Mary, Moses, Noah, Solomon, Saul, Zacharia.

3. A. Geiger, *Was hat Mohammed aus dem Judenthume aufgenommen?* Bonn, 1833. Translated by F. Young as *Judaism and Islam*, Bangalore, 1896.

4. H. Grimme, *Mohammed*, 2 vols., Münster, 1892–95.

5. J. Horovitz, *Koranische Untersuchungen*, Berlin and Leipzig, 1926.

6. A. Sprenger, *Das Leben und die Lehre des Mohammed*, 2nd ed., Berlin, 1869, vol. 2, I, pp. 13 ff.

7. H. Hirschfeld, *Jüdische Elemente im Koran*, Berlin, 1878; *Beiträge zur Erklärung des Koran*, Leipzig, 1886; *New Researches into the Composition and Exegesis of the Koran*, London, 1901.

8. H. Speyer, *Die biblischen Erzälungen im Qoran*, 2nd ed., Hildesheim, 1961.

9. D. Sidersky, *Les orgines des légendes musulmanes dans le Qoran et dans la vies des prophètes*, Paris, 1933.

10. V. Aptowitzer, *Kain und Abel in der Agada, den Apocryphen, der hellenistischen, christlichen und mohammedanischen Literatur*, Vienna and Leipzig, 1922.

11. C. C. Torrey, *The Jewish Foundation of Islam*, New York, 1933.

12. T. Andrae, *Les origines de l' Islam et le christianisme*, Paris, 1955.

13. G. Widengren, *Muhammad: The Apostle of God, and His Ascension* (King and Saviour V), Uppsala, 1955.

14. M. Philonenko, "Une tradition essénienne dans le Coran," *Revue de l'Histoire des Relgions* (1966): 143–57. Eng. translation in Ibn Warraq, ed., *What the Koran Really Says* (Amherst, NY: Prometheus Books, 2002): 268–82.

15. Especially Koran XXI, 78–80; XXXIV, 10–11; XXXVIII, 17–20.

16. Ṭabarī, *Ta'rīkh al-rusul wa-l-mulūk*, ed. M. J. de Goeje et al., 15 vols., Leiden, 1879–1901, vol. 1, p. 562. Cf. the translation of this passge by T. Fahd in the article by M. Philonenko, *art. cit.*, pp. 150–51.

17. Ḥujwīrī, *Kashf al-mahdjūb*, ed. Joukovski, Leningrad, 1926, pp. 524–25. Cf. the translation of this passage by M. G. Lazard in M. Philonenko, *art. cit.*, pp. 150–51.

18. Tha'labī, *Qiṣaṣ al-anbiyā'* [History of Prophets], Cairo, n. d., pp. 369–71.

19. This trait is found initially for the Islamic tradition in *Ṭabarī. Ta'rīkh al-rusul wa-l-mulūk*, Vol. 1 p. 562. Cf. for Orpheus, Virgil, *Georgics* 4, 510 and Ovid, *Metamorphosis* 10, 143–44.

20. This trait is found initially for the Islamic tradition in Ḥujwīrī, *Kashf al-mahdjūb*, p. 524. Cf. for Orpheus, Seneca, *Hercule sur l'Oeta*, 1036–47, trans. L. Hermann, ed. G. Budé, Paris, 1961.

21. Cf. for Orpheus, Horace, Odes I 12, 10, and Seneca, *Hercule sur l'Oeta* 1069, trans. L. Hermann, ed. G. Budé, Paris, 1961.

22. It concerns the murder of Uriah.

23. Wahb b. Munabbih, historian, born and died in *Ṣan'ā'* [34/654–114/732].

24. Cf. Bukhārī, *Ṣaḥīḥ* 60. 37. 1.

25. Abū Bakr al-Jawzaqī [316/928–388/998], traditionist of *Nīsābūr.*

26. Abū Mūsā al-Ash'arī [-21/602–44/665], companion of the Prophet.

27. Pun on the word *mizmār,* 1) Flute. 2) Psalm, and *āl* 1) lineage, progeny 2) instruments. One can equally legitimately understand it as: "You have received a psalm from among the psalms of the progeny of David. By God! I replied, O Apostle of God, if I thought that you would permit it, I would write for you in careful handwriting!"

28. Abū al-'Abbās al-Aṣamm [247/861–346/957], traditionist of N*īsābūr*

29. Barā' b. 'Azib [died 71/690], companion of the Prophet.

30. Cf. Bukhārī, *Ṣaḥīḥ* 66. 31

31. Koran XXXIV, 10

32. Koran XXXVIII, 18.

33. Koran XXXVIII, 18.

34. 'Abd Allāh Ibn al- 'Abbās [died 68/687], well-known companion of the Prophet and Koranic exegete.

35. Kisā'ī, *Qiṣaṣ al-anbiyā'. Vitae Prophetarum*, ed. I. Eisenberg, 2 vols., Leiden, 1923.

36. Idem, p. 259.

37. Cf. Koran XXXVIII, 26.

38. Kisā'ī, *Qiṣaṣ al-anbiyā'. Vitae Prophetarum*, ed. I. Eisenberg, 2 vols., Leiden, 1923, p. 261.

39. Ibn Kathīr, *Kitāb al-Bidāya wa-n-nihāya*, Cairo, 1932, vol. 2, pp. 9–16.

40. Muḥammad b. Isḥāq [died 151/768], author of the biography—*Sīra* of Muḥammad.

41. Psalm 151, of Essenian origin, makes an allusion to the short stature and sparse hair of David. This genre of physionomic details was usual in the portraits of the Messiah and the Anti-Christ. Cf. J. M. Rosentiehl, "Le Portait de l 'Antichrist," in *Pseudépigraphes de l'Ancien Testament et manuscrits de la Mer Morte*, I, Paris 1967, pp. 45–60.

42. This expression, so frequent in the manuscripts of Qumran, reminds one of *lammaskil*, which designates the initiated. Cf. A. Dupont-Sommer, *Les écrits esséniens découverts près de la Mer Morte*, 3rd ed. Paris, 1968, vol. 1, p. 88 n. 1.

43. The examination of conscience (*muḥāsaba*) was the custom in Sufi circles. Cf. Ghazālī, *Iḥyā' 'ulūm al-dīn*, 4 vols., Būlāq, 1289, vol. 4, pp. 379 ff., and Ghazālī, *Iḥyā' 'ulūm al-dīn*, ou Vivification des sciences de la din, analyse et index par G. H. Bousquet, Paris, 1955, p. 82. One remarks that the expression "family of David" designates here the monastic community. Could it thus already be in the Koran at XXXIV, 13?

44. 'Abd ar-Razzāq, traditionist and Koranic commentator born in 126/744 in Ṣan'ā'.

45. Ibn Jurayj [80/699–150/765], jurist [*faqīh*] of Mecca.

46. 'Atā' [27/647–14/732], muftī of Mecca, celebrated for his knowledge of pilgrimage.

47. 'Ubayd b. 'Umar b. Sajj, companion of the Prophet.

48. Awzā'ī [88/107–103/721], founder of a celebrated school of jurisprudence.

49. 'Abd Allāh b. 'Āmir al-Yaḥsubī [8/630–118/736], one of the seven readers of the Koran.

50. Mālik b. Anas [born between 90/708 and 97/715], author of one of the most celebrated collections of hadith, the *kitāb al –Muwatta'*.

51. Ja'far b. Sulaymān [died 178 AH], traditionist of Basra.

52. Mālik b. Dīnār [died 131/748], Tābi'ī [Muslim of second generation] of Basra.

53. Ibn Kathīr, op. cit, II, p. 14.

54. Koran, XXXIV, 13.

55. Those of [1] Bukhārī, *Ṣaḥīḥ*, ed. L. Krehl. Leiden, 1862–1868 (I–III) and

T. W. Juynboll, Leiden, 1907–1908 (IV) and French translation of O. Houdas and W. Marçais, 4 vols., Paris, 1903–1908; [2] Aḥmad b. Ḥanbal [died 241/855], *Musnad*, 6 vols., Cairo, 1913; [3] Muslim [died 261/875], *Ṣaḥīḥ*, 5 vols., Cairo, 1283 AH; [4] Nasā'ī [died 303/915], *Sunan*, 2 vols., Cairo, 1312. The hadith concerning vigils and fasting are comendably gathered together in two recent works: Shaykh Manṣūr 'Ali Nāsif, *at-tāj al-jāmi' lil- . . . fil aḥādith ar-rasūl*, 5 vols., 3rd ed, Beirut, 1961–62; Sayyid Sābiq, *Fiqh as –sunna*, 5 vols., Beirut, 1969, I, p. 453 ff. Cf. the classic work of the juriconsul Ibn Qudāma, *kitāb al-Mughnī*, 9 vols., Riyād, n.d, II, pp. 135 ff. and III, pp. 176 ff.

56. Celebrated companion of the Prophet.

57. Bukhārī, op. cit., 60. 37. 10 = Aḥmad b. Ḥanbal op. cit., II, p. 314.

58. 'Abd Allāh b. 'Amr al ' As [-7/616–65/684], companion of Prophet.

59. Bukhārī, op. cit., 60. 38. Parallel texts in Nasā'ī, op. cit., I, p. 242; Muslim, op. cit., III, p. 116, 118, 119; Aḥmad b. Ḥanbal, op. cit., II, p. 160, 164; Ibn Kathīr, op. cit., II, p. 10–11.

60. M. Philonenko, "Une tradition essénienne dans le Coran," *Revue de l'Histoire des Relgions*, 1966, p. 152, Eng. translation in Ibn Warraq, ed., *What the Koran Really Says* (Amherst, NY: Prometheus Books, 2002), pp. 268–82.

61. [An ancient stringed instrument resembling a dulcimer played by plucking with fingers or a plectrum.]

62. *Poverello* is due to A. Dupont-Sommer, *art. cit.*, p. 8.

63. Cf. Ghazāli [died 1111], op. cit., I, pp. 330–31 and G. H. Bousquet, op. cit., pp. 100–105. The tern used to designate vigil in Islamic tradition since the Koran, *qiyām al-layl*, recalls the Syriac *qeyomo*, which designates monastic obeservations. Cf. A. Vööbus, *History of Monasticism: A Contribution to the History of Culture in the Syrian Orient*, vol. 1, *The Origin of Ascetism. Early Monachism in Persia*, CSCO, vol. 184, suppl. 14, Louvain, 1958, pp. 13, 97 ff., 197 ff.; A. J. Wensinck, "Qejama und Benai Qejamen," *ZDMG* 64, 1910, p. 561 ff., and Weiteres, "Qejama und Benai Qejama," *ZDMG* 64, 1910, p. 812.

64. Ghazālī, *Iḥyā' 'ulūm al-dīn*, I, p. 227; cf. also Bousquet, op. cit., p. 82. The daily fast (*sawm ad-dahr*) is declared blameworthy in Islamic ethics. Cf. Ibn Qudāma, op. cit., III, p. 167 and H. Laoust, *Essai sur les doctrines sociales et politiques de Taki-d-dīn Aḥmad b. Taymīyya*, Cairo, 1933, p. 337.

65. Numerous traditions on this subject in particular, Nasā'ī, op. cit., 22, 70, 36, 83; Tirmidhī, *Ṣaḥīḥ* 6. 44, Ibn Māja, *Sunan* 7. 42, Abū Dāwud, *Sunan*, 14. 53, 59, 68, Dārimī, *Musnad*, 4. 41.

66. Cf. Strack-Billerbeck, *Kommentar zum Neuen Testament aus Talmud und Mischna*, vol. 3, Munich, 1924, p. 241, and vol. 4, Munich, 1928, p. 89.

67. Translation [French] A. Dupont-Sommer, op. cit., p. 101. On the Essenian vigils see also Josephus the Jew, *La prise de Jérusalem*, ed. and trans. V. Istrin, A. Vaillant, P. Pascal, 2 vols., Paris, 1934–38, I, p. 139 §5: "Towards the divinity, they are pious above all. They hardly ever have a rest, and get up at night to sing the praises of God, and pray. "

68. N. Wieder, *The Judaean Scrolls and Karaism*, London, 1962, pp. 96–102, which refers to Qirqisāni, *Kitāb al-Anwār*, ed. L. Nemoy, IV, p. 919. Cf. also A. Paul, *Écrits de Qumran et sected juives aux premiers siècles de l' Islam, Recherche sur l'origine du qaraïsme*, Paris, 1969, p. 122.

69. Cf. A. Dupont-Sommer, op. cit., p. 168.

70. A similar prescription is found in Jubilees 50. 12.

71. [Cf. English translation by M. Wise, Martin Abegg Jr., and Edward Cook, *The Dead Sea Scrolls: A New Translation*, Harper San Francisco, 1996, p. 68: "A man may not voluntarily cross Sabbath borders on the Sabbath day."]

72. A. Jaubert, *La date de la Cène, calendrier biblique et liturgie chrétienne*, Paris, 1957.

73. Luke 18, 12; Didache 8.

74. Didache 8, cf. also Tertullian, *De Jejunio*, 2.

75. A. Sprenger, op. cit., I, pp. 30 ff.

76. Epiphanius, *Haereses*, 33.

77. From the Semitic root SH-M-S, meaning *sun*.

78. F. Josephus, *Guerre des Juifs* [War of the Jews], § 128.

79. Bukhārī, *Ṣaḥīḥ*, 9. 30–32. Let us quote 9. 30: Ibn 'Abbās said: "Some honourable witnesses, and 'Umar has designated me as such a witness, confirmed to me that the Prophet forbade the saying of prayers from the morning until the moment the sun is in its splendor, and similarly, from the aftrenoon until sunset."

80. Other clues: an Essenian rule conserved by the Koran: M. Philonenko.

Part Three

Muhammad and the Koran

3.1

The Legend of Muhammad's Call to Prophethood[1]

Tor Andrae

As everybody knows, Sprenger[2] had already speculated that the accounts of Muhammad's call to prophethood as found in the works of Ibn Isḥāq, Muslim, and Ṭabarī were "a conglomerate of three or four traditions of 'Urwa." In fact, it is evident at first sight that the account has been welded together from several traditions that were arranged by different editors in different ways and that were adapted to each other with regard to the contents. It will be worthwhile to investigate further the problem suggested by Sprenger and to compare the various versions. Through the investigation the sometimes still-claimed unanimity of Muslim tradition will perhaps show itself in a new light.

The four traditions that are arranged in different ways by our authorities in their synoptical presentation/account are as follows:

1. The *taḥannuṯ* legend[3] (of Muhammad's prayers in solitude on mount Ḥirā').

2. The *iqra'* legend[4] (of the apparition of an angel in the cave on Mount Ḥirā' that forces Muhammad to recite sura 96:1–5 despite his three refusals).

3.The *ufuq* legend (of the apparition of an angel that, standing at the horizon [ufuq] or sitting on a throne between heaven and earth, declares himself to be Gabriel and addresses Muhammad as the prophet).

4. The *waraqa* legend.[5]

We leave the first and the last aside since they do not deal with the actual vocation. The first of our sources, Ibn Isḥāq,[6] begins with the legend of Muhammad's *taḥannuṯ* followed by the *iqra'* legend as a nightly vision (the silk cloth with letters is a characteristic of this version). Deeply disturbed by the vision, Muhammad fears to be obsessed and decides to jump down from the top of a mountain. After that we find the *ufuq* legend: Muhammad climbs the mountain halfway to the top, there he is called, he perceives the angel with his feet on the horizon, etc.

The seams where the legends are welded together are clearly perceptible. First a nightly vision, then the wandering about on the mountain and the apparition of the angel, which obviously takes place during daytime or at least at dawn.[7] The introduction and the *isnād* of Ibn Isḥāq's account already provide interesting information, which Sprenger[8] had certainly evaluated in the right way. When the legends of prophets—since almost everything that tradition knows of his life before the *hijra* can be considered a legend—have been used in the beginning by popular storytellers as material for devotional and entertaining stories. When the first scholars began to examine this material, they endeavored to lay bare the separate traditions, which had been used by the storytellers to compose their accounts, and to find, if possible, special guarantors for the individual traditions. Only by this means it seems understandable to me that the later compilers dealt with the material in such an impartial way. If there had really been a fixed version of the legend of vocation originating from such an honorable witness as 'Urwa (from 'Ā'isha), how could it have been possible for Ibn Hishām, Bukhārī, and Ṭabarī to tell the story in such a totally different order?

Proofs for the above-mentioned scientific ambition to separate the traditions and even for the fact that some of the separate traditions have been passed on independently and according to specific guarantors is provided by the state of affairs of our next witness, Ibn Sa'd.[9] He is more ambitious than Ibn Isḥāq in recording all variants which to him seem to be reliable or otherwise important.[10]

All separate traditions of the legend of vocation in Ibn Sa'd originate from the collections of Wāqidī, apart from the two "fragmentary traditions" (see below) and the second one about sura 96 as the first revelation.

The first of the separate traditions is the legend of *taḥannuṯ* according to

Zuhrī, etc. Then follows the legend of *ufuq*[11] with a new *isnād* (Ibrāhīm bin Ismā'il bin Abī Ḥabība from Dā'ud bin al-Ḥusain from 'Ikrima from Ibn 'Abbās) united with the legend of *Waraqa* as the actual inaugurating vision of the prophet. There is no trace of the *iqra'* legend, not even in an abridged form,[12] since the note communicated by Zuhrī, that sura 96 is said to be the first revelation "on the day on Mount Ḥirā'" does not need to be a fragment of the legend and besides does not originate from 'Urwa-'Ā'isha (see below). Ibn Sa'd had obviously known the two legends as different accounts of the call and then he had left out the one that seemed to him least credible, or he had not known the legend of *iqra'* at all or he had known it as insufficiently testified, which evidently is less probable.

It is remarkable that this account, that actually provides a completely different description of the proceedings of the call compared to the usual one, has not been taken into consideration in subsequent works of history, and that consequently this old and widespread tradition is only represented among the later ones by the account of Jābir. This will arise partly from the fact that Ibn Sa'd still regards sura 96 as the earliest one, which appears everywhere as the main point; then the discrepancy has just not been paid attention to, since the account could be recognized as a fragment from Ibn Isḥāq. But perhaps the judgement of the guarantors of the tradition had also contributed to that disregard. Of course, the Muslim authors had no objection to the first guarantor, the great "translator of the *Qur'ān*," "the sea of knowledge," "the head of the commentators."[13] Not so with 'Ikrima. Indeed he is mentioned unreservedly as one of the four followers of Ibn 'Abbās, each one of whom is said to be ('Ikrima in the *siyar*) the most learned of his time in his field,[14] and Ibn Khallikān[15] also praises his incomparable erudition; he only explains that people said about him that he followed Khārijite ideas. According to Ḏahabī[16] the opinions about him differ greatly. While Sa'īd bin Jubayr (a contemporary of his), Qatāda (his disciple) Ayyūb (bin Bušayr), Ša'bī, and others only know good things about him, just as many people have a very disparaging opinion of him. So by Yaḥyā bin Sa'īd, Sa'īd bin al Musayyib,[17] but especially by Mālik bin Anas, who had hated even to call his name and recited only one of his hadith. The son of Ibn 'Abbās, 'Alī, himself is said to have treated him very badly after his liberation "because he delivered the lies of his father." His Khārijite heresy had its effect on subsequent transmitters. Aḥmad bin Ḥanbal said about him: "He was the most learned human being of all, but he shared the conception of the Sufriyya."[18] Others associate him with the Ibadites or the Najdites.[19] His Khārijite remarks about the uselessness of the divine service of the laymen, who were only "confessors of the unity" or even unbelievers, have probably been distorted in the disdainful remarks about the religious exercises described by Ḏahabī. A slave of a foreign country, especially since he seems to have been distinguished more by his erudition than by his reverent sense of authority, must have appeared to men like Mālik as a very suspicious witness. It seems that this circumstance together with his heresy could partly explain the dislike of his traditions. Certainly, he is always quoted by the exegetes and apparently is held in honor. Dāwūd bin al-Ḥusayn,[20] the disciple of 'Ikrima, in whose house he died wanted by the authorities of Medina,[21] shared the Khārijite conception of his master and therefore he had to share sometimes his bad reputation. However, he is said to be reliable; some say that what he recited according to 'Ikrima is objectionable, but according to other authorities he is supposed to be reliable.

Ibn Sa'd related two traditions that obviously are fragments of the ones mentioned above.[22] Both originate from the famous Ḥammād bin Salama,[23] muftī of Baṣra, who was praised as someone reliable. But the first originates from 'Urwa, but not in the usual way via Zuhrī but from Hishām bin 'Urwa. The second is said to arise from Ibn 'Abbās. Ḥammād is supposed to have it from 'Ammār bin Abī 'Ammār; meanwhile he himself had a copy of sixty hadiths, which he had heard from Qatāda from 'Ikrima from Ibn 'Abbās, that Aḥmad bin Ḥanbal is said to have owned too.[24]

Moreover Ibn Sa'd gives (under a new title) two notes about sura 96 as the first revelation, the first from Zuhrī, from Muḥammad b. 'Abbād (unknown) from "one of the scholars." The second has as first guarantor 'Ubayd b. 'Umayr[25] to whom belongs the legend of the call in Ibn Isḥāq. On the way it went through the hands of Šu'ba (b.'Ayyāš). He—learned and reliable in the *tafsīr*, but often incorrect in the hadith[26]—had probably taken the note out of the account of 'Ubayd and passed it on as an evidence for his exegetic conception, without trusting the actual legend.

Finally we come across the legend of *ufuq* again, this time also from Dāwūd from 'Ikrima from Ibn 'Abbās, only with a new guarantor in the position next to the last. But now it has become the legend of the *fatra*. But it is obvious that we are dealing with the same legend as in Ibn Isḥāq. The prophet is very sad and wants to jump off from the top of a mountain (in Ibn Isḥāq because he saw Gabriel; here because he hadn't seen him for a couple of days); he is called, he sees the angel (certainly standing there; sitting here on the throne between heaven and earth, a difference that however can perhaps be explained by the quranic model of the whole tradition (see below), he is called with the same words, etc. Certainly the effect is a very different one, what is also due to the different enchainments of the legend: there the prophet remains restless [worried] just like before, here he is heartened immediately. Ibn Isḥāq[27] also knows a short passage of the *fatra,* but he only knows that it had ended with the revelation of sura 93.

In Bukhārī, as everybody knows, one misses the legend of *ufuq* as member of the synoptical account according to Zuhrī–'Urwa–'Ā'isha.[28] Instead it appears in two other forms,[29] the first from Zuhrī, the second from Yaḥyā b. Kathīr, but both in the last line from Jābir bin 'Abdallāh.[30] When we leave out the additions of the different editings, at first the account of Jābir had perhaps contained the following: Muhammad is in pious loneliness on Mt. Ḥirā'; wandering on the mountain, he is called, perceives an angel (sitting on the throne between heaven and earth), he returns shocked and calls Khadīja: "Cover me," followed by the revelation of sura 74 (resp. 73). Jābir had obviously wanted to describe hereby the call and the first revelation of the prophet. The deviating additions of Zuhrī's version namely want to explain away that fact through the transfer of the account to the end of the *fatra*; the ones in the version of Yaḥyā b. Kathīr are content with characterizing it as a remarkable contradiction against the already common acception of the priority of sura 96. The connection with the revelation of sura 74 is certainly secondary, the words "cover me" have not effected the connection,[31] but those words have been added to the tradition to explain the revelation of the sura. The tradition did not understand the purpose of the cover (which probably was in use in early times to receive the revelations[32]). The cover cannot be understood as the conscious intention to prepare himself for the reception of the divine message—Muhammad did not expect any revelation yet—but only as the expression of excessive fear of the prophet, explained several times by the supplement "and pour cold water over me." The explanations of the commentaries—actual and figurative ones—show that the custom was no longer understood by the oldest commentators. Besides, in favor of our assumption speaks the fact that Ibn 'Abbās and 'Ikrima, who tell the legend as the prophet's vision of vocation, have not linked it to the revelation of the sura. Ibn 'Abbās has regarded sura 96 as the oldest one,[33] and 'Ikrima is supposed to have explained sura 74 in a figurative sense.[34] Nevertheless some versions have *zammilūnī* [cover me] instead of *daṯṯirūnī*; therefore the legend can also be ended with the revelation of sura 73 (which is explainable out of 73: 4–5); this form of the legend can also be found in the commentaries.[35] Moreover, the legend has also been told with the revelation of the *fātiḥa* as the first revelation (see below). There will be no doubt that Jābir's legend is identical with our legend of *ufuq*. The only difference remaining is the fact that the angel in Ibn Isḥāq and in Ibn Sa'd's principal tradition is introduced standing on the horizon, but here sitting on the throne. For that reason Bukhārī (or his source) was able to cut it out of the synoptical presentation because he had provided a place for it elsewhere. Besides, in an earlier stage of this account the legend of *ufuq*, in Jābir's version, had probably followed the legend of *iqra'*; in remembrance of this connection the words *zammilūnī* have remained in Bukhārī. The alterations made to the legend of the *fatra* by simply adding "he (Muhammad) told from the *fatra*" and "the angel, who had come to him on Mt. Ḥirā'," all originate from Zuhrī. Whenever the legend is told as the vision of vocation with sura 74 as the first revelation, it originates with different *isnād*s from Yaḥyā b. Kathīr who is described as a reliable authority.[36] The remaining guarantors are thought to be reliable too.

In Bukhārī's there is also a second "conglomerate" of Zuhrī–'Urwa–'Ā'isha,[37] where the legend of *ufuq* has been incorporated into the synopsis as the end of the *fatra*, it's form reminiscent of Ibn Sa'd's legend of the *fatra*.

Ṭabarī[38] finally offers a synoptical account with a new combination, also from Zuhrī–'Urwa–'Ā'isha. Here, one version of the legend of *ufuq* is linked, just as in Ibn Isḥāq's case, to the legend of *iqra'*, but it precedes the latter in Ṭabarī instead of following it as in Ibn Isḥāq. The vision is repeated three times.[39] The prophet is on Mt. Ḥirā', the angel comes to him (his appearance is not described further), and he calls him: "You are the messenger of God!" The prophet was already sad before that, now he wants to jump off from the mountain, but new apparitions similar to the previous ones hinder him from carrying out his plan. He returns and calls "*zammilūnī*." When he is on the mountain again, the angel comes, and now the vision of *iqra'* follows.[40]

Ṭabarī also has a version where the legend of *iqra'* is the vision of vocation without the connection to the legend of *ufuq*. It originates from 'Abdallāh bin Šaddād, son of Ḥamza's widow and in any case born after the battle on Uḥud; he had a lot of hadith and is said to have been reliable. Besides this not much is known about him.[41]

Thus the oldest legends of Muhammad's call can be traced back to two main forms: the legend of *iqra'* and the legend of *ufuq*. the first one we find isolated in Bukhārī (*Bāb Bad' al-waḥī*) and Ṭabarī (from 'Abdallāh bin Šaddād). The legend of *ufuq* as an independent vision of vocation:

1. In Ibn Sa'd (from Ibn 'Abbās).

2. In Ibn Sa'd, fragmentary tradition II (from 'Urwa).

The enchainment, where the legend of *iqra'* is the actual vision of vocation followed by the legend of *ufuq*, as the legend of *fatra*, originates from Zuhrī. Certainly 'Urwa passed on both legends separately: 'Ā'isha has certainly been included into the *isnād* later on. Yet Ibn Isḥāq could attribute the whole to 'Ubayd; later on the authority of 'Urwa, who had included and worked on the account too, had been felt to be more reliable; of course now it is obvious to derive the account from his famous aunt. One recognizes that Ibn Hishām, who normally reproduces Ibn Isḥāq's account literally except for some parts that have seemed objectionable,[42] exchanged his *isnād* for the one of Zuhrī–'Urwa–'Ā'isha.

3. Linked to the revelation of sura 74 (from Jābir through Yaḥyā b. Kathīr) in Bukhārī and Ṭabarī.

4. Linked to the revelation of the *fātiḥa* (see below).

Moreover it appears as the legend of the *fatra* in Ibn Sa'd (from Ibn 'Abbās) and in Bukhārī and Ṭabarī (from Jābir through Zuhrī); finally with the revelation of sura 73, with the vague statement "not before Gabriel came to him," etc., in the commentaries (see above). Finally the two legends appear united in Ibn Isḥāq and Ṭabarī.

Certainly one cannot ascertain anything about the historicity or the historical authenticity of those legends out of what has been said so far. Both are of the same age, and one cannot conclude anything out of the judgement of the authorities[43] who passed on the accounts. Of course the only firm base of support remains the Qur'ān itself. As everybody knows, Muhammad twice mentioned visions that founded his mission: sura 81:15–26 and 53:1–19. As Sprenger[44] observes, the legend that is told in sura 81 and 53:6–10 is identical with the one that we have called the legend of *ufuq*. The general character of this vision corresponds to the the quranic one: a heavenly creature appears, obviously outdoors and during daylight, for it is probably that that "on a clear horizon" means,[45] the creature appears on the horizon (*ufuq*). Maybe it can be explained by the vague meaning of the term *istawā* ("to be harmonious," "to be upright," etc.), so that one can imagine the angel sometimes standing, sometimes sitting on a throne. It is possible that yet another feature of the quranic vision can be revealed in Jābir's version of the legend of *ufuq*. It has been supposed several times[46] that the object of the visions of sura 53 had been Allah himself. In fact, because of *'abdihi* [his servant] in verse 10 there is probably no other interpretation. Yet, even in the *Qur'ān* Muhammad cannot be called the servant of Gabriel. The commentaries offer despairing alternatives: "He (Gabriel) revealed to his servant (of Allah)" or "He (Allah) revealed to his servant (Gabriel)" and then this one to Muhammad.[47] Yet early, the second vision in sura 53 had been pointed to Allah himself; then certainly the same thing was assumed for the first one (because of verse 13).[48] A tradition of Bukhārī[49] vivaciously polemicizes against such unworthy conceptions. One has also tried to apply the suffixes to Allah, but then to abolish the improper part of the assumption by an allegorical explanation.[50] Possibly Muhammad himself, at least in the beginning, wanted to leave the question open as to who the witnessed creature was; later on he has corrected his assumption. Sura 81, which contains the shorter, so to speak paler, description would have emerged later than 53:1–18.[51] Since in the beginning the object of the vision has sometimes been said to be Allah himself, it is easier to understand that a being had been imagined sitting on the throne, since it seems to me that sitting on the throne is a strong, predominant trait of Muhammad's and his companions' conception of God and thus, in the beginning, not applicable to Gabriel. That is maybe the reason why in Zuhrī's versions and in Ibn Sa'd's legend of the *fatra* the word *'arạ* [throne], that Yaḥyā b. Kathīr uses twice, has been exchanged for *kursi* [chair]. One should also compare the reserved timidity in those cases (twice in Yaḥyā b. Kathīr) where it is only said "I saw something" instead of a more detailed description.[52] However that may be, it will be most probable that the legend of *ufuq* has been created out of sura 53:6–10, or at least that this passage of the Qur'ān decisively influenced the development of an already existing old tradition.

There seems to be a grave *argumentum e silentio* against the historicity or historical authenticity of the legend of *iqra'*. Muhammad, in order to defend himself from the accusation of being inspired by a *tābi'* [follower, disciple] of the jinns, tells the vision he has had of his *ṣāḥib* [master, commander] as a heavenly creature, but all the same he does not mention the actual vision of vocation. Could Muhammad really share that massive superstitious belief, that otherwise was used by the poets he hated, to explain the inspiration,[53] and thus have been guilty of a visionary imitation?

Obviously the historical value of the legend depends on the possibilty of accepting sura 96:1–5 as the first revelation, and that depends, because of 96:9f., on the possibility of proving the break between verses 5 and 6. Yet this is hardly possible. More likely there is every reason to believe that the sura was created of a piece. The sequence of thoughts, where at first the blessings of the Creation are pointed out, and then the ingratitude and the unbelief of the people are criticized in harsh contradiction to the grace of Allah, often appears in the Qur'ān. Compare especially 80:17–23 and 82:6–9; in sura 96:6, 80:23, and 82:9 the turning point is always introduced with *kallā* [No! or Nay!]

Finally some notes on the different views of the Muslims as far as the the first revelation is concerned may be given:

1. Sura 96:1–5. In the commentaries the assumption is sometimes attributed to the authority of Ibn 'Abbās, Mujāhid, and Abū Mūsā al-Aš'arī,[54] sometimes to the account of Zuhrī (resp. 'Ā'isha).[55] It is remarkable that the older exegetes still use terms like "Ibn 'Abbās and Mujāhid think it is the first" (*Kaššāf*), "it belongs to the first ones, that had been sent from the *Qur'ān*, in the opinion of most people,"[56] "the commentator thinks it is the

first" (*Mafātīḥ*), "it is said to be the first" (Ibn 'Arabī, *Tafsīr* II, 403), etc. Later on it is declared apodicticly.[57] Nawawī (died 676) said: "That is the right opinion, that is shared by the greatest number of the former and later ones."[58] In Yaqūbī[59] it is recounted as the first revelation with a new legend: the angel comes to Muhammad dressed in a silken coat, lets him sit on the lappet of the coat, tells him that he is the messenger of God, and teaches him *iqra'* and so on; thus a more intimate meeting than (the appearance of) the gloomy vision in the cave.

2. Sura 74. The statement is always based on Jābir's report only; only once[60] it is said "by Jābir and others." Kirmānī (died about 500) said: "Jābir himself has invented that, it does not belong to his account. 'Ā'isha's account is true because it has been passed on by her since tradition has to be preferred to fiction."[61] Nawawī:[62] "This is weak, yes even more, untrue or invented." Al Khaṭīb (al-Baghdādī?, died 403): "There is a long quarrel about the first thing that is revealed of the *Qur'ān*. The reliable truth and the way to the conciliation of the divergent opinions is, that *iqra'* is the first of all, muddaṯṯir [Sura 74] the first one after the *fatra*."[63] That is, as we have seen, Zuhrī's opinion that has gained the victory.

3. Sura 1. According to Zamakhsharī[64] most of the commentators of his time were of that opinion, which is named by Bāqillānī[65] as the third of the contradictory statements. The fact that the fātiḥa is the first revelation is told in a legend based on the legend of *ufuq* by Wāḥidī[66] from Yaḥyā b. Bukayr from Isrā'īl from Abū Isḥāq ('Amr bin 'Abdallāh) from Abū Maisara ('Amr bin Šuraḥbīl). At the end of the tradition it is said: "And that is the opinion of 'Ali bin Abī Tālib."[67] Otherwise it is not known that Abū Maisara was in contact with 'Ali. *Itqān*[68] gives the following *isnād*: Yūnus bin Bukayr from Yūnus bin 'Amr from Abū Isḥāq and so on (with the same *isnād* in *'Uyūn al-Āṯār* and *Iṣāba*[69]).[70] The guarantors are from Kufa, so it may be a kufan local tradition. Among them, Abū Isḥāq is known as a reliable and famous traditionalist.[71] As far as the two Yūnus are concerned the statements differ from one another. Yūnus bin Bukayr was a disciple of Ibn Isḥāq but he had "linked his kalām to hadith." Besides he also was a *murjit*,[72] so some regarded him as supicious.[73] Bayhaqī[74] incorporated the report into the *Dalā'il*, but he added: "The report is mursal [traditions of which the *isnād* is

defective in a certain sense]," [75] "but the guarantors are reliable, and if it has been passed on in the right way, so it refers to its revelation after *iqra'*." Nawawī explained about this tradition: "Its vanity is too obvious to point out." [76]

4. Sura 68. In an anonymous report in Ḥalabī.[77] He rejects the assumption referring to the words of Muhammad "I have not been able to read (up to now)" and the motive of the revelation of sura 68 in Wāḥidī.

5. The Basmala formula that is preceeded by the *schutzgebetformel* [literally: the formula of the prayer of protection] and followed by sura 96. Wāḥidī,[78] from aᵃ-Ḍaḥḥāk from Ibn 'Abbās, also included by Ṭabarī in *Tafsīr*.[79] It is certainly possible that this really was the opinion of Ibn 'Abbās. On the one hand we found that he thought *iqra'* was the first sura, on the other hand that he did not accept the legend of *iqra'*. The above-mentioned opinion does not seem to belong to the legend of *iqra'* either, where everything is built upon the sudden command: *iqra'*!

6. Sura 73. Zarqānī:[80] There is a weak tradition that says that sura 73, *al-mazzammil*, is the firt sura.

7. Sura 95. Ḥalabī:[81] Some commentators think the sura *wa-t-tin* [sura 95: The Fig] was the first one, but God knows best."

There were also such people who wanted to satisfy themselves with a more agnostical solution to the controversy. According to a tradition in Bukhārī[82] 'Ā'isha is supposed to have said—with regard to to the right order of the suras: "The first (sura) that has been revealed from the *Qur'ān* was one of the suras that are called *mufaṣṣal* which deals with paradise and hell. Then, when people had converted to Islam the permitted and the forbidden was sent." Suyūṭī comments:[83] "This has been thought to be doubtful because the first that was revealed is *iqra'*, where paradise and hell are not named. I answer that it deals with *al-muddaṯṯir* [sura 74] where at the end it is talks about paradise and hell, because it is possible that *al-muddaṯṯir* had been revealed as a whole before the end of the *iqra'*."

Whoever studies closely Muhammad's oldest revelations and finds how much Muhammad is dominated in the beginning by the practical object of his mission—the announcement of the Last Judgement, and how all the occasional statements about his prophetic mission and about the nature of his revelation, "all the confirmatory revelations," serve the one and only purpose to confirm this content, will concur with the above mentioned assumption according to 'Ā'isha's tradition and accept as the prophet's first revelation—if contained in our Qur'ān—as one of those passionate accounts of the upcoming Last Judgement, which still today fascinate us with their incomparable and thrilling originality, rather than *iqra'* or *muddaṯṯir.*

NOTES

1. [Originally published in German under the title "Die legenden von der berufung Muhammeds," in *Le Monde Oriental*, Uppsala, 6 (1912), pp. 5–18, translated by Hans-Jörg Döhla, with assistance from Christoph Heger, who also provided many of the footnotes below in square brackets.]

2. Leben I, 334. [A., Sprenger, *Das Leben und die Lehre des Moḥammad*, 3 vols., Berlin, 1861–65.] Cf. also Caetani, *Annali dell' Islam*, 10 vols., Milan, 1905–1926, Introduzione, § 208.

3. [*taḥannuṯ*, seeking expiation, exercise of penance.]

4. [*iqra'* is traditionally, though in surah XCVI, 1, "erreoneously, understood as "read!" See G. Lüling, *Über den Urkoran*, Erlangen, [1]1974, [2]1993, 29 ff.]

5. [Waraqa ibn Nawfal, relative of Muhammad's first wife Khadīja, is said to have greeted Muhammad as the prophet of his people. For this (distorted) tradition see Günter Lüling, *Über den Urkoran,* Erlangen, [1]1974, [2]1993, 293–95; and Günter Lüling, *Die Wiederentdeckung des Propheten Muhammad. Eine Kritik am christlichen Abendland*, Erlangen, 1981, 280–88.]

6. Ṭabarī, I, 1149.

7. In order to mediate between the contradictory statements about the vocation, if it happened during daytime or at night, the solution was indeed invented that Gabriel had come for the first time at dawn, when it is neither day nor night (Ḥalabī, *Insān al-'uyūn* I, 317 [a biography of the Prophet; *Insān al-'uyūn (al-sīra al-Ḥalabiyya)*, Būlāq, 1292, Cairo, 1280. Ḥalabī, died 1635 CE]).

8. Sprenger's correction of *qass* instead of *qādī* is confirmed Ibn al-Athīr, *Usd al-Ġāba fī ma'rifat al-ṣaḥāba* ([5 vols., Cairo, AH 1285–1286] III, 353) (loc. cit. I, 339).

9. I: 1, 129–31.

10. Compare for example the legend of the nightly journey, where Umm Hāni's account [as obviously the one that is closest to the truth] can be found again in Ibn

Sa'd (I:1, 143). This account is missing in Ibn Isḥāq—possibly also in the original one [see Zarqānī, *Šarḥ 'alā-l-mawāhib*]—although Umm Hāni is also named by him among the witnesses.

11. He sees the angel with crossed legs at the horizon, he is called as in Ibn Isḥāq (only that here the words "and you are the messenger of God" are omitted), he sees the angel everywhere he looks, etc.

12. Nöldeke-Schwally, *Gesch. d. Qorans*, 78 n. 2.

13. Suyūṭī, *Itqān fī 'ulūm al-Qur'ān*, 2 vols., Cairo, 1306, II, 197.

14. *Itqān* II, 189.

15. Cairo edition from 1299 I, 402; de Slane's translation II, 207f.

16. Ḏahabī [died 1348 or 1352/53 CE], *Mīzan al-i'tidāl fi naqd (or tarājim) al-rijāl*, II, 187–89. Lucknow, 1883–84 CE.

17. He is supposed to have said to somebody who had been set free: "Do not lie to me, as 'Ikrima had lied to Ibn 'Abbās."

18. A mediatory group of the Khārijite, Shahrastānī I, 77 (Būlāk, 1263 AH); 'Ikrima is also named there at the head of the best known Khārijite but he is not attributed to a special group. [Ṣufriyya, an early Islamic religious group defined by the heresiographers as the name of a Khārijite sect arising out of the breakup of the Khārijite community in Baṣra in the year 64/683–84. *E. I.*, 2nd ed.]

19. [Ibadites and Najdites were other factions of the Khārijite.]

20. *Mīzan* I, 281.

21. What certainly does not fit into the accounts on his funeral, Ibn Khallikān, *Ǐahabī*, loc. cit.

22. This is especially evident in the case of the second one.

23. *Mīzan* I, 245–46.

24. *Mīzan*. loc. cit.

25. *Usd al-Ghāba* III, 353.

26. *Mīzan* II, 637–39.

27. Ibn Hishām (Weil) I, 117; cf. Ṭabarī I, 1149.

28. *Bāb Bad' al-waḥī*.

29. *Bāb Bad' al-waḥī*, *tafsīr* on *sura* 74, *al-muddaṯṯir*; cf. *Ṭabarī* I, 1153.

30. Known comrade and hadith-teller, about the age of twenty when Muhammad died, *Usd al-Ghāba* I, 256.

31. Nöldeke-Schwally I, 87.

32. Nöldeke-Schwally, 87, n. 2.

33. Zamakhsharī. *Kaššāf*, Cairo, 1281, II, 479.

34. *Kaššāf* II, 434.

35. *Kaššāf* II, 430; *Mafātiḥ*, Būlāq, 1289, VIII, 332.

36. Although he is said to have recited from books that he had not heard personally, until—by request of his listeners/audience—he marked such hadith by the formula *balaghanī* [it was transmitted to me]. *Mīzan* II, 590.

37. *Kitāb al-ḥijal, bāb at-ta'bīr.*

38. I, 1147.

39. In Firūzābādī, *Sifr as-Sa'āda*, who otherwise seems to follow Ṭabarī's description, it only appears one time. It is emphasized that Muhammad witnessed everything, also the vision of *iqra,* while he was awake, Ḥalabī I, 319.

40. *Zammilūnī* certainly has come in through Jābir's version, which is another proof for our claim that that legend is identical with the legend of *ufuq*.

41. Ibn Sa'd VI, 86; *Usd al-Ghāba* III, 183.

42. The fear and the plans for suicide of the prophet.

43. [Translators' note: i.e., to judge them.]

44. Leben I, 306.

45. The fact that sura 81 has described a nightly face cannot be concluded from the oaths in v. 15–18; also not that the revelation of the sura happened at the end of the night, Nöldeke-Schwally I, 99 n. 4; in this case, when would sura 89 have been revealed?

46. Grimme, *Muhammed*, 2 vols., Münster, 1892, 1895, II, 101; H. P. Smith, *Bible and Islam*, London, 1897, 153.

47. *Mafātīḥ* VII, 733.

48. *Qāḍī, 'Ijāḍ, Šifā',* Konstantiopel, 1312, I, 159–64; cf. also *Mīzan* I, 256, with the strange tradition "I (Muhammed) saw my Lord as a young man without a beard wrapped in a pearl embroidered cloth," etc., from *Ḥammād* from *Qatāda* from 'Ikrima from Ibn 'Abbās. Ḏahabī says: "This is the worst that has come from H."

49. *Kitāb tafsīr,* on Sura 53, *an-najm*.

50. *Bayḍāwī* zur Stelle.

51. One may note here that Hirschfeld, *New Researches into the Composition and Exegesis of the Qoran*, London, 1902, p. 143, for totally different reasons traces sura 81 after sura 53, and following.

52. It is remarkable, that according to *Kaššāf* II, 434, Jābir's account is only supposed to have contained this; the words "on a throne" are said to have been in one of 'Ā'isha's accounts that is not further known. Maybe Zuhrī's version of Jābir has sometimes been traced back to 'Urwa-'Ā'isha?

53. Goldziher, *Abhandlungen zur arabischen Philologie*, 2 vols., Leiden, 1896–1899, I, 3.

54. *Kaššāf* II, 474. *Ṣiddīq al-Qanūjī*, Būlāq, 1300–1301, X, 311; also *Mawāhib* I, 257.

55. Abū-l-Fidā' bin Kathīr (*Ṣiddīq al-Qanūjī*, Būlāq, 1300–1301), X, 253, Abū Su'ūd referring to sura 96, etc.

56. Hibat Allāh, *An-nāsikh wa-l-mansūkh* (Wāḥidī, Cairo, 1315), 330.

57. Ibn *Kathīr*, *Abū Su'ūd*, *Ṣiddīq*, etc.

58. *Mawāhib* I, 257.

59. II, 21–22.

60. *Mawāhib* I, 257.

61. *Mawāhib* I, 258.

62. According to Zarqāni, *Šarh 'alā-l-mawāhib*, in his commentary on Bukhārī.

63. *Ṣiddīq* X, 103.

64. *Kitāb i'jāz* (*Itqān*, Cairo, 1306) II, 479.

65. II, 195.

66. *Asbāb an-Nuzūl*, 11–12.

67. 'Ali is one of the comrades who is especially regarded as an authority in the exegesis; in a sermon he is said to have assured that for every verse in the Qur'ān he knows the time and the location, *Itqān* II, 186–87.

68. I, 25.

69. [I. Ḥağar, *Al-Iṣāba fī tamyīz al-ṣaḥāba* (*A Biographical Dictionary of Persons Who Knew Mohammed*), ed. A. Sprenger et al., 4 vols., Calcutta, 1856–1888.]

70. Sprenger I, 344.

71. Ibn Sa'd VI, 219; *Mīzan* II, 263.

72. [Murjite: *Murji'a*: name of one of the early sects of Islam, the extreme opponents of the *Khārijites*.]

73. *Mīzan* II, 627.

74. *Ḥalabī* I, 328; *Mawāhib* I, 258.

75. According to *Usd al-Ghāba* IV, 114, 'Amr has not been a comrade.

76. *Mawāhib* loc. cit.

77. I, 328.

78. *Wāḥidī Ạsbāb an-Nuzūl*, Cairo, 1315, 10.

79. *Mawāhib* loc. cit.

80. *Šarḥ 'alā-l-mawāhibi* I, 258.

81. I, 348.

82. *Kitāb fadā'il al-qur'ān*.

83. *Itqān* I, 25.

3.2

An Example of Coptic Literary Influence on Ibn Isḥāq's *Sīrah*[1]

Gordon D. Newby

W. Montgomery Watt suggests in his article "The Materials Used by Ibn Isḥāq" that ". . . the chief task immediately ahead for scholars in this field is to look more closely at this *maghāzī* material and to study its relations to the various groups of anecdotes."[2] The most familiar form of the traditional biography of Muhammad, Ibn Hishām's edition of Muḥammad b. Isḥāq b. Yasār's *Sīrat rasūl Allāh*, introduces *maghāzī* material only into that section of Muhammad's life after he has received his prophetic call.[3] However, the material that Watt terms anecdotal is used throughout the biography, including in the introductory section before Muhammad's birth. It is this section that chiefly lays the ground for the anti-Judeo-Christian polemic and casts Muhammad into the mainstream of the hagiology of the past prophets.[4] As it does so it is not "historical" in the same sense as the *maghāzī* section. The controlling factors of the introductory section are: commentary on the Qur'ān; some glorification of the South Arabs, the ancestors of the *Anṣār*; and the above-mentioned polemic. The accounts of valorous raids that link Muhammad to the tradition of the *Aiyām al-ʿArab* come later. But the anecdotal material in the introductory section seems to stand in the same relation to these factors as it does later to the *maghāzī* material: it gives substance to the account and an air of plausibility. In all instances, the anecdotes are presented as historical traditions, whether from our point of view they are sheer fabrications, such as those that make up the account of the Prophet's conception and birth, or whether they are possibly historically true, such as the account of Muhammad's marriage to the rich widow Khadījah. It would be useful to determine the role of the anecdotal material throughout the biography, for it is in just this type of embellishing material that we can see the compositional criteria of the *Sīrah*. But before that task can be done, the nature, historicity, and sources of the individual anecdotes must be determined. That is to say insofar as possible the techniques of comparative literature must be applied thoroughly to the anecdotal portions of the *Sīrah* before we can adequately proceed to discuss their role in the composition.

A case in point is a section in the first part of the *Sīrah* that Guillaume titles "The Beginning of Christianity in Najrān." This section is the seventh in a series of accounts starting with the genealogy and leading up to an explanation of the events mentioned in *Sūrat al-fīl*, the Chapter of the Elephant. On the face of it, this account seems to present a somewhat fanciful but nevertheless plausible account of Christian missionary activity in Arabia. The account is as follows:[5]

> Al-Mughīra b. Abū Labīd, a freedman of al-Akhnās, on the authority of Wahb b. Munabbih the Yamanī,[6] told me that the origin of Christianity in Najrān was due to a man named Faymiyūn who was a righteous, earnest, ascetic man whose prayers were answered. He used to wander between towns: as soon as he became known in one town he moved to another, eating only what he earned, for he was a builder by trade using mud bricks. He used to keep Sunday as a day of rest and would do no work then. He used to go into a desert place and pray there until the evening. While he was following his trade in a Syrian village withdrawing himself from men, one of the people there called Ṣāliḥ perceived what manner of man he was and felt a violent affection for him, so that unperceived by Faymiyūn he used to follow him from place to place, until one Sunday he went as his wont was out into the desert followed by Ṣāliḥ. Ṣāliḥ chose a hiding place and sat down where he could see him, not wanting him to know where he was. As Faymiyūn stood to pray a tinnīn, a seven horned snake, came towards him and when Faymiyūn saw it he cursed it and it died. Seeing the snake but not knowing what had happened to it and fearing for Faymiyūn's safety, Ṣāliḥ could not contain himself and cried out: "Faymiyūn, a tinnīn is upon

you!" He took no notice and went on with his prayers until he had ended them. Night had come and he departed. He knew that he had been recognized and Ṣāliḥ knew that he had seen him. So he said to him: "Faymiyūn, you know that I have never loved anything as I love you; I want to be always with you and go wherever you go." He replied: "As you will. You know how I live and if you feel that you can bear the life well and good." So Ṣāliḥ remained with him, and the people of the village were on the point of discovering his secret. For when a man suffering from a disease came in his way by chance he prayed for him and he was cured; but if he was summoned to a sick man he would not go. Now one of the villagers had a son who was blind and he asked about Faymiyūn and was told that he never came when he was sent for, but that he was a man who built houses for people for a wage. Thereupon the man took his son and put him in his room and threw a garment over him and went to Faymiyūn saying that he wanted him to do some work for him in his house and would he come and look at it, and they would agree on a price. Arrived at the house Faymiyūn asked what he wanted done, and after giving the details the man suddenly whisked off the covering from the boy and said: "O Faymiyūn, one of God's creatures is in the state you see. So Pray for him." Faymiyūn did so and the boy got up entirely healed. Knowing that he had been recognized he left the village followed by Ṣāliḥ, and while they were walking through Syria they passed by a great tree and a man called from it saying: "I've been expecting you and saying, 'When is he coming?' until I heard your voice and knew it was you. Don't go until you have prayed over my grave for I am about to die." He did die and he prayed over him until they buried him. Then he left followed by Ṣāliḥ until they reached the land of the Arabs who attacked them, and a caravan carried them off and sold them in Najrān. At this time the people of Najrān followed the religion of the Arabs worshipping a great palm-tree there. Every year they had a festival when they hung on the tree any fine garment they could find and women's jewels. Then they sallied out and devoted the day to it. Faymiyūn was sold to one noble and Ṣāliḥ to another. Now it happened that when Faymiyūn was praying earnestly at night in a house which his master had assigned to him the whole house was filled with light so that it shone as it were without a lamp. His master was amazed at the sight and asked him about his religion. Faymiyūn told him and said that they were in error; as for the palm-tree it could neither help nor hurt; and if he were to curse the tree in the name of

> God, He would destroy it, for He was God Alone without companion. "Then do so," said his master, "for if you do that we shall embrace your religion, and abandon our present faith." After purifying himself and performing two *rak'as*, he invoked God against the tree and God sent a wind against it which tore it from its roots and cast it on the ground. Then the people of Najrān adopted his religion and he instructed them in the law of 'Isā b. Maryam. Afterwards they suffered the misfortunes which befell their co-religionists in every land. This was the origin of Christianity in Majrān in the land of the Arabs. Such is the report of Wahb B. Munabbih on the authority of the people of Najrān.

Following our above-stated dictum, we should now attempt to assess the historicity of the account, in this case to determine to what extent this tradition represents an actual case of missionary activity in Arabia, and, more important, we should try to determine the literary nature of this tradition, that is, to what degree this account follows traditional and literary motifs in Arabia and in the East Mediterranean generally.

On the whole, it is difficult to say with any surety much about the historical setting of this tradition. We know that Christianity prevailed in most of the countries surrounding Arabia, and the two countries that would have had the greatest influence in Southern Arabia, Egypt and Abyssinia, were both Monophysite. From at least A.D. 451, the Abyssinian Church to some extent depended on the Egyptian Coptic Church in clergy, liturgy, and tradition. Richard Bell speculates about the degree of penetration and types of Christianity that could have been found in Arabia at the time of the advent of Islam, but concludes, as most scholars have, that this must for now remain a moot point.[7] The problem is made more difficult when we realize that historical statements have often been made only from unanalyzed literary material.

A more profitable line of inquiry is the question of the literary nature of this tradition. It is clear that the account of Faymiyūn's adventures can be divided into several major thematic sections. Each one of these divisions has its own embellishments, but the outline is as follows:

1. The main character, a pious person, wishes to keep secret his spiritual achievements out of humility and goes to great pains to do so, even when he

must move away from a good income (in this case) and reject common intercourse with men.

2. The ascetic only accepts a disciple after that disciple has proved his sincerity and his ability to withstand the rigors of the ascetic life.

3. The ascetic is discovered when others use trickery against him and when charity and piety force him to reveal himself.

4. The ascetic possesses certain abilities by virtue of his spiritual achievements, such as knowledge of future events, the ability to cure illness through prayer, and the ability to call down God's curse or blessing for a righteous cause.

5. Severe trials, accepted humbly, allow the ascetic to further God's work and finally triumph in the end.

When the story is thus reduced to its component parts, it becomes immediately clear that we are dealing with a type of wisdom literature that has examples throughout the Mediterranean world but finds its best expression in that group of stories called the *Apophthegmata Patrum*, or Tales of the Coptic Fathers. In this group of tales we find the same themes with many variations that we find in the account of the beginning of Christianity in Najrān. The tales of the Coptic Fathers, dating primarily from the fourth and fifth centuries A.D., are not so much tales as they are short, pithy anecdotes that convey a moral or spiritual message.[8] As such, they correspond very closely to an item of *ḥadīth*, though, to be sure, without a chain of authority. These anecdotes spread with Christianity and Christian monasticism throughout the Western world, and individual anecdotes were often combined to form the basis for saints' lives and diversionary tales. It is this same stock of anecdotes that influences Hrotswitha of Gandersheim's *Paphnutius* and Anatole France's *Thais*.

The first thematic division of the account of the beginning of Christianity in Najrān is paralleled in tale number 31 of the Sahidic version of the *Apophthegmata Patrum*:[9]

> There was a certain saint named Philagrios living in Jerusalem who worked hard so that he acquired his own bread. As he stood in the market to sell his handwork, he suddenly found a purse containing a thousand small coins. He stood in his place saying, "It is right for the one who has lost it to

> come." And behold, that one came weeping. The elder after having taken it took him aside and gave it to him. That one took hold of him, wishing to give him some, but the elder did not want to take any. Then he began to cry out saying, "Come, see what a man of God has done." The elder swiftly ran away and left the city in order that they might not recognize him.

Faymiyūn follows this ideal of humility, moving from place to place as his spiritual virtues become known, thus conforming to the rule, which becomes general in monasticism, that he live on what comes to him or what he earn with his hands, and that not too much, for it was widely believed that the "Devil multiplies the needs of the monk."[10]

The second theme concerns Ṣāliḥ, i.e., Good, Righteous, who becomes the companion and disciple of Faymiyūn. Faymiyūn is not at all anxious to accept a companion, and Ṣāliḥ must bear with rejection for a time so that both he and Faymiyūn can be sure that Ṣāliḥ is cut out for the ascetic life. It is common among the tales of the Coptic Fathers to find accounts of disciples rejected at first, and later becoming as great or greater than the master who rejected them, and a period of trial was the rule rather than the exception. The most noted example involves Saint Anthony and his disciple Paul the Simple.[11] Paul, wishing to become a monk, went to the door of Saint Anthony's cell and made his request, but Saint Anthony refused him and made him wait outside for four days without food or water. When he finally let Paul in, he made him weave and take out and reweave palm fibers into mats so many times that the normal man would have become disgusted with the regimen and quit, as he was advised to do in the first place. Paul, however, persevered and finally became a monk.

The reference to the *tinnīn*, the seven-horned snake, in this sequence is, of course, a reference to the Devil, and this theme recurs constantly throughout the Coptic tales. Taking imagery from both Old and New Testaments, the text that is often cited in this regard is from Luke 10:19: "Behold, I give unto you power to tread on serpents and scorpions, and over all the power of the enemy: and nothing shall by any means hurt you."[12] Monks in the desert were constantly plagued by snakes and scorpions, and, according to the accounts, could vanquish them by prayer, as does Faymiyūn in this story.

The next two themes, essentially combined in this account, involve the power to heal through prayer and faith and the reluctance to do so for reasons of humility (see theme one above). Egypt was long regarded as the source for cures, and it was no less so during the height of Coptic monasticism. But with the desert fathers, healing was a miracle from God, and the privilege to act as the medium through which He acted was a reward for good works and long spiritual trials. Since one slip, one small sin, such as being proud, could remove this privilege, the monks preferred to heal secretly, if at all, so as not to be tempted. A clever man could trick a monk, however, as in the Faymiyūn account, but usually with the ultimate displeasure of the monk. There are many tales that are similar to the one in the account, and they all follow much the same theme, so one will suffice:[13]

> Once a layman came with his son to Apa Jijoi, who lived in the mountain of Apa Anthony. Along the way his son died in his hands. He was not disturbed but took him to the elder in faith and bowed with his son that they might do penance to the elder so that he might bless them. Then the father arose and left his son at the feet of the elder, and he departed from the cell. The elder, thinking that he bowed to him to receive absolution, said to him, "Rise, depart," for he did not know that he was dead. Immediately he arose and departed, and when his father saw this, he marvelled and entered and bowed to the elder. He told him of the deed, and the elder heard and was grieved, for he did not wish to do things in this way. Then his disciple commanded them. "Do not tell this to anyone while the elder is alive."

Faymiyūn, recognizing the popularity that would follow his cure of the blind boy, decided to leave the village rather than remain in a prideful situation. His journey took him past a person who appears to be a monk, for this person had foreknowledge of his own death and of Faymiyūn's coming, another of the accomplishments of the desert ascetics. Following the passage from Psalms 146:8: "The Lord openeth the eyes of the blind," there are many stories of monks who were able to "declare things before they came to pass,"[14] as with John of Lycus who predicted events concerning the emperor Theodosius,[15] and with Abbā Pachomius who foretold the death of a brother at a distant monastery while journeying to that monastery to bless him before his death.[16]

Faymiyūn and his companion are next captured and carried off with a caravan to the land of Najrān. This seems to be a plausible motif to introduce at this point, for it would probably reflect an actual active slave trade. This sequence too has its parallels in Coptic literature, at least in part, with the tale of Mark the Monk, who is captured, along with a certain woman, and made a slave by the Arab chief.[17] Faymiyūn perseveres in his devotion, and such acceptance of whatever befalls is the standard pattern in the lives of the desert fathers. While they are termed the "athletes of God" striving against the forces of Evil, they are remarkably passive about their living conditions.

Faymiyūn is next found out not by trickery this time but by piety, for he is reported to have been surrounded by a light when he prayed. This is the nimbus of traditional iconography. His destruction of the palm tree of the Arabs because that tree was an idol and a false object of worship is much like the story of Pachomius and the gardener Yawnan:[18]

> To this man came the blessed Pachomius, and told him to cut down this fig tree, and when Yawnan heard this, he said unto Rabbā, "Nay, O father, for we are accustomed to gather a large crop of fruit from this fig tree for the brethren"; now although Rabbā was greatly grieved because of this matter, he did not wish to urge the old gardener any further, and he was the more grieved because he knew that Yawnan lived a great and marvellous life, and that he was held to be wonderful by many, and by great and small alike. And it came to pass on the day following that the fig tree was found to have become withered so completely that not one soft leaf or fruit was found upon it. Now when the blessed man saw these things, he was greatly grieved, not for the sake of the fig tree, but because of his own disobedience, when Rabbā told him to cut down the fig tree, and he did not act according to his word.

Conversion follows Faymiyūn as repentance follows the acts of Pachomius, in both stories the point being the same: the tree represents the temptations of this life which are overcome by piety and acts of faith and good works.

From the above analysis, it is clear that the account of the beginning of Christianity in Najrān parallels numerous Coptic tales thematically, and the all too frequent points of correspondence between this tale and the *Apoph-*

thegmata Patrum indicate that the Coptic tales were known and well circulated in Arabia around the time of the rise of Islam. A further point of correspondence is with the name Faymiyūn. One of the most prominent of the later desert fathers, and the last to be systematically included in the *Apophthegmata Patrum*, was Apa Poimen (fl. fifth century A.D.). It is speculated that the systematic collecting of the traditions of the Coptic Fathers began with him, or his school, and in some versions, sayings attributed to him constitute as much as twenty percent of the collections.[19] It is not unlikely that such a famous name would remain associated with these traditions, even when the traditions were translated into Arabic.[20]

This obviously literary account of Faymiyūn follows, or is rather placed within, the account of Dhū Nuwās, the Jewish ruler of Yemen. With the recent discovery of G. Ryckmans of the inscription at Qāra, Dhū Nuwās, his Jewish name Joseph, has become an historical figure, so it is ill-advised to reject the historicity of Faymiyūn out of hand.[21] But factual or not at its root, these Coptic tales serve an important literary function in this section of the *Sīrah*. Hagiologic tales were undoubtedly a part of the stock repertory of the storytellers, *quṣṣāṣ*, in Arabia as they were in the rest of the Mediterranean world. These storytellers occupied prominent positions in early Islam, and some rose to prominence as preachers and judges.[22] They fashioned moralistic tales around Qur'ānic themes and embellished them with tales from the Bible and from ancient folklore, and were soon occupying regularized positions in the Islamic community. Their art, as preachers in the community, was primarily moralistic and propagandistic, and no matter how embellished, their stories usually had a point or goal. Such seems the case with these Coptic tales in the first part of the *Sīrah*. The climax of the first part of the *Sīrah*, excluding the genealogy, which is reminiscent of the opening of the Gospel according to Saint Matthew, is an explanation of the events alluded to in *Sūrat al-fīl*, The Chapter of the Elephant, where the Abyssinian Abraha was supposed to have attacked Mecca unsuccessfully during the year Muhammad was born. In order to fully explain this event, it was necessary to present accounts of Jewish and Christian settlement and conflict, with the subsequent intervention of the Abyssinians, in southern Arabia. This account explains the Christian presence.

But *tafsīr* is not the only point to the group of traditions in the first part of the *Sīrah*. They are also etiological, when they explain the prohibition of blood around the *Kaʿbah*, for example,[23] and they present some of the history of the *Anṣār* of Medina and their ancestors the South Arabs. Further, it seems clear at this point that one of the major functions of the *Sīrah* is to present a biography of Muhammad that would fit into the already existent and revered patterns of Christian hagiology. It is not surprising, then, to find older hagiologic material used in its composition.

Although we do not possess a complete picture of Christian literature, oral or written, from Arabia around the time of the advent and early development of Islam, it is likely that further investigation of the nature of the anecdotal portions of the *Sīrah* will demonstrate that the early Arab compilers of biographic traditions were acquainted at least with some of the Gospels and an extensive hagiologic tradition. It seems that it is this material that has strongly influenced our present picture of Muhammad.

NOTES

1. [Gordon D. Newby, "An Example of Coptic Literary Influence on Ibn Isḥāq's Sīrah," *Journal of Near Eastern Studies* 31 (1972): 22–28.]

2. W. Montgomery Watt, "The Materials Used by Ibn Isḥāq," *Historians of the Middle East*, B. Lewis and P. Holt, eds. (London, 1962), p. 34.

3. Likewise, al-Wāqidī's *Kitāb al-Maghāzī*, edited by M. Jones (London, 1966), begins with the *hijrah*. A most useful aid in this study is A. Guillaume's reconstruction of Ibn Isḥāq's lost work in *The Life of Muhammad* (London, 1955).

4. Watt modifies the "Lammens-Becker" position on this point and adds that it ". . . might arise from a desire to assimilate Muḥammad to the conception of a religious leader current in the heartlands of the Islamic empire" (Watt, "Materials," p. 25).

5. Ibn Isḥāq, *The Life of Muhammad*, A. Guillaume, trans. (London, 1955), pp. 14–16.

6. Wahb. b. Munabbih, whose father was probably a Jew, is the most prominent traditionist concerned with Jewish and Christian scriptures and traditions and his *Kitāb al-Mubtadaʾ* had a profound influence on Islamic tradition.

7. R. Bell, *Introduction to the Qurʾān* (Edinburgh, 1963), pp. 10–14.

8. The two versions used for this study are J. Hartley, *Studies in the Sadhidic*

Version of the Apophthegmata Patrum (Ann Arbor, 1969), and E. A. Wallis Budge, *The Book of Paradise*, 2 vols. (London, 1904).

9. Hartley, *Studies*, pp. 36–37.

10. Budge, *Book of Paradise*, p. 748.

11. Ibid., pp. 183–89.

12. Ibid., p. 538.

13. Hartley, *Studies*, p. 149.

14. Budge, *Book of Paradise*, p. 256.

15. Ibid.

16. Ibid., p. 442.

17. Ibid., p. 344 ff.

18. Ibid., p. 472. It should be noted that the account of Pachomius and the account of Faymiyūn do not at this point stand in direct relation to each other, but rather seem to hark back to a common source. The most obvious source is, of course, the Gospel accounts of Christ's cursing the barren fig tree. The particular deviations of both of these accounts from the Gospel stories have led to the admission of possible Gnostic influence on either the Coptic or the Arabic account or both. It would seem that a possible line of future inquiry might be to attempt to re-examine these traditions in light of the Nag-Hamâdi papyri.

19. W. Bousset, *Apophthegmata Patrum, Studien zur Geschichte des ältesten Mönchtums* (Tübingen, 1923), pp. 68–71.

20. Also the name Ṣāliḥ might well be a Christian name if we are to accept A. Baumstark's analysis of Sūrah 21, verse 105, in "Das Problem eines vorislamischen Christlich-Kirchlichen Schrifttums in arabischer Sprache," *Islamica* 4 (1931): 566, where he equates the Greek *dikaioi* with the Arabic *ṣāliḥūn*.

21. See Guillaume, op. cit., p. 799, for a bibliography.

22. N. Abbott, *Studies in Arabic Literary Papyri*, vol. 2 (Chicago, 1967), p. 15.

23. Guillaume, op. cit., p. 9.

3.3

The Biography of the Prophet and Its Scriptural Basis[1]

Wim Raven

Whoever may want to write a biography of Nadjib Maḥfūẓ will have a difficult task. The novelist has been so discreet about his private life that almost nothing is known about it. However, since he is famous and has written an extended oeuvre, one may guess what will happen one day: a biography will appear, mainly based on his *works*. This, I suppose, is what has happened with biographies of authors of all times and cultures.

In ancient Arabic literature, the situation was similar, as some examples may show. In the case of the pre-Islamic poet Ta'abbata Sharran a question which apparently cried for an answer was, how he had got that peculiar nickname, which means: "he carried something evil under his arm." Several anecdotes (*akhbār*) adduce explanations; one of them recounts that the poet had a fight with a *ghūl*, which he killed and carried home under his arm. Since he composed some lines of poetry about a fight with a *ghūl*, it is obvious that this particular anecdote was inspired not only by the desire to explain his name, but also by that poetic text.[2]

Another example: the little that is supposed to be known about the life of the Umayyad poet al-Shamardal was almost completely distilled from his *dīwān*, as Seidensticker pointed out.[3]

Of the anecdotes about the life and death of Muḥammad ibn Dāwūd al-Ẓāhirī (255–297/868–910), a good deal is directly based on his *Kitāb al-Zahra*.[4]

Narrators who rely on texts by the very authors they want to write about may have various starting points. Their primary interest may be the author's life, which they find so important or fascinating that they start collecting text fragments, to exploit them for their purpose and knit them into a coherent, marketable narration. Their activity can also start from the author's text itself. They may, for instance, wish to explain an enigmatic passage by weaving a story around it. Or they may search for the circumstances in which the text came into being. Many a piece of ancient Arabic poetry would be incomprehensible, had it not been embedded in an explicatory narration.

"The assessment of fictitious elements in historiographical *akhbār* may draw attention to their literary quality, but it does not necessarily invalidate them as historical sources." Whether we like it or not, we have to agree with this statement of Stefan Leder,[5] since neither fact nor fiction ever occurs in an unadulterated form. But what about intertextuality? When an element in an anecdote is not only fictitious, but can demonstrably be reduced to some earlier text fragment, can it still be used as a historical source? Whoever believes that the historical Ta'abbata Sharran really carried a *ghūl* home under his arm may see his belief already shaken when he understands how aetiological legends work, but he will loose it completely as soon as he reads Taʾabbaṭa's verse about his fight with that *ghūl*.

Does this have any relevance in the case of Muḥammad? The Prophet was not considered to be the author of the Koran, but he was so closely connected with that scripture that, for practical purposes, he was treated like an author. His biography is largely dependent on the scripture he spread. The situation with Muḥammad is even more complicated than with other authors, because the biographical elements are not only connected with his "own" text, the Koran, but also with biblical narrations,[6] and perhaps with other literary sources, such as Christian legends of the saints.[7]

The perception that the *vita* of the Prophet is useless for historiograph: inasmuch it is dependent on scripture is by no means new. However, it seems to have been persistently forgotten, and then rediscovered. Rather than with developments in science, this is due to the personal background and persuasion of the researcher, as well as with the *Zeitgeist*. Some people happen to be "sceptics"; others are not. Although non-Muslim scholars have no religious reason to believe what was written about Muḥammad, many of them simply feel at home with the traditional stories, whereas others seem to know no greater pleasure than debunking them.

In the early fifties the "conservative" scholar W. M. Watt wrote an extensive biography of the Prophet, which turned out to be the last one.[8] With Wansbrough, Cook and Crone,[9] and others, a new wave of "scepticism" came. Their works, although not generally accepted, at least spread the idea that writing a scholarly biography is no longer possible. After the 1980 Strasbourg colloquium on the *sīra*, a period of silence on the matter set in.[9]

This silence was broken recently, when Uri Rubin and Gregor Schoeler published sizable monographs on the *sīra*.[11] I was curious to see how these scholars would handle the use of scripture in the *sīra*.

In the introduction to his *Charakter and Authentic*, Schoeler deals with the history of the research and the fluctuations of scepticism and counter-scepticism. In his important first chapter he discusses the character of the sources and their development from oral *ḥadīth* and *qiṣṣa* to fixed literary works meant for a general public (from about 800 AD onwards), with their intermediate stages such as mnemotechnic aids, notebooks for private use, and fully-fledged books for internal use both in school and at court. Then he focuses on two narratives from the *sīra*,: that of the first revelation (with the *iqraʾ* and *ufuq* episodes as central motifs), and that of ʿĀʾisha's alleged adultery (*ifk*).

For Schoeler, authentic (*echte*) traditions are traditions which were really transmitted, whereas inauthentic (*unechte*) traditions were consciously modified, embellished, ascribed to false authorities and/or contaminated. Applying these definitions enables him to declare many traditions authentic, for "contradictions between various transmitted versions are not necessarily an argument against the authenticity (in this sense)." When a story is transmitted orally, it is no wonder that already at an early stage *topoi* appear, to meet with both the expectations of the hearers and the inner logic of "what must have happened." We should not expect, then, not even in the case of "authentic" traditions, that we have matter-of-fact reports about real events before us. What we have are at best "memories" (*Erinnenzngen*), or even more frequently, "memories of memories."[12]

Yet, this concept of authenticity obtains another ring when we read immediately after this expose, with reference to the *ifk* story, that too much scepsis is out of place, and that there is no reason to doubt the outline of the story, because:

- in oral transmission one or two generations after the event can be bridged without distorting the facts too much,
- the plurality in transmission is almost a recommendation (a variant of the traditional muslim *mutawātir* argument?),
- the anecdotes have resisted the usual pattern of idealisation, in this case of ʿĀʾisha as the mother of the faithful.

In my view early Muslims were by no means shy when it came to writing fiction. They did not even hesitate to describe the *allzumenschliche* characteristics of the Prophet. Besides, ʿĀʾisha does not always have a good press in Tradition. Often enough she is depicted as jealous and bothersome. In the *ifk* story she is dripping with so much innocence that one is almost inevitably convinced of her guilt. However, Schoeler would agree that scepticism is a matter of taste, and I should not allow myself to be carried away into a discussion of a type which Schoeler is right in avoiding carefully.

Schoeler's method has various great merits: 1) He uses *all* versions of a story he can lay hands on. That this is necessary has also been seen and said by others, but who else brought this principle into practice? — 2) He studies the relationship between the various transmissions and establishes where every version of a story belongs on the scale between orally transmitted and fixed literary text. — 3) On this base, he convincingly assigns dates to the various stages of a text, with the help of *isnād* analysis according to the common link method designed by J. Schacht and further developed by G. H. A. Juynboll. This is one of the first serious attempts to apply that method, outside the works of Juynboll himself.

The "character," then, is the oral, written or literary character of a tradition; an important aspect indeed. Besides, Schoeler sometimes characterises a given version of a narrative in a few words, by summarising its tenor. However, one looks in vain for an investigation into the impact of the Scripture on the narratives. Next to textuality lies intertextuality, but the latter is not discussed at all, in spite of the fact that koranic text plays an eminent part in both the *iqra'* and the *ifk* story. Schoeler is of course aware of this, but leaves it simply outside the scope of his book. This remains to be studied, because there would indeed be reason to doubt the outline of a story, if koranic text were at the origin of it. And, more interesting, koranic text may have been applied differently in the various versions of a narrative, which affects their character.

In *The Eye of the Beholder*, Rubin studied eleven motifs and episodes from the *sīra* which refer to Muḥammad's Meccan period, and we can only hope that he will continue with the materials about Medina. In his introduction, he declares not to be interested in finding out "what really happened," which is a great relief. The study of Muḥammad's biography as literature, which is long overdue, has always been impeded by the obsession with the "historical Muḥammad." From Rubin's revealing chapter on chronology in the *sīra*, which leaves few illusions about the "historical Muḥammad," I deduce that he may well be a "sceptic." On the other hand, his dating of traditions (*ḥadīth*) is conservative, or at least vague: traditions are earlier than the *sīra*, if I understand him right, and he speaks about earlier and later traditions without explaining why they are so. There is no attempt to assign dates to the traditions or to establish a relative chronology for them, except on the base of their contents. This does not distract much from the value of the book, which is above all an eye-opener for the possible scriptural origins of the stories, and how these were removed, manipulated or enriched. In fact, the scriptural base of Muḥammad's biography is the main subject of his book.

I will try to summarise Rubin's view of the development of narratives abot the Prophet:

In the beginning there is something like a "basic narrative framework,"[13] describing the bare facts or wording a universal theme. Since the Prophet was modelled on his biblical predecessors, this framework was likely to be padded with biblical materials. Or the original stage of a narrative was biblical in the first place. The basic narrative framework is always independent of koranic verses and ideas.

Somewhat later, the biblical elements were found embarrassing. Therefore themes found (also) their way into narratives with an Arabian atmosphere, a Meccan decor, pre-Islamic poetry and pagan actors.

The next step was the islamisation of the stories. Unislamic details, e.g. allusions to the Bible, were eliminated. Adaptations to koranic models were made, and koranic texts were woven into the framework, to embellish it and make it acceptable for the increasingly islamised environment. This is what Rubin calls koranisation.[14] It took place in *sīra* works.

In the last stage, these koranised *sīra* fragments were turned into "occasions for the revelation," *asbāb al-nuzūl* stories. This happened only in *tafsīr* works, which are essentially later than and separate from *sīra* texts.

As a matter of fact, Rubin does not claim that all narrations actually go through all these stages. It is merely a model of what happened to *sīra* materials during their development, that can be distilled from his investigations.

I will briefly mention two convincing illustrations of Rubin's way of looking at things here:

It is fascinating to see how a biblical description of the expected Prophet: "He shall not cry, nor lift up, nor cause his voice to be heard in the street [...]" (*Isaiah* 42:2), turns into a fully-fledged Islamic Tradition without any biblical reference, about a prophet who "is not crude nor coarse, and does not raise his voice in the streets."[15] This indeed is a clear case of islamisation by eliminating an embarrassing biblical element.

The Traditions about the splitting of Muḥammads belly (*shaqq al-baṭn*), which were adulterated, in their later stages, with the wordings of sura 94 (opening of the breast, *sharḥ al-ṣadr*), are a convincing example of koranisation of an ancient Arabian motif.[16]

How does Rubin's scheme of koranisation work out with a narrative which he did not discuss? I tried it with the story of how Quraysh plotted to starve out, expel or kill Muḥammad, just before the *hidjra*, and how the latter had ʿAlī sleep in his bed and left unseen; which I read in the version of Ibn Hishām and al-Ṭabarī[17] and that of Wahb ibn Munabbih.[18]

Both versions are elaborations of Q 8:30: "And [remember] when the unbelievers plotted against you, so as to confine you, kill or expel you. They schemed, and Allah schemed, but Allah is the best of schemers."[19]

The three possible lines of action against the Prophet mentioned in the Koran verse all find a parallel, in the narration,[20] as does God's counter-plot. So at least about this particular narrative it is obvious that it was generated by the Koran. There are too many correspondences to suppose anything else. Now Rubin would probably like to see an earlier, non-koranised version of this episode, but apparently there is none. It seems that, for lack of an older layer to be koranised, the narrator could only start from the bare fact of that plot, then looked for an appropriate Koran passage to apply, found Q 8:30, and built his plot—and counter-plot—story on it. But was there ever such a bare fact, outside this story? Did the event really take place? Or did the plot of Quraysh take place, whereas God's counterplot did not? Here we are back at the tiresome question of "what really happened," which Rubin, sympathetically, wished to avoid.

The idea of koranisation of an initially non-koranic "basic narrative framework" seems simply not to work here. Besides, the narration presents itself explicitly as an *asbāb al-nuzūl* story,[21] and it does so in *sīra* contexts, not in *tafsīr* work, as Rubin would have liked.

However, for part of the story Rubin's line of thought is applicable. God's counter-plot consists, among other things, in His making the Quraysh enemies temporarily blind. Muḥammad spreads dust on their heads and walks away without being seen by them. In the version of Wahb this part of the story comes with a piece of poetry. Rubin would recognise here a non-koranic, Arabia-centered "basic narrative framework." In Ibn Hishām's edition of Ibn Isḥāq, however, the motif is grafted onto Q 36:8: "[...] and We have covered them, so they do not see." From the eight quoted verses of sura 36, only these words were, with some effort, applicable to the narrative. So this is indeed an interesting case of attempted koranisation as meant by Rubin. It seems fruitful, in any case, to read the sira with Rubin's scheme of koranisation in mind. Sometimes it works, sometimes it does not, but for every time it does we owe him gratitude.

The way Rubin handles the story of the Satanic verses I cannot find convincing. He considers the episode with these verses secondary and sees it embedded in the theme of isolation by rejection. So far so good. First he adduces a non-Koran tradition of al-Zuhri about this theme:

al-Wāqidī *ʿan* Maʿmar *ʿan* al-Zuhrī: The Prophet calls to Islam in secret; many young and weak men follow him. The Quraysh admit that he is spoken to from heaven. But when he attacks their idols, and states that their fathers have perished in unbelief, they resent it and persecute the Prophet.[22]

Then he presents three versions of the story which are attributed to ʿUrwa ibn al-Zubayr. According to Rubin,[23] "Versions 1 and 2 represent the non-Quranic level, whereas version 3 is Quranic." I summarise:

V.1. Hisham 'an 'Urwa in his "letter" to 'Abd al-Malik:[24] The Meccans believe the Prophet and listen to him. When he attacks their idols, some Meccan leaders torment him. Most people abandon him, except a few. The Meccan leaders plot to tempt (*iflatana*) their relatives away from God's religion. "*It was a vehement fitna*." Then the Prophet orders the Muslims to set off for Abyssinia [...].

- The Prophet remains in Mecca for several years; Meccans continue torment converts. Yet, Islam spreads and even notables convert, so that the leaders moderate their persecution. "*This was the first fitna*, the one which compelled the Muslims to leave for Abyssinia."
- When the *fitna* calms down and Islam spreads in Mecca, this becomes known in Abyssinia and the Muslims return, feeling nearly safe in Mecca now. Islam spreads also in Medina. When the Meccan opponents see that, they plot to tempt them and to persecute them. "*This was the last fitna*, and they were two: a fitna which caused some to go to Abyssinia [...], and a fitna when they had returned [...]."

V.2. Ibn Lahīʿa *ʿan* Abū l-Aswad *ʿan* ʿUrwa *ʿan* Miswar ibn Makhrama *ʿan* Makhrama ibn Nawfal:[25] All(!) Meccans become Muslims. The Muslims grow so numerous that they cannot perform prostration during the recitation of the Koran, because of the crowds. When the Meccan leaders return from Ṭāʾif, they reprove the Meccans for having abandoned the religion of their ancestors. The people renounce Islam and break up with the Prophet.

V.3. Ibn Lahīʿa *ʿan* Abū l-Aswad *ʿan* ʿUrwa:[26] [Muslims fled to Abyssinia due to persecution][27] [...] The polytheists say: If this man only mentioned our idols in a favourable manner [...]. Then God reveals sura 53. Satan introduces his own false words. "This was the *fitna* of Satan." The polytheists rejoice. At the end of the sura, Muḥammad prostrates himself, and everyone with him, except old al-Walīd ibn al-Mughīra. The polytheists are pleased with what Satan had thrown into the recitation of the Prophet. Their participation in the *ṣalāt* reaches the Muslims in Abyssinia; these return to Mecca. Gabriel comes in the evening to review the revelation. When checking sura 53, he flares up. Muḥammad becomes aware that he has spoken the words of Satan. God abrogates the Satanic verses and reveals Q 22:52.

It is obvious that V.3 is permeated with koranic materials, but is it therefore the koranised elaboration of something like al-Zuhrī's tradition, or of ʿUrwa's V.1? The first one looks like a short epitome, and V.1 looks far from being a "basic narrative framework" to me. It twice repeats the same motif: "after initial success, a *fitna* arose," and a third time in a different way. One gains the impression that the compiler knew two or three conflicting variants of the same story, none of which he wanted to discard; so he combined them in one report. Of what had been essentially one *fitna*, he made two-and-a-half *fitna*s, two with a number and one without. The resulting report is clumsy, and by no means a narration. The compiler wanted, or had to be, very concise. Apparently he wrote for an addressee already acquainted with the subject matter, who may have needed a mnemonic device, or a politically correct compendium.

And this hybrid, incomprehensible, condensed triple report would be the real thing, the narrative starting point? That seems very unlikely. Why would not Q 17:73–75 have been the starting point of the whole episode, with its keyword *iflatana*, a golden opportunity for every story-teller? Maybe it was recounted in a period of real *fitna*s (civil wars), which made it attractive to project the *fitna* phenomenon into the past. Or otherwise the origin of the story may have been Q 22:52, which, by the way, was presented as a *sabab al-nuzūl* as early as Ibn Bukayr's edition of Ibn Isḥāq.[28] Is it not just as well conceivable that the compilers of the short versions were familiar with all the koranic materials, but omitted them because they were irrelevant for their purposes?

And what about V.2? Is this an early, not-yet-koranised version of the story, or is it a late, *de-koranised* version with the emphasis on prostration, the remains of a longer text in which sura 53 once figured, as suggested by Rubin himself?[29] And would this not indicate an early rather than a late koranisation?

We simply cannot know how it started, and certainly not from such a small number of texts. Here I would have liked to see Schoeler at work before Rubin! The latter mostly uses only a few versions of the story—although his footnotes show that he knows many more—and he does not look at the type of text he has before him. Schoeler would use them all, and establish their interdependence and relative dates. Rubin's discourse remains rather impressionistic, meant to support his schedule: non-koranic traditions are original, koranised stories are later, and *asbāb* stories are the final stage. As long as no research is done about the relative dating of *all* the reports and into their character, in the Schoelerian sense of the word, we cannot be sure at all.

Schoeler and Rubin have reopenend the discussion in different ways, both of which are worth to be continued. It is as if with their books the research into the *sīra* as literature has only begun.

I am still wondering, however, what the exact relations are between *sīra* and Koran or other Scripture. Rubin answered many, but not all questions. It seems that these relations are manifold, and a next step should be to establish a detailed survey of the various possibilities.

For the moment I only suggest some points for further investigation.

- What is the precise nature of an *asbāb al-nuzūl* story? It claims that first some event took place, on account of which a piece of Koran was revealed. In reality the koranic fragment was there first. After it, and because of it, the story came into existence. Henri Lammens without doubt went too far by suggesting that the whole *sīra* amounts to *asbāb al-nuzūl*. However, Rubin goes to the other extreme in claiming that *no* part of the *sīra* is such a story: "no process of spinning a narrative framework round a Quranic verse seems to have taken place."[30] Or is a *sabāb* only a *sabāb* when it features the words: "And thereupon God revealed . . ."? There is probably something like a gliding scale between a koranised story and an *asbāb al-nuzūl* story.
- The two narrations about the Satanic Verses in al-Ṭabari's *Tarīkh* are briefly mentioned by Rubin, but not discussed. The first version[31] presents itself an *asbāb al-nuzūl* story for Q 22:52. The other one[32] is more interesting, as it shows the Satanic Verses episode as an *asbāb al-nuzūl* story for Q 17:73–75, but in the end, albeit somewhat less clearly, *also* as the occasion for the revelation of Q 22:52. Two *asbāb* in one story, that seems to be worth investigating. Should we assume, with Rubin, that there was a basic story to which koranic verses, including their *asbāb*, could be added to taste? And how do these stories relate to those which Rubin did discuss?

- When a koranic verse forms the inspiration of a narrative, the verse need not, or hardly, be quoted. Rubin himself points to a short version of the first revelation story which had at least the key word *ufuq* in common with sura 53:7.[33] The more elaborated versions of the *ufuq* episode do not have more words in common with sura 53, but the whole setting reminds of the beginning of that sura: *dhū mirra*; *istawā* (either standing, or sitting on a throne or chair, or throwing one leg over another (while sitting?); the difference in height, the vision. Was the intention of the story to casually explain away the embarrassing presence of Allah, and replacing Him by an angel? Or did Allah Himself sit on His throne, in some primal version? I cannot help surmising that the whole story was inspired by sura 53 in the first place.
- The story about the reception of Muslim emigrants by the Negus of Abyssinia seems to be built around Koran 3:191.[34]
- In Ibn Isḥāq the Ascension story is both preceded and followed by passages about revilers and mockers.[35] These have no connection with the Ascension story, unless one thinks of Q 17:90–93: "We will not believe in you until you [...] ascend to heaven [...]." When this miracle had happened indeed, they still refused to believe; that is what Ibn Isḥāq apparently intends to express. The unquoted koranic verse may well play a part in the background.
- The first half of the *ifk* story is non-koranic, the second half is very firmly embedded in part of sura 24. This cries for an explanation.

All these, and without any doubt many more, ways of handling of koranic texts in the *sīra* deserve further study.

Notes

1. [Wim Raven, "The Biography of the Prophet and Its Scriptual Basis," in Stefan Leder, ed., *Story-Telling in the Framwork of Non-fictional Arabic Literature* (Wiesbaden: Otto Harrassowitz Verlag, 1998), pp. 421–31.
2. Abū l-Faradj al-Iṣbahāni: *K. al-Aghāni*. Cairo 1927–61, XXI, 128–29.
3. Tilman Seidensticker: *Die Gedichte des Šamardal ibn Šarik. Neuedition,*

Übersetzung, Kommentar. Wiesbaden 1983, 4–9.

4. W. Raven: *Ibn Dâwûd al-Iṣbahânî and his Kitāb al-Zahra.* Diss. Leiden 1989, 53.

5. Stefan Leder: The Literary Use of the *Khabar*. A Basic Form of Historical Writing. In: Averil Cameron and Lawrence Conrad (eds.): *The Byzantine and Early Islamic Near East.* I. *Problems in the Literary Source Material.* Princeton 1992 (Studies in Late Antiquity and Early Islam, 1), 277–315, at 306.

6. See e.g. Hans von Mžik: Die Gideon-Saul-Legende and die Überlieferung der Schlacht bei Badr. Ein Beitrag zur ältesten Geschichte des Islam. In: *WZKM* 29 (1915), 371–83.

7. G. D. Newby: An Example of Coptic Literary Influence on Ibn Isḥāq's *Sīrah.* In: *JNES* 31 (1972), 22–28, establishes a parallel between the story about the Nadjrāni Christian sect. [See page 417 in present volume.]

Faymiyūn (lbn Hishām: *Das Leben Muhammed's nach Muhammed Ibn Ishâk, bearbeitet von Abd el-Malik Ibn Hischâm.* Ed. F. Wüstenfeldt. Göttingen 1858, 20–22) and a Coptic hagiology about Pachomius. In this story the Prophet does not occur; yet saints" legends may well have contributed to other parts of the *sīra.*

8. *Muhammad at Mecca.* Oxford 1953; *Muhammad at Medina.* Oxford 1956.

9. E.g. J. Wansbrough: *The Sectarian Milieu. Content and Composition of Islamic Salvation History.* Oxford 1978; P. Crone & M. Cook: *Hagarism. The making of the Islamic World Cambridge* 1977.

10. *La vie du prophète Mahomet.* Colloque de Strasbourg (Octobre 1980). Ed. T. Fahd. Paris 1983. F. E. Peters: The quest of the historical Muhammad. In: *IJMES* 23 (1991), 291–315, surveys the debris left by the "sceptics" and what there is left to do on Muhammad's biography.

11. Uri Rubin: *In the Eye of the Beholder. The Life of Muhammad as viewed by the Early Muslims. A Textual Analysis.* Princeton 1995. Gregor Schoeler: *Charakter und Authentie der muslimischen Überlieferung über das Leben Mohammeds.* Berlin/New York 1996.

12. Schoeler: *Charakter*, 163–64.

13. This expression reminds of Sellheim's *Grundschich*, albeit that Rubin is not interested in "what really happened." In his view, these basic stories only deal with facts *as told.*

14. He writes *Quranisation*; I homogenised the orthography.

15. Rubin: *Eye*, 30ff.

16. Rubin: *Eye*, 59ff.

17. Ibn Hishām: Ed. F. Wüstenfeld, 1, 1–2, II. Göttingen, 1858, 1860, I, 1, 326;

al-Ṭabarī: *Ta'rikh al-rusul wal-mulūk.* Ed. M. J. De Goeje. Series I–III. Leiden 1879–1901, I, 1229–34.

18. R. G. Khoury: *Wahb b. Munabbih. Teil 1. Der Heidelberger Papyrus PSR Herd. Arab. Leben und Werk des Dichters*. Wiesbaden 1972, 23, 136–44.

19. *The Qur''an. A modern English Version*. Trsl. Majid Fakhry. Reading 1997.

20. The order in the narration has been changed, however, to build up more suspense.

21. Wahb ibn Munabbih, ed. Khoury, 138; al-Ṭabarī: *Ta'rikh*, I, 1234; Ibn Hishām, 326.

22. Rubin: *Eye*, 156; the summary was done by me.

23. Rubin: *Eye*, 157, quoting al-Ṭabarānī: *al-Mu'djam al-kabīr.* Since I do not have this work at my disposal, I must rely on his excerpts.

24. This story exists in two versions. Rubin presents on p. 157 the version of al-Ṭabarī: *Djāmi' al-bayān fī tafsīr al-Qur'ān*. Būlāq 1323–29, IX, 162–63. The other version is in al-Ṭabarī: *Ta'rikh*, I, 1180–81.

25. Rubin: *Eye*, 158, quoting al-Ṭabarānī.

26. Rubin: *Eye*, 158–61, quoting al-Ṭabarānī.

27. Rubin calls this "the first *fitna* of version P." I would be curious to see whether the word *fitna* is used in the text itself.

28. Ibn Isḥāq: *Sīrat ibn Isḥāq al-musammāt al-mubtada' wal-mab'ath wal-maghāzi*. Ed Hamidullah. Rabat 1976, no. 219.

29. Rubin: *Eye*, 165–66.

30. Rubin: *Eye*, 227.

31. al-Ṭabarī: *Ta'rikh*, I, 1192–93.

32. al-Ṭabarī: *Ta'rikh*, I, 1195–96.

33. Rubin: *Eye*, 110.

34. W. Raven: Some Early Islamic Texts on the Negus of Abyssinia, In: *JSS33* (1988), 197–218, at 201.

35. Ibn Hishām, 262–72.

Appendix A

Abbreviations

AcO	*Acta Orientalia*. Copenhagen.
AO	*Ars Orientalis*. Washington, DC, Ann Arbor, 1954–.
BSOAS	*Bulletin of the School of Oriental and African Studies*. London, 1917–.
CODCH	*The Concise Oxford Dictionary of the Christian Church*. Edited by E. A. Livingstone. Oxford, 1980.
CSCO	*Corpus scriptorum christianorum orientalium*. Edited by J. B. Chabot, I. Guidi, et al. In six sections: Scriptores Aethiopici; Scriptores Arabici; Scriptores Armeniaci; Scriptores Coptici; Scriptores Iberici; Scriptores Syri (various publishers). Paris, Leuven, 1903–.
EI	*Encyclopaedia of Islam*. Edited by M. T. Houtsma et al. 4 vols. Leiden and London, 1913–1934.
EI^2	*Encyclopaedia of Islam*, 2d ed. Edited by H. A. R. Gibb et al. Leiden and London, 1960–.
EQ	*Encyclopaedia of the Qur'ān*, 6 volumes. Leiden, Netherlands: Brill, 2001–.

ER	*Encyclopedia of Religion*. Edited by M. Eliade. New York: Macmillan, 1993.
GAL	C. Brockelmann. *Geschichte des Arabischen Literatur*, 2d ed. 2 vols. Leiden, 1943–49; Supplementbände. 3 vols. Leiden, 1937–42.
GAS	Fuat Sezgin. *Geschichte des arabischen Schriftums*. Leiden, 1967–.
GdQ/GdK	Theodor Nöldeke. *Geschichte des Qorans*. Göttingen, 1860. 2d ed. Edited by Friedrich Schwally, G. Bergstrasser, and O. Pretzl. 3 vols. Leipzig, 1909–1938.
IC	*Islamic Culture*. Hyderabad, 1927–.
IJMES	*International Journal of Middle East Studies*. Middle East Studies Association of North America, New York. Vol. 1, 1970–.
JA	*Journal asiatique*. Paris, 1822–.
JAATA	*Journal of the American Association of Teachers of Arabic*.
JAL/ZAL	*Journal for Arabic Linguistics*. Wiesbaden.
JAOS	*Journal of the American Oriental Society*. New Haven, Ann Arbor, 1842–.
JESHO	*Journal of the Economic and Social History of the Orient*. Paris, 1957–.
JNES	*Journal of Near Eastern Studies*. Oriental Institute, University of Chicago. Vol. 1, 1942–. Supersedes *American Journal of Semitic Languages and Literatures*.

JPHS	*Journal of the Pakistan Historical Society*
JRAS	*Journal of the Royal Asiatic Society.* London, 1834–.
JSAI	*Jerusalem Studies in Arabic and Islam.* Jerusalem, 1979–.
JSS	*Journal of Semitic Studies.* Oxford, 1956–.
MW	*Muslim World.* Hartford Seminary Foundation, Hartford, CT. Vol. 1, 1911–. Published as *Moslem World*, 1911–1947.
Or.Ltz.	*Orientalistische Literaturzeitung*, Berlin. Vols. 1–8, 1898–1905.
REI	*Revue des Etudes Islamiques.* Paris.
REJ	*Revue des Etudes Juives.*
RHPR	*Revue d'Histoire et de Philosophie Religieuses.* Strasbourg.
RHR	*Revue de l'histoire des religions. Annales du Muséé Guimet.* Paris. Vol. 1, 1880–.
RSO	*Rivista degli studi orientali.* Rome. Vol. 1, 1907–.
RSPT	*Revue des Sciences Philosophiques et Théologiques.* Paris.
RSR	*Revue des sciences religieuses.* Strasbourg, 1921–.
SBWA	*Sitzungsberichte der Philosophisch-Historischen Klasse der Kaiserlichen Akademie der Wissenschaften.* Vienna, 1848–.

SEI	*Shorter Encyclopaedia of Islam.* Edited by H. A. R. Gibb and J. H. Kramers. Leiden, 1953.
SI	*Studia Islamica.* Paris, 1953–.
TGUOS	*Transactions of the Glasgow University Oriental Society.* Glasgow.
THES	*Times Higher Education Supplement.* London.
TLS	*Times Literary Supplement.* London.
Wellhausen *Reste*	J. Wellhausen. *Reste arabischen Heidentums*, 2d ed. Berlin, 1897.
WI	*Die Welt des Islams.* Berlin, 1913–.
WZKM	*Wiener Zeitschrift für die Kunde des Morgenlandes.* Vienna.
ZA	*Zeitschrift für Assyriologie und verwandte Gebiete.* Vols. 1–19, Berlin 1886–1905/06.
ZAL/JAL	*Zeitschrift für Arabische Linguistik.* Wiesbaden.
ZATW	*Zeitschrift für alttestamentliche Wissenschaft.*
ZDMG	*Zeitschrift der deutschen Morgenlandischen Gesellschaft.* Leipzig, Wiesbaden, 1847–.

Appendix B

Glossary

Abū l -Qāsim. Father of Qasim, that is, Muhammad, the Prophet; a **kunya** for Muhammad, the Prophet.

adab. *Belles-lettres*; refinement, culture.

'adālah. Probity; synonym of **ta'dīl**.

adīb. Writer of **adab**; man of letters.

'ahd. Covenant, treaty, engagement.

Ahl al-Bayt. The people of the house, Muhammad's household (the family of the Prophet).

ahl al-Ḥadīth. Those collecting and learned in the **Ḥadīth**.

Ahl al-Kitāb. "People of the Book," especially Christians and Jews.

ahl al-ra'y. People of reasoned opinion; those using their own opinion to establish a legal point.

ahl as-ṣuffa. The people of the bench, of the temple at Mecca; they were poor strangers without friends or place of abode who claimed the promises of the Apostle of God and implored his protection.

akhbār. Reports, anecdotes, history.

'alām. Signs, marks, badges.

amān. Safe conduct.

amārāt al-nubūwwa. Marks of prophethood.

ʿāmm. Collective or common words.

anṣār. The helpers; early converts of Medina, and then later all citizens of Medina converted to Islam; in contrast to the Muhajirun, or exiles, those Muslims who accompanied the Prophet from Mecca to Medina.

ʿaqīqah. The custom, observed on the birth of a child, of leaving the hair on the infant's head until the seventh day, when it is shaved and animals are sacrificed.

ʿarabiyyah. The standard of correct Arabic usage of the sixth and seventh centuries CE, as envisaged by the eighth-century grammarians.

ʿaṣabiyyah. Tribal solidarity.

asbāb al-nuzūl. The occasions and circumstances of the Koranic revelations.

aṣḥā b al-nabī. Companions of the Prophet. (A single companion is a **sahabi**.)

assonance. A repeated vowel sound, a part rhyme, which has great expressive effect when used internally (within lines), for example, "An old, mad, blind, despised and dying king," Shelley, "Sonnet: England in 1819." It consists in a similarity in the accented vowels and those which follow, but not in the consonants, for example, creep/feet skin/swim. Examples in the Koran at VI, 164; XVII,15; and so on, for example, *wa-lā taziru wāzir -atun wizra ukhrā.*

Awāʾil. The ancients; the first people to do something.

āyah (pl. **āyāt**). Sign, miracle; verse of the Koran.

ayyām al-ʿArab. "Days" of the Arabs; pre-Islamic tribal battles.

bāb. Subchapter, especially in **Ḥadīth** literature.

basmalah. The formula "In the name of God, the Merciful, the Compassionate" (*bi-ʿsmi ʿillahi ʿl-Rahmani ʿ l-Rahim*).

bint. Girl; daughter of.

ḍaʿīf (pl. **ḍuʿafāʾ**). Weak, as classification of a **Ḥadīth**; traditionist of dubious reliability.

dalāʾil. Proofs, signs, marks.

dār. Abode.

Dār al-Ḥarb. The Land of Warfare, a country belonging to infidels not subdued by Islam.

Dār al-Islām. The Land of Islam, the Islamic world.

dhimmah. Security, pact.

dhimmī. Non-Muslim living as a second-class citizen in an Islamic state; Christian or Jew.

diglossia. A situation where two varieties of the same language live side by side. The two variations are high and low: High Arabic and Low Arabic.

dīn. Religion.

dīwān. Register; collection of poetry by a single author or from a single tribe.

du'ā'. Prayer; generally used for supplication as distinguished from ṣalāt, or liturgical form of prayer.

faḍā'il. Merits.

fakhr. Boasting, self-glorification, or tribal vaunting.

faqīh (pl. **fuqahā'**)**.** One learned in **fiqh**.

fātiḥah. The first **sura** of the Koran.

fiqh. Islamic jurisprudence.

al-fiṭaḥl. The time before the Flood.

fitnah. Dissension, civil war; particularly the civil war ensuing on the murder of the Caliph 'Uthmān.

fuṣḥā. The pure Arabic language.

futūḥ. Conquests; the early Islamic conquests.

ghārāt. Raids.

gharīb. Rare, uncommon word or expression; a rare tradition, or such traditions as are isolated, do not date from one of the companions of the Prophet, and are only from a later generation.

ghazwah (pl. **ghazawāt**)**.** Early Muslim military expeditions or raiding parties in which the Prophet took part; synonym of **maghāzī**.

ḥabl. Covenant, treaty, engagement.

Ḥadīth. The corpus of traditions of the sayings and doings of the Prophet.

ḥadīth (with a small initial)**.** Such a tradition.

ḥajj. The annual pilgrimage to Mecca in the month of Dhu 'l-Hijjah.

ḥalāl. Licit, permitted; opposite of **ḥarām**.

ḥanīf. A Koranic term applying to those of true religion; seeker of religious truth.

ḥaram. Sacred enclave; especially those of Mecca and Medina.

ḥarām. Forbidden, illicit; opposite of **ḥalāl**.

ḥarakāt. Vowels.

ḥasan. Category of **ḥadīth** between sound (ṣaḥīḥ) and weak (ḍaʿīf).

hijrah (hijra). Muhammad's migration from Mecca to Medina in 622 CE.

ḥukm. Judgment.

ibn. Son of.

i ʿjāz. Inimitability of the Koran.

ijāzah. License given by a scholar to his pupil, authorizing the latter to transmit and teach a text.

ijmāʿ. Consensus; the consensus of the Islamic community.

illah (pl. **ilal**). Cause; defect; especially a gap in the chain of authentic transmission of a **ḥadīth**.

imām. Leader, especially a religious leader; leader in communal prayer.

Injīl. The Gospel.

Iʿrāb. Usually translated as "inflection," indicating case and mood, but the Arab grammarians define it as the difference that occurs, in fact or virtually, at the end of a word, because of the various antecedents that govern it.

isnād. Chain of authorities; in particular in **Ḥadīth** and historical writings.

isrāʿ. Journey by night; the famous night journey of Muhammd to Jerusalem.

Jāhiliyyah. Period before Muhammad's mission; era of ignorance; pre-Islamic period.

jihād. Holy war.

jizyah. Poll tax; capitation tax.

kāfir. Unbeliever.

kāhin. Pre-Islamic soothsayer.

kalāla. (a) one who dies leaving neither parent nor child, or, all the heirs with the exception of parents and children; (b) a bride, daughter-in-law, or sister-in-law.

kalām. Scholastic theology.

karshūnī. Syriac alphabet adapted to suit the Arabic language.

khabar (pl. **akhbār**). Discrete anecdotes, reports.

khafī. Sentences whose meanings are hidden.

khajī. Sentences in which other persons or things are hidden beneath the plain meaning of a word or expression contained therein.

khāṣṣ. Words used in a special sense.

khāṣṣīya (pl. **khaṣā'iṣ**). Privilege, prerogative, feature, trait.

khaṭīb. Orator; person pronouncing the Friday **khuṭbah**.

khulq. Disposition, temper, nature.

khuṭbah. Oration; address in the mosque at Friday prayers.

kiblah. *See* **qiblah**.

kissa. *See* **qiṣṣah**.

kitāb (pl. **kutub**). Writing, Scripture, book; in **Ḥadīth**, a division approximating a chapter.

kufic. Style of Arabic script, used in early Koran codices.

kunya (konia, kunyah). A patronymic or name of honor of the form Abu N or Umm N (father or mother of N).

kussas. *See* **quṣṣāṣ**.

mab 'ath. Sending; the Call, when Muhammad was summoned to act as God's Prophet.

maghāzī. Early Muslim military expeditions or raiding parties in which the Prophet took part.

majlis (pl. **majālis**). Meeting, session, scholarly discussion.

manāqib. Virtues, good qualities.

mansūkh. Abrogated.

mashhūr. Well known, widely known; a statement handed down by at least three different reliable authorities.

mathālib. Defects.

matn. Main text; narrative content.

mawlā (pl. **mawālī**). Client, non-Arab Muslim.

Midrash (Hebrew for "exposition or investigation"). A Hebrew term for the method of biblical investigation or exegesis by which oral tradition interprets and elaborates on the scriptural text. This investigation became necessary because the written law in the Pentateuch (the first five books of the Old Testament) needed to be reinterpreted in the light of later situations and disagreements. The Midrashim are usually divided into two broad groups:

1. **Halakha Midrash**, which is the scholastic deduction of the oral law (Halakha) from the written law; the totality of laws that have evolved since biblical times regulating religious observances and conduct of the Jewish people; they tend to be rather dry and legalistic.

2. **Haggada Midrash**, which consists of homiletic works whose purpose is edification rather than legislation; while less authoritative than halakhic ones, they are often highly imaginative stories, with a great deal of charm.

mi 'rāj. Ascent; the Prophet's vision of heaven.

Mu'allaqah (pl. **Mu'allaqāt**). A collection of supposedly pre-Islamic poems.

mu'awwal. Words that have several significations, all of which are possible.

mubtada'. Beginnings.

mufakharah. Contests of vaunting; a war of words constituting a literary genre.

mufaṣṣal. Set forth or described minutely or in great detail.

mufassar. Explained. A sentence that needs some word in it to explain it and make it clear.

muḥaddith Ḥadīth. Scholar, collecting and studying the **Ḥadīth**.

muhājirūn. Those who went with the Prophet from Mecca to Medina at the time of the *hijrah*.

muḥkam. Perspicuous; a sentence the meaning of which there is no doubt.

mujmal. Sentences that may have a variety of interpretations.

muruwwah. Manliness, chivalry, prowess; the qualities of the ideal pre-Islamic Arab.

musannaf. Classified, systemized compilation. **Ḥadīth** compilations arranged according to subject matter.

muṣḥaf. Koran codex.

mushkil. Sentences that are ambiguous.

mushtarak. Complex words that have several significations.

musnad. Work of **ḥadīth** in which individual **ḥadīth** can be attributed to the Prophet himself.

mutʿah. Temporary marriage.

mutakallim. Scholastic theologian.

mutashābih. Intricate sentences or expressions, the exact meaning of which it is impossible for man to ascertain.

mutawātir. A report handed down successively by numerous companions, which was generally known from early times and to which objections have never been raised.

Muʿtazilah. Theological school that created speculative dogmatics of Islam.

nabī. Prophet.

nahḍah. Renaissance.

nasab (pl. **ansāb**). Genealogy.

nāsikh. Passage in the Koran or Sunnah that abrogates another passage.

nuqaṭ. The diacritical points, the function of which is to differentiate letters of the basic ***rasm***; there are seven letters that are the unmarked members of pairs where the other member has over-dotting.

Peshitta (Pšiṭṭā). The official text of the Bible in Syriac.

Poetical koinē. The written but not spoken language common to pre-Islamic poetry. (Not a happy term, as Rabin says (chap. 3.4) since the Greek *koinē* was a spoken language; thus Classical Arabic resembles more closely the status of Homeric Greek.)

Qaddarites. A group of teachers during ther Abbasid period who championed free will against the theory of predestination.

Qāḍī. Judge of a sharīʿah court.

qara'a 'alā. Literally, read aloud to; study under.

qāri' (pl. **qurrā'**). Reader, reciter of the Koran.

qiblah. Direction of prayer.

qirā'ah. Recitation of the Koran; variant reading of the Koran.

qiṣṣah (pl. **qiṣaṣ**). Story, fable, narrative tale; the narrative tales of the Koran.

qiyās. Analogy; the process of arriving at a legal decision by analogy.

quṣṣāṣ. Storytellers, relaters of **qiṣaṣ**.

Rāshidūn. The first four caliphs (the orthodox or rightly guided caliphs), that is, Abū Bakr, ʿUmar, 'Uthmān, and ʿAlī.

rasm. The basic (unpointed) form, shape, or drawing of the individual word.

rasūl. Messenger; apostle.

rāwī (pl. **ruwāh**). Reciter, transmitter.

ra'y. Opinion.

rijāl (sing. **rajul**). Men; trustworthy authorities in **Ḥadīth** literature.

risālah (pl. **rasā'il**). Epistle.

riwāyah. Transmission (of a nonreligious text); recension; variant reading in poetry.

Ṣadaqa. Alms, charitable gift; almsgiving, charity; legally prescribed alms tax.

Ṣaḥābah. The group of the Companions of the Prophet.

ṣaḥīfah (pl. **ṣuḥuf**). Page leaf; in the plural: manuscripts, documents containing **Ḥadīth** material.

ṣaḥīḥ. Sound (category of **Ḥadīth**); name of the **Ḥadīth** collections of al-Bukhārī and Muslim.

sajʿ. Balanced and rhyming prose.

sarāyā. Early Muslim military expeditions at which the Prophet was not present.

shādhdh. Peculiar; especially unacceptable variants of the Koranic text.

shamā'il. Good qualities; character, nature.

sharīʿah. The corpus of Islamic law.

shawāhid. Piece of evidence or quotation serving as textual evidence.

Shīʿah. Sect that holds that the leadership of the Islamic community belongs only to the descendants of ʿAlī and Fāṭima.

Shuʿūbiyyah. Anti-Arab political and literary movement, especially strong in Iranian circles.

sīra/sīrah (pl. **siyar**)**.** Biography, especially of the Prophet.

Sitz im leben (German: situation or place in life)**.** A term used initially in biblical criticism to signify the circumstances (often in the life of a community) in which a particular story, saying, and so on, was created or preserved and transmitted.

stanza/strophe. Some poems are divided into groups of lines that stricly speaking are called "stanzas"; though in popular language they are often called "verses." The stanza will have a predominating meter and pattern of rhyme. For example, the Omar Khayyam stanza has four iambic pentameters, rhyming AABA; it receives its name from its use by E. Fitzgerald in his translation of the *Rubaiyat.*

sunnah. Way, path; customary practice; usage sanctioned by tradition; the sayings and doings of the Prophet that have been established as legally binding.

sura/sūrah. A chapter of the Koran.

ṭabaqāt. Historical works organized biographically.

tābiʿūn (sing. **tābiʿ**)**.** Followers, the generation after the Prophet's companions (**ṣaḥā bah**).

ta ʿdīl. Confirming the credibility of a **muḥaddith**.

tafsīr. Koranic exegesis.

tafsīr bi'l-ma'thūr. Interpretation or exegesis of the Koran following tradition.

tafsīr bi'l-ra'y. Interpretation or exegesis of the Koran by personal opinion.

tajwīd. The art of reciting the Koran, giving each consonant its full value, as much as it requires to be well pronounced without difficulty or exaggeration.

tanzīl. The divine revelation incorporated in the Koran; occasionally, the inspiration of soothsayers.

ta'rīkh. History.

tawḥīd. The doctrine of the unity of God.

ta'wīl. Interpretation; sometimes used as a synonym for **tafsīr**; later acquired specialized sense of exposition of the subject matter of the Koran, in contrast to the more external philological exegesis of the Koran, which was now distinguished as **tafsīr**.

ummah. Folk; the Islamic community.

Ur- (German origin; prefix). Primitive, original.

uṣūl. The fundamentals of jurisprudence.

waḍū'. Ablution.

warrāq. Paper seller, stationer, bookseller, copyist.

zakāh. Alms tax of prescribed amount.

zuhd. Asceticism.

Appendix C

Conversion Chart

The left-hand column gives Flügel's numbers; the corresponding numbers in the Egyptian text are obtained by adding or subtracting as shown. At the points of transition this applies only to part of a verse in one of the editions.

I	1–6	+1	III *cont.*	180–90	+3	VII *cont.*	28–103	+2
II	1–19	+1		191–93	+2		103–31	+3
	19–38	+2		194	+1		131–39	+4
	38–61	+3		196–98	+1		140–43	+3
	61–63	+4	IV.	3–5	+1		144–46	+2
	63–73	+5		7–13	–1		147–57	+1
	73–137	+6		14	–2		166–86	+1
	138–72	+5	–	15	–3		191–205	+1
	173–212	+4		16–29	–4	VIII1	37–43	–1
	213–16	+3		30–32	–5		44–64	–2
	217–18	+2		32–45	–4		64–76	–1
	219–20	+1		45–47	–3	IX	62–130	–1
	236–58	–1		47–48	–2	X	11–80	–1
	259–69	–2		49–70	–3	XI	6	–1
	270–73	–3		70–100	–2		7–9	–2
	273–74	–2		100–106	–1		10–22	–3
	274–77	–1		118–56	+1		22–54	–2
III	1–4	+1		156–70	+2		55–77	–3
	4–18	+2		171–72	+1		77–84	–2
	19–27	+1		174–75	+1		84–87	–1
	27–29	+2	V	3–4	–1		88–95	–2
	29–30	+3		5–8	–2		96–99	–3
	30–31	+4		9–18	–3		99–120	–2
	31–43	+5		18–19	–2		120–22	–1
	43–44	+6		20–35	–3	XII	97–103	–1
	44–68	+7		35–52	–4	XIII	6–18	–1
	69–91	+6		53–70	–5		28–30	+1
	92–98	+5		70–82	–4	XIV	10–11	–1
	99–122	+4		82–88	–3		12–13	–2
	122–26	+5		88–93	–2		14–24	–3
	126–41	+6		93–98	–1		25–26	–4
	141–45	+7		101–109	+1		27–37	–5
	146–73	+6	VI	66–72	+1		37	–4
	174–75	+5		136–63	–1		37–41	–3
	176–79	+4	VII	1–28	+1		41–42	–2

XIV *cont.*	42–45	–1
	46–47	–2
	47–51	–1
XVI	22–24	–1
	25–110	–2
	110–28	–1
XVII	10–26	–1
	27–48	–2
	49–53	–3
	53–106	–2
	106–108	–1
XVIII	2–21	+1
	23–31	+1
	31–55	+2
	56–83	+1
	83–84	+2
	85–97	+1
XIX	1–3	+1
	8–14	–1
	27–76	–1
	77–78	–2
	79–91	–3
	91–93	–2
	93–94	–1
XX	1–9	+1
	16–34	–1
	40–41	–1
	42–63	–2
	64–75	–3
	75–79	–2
	80–81	–3
	81–88	–2
	89–90	–3
	90–94	–2
	94–96	–1
	106–15	+1
	115–21	+2
	122–23	+1
XXI	29–67	–1
XXII	19–21	–1
XXII *cont.*	26–43	–1
	43–77	+1
XXIII	28–34	–1
	35–117	–2
	117	–1
XXIV	14–18	+1
	44–60	+1
XXV	4–20	–1
	21–60	–2
	60–66	–1
XXVI	1–48	+1
	228	–1
XXVII	45–66	–1
	67–95	– 2
XXVIII	1–22	+1
XXIX	1–5I	+1
XXX	1–54	+1
XXXI	1–32	+1
XXXII	1–9	+1
XXXIII	41–49	+1
XXXIV	10–53	+1
XXXV	8–20	–1
	20–21	+1
	21–25	+2
	25–34	+3
	35–41	+2
	42–44	+1
XXXVI	1–30	+1
XXXVII	29–47	+1
	47–100	+2
	101	+1
XXXVIII	1–43	+1
	76–85	–1
XXXIX	4	–1
	5–9	–2
	10–14	–3
	14–19	–2
	19–63	–1
XL	1–2	+1
	19–32	–1
XL *cont.*	33–39	–2
	40–56	–3
	56–73	–2
	73–74	–1
XLI	1–26	+1
XLII	1–11	+2
	12–31	+1
	31–42	+2
	43–50	+1
XLIII	1–51	+1
XLIV	1–36	+1
XLV	1–36	+1
XLVI	1–34	+1
XLVII	5–16	–1
	17–40	–2
L	13–44	+1
LIII	27–58	–1
LV	1–16	+1
LVI	22–46	+1
	66–91	+1
LVII	13–19	+1
LVIII	3–21	–1
LXXI	5–22	+1
	26–29	–1
LXXII	23–26	–1
LXXXIV	32	–1
	33	–2
	34–41	–3
	41–42	–2
	42–51	–1
	54–55	+1
LXXVIII	41	–1
LXXX	15–18	+1
LXXXIX	1–14	+1
	17–25	–1
XCVIII	2–7	+1
CI	1–5	+1
	5–6	+2
	6–8	+3
CVI	3	+1

Appendix D

List of Contributors

Tor Andrae, born July 9, 1885, at Vena, Sweden, studied Semitic languages and history of religion at Uppsala Universitet, where he received a doctorate in 1947 for his thesis "Die Person Muhammeds in Lehre und Glauben seiner Gemeinde." His writings include *Mohammed: The Man and His Faith* (1936; German ed., 1932; Spanish ed., 1933; French ed., 1945; Swedish ed., 1967), *Islamische Mystiker* (1960), and *In the Garden of Myrtles* (1987). He died in Vena, Sweden, July 9, 1947. In the same year was published *Tor Andrae in Memoriam*. Geo Widengren wrote *Tor Andrae* (1947).

Edmund Beck was born November 6, 1902, in Huldessen, Germany, and died June 12, 1991, in Metten. He was a German Benedictine monk at the Abbey of Metten and professor of scripture at the Pontifical Athenaeum San Anselmo, Rome. He received a doctorate in philosophy in 1959 from the Universität München for his thesis "Die Koranzitate bei Sibawaih." Recognized as one of the greatest scholars of the works of Ephrem the Syrian, he wrote between 1955 and 1979 a monumental critical edition with translations of the work of Ephrem in Corpus Scriptorum Christianorum Orientalium. His other writings include *Ephräms Polemik gegen Mani und die Manichäer* (Louvain: Scriptorum Christianorum Orientalium, 1978).

The Reverend E. F. F. Bishop (1891–1976) was formerly principal of the Newman School of Missions in Jerusalem, from 1927 to 1948. He was senior lecturer in Arabic at the University of Glasgow from 1949 to 1956. He was author of the *Prophets of Palestine* (1962), among other works.

G. Borg, born 1953, Enschede, the Netherlands, studied Semitic languages at the University of Nijmegen, including Arabic language and literature, Ugaritic, and literary theory. He taught Arabic at Nijmegen University from 1979 to 1989 and is at present the director of the Netherlands-Flemish Institute in Cairo, Egypt.

Jean-Louis Déclais, born 1935, came to Islamic studies after years of biblical studies. Déclais has been a lay priest since 1978, living in Oran, Algeria. He is the author of *Les Premiers Musulmans Face à la Tradition Biblique*, *Trois Récits sur Job* (Paris: L'Harmattan, 1996), *David Raconté par les Musulmans* (Paris: Éditions du Cerf, 1999), and *Un Récit Musulman sur Isaie* (Paris: Éditions du Cerf, 2001).

Clement Huart (1854–1926) was an eminent scholar of Arabic, Persian, and Turkish, from the Ecole des Langues Orientales Vivantes, who was widely published in the late nineteenth and early twentieth centuries. Some of his major works include *A History of Arabic Literature* (1901), *Histoire de Bagdad dans les Temps Modernes* (1901), *Histoire des Arabes* (1912–13), and *La Perse Antique et la Civilisation Iranienne* (1925). Earlier in his career, he was the chancellor at the French Consulate in Damascus, and he subsequently served as dragoman (interpreter), then consul, for the French Embassy in Constantinople.

David S. Margoliouth (1858–1940) was professor of Arabic at the University of Oxford and a member of the Council of the Royal Asiatic Society. He was the author of numerous articles and books on Islam, including *Muhammad and the Rise of Islam* (London, 1905) and *The Early Development of Mohammedanism* (London, 1914). His research into the history of early Islam led him to compare the life of Joseph Smith, the founder of Mormonism, to that of the Prophet of Islam, and it forced him to conclude that human beings with unusual powers fall easily into dishonesty.

Hans Mzik (1876–1961), of Czech origin, was a scholar of Greek and Arabic geography. He editd *Klaudios Ptolemaios: Einführung in die darstellende Erdkund* (Vienna, 1938) and *Die Reise des Arabers Ibn Batuta durch Indien und China* (Hamburg, 1911). Mzik was a member of the Academy of the Arabic Language in Damascus, Syria.

Gordon Darnell Newby, born December 16, 1939, at Salt Lake City, graduated in 1962 from the University of Utah and received a PhD in 1966 from Brandeis University, Waltham, MA, for "Ibn Asbat's Ta'rikh." He has been affiliated, since 1976, with North Carolina State University, Raleigh, and since about 1990 with the Department of Near Eastern Languages and Literatures at the University of Illinois at Urbana. His writings include *A History of the Jews of Arabia* (1988), and he translated from the Arabic of Muhammad Ibn Ishāq *The Making of the Last Prophet: A Reconstruction of the Earliest Biography of Muhammad* (1989).

Hugh Nibley is a professor of history and religion at Brigham Young University, Provo, UT.

Marc Philonenko is a professor at the University of Strasbourg and one of the directors of the journal *Revue d'Histoire et de Philosophie Religieuses*. He is the author of many articles on the Dead Sea Scrolls, and he edited *La Bible: Ecrits Intertestamentaires* (Paris: Gallimard, 1987), for which he also translated from the Hebrew into French the Testament of Job, the Apocalypse of Abraham, and the Book of Secrets of Enoch, among others.

Edmond Power, born in the nineteenth century, was a Jesuit priest who received a doctorate from the Université Saint-Joseph de Beyrouth with a thesis on the poetry of Umayya ibn Abī ṣ-Ṣalt.

Wim Raven was born in 1947. He pursued Oriental studies from 1965 to 1974 in Amsterdam and Leiden, focusing on Arabic poetry criticism and Hadith. From 1974 to 1977 he was an assistant at Leiden University and took part in the Concordance et indices de la tradition musulmane; he was joint author of the eighth and final volume. Subsequently he taught until 1996

Arabic and Islamic studies at the Free University of Amsterdam. In 1989 he received his doctorate with a dissertation on Ibn al- Dâwûd al-Isbahânî. From 1996 to 2007 he worked as a teacher at the Oriental Institute of the J. W. Goethe University in Frankfurt. Since 2007 he has been a teacher at the Center for Near and Middle Eastern Studies at Philipps-University Marburg. His teaching interests include Arabic syntax, early Islamic texts (Hadith, biography of the Prophet, law), the Koran and Koranic exegesis, classical Arabic literature, and Islamic apocalyptic and intellectual history of the nineteenth and twentieth centuries.

A. Regnier is the author of "La Terminologie mystique des Ibn 'Arabi," *Le Muséon* 48 (1935): 145–62.

Martiniano P. Roncaglia was born in 1923. His writings include *Histoire de l'Église copte* (1966), *Essai bibliographique de diplomatique islamique* (1979), Les Freres Mineurs et l'Eglise grecque orthodoxe au XIII siecle (1231–1274) (Cairo, 1954). A Franciscan, Roncaglia wrote regularly for the journal Studia Christiana Orientalia articles such as "Giovanni Duns Scoto e l'Islam" (II, 52–58), and "Les Franciscains et les Armenians Catholiques" (II, 59–64).

Michael Schub, PhD, was born in 1944. Before retiring he taught classical Arabic, Hebrew, and comparative religion for four years each at Yale University, Cornell University, and the University of Miami (Coral Gables, FL); and he taught for ten years at Trinity College, Hartford, CT. Dr Schub was senior Fulbright research scholar at University of Saarland, Saarlands, Germany, from 1979 to 1980. He has published numerous articles in learned journals such as the *Journal of Semitic Studies*, the *Journal of Arabic Linguistics*, and *al-Andalus*. Dr. Schub is one of three translators of Suyūṭī's *Al-Itq n f 'Ul m al-Qur' n*, which was one of the books in the Great Books of Islamic Civilization series.

Friedrich Schulthess (1878–1922) studied theology and Oriental languages at Basel, Göttingen, Strasbourg, and Zurich, and became a professor of Semitic philology successively at Göttingen, Königsberg, Strasbourg, and

Basel. His writings include *Christlich-palästinische Fragmente aus der Omajjaden-Moschee zu Damaskus* (1905), *Kalila und Dimna, syrisch und deutsch* (1911), and *Die Machtmittel des Islams* (1922), and he edited and translated *Diwan des arabischen Dichters Hatim Tej nebst Fragmenten* (1897).

Tilman Seidensticker was born in 1955 at Göttingen. He received a doctorate in philosophy in 1982 with a thesis entitled "Die Gedichte des Šarmadalibn Šarīk," and a doctorate in habilitation in 1990 at Giessen, where he subsequently lectured in Islamic studies.

Aloys Sprenger (1813–1893), of Austrian origin, studied at the exclusive Orientalische Akademie. After studies in Zurich and Paris, he went in 1836 to London where he collaborated on "History of the Art of War among Eastern Nations." After acquiring a doctorate in medicine in 1840 at Leiden, Sprenger went in 1843 to Calcutta in the service of the East India Company. In India he became a prolific writer, editor, and collector of Islamic literature. He left India in 1857 with a large collection of Arabic books and manuscripts, which in 1858 was acquired by the Prussian Library, Berlin. From 1858 to his retirement in 1881 he was a professor of Oriental languages at Bern.

Ralph Stehly, Islamologue, is professor of history of religions at the Faculty of Protestant Theology at Strasbourg and president of L'Association pour la Création de la Faculté de Théologie Musulmane de Strasbourg. His publications include *Le Sahîh de Bukhârî, texte arabe avec versions parallèles, traduction et commentaire des hadiths 1 à 25, contribution à l'étude du hadith*, and "Un problème de théologie islamique: la définition des fautes graves (kabâ'ir)," *Revue des Etudes Islamiques* (1979): 185–201.